SOLIDWORKS 2018: A Tutorial Approach

(4th Edition)

Sham Tickoo
Professor
Purdue University Northwest
Hammond, Indiana, USA

Contributing Authors
Tickoo Institute of Emerging Technologies (TIET)
Gurgaon, India

CADCIM Technologies
Indiana, USA

BPB PUBLICATIONS

ISBN: 978-9-3881763-1-6
4th Revised and Updated Edition
(For distribution in SAARC countries only)

Limits of Liability and Disclaimer of Warranty

The information contained in this book is the best of Author's & Publisher's knowledge. We are committed to serve students with best of our knowledge and resources. We have taken utmost care and attention while editing and printing of this book but Author and Publisher should not be held responsible for errors, omissions and any other unintentional mistake that might have crept in. However, errors brought to our notice shall be gratefully acknowledged and attended to.

All trademarks referred to in the book are acknowledged as properties of their respective owners. This book is written solely for the benefit and guidance of the students.

Distributors

COMPUTER BOOK CENTRE
12, Shrungar Shopping Centre
M.G. Road
BENGALURU–560001
Ph: 25587923/25584641

DECCAN AGENCIES
4-3-329, Bank Street
HYDERABAD-500195
Ph: 24756967/24756400

MICRO MEDIA
Shop No. 5, Mahendra Chambers
150 DN Rd. Next to Capital Cinema
V.T (C.S.T.) Station
MUMBAI-400001

BPB BOOK CENTRE
376 Old Lajpat Rai Market
DELHI-110006
Ph: 23861747

INFOTECH
G-2, Sidhartha Building, 96 Nehru Place
NEW DELHI-110019
Ph: 26438245

BPB PUBLICATIONS
20, Ansari Road, Darya Ganj
New Delhi-110002
Ph: 23254990/23254991

Published by Manish Jain for BPB Publications, 20 Ansari Road, Darya Ganj
New Delhi-110002 and Printed Repro India Pvt. Ltd, Mumbai

DEDICATION

To teachers, who make it possible to disseminate knowledge to enlighten the young and curious minds of our future generations

To students, who are dedicated to learning new technologies and making the world a better place to live in

THANKS

To the faculty and students of the MET Department of Purdue University Northwest for their cooperation

To employees of CADCIM Technologies for their valuable help

Note

If you are a faculty member, you can register by clicking on the following link to access the teaching resources: ***http://www.cadcim.com/Registration.aspx***. The student resources are available at ***http://www.cadcim.com***.

Table of Contents

This page is intentionally left blank

Preface

SOLIDWORKS 2018

SOLIDWORKS, originally developed by the SOLIDWORKS Corporation, USA, was acquired by Dassault Systemes, France, in 1997. Dassault Systemes is world's leading developer of product life cycle management solutions. It is one of the fastest growing solid modeling software. It is a parametric, feature-based solid modeling tool that not only unites the three-dimensional (3D) parametric features with two-dimensional (2D) tools, but also addresses every design-through-manufacturing needs. SOLIDWORKS 2018 includes a number of customer requested enhancements, substantiating that it is completely tailored to address customers needs. Based mainly on the user feedback, this solid modeling tool is remarkably user-friendly and allows you to be productive from day one.

In SOLIDWORKS , you can easily generate the 2D drawing views of the components. The drawing views that can be generated include detailed, orthographic, isometric, auxiliary, section, and other views. You can use any predefined standard drawing document to generate the drawing views. Besides displaying the model dimensions in the drawing views or adding reference dimensions and other annotations, you can also add the parametric Bill of Materials (BOM) and balloons in the drawing view. If a component in the assembly is replaced, removed, or a new component is assembled, the modification will automatically reflect in the BOM placed in the drawing document. The bidirectional associative nature of this software ensures that any modification made in the model is automatically reflected in the drawing views and any modification made in the dimensions in the drawing views automatically updates the model.

In addition to creating solid models, assembly features, and drawing views, SOLIDWORKS enables you to effectively and easily create complex sheet metal components using a number of tools.

SOLIDWORKS 2018: A Tutorial Approach textbook has been written to help the users who are interested in learning 3D design and basics of FEA. This textbook has been written with the tutorial point of view and the learn-by-doing theme to help the users who are interested in learning 3D design and basics of FEA. Real-world mechanical engineering industry examples and tutorials have been used to ensure that the users can relate the knowledge of this book with the actual mechanical industry designs. The main features of the book are as follows:

- **Tutorial Approach**
  The author has adopted the tutorial point-of-view and the learn-by-doing approach throughout the book. This approach guides the users through the process of creating the models in the tutorials.

- **Real-world Mechanical Engineering Projects as Tutorials**
  The author has used the real-world mechanical engineering projects as tutorials in this textbook so that the readers can correlate the tutorials with the real-time models in the mechanical engineering industry.

- **Coverage of Major SOLIDWORKS Modes**
  All major modes of SOLIDWORKS are covered in this book. These include the **Part** mode, the **Assembly** mode, and the **Drawing** mode.

- **Tips and Notes**
  Additional information related to various topics is provided to the users in the form of tips and notes.

- **Learning Objectives**
  The first page of every chapter summarizes the topics that are covered in the chapter.

- **Self-Evaluation Test, Review Questions, and Exercises**
  Each chapter ends with Self-Evaluation Test that enables the users to assess their knowledge of the chapter. The answers to Self-Evaluation Test are given at the end of the chapter. Also, the Review Questions and Exercises are given at the end of each chapter and they can be used by the instructors as test questions and exercises.

Symbols Used in this Textbook

Note

The author has provided additional information to the users about the topic being discussed in the form of Notes.

Tip

Special information on various techniques is provided in the form of Tips that will increase the efficiency of the users.

Formatting Conventions Used in the Textbook

Please refer to the following list for the formatting conventions used in this book.

- Names of tools, buttons, options, toolbars, and are written in boldface. Example: The **Extrude Boss/Base** tool, the **Mid-Plane** option, the **OK** button, the **Features** toolbar, and so on.

- Names of CommandManager, PropertyManager, rollouts, dialog box, drop-down lists, spinners, selection boxes, areas, edit boxes, check boxes, and radio buttons are written in boldface. Example: The **Features CommandManager**, the **Boss-Extrude PropertyManager**, the **Open** dialog box, the **End Condition** drop-down list, the **Depth** spinner, the **Direction of Extrusion** selection box, the **Draft outward** check box, and so on.

- Values entered in edit boxes are written in boldface. Example: Enter **5** in the **Radius** edit box.

- Names and paths of the files are written in italics. Example: *C:\Documents\SOLIDWORKS\c08\c08_tut01* and so on

Naming Conventions Used in the Textbook

Tool

If you click on an item in a toolbar and a command is invoked to create/edit an object or perform some action, then that item is termed as tool.

For example:
To Create: **Line** tool, **Smart Dimension** tool, **Extruded Boss/Base** tool
To Modify: **Fillet** tool, **Draft** tool, **Trim Surface** tool
Action: **Zoom to Fit** tool, **Pan** tool, **Copy** tool

If you click on an item in a toolbar and a dialog box is invoked wherein you can set the properties to create/edit an object, then that item is also termed as tool, refer to Figure 1.

For example:
To Create: Extruded Boss/Base tool, **Mirror** tool, **Rib** tool
To Modify: Flex tool, **Deform** tool

In this book, the path to invoke a tool is given as:

CommandManager:	Features > Extruded Boss/Base
SOLIDWORKS Menus:	Insert > Boss/Base > Extrude
Toolbar:	Features > Extruded Boss/Base

Flyout

A flyout is the one in which a set of tools are grouped together. You can identify a flyout with a down arrow on it. A flyout is given a name based on the types of tools grouped in it. For example, **Line** flyout, **View Settings** flyout, **Fillet** flyout, and so on; refer to Figure 1.

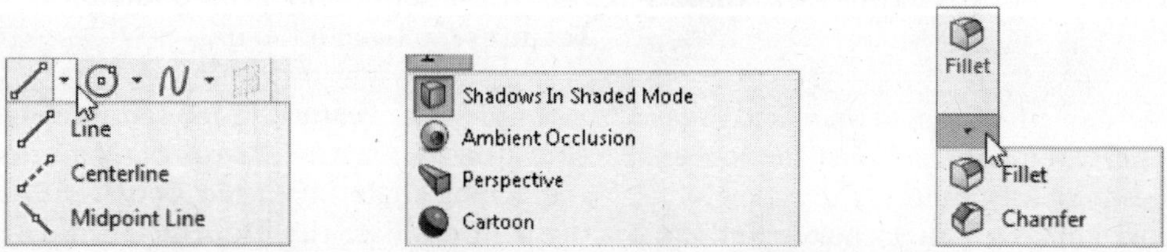

*Figure 1 The **Line**, **View Settings**, and **Fillet** flyouts*

PropertyManager

The naming conventions for the components in a PropertyManager are mentioned in Figure 2.

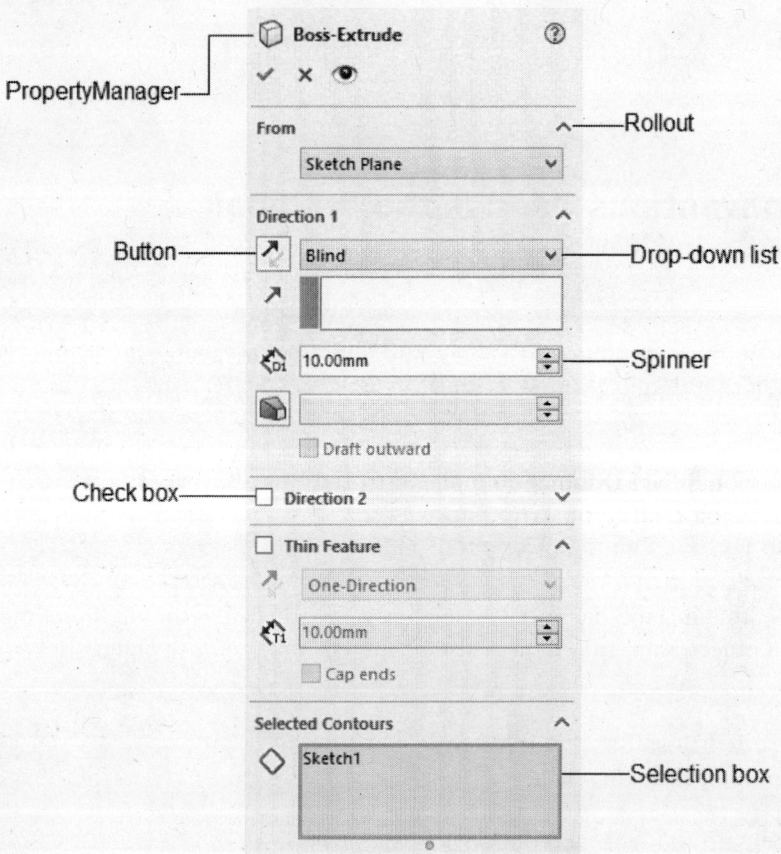

*Figure 2 The **Boss-Extrude PropertyManager***

Button

The items in a dialog box that has a 3D shape like a button is termed as **Button**. For example, **OK** button, **Cancel** button, and so on.

Free Companion Website

It has been our constant endeavor to provide you the best textbooks and services at affordable price. In this endeavor, we have come out with a Free Companion website that will facilitate the process of teaching and learning of SOLIDWORKS 2018. If you purchase this book, you will get access to the files on the Companion website.

The following resources are available for the faculty and students in this website:

Faculty Resources

- **Technical Support**
  You can get online technical support by contacting ***techsupport@cadcim.com***.

- **Instructor Guide**
  Solutions to all review questions and exercises in the book are provided in the instructor guide to help the faculty members test the skills of the students.

- **PowerPoint Presentations**
  The contents of the book are arranged in PowerPoint slides that can be used by the faculty for their lectures.

- **Part Files**
  The part files used in illustrations, examples, and exercises are available for free download.

Student Resources

- **Technical Support**
  You can get online technical support by contacting ***techsupport@cadcim.com***.

- **Part Files**
  The part files used in illustrations and examples are available for free download.

- **Additional Students Projects**
  Various projects are provided for the students to practice.

If you face any problem in accessing these files, please contact the publisher at ***sales@cadcim.com*** or the author at ***stickoo@pnw.edu*** or ***tickoo525@gmail.com***.

Stay Connected

You can now stay connected with us through Facebook and Twitter to get the latest information about our textbooks, videos, and teaching/learning resources. To stay informed of such updates, follow us on Facebook ***(www.facebook.com/cadcim)*** and Twitter (***@cadcimtech***). You can also subscribe to our YouTube channel ***(www.youtube.com/cadcimtech)*** to get the information about our latest video tutorials.

This page is intentionally left blank

Chapter 1

Introduction to SOLIDWORKS 2018

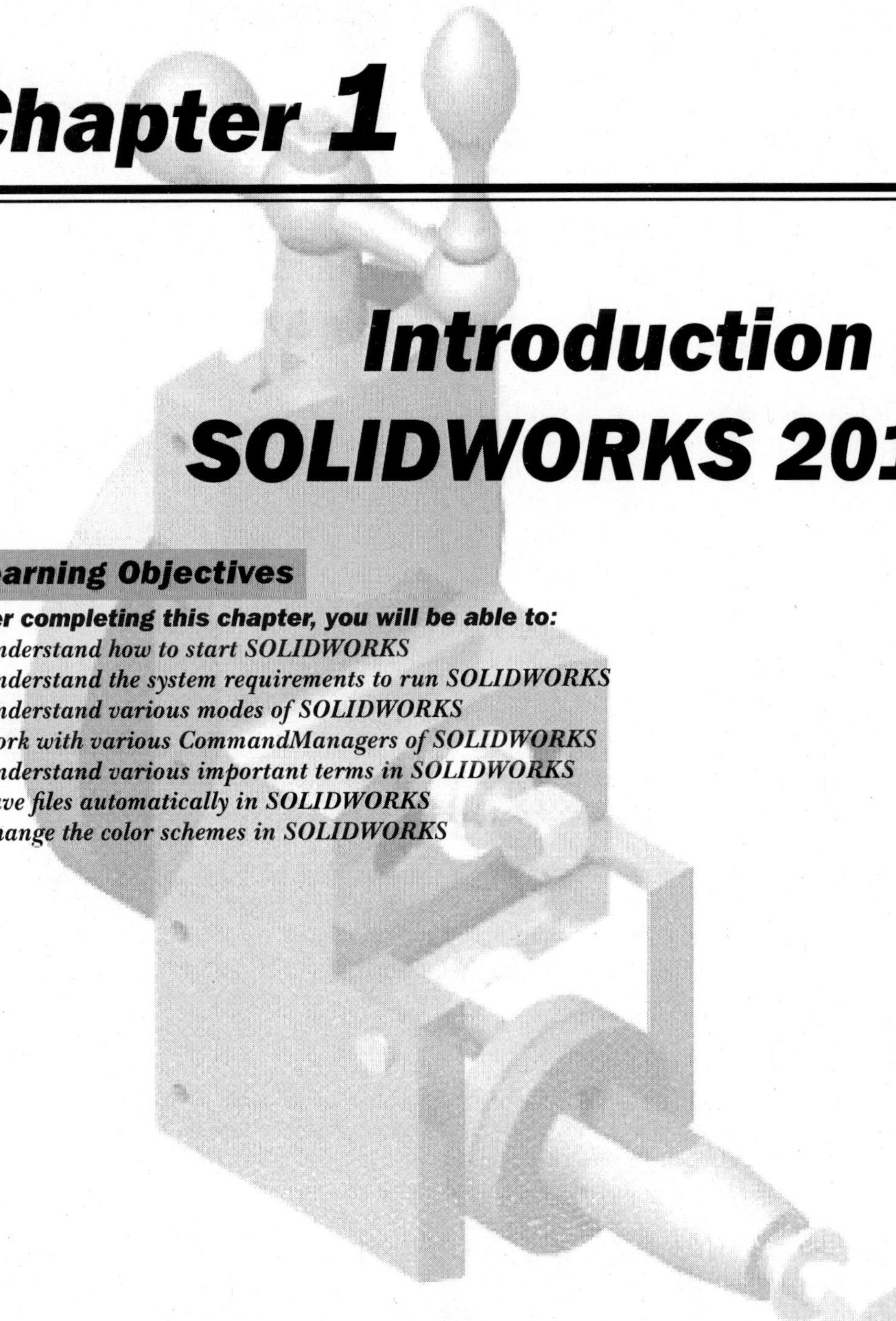

Learning Objectives

After completing this chapter, you will be able to:

- *Understand how to start SOLIDWORKS*
- *Understand the system requirements to run SOLIDWORKS*
- *Understand various modes of SOLIDWORKS*
- *Work with various CommandManagers of SOLIDWORKS*
- *Understand various important terms in SOLIDWORKS*
- *Save files automatically in SOLIDWORKS*
- *Change the color schemes in SOLIDWORKS*

INTRODUCTION TO SOLIDWORKS 2018

Welcome to the world of Computer Aided Design (CAD) with SOLIDWORKS. If you are a new user of this software package, you will be joining hands with thousands of users of this parametric, feature-based, and one of the most user-friendly software packages. If you are familiar with the previous releases of this software, you will be able to upgrade your designing skills with this improved release of SOLIDWORKS.

SOLIDWORKS, developed by the SOLIDWORKS Corporation, USA, is a feature-based, parametric solid-modeling mechanical design and automation software. SOLIDWORKS is the first CAD package to use the Microsoft Windows graphic user interface. The use of the drag and drop (DD) functionality of Windows makes this CAD package extremely easy to learn. The Windows graphic user interface makes it possible for the mechanical design engineers to innovate their ideas and implement them in the form of virtual prototypes or solid models, large assemblies, subassemblies, and detailing and drafting.

SOLIDWORKS is one of the products of SOLIDWORKS Corporation, which is a part of Dassault Systemes. SOLIDWORKS also works as platform software for a number of software. This implies that you can also use other compatible software within the SOLIDWORKS window. There are a number of software provided by the SOLIDWORKS Corporation, which can be used as add-ins with SOLIDWORKS. Some of the software that can be used on SOLIDWORKS's work platform are listed below:

SOLIDWORKS Motion	SOLIDWORKS Routing	ScanTo3D	eDrawings
SOLIDWORKS Simulation	SOLIDWORKS Toolbox	PhotoView 360	CircuitWorks
SOLIDWORKS Plastics	SOLIDWORKS Inspection	TolAnalyst	

As mentioned earlier, SOLIDWORKS is a parametric, feature-based, and easy-to-use mechanical design automation software. It enables you to convert the basic 2D sketch into a solid model by using simple but highly effective modeling tools. It also enables you to create the virtual prototype of a sheet metal component and the flat pattern of the component. This helps you in the complete process planning for designing and creating a press tool. SOLIDWORKS helps you to extract the core and the cavity of a model that has to be molded or cast. With SOLIDWORKS, you can also create complex parametric shapes in the form of surfaces. Some of the important modes of SOLIDWORKS are discussed next.

Part Mode

The **Part** mode of SOLIDWORKS is a feature-based parametric environment in which you can create solid models. In this mode, you are provided with three default planes named as **Front Plane**, **Top Plane**, and **Right Plane**. First, you need to select a sketching plane to create a sketch for the base feature. On selecting a sketching plane, you enter the sketching environment. The sketches for the model are drawn in the sketching environment using easy-to-use tools. After drawing the sketches, you can dimension them and apply the required relations in the same sketching environment. The design intent is captured easily by adding relations and equations and using the design table in the design. You are provided with the standard hole library known as the **Hole Wizard** in the **Part** mode. You can create simple holes, tapped holes, counterbore holes, countersink holes, and so on by using this wizard. The holes can be of any standard such as ISO, ANSI, JIS, and so on. You can also create complicated surfaces by using the surface modeling tools available in the **Part** mode. Annotations such as weld symbols, geometric tolerance, datum references, and surface finish symbols can be added to the model within the **Part** mode. The standard features that are used frequently can be saved as library features and retrieved when needed. The palette feature library of SOLIDWORKS contains a number of standard mechanical parts and features. You can also create the sheet metal components in this mode of SOLIDWORKS by using the related tools. Besides this, you can also analyze the part model for various stresses applied to it in the real physical conditions by using an easy and user-friendly tool called SimulationXpress. It helps you reduce the cost and time in physically testing your design in real testing conditions (destructive tests). You can also analyze the component during modeling in the SOLIDWORKS windows. In addition, you can work with the weld modeling within the **Part** mode of SOLIDWORKS by creating steel structures and adding weld beads. All standard weld types and welding conditions are available for your reference. You can extract the core and the cavity in the **Part** mode by using the mold design tools.

Assembly Mode

In the **Assembly** mode, you can assemble components of the assembly with the help of the required tools. There are two methods of assembling the components:

1. Bottom-up assembly
2. Top-down assembly

In the bottom-up assembly method, the assembly is created by assembling the components created earlier and maintaining their design intent. In the top-down method, the components are created in the assembly mode. You may begin with some ready-made parts and then create other components in the context of the assembly. You can refer to the features of some components of the assembly to drive the dimensions of other components. You can assemble all components of an assembly by using a single tool, the **Mate** tool. While assembling the components of an assembly, you can also animate the assembly by dragging. Besides this, you can also check the working of your assembly. Collision detection is one of the important features in this mode. Using this feature, you can rotate and move components as well as detect the interference and collision between the assembled components. You can see the realistic motion of the assembly by using physical dynamics. Physical simulation is used to simulate the assembly with the effects of motors, springs, and gravity on the assemblies.

Drawing Mode

The **Drawing** mode is used for the documentation of the parts or the assemblies created earlier in the form of drawing views. The procedure for creating drawing views is called drafting. There are two types of drafting done in SOLIDWORKS:

1. Generative drafting
2. Interactive drafting

Generative drafting is a process of generating drawing views of a part or an assembly created earlier. The parametric dimensions and the annotations added to the component in the **Part** mode can be generated in the drawing views. Generative drafting is bidirectionally associative in nature. Automatic BOMs and balloons can be added to an assembly while generating the drawing views of it.

In interactive drafting, you have to create the drawing views by sketching them using normal sketching tools and then add dimensions to them.

SYSTEM REQUIREMENTS

The system requirements to ensure the smooth functioning of SOLIDWORKS on your system are as follows:

- Microsoft Windows 10, Windows 8.1 or Windows 8 (64 bit only) or Windows 7 (SP1 required).
- Intel or AMD Processor with SSE2 support.
- 2 GB RAM minimum (8 GB recommended).
- Hard disk space 5 GB minimum (10 GB recommended).
- A certified graphics card and driver.
- Microsoft Office 2007 or later.
- Adobe Acrobat higher than 8.0.7.
- DVD drive and Mouse or any other compatible pointing device.
- Internet Explorer version 8 or higher.

GETTING STARTED WITH SOLIDWORKS

Install SOLIDWORKS 2018 on your system; the shortcut icon of SOLIDWORKS 2018 will automatically be created on the desktop. Double-click on this icon; the system will prepare to start SOLIDWORKS and after sometime, the SOLIDWORKS window will be displayed on the screen. On opening SOLIDWORKS for the first time, the **SOLIDWORKS License Agreement** dialog box will be displayed, as shown in Figure 1-1. Choose the **Accept** button in this dialog box; the SOLIDWORKS 2018 interface window will open and the **SOLIDWORKS Resources** task pane will be displayed on the right. Also, the **Welcome - SOLIDWORKS 2018** dialog box is invoked simultaneously, as shown in Figure 1-2. This window can be used to open a new file or an existing file.

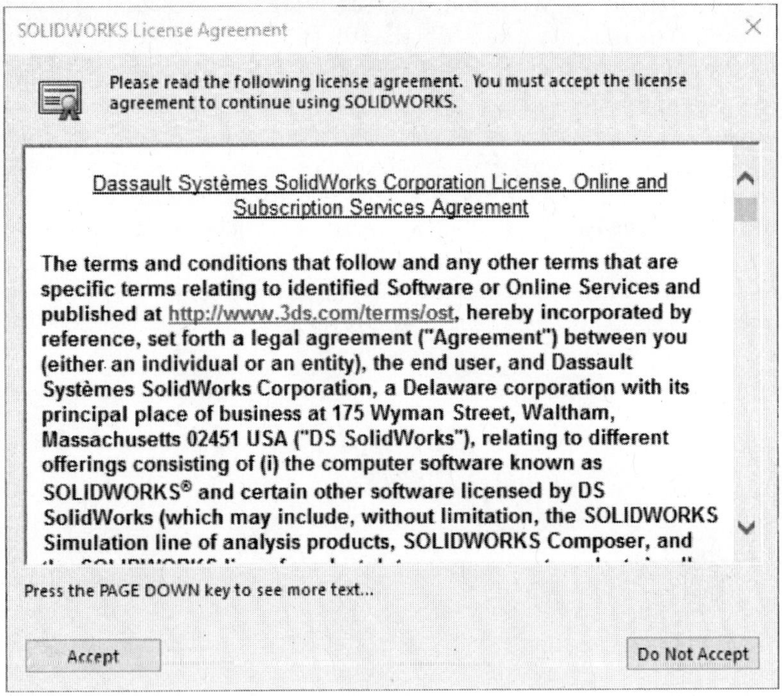

***Figure 1-1** The **SOLIDWORKS License Agreement** dialog box*

***Figure 1-2** The SOLIDWORKS 2018 window and the **SOLIDWORKS Resources** task pane*

If the **SOLIDWORKS Resources** task pane is not displayed or expanded, choose the **SOLIDWORKS Resources** button located on the right side of the window to display it. This task pane can be used to open online tutorials and to visit the website of SOLIDWORKS partners. Choose the **Part** button from the **Welcome - SOLIDWORKS 2018** dialog box or the **New** button from the Menu Bar to create a new document. If you start a new document using the **New** button from the Menu Bar then the **New SOLIDWORKS Document** dialog box will be displayed, as shown in Figure 1-3.

Note

If you are starting SOLIDWORKS 2018 for the first time, then on invoking the ***New SOLIDWORKS Document*** *dialog box, the* ***Units and Dimension Standard*** *dialog box will be displayed, as shown in Figure 1-4. Using this dialog box, you can specify the default units and dimension standards for SOLIDWORKS. In this book, the unit system used is MMGS (millimeter, gram, second) and the dimension standard used is ISO.*

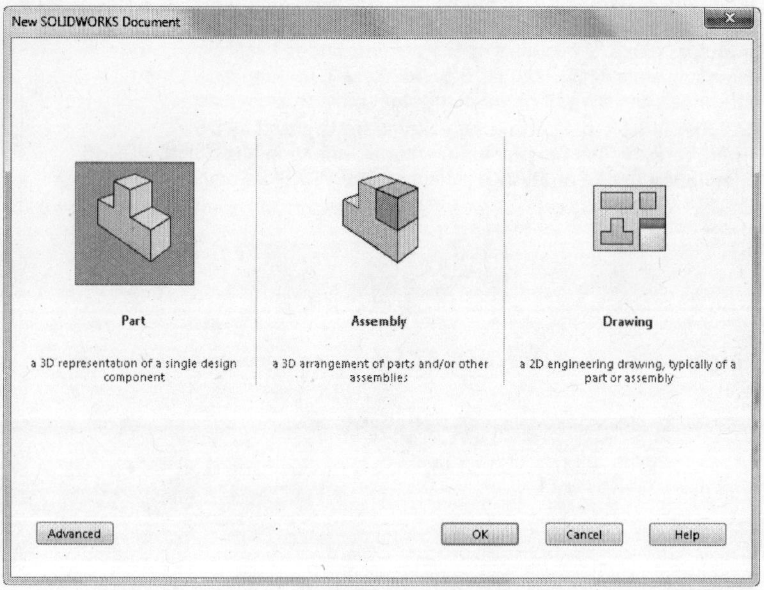

Figure 1-3 *The* ***New SOLIDWORKS Document*** *dialog box*

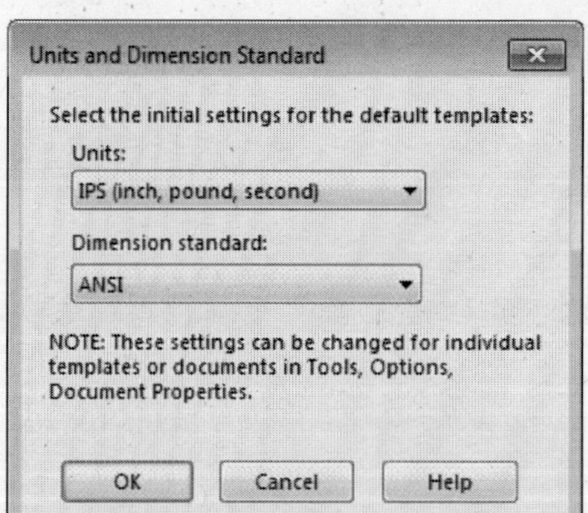

Figure 1-4 *The* ***Units and Dimension Standard*** *dialog box*

Choose the **Part** button to create a part model and then choose **OK** from the **New SOLIDWORKS Document** dialog box to enter the **Part** mode of SOLIDWORKS. Move the cursor to the arrow on the right of the SOLIDWORKS logo; the SOLIDWORKS menus will be displayed. Note that the task pane is automatically closed once you start a new file and click in the drawing area. The initial screen display on starting a new part file of SOLIDWORKS using the **New** button in the Menu Bar is shown in Figure 1-5.

Tip

*In SOLIDWORKS, the tip of the day is displayed at the bottom of the task pane. You can choose **Next Tip** to view additional tips. These tips help you use SOLIDWORKS efficiently. It is recommended that you view at least 2 or 3 tips every time you start a new session of SOLIDWORKS 2018.*

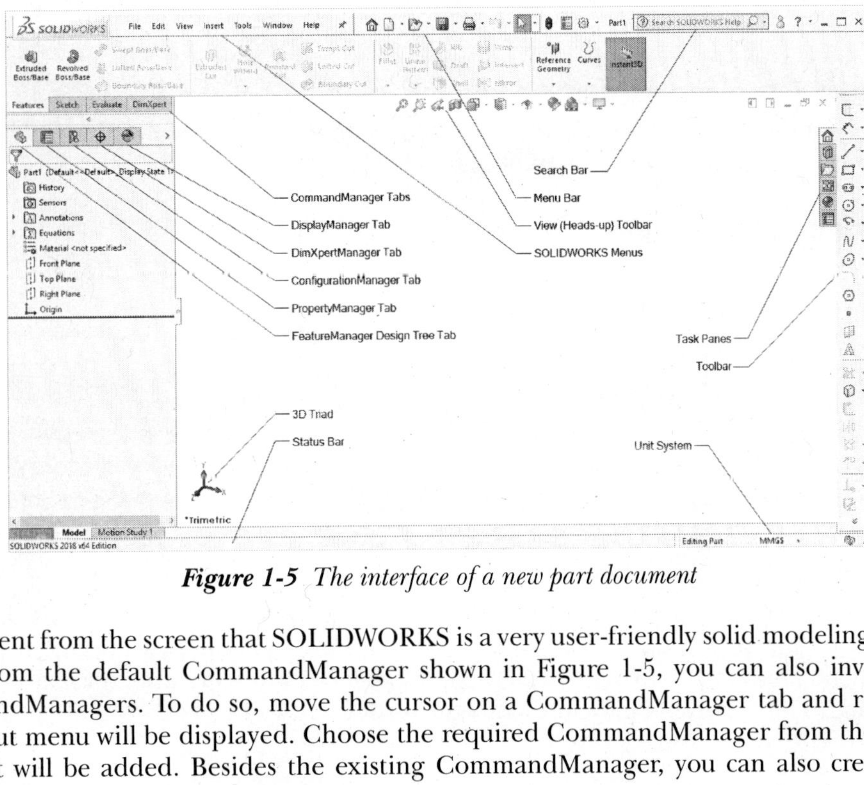

***Figure 1-5** The interface of a new part document*

It is evident from the screen that SOLIDWORKS is a very user-friendly solid modeling software. Apart from the default CommandManager shown in Figure 1-5, you can also invoke other CommandManagers. To do so, move the cursor on a CommandManager tab and right-click; a shortcut menu will be displayed. Choose the required CommandManager from the shortcut menu; it will be added. Besides the existing CommandManager, you can also create a new CommandManager.

MENU BAR AND SOLIDWORKS MENUS

In SOLIDWORKS, the display area of the screen has been increased by grouping the tools that have similar functions or purposes. The tools that are in the **Standard** toolbar are also available in the Menu Bar, as shown in Figure 1-6. This toolbar is available above the drawing area. When you move the cursor to the arrow on the right of the SOLIDWORKS logo, the SOLIDWORKS menus will be displayed, as shown in Figure 1-7. You can also fix them by choosing the push-pin button.

Figure 1-6 The Menu Bar

Figure 1-7 The SOLIDWORKS menus

CommandManager

You can invoke a tool in SOLIDWORKS from four locations, CommandManager, SOLIDWORKS menus on top of the screen, toolbar, and shortcut menu. The CommandManagers are docked above the drawing area. While working with CommandManager, you will realize that invoking a tool from the CommandManager is the most convenient method to invoke a tool. Different types of CommandManagers are used for different design environments. These CommandManagers are discussed next.

Part Mode CommandManagers

A number of CommandManagers can be invoked in the **Part** mode. The CommandManagers that are extensively used during the designing process in this environment are described next.

Sketch CommandManager

This CommandManager is used to enter and exit the 2D and 3D sketching environments. The tools available in this CommandManager are used to draw sketches for features. This CommandManager is also used to add relations and smart dimensions to the sketched entities. The **Sketch CommandManager** is shown in Figure 1-8.

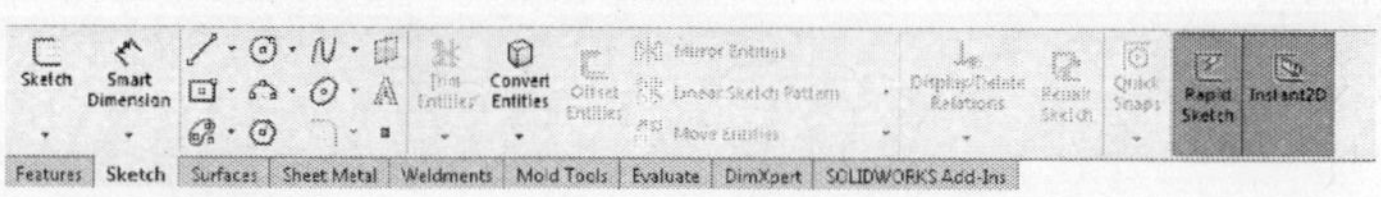

*Figure 1-8 The **Sketch CommandManager***

Features CommandManager

This is one of the most important CommandManagers provided in the **Part** mode. Once the sketch has been drawn, you need to convert the sketch into a feature by using the modeling tools. This CommandManager contains all the modeling tools that are used for feature-based solid modeling. The **Features CommandManager** is shown in Figure 1-9.

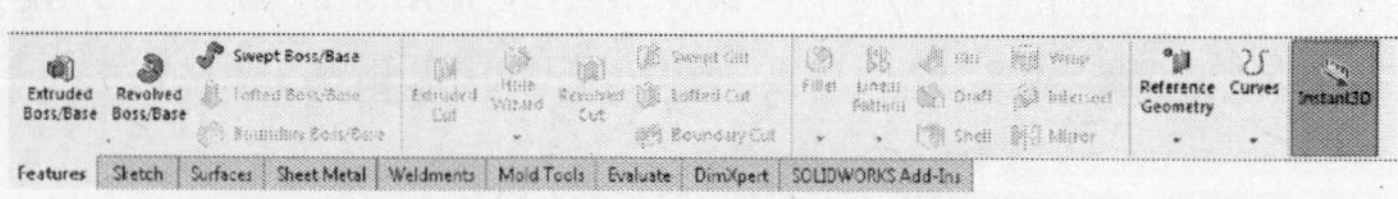

*Figure 1-9 The **Features CommandManager***

DimXpert CommandManager

This CommandManager is used to add dimensions and tolerances to the features of a part. The **DimXpert CommandManager** is shown in Figure 1-10.

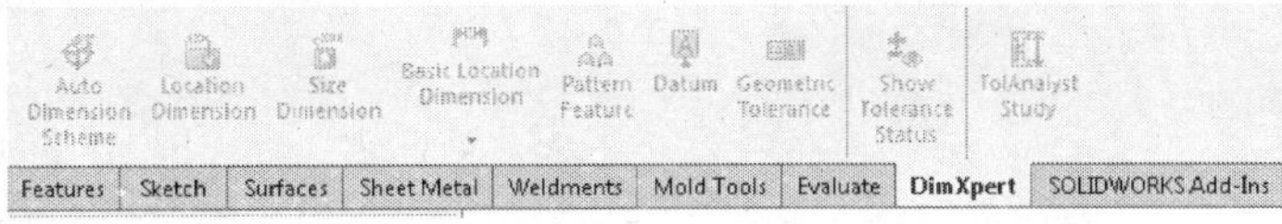

*Figure 1-10 The **DimXpert CommandManager***

Sheet Metal CommandManager

This CommandManager provides you the tools that are used to create the sheet metal parts. In SOLIDWORKS, you can also create sheet metal parts while working in the **Part** mode. This is done with the help of the **Sheet Metal CommandManager** shown in Figure 1-11.

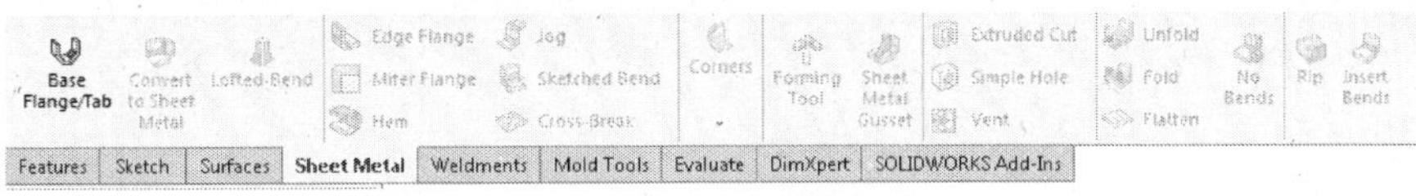

*Figure 1-11 The **Sheet Metal CommandManager***

Mold Tools CommandManager

The tools in this CommandManager are used to design a mold and to extract its core and cavity. The **Mold Tools CommandManager** is shown in Figure 1-12.

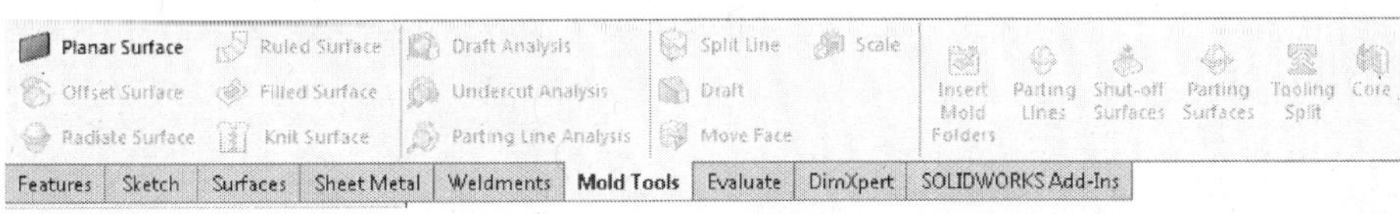

*Figure 1-12 The **Mold Tools CommandManager***

Evaluate CommandManager

This CommandManager is used to measure the distance between two entities, add equations in the design, calculate the mass properties of a solid model, and so on. The **Evaluate CommandManager** is shown in Figure 1-13.

*Figure 1-13 The **Evaluate CommandManager***

Surfaces CommandManager

This CommandManager is used to create complicated surface features. These surface features can be converted into solid features. The **Surfaces CommandManager** is shown in Figure 1-14.

*Figure 1-14 The **Surfaces CommandManager***

Direct Editing CommandManager

This CommandManager consists of tools (Figure 1-15) that are used for editing a feature.

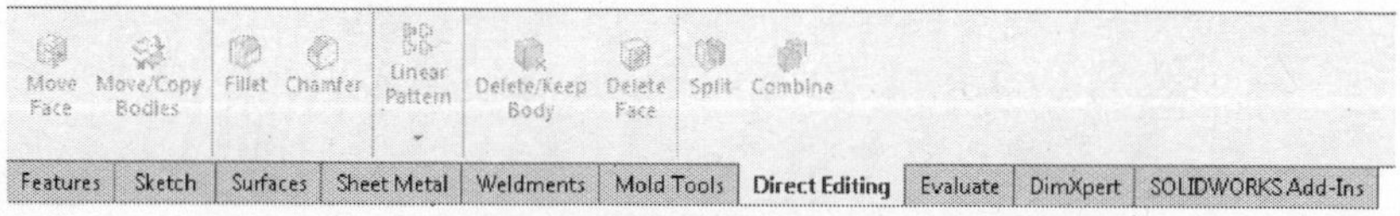

Figure 1-15** The **Direct Editing CommandManager

Data Migration CommandManager

This CommandManager consists of tools (Figure 1-16) that are used to work with the models created in other packages or in different environments.

Figure 1-16** The **Data Migration CommandManager

Assembly Mode CommandManagers

The CommandManagers in the **Assembly** mode are used to assemble the components, create an explode line sketch, and simulate the assembly. The CommandManagers in the **Assembly** mode are discussed next.

Assembly CommandManager

This CommandManager is used to insert a component and apply various types of mates to the assembly. Mates are the constraints that can be applied to components to restrict their degrees of freedom. You can also move and rotate a component in the assembly, change the hidden and suppression states of the assembly and individual components, edit the component of an assembly, and so on. The **Assembly CommandManager** is shown in Figure 1-17.

Figure 1-17** The **Assembly CommandManager

Layout CommandManager

The tools in this CommandManager (Figure 1-18) are used to create and edit blocks.

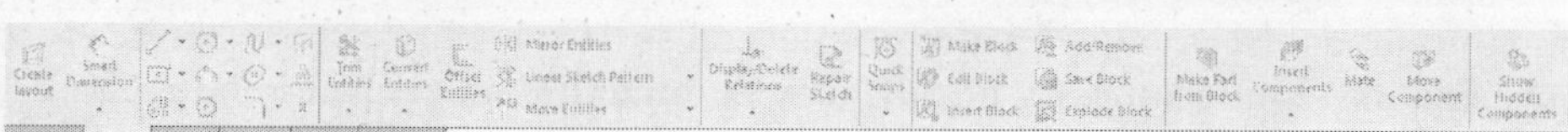

Figure 1-18** The **Layout CommandManager

Drawing Mode CommandManagers

You can invoke a number of CommandManagers in the **Drawing** mode. The CommandManagers that are extensively used during the designing process in this mode are discussed next.

View Layout CommandManager

This CommandManager is used to generate the drawing views of an existing model or an assembly. The views that can be generated using this CommandManager are model view, three standard views, projected view, section view, aligned section view, detail view, crop view, relative view, auxiliary view, and so on. The **View Layout CommandManager** is shown in Figure 1-19.

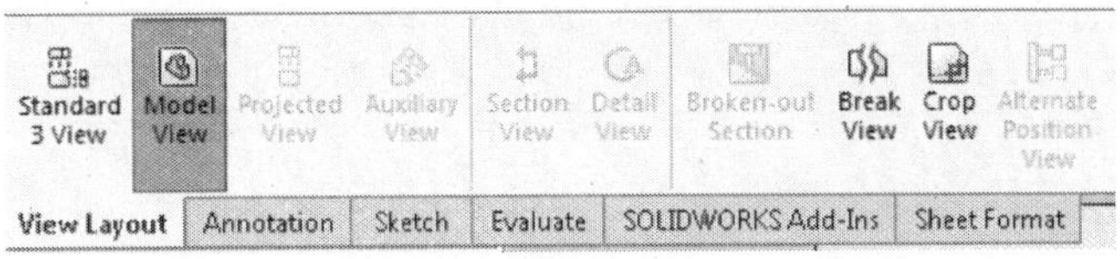

***Figure 1-19** The View Layout CommandManager*

Annotation CommandManager

The **Annotation CommandManager** is used to generate the model items and to add notes, balloons, geometric tolerance, surface finish symbols, and so on to the drawing views. The **Annotation CommandManager** is shown in Figure 1-20.

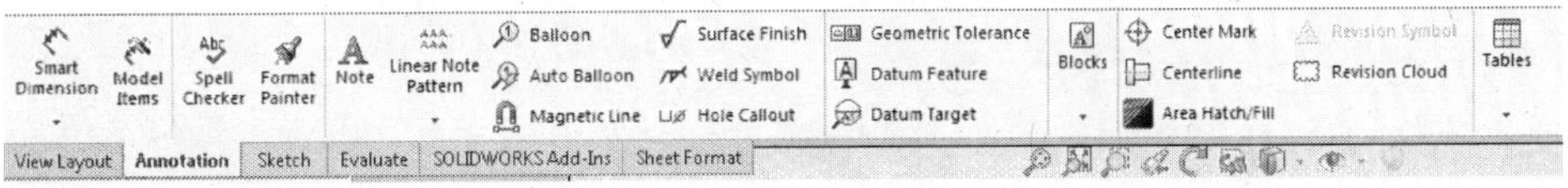

***Figure 1-20** The Annotation CommandManager*

Customized CommandManager

If you often work on a particular set of tools, you can create a customized CommandManager to cater to your needs. To do so, right-click on a tab in the CommandManager; a shortcut menu will be displayed. Choose the **Customize CommandManager** option from the shortcut menu; the **Customize** dialog box will be displayed. Also, a new tab will be added to the CommandManager. Click on this tab; a flyout will be displayed with **Empty Tab** as the first option and followed by the list of toolbars. Choose the **Empty Tab** option; another tab named **New Tab** will be added to the CommandManager. Rename the new tab. Next, choose the **Commands** tab from the **Customize** dialog box. Select a command from the **Categories** list box; the tools of the corresponding command will be displayed in the **Buttons** area. Select a tool, press and hold the left mouse button, and drag the tool to the customized CommandManager; the tool will be added to the customized CommandManager. Choose **OK** from the **Customize** dialog box.

To add all the tools of a toolbar to the new CommandManager, invoke the **Customize** dialog box and click on the new tab; a flyout will be displayed with **Empty Tab** as the first option followed by the list of toolbars. Choose a toolbar from the flyout; all tools in the toolbar will be added to the **New Tab** and its name will be changed to that of the toolbar.

To delete a customized CommandManager, invoke the **Customize** dialog box as discussed earlier. Next, choose the CommandManager tab to be deleted and right-click; a shortcut menu will be displayed. Choose the **Delete** option from the shortcut menu; the CommandManager will be deleted.

TOOLBAR

In SOLIDWORKS, you can choose most of the tools from the CommandManager or from the SOLIDWORKS menus. However, if you hide the CommandManager to increase the drawing area, you can use the toolbars to invoke a tool. To display a toolbar, right-click on a CommandManager; the list of toolbars available in SOLIDWORKS will be displayed. Select the required toolbar.

Pop-up Toolbar

A pop-up toolbar will be displayed when you select a feature or an entity and do not move the mouse. Figure 1-21 shows a pop-up toolbar displayed on selecting a feature. Remember that this toolbar will disappear if you move the cursor away from the selected feature or entity.

Figure 1-21 *The pop-up toolbar*

You can switch off the display of the pop-up toolbar. To do so, invoke the **Customize** dialog box. In the **Context toolbar Settings** area in the **Toolbars** tab, the **Show on selection** check box will be selected by default. It means that the display of the pop-up toolbar is on, by default. To turn off the display of the pop-up toolbar, clear this check box and choose the **OK** button.

View (Heads-Up) Toolbar

In SOLIDWORKS, some of the display tools have been grouped together and are displayed in the drawing area in a toolbar, as shown in Figure 1-22. This toolbar is known as **View (Heads-Up)** toolbar.

Figure 1-22 *The* ***View (Heads-Up)*** *toolbar*

Customizing the CommandManagers and Toolbars

In SOLIDWORKS, all buttons are not displayed by default in toolbars or CommandManagers. You need to customize and add buttons to them according to your need and specifications. Follow the procedure given below to customize the CommandManagers and toolbars:

1. Choose **Tools > Customize** from the SOLIDWORKS menus or right-click on a CommandManager and choose the **Customize** option to display the **Customize** dialog box.
2. Choose the **Commands** tab from the **Customize** dialog box.
3. Select a name of the toolbar from the **Categories** area of the **Customize** dialog box; the tools available in the toolbars will be displayed in the **Buttons** area.
4. Click on a button in the **Buttons** area; the description of the selected button will be displayed in the **Description** area.
5. Press and hold the left mouse button on a button in the **Buttons** area of the **Customize** dialog box.

6. Drag the mouse to a CommandManager or a toolbar and then release the left mouse button to place the button on that CommandManager or toolbar. Next, choose **OK**.

To remove a tool from the CommandManager or toolbar, invoke the **Customize** dialog box and drag the tool that you need to remove from the CommandManager to the graphics area.

Shortcut Bar

On pressing the S key on the keyboard, some of the tools that can be used in the current mode will be displayed near the cursor. This is called as shortcut bar. To customize the tools in the shortcut bar, right-click on it, and choose the **Customize** option. Then, follow the procedure discussed earlier.

Mouse Gestures

In SOLIDWORKS, when you press the right mouse button and drag the cursor in any direction, a set of tools that are arranged radially will be displayed. This is called as Mouse Gesture. After displaying the tools by using the Mouse Gesture, move the cursor over a particular tool to invoke it. By default, four tools will be displayed in a Mouse Gesture. However, you can customize the Mouse Gesture and display 2, 3, 4, 8, or 12 tools. To customize a Mouse Gesture, invoke the **Customize** dialog box and choose the **Mouse Gestures** tab; the **Mouse Gesture Guide** window will be displayed, showing various tools that are used in different environments, refer to Figure 1-23. Now you can drag and drop the required tools to this window. Next, specify the options in the appropriate field and choose the **OK** button.

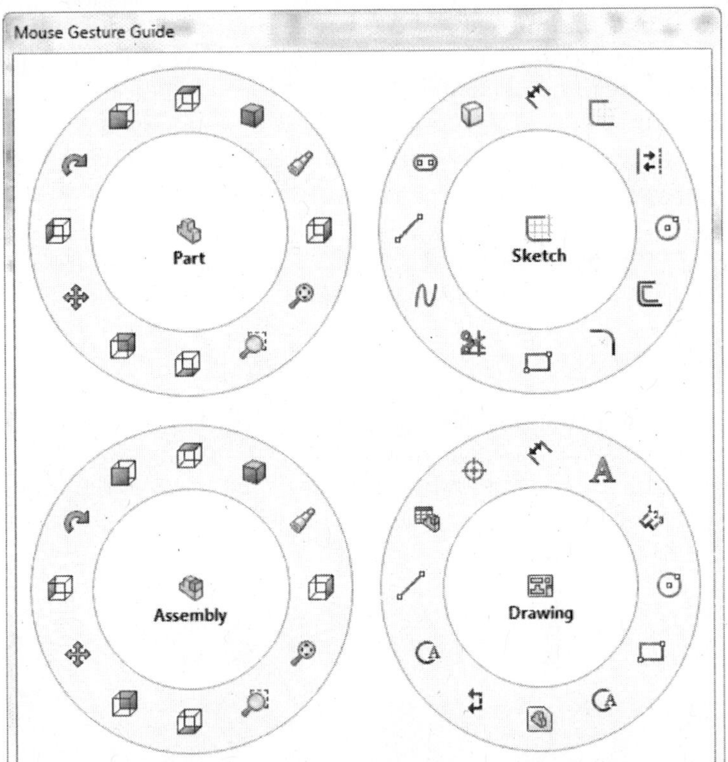

Figure 1-23 *Tools displayed by using Mouse Gesture in different environment*

Tip

*You can display some of the tools by pressing a key on the keyboard. To assign a shortcut key to a tool, invoke the **Customize** dialog box and choose the **Keyboard** tab. Enter the key in the **Shortcut** column for the corresponding tool and choose **OK**.*

DIMENSIONING STANDARDS AND UNITS

While installing SOLIDWORKS on your system, you can specify the units and dimensioning standards for dimensioning the model. There are various dimensioning standards such as ANSI, ISO, DIN, JIS, BSI, and GOST that can be specified for dimensioning a model and units such as millimeters, centimeters, inches, and so on. This book follows millimeters as the unit for dimensioning and ISO as the dimension standard. Therefore, it is recommended that you install SOLIDWORKS with ISO as the dimensioning standard and millimeter as units.

IMPORTANT TERMS AND THEIR DEFINITIONS

Before you proceed, it is very important to understand the following terms as they have been widely used in this book.

Feature-based Modeling

A feature is defined as the smallest building block that can be modified individually. In SOLIDWORKS, the solid models are created by integrating a number of these building blocks. A model created in SOLIDWORKS is a combination of a number of individual features that are related to one another, directly or indirectly. These features understand their fits and functions properly and therefore can be modified at any time during the design process. If proper design intent is maintained while creating the model, these features automatically adjust their values to any change in their surrounding. This provides greater flexibility to the design.

Parametric Modeling

The parametric nature of a software package is defined as its ability to use the standard properties or parameters in defining the shape and size of a geometry. The main function of this property is to drive the selected geometry to a new size or shape without considering its original dimensions. You can change or modify the shape and size of any feature at any stage of the design process. This property makes the designing process very easy.

For example, consider the design of the body of a pipe housing shown in Figure 1-24. In order to change the design by modifying the diameter of the holes and the number of holes on the front, top, and bottom faces, you need to select the feature and change the diameter and the number of instances in the pattern. The modified design is shown in Figure 1-25.

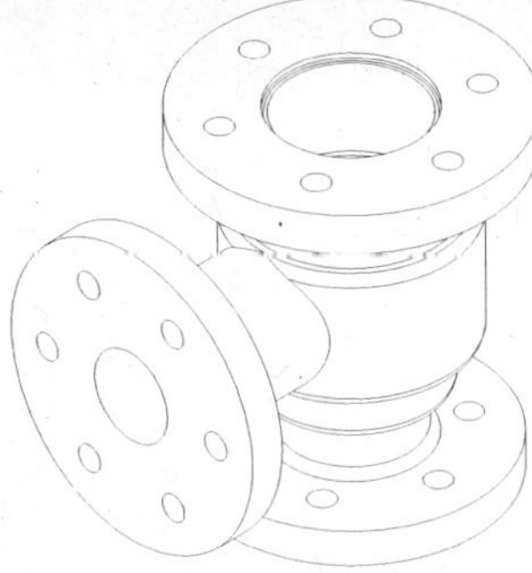

Figure 1-24 Body of pipe housing

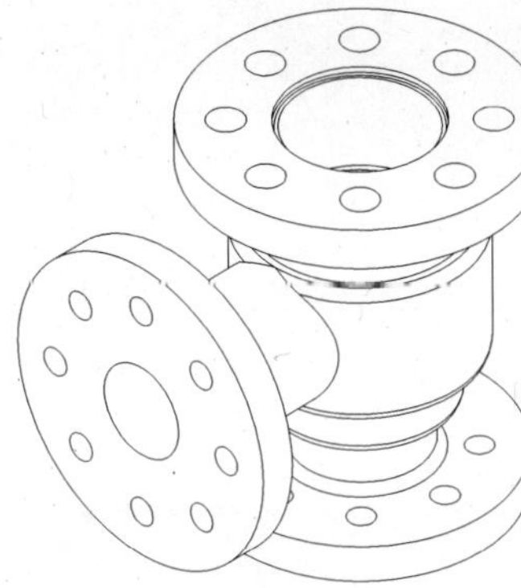

Figure 1-25 Design after modifications

Bidirectional Associativity

As mentioned earlier, SOLIDWORKS has different modes such as **Part**, **Assembly**, and **Drawing**. There exists bidirectional associativity among all these modes. This associativity ensures that any modification made in the model in any one of these modes of SOLIDWORKS is automatically reflected in the other modes immediately. For example, if you modify the dimension of a part in the **Part** mode, the change will reflect in the **Assembly** and **Drawing** modes as well. Similarly, if you modify the dimensions of a part in the drawing views generated in the **Drawing** mode, the changes will reflect in the **Part** and **Assembly** modes. Consider the drawing views shown in Figure 1-26 of the body of the pipe housing shown in Figure 1-24. Now, when you modify the model of the body of the pipe housing in the **Part** mode, the changes will reflect in the **Drawing** mode automatically. Figure 1-27 shows the drawing views of the pipe housing after increasing the diameter and the number of holes.

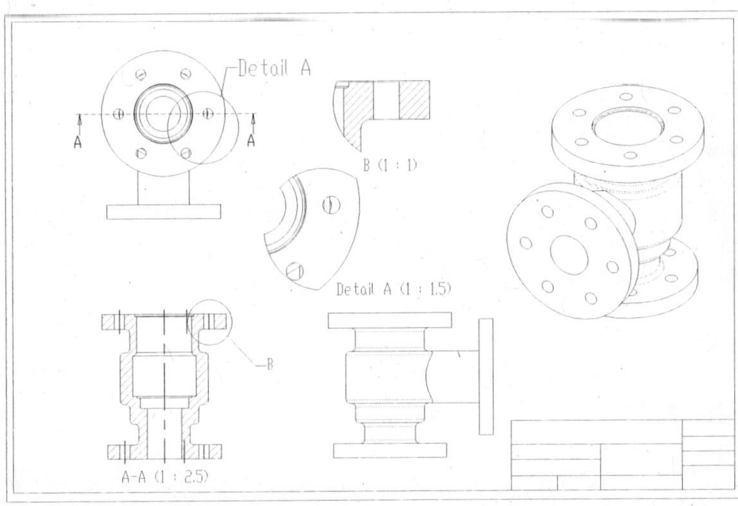

Figure 1-26 Drawing views of the body part

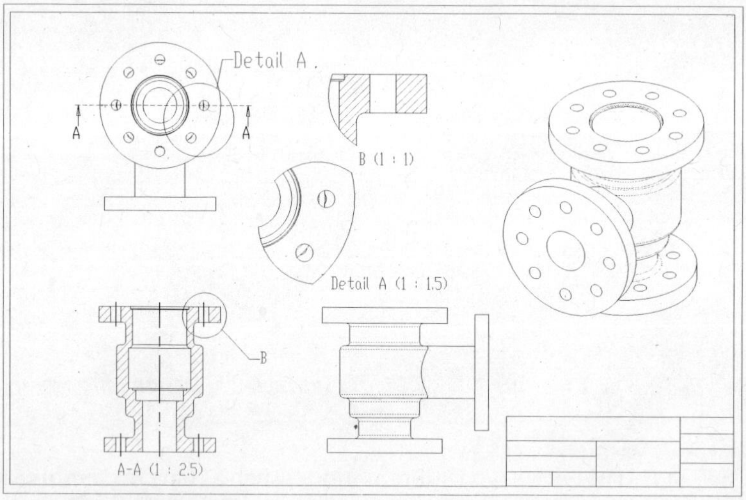

Figure 1-27 Drawing views after modifications

Windows Functionality

SOLIDWORKS is a Windows-based 3D CAD package. It uses Window's graphical user interface and the functionalities such as drag and drop, copy paste, and so on. For example, consider that you have created a hole feature on the front planar surface of a model. Now, to create another hole feature on the top planar surface of the same model, select the hole feature and press CTRL+C (copy) on the keyboard. Next, select the top planar surface of the base feature and press CTRL+V (paste); the copied hole feature will be pasted on the selected face. You can also drag and drop the standard features from the **Design Library** task pane to the face of the model on which the feature is to be added.

SWIFT Technology

SWIFT is the acronym for SOLIDWORKS Intelligent Feature Technology. This technology makes SOLIDWORKS more user-friendly. This technology helps the user think more about the design rather than the tools in the software. Therefore, even the novice users find it very easy to use SOLIDWORKS for their design. The tools that use SWIFT Technology are called as *Xperts*. The different *Xperts* in SOLIDWORKS are **SketchXpert**, **FeatureXpert**, **DimXpert**, **AssemblyXpert**, **FilletXpert**, **DraftXpert**, and **MateXpert**. The **SketchXpert** in the sketching environment is used to resolve the conflicts that arise while applying relations to a sketch. Similarly, the **FeatureXpert** in the Part mode is used when the fillet and draft features fail. You will learn about these tools in the later chapters.

Geometric Relations

Geometric relations are the logical operations that are performed to add a relationship (like tangent or perpendicular) between the sketched entities, planes, axes, edges, or vertices. When adding relations, one entity can be a sketched entity and the other entity can be a sketched entity, or an edge, face, vertex, origin, plane, and so on. There are two methods to create the geometric relations: Automatic Relations and Add Relations.

Automatic Relations

The sketching environment of SOLIDWORKS has been provided with the facility of applying auto relations. This facility ensures that the geometric relations are applied to the sketch automatically while creating it. Automatic relations are also applied in the **Drawing** mode while working with interactive drafting.

Add Relations

Add relations is used to add geometric relations manually to the sketch. The sixteen types of geometric relations that can be manually applied to the sketch are as follows:

Horizontal

This relation forces the selected line segment to become a horizontal line. You can also select two points and force them to be aligned horizontally.

Vertical

This relation forces the selected line segment to become a vertical line. You can also select two points and force them to be aligned vertically.

Collinear

This relation forces the two selected entities to be placed in the same line.

Coradial

This relation is applied to any two selected arcs, two circles, or an arc and a circle to force them to become equi-radius and also to share the same center point.

Perpendicular

This relation is used to make selected line segment perpendicular to another selected segment.

Parallel

This relation is used to make the selected line segment parallel to another selected segment.

Tangent

This relation is used to make the selected line segment, arc, spline, circle, or ellipse tangent to another arc, circle, spline, or ellipse.

Note

In case of splines, relations are applied to their control points.

Concentric

This relation forces two selected arcs, circles, a point and an arc, a point and a circle, or an arc and a circle to share the same center point.

Midpoint

This relation forces a selected point to be placed on the mid point of a selected line.

Intersection

This relation forces a selected point to be placed at the intersection of two selected entities.

Coincident
This relation is used to make two points, a point and a line, or a point and an arc coincident.

Equal
The equal relation forces the two selected lines to become equal in length. This relation is also used to force two arcs, two circles, or an arc and a circle to have equal radii.

Symmetric
The symmetric relation is used to force the selected entities to become symmetrical about a selected center line, so that they remain equidistant from the center line.

Fix
This relation is used to fix the selected entity to a particular location with respect to the coordinate system. The endpoints of the fixed line, arc, spline, or elliptical segment are free to move along the line.

Pierce
This relation forces the sketched point to be coincident to the selected axis, edge, or curve where it pierces the sketch plane. The sketched point in this relation can be the end point of the sketched entity.

Merge
This relation is used to merge two sketched points or end points of entities.

Blocks
A block is a set of entities grouped together to act as a single entity. Blocks are used to create complex mechanisms as sketches and check their functioning before developing them into complex 3D models.

Library Feature
Generally, in a mechanical design, some features are used frequently. In most of the other solid modeling tools, you need to create these features whenever you need them. However, SOLIDWORKS allows you to save these features in a library so that you can retrieve them whenever you want. This saves a lot of designing time and effort of a designer.

Design Table
Design tables are used to create a multi-instance parametric component. For example, some components in your organization may have the same geometry but different dimensions. Instead of creating each component of the same geometry with a different size, you can create one component and then using the design table, create different instances of the component by changing the dimension as per your requirement. You can access all these components in a single part file.

Equations
Equations are the analytical and numerical formulae applied to the dimensions during the sketching of the feature sketch or after sketching the feature sketch. The equations can also be applied to the placed features.

Collision Detection

Collision detection is used to detect interference and collision between the parts of an assembly when the assembly is in motion. While creating the assembly in SOLIDWORKS, you can detect collision between parts by moving and rotating them.

What's Wrong Functionality

While creating a feature of the model or after editing a feature, if the geometry of the feature is not compatible and the system is not able to construct that feature, then the **What's Wrong** functionality is used to detect the possible error that may have occurred while creating the feature.

2D Command Line Emulator

The 2D command line emulator is an add-in of SOLIDWORKS. You can activate this by choosing **Tools > Add-Ins** from the SOLIDWORKS menus. On doing so, the **Add-Ins** dialog box will be displayed. Select the **SOLIDWORKS 2D Emulator** check box and choose **OK** from the **Add-Ins** dialog box; a command section will be displayed at the bottom of the graphics area. This 2D Command line emulator is useful for invoking the commands by typing them. You can type the commands in the 2D Command line emulator.

SimulationXpress

In SOLIDWORKS, you are provided with an analysis tool named as SimulationXpress, which is used to execute the static or stress analysis. In SimulationXpress, you can only execute the linear static analysis. Using the linear static analysis, you can calculate the displacement, strain, and stresses applied on a component with the effect of material, various loading conditions, and restraint conditions applied on a model. A component fails when the stress applied on it reaches beyond a certain permissible limit. The Static Nodal stress plot of the crane hook designed in SOLIDWORKS and analyzed using SimulationXpress is shown in Figure 1-28.

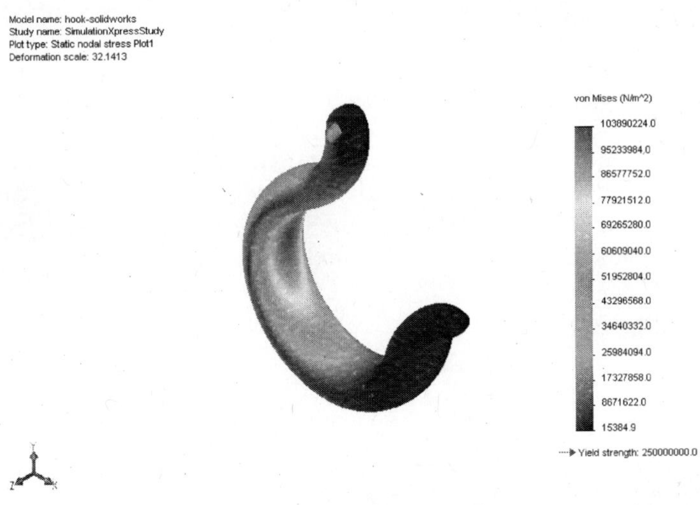

Figure 1-28 *The crane hook analyzed using SimulationXpress*

Physical Dynamics

The Physical Dynamics is used to observe the motion of the assembly. With this option selected, the component dragged in the assembly applies a force to the component that it touches. As a result, the other component moves or rotates within its allowable degrees of freedom.

Physical Simulation

The Physical Simulation is used to simulate the assemblies created in the assembly environment of SOLIDWORKS. You can assign and simulate the effect of different simulation elements such as linear, rotary motors, and gravity to the assemblies. After creating a simulating assembly, you can record and replay the simulation.

Seed Feature

The original feature that is used as the parent feature to create any type of pattern or mirror feature is known as the seed feature. You can edit or modify only a seed feature. You cannot edit the instances of the pattern feature.

FeatureManager Design Tree

The **FeatureManager Design Tree** is one the most important components of SOLIDWORKS screen. It contains information about default planes, materials, lights, and all the features that are added to the model. When you add features to the model using various modeling tools, the same are also displayed in the **FeatureManager Design Tree**. You can easily select and edit the features using the **FeatureManager Design Tree**. When you invoke any tool to create a feature, the **FeatureManager Design Tree** is replaced by the respective PropertyManager. At this stage, the **FeatureManager Design Tree** is displayed in the drawing area.

Absorbed Features

Features that are directly involved in creating other features are known as absorbed features. For example, the sketch of an extruded feature is an absorbed feature of the extruded feature.

Child Features

The features that are dependent on their parent feature and cannot exist without their parent features are known as child features. For example, consider a model with extrude feature and filleted edges. If you delete the extrude feature, the fillet feature will also get deleted because its existence is not possible without its parent feature.

Dependent Features

Dependent features are those features that depend on their parent feature but can still exist without the parent feature with some minor modifications. If the parent feature is deleted, then by specifying other references and modifying the feature, you can retain the dependent features.

AUTO-BACKUP OPTION

SOLIDWORKS also allows you to set the option to save the SOLIDWORKS document automatically after a regular interval of time. While working on a design project, if the system crashes, you may lose the unsaved design data. If the auto-backup option is turned on, your data will be saved automatically after regular intervals. To turn this option on, choose **Tools > Options** from the SOLIDWORKS menus; the **System Options - General** dialog box will be displayed. Select the **Backup/Recover** option from the display area provided on the left of this dialog box. Next, choose the **Save auto-recover information every** check box in the **Auto-recover** area, if it is not chosen by default. On doing so, the spinner and the drop-down list provided on the right of the check box will be enabled. Use the spinner and the drop-down list to set the number of changes or minutes after which the document will be saved automatically. By default, the backup files are saved at the location *X:\Users\<name of your machine>AppData\Local\TempSWBackupDirectory\swxauto* (where *X* is the drive in which you have installed SOLIDWORKS 2018 and the *AppData* folder is a hidden folder). You can also change the path of this location. To change this path, choose the button provided on the right of the edit box; the **Browse For Folder** dialog box will be displayed. You can specify the location of the folder to save the backup files using this dialog box. If you need to save the backup files in the current folder, select the **Number of backup copies per document** check box and then select the **Save backup files in the same location as the original** radio button. You can set the number of backup files that you need to save using the **Number of backup copies per document** spinner. After setting all options, choose the **OK** button from the **System Options - Backup/Recover** dialog box.

SELECTING HIDDEN ENTITIES

Sometimes, while working on a model, you need to select an entity that is either hidden behind another entity or is not displayed in the current orientation of the view. SOLIDWORKS allows you to select these entities using the **Select Other** option. For example, consider that you need to select the back face of a model, which is not displayed in the current orientation. In such a case, you need to move the cursor over the visible face such that the cursor is also in line with the back face of the model. Now, click on the front face and choose the **Select Other** button from the pop-up toolbar; the cursor changes to the select other cursor and the **Select Other** list box will be displayed. This list box displays all entities that can be selected. The item on which you move the cursor in the list box will be highlighted in the drawing area. You can select the hidden face using this box.

HOT KEYS

SOLIDWORKS is more popularly known for its mouse gesture functionality. However, you can also use the keys of the keyboard to invoke some tools, windows, dialog boxes, and so on. These keys are known as hot keys. Some hot keys along with their functions are given next.

Hot Key	Function
F11	Full screen
S	Invokes the shortcut bar
R	Invokes the recent documents
F	Fits the object in the drawing over the screen
Z	Zooms out

SPACE BAR	Invokes the **Orientation** menu
CTRL+1	Changes the current view to the Front View
CTRL+2	Changes the current view to the Back View
CTRL+3	Changes the current view to the Left View
CTRL+4	Changes the current view to the Right View
CTRL+5	Changes the current view to the Top View
CTRL+6	Changes the current view to the Bottom View
CTRL+7	Changes the current view to the Isometric View
CTRL+8	Changes the current view to the Normal View
CTRL+SHIFT+Z	Changes the current view to the Previous View
CTRL+Arrows	Moves the feature along the arrows direction
SHIFT+Arrows	Rotates the feature along the arrows direction
CTRL+B	Rebuilds the model
CTRL+Z	Invokes the **Undo** tool
CTRL+N	Invokes the **New SOLIDWORKS Document** dialog box
CTRL+O	Invokes the **Open** window
CTRL+S	Saves the document
CTRL+P	Prints the document
CTRL+A	Selects all the parts in the document
CTRL+C	Copies the selected feature
CTRL+V	Pastes the selected feature
CTRL+X	Cuts the selected feature
ALT+F	Opens the **File** menu
ALT+E	Opens the **Edit** menu

ALT+V	Opens the **View** menu
ALT+I	Opens the **Insert** menu
ALT+T	Opens the **Tool** menu
ALT+W	Opens the **Window** menu
ALT+H	Opens the **Help** menu
CTRL+W	Closes the current document

COLOR SCHEME

SOLIDWORKS allows you to use various color schemes as the background color of the screen, color and display style of **FeatureManager Design Tree**, and for displaying the entities on the screen. Note that the color scheme used in this book is neither the default color scheme nor the predefined color scheme. To set the color scheme, choose **Tools > Options** from the SOLIDWORKS menus; the **System Options - General** dialog box will be displayed. Select the **Colors** option from the left of this dialog box; the option related to the color scheme will be displayed in the dialog box and the name of the dialog box will change to **System Options - Colors**. In the list box available in the **Color scheme settings** area, the **Viewport Background** option is available. Select this option and choose the **Edit** button from the preview area on the right. Select white color from the **Color** dialog box and choose the **OK** button. After setting the color scheme, you need to save it so that next time if you need to set this color scheme, you do not need to configure all the settings. You just need to select the name of the saved color scheme from the **Current color scheme** drop-down list. To save the color scheme, choose the **Save As Scheme** button; the **Color Scheme Name** dialog box will be displayed. Enter the name of the color scheme as **SOLIDWORKS 2018** in the edit box in the **Color Scheme Name** dialog box and choose the **OK** button. Now, choose the **OK** button from the **System Options - Colors** dialog box.

Note

In this book, the description of the color has been given considering Windows 7/Windows 8 as the operating system. So if you are working on a system with operating system other than Windows 7/ Windows 8, the color of the entities may be different.

Self-Evaluation Test

Answer the following questions and then compare them to those given at the end of this chapter:

1. The __________ property ensures that any modification made in a model in any of the modes of SOLIDWORKS is also reflected in the other modes immediately.

2. The __________ relation forces two selected arcs, two circles, a point and an arc, a point and a circle, or an arc and a circle share the same centerpoint.

3. The __________ relation is used to make two points, a point and a line, or a point and an arc coincident.

4. The __________ relation forces two selected lines to become equal in length.

5. The __________ is used to detect interference and collision between the parts of an assembly when the assembly is in motion.

6. __________ are the analytical and numerical formulae applied to the dimensions during or after sketching of the feature sketch.

7. The **Part** mode of SOLIDWORKS is a feature-based parametric environment in which you can create solid models. (T/F)

8. Generative drafting is the process of generating drawing views of a part or an assembly created earlier. (T/F)

9. The tip of the day is displayed at the bottom of the task pane. (T/F)

10. In SOLIDWORKS, solid models are created by integrating a number of building blocks called features. (T/F)

Answers to Self-Evaluation Test

1. bidirectional associativity, **2.** concentric, **3.** coincident, **4.** equal, **5.** collision detection, **6.** Equations, **7.** T, **8.** T, **9.** T, **10.** T

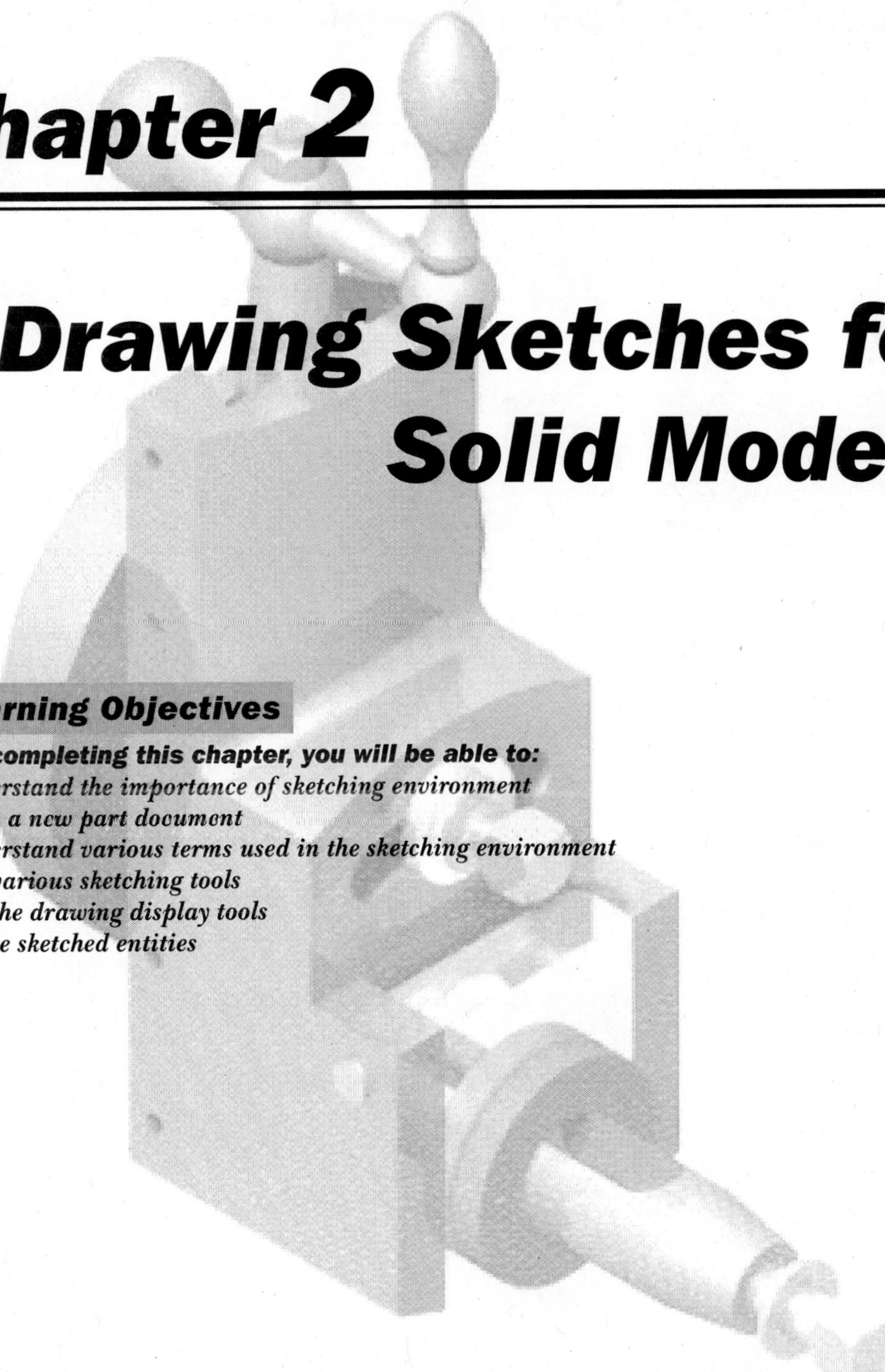

Chapter 2

Drawing Sketches for Solid Models

Learning Objectives

After completing this chapter, you will be able to:

- *Understand the importance of sketching environment*
- *Open a new part document*
- *Understand various terms used in the sketching environment*
- *Use various sketching tools*
- *Use the drawing display tools*
- *Delete sketched entities*

THE SKETCHING ENVIRONMENT

Most of the products designed by using SOLIDWORKS are a combination of sketched, placed, and derived features. The placed and derived features are created without drawing a sketch, but the sketched features require a sketch to be drawn first. Generally, the base feature of any design is a sketched feature and is created using the sketch. Therefore, while creating any design, the first and foremost requirement is to draw a sketch for the base feature. Once you have drawn the sketch, you can convert it into the base feature and then add the other sketched, placed, and derived features to complete the design. In this chapter, you will learn to create the sketch for the base feature using the various sketching tools.

In general terms, a sketch is defined as the basic contour of a feature. For example, consider the solid model of a spanner shown in Figure 2-1.

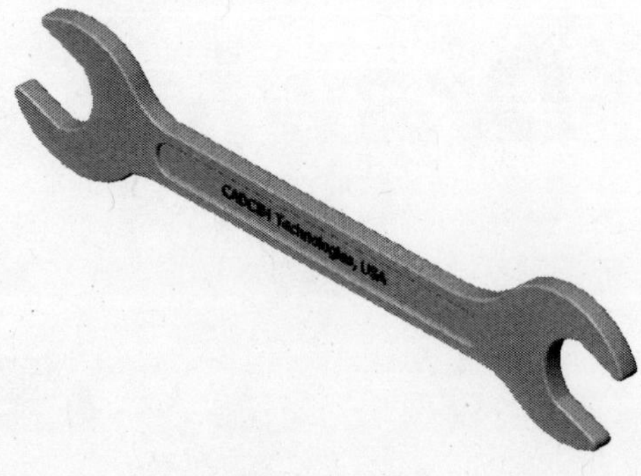

Figure 2-1 *Solid model of a spanner*

This spanner consists of a base feature, cut feature, mirror feature (cut on the back face), fillets, and an extruded text feature. The base feature of this spanner is shown in Figure 2-2. It is created using a single sketch drawn on the **Front Plane**, as shown in Figure 2-3. This sketch is drawn in the sketching environment using various sketching tools. Therefore, to draw the sketch of the base feature, first you need to invoke the sketching environment where you will draw the sketch.

Figure 2-2 *Base feature of the Spanner*

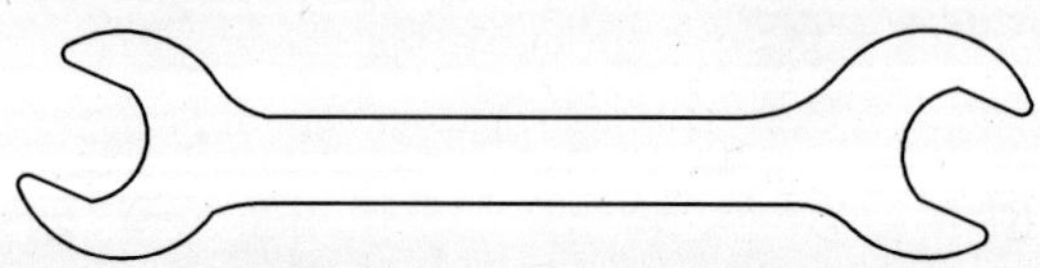

Figure 2-3 *Sketch for the base feature of the Spanner*

Note

The sketching environment of SOLIDWORKS can be invoked at any time in the ***Part*** *or* ***Assembly*** *mode. You will learn more about invoking sketcher environment later in this chapter.*

TUTORIALS

Tutorial 1

In this tutorial, you will start a new part document in SOLIDWORKS 2018 and then invoke the sketcher environment to draw the sketch of the solid model shown in Figure 2-4. The sketch of the model is shown in Figure 2-5. While drawing the sketch, you will modify the Snap, Grid, and Units settings for the active document. Note that the solid model and dimensions given in Figures 2-4 and 2-5 are for your reference only. You will learn to apply dimensions and creating solid models in the later chapters.

(Expected time: 30 min)

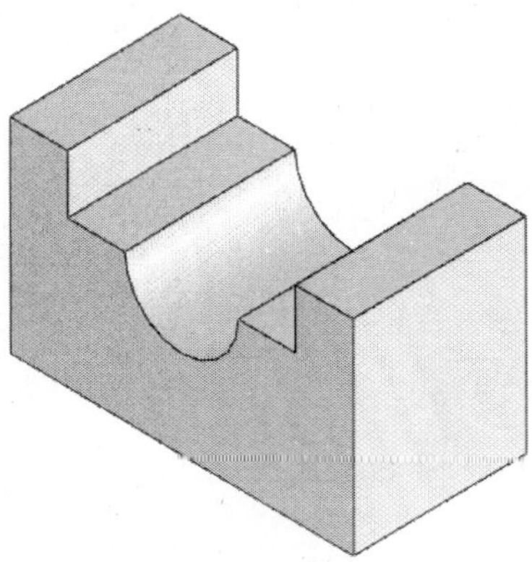

Figure 2-4 *Solid model for Tutorial 1*

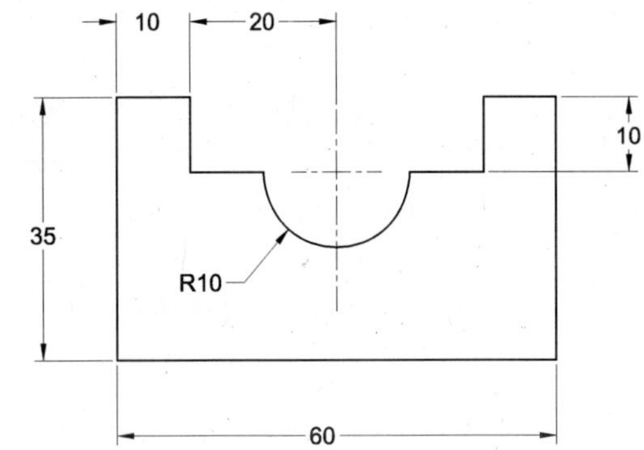

Figure 2-5 *Sketch for Tutorial 1*

The following steps are required to complete this tutorial:

a. Start SOLIDWORKS 2018 and then start a new part document.
b. Invoke the sketching environment.
c. Modify the settings of the snap, grid, units so that the cursor jumps through a distance of 5 mm.
d. Draw the sketch using the **Line** tool, refer to Figure 2-15.
e. Save the sketch and then close the file.

Starting SOLIDWORKS 2018

Once you have installed SOLIDWORKS 2018, an icon is displayed on the windows desktop and a folder is added to the **Start** menu.

1. Choose **Start > SOLIDWORKS 2018** from the **Start** menu or double-click on the **SOLIDWORKS 2018** icon on the desktop of your computer; the SOLIDWORKS 2018 window will be displayed. If you are starting the SOLIDWORKS application for the first time after installing it, the **SOLIDWORKS License Agreement** dialog box will be displayed, as shown in Figure 2-6. Choose the **Accept** button from the dialog box; the **SOLIDWORKS 2018** interface window will be displayed, as shown in Figure 2-7.

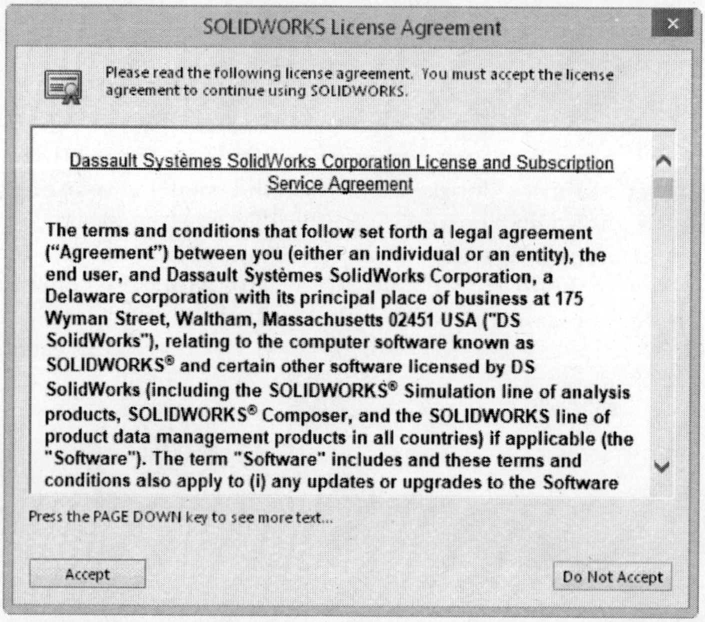

*Figure 2-6 The **SOLIDWORKS License Agreement** dialog box*

The initial interface of the **SOLIDWORKS 2018** interface window consists of SOLIDWORKS menus, Menu bar, and Task Pane, refer to Figure 2-7.

*Figure 2-7 The **SOLIDWORKS** interface window*

The Task Pane is displayed on the right in the **SOLIDWORKS 2018 interface** window. It contains various options that are used to start a new file, open an existing file, browse the related links of SOLIDWORKS, and so on. Various Task Pane in SOLIDWORKS are discussed next.

SOLIDWORKS Resources Task Pane

By default, the **SOLIDWORKS Resources** task pane is displayed when you start a SOLIDWORKS session. Different options available in this task pane are discussed next.

SOLIDWORKS Tools Rollout: The options in this rollout are **SOLIDWORKS files**, **SOLIDWORKS Rx**, **Compare My Score**, **Copy Settings Wizard,** and **My Products**. These options are used to control custom properties and attributes of the files. SOLIDWORKS Rx can be used to help diagnose issues with your computer.

Online Resources Rollout: The options in this rollout are used to participate in discussion forum of SOLIDWORKS, buy subscription services, avail partner solutions, join manufacturing network, and print 3D websites.

Subscription Services Rollout: The options in this rollout are used to access various software releases, service packs, and value added resources provided by SOLIDWORKS Corporation and its global network.

Design Library Task Pane

The **Design Library** task pane is invoked by choosing the **Design Library** tab from the Task Panes. This task pane is used to browse the default **Design Library** and the toolbox components available in SOLIDWORKS. Also, it allows you to access the **3D ContentCentral** website. To access the toolbox components, you need to add **Toolbox Add-Ins** in your computer. To do so, choose **Tools > Add-Ins** from the SOLIDWORKS menu; the **Add-Ins** dialog box will be displayed. Select the **SOLIDWORKS Toolbox Library** check box in this dialog box and then choose **OK**. To access the **3D ContentCentral** website, your computer needs to be connected to the Internet.

File Explorer Task Pane

The **File Explorer** task pane is used to explore the files and folders that are saved in the hard disk of your computer.

View Palette Task Pane

The **View Palette** task pane is used to drag and drop the drawing views into a drawing sheet.

Appearances, Scenes, and Decals Task Pane

The **Appearances, Scenes, and Decals** task pane is used to change the appearance of models or drawing display area. On choosing the **Appearances**, **Scenes**, **and Decals** tab from the Task Panes; the **Appearances, Scenes, and Decals** task pane will be invoked with three nodes: **Appearances(color)**, **Scenes**, and **Decals**. The **Appearances(color)** node is used to change the appearance of a model. The **Scenes** node is used to change the background of the drawing area and the **Decals** node is used to apply decals to a model.

Custom Properties Task Pane

The **Custom Properties** task pane is displayed on choosing the **Custom Properties** tab from the Task Panes. This task pane is used to view the properties of the files.

In SOLIDWORKS, the tools that are in the **Standard** toolbar are also available in the Menu Bar, as shown in Figure 2-8. This toolbar is available above the drawing area. When you move the cursor over the SOLIDWORKS logo at the top left corner of the display area, the SOLIDWORKS menus will be displayed as a cascading menu, as shown in Figure 2-9. You can also fix this menu by choosing the push-pin button.

Figure 2-8 *The Menu Bar*

Figure 2-9 *The SOLIDWORKS menus*

Starting a New Part Document in SOLIDWORKS 2018

1. Select the **New** option from the SOLIDWORKS menu; the **New SOLIDWORKS Document** dialog box will be displayed, as shown in Figure 2-10.

2. Make sure that the **Part** button is chosen in the **New SOLIDWORKS Document** dialog box. Next, choose the **OK** button to invoke the **Part** mode, refer to Figure 2-11.

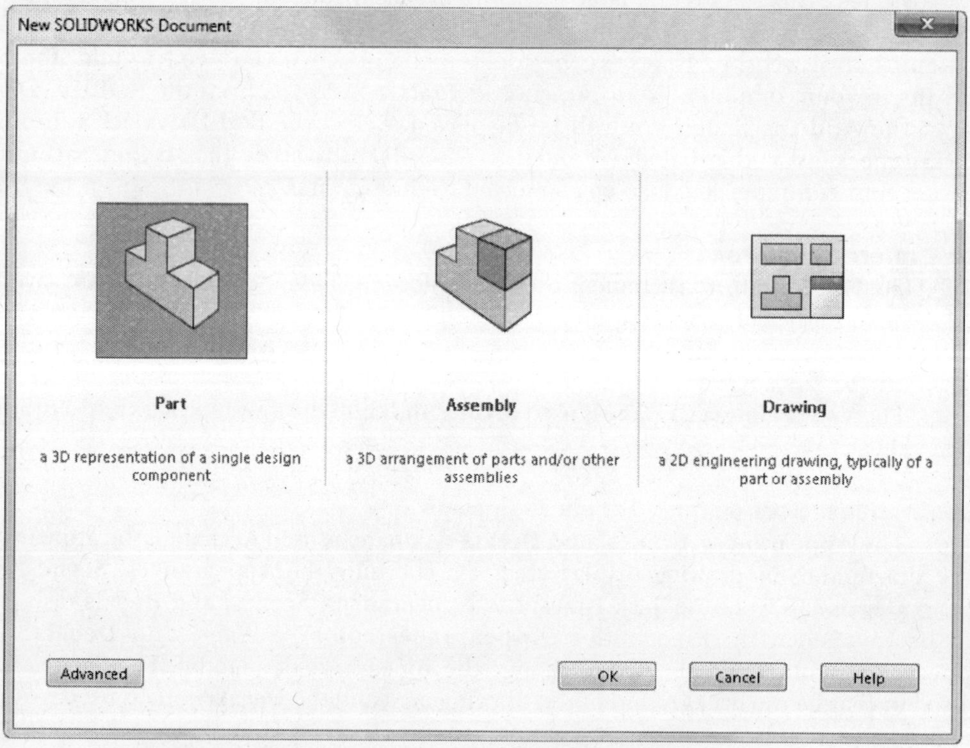

Figure 2-10 *The **New SOLIDWORKS Document** dialog box*

***Figure 2-11** The initial interface displayed on invoking the **Part** document*

Note

*To start a new assembly document, you need to choose the **Assembly** button and then the **OK** button from the **New SOLIDWORKS Document** dialog box. In an assembly document, you can assemble the components created in the part documents. You can also create components in the assembly documents. You will learn more about the assembly document in the later chapters.*

*To start a new drawing document, you need to choose the **Drawing** button and then the **OK** button from the **New SOLIDWORKS Document** dialog box. In a drawing document, you can generate or create different drawing views of the parts created in the part documents or the assemblies created in an assembly document. You will learn more about drawing document in the later chapters.*

Whenever you start a new part document, by default, you are in the part modeling environment, but you need to start the design by first creating the sketch of the base feature. You need to invoke the sketcher environment to create the sketch of the model shown in the Figure 2-4.

3. Click on the **Sketch** tab of the **CommandManager** to display the **Sketch CommandManager** tools.

4. Choose the **Sketch** button from the **Sketch CommandManager**; the **Edit Sketch PropertyManager** is displayed on the left in the graphic area and you are prompted to select the sketching plane on which the sketch is to be created. Also, the three default planes (**Front Plane**, **Right Plane**, and **Top Plane**) are available in SOLIDWORKS, and are temporarily displayed on the screen, as shown in Figure 2-12.

You can select a plane to draw the sketch of the base feature depending on the requirement of the design. The selected plane will automatically be oriented normal to the view, so that you can easily create the sketch. Also, the **CommandManager** will display various sketching tools to draw the sketch.

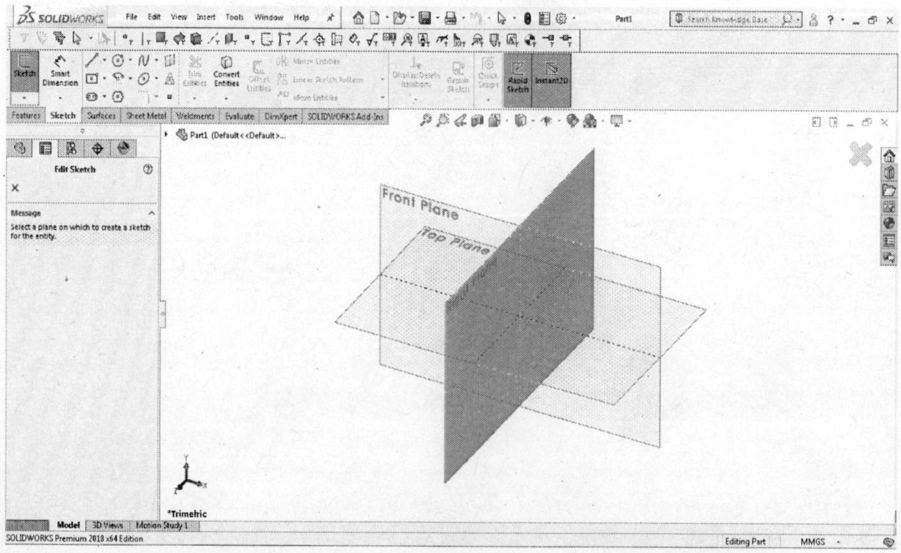

Figure 2-12 *The three default planes displayed on the interface*

5. Select the **Front Plane** from the graphics area; the sketching environment is invoked and the selected plane gets oriented normal to the view. You will notice that the red colored arrows are displayed at the center of the interface window, indicating that you are in the sketching environment. Also, the confirmation corner with the **Exit Sketch** and **Cancel Sketch** options at the upper right corner in the drawing area is displayed. The window display in the sketching environment of SOLIDWORKS is shown in Figure 2-13.

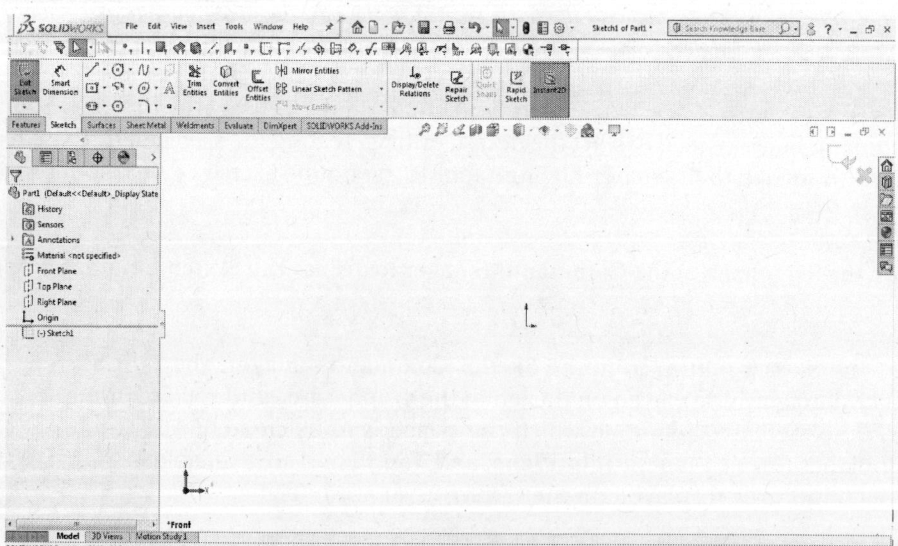

Figure 2-13 *Default interface of a part document in the sketching environment*

Modifying the Snap, Grid, and Units Settings

It is assumed that while installing SOLIDWORKS, you have selected the **MMGS (millimeters, gram, second)** option for measuring the length. Therefore, the length of an entity will be measured in millimeters in the current file. But, if you select some other unit at the time of installation, you need to change the linear and angular units before drawing the sketch. For this tutorial, you need to modify the grid and snap settings so that the cursor jumps through a distance of 5 mm.

1. Choose the **Options** button from the Menu Bar; the **System Options - General** dialog box is displayed.

2. Choose the **Document Properties** tab; the name in the dialog box changes to the **Document Properties - Drafting Standard**.

Note
If you have selected millimeters as the unit of measurement while installing SOLIDWORKS, skip steps 3 and 4 in this section.

3. Select the **Units** option from the area on the left of the dialog box; the options related to linear and angular units are displayed.

4. Select the **MMGS (millimeter, gram, second)** radio button in the **Unit system** area. Also, select the **degrees** option from the **Angle** area in the **Unit** column.

Tip
*In SOLIDWORKS, you can also change the units for the current document by using the **Unit system** that is located towards right in the Status Bar, refer to Figure 2-11. To do so, click on the **Unit system**; a flyout will be displayed with a tick mark on the left of the activated unit system, refer to Figure 2-14. Now, you can select the required unit system for the activated unit system from this flyout. You can also invoke the **Document Properties-Units** dialog box by selecting the **Edit Document Units** from this flyout.*

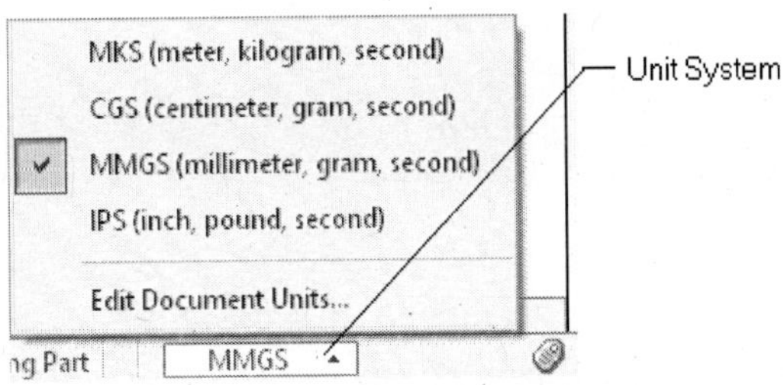

***Figure 2-14** The flyout showing the currently selected unit system*

Note
*Note that the short form of the current unit system of the activated document will be displayed in the **Status Bar**. For example, if the **MMGS (millimeter, gram, second)** is the current unit system then **MMGS** will be displayed in the **Status Bar**.*

As evident from Figure 2-5, the dimensions in the sketch are multiple of 5. Therefore, you need to modify the grid and snap settings so that the cursor jumps through a distance of 5 mm.

5. Select the **Grid/Snap** option from the area on the left in the dialog box; the options related to the grid and snap are displayed. Also, the name of the dialog box is modified to **Document Properties - Grid/Snap**.

6. In this dialog box, set the value in the **Major grid spacing** and **Minor-lines per major** spinners to **50** and **10**, respectively.

Note

The distance through which the cursor jumps depends on the ratio between the values in the ***Major grid spacing*** *and* ***Minor-lines per major*** *spinners available in the* ***Grid*** *area. For example, if you want the coordinates to increment by 10 mm, you will have to set the ratio of the major and minor lines to 10. This can be done by setting the value of the* ***Major grid spacing*** *spinner to 100 and the* ***Minor-lines per major*** *spinner to 10. Similarly, to make the cursor jump through a distance of 5 mm, set the value of the* ***Major grid spacing*** *spinner to 50 and the* ***Minor-lines per major*** *spinner to 10.*

Tip

If you want to display the grid in the sketching environment, select the ***Display grid*** *check box from the* ***Grid*** *area of the* ***Document Properties - Grid/Snap*** *dialog box. Alternatively, choose* ***Hide/Show Items > View Grid*** *from the* ***View (Heads-Up)*** *toolbar.*

While drawing a sketched entity by snapping through grips, the grips symbol will be displayed below the cursor on the right.

7. Make sure that the **Grid** check box is selected in the **System Options - Relations/Snaps** dialog box. To invoke this dialog box, choose the **Go To System Snaps** button from the **Document Properties - Grid/Snap** dialog box.

8. Choose the **OK** button to exit the dialog box.

Now, when you move the cursor, the coordinates displayed close to the lower right corner of the drawing area show an increment of 5 mm.

Drawing the Sketch

The sketch will be drawn using the **Line** tool. The arc in the sketch will also be drawn using the same tool. You need to start the drawing from the lower left corner of the sketch to be drawn.

1. Choose the **Line** tool from the **Sketch CommandManager**; the arrow cursor is changed into line cursor. Also, the **Insert Line PropertyManager** is displayed at the left in the drawing area.

The line cursor is actually a crosshairs-like cursor with a small inclined line below the crosshairs. You can also invoke the **Line** tool by pressing the L key.

The line is the basic sketching entity available in SOLIDWORKS. In general terms, a line is defined as the shortest distance between two points.

In SOLIDWORKS, the **Line** tool is used to draw a chain of continuous lines which is a default method of drawing lines. In this method, you have to specify the start point and the endpoint of the line using the left mouse button. As soon as you specify the start point of the line, the **Insert Line PropertyManager** will disappear and the **Line Properties PropertyManager** will be displayed. However, the options available in this PropertyManager are not activated at this stage. These options will be activated after the line is created. As soon as, you specify the end point of the line by using the left mouse button, a line will be drawn between two points. Now, when you move the cursor away from the end point of the line, you will notice that another line is attached with the cursor. It means that you can create a chain of continuous line one after other. You can end the process of drawing the continuous line by pressing the ESC key, by double-clicking on the screen, or by invoking the **Select** tool from the Menu Bar. You can also right-click to display the shortcut menu and choose the **End chain** or **Select** option to terminate the process of drawing the line.

Note

When you terminate the process of drawing a line by double-clicking on the screen or by choosing the ***End chain*** *from the shortcut menu, the current chain ends but the* ***Line*** *tool still remains active. As a result, you can draw other lines. However, if you choose* ***Select*** *from the shortcut menu, the* ***Line*** *tool will be deactivated.*

You can also draw an individual line by using the **Line** tool. To do so, invoke the **Line** tool. Next, press and hold the left mouse button to specify the start point of the line and then drag the cursor toward the required direction. After getting the required direction and length, release the left mouse button.

2. Move the line cursor to a point whose coordinates are 30 mm, 0 mm, and, 0 mm.

3. Click at this point to specify the start point of the line; the **Line Properties PropertyManager** will be displayed.

4. Move the cursor horizontally toward the right. Click again when the length of the line above the line cursor displays 60; a bottom horizontal line of 60 mm length is drawn.

5. Move the line cursor vertically upward and click when the length of the line above the line cursor displays 35.

6. Choose the **Zoom to Fit** button from the **View (Heads-Up)** toolbar to fit the sketch into the screen.

Note

You can invoke the drawing display tools when any other tool is active in the drawing area. After modifying the drawing display area, the tool that was active before invoking the drawing display tool will be restored and you can continue using that tool.

7. Move the line cursor horizontally toward the left and press the left mouse button when the length of the line above the line cursor shows the value 10.

8. Move the line cursor vertically downward and click when the length of the line above the line cursor is displayed as 10.

9. Move the line cursor horizontally toward the left and click when the length of the line above the line cursor is displayed as 10.

   Next, you need to draw an arc normal to the last line. As mentioned earlier, you can also draw an arc using the **Line** tool. Drawing arcs using the **Line** tool is a recommended method to draw a sketch that is a combination of lines and arcs. This increases the productivity by reducing the time taken in invoking tools for drawing an arc and then invoking the **Line** tool to draw lines.

10. Move the line cursor away from the endpoint of the last line and then move it back close to the endpoint; the arc mode is invoked. Also, the **Line Properties PropertyManager** disappears and the **Arc PropertyManager** is displayed at the left in the drawing area.

11. Move the arc cursor vertically downward to the next grid point.

12. Move the arc cursor toward the left.

    You will notice that a normal arc is being drawn and the angle and radius of the arc are displayed above the line cursor.

13. Move the cursor to the left and click when the angle value on the arc cursor is displayed as 180 and the radius value is displayed as 10. An arc normal to the last line is drawn and again the line mode is invoked automatically.

14. Move the line cursor horizontally toward the left and click when the length of the line on the line cursor is displayed as 10.

15. Move the line cursor vertically upward and click when the length of the line on the line cursor is displayed as 10.

16. Move the line cursor horizontally toward the left and click when the length of the line on the line cursor is displayed as 10.

17. Move the line cursor to the start point of the first line and click when the orange circle is displayed.

18. Press the ESC key to exit the **Line** tool.

    This completes the sketch. However, you need to modify the drawing display area such that the sketch fits the screen.

19. Press the F key; the drawing display area is modified and sketch fits into the screen. The final sketch for Tutorial 1 with the grid display turned off is shown in Figure 2-15.

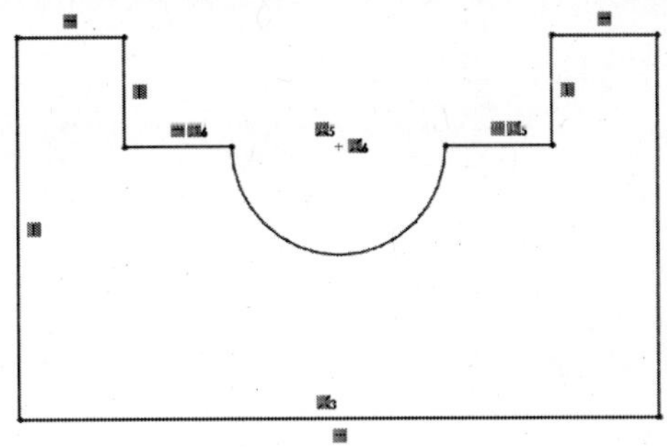

Figure 2-15 *Final sketch for Tutorial 1*

Note

Figure 2-15 shows the relation symbols that are applied automatically while drawing the sketch. To control the display of relations on and off, choose the ***Hide/Show Items*** *button in the* ***View (Heads-Up)*** *toolbar; the flyout will be displayed, refer to Figure 2-16. Next, choose the* ***View Sketch Relations*** *button which is a toggle button from this flyout.*

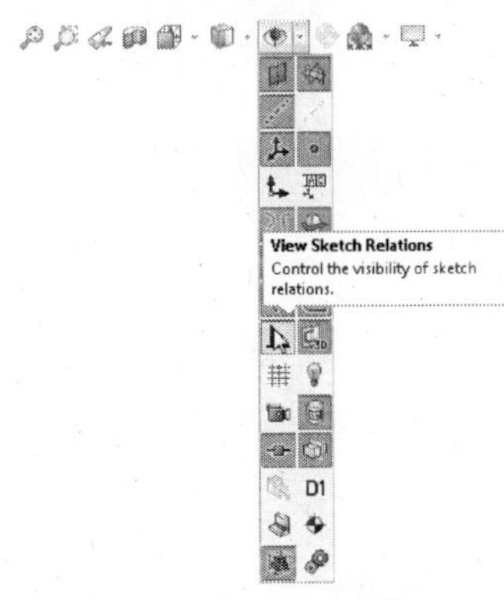

Figure 2-16 *The* ***Hide/Show Items*** *flyout*

Saving the Sketch

It is recommended that you create a separate folder to save the tutorial files of this book. You will create a folder with the name *SOLIDWORKS Tutorials* in the *Documents* folder and then create the sub-folder of each chapter inside the *SOLIDWORKS Tutorials* folder. Next, you can save the tutorials of a chapter in the folder of that chapter.

1. Choose the **Save** button from the Menu Bar to invoke the **Save As** dialog box. Create the *SOLIDWORKS Tutorials* folder inside the *\Documents* folder and then create the *c02* folder inside the *SOLIDWORKS Tutorials* folder.

2. Enter **c02_tut01** as the name of the document in the **File name** edit box. Choose the **Save** button to save the file at the location *\Documents\SOLIDWORKS Tutorials\c02*.

3. Close the document by choosing **File > Close** from the SOLIDWORKS menus.

Tutorial 2

In this tutorial, you will draw the basic sketch of the revolved solid model shown in Figure 2-17. The sketch of this model is shown in Figure 2-18. Do not dimension the sketch. The solid model and its dimensions are given for your reference only. **(Expected time: 30 min)**

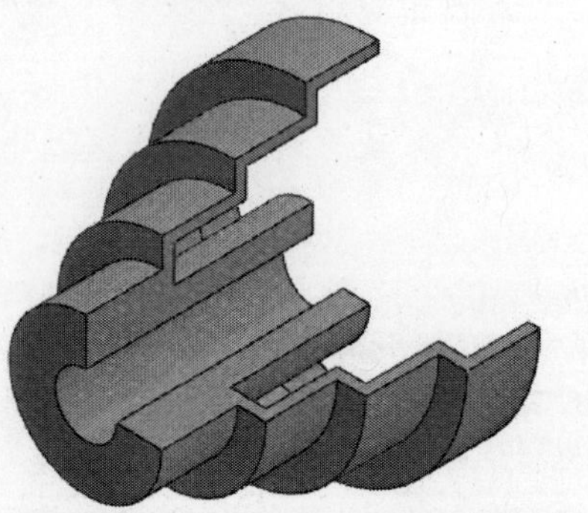

Figure 2-17 *Revolved solid model for Tutorial 1*

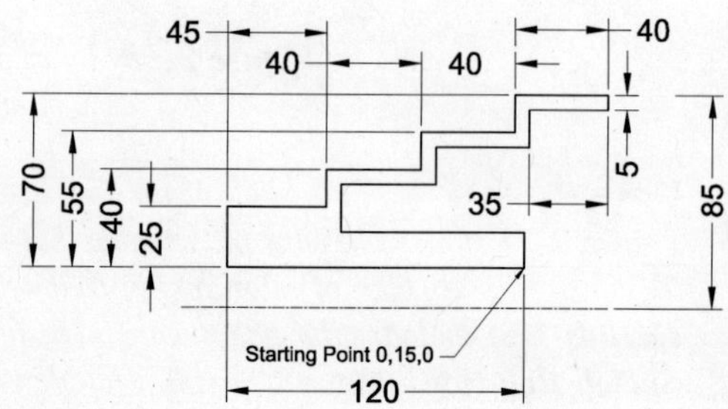

Figure 2-18 *Sketch of the revolved solid model*

The following steps are required to complete this tutorial:

a. Invoke a new part document.
b. Invoke the sketching environment.
c. Modify the settings of the snap, grid, and units settings so that the cursor jumps through a distance of 5 mm.
d. Draw the sketch using the **Line** and **Centerline** tools, refer to Figure 2-21.
e. Save the sketch and then close the file.

Invoking a New Part Document

1. Choose the **New** button from the Menu Bar to invoke the **New SOLIDWORKS Document** dialog box.

2. In the **New SOLIDWORKS Document** dialog box, the **Part** button is chosen by default. Choose the **OK** button in this dialog box; a new SOLIDWORKS part document starts in part modeling environment.

You need to invoke the sketching environment to draw the sketch.

3. Choose the **Sketch** tab from the CommandManager and then the **Sketch** button from the **Sketch CommandManager**; the **Edit Sketch PropertyManager** is displayed and you are prompted to select a plane on which you want to draw the sketch.

4. Select the **Right Plane** from the drawing area; the sketching environment is invoked and the plane gets oriented normal to the view. You will notice that the red colored arrows are now displayed at the center of the screen indicating that you are in the sketching environment.

Modifying the Snap, Grid, and Units Settings

It is assumed that while installing SOLIDWORKS, you have selected the **MMGS (millimeters, gram, second)** option for measuring the length. Therefore, the length of an entity will be measured in millimeters in the current file. But, if you select some other unit at the time of installation, you need to change the linear and angular units before drawing the sketch. For this tutorial, you need to modify the grid and snap settings so that the cursor jumps through a distance of 5 mm.

1. Click on the **Unit system** that is located towards right in the Status Bar; a flyout is displayed with a tick mark next to the unit system of the current document, refer to Figure 2-19.

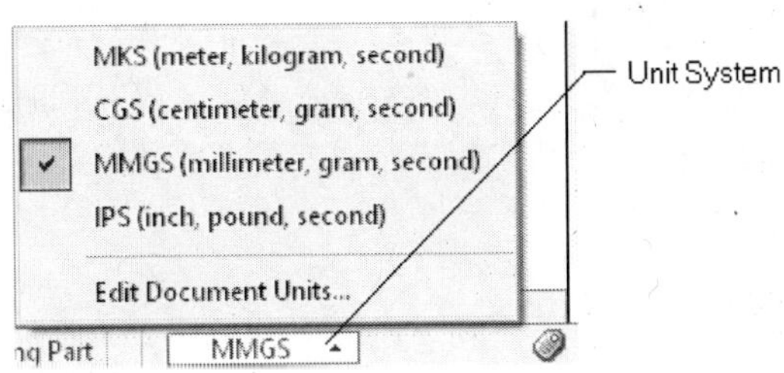

***Figure 2-19** The flyout showing the currently selected unit system*

2. Choose the **Edit Document Units** option from this flyout; the **Document Properties - Units** dialog box is displayed.

Note

If you have selected millimeters as the unit of measurement while installing SOLIDWORKS, you can skip step 3.

3. Select the **MMGS (millimeter, gram, second)** radio button in the **Unit system** area. Also, select the **degrees** option from the **Angle** area in the **Units** column.

Note

*You can also select the required unit system directly for the current document by selecting the respective option from the **Unit System** flyout. However, if you are in the sketching environment, on selecting the unit system from the unit system flyout, you will automatically exit the sketching environment.*

As evident from Figure 2-18, the dimensions in the sketch are multiples of 5. Therefore, you need to modify the grid and snap settings so that the cursor jumps through a distance of 5 mm.

4. Select the **Grid/Snap** option from the area on the left of the **Document Properties - Units** dialog box to display the options related to the grid and snap. Also, note that name of the dialog box is modified to **Document Properties - Grid/Snap**.

5. In this dialog box, set the value in the **Major grid spacing** and **Minor-lines per major** spinners to **50** and **10**, respectively.

6. Choose the **Go To System Snap** button from the dialog box; the name of the dialog box is modified to **System Options - Relations/Snaps**.

7. Make sure that the **Grid** check box is selected in this dialog box. Next, choose the **OK** button to exit the dialog box.

   Now, when you move the cursor, the coordinates displayed close to the lower right corner of the drawing area show an increment of 5 mm.

Drawing the Sketch

As evident from the Figure 2-18, the sketch will be drawn using the **Line** tool and you need to start drawing the sketch from the lower left corner of the sketch. As the model of the sketch is a revolved feature, you first need to create its axis by using the **Centerline** tool, so that while converting the sketch you can use this as an axis of revolution. You will learn more about the revolve features in later chapters.

1. Click on the down arrow next to the **Line** tool; the **Line** flyout is displayed, refer to Figure 2-20.

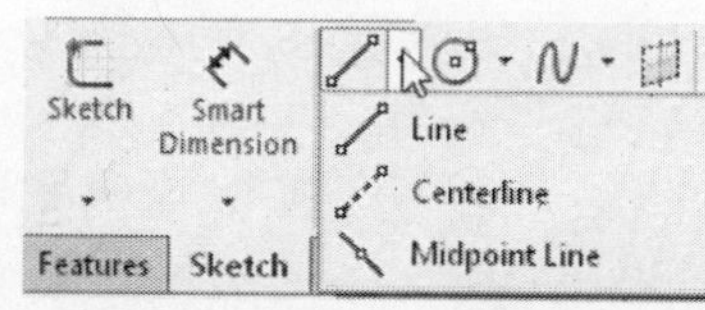

***Figure 2-20** The **Line** flyout*

2. Choose the **Centerline** button form the **Line** flyout; the **Insert Line PropertyManager** is displayed at the left of the drawing area. Note that in the **Options** rollout of this PropertyManager, the **For construction** check box is selected.

If the **For construction** check box of the **Insert Line PropertyManager** is selected, you can draw a construction line or a centerline. The construction lines or the centerlines are drawn only for the aid of sketching and are not considered while converting the sketches into features. You can draw a construction line similar to the sketched line by using the **Centerline** tool.

3. Move the cursor towards the origin and specify the start point of the centerline when the cursor snaps to the origin and the coincident relation is displayed below the cursor.

4. Move the cursor horizontally toward the left and specify the end point of the centerline when the length of the centerline above the cursor is displayed close to 120. Note that, you may need to scroll the wheel of the mouse to zoom in/out of the drawing. You can also invoke the **Zoom In/Out** tool by choosing the **View > Modify > Zoom In/Out** from the SOLIDWORKS menus to zoom in/out of the drawing.

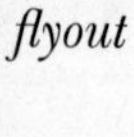

The **Zoom In/Out** tool is used to dynamically zoom in or out of the drawing. When you invoke this tool, cursor changes to zoom cursor. To zoom out of a drawing, press and hold the left mouse button and drag the cursor to the downward direction. Similarly, to zoom in a drawing, press and hold the left mouse button and drag the cursor in upward direction. As you drag the cursor, the drawing display area will be modified dynamically. After getting the desired view, exit this tool by right-clicking and choosing the **Zoom In/Out** button from the shortcut menu displayed.

5. Right-click in the drawing area; a shortcut menu is displayed. Choose the **Select** option from it to exit the **Centerline** tool.

6. Press the F key; the sketch is zoomed and it fits on the screen.

7. Choose the **Line** button from the **Sketch CommandManager**; the arrow cursor changes to line cursor. Also, the **Insert Line PropertyManager** is displayed on the left of the drawing area.

Tip

You can also draw a construction line using the ***Line*** *tool. To do so, invoke the* ***Insert Line PropertyManager*** *by chosing the* ***Line*** *tool. Next, select the* ***For construction*** *check box from the* ***Options*** *rollout of the PropertyManager to draw the construction line.*

8. Move the line cursor to a location whose coordinates are 0 mm, 15 mm, and 0 mm.

9. Left-click at this point and move the cursor horizontally toward the left. You will notice that the symbol of the **Horizontal** relation is displayed below the line cursor and the length and angle of the line are displayed above the line cursor.

Note

You will learn more about adding relations in the later chapters.

10. Left-click again when the length of the line above the line cursor is displayed as 120.

    The first horizontal line is drawn. As you are drawing continuous lines, the endpoint of the line drawn is automatically selected as the start point of the next line.

11. Move the line cursor vertically upward. The symbol of the **Vertical** relation is displayed on the right of the line cursor and the length of the line is displayed above the line cursor. Click when the length of the line on the line cursor is displayed as 25.

12. Move the cursor horizontally toward the right and click when the length of the line on the line cursor is displayed as 45.

13. Move the line cursor vertically upward and press the left mouse button when the length of the line on the line cursor is displayed as 15.

14. Move the line cursor horizontally toward the right and click when the length of the line on the line cursor is displayed as 40.

15. Move the line cursor vertically upward and click when the length of the line on the line cursor is displayed as 15.

16. Press F on the keyboard to fit the sketch on the screen.

17. Move the line cursor horizontally toward the right and click when the length of the line on the line cursor is displayed as 40.

18. Move the line cursor vertically upward and click when the length of the line on the line cursor is displayed as 15.

19. Move the line cursor horizontally toward the right and click when the length of the line on the line cursor displays as 40.

20. Move the line cursor vertically downward and click when the length of the line on the line cursor is displayed as 5.

21. Move the line cursor horizontally toward the left and click when the length of the line on the line cursor is displayed as 35.

22. Move the line cursor vertically downward and click when the length of the line on the line cursor is displayed as 15.

23. Move the line cursor horizontally toward the left and click when the length of the line on the line cursor is displayed as 40.

24. Move the line cursor vertically downward and click when the length of the line on the line cursor is displayed as 15.

25. Move the line cursor horizontally toward the left and click when the length of the line on the line cursor is displayed as 40.

26. Move the line cursor vertically downward and click when the length of the line on the line cursor is displayed as 20.

27. Move the line cursor horizontally toward the right and click when the length of the line on the line cursor is displayed as 70.

28. Move the line cursor vertically downward to the start point of the first line. Click when an orange or yellow circle is displayed; the final sketch for Tutorial 2 is created, as shown in Figure 2-21. In this figure, the grid display is turned off for clarity.

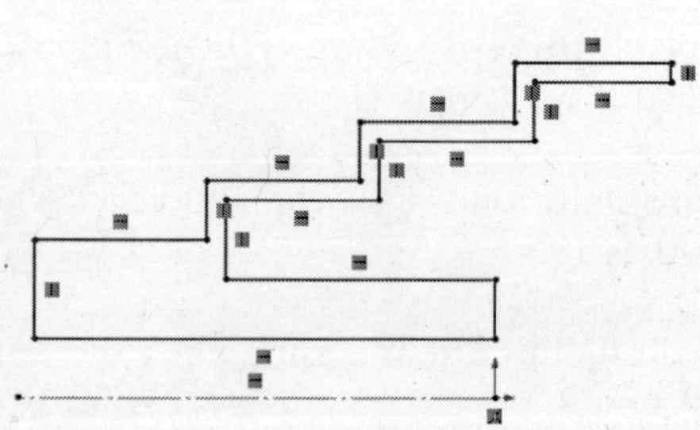

Figure 2-21 *Final sketch for Tutorial 2*

29. Right-click and then choose **Select** from the shortcut menu displayed to exit the **Line** tool.

Note

*The display of relations shown in Figure 2-21, can be turned on or off by choosing the **View Sketch Relations** button from the **View (Heads-Up) > Hide/Show items** flyout.*

Tip

*In case, you have drawn wrong sketch entities, you can delete them. To do so, select the entities to be deleted by using the **Select** tool (cursor) and then press the DELETE key. You can select the entities individually or more than one by defining a window around the entities. When you select the entities, they turn light blue. When they turn light blue, press the DELETE key. You can also delete the sketched entities by selecting them and choosing the **Delete** option from the shortcut menu that is displayed on right-clicking.*

Saving the Sketch

1. Choose the **Save** button from the Menu Bar to invoke the **Save As** dialog box. Create the *SOLIDWORKS Tutorials* folder inside the *\Documents* folder and then create the *c02* folder inside the *SOLIDWORKS Tutorials* folder, if it is not created in Tutorial 1 of this chapter.

2. Enter **c02_tut02** as the name of the document in the **File name** edit box and choose the **Save** button. The document is saved at the location *\Documents\SOLIDWORKS Tutorials\c02*.

3. Close the document by choosing **File > Close** from the SOLIDWORKS menus.

Tip

*If you save a file in the sketching environment and then open it next time by using the **Open** button available in the Menu Bar, it will open in the sketcher environment only.*

Tutorial 3

In this tutorial, you will draw the basic sketch of the model shown in Figure 2-22. The sketch to be drawn is shown in Figure 2-23. Do not dimension the sketch; the solid model and its dimensions are given for your reference only. **(Expected time: 30 min)**

Figure 2-22 *Solid model for Tutorial 3*

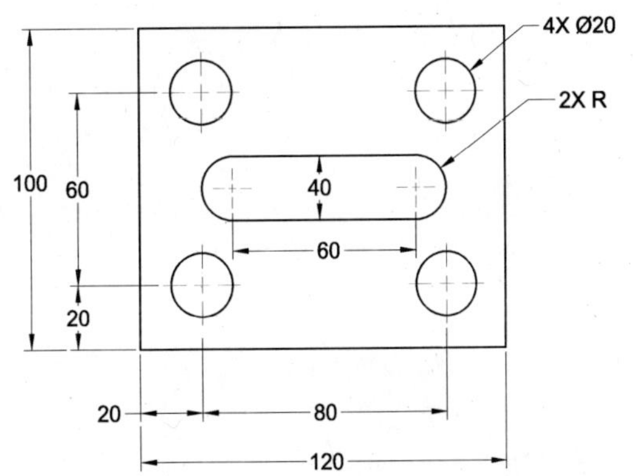

Figure 2-23 *Sketch for Tutorial 3*

The following steps are required to complete this tutorial:

a. Invoke a new part document.
b. Modify the settings of the snap, grid, and units settings so that the cursor jumps through a distance of 10 mm.
c. Invoke the sketching environment.
d. Draw the sketch using the sketching tools, refer to Figures 2-26 through 2-31.
e. Save the sketch and then close the file.

Invoking a New Part File

1. Choose the **New** button from the Menu Bar; the **New SOLIDWORKS Document** dialog box is displayed with the **Part** button chosen by default.

2. Choose the **OK** button from this dialog box; a new SOLIDWORKS part document is started.

   Now, you need to invoke the sketching environment to draw the sketch of the model.

3. Choose the **Sketch** button from the **Sketch CommandManager**; the **Edit Sketch PropertyManager** is displayed.

4. Select the **Front Plane** from the drawing area; the sketching environment is invoked.

Modifying the Snap, Grid, and Units Settings

As the dimensions in the sketch are multiples of 10, you need to modify the grid and snap settings so that the cursor jumps through a distance of 10 mm.

1. Click on the **Unit system** that is located in the Status Bar; a flyout is displayed with a tick mark next to the unit system of the current document, refer to Figure 2-24.

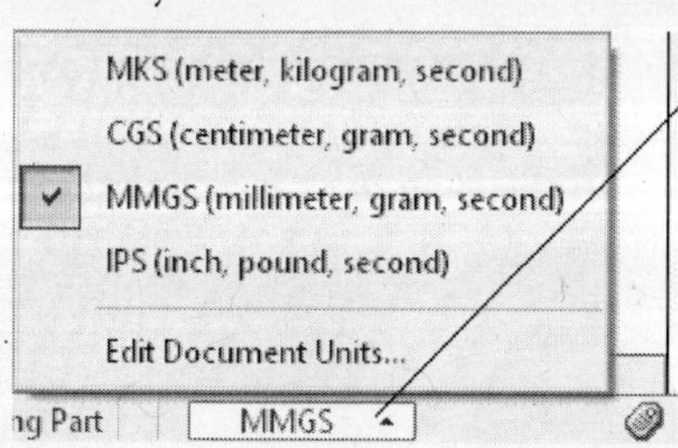

***Figure 2-24** The flyout showing the currently selected unit system*

2. Choose the **Edit Document Units** option from this flyout; the **Document Properties - Units** dialog box is displayed.

Note
If you have selected millimeter as the unit of measurement while installing SOLIDWORKS, you can skip step 3 in this section.

3. Select the **MMGS (millimeter, gram, second)** radio button in the **Unit system** area. Also, select the **degrees** option from the **Angle** area in the **Unit** column.

Note

You can also directly select the required unit system for the current document by selecting the respective option from the ***Unit system*** *flyout. However, in this case, if you are in the sketcher environment, you will automatically exit from the sketcher environment.*

As evident from Figure 2-23, the dimensions in the sketch are multiple of 10. Therefore, you need to modify the grid and snap settings so that the cursor jumps through a distance of 10 mm.

4. Select the **Grid/Snap** option from the area on the left of the **Document Properties - Units** dialog box; the options related to the grid and snap are displayed. Also, note that the name of the dialog box is modified to **Document Properties - Grid/Snap**.

5. In this dialog box, set the value in the **Major grid spacing** and **Minor-lines per major** spinners to **100** and **10**, respectively.

6. Choose the **Go To System Snap** button from the **Document Properties - Grid/Snap** dialog box; the name of the dialog box is modified to **System Options - Relations/Snaps**. Now, make sure that the **Grid** check box is selected in it.

7. Choose the **OK** button to exit the dialog box.

Now, when you move the cursor, the coordinates displayed close to the lower right corner of the drawing area are showing an increment of 10 mm.

Drawing the Sketch

In this tutorial, you need to draw the sketch in two parts. Initially, you need to draw the outer loop of the sketch which is a rectangle. Next, you need to draw the inner loops of the sketch which consist of four simple holes and an elongated hole.

1. Choose the **Corner Rectangle** tool from the **Rectangle** flyout of the **Sketch CommandManager** to draw a rectangle by specifying the two diagonally opposite corners; the **Rectangle PropertyManager** is displayed on the left of the drawing area. Also, the arrow cursor changes to the rectangle cursor.

In SOLIDWORKS, the tools that are used to draw rectangles are grouped together in the **Rectangle** flyout. To invoke this flyout, click on the down arrow located on the right of the **Rectangle** flyout, refer to Figure 2-25. From this flyout, you can select an appropriate method to draw a rectangle.

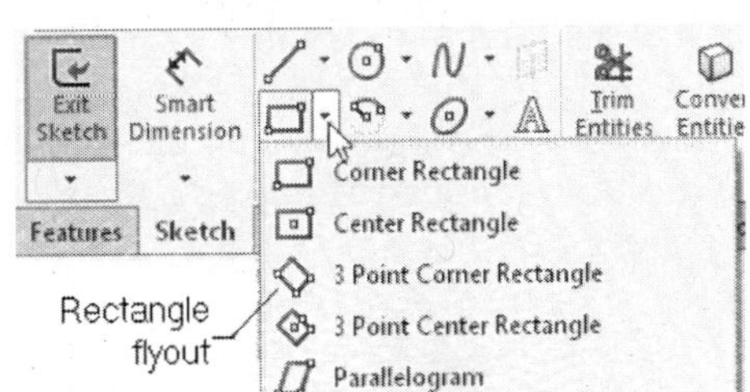

Figure 2-25 *The* ***Rectangle*** *flyout*

The **Corner Rectangle** tool is used to draw a rectangle by specifying the two diagonally opposite corners. To draw a rectangle by specifying the center and one of the corners, use the **Center Rectangle** tool. To draw a rectangle at an angle by specifying its three corners, use the **3 Point Corner Rectangle** tool. In this case, the first two corners will define the length and angle of the rectangle and the third corner will define the width of the rectangle. Similarly, the **3 Point Center Rectangle** tool of the **Rectangle** flyout is use to draw a centerpoint rectangle at an angle. The last tool of the **Rectangle** flyout is the **Parallelogram** tool. This tool is used to draw a parallelogram.

Note

You can also select an appropriate method to draw a rectangle from the ***Rectangle Type*** *rollout of the* ***Rectangle PropertyManager****.*

2. Move the rectangle cursor toward the origin and specify the first corner of the rectangle when it snaps to the origin and the symbol of coincident relation is displayed below the cursor.

Note

You will learn more about adding relations to the sketch in the later chapters.

3. Move the cursor toward right direction and specify the second corner of the rectangle when the X and Y length value of the rectangle displayed above the cursor are 120 and 100. Note that, you may need to scroll the wheel of the mouse to zoom in/out of the drawing. You can also invoke the **Zoom In/Out** tool by choosing the **View > Modify > Zoom In/Out** from the SOLIDWORKS menus to zoom in/out of the drawing.

The **Zoom In/Out** tool is used to dynamically zoom in or out the drawing. When you invoke this tool, cursor changes to by zoom cursor. To zoom out of a drawing, press and hold the left mouse button and drag the cursor to downward direction. Similarly, to zoom in a drawing, press and hold the left mouse button and drag the cursor to upward direction. Now, when you drag the cursor, the drawing display area gets modified dynamically. After getting the desired view, exit this tool by right-clicking and choosing the **Zoom In/Out** button from the shortcut menu displayed.

4. Exit the **Corner Rectangle** tool by right-clicking and choosing the **Select** option from the shortcut menu, displayed. Figure 2-26 shows the outer loop of the sketch drawn using the **Corner Rectangle** tool.

   You have drawn the outer loop of the sketch. Now, you need to draw the inner loops, which consist of four holes and an elongated hole. First, draw an elongated hole by using the **Straight Slot** tool and then the four holes by using the **Circle** tool.

5. Choose the **Straight Slot** button from the **Slot** flyout of the **Sketch CommandManager**; the **Slot PropertyManager** is displayed on the left of the drawing area, refer to Figure 2-27.

In SOLIDWORKS, the tools that are used to draw a slot profile are grouped together in the **Slot** flyout. To display this flyout, click on the down arrow located next to the **Straight Slot** tool; the **Slot** flyout will be displayed; as shown in Figure 2-28. From this flyout, you can choose the appropriate method to draw a slot profile. Alternatively, invoke the **Slot PropertyManager** by choosing the **Straight Slot** button from the **Sketch CommandManager**. Next, select an appropriate method to draw a slot profile from the **Slot Type** rollout.

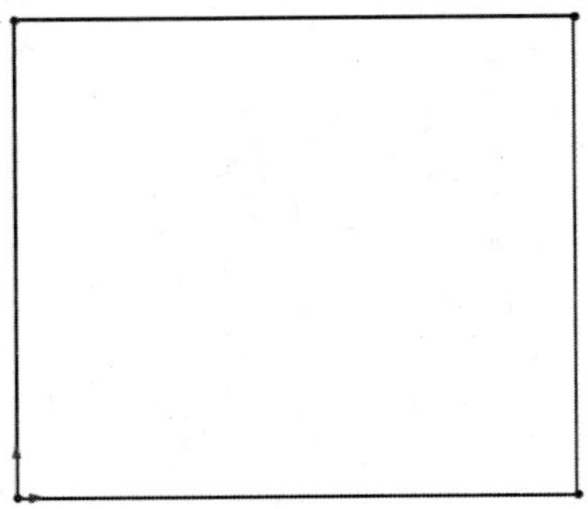

Figure 2-26 The outer loop of the sketch

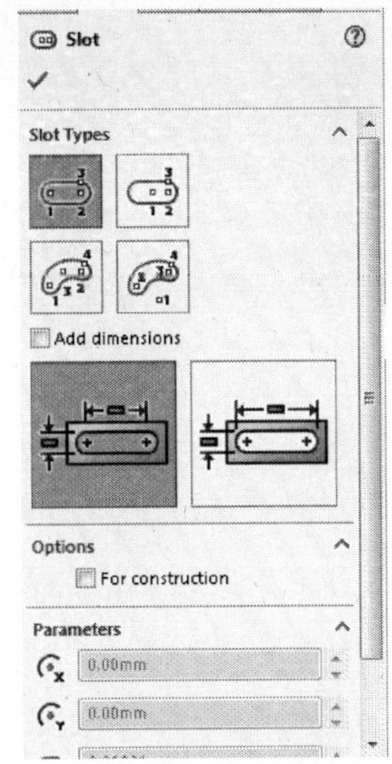

*Figure 2-27 The **Slot PropertyManager***

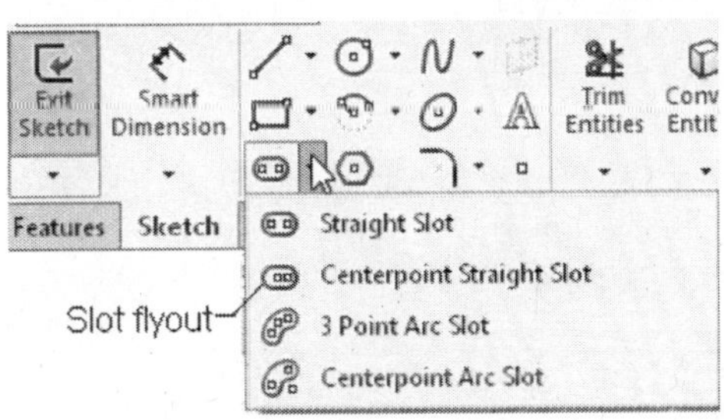

*Figure 2-28 The **Slot** flyout*

Tip
*The tool selected from the **Slot** flyout will be displayed as default tool in the **Sketch CommandManager**.*

6. Make sure that the **Straight Slot** and **Center to Center** buttons are chosen in the **Slot Type** rollout of the **Slot PropertyManager**.

The **Slot Type** rollout of the PropertyManager displays different types of methods to create a slot profile. You can choose the appropriate method from this rollout to draw a slot profile. The **Center to Center** button of this rollout is used to measure the slot length from its center to center. You can also choose the **Overall Length** button from this rollout to measure the overall length of the slot. Note that, by default the **Add dimensions** check box of this rollout is clear. If you select this check box, the current dimensions of the slot will be added to it automatically in the drawing area.

7. Move the cursor to the point whose coordinates are 30 and 50 and then specify the first point of the slot.

Note
The coordinates are displayed in the Status Bar that is located at the bottom of the drawing area.

8. Move the cursor horizontally toward right. You will notice that the symbol of the horizontal relation is displayed below the cursor and the length and angle values are displayed above the cursor.

9. Left-click when the length above the cursor shows the value 60; a reference slot is attached to the cursor.

10. Specify a point in the drawing area, when the width value of the slot is displayed closer to 20 mm in the **Parameters** rollout of the **Slot PropertyManager**.

The **Parameters** rollout of the **Slot PropertyManager** displays the parameters of the slot. The parameters displayed in this rollout will be enabled for modification once the slot is created.

11. Set the value of the **Slot Width** spinner in the **Parameters** rollout of the PropertyManager to **20 mm**.

12. Exit the tool by right-clicking and choosing the **Select** option from the shortcut menu displayed. Figure 2-29 shows the sketch after creating the sketch of the elongated hole by using the **Straight Slot** tool.

13. Choose the **Circle** tool from the **Circle** flyout of the **Sketch CommandManager**; the **Circle PropertyManager** is displayed on the left side of the drawing area. Also, the cursor is changed to a circle cursor.

In SOLIDWORKS, there are two methods to draw circles. The first method is by specifying the center point of a circle and then defining its radius. The second method is drawing a circle by defining the three points that lie on its periphery. The tools used to create circle are grouped together in the **Circle** flyout in the **Sketch CommandManager**. To invoke this flyout, click on the down arrow located next to the **Circle** tool, refer to Figure 2-30.

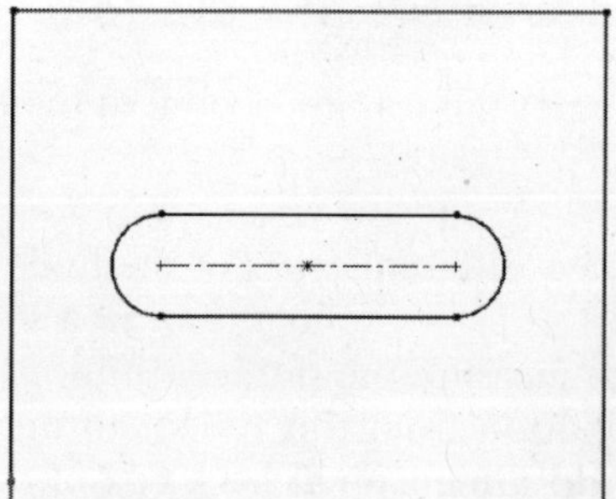

Figure 2-29 The sketch after creating the elongated hole

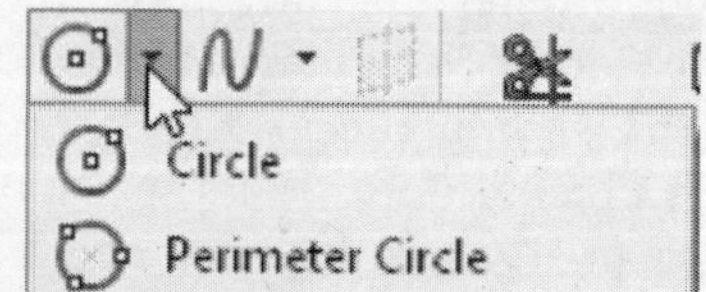

*Figure 2-30 The **Circle** flyout*

Note

You can also select an appropriate method to draw a circle from the ***Circle Type*** *rollout of the* ***Circle PropertyManager****.*

14. Move the circle cursor to the location whose coordinates are 20 and 20 and then specify the center point of the circle at this location; the rubber band circle is attached with the circle cursor. The circle cursor consists of a crosshairs and a circle with snap grid below it.

15. Move the circle cursor horizontally toward the right and click when the radius of the circle on the circle cursor is displayed as 10. The circle of radius 10 mm has been drawn. Note that the **Circle** tool is still active.

16. Move the circle cursor to the location whose coordinates are 100 and 20 and then specify the center point of the circle at this location; the rubber band circle is attached with the circle cursor.

17. Move the circle cursor horizontally toward the right and click when the radius of the circle on the circle cursor is displayed as 10. The circle of radius 10 mm has been drawn. Note that the circle tool is still active.

18. Similarly, draw the other two circles. The coordinates of the center point of the other two circles are 20, 80 and 100, 80.

19. Right-click in the drawing area; a shortcut menu is displayed. Choose the **Select** option from the shortcut menu to exit the **Circle** tool.

20. Choose the **Zoom to Fit (F)** button from the **View (Heads Up) > Hide/Show items** toolbar to fit the sketch on the screen. The final sketch with the display of relations turned on, is shown in Figure 2-31.

Note

To turn on/off the display of relations, choose the ***View Sketch Relations*** *button from the* ***View (Heads-Up)*** *flyout.*

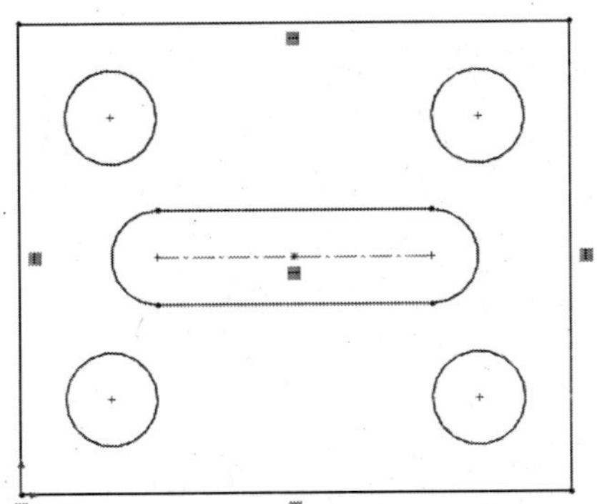

Figure 2-31 *Final sketch for Tutorial 3*

Saving the Sketch

After creating the sketch, save it in the *SOLIDWORKS Tutorials* folder.

1. Choose the **Save** button from the Menu Bar to invoke the **Save As** dialog box. Browse to the *c02* folder inside the *SOLIDWORKS Tutorials* folder.

2. Enter **c02_tut03** as the name of the document in the **File name** edit box and choose the **Save** button. The document is saved at the location *\Documents\SOLIDWORKS Tutorials\c02*.

3. Close the document by choosing **File > Close** from the SOLIDWORKS menus.

Self-Evaluation Test

Answer the following questions and then compare them to those given at the end of this chapter:

1. You can convert a sketched entity into a construction entity by selecting the __________ check box provided in the PropertyManager.

2. To draw a rectangle at an angle, you need to use the __________ tool.

3. You can invoke the __________ tool or press the ESC key to exit the sketching tool.

4. In SOLIDWORKS, a rectangle is considered as a combination of individual __________.

5. The base feature of any design is a sketched feature and is created by drawing a sketch. (T/F)

6. You can invoke the arc mode using the **Line** tool. (T/F)

7. If the value of the **Major grid spacing** and **Minor-lines per major** spinners is set to **100** and **10**, respectively, then the cursor will jump through a distance of 5 mm. (T/F)

8. If you save a file in the sketching environment and then open it next time, it will open in the part modeling environment. (T/F)

Review Questions

Answer the following questions:

1. In SOLIDWORKS, a rectangle is considered as a combination of which of the following entities?

   (a) Lines (b) Arcs
   (c) Splines (d) None of these

2. Which of the following options is displayed in the **New SOLIDWORKS Document** dialog box?

   (a) **Part** (b) **Assembly**
   (c) **Drawing** (d) All of these

3. Which of the following entities is not considered while converting a sketch into a feature?

   (a) Sketched circles (b) Sketched lines
   (c) Construction lines (d) None of these

4. Which of the following PropertyManagers is displayed when you select a line of a rectangle?

   (a) **Line Properties PropertyManager** (b) **Line/Rectangle PropertyManager**
   (c) **Rectangle PropertyManager** (d) None of these

5. Which of the following PropertyManagers is displayed while drawing a parallelogram?

   (a) **Parallelogram PropertyManager** (b) **Rectangle PropertyManager**
   (c) **Elliptical Arc PropertyManager** (d) None of these

6. You can draw a construction line by invoking the **Line** tool. (T/F)

7. You can delete the sketched entities by right-clicking on them and then choosing the **Delete** option from the shortcut menu. (T/F)

8. In sketching environment of SOLIDWORKS, the origin is displayed as a blue icon in the middle of the sketcher screen. (T/F)

9. In SOLIDWORKS, circles are drawn by specifying their centerpoint and radius in the **Circle** dialog box. (T/F)

10. When you open a new SOLIDWORKS document, it is not maximized in the SOLIDWORKS window. (T/F)

EXERCISES

Exercise 1

Draw the sketch of the model shown in Figure 2-32. The sketch to be drawn is shown in Figure 2-33. Do not dimension the sketch. The solid model and its dimensions are given for your reference only. **(Expected time: 30 min)**

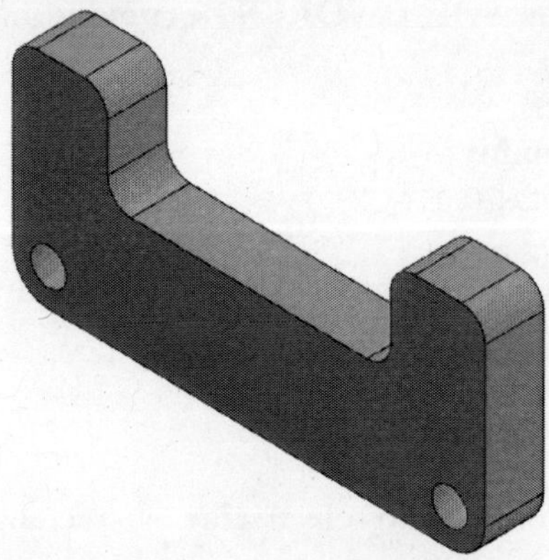

Figure 2-32 Solid model for Exercise 1

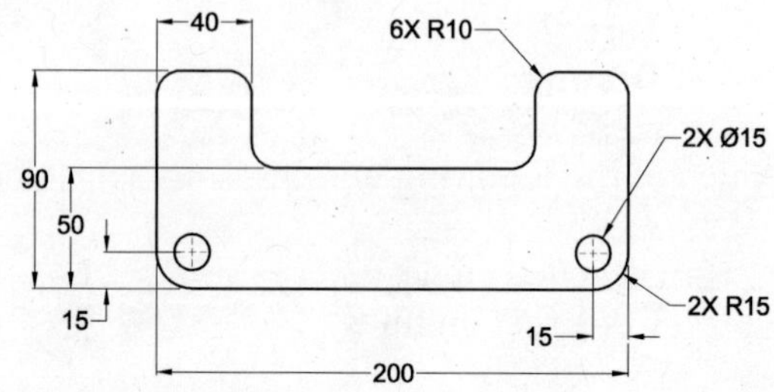

Figure 2-33 Sketch for Exercise 1

Exercise 2

Draw the sketch of the model shown in Figure 2-34. The sketch to be drawn is shown in Figure 2-35. Do not dimension the sketch. The solid model and its dimensions are given for your reference only. **(Expected time: 30 min)**

Figure 2-34 Solid model for Exercise 2

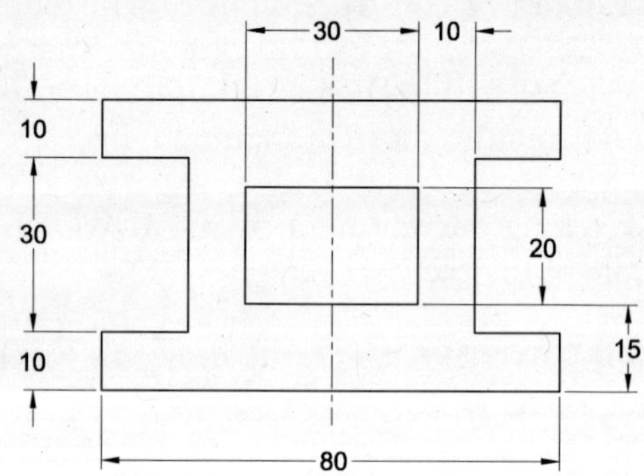

Figure 2-35 Sketch for Exercise 2

Exercise 3

Draw the sketch of the model shown in Figure 2-36. The sketch to be drawn is shown in Figure 2-37. Do not dimension the sketch. The solid model and its dimensions are given for your reference only. **(Expected time: 30 min)**

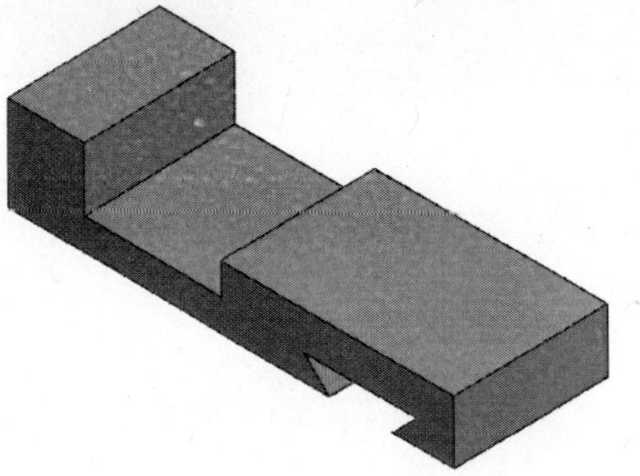

Figure 2-36 *Solid model for Exercise 3*

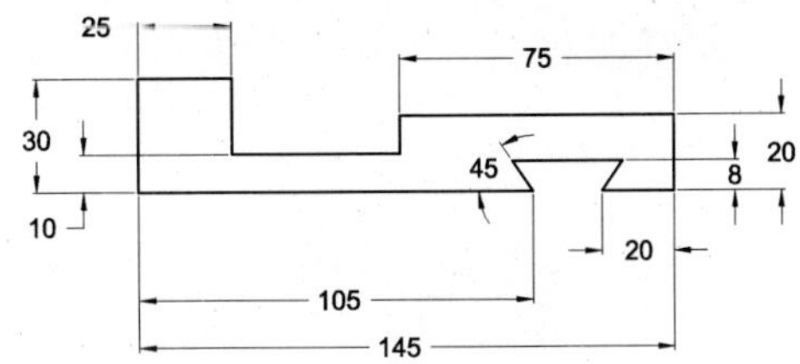

Figure 2-37 *Sketch for Exercise 3*

Answers to Self-Evaluation Test

1. **For construction**, **2.** **Point Corner Rectangle**, **3.** **Select**, **4.** lines **5.** T, **6.** T, **7.** F, **8.** F

This page is intentionally left blank

Chapter 3

Editing and Modifying Sketches

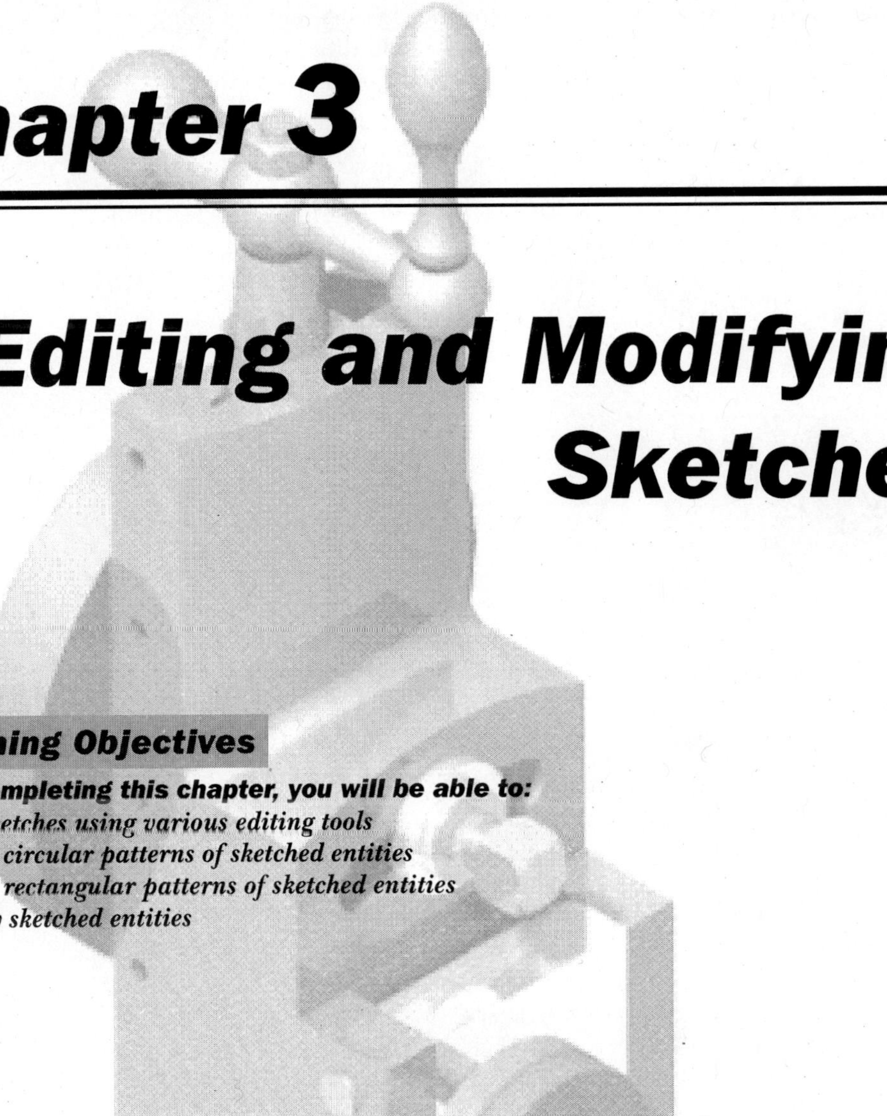

Learning Objectives

After completing this chapter, you will be able to:

- *Edit sketches using various editing tools*
- *Create circular patterns of sketched entities*
- *Create rectangular patterns of sketched entities*
- *Modify sketched entities*

EDITING SKETCHED ENTITIES

SOLIDWORKS provides you with a number of tools that can be used to edit the sketched entities. You can trim, extend, offset, or mirror the sketched entities using these tools. You can also perform various other editing operations by using these tools. Various editing operations and the tools used to perform them are discussed in this chapter.

Tutorial 1

In this tutorial, you will create the base sketch of the model shown in Figure 3-1. The sketch of the model is shown in Figure 3-2. You will create the sketch of the base feature by using the sketch tools. Also, you will modify and edit the sketch using various modifying options. Do not create the center marks and centerlines, as they are for your reference only.

(Expected time: 30 min)

Figure 3-1 *Solid model for Tutorial 1*

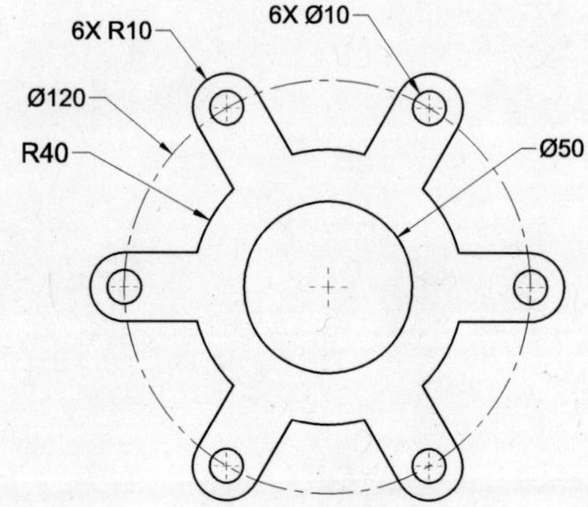

Figure 3-2 *Sketch for Tutorial 1*

The following steps are required to complete this tutorial:

a. Start SOLIDWORKS and then a new part document.
b. Invoke the sketching environment.
c. Modify the snap, grid, and units settings.
d. Draw outer loop of the sketch, refer to Figures 3-5 through 3-11.
e. Draw the inner cavity of the sketch by using the **Circle** and **Circular Sketch Pattern** tools, refer to Figure 3-12.
f. Save the sketch.

Starting SOLIDWORKS and a New SOLIDWORKS Document

1. Start SOLIDWORKS by choosing **Start > All Programs > SOLIDWORKS 2018 > SOLIDWORKS 2018** or by double-clicking on the shortcut icon of SOLIDWORKS 2018 on the desktop of your computer; the SOLIDWORKS window is displayed.

2. Choose the **New** tool from the Menu Bar; the **New SOLIDWORKS Document** dialog box is displayed.

3. In this dialog box, the **Part** button is chosen by default. Choose the **OK** button from this dialog box; a new SOLIDWORKS part document is invoked.

Invoking the Sketching Environment

Next, you need to invoke the sketching environment.

1. Choose the **Sketch** tab from the CommandManager. Next, choose the **Sketch** tool from the **Sketch CommandManager**; the **Edit Sketch PropertyManager** is invoked and you are prompted to select a plane to create the sketch. Also, the three default planes (**Front Plane**, **Right Plane**, and **Top Plane**) available in SOLIDWORKS are temporarily displayed on the screen.

2. Select the **Front Plane** as the sketching plane; the sketching environment is invoked and the plane is oriented normal to the view.

Modifying the Snap, Grid, and Unit Settings

It is assumed that while installing SOLIDWORKS, you have selected the **MMGS (millimeters, gram, second)** option for measuring the length. Therefore, the length of an entity will be measured in millimeters in the current file. But, if you select some other unit at the time of installation, you need to change the linear and angular units before drawing the sketch. For this tutorial, you need to modify the grid and snap settings so that the cursor jumps through a distance of 10 mm.

1. Choose the **Unit system** button located in the Status Bar; a flyout is displayed with a tick mark next to the unit system of the current document, as shown in Figure 3-3.

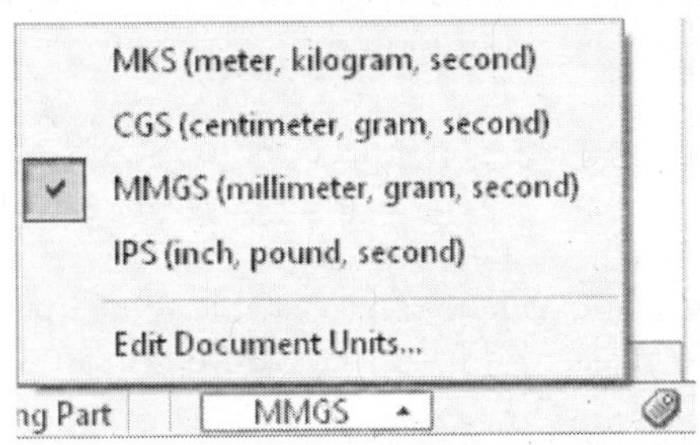

Figure 3-3 *The flyout showing the currently selected unit system*

2. Choose the **Edit Document Units** option from this flyout; the **Document Properties - Units** dialog box is displayed.

Note

If you have selected millimeters as the unit of measurement while installing SOLIDWORKS, you can skip step 3 in this section.

3. Select the **MMGS (millimeter, gram, second)** in the **Unit system** area. Also, select the **degrees** option from the **Angle** area in the **Units** column.

Note

You can also select the required unit system for the current document by selecting the required unit system from the ***Unit system*** *flyout directly. However, in this case, if you are in the sketcher environment, you will automatically exit the sketcher environment.*

As evident from Figure 3-2, the dimensions in the sketch are multiples of 10. Therefore, you need to modify the grid and snap settings such that the cursor jumps through a distance of 10 mm.

4. Select the **Grid/Snap** option on the left of the **Document Properties - Units** dialog box to display all the options related to the grid and snap. Also, note that the name of the dialog box is modified to the **Document Properties - Grid/Snap** dialog box.

5. In this dialog box, set the value in the **Major grid spacing** and **Minor-lines per major** spinner to **100** and **10**, respectively.

6. Invoke the **System Options - Relations/Snaps** dialog box by choosing the **Go To System Snaps** button from the **Document Properties - Grid/Snap** dialog box. Next, make sure that the **Grid** check box is selected in it.

7. Choose the **OK** button to exit from the dialog box.

Now, when you move the cursor, the coordinates that are displayed closer to the lower right corner of the drawing area show an increment of 10 mm.

As evident from Figure 3-2, the sketch consists of the outer loop and inner cavities. It is recommended that you create the outer loop of the sketch first and then the inner cavities.

Drawing the Outer Loop of the Sketch

The outer loop of the sketch will be drawn by using the **Circle**, **Line**, and **Trim Entities** tools.

1. Choose the **Circle** tool from the **Circle** flyout in the **Sketch CommandManager**; the **Circle PropertyManager** is displayed with the **Circle** button chosen in the **Circle Type** rollout.

Tip

You can also choose an appropriate method to create a circle from the ***Circle Type*** *rollout of the* ***Circle PropertyManager****. The* ***Circle*** *tool of this rollout is used to create a circle by specifying the center point of the circle and then defining its radius. The* ***Perimeter Circle*** *tool in this rollout is used to draw a circle by defining three points that lie on its periphery.*

2. Move the cursor toward the origin and specify the center point of the circle when it snaps to the origin and the symbol of coincident relation is displayed below the cursor.

3. Move the cursor horizontally toward the right and click when the radius of the circle above the cursor shows the value 40.

4. Right-click in the drawing area to invoke the shortcut menu. Now, choose the **Select** option from the shortcut menu to exit the **Circle** tool.

5. Choose the **Zoom to Area** tool from the **View (Heads-Up)** toolbar. Press and hold the left mouse button and drag the cursor to define a window such that the sketched circle is placed in the window. Next, release the left mouse button to increase the display area of the sketch.

The **Zoom to Area** tool is used to magnify a specified area of the drawing window. The portion of the drawing that is inside the magnified area can be viewed in the current window.

6. Exit the tool by choosing the **Select** option from the shortcut menu that is displayed after right-clicking in the drawing area.

7. Press the right mouse button and drag the cursor; the Mouse Gesture is displayed in the drawing area, refer to Figure 3-4. Move the cursor over the **Circle** tool; the **Circle** tool is invoked and the cursor is changed to a circle cursor.

Note

You can also invoke the ***Circle*** *tool from the* ***Sketch CommandManager****, as discussed earlier.*

In SOLIDWORKS, when you press the right mouse button and drag the cursor in a direction, a set of radially arranged tools are displayed. This action is called Mouse Gesture. After displaying the tools by using the Mouse Gesture, you can move the cursor over a particular tool to invoke it.

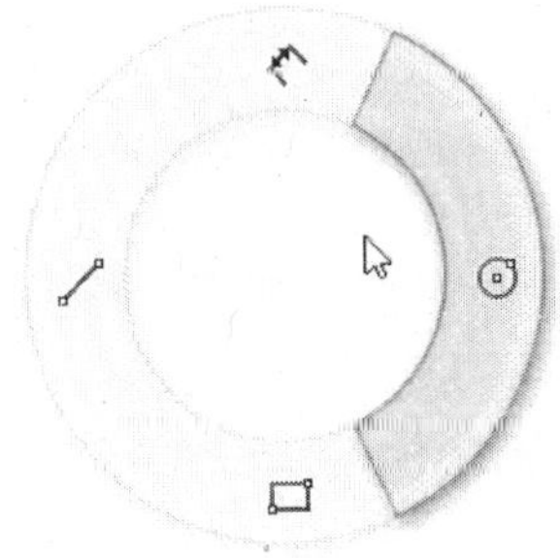

Figure 3-4 *Tools displayed in the Mouse Gesture in the sketching environment*

By default, four tools are displayed in the Mouse Gesture. However, you can customize the Mouse Gesture and display eight tools. To customize the Mouse Gesture, invoke the **Customize** dialog box by choosing the **Tools > Customize** from the SOLIDWORKS menus and then choose the **Mouse Gestures** tab. Next, select the **12 gestures** radio button from the top right corner of the dialog box to display the Mouse Gesture with 12 tools. The **Enable mouse gestures** check box in this dialog box is used to enable or disable the Mouse Gesture.

Note

The tools displayed by Mouse Gesture are different for different environments. For example, when you invoke the Mouse Gesture in the ***Part*** *environment, it displays the tools of the* ***Part*** *environment. Similarly, when you invoke the Mouse Gesture in the* ***Sketching*** *environment, it displays the tools of the* ***Sketch*** *environment.*

8. Move the cursor to the location whose coordinates are 60, 0, 0 and specify the center point of the circle at this location by clicking the left mouse button.

9. Move the cursor horizontally toward the right and click the left mouse button when the radius above the cursor shows 10 mm. Next, exit the tool by right-clicking in the drawing area and choosing the **Select** option from the shortcut menu. Figure 3-5 shows the sketch after drawing the circles of 80 mm and 20 mm diameters.

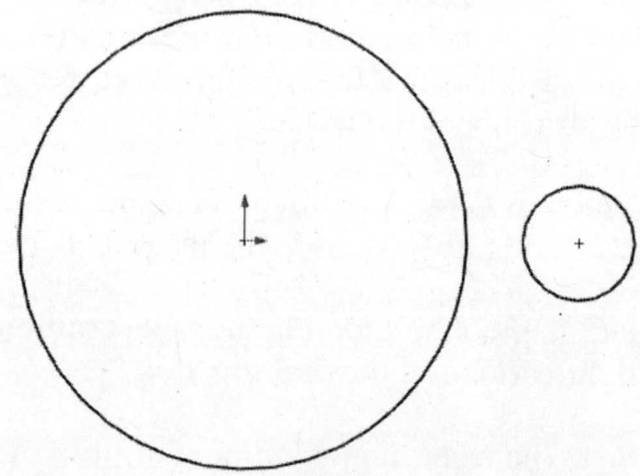

Figure 3-5 *Sketch after drawing circles*

10. Invoke the **Line** tool from the Mouse Gesture. To do so, press and hold the right mouse button and drag the cursor to a small distance; a set of sketching tools is displayed. Move the cursor over the **Line** tool; the **Line** tool is invoked and the cursor is converted into a line cursor.

Note

*You can also invoke the **Line** tool from the **Sketch CommandManager**, as discussed earlier.*

11. Move the line cursor to the location whose coordinates are 60, 10, 0. Next, specify the start point of the line when the line cursor snaps to the circle of diameter 20 mm and displays the symbol of coincident relation below the line cursor.

12. After specifying the first point of the line, move the line cursor horizontally toward the circle of diameter **80** mm; a rubber band line is attached to the cursor.

13. Specify the end point of the line when the line cursor snaps to the circle of diameter 80 mm and the symbol of coincident and horizontal relations are displayed below the line cursor.

14. Right-click in the drawing area and choose the **End Chain** option from the shortcut menu; the current chain ends but the **Line** tool still remains active.

Note

*When you terminate the process of drawing a line by double-clicking on the screen or by choosing the **End Chain** from the shortcut menu, the current chain would end. However, the **Line** tool would remain active.*

15. Move the line cursor to the location whose coordinates are 60, -10, 0. Now, specify the start point of the line when the line cursor snaps to the circle of diameter 20 mm and the symbol of coincident relation is displayed below the line cursor.

16. Move the line cursor horizontally towards the circle of diameter 80 mm; a rubber band line is attached to the cursor.

17. Specify the end point of the line when the line cursor snaps to the circle of diameter 80 mm and the symbols of coincident and horizontal relations are displayed below the line cursor.

18. Right-click in the drawing area and choose the **Select** option from the shortcut menu to exit the **Line** tool. Figure 3-6 shows the sketch after drawing the horizontal lines.

    Now, you need to trim the unwanted entities of the sketch by using the **Trim Entities** tool.

19. Choose the **Trim Entities** tool from the **Sketch CommandManager**; the **Trim PropertyManager** is displayed on the left of the drawing area, refer to Figure 3-7.

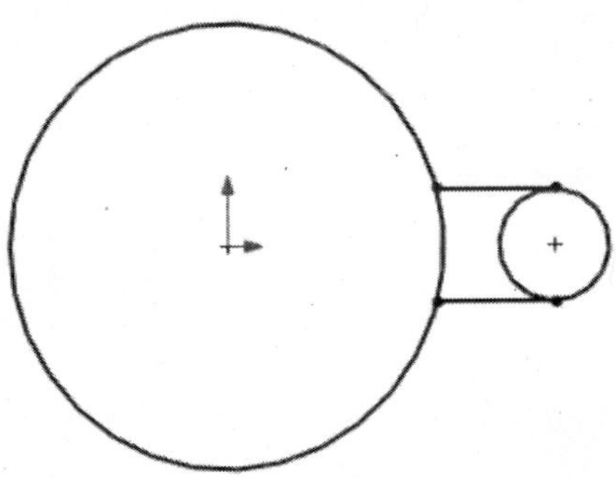

Figure 3-6 Sketch after drawing the lines

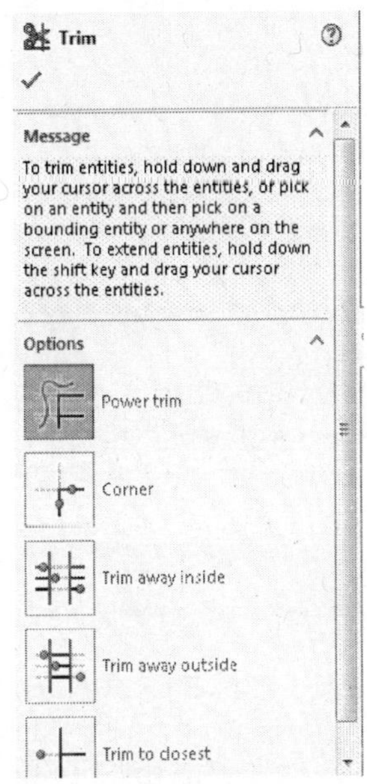

Figure 3-7** The **Trim PropertyManager

The **Trim Entities** tool is used to trim the unwanted entities in a sketch. You can use this tool to trim a line, arc, ellipse, parabola, circle, spline, centerline intersecting another line, arc, ellipse, parabola, circle, spline, or centerline. You can also extend the sketched entities using the **Trim Entities** tool.

The options of the **Trim PropertyManager** are discussed next.

Message Rollout

The **Message** rollout in the **Trim PropertyManager** informs you about the procedure of trimming and extending the sketched elements, depending upon the option selected in the **Options** rollout.

Options Rollout

The **Options** rollout displays all options that are used to trim the sketched entities. These options are discussed next.

Power trim: When the **Power trim** button is chosen in the **Options** rollout, the **Message** rollout of the **Trim PropertyManager** will inform you about the procedure of trimming and extending the sketched elements. To trim the unwanted portion of a sketch using this option, press and hold the left mouse button and drag the cursor. You will notice that a gray-colored drag trace line is displayed along the path of the cursor. When you drag the cursor across the unwanted sketched entity, it will be trimmed and a small red-colored box will be displayed in its place. You can continue trimming the entities by dragging the cursor across them. After trimming all unwanted entities, release the left mouse button.

To extend or shorten an entity dynamically when the **Power trim** button is chosen in the **Trim PropertyManager**, click once on the entity and then move the cursor; the entity will extend or shorten dynamically depending upon the direction of movement. Move the cursor up to a level to which the entity has to be extended or shortened. Press the left mouse button to complete the operation.

To extend a line or a curve such that it intersects the other entity, select the first entity and then the second entity; the first entity will extend and intersects the second entity. While extending, if the first entity cannot intersect the second entity, then the first entity will extend up to the apparent intersection point.

Note

If the first entity cannot be extended to intersect the second entity, then a tooltip will be displayed stating that the selected entity cannot be extended to intersect the second entity.

Corner: The **Corner** button in the **Options** rollout is used to trim or extend the sketched entities in such a way that the resulting entities form a corner. To trim the unwanted elements using this option, choose the **Corner** button from the **Options** rollout; you will be prompted to select an entity. Select the entity from the geometry area; you will be prompted to select another entity. When you move the cursor over the second entity, the preview of the resulting entity will be displayed in a different color. In the second entity, select the portion to be retained.

You can also extend the entities using this tool. To do so, choose the **Corner** button from the **Options** rollout and select the entities to be extended; the selected entities will be extended to their apparent intersection.

Trim away inside: The **Trim away inside** button in the **Options** rollout is used to trim the portion of the selected entity that lies inside two bounding entities. To do so, invoke the **Trim PropertyManager** and choose the **Trim away inside** button from the **Options**

rollout; the **Message** rollout will be displayed informing you to select the two bounding entities, and then to select the entities to be trimmed. Select the bounding entities from the drawing area. Now, select the entities to be trimmed from the drawing area; the portion of the entity inside the bounding entities will be removed and the portion outside the bounding entities will be retained.

Trim away outside: The **Trim away outside** button in the **Options** rollout is used to trim the portion of an entity outside the bounding entities. To do so, invoke the **Trim PropertyManager** and choose the **Trim away outside** button from the **Options** rollout; the **Message** rollout will inform you to select the two bounding entities, and then to select the entities to be trimmed.

Trim to closest: The **Trim to closest** button is used to trim the selected entity to its closest intersection. To do so, invoke the **Trim PropertyManager** and then choose the **Trim to closest** button from the **Options** rollout; the cursor will be replaced by the trim cursor. Move the trim cursor near the portion of the sketched entity to be removed; the entity or the portion of the entity to be removed will be highlighted in orange. Press the left mouse button to remove the highlighted entity.

You can also extend the sketched entities when the **Trim to closest** button is chosen in the **Trim PropertyManager**. To do so, move the trim cursor to the entity to be extended; the sketched entity will turn orange. Now, press the left mouse button and drag the cursor to the entity up to which it has to be extended. You will notice the preview of the extended entity. Release the left mouse button when the preview of the extended entity appears; the entity will be extended.

20. Choose the **Trim to closest** button from the **Options** rollout of the **Trim PropertyManager**; the cursor is replaced by the trim cursor.

21. Move the trim cursor near the sketched entities to be removed one by one. Refer to Figure 3-8 for the entities to be trimmed. Next, click the left mouse button to trim them. Figure 3-9 shows the sketch after trimming the entities.

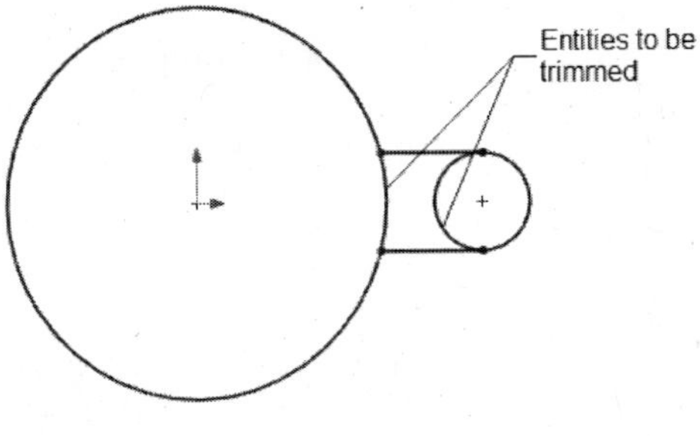

Figure 3-8 *Entities to be trimmed*

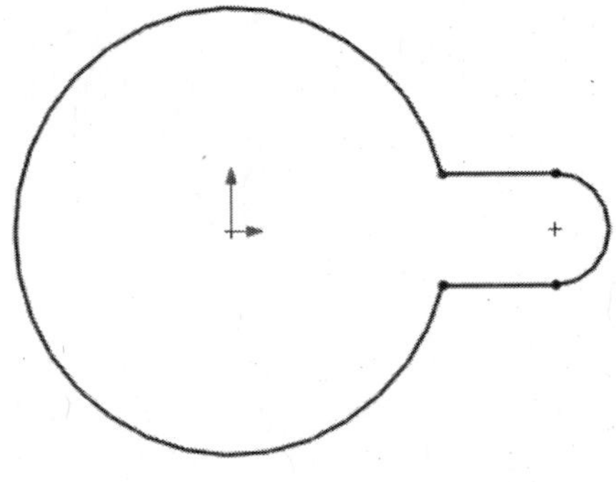

Figure 3-9 *Sketch after trimming the entities*

22. Next, choose the **Close Dialog** button from the **Trim PropertyManager** to exit it.

23. Press the CTRL key and select both the horizontal lines and the arc of radius 10 mm. Next, choose the **Circular Sketch Pattern** tool from the **Linear Sketch Pattern** flyout in the **Sketch CommandManager**; the **Circular Pattern PropertyManager** is displayed, refer to Figure 3-10 and the preview of the circular pattern with default settings is displayed in the drawing area.

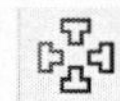

Also, you will notice that the center of the circular pattern is placed at the origin and an arrow is displayed, indicating that the origin is the center of the circular pattern. If required, you can modify the center of the circular pattern by setting the coordinates of the point in the **Center X** and **Center Y** spinners in the **Parameters** rollout of the PropertyManager. Alternatively, drag the arrow displayed at the center of the pattern to the required location.

The **Circular Sketch Pattern** tool is used to create a circular pattern of the selected entities. You can also create linear pattern of the selected entities. To do so, you need to choose the **Linear Sketch Pattern** tool from the **Sketch CommandManager**. Next, you need to define the first and second linear directions for creating the linear pattern. Also, you can define the number of instances in respective direction and spacing between each instance.

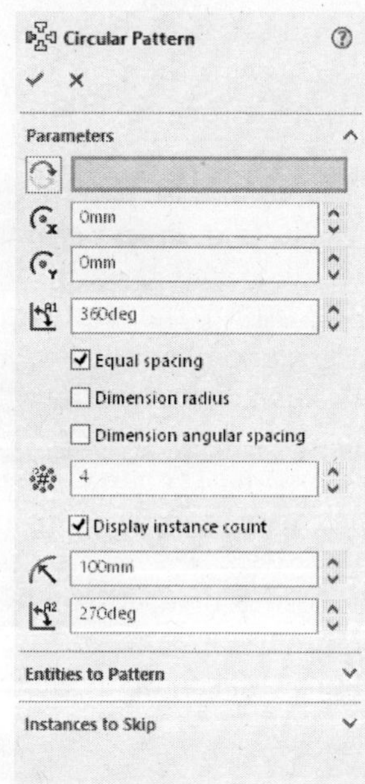

*Figure 3-10 The **Circular Pattern PropertyManager***

24. Set the value of the **Number of Instances** spinner to **6**.

25. Make sure that the **Equal spacing** check box is selected. Next, clear the **Dimension radius** and **Dimension angular spacing** check boxes.

26. Select the **Display instance count** check box, if it is not selected by default. Accept the other default values and choose the **OK** button to create a pattern.

The **Display instance count** check box is used to display the number of instances in the resulting sketch pattern.

27. Trim the unwanted portion of the 80 mm diameter circle using the **Trim Entities** tool. You need to use the **Trim to closest** button for this trimming.

28. Choose **Close Dialog** after trimming. The outer loop of the sketch is created, as shown in Figure 3-11.

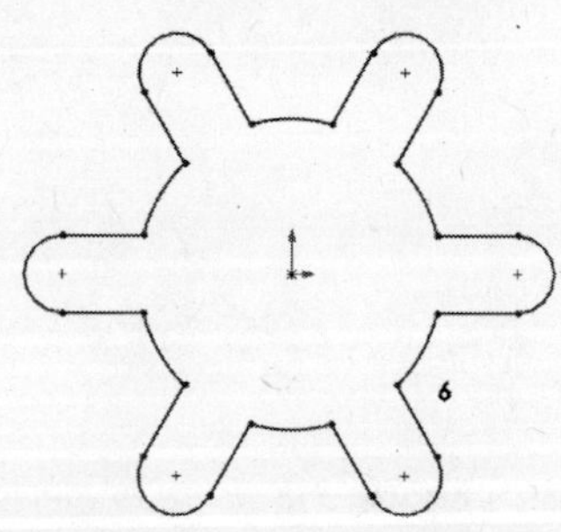

***Figure 3-11** Sketch after drawing the outer loop*

Drawing Inner Cavities of the Sketch

As is evident from Figure 3-2, you need to create seven circles. Out of seven circles, six are to be of 10 mm diameter. Therefore, after drawing the first circle of 10 mm diameter, you need to create the other five circles of same diameter by creating a circular pattern of the parent circle.

1. Invoke the **Circle** tool by using the Mouse Gesture. As soon as you invoke the **Circle** tool, the **Circle PropertyManager** is displayed.

2. Select the center point of the 10 mm radius arc on the left quadrant of the larger circle as the center point of the new circle.

3. Press and hold the CTRL key and draw a circle of radius close to 5. Make sure you press the CTRL key so that the cursor does not snap to the points or grid.

4. Set **5** in the **Radius** spinner in the **Circle PropertyManager**. Next, choose the **Close Dialog** button to exit the **Circle PropertyManager**.

   Now, you need to create the other five instances of the circle by using the **Circular Sketch Pattern**.

5. Choose the **Circular Sketch Pattern** tool from the **Linear Sketch Pattern** flyout in the **Sketch CommandManager**; the **Circular Pattern PropertyManager** is displayed and a preview of the circular pattern is displayed with an arrow at the center.

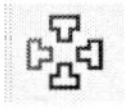

6. Set **6** in the **Number of Instances** spinner.

7. Make sure that the **Equal spacing** check box is selected. Next, clear the **Dimension radius** and **Dimension angular spacing** check boxes.

8. Select the **Display instance count** check box. Accept the remaining default values and choose the **OK** button to create the pattern.

9. Choose the **Circle** tool from the **Sketch CommandManager**; the **Circle PropertyManager** is invoked. Specify the center point of the circle at the origin. Next, press and hold the CTRL key and draw a circle of radius close to 25 mm.

10. Enter **25** in the **Radius** spinner in the **Circle PropertyManager**. Next, choose the **Close Dialog** button to exit the **Circle PropertyManager**. The final sketch of the model is shown in Figure 3-12. In this figure, all relations are hidden for clarity.

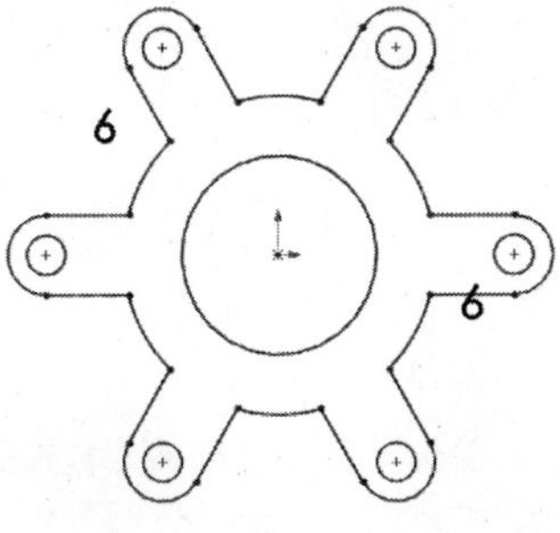

Figure 3-12 *Final sketch*

Saving the Sketch

1. Choose the **Save** button from the Menu Bar; the **Save As** dialog box is displayed.

2. Browse to the *SOLIDWORKS Tutorials* folder, choose the **New Folder** button from the **Save As** dialog box, specify the name of the new folder as *c03*, and then press ENTER twice. Next, enter the name of the document as **c03_tut01** in the **File name** edit box and choose the **Save** button; the document is saved at the location */Documents/SOLIDWORKS Tutorials/c03*.

3. Close the file by choosing **File > Close** from the SOLIDWORKS menus.

Tutorial 2

In this tutorial, you will create the base sketch of the model shown in Figure 3-13. The sketch of the model is shown in Figure 3-14. You will draw the sketch with a mirror line. The dimensions given in Figure 3-14 are for your reference only. **(Expected time: 30 min)**

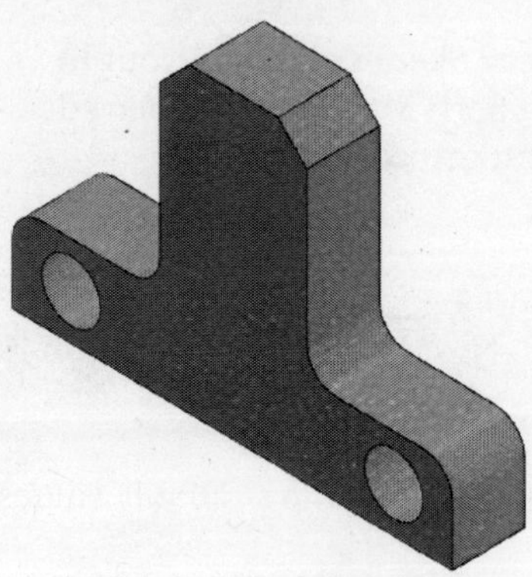

Figure 3-13 *Solid model for Tutorial 2*

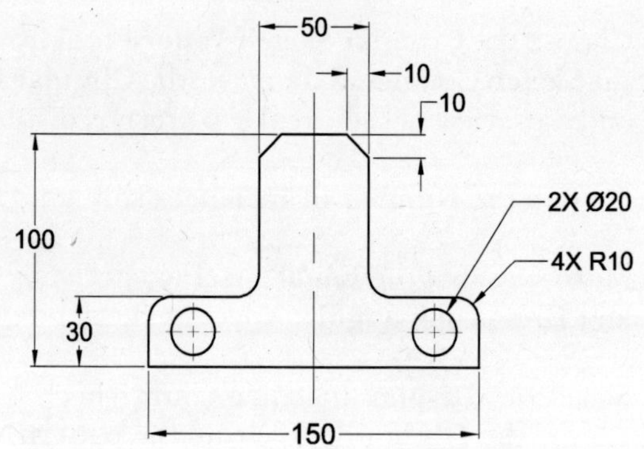

Figure 3-14 *Sketch for Tutorial 2*

The following steps are required to complete this tutorial:

a. Start SOLIDWORKS and then a new part document.
b. Invoke the sketching environment.
c. Modify the snap, grid, and units settings.
d. Create vertical centerline and convert it into a mirror line using the **Dynamic Mirror** tool.
e. Create the left side sketch; the sketch will automatically be mirrored on the right side of the mirror line, refer to Figure 3-17.
f. Apply fillets, refer to Figure 3-20.
g. Apply chamfers, refer to Figure 3-23.
h. Save the sketch.

Starting SOLIDWORKS and a New SOLIDWORKS Document

1. Start SOLIDWORKS and then invoke the **New SOLIDWORKS Document** dialog box by choosing the **New** tool from the Menu Bar. Next, invoke the **Part** environment.

Invoking the Sketching Environment

Now, you will invoke the sketching environment.

1. Choose the **Sketch** tab from the **CommandManager**. Next, choose the **Sketch** tool from the **Sketch CommandManager**; the **Edit Sketch PropertyManager** is invoked and you are prompted to select the plane to create the sketch.

2. Select the **Front Plane**; the sketching environment is invoked and the plane is oriented normal to the view.

Modifying the Snap, Grid, and Unit Settings

Before drawing the sketch, you need to modify the grid and snap settings to make the cursor jump through a distance of 5 mm.

1. Choose the **Options** button from the Menu Bar; the **System Option - General** dialog box is displayed.

2. Choose the **Document Properties** tab and select the **Grid/Snap** option from the area on the left of the dialog box. Set the values **50** and **10** in the **Major grid spacing** and the **Minor-lines per major** spinners, respectively.

3. If on invoking the sketching environment, the grid is displayed, you can turn off its display by clearing the **Display grid** check box in the **Grid** area.

4. Choose the **Go To System Snaps** button and select the **Grid** check box. Next, clear the **Snap only when grid is displayed** check box, if it is already selected.

   If you have selected a unit other than millimeter to measure the length while installing SOLIDWORKS, you need to select millimeter as the unit for the current drawing by following the next two steps.

5. Choose the **Document Properties** tab and select the **Units** option from the area on the left of the **Document Properties - Grid/Snap** dialog box.

6. Select the **MMGS (millimeter, gram, second)** radio button in the **Unit system** area. Next, select **degrees** from the drop-down list in the cell corresponding to the **Angle** row and the **Unit** column.

7. After modifying the necessary settings, choose the **OK** button.

   The coordinates displayed close to the lower right corner of the SOLIDWORKS window show an increment of 5 mm when you move the cursor in the drawing area after exiting the dialog box.

Drawing the Centerline and Converting it into a Mirror Line

It is recommended that you draw symmetrical sketches about the centerline that is created by using the **Centerline** tool.

1. Choose the **Centerline** tool from the **Line** flyout in the **Sketch CommandManager**; the **Insert Line PropertyManager** is displayed. Note that the **For construction** check box is selected in this PropertyManager.

2. Move the line cursor toward the origin and specify the start point of the centerline when it snaps to the origin and the symbol of coincident relation is displayed above the cursor.

3. Move the cursor vertically upward and click to specify the end point of the centerline when the length of the centerline above the cursor is displayed close to 110. You may have to zoom and pan the drawing to draw a line of this length.

4. Press F to fit the drawing on the screen. Next, right-click and choose the **Select** option from the shortcut menu; the line cursor is replaced by the select cursor.

5. Select the centerline and choose **Tools > Sketch Tools > Dynamic Mirror** from the SOLIDWORKS menus; the selected centerline is converted into mirror line and the dynamic mirror option is activated.

   You can confirm the creation of the mirror line and the activation of the dynamic mirror option by observing the symmetrical symbol displayed on both ends of the centerline.

Drawing the Sketch

Next, you need to draw the sketch of the model. You will draw the sketch on the left of the mirror line and the same sketch will be created automatically on the right side of the mirror line. The symmetrical relation is applied between the parent entity and the mirrored entity.

1. Press the L key on the keyboard; the **Line** tool is invoked.

2. Move the line cursor towards the origin and specify the start point of the line when it snaps to the origin and the symbol of coincident relation is displayed above the cursor.

3. Move the cursor horizontally toward the left and specify the endpoint of the line when 75 is displayed above the cursor.

   You will notice that as soon as you specify the endpoint of the line, a mirror image is automatically created on the right of the mirror line. The line drawn as the mirrored entity is merged with the line drawn on the left. Therefore, the entire line becomes a single entity. Remember that the lines will merge only if one of the endpoints of the line drawn is coincident with the mirror line.

4. Move the cursor vertically upward and click to specify the endpoint of the line when the length of the line above the cursor is displayed as 30.

   You will notice that as soon as you specify the endpoint of the line, a mirror image is created automatically on the other side of the mirror line.

5. Move the cursor horizontally toward the right and click to specify the endpoint of the line when the length of the line above the cursor is displayed as 50; a mirror image is created automatically on the other side of the mirror line.

6. Move the cursor vertically upward and click to specify the endpoint of the line when the length of the line above the cursor is displayed as 70; a mirror image is created automatically on the other side of the mirror line.

7. Move the cursor horizontally toward the right and click to specify the endpoint of the line when the cursor snaps to the centerline; a mirror image is created automatically on the other side of the mirror line. The sketch after drawing the lines is shown in Figure 3-15.

8. Right-click in the drawing area to display a shortcut menu. Next, choose the **Select** option from the shortcut menu to exit the **Line** tool.

   Note that the symmetrical symbol is still displayed on both ends of the centerline. It indicates that the dynamic mirror option is still activated. Since this tool is activated, you will create left side circle of the sketch and the right side circle will be created automatically.

9. Choose the **Circle** tool from the **Circle** flyout in the **Sketch CommandManager**; the **Circle PropertyManager** is displayed, as shown in Figure 3-16.

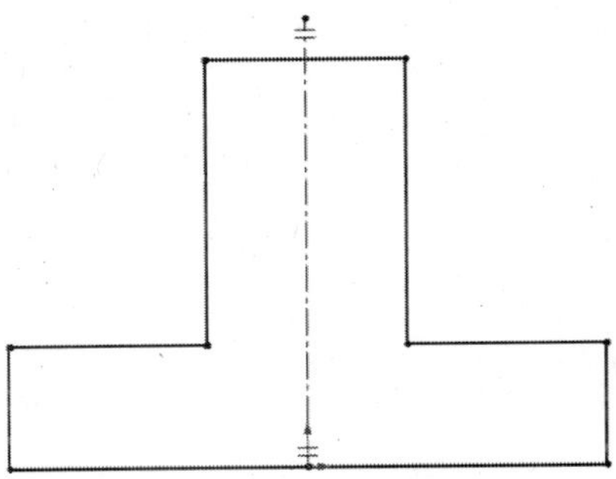

Figure 3-15 *Sketch after drawing lines*

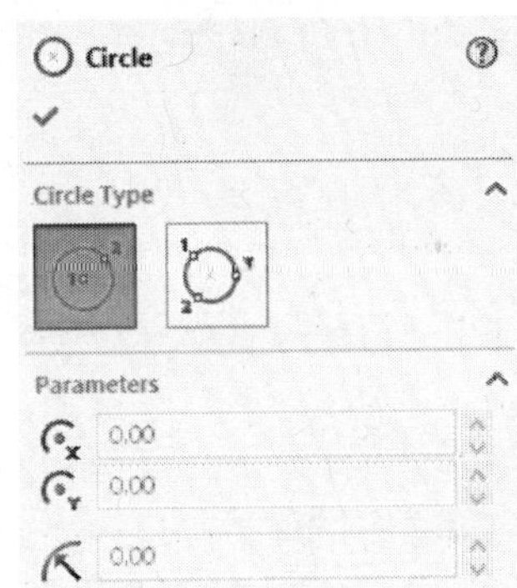

Figure 3-16 *The* ***Circle PropertyManager***

10. Move the cursor to the location whose coordinates are -55 mm, 15 mm, 0 mm and specify it as the center point of the circle.

11. Move the cursor horizontally toward right to draw a circle and click the left mouse button when the radius of the circle above the cursor shows 10; a circle of 10 mm radius is drawn. Also, a mirror image is created automatically on the right side of the mirror line, refer to Figure 3-17.

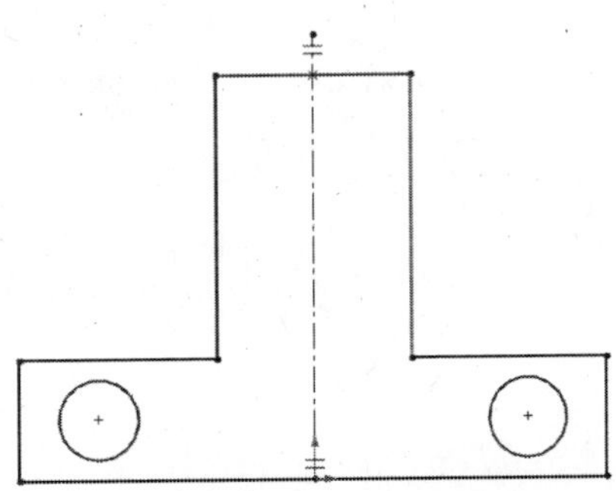

Figure 3-17 *Sketch after drawing circles*

12. Exit the **Circle** tool by pressing the ESC key or choosing the **Select** option from the shortcut menu.

Now, you need to disable the dynamic mirroring.

13. Right-click in the drawing area and then choose **Recent Commands > Dynamic Mirror Entities** from the shortcut menu to disable dynamic mirroring.

Filleting Sketched Entities

Now, you need to fillet the sketched entities by using the **Sketch Fillet** tool.

1. Choose the **Sketch Fillet** tool from the **Sketch CommandManager**; the **Sketch Fillet PropertyManager** is displayed, as shown in Figure 3-18. Also, you are prompted to select the sketched entities or sketched vertex to be filleted.

The **Sketch Fillet** tool is used to create a fillet or a tangent arc at the intersection of two sketched entities. It trims or extends the entities to be filleted, depending on the geometry of the sketched entity. You can apply a fillet to two nonparallel lines, two arcs, two splines, an arc and a line, a spline and a line, or a spline and an arc. A fillet between two arcs and a line depends on the compatibility of the geometry to be extended or filleted along the given radius.

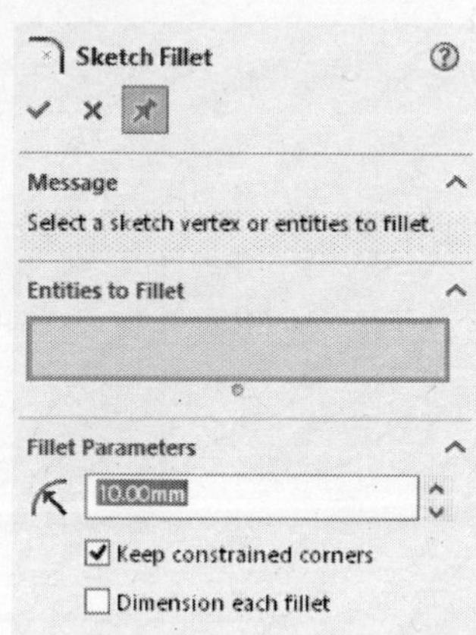

Figure 3-18 The Sketch Fillet PropertyManager

2. Select the first set of entities to be filleted, refer to Figure 3-19; the preview of the fillet with the default radius is displayed. Next, select the second, third, and forth set of entities to be filleted one by one, refer to Figure 3-19.

3. Set the value of the **Fillet Radius** spinner in the **Fillet Parameters** rollout of the PropertyManager to **10**.

4. Ensure that the **Dimension each fillet** check box in the **Fillet Parameters** rollout of the PropertyManager is cleared.

If the **Dimension each fillet** check box is selected, it will apply dimensions individually to all set of entities to be filleted. Therefore, you can control the dimension of each entities of the selected set individually and create multiple fillets of different radii. However, if this check box is cleared, the dimensions will be applied to the last selected entity only and equal radii relation with the other entities of the selected set to be filleted. Therefore, while modifying the radii of the first set of entities, the radii of all the other set of entities will be modified automatically.

> **Tip**
> *You can also select the vertex formed at the intersection of the two entities to be filleted.*

5. Choose the **OK** button twice from the **Sketch Fillet PropertyManager** to exit from it. The sketch after creating the fillets is shown in Figure 3-20.

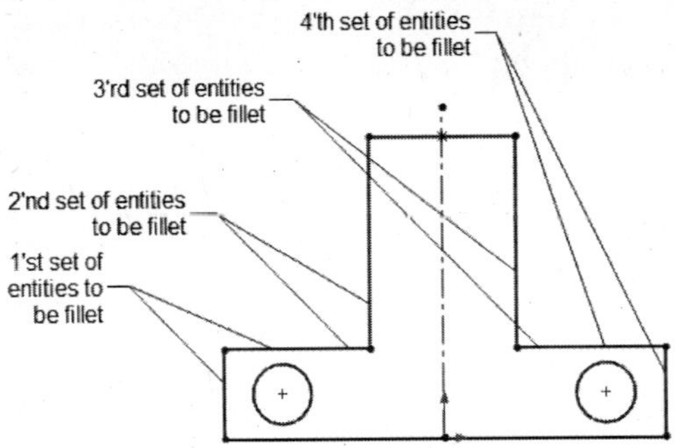

Figure 3-19 Sets of entities to be filleted

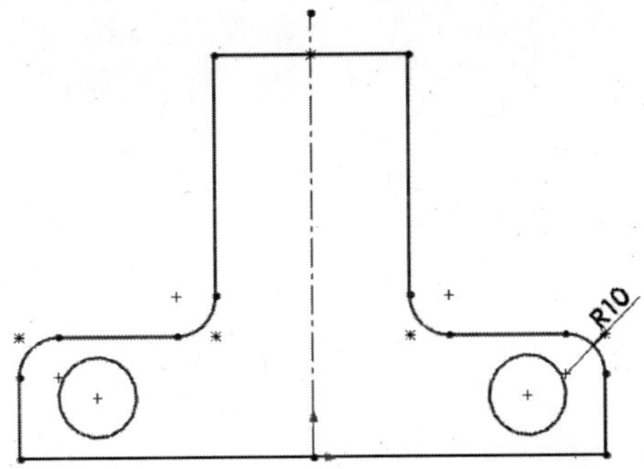

Figure 3-20 Sketch after creating the fillets

Chamfering Sketched Entities

Now, you need to chamfer the sketched entities by using the **Sketch Chamfer** tool.

1. Choose the **Sketch Chamfer** tool from the **Sketch Fillet** flyout in the **Sketch CommandManager**; the **Sketch Chamfer PropertyManager** is displayed, as shown in Figure 3-21.

The **Sketch Chamfer** tool is used to apply a chamfer to the adjacent sketched entities at the point of intersection. A chamfer can be specified by two lengths or angle and length from the point of intersection. You can apply a chamfer between two nonparallel lines that may be intersecting or non-intersecting. The creation of a chamfer between two non-intersecting lines depends on the length of the lines and the chamfer distance.

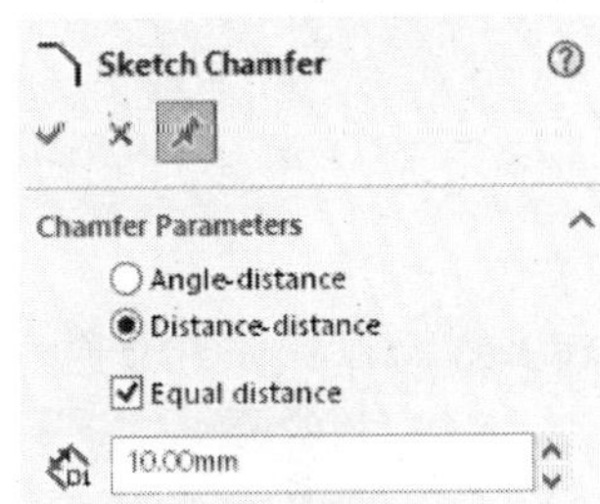

*Figure 3-21 The **Sketch Chamfer PropertyManager***

2. Make sure that the **Distance-distance** radio button and **Equal distance** check box are selected in the **Chamfer Parameters** rollout of the PropertyManager.

The **Distance-distance** radio button allows you to create chamfer by specifying the distance value. If the **Equal distance** check box is selected, only the **Distance 1** spinner is available in the PropertyManager to specify the distance value for creating chamfer. The distance entered in this spinner will also be applied as the distance of the second direction for creating chamfer. However, if you clear this check box, it allows you to specify two different distances for creating a chamfer. As soon as you clear the **Equal distance** check box, the **Distance 2** spinner will also be displayed below the **Distance 1** spinner of the **Sketch Chamfer PropertyManager** to set the value of the distance in the second direction.

Tip

*You can also create a chamfer by specifying the angle and distance values. To do so, you need to select the **Angle-distance** radio button from the **Sketch Chamfer PropertyManager**. When you select this radio button, the **Distance 1** and **Direction 1 Angle** spinners will be activated in the PropertyManager where you can specify the distance and angle value for creating chamfer.*

3. Set the value of the **Distance 1** spinner to **10**. Next, select the first set of entities to be chamfered, refer to Figure 3-22; the **SOLIDWORKS** message window is displayed with the message that **At least one sketch constraint is about to be lost. Chamfer anyway?**.

4. Choose the **Yes** button in the message window; the chamfer between the selected set of entities is created.

5. Select the second set of entities to be chamfered and then exit the PropertyManager by choosing the **OK** button. Figure 3-23 shows the final sketch after creating the chamfers.

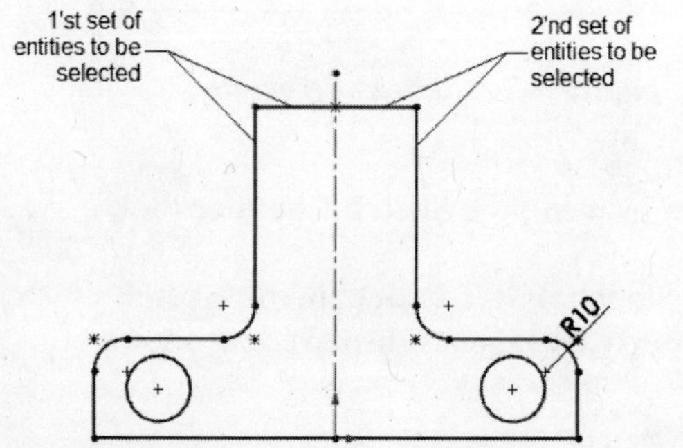

Figure 3-22 Entities to be selected for chamfering

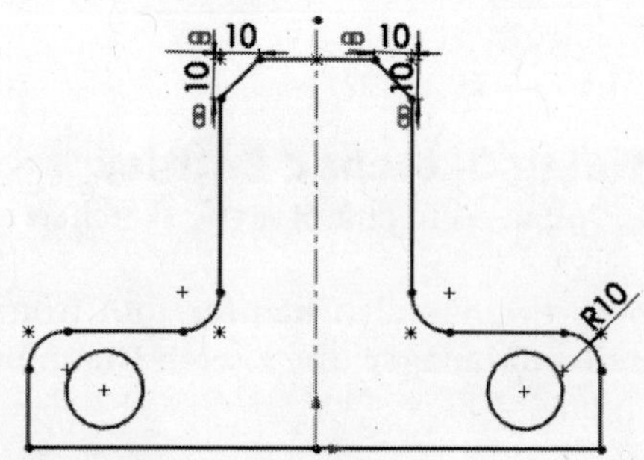

Figure 3-23 Final sketch after creating chamfers

Saving the Sketch

1. Choose the **Save** button from the Menu Bar to invoke the **Save As** dialog box.

2. Browse to the *c03* folder and enter the name of the document as **c03_tut02** in the **File name** edit box and choose the **Save** button.

3. Press CTRL+W to close the file.

Tutorial 3

In this tutorial, you will create the base sketch of the model shown in Figure 3-24. The sketch of the model is shown in Figure 3-25. The dimensions in Figure 3-25 are given for your reference only. **(Expected time: 30 min)**

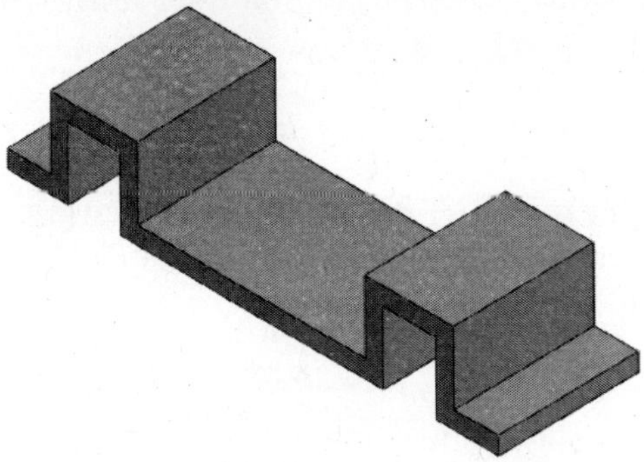

Figure 3-24 Solid model for Tutorial 3

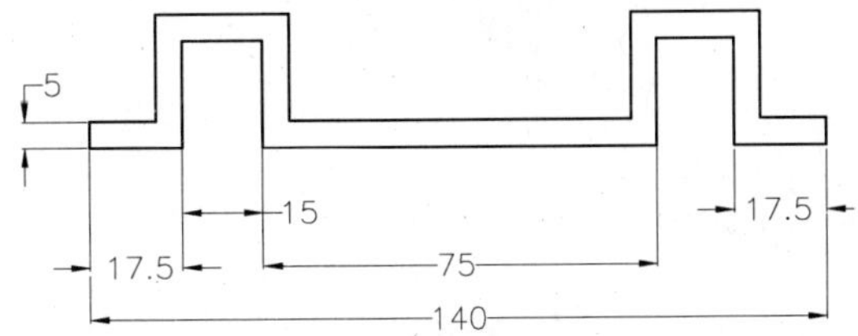

Figure 3-25 Sketch for Tutorial 3

The following steps are required to complete this tutorial:

a. Start SOLIDWORKS and then a new part document.
b. Invoke the sketching environment.
c. Modify the snap, grid, and units settings.
d. Draw the sketch, refer to Figure 3-26.
e. Offset the entire sketch bidirectionally, refer to Figure 3-28.
f. Save the sketch.

Starting SOLIDWORKS and then a New SOLIDWORKS Document

1. Start SOLIDWORKS and then invoke the **Part** environment by choosing the **Part** button from the **New SOLIDWORKS Document** dialog box.

Invoking the Sketching Environment

Next, you need to invoke the sketching environment by selecting the **Front Plane** as the sketching plane.

1. Choose the **Sketch** tab from the **CommandManager**. Next, choose the **Sketch** tool from the **Sketch CommandManager**; the **Edit Sketch PropertyManager** is invoked and you are prompted to select the plane to create the sketch.

2. Select the **Front Plane**; the sketching environment is invoked and the plane is oriented normal to the view.

Modifying the Snap, Grid, and Unit Settings

Before drawing the sketch, you need to modify the grid and snap settings to make the cursor jump through a distance of 5 mm.

1. Invoke the **Document Properties - Grid/Snap** dialog box and then set the value as **50** and **10** in the **Major grid spacing** and **Minor-lines per major** spinners, respectively.

2. Make sure that the **Grid** check box is selected in the **System Option - Relations/Snaps** dialog box. Also, make sure that the unit system is set to **MMGS (millimeter, gram, second)** in the **Document Properties - Units** dialog box.

3. After making the necessary settings, choose the **OK** button from the dialog box.

   The coordinates displayed close to the lower right corner of the SOLIDWORKS window show an increment of 5 mm when you move the cursor in the drawing area after exiting the dialog box.

Drawing the Sketch

Next, you need to draw the sketch using the sketch tools. In this tutorial, you will create the sketch by using the **Line** and **Offset Entities** tools. First, you will create a symmetric line for the sketch and then offset it bidirectionally. After offsetting the symmetric line, you need to convert it into a construction line.

1. Invoke the **Line** tool and specify the start point of the line at the origin. Next, move the cursor horizontally toward right and specify the end point of the line when the length of the line displayed above the cursor is 15.

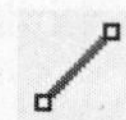

2. Move the cursor vertically upward and specify the end point of the line when the length of the line displayed above the cursor is 20.

3. Move the cursor horizontally toward the right and specify the end point of the line when the length of the line displayed above the cursor is 20.

4. Move the cursor vertically downward and specify the end point of the line when the length of the line displayed above the cursor is 20.

5. Move the cursor horizontally toward the right and specify the end point of the line when the length of the line displayed above the cursor is 70.

6. Move the cursor vertically upward and specify the end point of the line when the length of the line displayed above the cursor is 20.

7. Move the cursor horizontally toward the right and specify the end point of the line when the length of the line displayed above the cursor is 20.

8. Move the cursor vertically downward and specify the end point of the line when the length of the line displayed above the cursor is 20.

9. Move the cursor horizontally toward the right and specify the end point of the line when the length of the line displayed above the cursor is 15. Next, exit the **Line** tool. Figure 3-26 shows the sketch after creating its symmetric line.

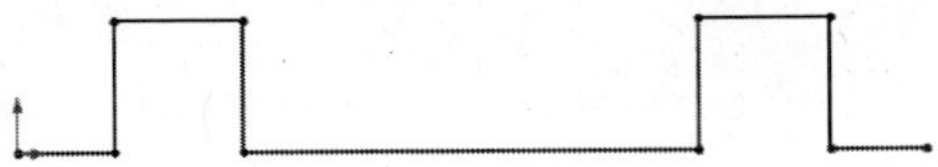

Figure 3-26 The sketch after creating its symmetric line

Offsetting the Entities

Next, you need to offset the sketch in both directions of the sketched entities using the **Offset Entities** tool.

1. Choose **Offset Entities** tool from the **Sketch CommandManager**; the **Offset Entities PropertyManager** is displayed, as shown in Figure 3-27. Also, you are prompted to select faces, edges, or curves to offset.

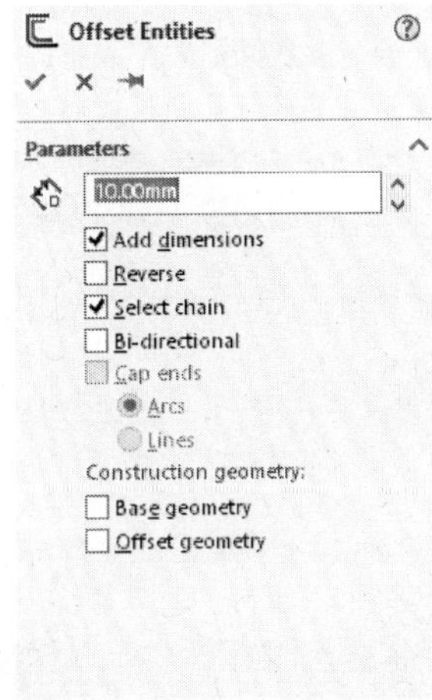

*Figure 3-27 The **Offset Entities PropertyManager***

The **Offset Entities** tool is used to offset selected entities such as sketches, edges, or faces by a specified distance. This tool cannot be used on fit splines, already offset splines, or if the resultant is an intersecting geometry.

2. Set the value of the **Offset Distance** spinner to **2.5** and then press ENTER.

3. Make sure that the **Select chain** check box is selected in the **Parameters** rollout of the PropertyManager.

The **Select chain** tool is used to select the entire chain of continuous sketched entities that are in contact with the selected entity. When you invoke the **Offset Entities PropertyManager**, the **Select chain** check box is selected by default. If you clear this check box, only the selected sketched entity will be offset.

4. Select any one entity of the sketch from the drawing area; the entire sketch gets selected and the preview of the offset sketch is displayed in the drawing area. Note that, by default, the offset is in one direction.

   Now, you need to change the direction of the offset to both sides of the sketched entities.

5. Select the **Bi-directional** check box from the **Parameters** rollout of the **Offset Entities PropertyManager**; the **Cap ends** check box is enabled in the PropertyManager. Also, the preview of the offset sketch is modified accordingly.

The **Bi-directional** check box is used to create the offset of a selected entity in both directions of the sketched entity. If you select this check box, the **Reverse** check box that is used to flip the direction of the offset entity will not be displayed in the **Parameters** rollout of the PropertyManager.

As is evident from Figure 3-25 that the ends of the sketch are closed with lines. Therefore, you need to close the ends of the sketch.

6. Select the **Cap ends** check box from the **Parameters** rollout of the PropertyManager; the **Arcs** and **Lines** radio buttons are enabled below the check box.

The **Cap ends** check box is available only if the **Bi-directional** check box is selected. This check box is used to close the ends of the bidirectionally offset entities. The **Arcs** and **Lines** radio buttons are used to specify the type of cap required to close the ends.

7. Select the **Lines** radio button from the **Parameters** rollout of the PropertyManager; the preview of the offset sketch is modified accordingly.

   As discussed earlier, you need to convert the parent sketch into a construction sketch.

8. Select the **Base geometry** check box under **Construction geometry** in the **Parameters** rollout of the PropertyManager.

The **Base geometry** check box is used to convert the parent entity into a construction entity.

9. Choose the **OK** button from the PropertyManager. The final sketch is shown in Figure 3-28.

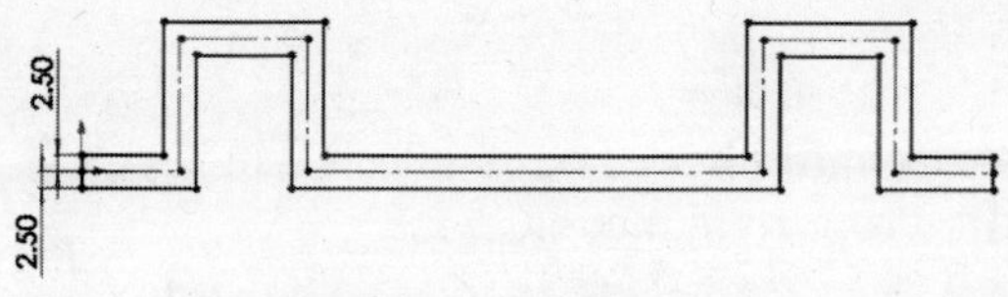

Figure 3-28 The final sketch

Saving the Sketch

1. Choose the **Save** button from the Menu Bar to invoke the **Save As** dialog box.

2. Browse to the *c03* folder and enter the name of the document as **c03_tut03** in the **File name** edit box and choose the **Save** button.

   The document is saved at the location */Documents/SOLIDWORKS Tutorials/c03*.

3. Close the file by choosing **File > Close** from the SOLIDWORKS menus.

Self-Evaluation Test

Answer the following questions and then compare them to those given at the end of this chapter:

1. The __________ tool is used to create a circular pattern in the sketching environment of SOLIDWORKS.

2. To modify a sketched circle, you need to select it using the __________ tool.

3. The __________ tool is used to invoke dynamic mirroring.

4. The **Trim Entities** tool is also used to trim the sketched entities. (T/F)

5. In the sketching environment, you can apply fillets to two parallel lines. (T/F)

6. You can apply a fillet to two nonparallel and non-intersecting entities. (T/F)

7. You cannot offset a single entity using the **Offset Entities** tool. (T/F)

8. You can choose **Insert > Customize Menu** from the SOLIDWORKS menus to display the **Customize** dialog box. (T/F)

9. You can select the vertex formed at the intersection of two entities to be filleted. (T/F)

Review Questions

Answer the following questions:

1. Which PropertyManager is displayed when you choose the **Sketch Fillet** tool from the **Sketch CommandManager**?

   (a) **Sketch Fillet** (b) **Fillet**
   (c) **Surface Fillet** (d) **Sketching Fillet**

2. Which PropertyManager is displayed on the left of the drawing area when you choose the **Sketch Chamfer** tool from the **Sketch Fillet** flyout in the **Sketch CommandManager**?

   (a) **Sketch Chamfer** (b) **Sketcher Chamfer**
   (c) **Sketching Chamfer** (d) **Chamfer**

3. Which of the following tools is used to create an automatic mirror line?

   (a) **Dynamic Mirror Entities** (b) **Mirror**
   (c) **Automatic Mirror** (d) None of these

4. Which of the following tools is used to extend the sketch entities?

   (a) **Split Entities** (b) **Extend Entities**
   (c) **Break Curve** (d) **Trim Curve**

5. Which of the following tools is used to create a circular pattern in SOLIDWORKS?

   (a) **Pattern** (b) **Circular Sketch Pattern**
   (c) **Array** (d) None of these

6. You cannot extend the sketched entity using the **Trim** tool. (T/F)

7. There are four type of slot tools available in SOLIDWORKS. (T/F)

8. The sketched entities can be mirrored without using a centerline. (T/F)

9. The **Display instance count** check box in the **Circular Pattern PropertyManager** is used to display the number of instances in the resulting sketch pattern. (T/F)

EXERCISES

Exercise 1

Create the sketch of the model shown in Figure 3-29. The sketch of the model is shown in Figure 3-30. The solid model and dimensions are given for your reference only.

(Expected time: 30 min)

Figure 3-29 Solid model for Exercise 1

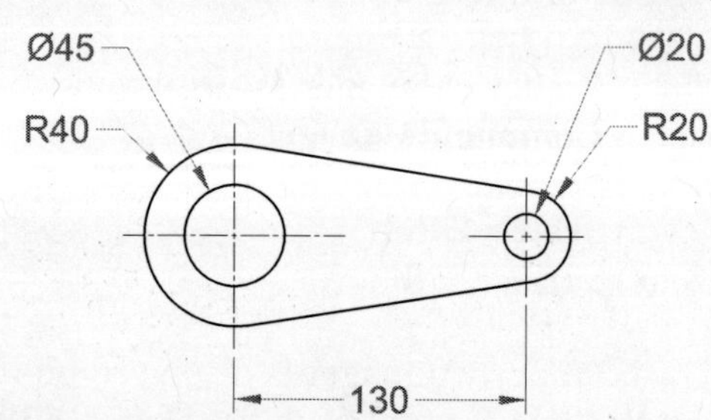

Figure 3-30 Sketch for Exercise 1

Exercise 2

Create the sketch of the model shown in Figure 3-31. The sketch of the model is shown in Figure 3-32. Do not dimension the sketch. The solid model and dimensions are given for reference only. **(Expected time: 30 min)**

Figure 3-31 Solid model for Exercise 2

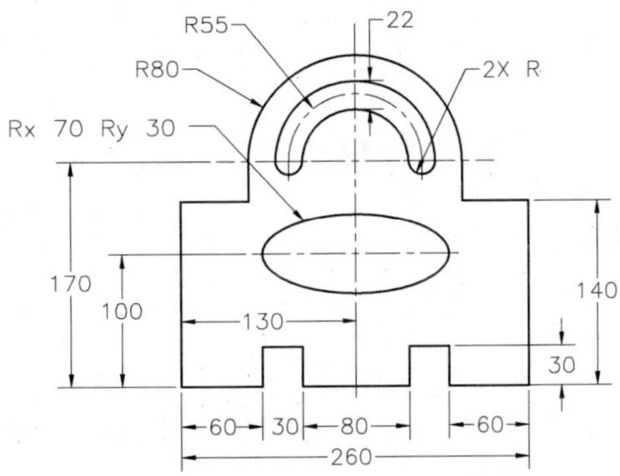

Figure 3-32 Sketch for Exercise 2

Exercise 3

Create the sketch of the model shown in Figure 3-33. The sketch of the model is shown in Figure 3-34. The solid model and dimensions are given only for your reference. Create the sketch on one side and then mirror it on the other side. Make sure you do not use the **Dynamic Mirror** tool to draw this sketch. This is because if you draw the sketch using this tool, some relations are applied to the sketch. These relations interfere while creating fillets.

(Expected time: 30 min)

Figure 3-33 Solid model for Exercise 3

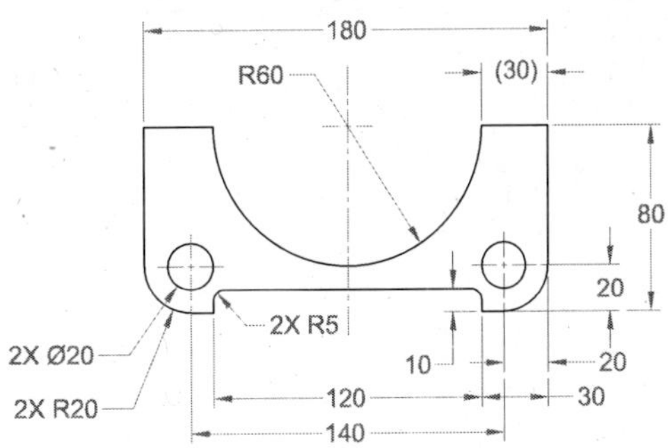

Figure 3-34 Sketch for Exercise 3

Exercise 4

Create the sketch of the model shown in Figure 3-35. The sketch of the model is shown in Figure 3-36. The solid model and dimensions are given for your reference only.

(Expected time: 30 min)

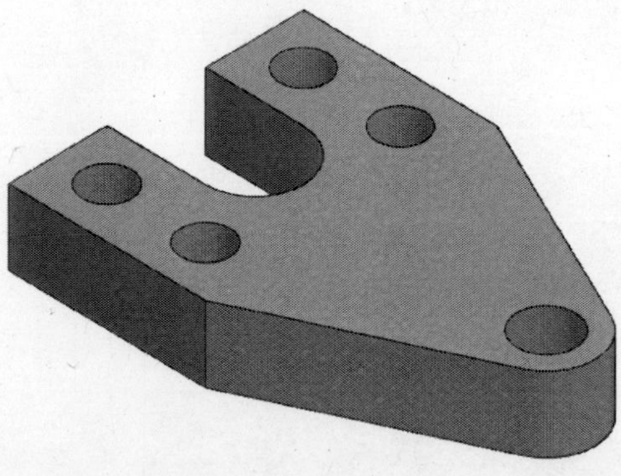

Figure 3-35 Solid model for Exercise 4

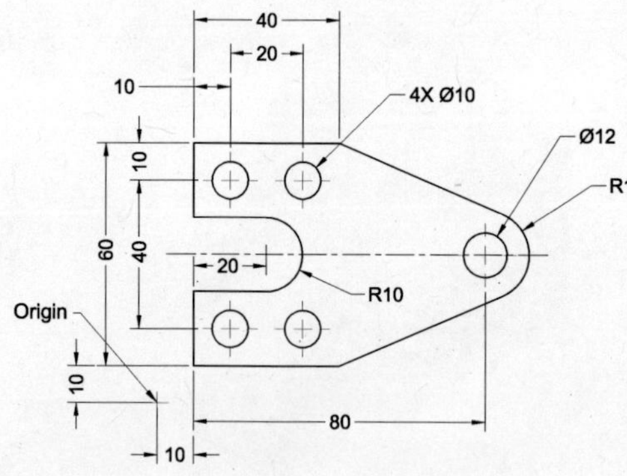

Figure 3-36 Sketch for Exercise 4

Answers to Self-Evaluation Test

1. **Circular Sketch Pattern**, **2.** **Select**, **3.** **Dynamic Mirror Entities**, **4.** T, **5.** F, **6.** T, **7.** F, **8.** F, **9.** T

Chapter 4

Adding Relations and Dimensions to Sketches

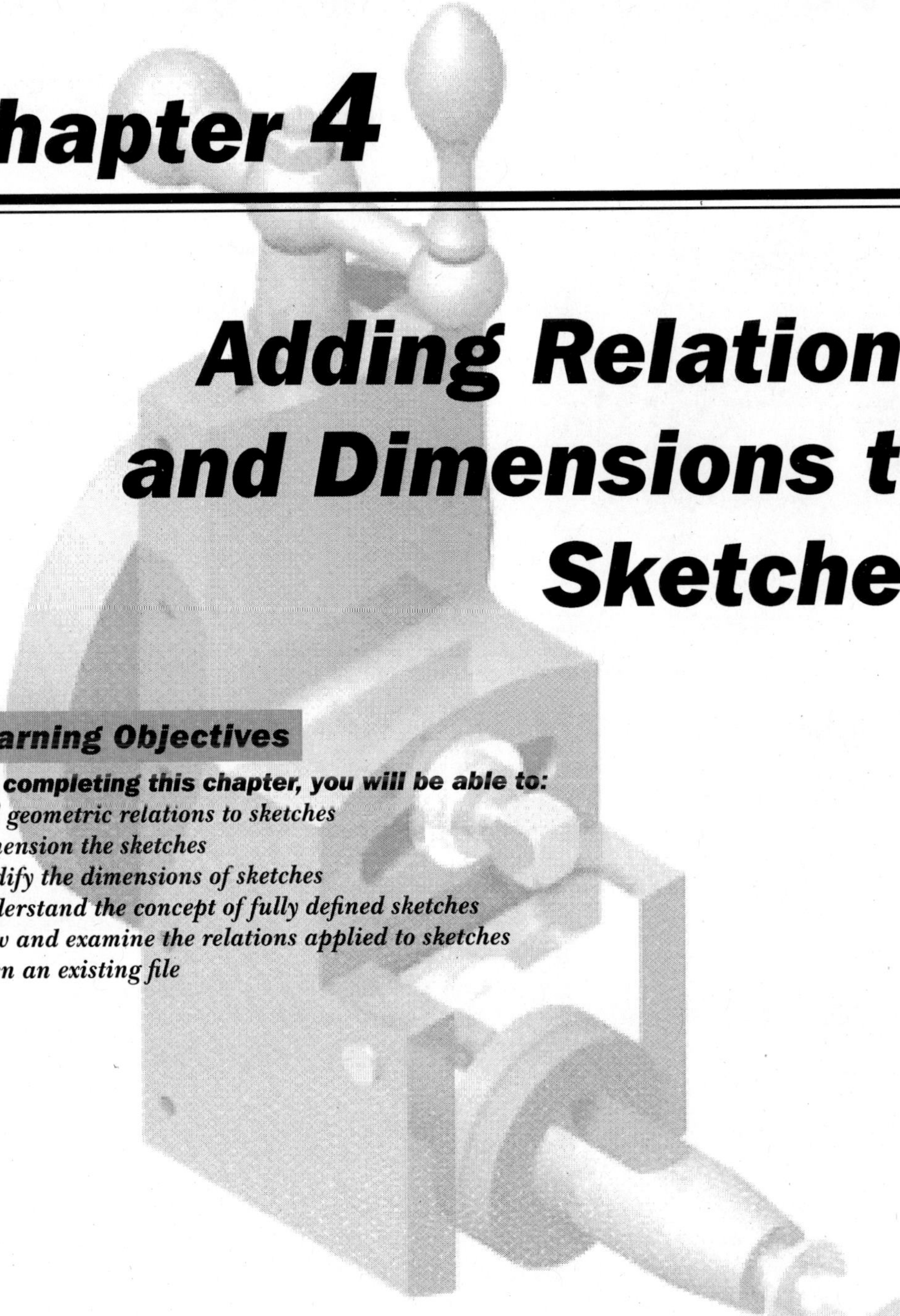

Learning Objectives

After completing this chapter, you will be able to:

- *Add geometric relations to sketches*
- *Dimension the sketches*
- *Modify the dimensions of sketches*
- *Understand the concept of fully defined sketches*
- *View and examine the relations applied to sketches*
- *Open an existing file*

TUTORIALS

Tutorial 1

In this tutorial, you will draw the sketch of the model shown in Figure 4-1. You will draw the sketch using the mirror line and then add required relations and dimensions to it. The sketch is shown in Figure 4-2. The solid model is given for your reference only.

(Expected time: 30 min)

Figure 4-1 *Solid model for Tutorial 1*

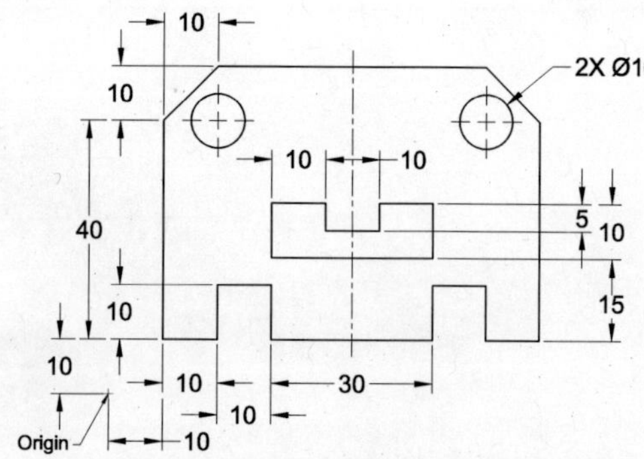

Figure 4-2 *Sketch of the model*

The following steps are required to complete this tutorial:

a. Start SOLIDWORKS and then start a new part document.
b. Create a mirror line using the **Centerline** tool.
c. Invoke the **Dynamic Mirror** tool.
d. Draw the sketch of the model on one side of the mirror line so that it is automatically drawn on the other side, refer to Figures 4-3 through 4-8.
e. Add relations to the sketch, refer to Figure 4-16.
f. Add dimensions to the sketch and fully define the sketch, refer to Figures 4-20 through 4-22.
g. Save the sketch and then close the document.

Starting SOLIDWORKS and a New Part Document

1. Start SOLIDWORKS and then invoke the **Part** environment by choosing the **Part** button from the **New SOLIDWORKS Document** dialog box.

   Next, you need to invoke the sketching environment.

2. Choose the **Sketch** tab from the **CommandManager**. Next, choose the **Sketch** button from the **Sketch CommandManager**; the **Edit Sketch PropertyManager** is invoked and you are prompted to select the plane to create the sketch.

3. Select the **Front Plane** as the sketching plane to invoke the sketching environment.

In previous chapters, you used the grid and snap settings to create sketches. From this chapter onward, you are recommended not to use those settings. Now, you can draw the sketches at arbitrary locations and then apply dimensions and relations to them.

4. If the grid is displayed, invoke the **Document Properties - Grid/Snap** dialog box by choosing **Tools > Options** from the SOLIDWORKS menus and then clear the **Display grid** check box from the **Grid** area to hide the grids. Also, clear the **Grid** check box from the **Sketch snaps** area in the **System Options - Relations/Snaps** dialog box.

5. Invoke the **Document Properties - Units** dialog box and set the units to millimeters and degree for measuring linear and angular dimensions, respectively. However, if you have selected millimeters as unit while installing SOLIDWORKS, you can skip this step.

Drawing the Mirror Line

In this section, you will draw the sketch of the given model with the help of the **Dynamic Mirror** tool. So, when you draw an entity on one side of the centerline, the same entity will be drawn automatically on its other side. Also, the symmetric relation will be applied to the entities on both sides of the centerline. Therefore, if you modify an entity on one side of the centerline, the same modification will be reflected in the mirrored entity on the other side and vice versa.

The origin of the sketching environment is placed at the center of the drawing area and as is evident from Figure 4-2, you need to create the sketch in the first quadrant. Therefore, it is recommended that you modify the drawing area such that the area in the first quadrant is increased. This can be done by using the **Pan** tool.

1. Press the CTRL key and the middle mouse button to invoke the **Pan** tool and then drag the cursor toward the bottom left corner of the drawing area to increase the drawing area in the first quadrant. While dragging the cursor, you will notice that the origin is also moving toward the bottom left corner of the drawing area. Next, release the CTRL key and the middle mouse button.

The **Pan** tool is used to drag the view in the current display. You can also invoke the **Pan** tool by choosing **View > Modify > Pan** from the SOLIDWORKS menus.

2. Choose the **Centerline** button from the **Line** flyout in the **Sketch CommandManager**; the **Insert Line PropertyManager** is displayed.

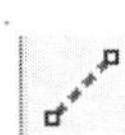

3. Move the line cursor to a location whose coordinates are close to 45 mm, 70 mm, and 0 mm. Now, specify the start point of the centerline at this location.

4. Move the line cursor vertically downward to draw a line of length close to 80 mm. As soon as you specify the endpoint of the centerline, a rubber-band line is attached to the line cursor.

5. Right-click to display the shortcut menu and then choose the **Select** option from the shortcut menu to exit the **Centerline** tool.

6. Press the F key; the sketch is zoomed and fits the screen.

7. Select the centerline and choose **Tools > Sketch Tools > Dynamic Mirror** from the SOLIDWORKS menus; the centerline is converted into a mirror line.

Drawing the Sketch

You will draw the sketch on the right of the mirror line and the same sketch will automatically be drawn on the other side of the mirror line.

1. Choose the **Line** button from the **Sketch CommandManager**; the arrow cursor is replaced by the line cursor.

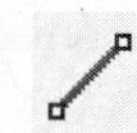

2. Move the line cursor towards the centerline. Next, specify the start point of the line when the cursor snaps to the centerline; a coincident symbol is displayed below the cursor, and coordinate values are displayed close to 45 mm, 10 mm, and 0 mm.

Note

If the cursor does not snap to the centerline at the location whose coordinates are 45 mm, 10 mm, and 0 mm, you need to enable the snapping for the nearest point. To do so, invoke the ***System Options - Relations/Snaps*** *dialog box and then select the* ***Nearest*** *check box from it.*

3. Move the cursor horizontally toward the right and specify the endpoint of the line when its length above the line cursor shows a value close to 15. As soon as you press the left mouse button to specify the endpoint of the line, a line of the same length is drawn automatically on the other side of the mirror line, refer to Figure 4-3.

   In Figure 4-3, the display of relations has been turned off by choosing the **View Sketch Relations** button in the **Hide/Show Items** flyout in the **View (Heads-Up)** toolbar.

Note

The mirrored entity that is automatically created on the left of the mirror line gets merged with the line drawn on the right. Therefore, the entire line becomes a single entity. The mirror image of the line will merge with the line that you draw only if one of the endpoints of the line is coincident with the mirror line.

4. Move the cursor vertically upward. Specify the endpoint of the line when the length of the line on the line cursor displays a value close to 10. Figure 4-4 shows the sketch after drawing the vertical lines.

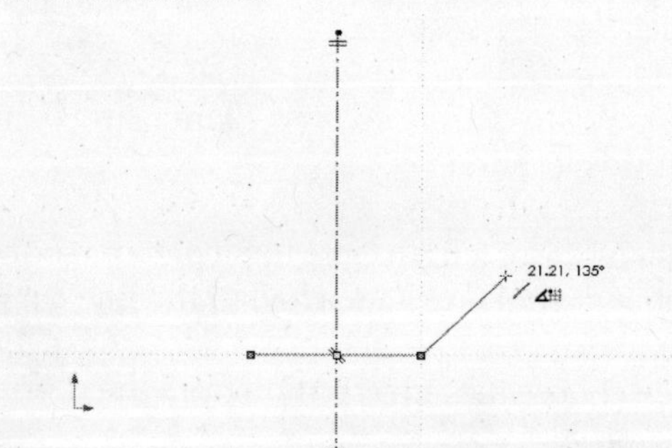

Figure 4-3 *Line drawn automatically on the other side of the mirror line*

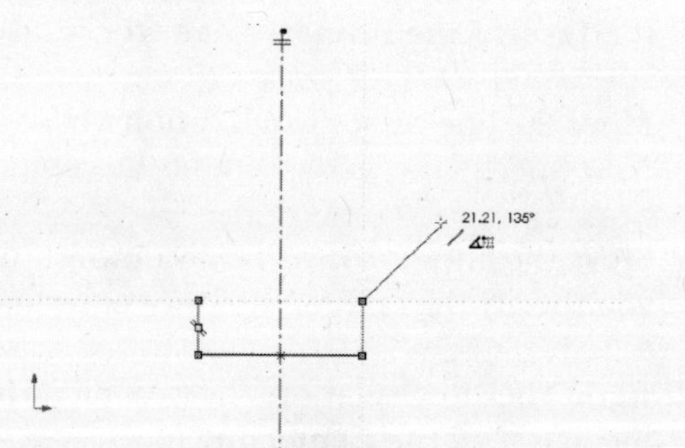

Figure 4-4 *Left line drawn by mirroring*

5. Move the line cursor horizontally toward the right. Specify the endpoint of the line when the length of the line on the line cursor displays a value close to 10.

6. Move the line cursor vertically downward. Specify the endpoint when the length of the line on the line cursor displays a value close to 10.

7. Move the line cursor horizontally toward the right. Specify the endpoint when the length of the line on the line cursor displays a value close to 10.

8. Move the line cursor vertically upward. Specify the endpoint when the length of the line on the line cursor displays a value close to 40.

9. Move the line cursor at an angle close to 135-degree from the horizontal reference and specify the endpoint of the line when length of the line above the line cursor displays a value close to 14. For angle value refer to the **Angle** spinner in the **Parameters** rollout of the PropertyManager. Figure 4-5 shows the sketch after drawing the inclined line.

10. Move the line cursor horizontally toward the left. Specify the endpoint when the cursor snaps to the mirror line and the mirror line is highlighted. Double-click anywhere in the drawing area to end the creation of line. The sketch after completing the outer profile is shown in Figure 4-6.

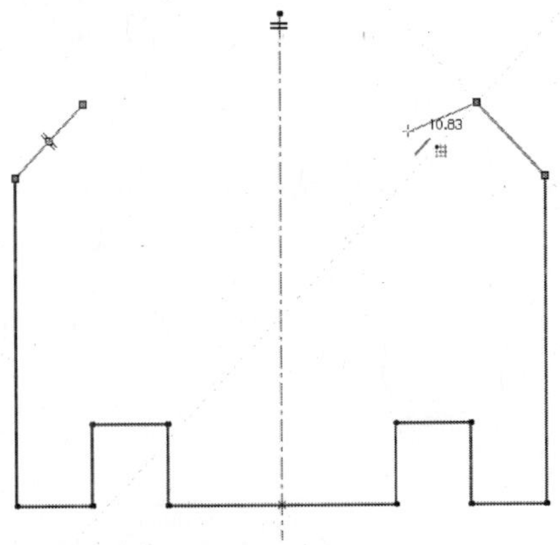

Figure 4-5 *Sketch after drawing the inclined line*

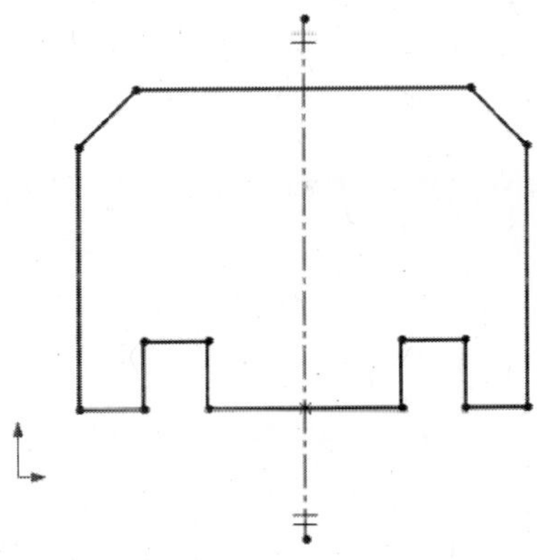

Figure 4-6 *Sketch after completing the outer profile of the sketch*

Next, you will draw the sketch of the inner cavity. To draw the sketch of the inner cavity, you need to start with the lower horizontal line.

11. Specify the start point of the line when the coordinates display as 45, 25, 0 in the status bar. Next, move the cursor horizontally toward the right. Specify the endpoint when the length of the line above the line cursor displays a value close to 15.

12. Move the line cursor vertically upward. Specify the endpoint when the length of the line on the line cursor displays a value close to 10.

13. Move the line cursor horizontally toward the left. Specify the endpoint when the length of the line on the line cursor displays a value close to 10.

14. Move the line cursor vertically downward. Specify the endpoint when the length of the line on the line cursor displays a value close to 5.

15. Move the line cursor horizontally toward the left. Specify the endpoint when the line cursor snaps to the mirror line.

16. Double-click anywhere in the drawing area to end the creation of the line. The sketch after completing the inner cavity is shown in Figure 4-7.

17. Choose the **Circle** button from the **Sketch CommandManager** to invoke the **Circle** tool.

18. Move the circle cursor to the point where the inferencing lines that are originating from the endpoints of the right inclined line are intersecting.

19. Specify the center of the circle when the coordinates display as 70, 50, 0 in the status bar. Next, move the circle cursor toward the left to define the radius of the circle. Press the left mouse button when the radius of the circle above the circle cursor displays a value close to 5.

    The circle is automatically mirrored on the other side of the mirror line, refer to Figure 4-8.

20. Exit the **Dynamic Mirror** tool by choosing **Tools > Sketch Tools > Dynamic Mirror** from the SOLIDWORKS menus.

21. As the circles created previously are still selected, press the ESC key to remove the circles from the selection set. The sketch after drawing the circle is shown in Figure 4-8.

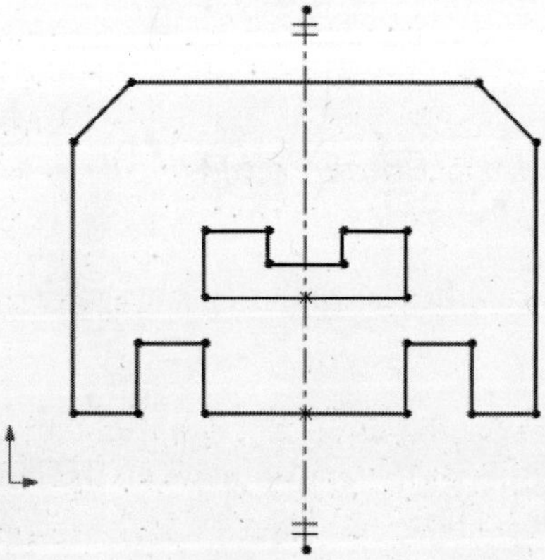

Figure 4-7 *Sketch after drawing the inner cavity*

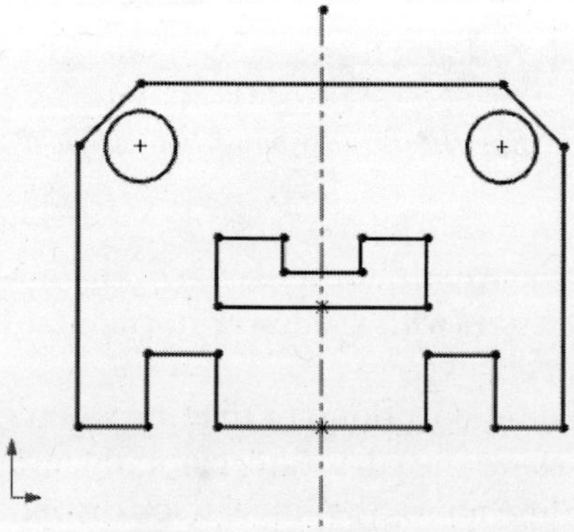

Figure 4-8 *Sketch after drawing the circles*

Adding Geometric Relations to the Sketch

After drawing the sketch, you need to add geometric relations to it by using the **Add Relations PropertyManager**. Relations are applied to a sketch to constrain its degree of freedom, reduce the number of dimensions in the sketch, and capture the design intent of the sketch.

1. Choose the **Add Relation** button from the **Display/Delete Relations** flyout in the **Sketch CommandManager**, refer to Figure 4-9; the **Add Relations PropertyManager** is displayed, as shown in Figure 4-10. Also, the confirmation corner is displayed at the upper right corner of the drawing area.

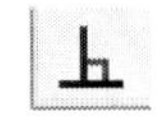

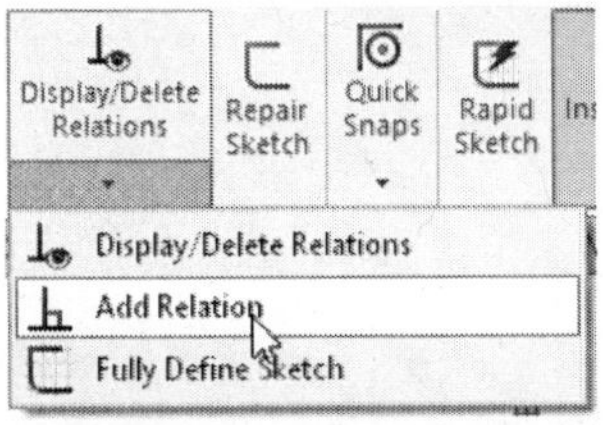

*Figure 4-9 The **Add Relation** button in the **Display/Delete Relations** flyout*

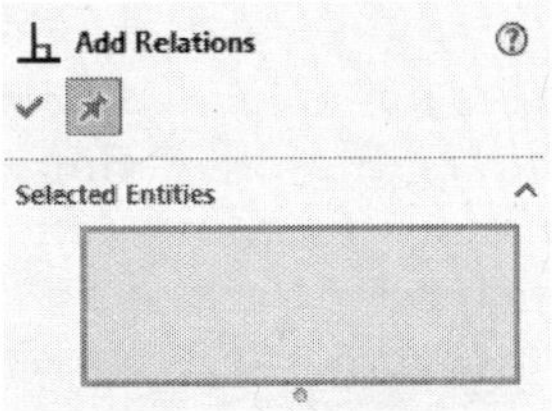

Figure 4-10** The **Add Relations PropertyManager

Geometric relations are logical operations that are performed to add relationships (such as tangent or perpendicular) between the sketched entities, planes, axes, edges, or vertices. The relations applied to the sketched entities are used to capture the design intent. Geometric relations constrain the degree of freedom of the sketched entities. You can apply relations to a sketch by using the **Add Relations PropertyManager**.

The **Add Relations PropertyManager** is widely used to apply relations to a sketch in the sketching environment of SOLIDWORKS.

In SOLIDWORKS, some of the relations are applied automatically to the sketch entities while drawing. For example, when you specify the start point of a line and move the cursor horizontally toward the right or left, you will notice that the horizontal line symbol is displayed below the line cursor. This is the symbol of the **Horizontal** relation that is applied to the line while drawing. If you move the cursor vertically downward or upward, the vertical line symbol for the **Vertical** relation will be displayed below the line cursor. If you move the cursor to the intersection of two or more sketched entities, the intersection symbol will appear below the cursor. Similarly, other relations are also applied automatically to the sketch when you draw it. These automatically applied relations are called Automatic Relations.

Tip

*You can activate or deactivate the **Automatic Relations** option. To do so, choose the **Options** button from the Menu Bar; the **System Options - General** dialog box will be displayed. Select the **Relations/Snaps** option from the area on the left and select the **Automatic relations** check box from this dialog box. Next, choose the **OK** button. Alternatively, choose **Tools > Sketch Settings > Automatic Relations** from the SOLIDWORKS menu. This is a toggle button.*

The relations that can be applied automatically are listed next:

Horizontal	Vertical	Coincident	Midpoint
Intersection	Tangent	Perpendicular	

Tip

While drawing a sketch, you will observe that two types of inferencing lines are displayed: blue and yellow. The yellow inferencing line indicates that a relation has been applied automatically to the sketch, whereas the blue inferencing line indicates that no automatic relation has been applied.

2. Select the center point of the circle on the right and then the lower endpoint of the right inclined line; the **Add Relations PropertyManager** is modified and the names of the selected entities are displayed in the **Selected Entities** rollout of the PropertyManager, refer to Figure 4-11. Also, the relations that can be applied to the two selected entities are displayed in the **Add Relations** rollout of the PropertyManager, refer to Figure 4-11. Note that the **Horizontal** button is highlighted, suggesting that the horizontal relation is the most appropriate relation for the selected entities.

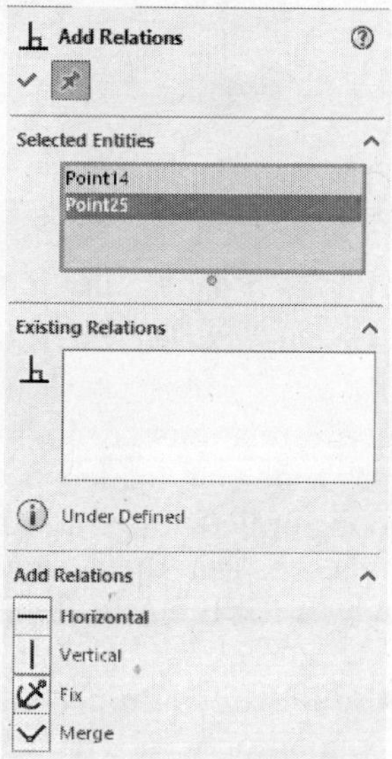

***Figure 4-11** The **Add Relations PropertyManager** displayed after selecting the entities*

Note

*The names of the entities displayed in the **Selected Entities** rollout of the **Add Relations PropertyManager** may be different from those displayed on your computer screen.*

The **Selected Entities** rollout of the PropertyManager is used to display the name of the entities selected to apply relations. In case you have selected the wrong entity to apply relation, you can remove it from the selection set of the **Selected Entities** rollout by selecting it again from the drawing area. Alternatively, select the entity from the **Selected Entities** rollout and then right-click to display the shortcut menu. Next, choose the **Delete** option from the shortcut menu. If you choose the **Clear Selections** option from the shortcut menu, all the entities will be removed from the selection set.

The **Add Relations** rollout of the PropertyManager is used to display the list of all the relations that can be applied to a selected entity or entities. Also, it displays the most appropriate relation for the selected entities in bold letters.

The relations that can be applied to the sketches using the **Add Relations** rollout are discussed next.

Horizontal

The **Horizontal** relation forces one or more selected lines or centerlines to become horizontal. You can also select an external entity such as an edge, plane, axis, or sketch curve on an external sketch that will act as a line to apply this relation. You can also force two or more points to become horizontal using the **Horizontal** relation. The point can be a sketch point, a center point, an endpoint, a control point of a spline, or an external entity such as origin, vertex, axis, or point in an external sketch. To apply this relation, invoke the **Add Relations PropertyManager**. Select the entity or entities and then choose the **Horizontal** button from the **Add Relations** rollout in the **Add Relations PropertyManager**. You will notice that the name of the horizontal relation will be displayed in the **Existing Relations** rollout.

Vertical

The **Vertical** relation forces one or more selected lines or centerlines to become vertical. You can force two or more points to become vertical using the **Vertical** relation. To apply this relation, invoke the **Add Relations PropertyManager** and then select the entity or entities on which relation has to be applied. Next, choose the **Vertical** button from the **Add Relations** rollout. You will notice that the name of the vertical relation is displayed in the **Existing Relations** rollout.

Collinear

The **Collinear** relation forces the selected lines to lie on the same infinite line. To apply this relation, select the lines on which the **Collinear** relation has to be applied. Next, choose the **Collinear** button from the **Add Relations** rollout.

Coradial

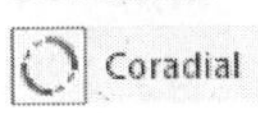

The **Coradial** relation forces the selected arcs or circles to share the same radius and center point. You can also select an external entity that projects as an arc or a circle in the sketch to apply this relation. To apply this relation, invoke the **Add Relations PropertyManager** and select two arcs or circles, or an arc and a circle. Next, choose the **Coradial** button from the **Add Relations** rollout.

Perpendicular

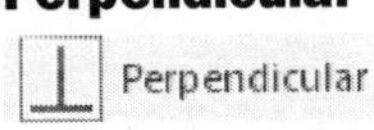

The **Perpendicular** relation forces the selected lines to become perpendicular to each other. To apply this relation, invoke the **Add Relations PropertyManager**. Then, select two lines and choose the **Perpendicular** button from the **Add Relations** rollout. Figure 4-12 shows two lines before and after applying the **Perpendicular** relation.

Parallel

The **Parallel** relation forces the selected lines to become parallel to each other. To apply this relation, invoke the **Add Relations PropertyManager**. Then, select two lines and choose the **Parallel** button from the **Add Relations** rollout. Figure 4-13 shows two lines before and after applying this relation.

ParallelYZ

The **ParallelYZ** relation forces a line in the three-dimensional (3D) sketch to become parallel to the YZ plane with respect to the selected plane. To apply this relation, invoke the **Add Relations PropertyManager**. Next, select a line in the 3D sketch and then select a plane. Next, choose the **ParallelYZ** button from the **Add Relations** rollout.

Note

You will learn more about the 3D sketch in the later chapters.

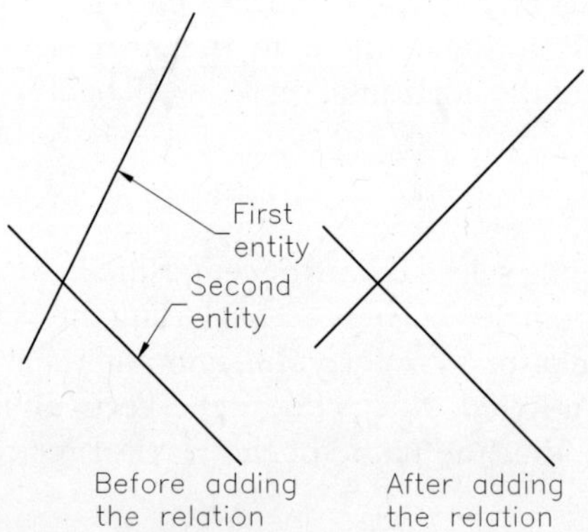

Figure 4-12 *Entities before and after applying the* ***Perpendicular*** *relation*

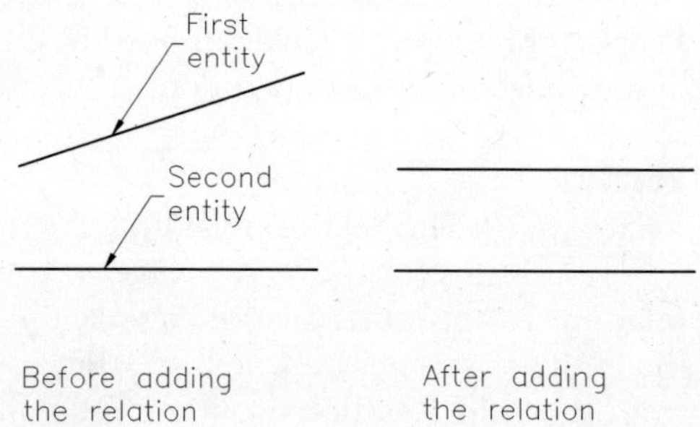

Figure 4-13 *Entities before and after applying the* ***Parallel*** *relation*

ParallelZX

The **ParallelZX** relation forces a line in the 3D sketch to become parallel to the ZX plane with respect to the selected plane. To apply this relation, invoke the **Add Relations PropertyManager**. Select a line in the 3D sketch and then select a plane. Next, choose the **ParallelZX** button from the **Add Relations** rollout.

AlongZ

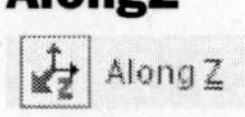

The **AlongZ** relation forces a line in the 3D sketch to become normal to a selected plane. To apply this relation, invoke the **Add Relations PropertyManager**. Select a line in the 3D sketch and then select a plane. Next, choose the **AlongZ** button from the **Add Relations** rollout.

Tangent

The **Tangent** relation forces a selected arc, circle, spline, or ellipse to become tangent to the other arc, circle, spline, ellipse, line, or edge. To apply this relation, invoke the **Add Relations PropertyManager**. Select the two entities and choose the **Tangent** button from the **Add Relations** rollout. Figure 4-14 shows a line and a circle before and after applying the **Tangent** relation. Figure 4-15 shows two arcs after applying the **Tangent** relation.

Concentric

The **Concentric** relation forces a selected arc or circle to share the same center point with the other arc, circle, point, vertex, or circular edge. To apply this relation, invoke the **Add Relations PropertyManager**. Next, select the required entity and then choose the **Concentric** button from the **Add Relations** rollout.

Equal

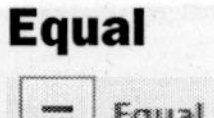

The **Equal** relation forces the selected lines to have equal length and the selected arcs, circles, or arc and circle to have equal radii. To apply this relation, invoke

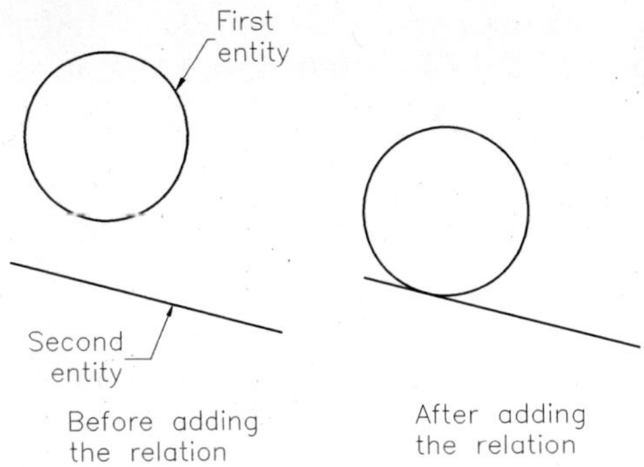

***Figure 4-14** Applying the **Tangent** relation to a line and a circle*

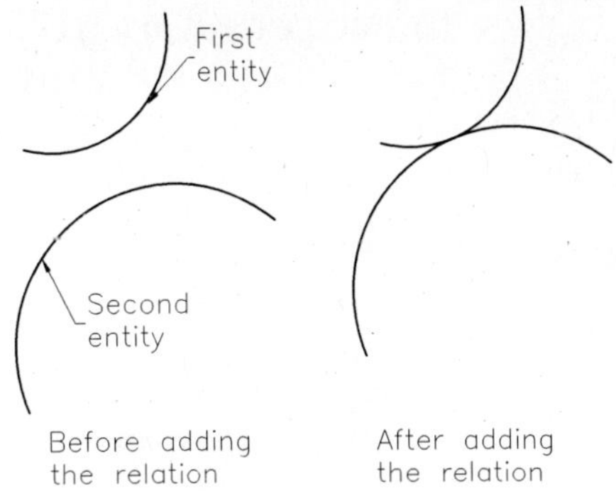

***Figure 4-15** Applying the **Tangent** relation to two arcs*

the **Add Relations PropertyManager**. Next, select the required entity and choose the **Equal** button.

Intersection

The **Intersection** relation forces a selected point to move at the intersection of two selected lines. To apply this relation, invoke the **Add Relations PropertyManager**. Next, select the required entity and then choose the **Intersection** button from the **Add Relations** rollout.

Coincident

The **Coincident** relation forces a selected point to be coincident with a selected line, arc, circle, or ellipse. To apply this relation, invoke the **Add Relations PropertyManager**. Select the required entity and then choose the **Coincident** button from the **Add Relations** rollout.

Midpoint

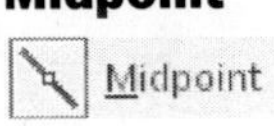

The **Midpoint** relation forces a selected point to move to the midpoint of a selected line. To apply this relation, invoke the **Add Relations PropertyManager**. Select the point and the line. Next, choose the **Midpoint** button from the **Add Relations** rollout.

Symmetric

The **Symmetric** relation forces two selected lines, arcs, points, and ellipses to remain equidistant from the centerline. This relation also forces the entities to have the same orientation. To apply this relation, invoke the **Add Relations PropertyManager**. Select the required entity and then select a centerline. Choose the **Symmetric** button from the **Add Relations** rollout.

Fix

The **Fix** relation forces the selected entity to be fixed at the specified position. If you apply this relation to a line or an arc, its location will be fixed but you can change its size by dragging the endpoints. To apply this relation, invoke the **Add Relations PropertyManager**. Next, select the required entity and choose the **Fix** button.

Merge

The **Merge** relation forces two sketch points or endpoints to merge at a single point. To apply this relation, invoke the **Add Relations PropertyManager**. Next, select the required entities and choose the **Merge** button from the **Add Relations** rollout.

Pierce

The **Pierce** relation forces a sketch point or the endpoint of an entity to be coincident with an entity of another sketch. To apply this relation, invoke the **Add Relations PropertyManager**. Next, select the required entities and choose the **Pierce** button from the **Add Relations** rollout.

> **Tip**
>
> *You can also apply the relations using the **Properties PropertyManager**. This PropertyManager is automatically invoked, if you select more than one entity from the drawing area. The possible relations for the selected geometry will be displayed in the **Add Relations** rollout. Choose the relation you need to apply to the selected geometry.*
>
> *Alternatively, select the entity or entities to which you need to apply the relation and do not move the mouse for a while; a pop-up toolbar will be displayed with possible relations. Select the required relation from the pop-up toolbar. You can also select the entity or entities and invoke the shortcut menu to display these relations.*

3. Choose the **Horizontal** button from the **Add Relations** rollout; the **Horizontal** relation is applied to the selected set of entities. Also, the name of the entities are displayed in the **Existing Relations** rollout of the PropertyManager.

The **Existing Relations** rollout of the PropertyManager displays the relations that are already applied to the selected sketched entities. It also shows the status of the sketched entities. You can delete the existing relation from this rollout. To do so, select the existing relation from the selection box and right-click to display the shortcut menu. Choose the **Delete** option from this shortcut menu to delete the selected relation. If you choose the **Delete All** option, all relations displayed in the selection box of the **Existing Relations** rollout will be deleted.

4. After applying the **Horizontal** relation, move the cursor to the drawing area and right-click to display a shortcut menu. Choose the **Clear Selections** option from the shortcut menu to remove the selected entities from the selection set.

5. Select the center point of the circle on the right and then the upper endpoint of the right inclined line.

   The relations that can be applied to the selected entities are displayed and the **Vertical** button is highlighted in the **Add Relations** rollout.

6. Choose the **Vertical** button from the **Add Relations PropertyManager** to apply the **Vertical** relation to the selected entities. Next, right-click in the drawing area and choose the **Clear Selections** option.

7. Select the entities, as shown in Figure 4-16. Choose the **Equal** button from the **Add Relations** rollout in the **Add Relations PropertyManager** to apply the **Equal** relation between them.

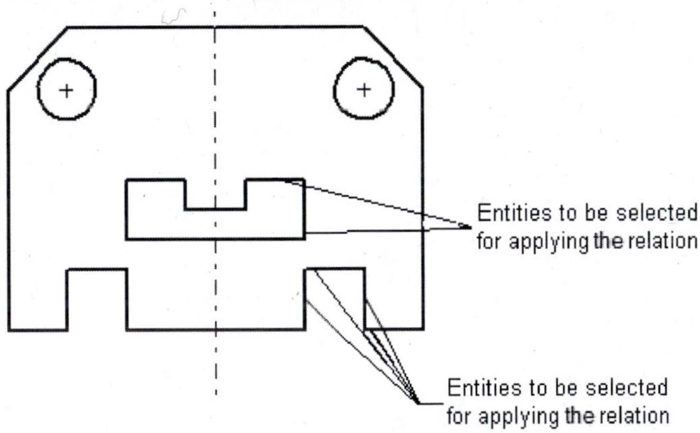

Figure 4-16 *Entities to be selected to apply the **Equal** relation*

8. Choose the **OK** button from the **Add Relations PropertyManager** or choose **OK** from the confirmation corner to close the PropertyManager. Click anywhere in the drawing area to clear the selected entities.

Applying Dimensions to the Sketch

Next, you will apply dimensions to the sketch and fully define it. After drawing the sketch and adding relations, the most important step in creating a design is dimensioning.

1. Choose **Options** from the Menu Bar; the **System Options - General** dialog box is displayed. Select the **Input dimension value** check box, if it is cleared, and then choose **OK** from the **System Options - General** dialog box. This check box is selected to invoke the **Modify** dialog box.

The **Modify** dialog box is used to enter a new dimension value. SOLIDWORKS being a parametric software, the entity on dimensioning is driven by the specified value, irrespective of the original size. Therefore, when you apply and modify the dimension of an entity, it is forced to change its size in accordance with the specified dimension value.

2. Choose the **Smart Dimension** button from the **Sketch CommandManager** to apply dimensions. You can also right-click in the drawing area and choose the **Smart Dimension** option from the shortcut menu or use the Mouse Gesture to invoke this tool. As soon as you invoke the **Smart Dimension** tool, the select cursor is replaced by the dimension cursor.

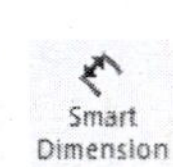

In SOLIDWORKS, you can dimension any kind of entity by using the **Smart Dimension** tool, which is available in the **Sketch CommandManager**. If you use the **Smart Dimension** tool, the type of dimension to be applied will depend on the type of entity selected. For example, if you select a line, then a horizontal, vertical, or aligned dimension will be applied. If you select a circle; a diametric dimension will be applied. Similarly, if you select an arc, a radius dimension will be applied. However, if you want to apply a particular dimension, then you need to choose the required tool from the **Smart Dimension** flyout in the **Sketch CommandManager**, refer to Figure 4-17.

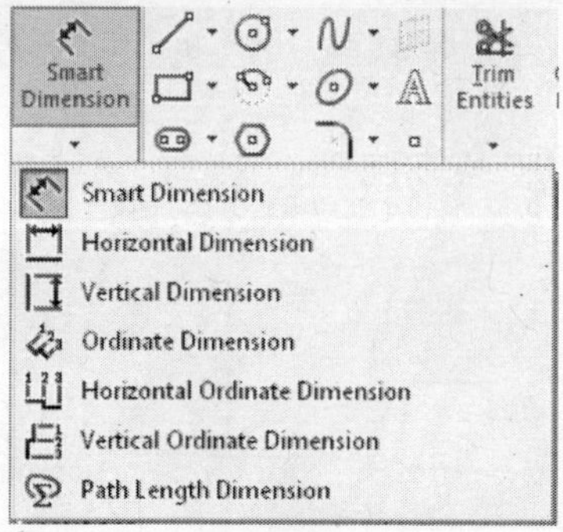

***Figure 4-17** Tools in the **Smart Dimension** flyout*

The tools in the **Smart Dimension** flyout are discussed next.

Horizontal Dimension

The **Horizontal Dimension** tool is used to apply the horizontal dimension on a selected line or between two points. The points can be the endpoints of lines or arcs, or the center points of circles, arcs, ellipses, or parabolas.

Vertical Dimension

The **Vertical Dimension** tool is used to apply the vertical dimension on a selected line or between two points. The points can be the endpoints of lines or arcs, or the center points of circles, arcs, ellipses, or parabolas.

Ordinate Dimension

The **Ordinate Dimension** tool is used to dimension a sketch with respect to a specified datum. Depending on the requirement of the design, the datum can be an entity in the sketch or the origin. The ordinate dimensions are of two types, horizontal and vertical.

Horizontal Ordinate Dimension

The **Horizontal Ordinate Dimension** tool is used to dimension the horizontal distances of the selected entities from the specified datum, refer to Figure 4-18. Note that when you apply the ordinate dimensions, the **Modify** dialog box will not be displayed to modify the dimension values. After placing all the ordinate dimensions, you need to exit the ordinate dimensioning tool and then double-click on the dimensions to modify their values.

Vertical Ordinate Dimension

The **Vertical Ordinate Dimension** tool is used to dimension the vertical distances of the selected entities from the specified datum, refer to Figure 4-19.

Path Length Dimension

The **Path Length Dimension** tool is used to dimension a chain of sketch entities which are coincident. You can set the dimension as a driving dimension, so that when you drag the entities, the shape of the path changes but its length remains same.

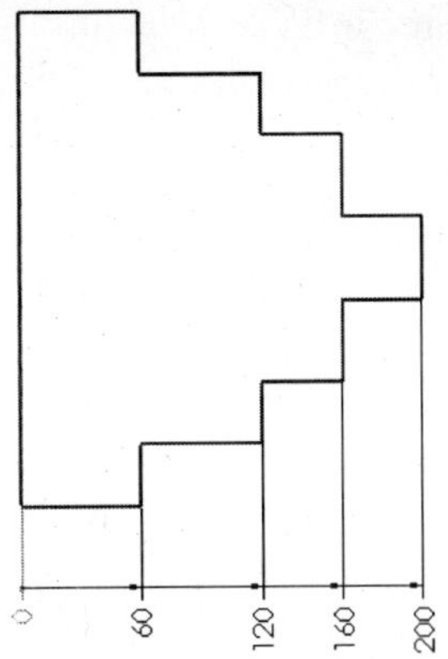

Figure 4-18 *Horizontal ordinate dimensions*

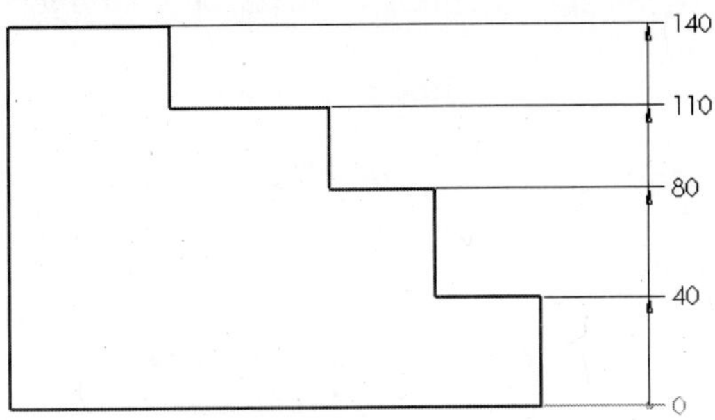

Figure 4-19 *Vertical ordinate dimensions*

After invoking the **Smart Dimension** tool, you need to apply dimensions.

3. Move the cursor to the origin and click when an orange circle is displayed.

4. Select the outer left vertical line (Figure 4-20, line 1); a horizontal dimension is attached to the cursor.

5. Place it at a suitable location; the **Modify** dialog box is displayed, refer to Figure 4-21. Enter **10** in the edit box of this dialog box and press ENTER.

> **Tip**
> *If the **Modify** dialog box is not displayed on placing the dimension, you need to set its preference manually. To do so, invoke the **System Options - General** dialog box and select the **Input dimension value** check box.*

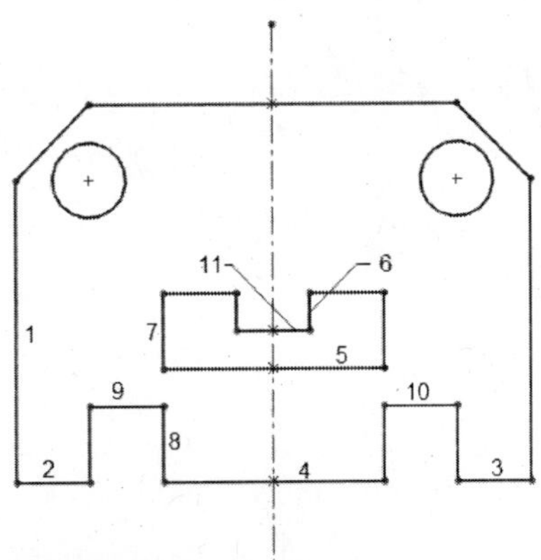

Figure 4-20 *The lines to be dimensioned are numbered for your reference*

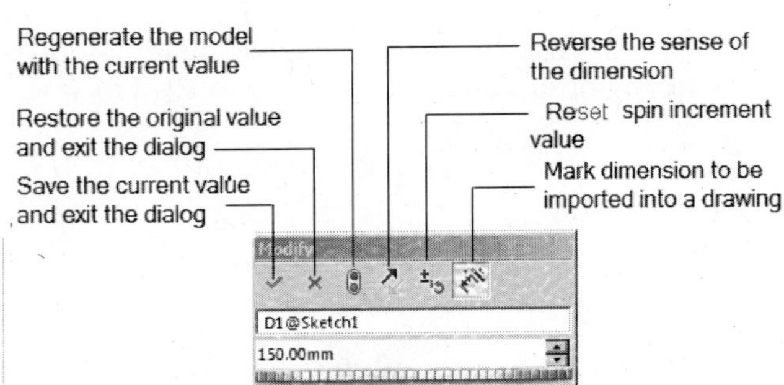

Figure 4-21 *The **Modify** dialog box*

You can modify the default dimension value by using the spinner or by entering a new value in the edit box available in the **Modify** dialog box. You can also drag the thumbwheel provided below the spinner, to the right and left to increase and decrease the dimension value.

The buttons in the **Modify** dialog box are discussed next.

The **Save the current value and exit the dialog** button is used to accept the current value and exit the dialog box. The **Restore the original value and exit the dialog** button is used to restore the last dimensional value applied to the sketch and exit the dialog box. The **Regenerate the model with the current value** button is used to preview the geometry of the sketch with the modified dimensional value. The **Reverse the sense of the dimension** button is used to flip the dimension value of an entity. This button will be available in the **Modify** dialog box when the selected dimension is a linear dimension. The **Reset spin increment value** button is used to modify the increment value of the spinner. If you choose this button, the **Increment** dialog box will be displayed. Enter a value and press ENTER. This new value will be added to or subtracted from the current value when you click on the spinner arrow. The **Mark dimensions to be imported into a drawing** button is chosen to make sure that the selected dimension is generated as a model annotation in the drawing views. If this button is not chosen, the selected dimension will not be generated in the drafting environment.

Tip

You can also enter the arithmetic symbols directly in the edit box of the ***Modify*** *dialog box to calculate the dimension. For example, if you need to enter a dimension after solving a complex arithmetic function such as (220*12.5)-3+150, which is equal to 2897, there is no need to calculate this function using the calculator. Just enter the statement in the edit box and press ENTER; SolidWorks will automatically solve the mathematical expression to get the value of the dimension.*

Next, you need to create a vertical dimension between the origin and the left horizontal line.

6. Select the origin and the left horizontal line with the dimension cursor (Figure 4-20, line 2); a vertical dimension is attached to the cursor.
7. Place the dimension at a suitable location; the **Modify** dialog box is displayed. Enter **10** in the edit box of this dialog box and press ENTER.
8. Move the dimension cursor to the lower right horizontal line (Figure 4-20, line 3); the line is highlighted.
9. Select the line; a horizontal dimension is attached to the cursor.
10. Move the cursor downward and click to place the dimension below the line, refer to Figure 4-22. As you place the dimension, the **Modify** dialog box is displayed.
11. Enter **10** as the value of dimension in this dialog box and press ENTER; the dimension is placed and the length of line is modified to **10**.

12. Select the lower-middle horizontal line (Figure 4-20, line 4) by using the dimension cursor; a dimension is attached to the cursor.

13. Move the cursor downward and click to place the dimension. Enter **30** in the **Modify** dialog box and press ENTER.

14. Select the left vertical line (Figure 4-20, line 1) by using the dimension cursor; a dimension is attached to the cursor.

15. Move the cursor to the left and then click to place the dimension. Enter **40** in the **Modify** dialog box and press ENTER.

16. Select the right inclined line; a dimension is attached to the cursor. Move the cursor vertically upward to apply the horizontal dimension to the selected line. Click to place the dimension at an appropriate place, refer to Figure 4-22.

17. Enter **10** in the **Modify** dialog box and press ENTER.

18. Again, select the right inclined line; a dimension is attached to the cursor. Move the cursor horizontally toward the right to apply the vertical dimension to the selected line. Click to place the dimension at an appropriate place, refer to Figure 4-22.

19. Enter **10** in the **Modify** dialog box and press ENTER.

20. Move the cursor towards the left circle, and when the circle is highlighted, select it; a diameter dimension is attached to the cursor. Next, move the cursor outside the sketch.

21. Place the diameter dimension. Next, enter **10** in the **Modify** dialog box and press ENTER.

22. Select the lower horizontal line (Figure 4-20, line 5) of the inner cavity; a horizontal dimension is attached to the cursor. Next, select the lower middle horizontal line (Figure 4-20, line 4) of the outer loop; a vertical dimension is attached to the cursor between the lower horizontal line of the inner cavity and the lower right horizontal line of the outer sketch.

23. Move the cursor horizontally toward the right and place the dimension. Enter **15** in the **Modify** dialog box and press ENTER.

24. Select the inner right vertical line (Figure 4-20, line 6) of the inner cavity and place the dimension outside the sketch. Enter **5** in the **Modify** dialog box and press ENTER.

25. Select the upper-middle horizontal line (Figure 4-20, line 11) of the inner cavity and place the dimension above the slot. Enter **10** in the **Modify** dialog box and press ENTER.

    Note that the color of all theentities is changed from blue to black, which indicates that the sketch is fully defined. If the sketch is not fully defined, you may need to apply collinear relation between lines 7 and 8, or between lines 9 and 10, or between lines 2, 3, and 4. The fully defined sketch after applying all required relations and dimensions is shown in Figure 4-22.

It is important for you to understand the concept of fully defined sketches. A fully defined sketch is the one in which all entities of the sketch and their positions are completely defined by the relations or dimensions, or both. Also, all degrees of freedom of a sketch are constrained. Therefore, the sketched entities cannot move or change their size and location unexpectedly. If a sketch is not fully defined, it can change its size or position at any time during the design because all degrees of freedom are not constrained. All entities in a fully defined sketch are displayed in black.

Tip

In SOLIDWORKS, it is not necessary to fully dimension or define the sketches before you use them to create the features of a model. However, it is recommended that you fully define the sketches before you proceed further to create the feature.

If you always want to use fully defined sketches before proceeding further, you can do so by choosing ***Tools > Options*** *from the SOLIDWORKS menus to display the* ***System Options - General*** *dialog box. Select the* ***Sketch*** *option from the area on the left. Next, select the* ***Use fully defined sketches*** *check box and choose* ***OK*** *from this dialog box.*

Note

You can also dimension the sketch while creating it. To do so, choose ***Tools > Options*** *from the SOLIDWORKS menus to display the* ***System Options- General*** *dialog box. Select the* ***Sketch*** *option from the area on the left. Select the* ***Enable on screen numeric input on entity creation*** *check box and then the* ***Create dimension only when value is entered*** *check box. Next,choose the* ***OK*** *button from the dialog box.*

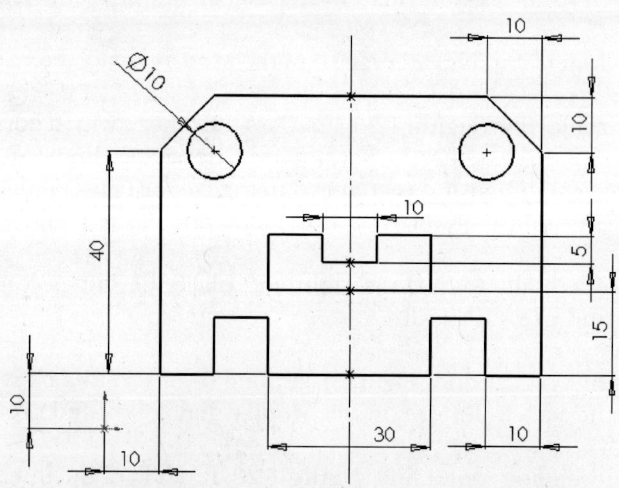

Figure 4-22 *Fully defined sketch after applying all the required relations and dimensions*

Saving the Sketch

1. Choose the **Save** button from the Menu Bar to invoke the **Save As** dialog box. Browse to the *\Documents\SOLIDWORKS Tutorials* folder. Next, create a new folder with the name *c04*.

2. Enter **c04_tut01** as the name of the document in the **File name** edit box and choose the **Save** button. The document will be saved at the location *\Documents\SOLIDWORKS Tutorials\c04*.

3. Close the document by choosing **File > Close** from the SOLIDWORKS menus.

Tutorial 2

In this tutorial, you will draw the sketch of the revolved model shown in Figure 4-23. The sketch to be drawn is shown in Figure 4-24. The solid model is given for your reference only.

(Expected time: 30 min)

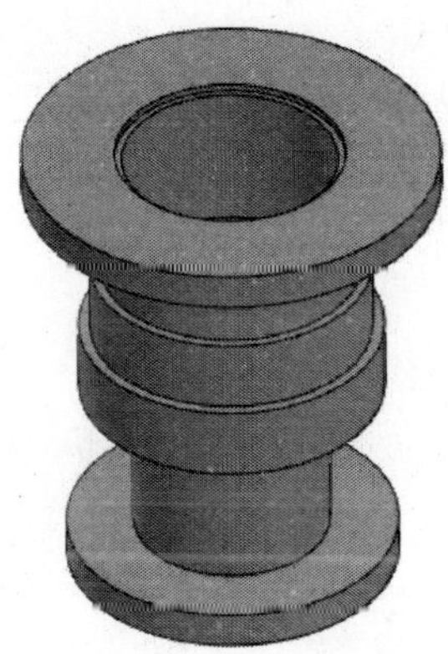

Figure 4-23 Solid model for Tutorial 2

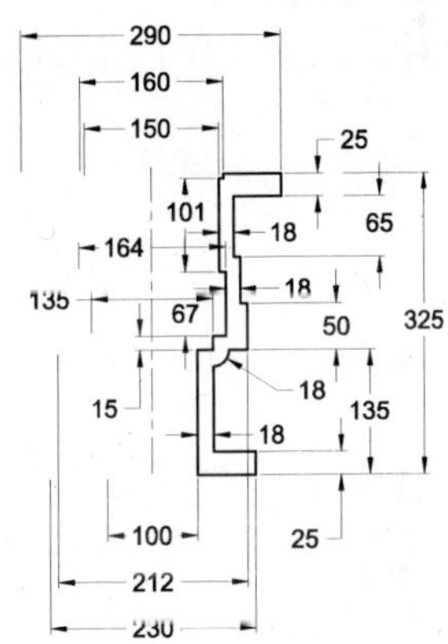

Figure 4-24 Sketch of the model

The following steps are required to complete this tutorial:

a. Start a new part document and then invoke the sketching environment.
b. Draw a centerline to add the linear diameter dimensions to the sketch of the model.
c. Create the sketch by using various sketching tools, refer to Figures 4-25 and 4-26.
d. Add relations to the sketch.
e. Add dimensions to the sketch to fully define it, refer to Figure 4-29.

Starting a New Part Document

1. Choose the **New** button from the Menu Bar; the **New SOLIDWORKS Document** dialog box is displayed with the **Part** button chosen by default.

2. Choose the **OK** button from this dialog box; a new SOLIDWORKS part document is started.

3. Choose the **Sketch** button from the **Sketch CommandManager** and select the **Front Plane** as the sketching plane; the sketching environment is invoked and the selected plane is oriented normal to the view.

4. If the grid is displayed, invoke the **Document Properties - Grid/Snap** dialog box and then clear the **Display grip** check box from the **Grid** area to hide the grids. Next, invoke the **System Options - Relations/Snaps** dialog box and clear the **Grid** check box from the **Sketch snaps** area.

5. Invoke the **Document Properties - Units** dialog box and set the units to millimeters and degree for measuring linear and angular dimensions, respectively. However, if you have selected millimeters as unit while installing SOLIDWORKS, you can skip this step.

Drawing the Sketch

To draw the sketch of the revolved model, you need to draw a centerline around which the sketch of the base feature will be revolved.

1. Invoke the **Centerline** tool from the **Sketch CommandManager**.

2. Draw a vertical centerline of length close to 325 mm starting from the origin.

Next, you need to draw the sketch of the model.

3. Right-click in the drawing area and then choose the **Line** tool from the **Sketch Entities** in the shortcut menu. Move the cursor where coordinates are close to 50 mm, 0 mm, and 0 mm. Click at this point to specify the start point of the line.

4. Move the cursor vertically upward and left-click when the length of the line displayed above the cursor is close to 135 mm, refer to Line 1 in Figure 4-25.

5. Move the cursor horizontally toward the right and draw a horizontal line of length close to 17.5 mm, refer to Line 2 in Figure 4-25.

6. Move the cursor vertically upward and draw a vertical line of length close to 15, refer to Line 3 in Figure 4-25.

7. Move the cursor horizontally toward the right and draw a horizontal line of length close to 14.5 mm, refer to Line 4 in Figure 4-25.

8. Move the line cursor vertically upward and draw a vertical line of length close to 67 mm, refer to Line 5 in Figure 4-25.

9. Move the line cursor horizontally towards the left and draw a horizontal line of length close to 7 mm, refer to Line 6 in Figure 4-25.

10. Move the line cursor vertically upward and draw a vertical line of length close to 101 mm, refer to Line 7 in Figure 4-25.

11. Similarly, draw other entities of the sketch. For dimensions, refer to Figure 4-24. The sketch after drawing all the entities is shown in Figure 4-26.

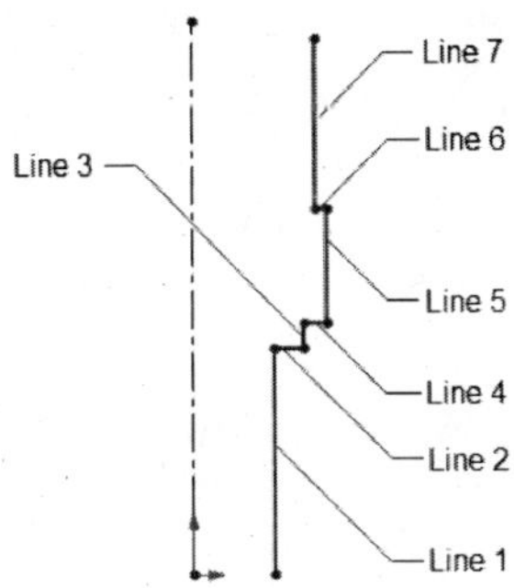

Figure 4-25 *Solid model for Tutorial 2*

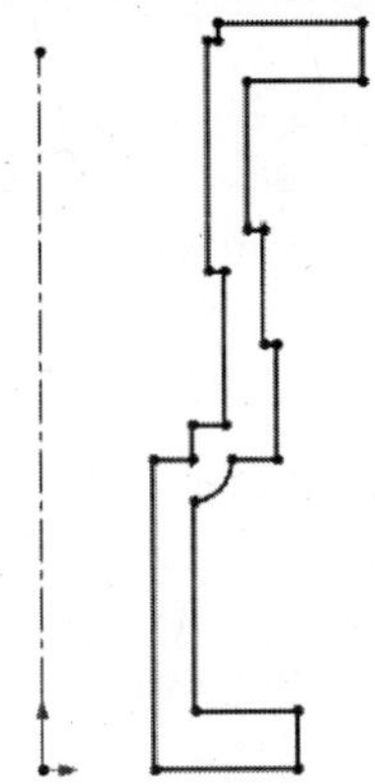

Figure 4-26 *Sketch of the model*

Adding Relations to the Sketch

Next, you will add the required relations to the sketched entities.

1. Right-click in the drawing area and then choose the **Select** option from the shortcut menu displayed. Next, press and hold the CTRL key and select the start point of the Line 1 and then select the origin for applying the horizontal relation, refer to Figure 4-27. Release the CTRL key after the selection; a pop-up toolbar is displayed, refer to Figure 4-28. Choose the **Make Horizontal** button from the pop-up toolbar; the horizontal relation is applied to the selected entities. Click anywhere in the drawing area to clear the selection set.

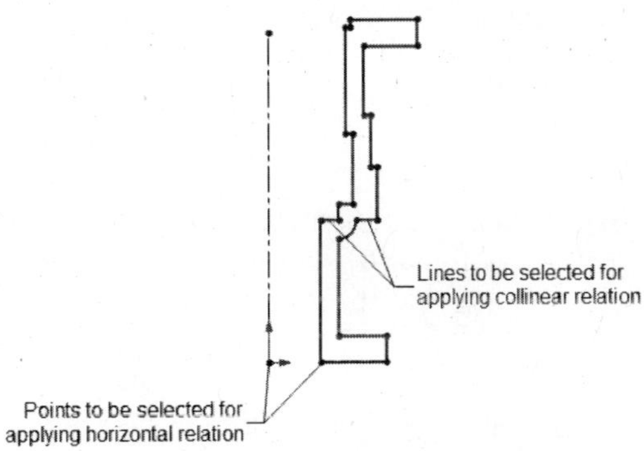

Figure 4-27 *Points and lines to be selected*

Figure 4-28 *The pop-up toolbar displayed after selecting two points*

If you select an entity, group of entities, or feature and do not move the cursor, a pop-up toolbar will be displayed. Remember that this toolbar will disappear if you move the cursor away from the selected entity or feature.

2. Press and hold the CTRL key and then select the horizontal lines one by one, refer to Figure 4-27. Next, release the CTRL key after selecting the lines; a pop-up toolbar is displayed. Choose the **Make Collinear** button from it to apply the collinear relation.

3. Press and hold the CTRL key and select the intersection point of the lines 2 and 3, refer to Figure 4-25. Next, select the center point of the arc and then release the CTRL key; a pop-up toolbar is displayed.

4. Choose the **Merge Points** button from the pop-up toolbar; the selected points are merged together.

   As discussed earlier, some of the relations such as horizontal, vertical, tangent, and so on are automatic relations and are therefore applied automatically to a sketch while drawing. This means, you need not to apply horizontal relation to the horizontal lines and vertical relation to the vertical lines of the sketch. However, if it is not applied automatically, you need to apply them manually by using the pop-up toolbar or the **Add Relations PropertyManager**.

Adding Dimensions to the Sketch

After drawing and applying relations to the sketch, you need to add dimensions to fully define the sketch. As is evident from Figures 4-23 and 4-24 that this is a sketch of revolve model, therefore, you need to apply the linear diameter dimensioning to it.

1. Invoke the **Smart Dimension** tool by using the Mouse Gesture. Next, select the inner vertical line of length 135 mm (refer to Line 1 in Figure 4-25).

2. Select the vertical centerline and move the cursor to the other side of the centerline; the preview of linear diameter dimensioning is attached to the cursor. Next, click to place the dimension below the sketch, refer to Figure 4-29 for the placement of dimension. As soon as you click the left mouse button to place the dimension, the **Modify** dialog box is displayed.

3. Enter **100** in the **Modify** dialog box and press ENTER; the linear diameter dimension is applied between the selected entities. Also, note that the symbol of centerline is displayed above the cursor. It indicates that the centerline is still selected and you can directly select the other entities of the sketch to apply linear diameter dimension with respect to the selected centerline.

The linear diameter dimensioning is used to dimension the sketch of a revolved component. If you dimension the sketch of the base feature of the given model using the linear dimensioning method, the same dimensions will be generated in the drawing views. This may be confusing because in the shop floor drawing, you need the diameter dimension of a revolved model. To overcome this problem, it is recommended that you apply the linear diameter dimension to the revolved components.

4. Select the inner vertical line of length 15 mm, refer to Line 3 in Figure 4-25. As soon as you select the vertical line, the preview of the linear diameter dimension between the selected vertical line and the centerline is attached to the cursor. Next, click to place the dimension below the sketch, refer to Figure 4-29 for the placement of dimension. On doing so, the **Modify** dialog box is displayed.

5. Enter the value **135** in the **Modify** dialog box and press ENTER.

6. Similarly, apply linear diameter dimensioning and linear dimensioning to the remaining entities of the sketch, respectively. The final sketch after applying all the dimensions is shown in Figure 4-29.

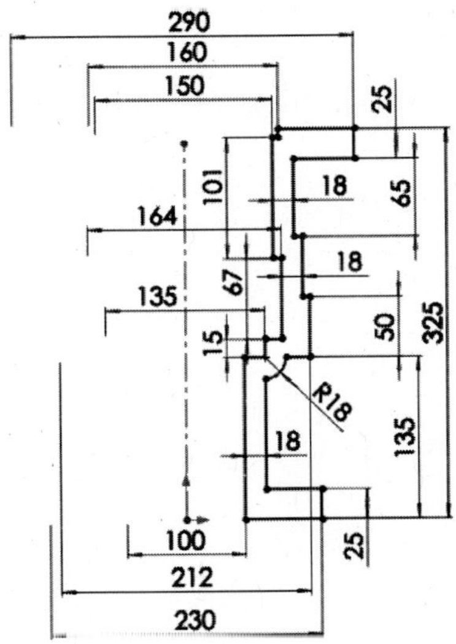

***Figure 4-29** Final sketch for Tutorial 2*

Note
You can also dimension the sketch while creating it as discussed in Tutorial 1.

Saving the Sketch

1. Choose the **Save** button from the Menu Bar and save the sketch with the name *c04_tut02* at the location *\Documents\SOLIDWORKS Tutorials\c04*

2. Choose **File > Close** from the SOLIDWORKS menus to close the document.

Self-Evaluation Test

Answer the following questions and then compare them to those given at the end of this chapter:

1. The __________ relation forces the selected arcs or circles to share the same radius and the same center point.

2. The __________ **PropertyManager** is displayed on invoking the **Dynamic Mirror Entities** tool.

3. The __________ dimension is used to dimension a line that is at an angle with respect to the X or Y axes.

4. A __________ sketch is the one in which all entities and their positions are described by relations or dimensions, or both.

5. Some relations are automatically applied to a sketch while it is being drawn. (T/F)

6. When you choose the **Add Relation** button, the **Apply Relations PropertyManager** is displayed. (T/F)

7. In SOLIDWORKS, you can dimension any entity by using the **Smart Dimension** tool. (T/F)

8. In SOLIDWORKS, you cannot enter the arithmetic symbols directly in the edit box of the **Modify** dialog box to calculate the dimension. (T/F)

Review Questions

Answer the following questions:

1. Which of the following relation forces a selected arc to share the same center point with another arc or point?

   (a) **Concentric** (b) **Coradial**
   (c) **Merge points** (d) **Equal**

2. Which of the following types of dimension changes the color of entities to red?

   (a) Underdefined (b) Overdefined
   (c) Dangling (d) None of these

3. Which of the following dialog boxes is displayed when you modify a dimension?

   (a) **Modify Dimensional Value** (b) **Insert a value**
   (c) **Modify** (d) None of these

4. Which of the following dialog boxes is displayed when you add an extra dimension or an extra relation that overdefines the sketch?

   (a) **Over defining** (b) **Delete relation**
   (c) **Make Dimension Driven?** (d) **Add Geometric Relations**

5. You can invoke the **Display/Delete Relations PropertyManager** by using the **Display/Delete Relations** button from the __________ **CommandManager**.

6. The linear diameter dimensions are applied to the sketches of __________ features.

7. The __________ sketch geometry is constrained by too many dimensions and/or relations. Therefore, you must delete the extra and conflicting relations or dimensions.

8. The __________ relation forces two selected lines, arcs, points, or ellipses to remain equidistant from a centerline.

EXERCISES

Exercise 1

Create the sketch of the model shown in Figure 4-30. Apply the required relations and dimensions to the sketch and fully define it. The sketch of the model is shown in Figure 4-31. The solid model is given for your reference only. **(Expected time: 30 min)**

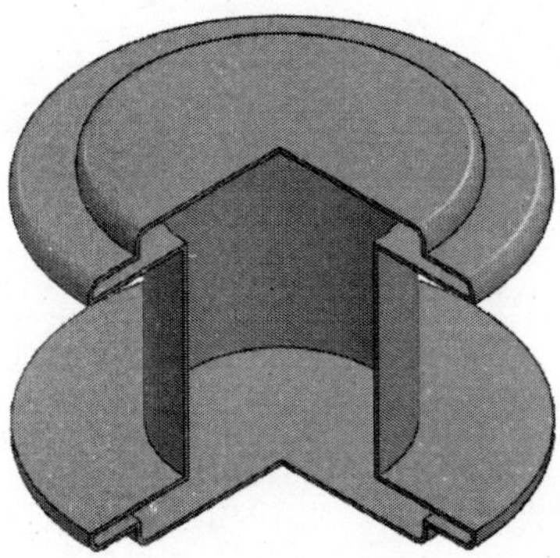

Figure 4-30 Solid model for Exercise 1

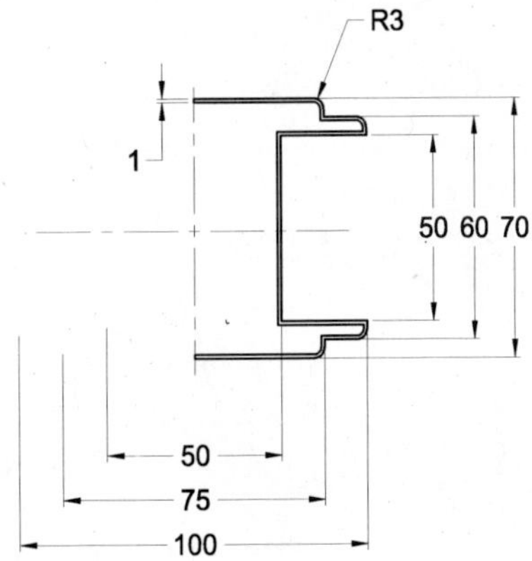

Figure 4-31 Sketch for Exercise 1

Exercise 2

Create the sketch of the model shown in Figure 4-32. Apply the required relations and dimensions to the sketch and fully define it. The sketch of the model is shown in Figure 4-33. The solid model is given for your reference only. **(Expected time: 30 min)**

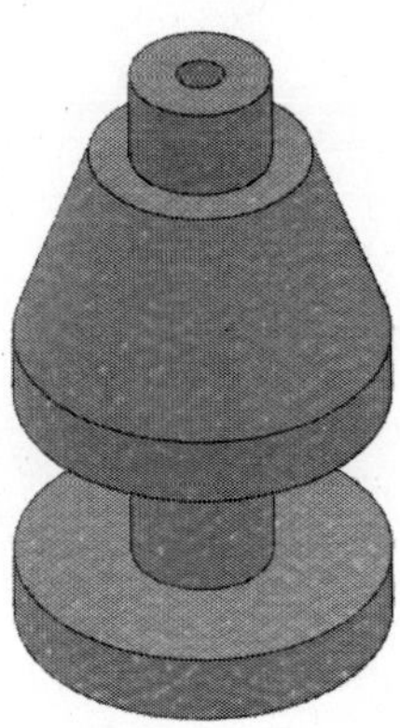

Figure 4-32 Solid model for Exercise 2

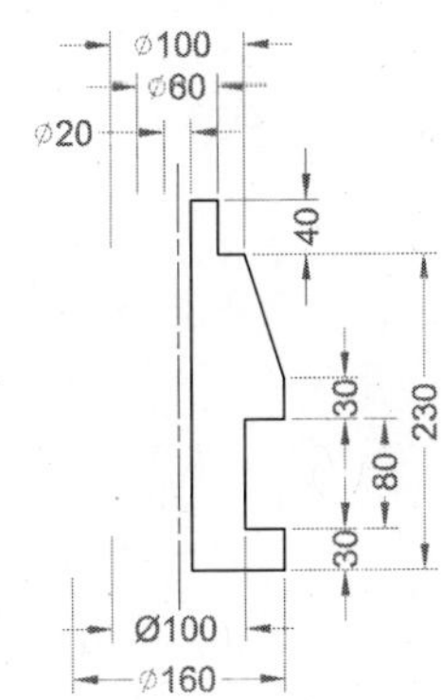

Figure 4-33 Sketch for Exercise 2

Exercise 3

Create the sketch of the model shown in Figure 4-34. Apply the required relations and dimensions to the sketch and fully define it. The sketch of the model is shown in Figure 4-35. The solid model is given for your reference only. **(Expected time: 30 min)**

Figure 4-34 Solid model for Exercise 3

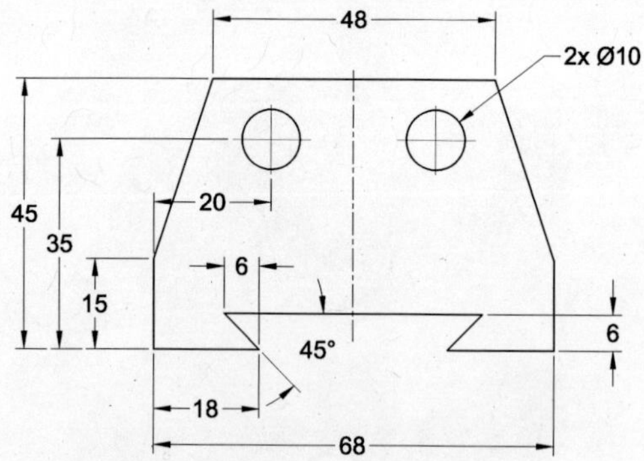

Figure 4-35 Sketch for Exercise 3

Answers to Self-Evaluation Test

1. **Coradial**, **2.** **Mirror**, **3.** aligned, **4.** fully defined, **5.** T, **6.** T, **7.** **T**, **8.** **F**

Chapter 5

Advanced Dimensioning Techniques and Base Feature Options

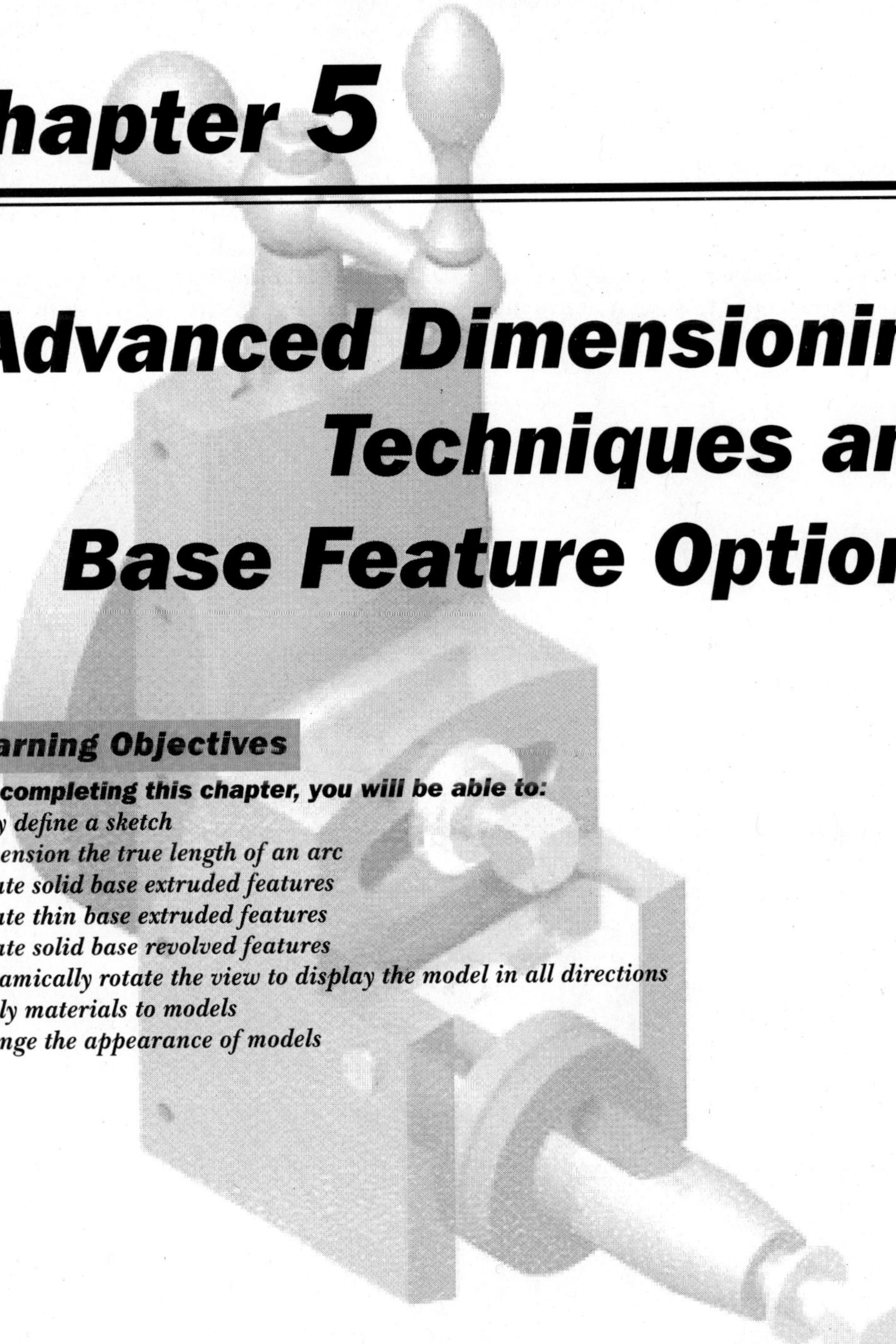

Learning Objectives

After completing this chapter, you will be able to:

- *Fully define a sketch*
- *Dimension the true length of an arc*
- *Create solid base extruded features*
- *Create thin base extruded features*
- *Create solid base revolved features*
- *Dynamically rotate the view to display the model in all directions*
- *Apply materials to models*
- *Change the appearance of models*

In this chapter, you will learn about the advanced dimensioning techniques that are used to dimension the sketches. In SOLIDWORKS, you can apply all possible relations and dimensions to a sketch by using a single tool. Also, you will learn about the tools that are used to convert a sketch into the base feature of a model in the **Part** environment.

TUTORIALS

Tutorial 1

In this tutorial, you will create the model shown in Figure 5-1. The sketch of the model is shown in Figure 5-2. First, you will draw the sketch of the model and make it fully defined by applying the required relations and dimensions in the sketching environment. Next, you will convert the sketch into a model by extruding it in two directions. The parameters for extruding the sketch are given next.

Direction 1
Depth = 10 mm
Draft angle = 35 degrees

Direction 2
Depth = 15 mm
Draft angle = 0 degree

After creating the model, you will turn on the option to display shadows and also apply Alloy Steel (SS) material to the model. Additionally, you will determine the mass properties of the model.
(Expected time: 30 min)

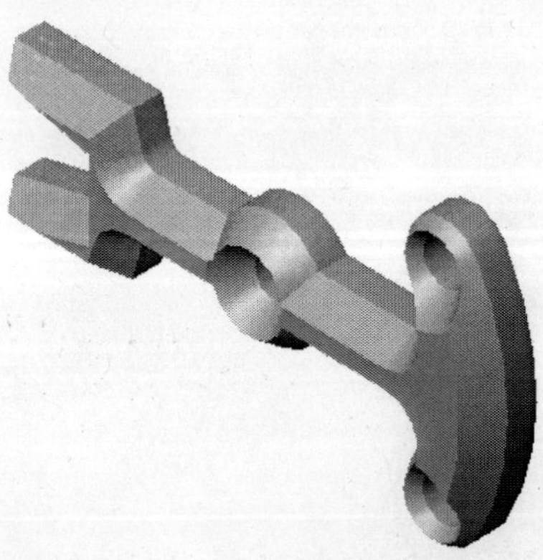

Figure 5-1 Solid Model for Tutorial 1

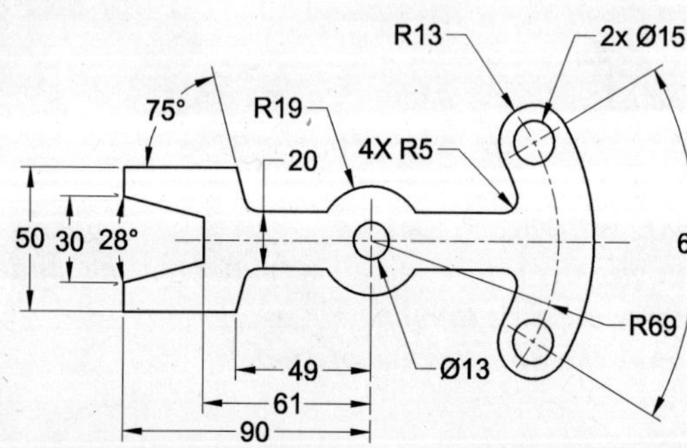

Figure 5-2 Sketch of the model

The following steps are required to complete this tutorial:

a. Create the sketch of the model using the sketching tools, refer to Figures 5-3 through 5-14.
b. Apply dimensions to the sketch and make it fully defined, refer to Figure 5-15.
c. Invoke the **Extruded Boss/Base** tool and convert the sketch into a model, refer to Figures 5-30 through 5-33.

d. Display the shadow of the model, refer to Figure 5-35.
e. Assign materials to the model, refer to Figure 5-36.
f. Determine the mass properties of the model, refer to Figure 5-37.

Drawing the Sketch

1. Start SOLIDWORKS and then invoke a new Part document. Next, choose the **Sketch** button from the **Sketch CommandManager** and then select the **Front Plane** as the sketching plane to invoke the sketching environment.

   As evident from Figure 5-2, the sketch of the model is symmetric about its centerline, therefore, you need to draw it with the help of a mirror line.

2. Increase the display of the drawing area by using the **Zoom In/Out** tool and invoke the **Centerline** tool from the **Line** flyout of the **Sketch CommandManager**.

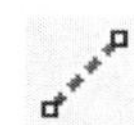

3. Move the line cursor to a location whose coordinates are close to -102 mm, 0 mm, and 0 mm and click to specify the start point of the centerline at this point.

4. Move the line cursor horizontally toward the right and specify the endpoint of the centerline when the length of the line shows a value close to 204.

5. Exit the **Centerline** tool.

6. Choose the **Zoom to Fit** button from the **View (Heads-Up)** toolbar to fit the sketch into the drawing area. Alternatively, you can also press the F key.

7. Choose the **Centerpoint Arc Slot** button from the **Slot** flyout; the arrow cursor is replaced by the arc cursor and the **Slot PropertyManager** is displayed.

8. Move the arc cursor close to the origin. Click to specify the center point of the slot, when the cursor snaps to the origin. Next, move the cursor toward the right direction and click when the arc cursor displays a value close to 69, refer to Figure 5-3.

9. Move the arc cursor in a counterclockwise direction. Click to specify the endpoint of the arc slot when the value of the angle above the arc cursor is close to 60 degrees; a reference slot is attached to the cursor. Specify a point in the drawing area where the value of the width of the slot is close to 26 mm, refer to Figure 5-4.

10. Choose the **Add Relation** button from the **Display/Delete Relations** flyout; the **Add Relations PropertyManager** is invoked.

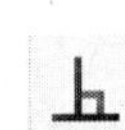

11. Right-click in the drawing area and then choose the **Clear Selections** option from the shortcut menu to clear selections from the selection set. Select the centerline and the coordinate point of the slot, as shown in Figure 5-5; the **Coincident** button is highlighted in bold in the **Add Relations** rollout of the **Add Relation PropertyManager**. This indicates that the coincident relation is the most appropriate relation for the selected entities.

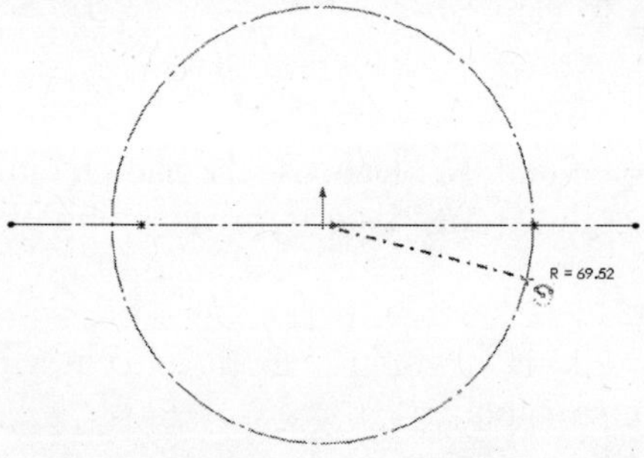

Figure 5-3 Specifying the start point of the slot

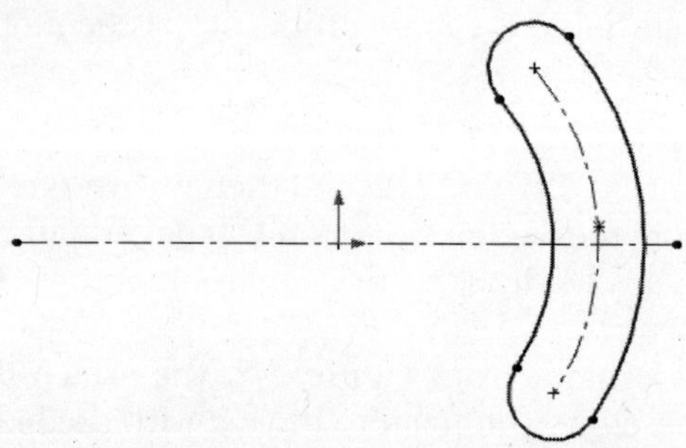

Figure 5-4 The sketch after drawing the slot

12. Choose the **Coincident** button from the **Add Relations PropertyManager**.

13. Choose the **OK** button from the **Add Relations PropertyManager** or choose **OK** from the confirmation corner. The sketch after applying the coincident relation is shown in Figure 5-6.

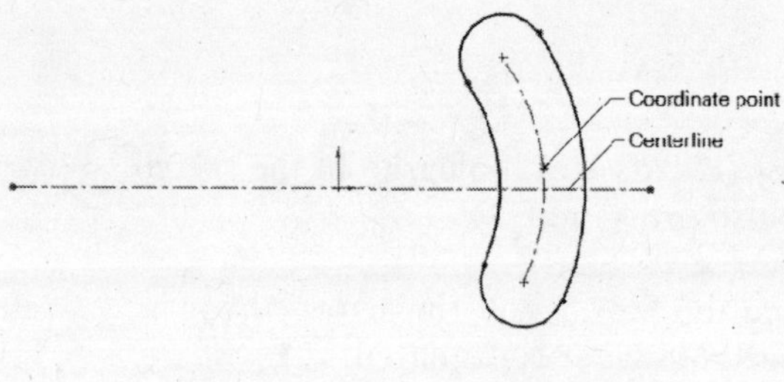

Figure 5-5 The centerline and the coordinate point to be selected

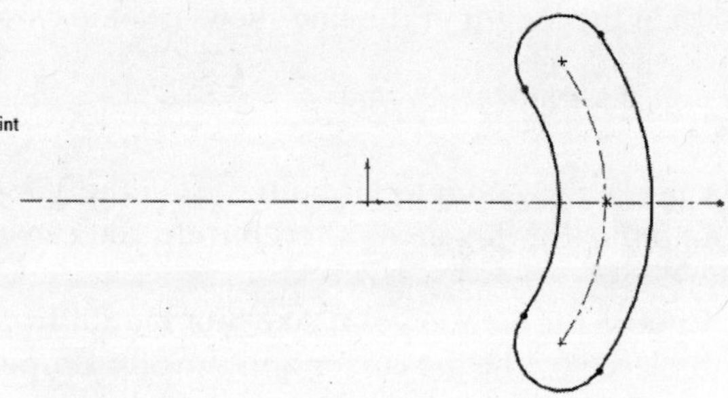

Figure 5-6 The sketch after applying the coincident relation

Next, you need to make the centerline as the mirror line and draw the sketch on the upper side of the mirror line. On doing so, the same sketch is reflected on the other side of the mirror line.

14. Choose **Tools > Sketch Tools > Dynamic Mirror** from the SOLIDWORKS menu and select the centerline; the centerline is converted into a mirror line.

15. Invoke the **Line** tool from the **Sketch CommandManager**. Next, move the cursor to the point whose coordinates are close to -61, 0, and 0 and then click to specify the start point of the line.

16. Move the cursor vertically upward and draw a line of length close to 7.

17. Move the cursor toward the left at an angle of 166-degree with the horizontal axis. Refer to the **Parameters** rollout of the PropertyManager for the angle measurement. Next, click to specify the endpoint of the line where the length of the line is close to 30; the mirrored entities are created on the other side.

18. Move the cursor vertically upward and specify the endpoint of the vertical line where the length of the line above the line cursor displays a value close to 10.

19. Move the cursor horizontally toward right and specify the endpoint where the length of the line above the line cursor displays a value close to 42.

20. Move the cursor downward at an angle of 285-degree; refer to the **Parameters** rollout of the PropertyManager for angle measurement. Next, specify the endpoint of the line where the length is close to 15. The sketch after drawing the inclined line is shown in Figure 5-7.

21. Move the cursor horizontally toward the right and specify the endpoint when the line cursor snaps to the left arc of the slot, refer to Figure 5-8. Next, exit the **Line** tool.

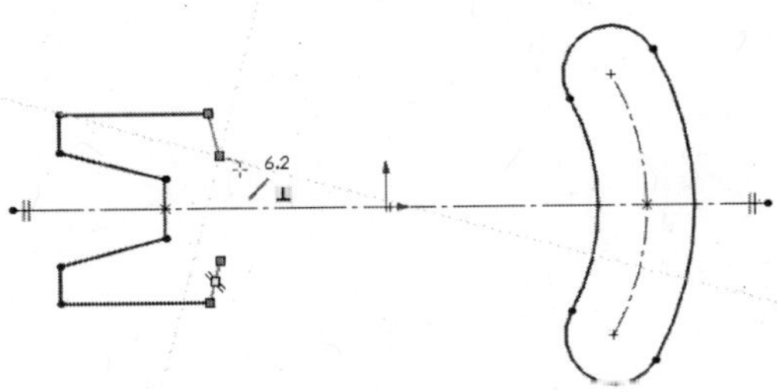

Figure 5-7 *Sketch after drawing the inclined line*

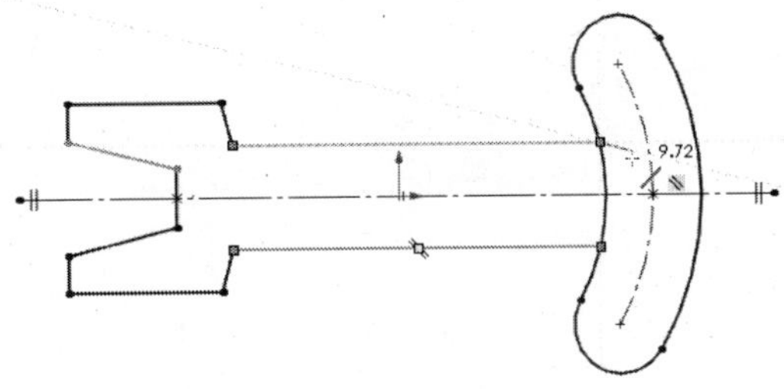

Figure 5-8 *Sketch after creating the horizontal lines*

22. Choose the **Circle** button from the **Sketch CommandManager**.

23. Move the cursor to the endpoint of the slot and specify the center point of the circle when the center point is highlighted. Next, move the cursor horizontally toward the right and click the left mouse button when the radius of the circle above the circle cursor is close to 7.5. Similarly, draw the other circle of diameter 7.5. Figure 5-9 shows the sketch after drawing circles.

24. Right-click in the drawing area and then choose **Recent Commands > Dynamic Mirror Entities** to exit the **Dynamic Mirror** tool.

25. Invoke the **Circle** tool again from the **Sketch CommandManager**.

26. Move the cursor to the origin and click to specify the center point of the circle when the cursor snaps to the origin. Next, move the cursor horizontally toward the right and click the left mouse button when the radius of the circle above the circle cursor shows a value close to 6.5.

27. Similarly, create one more circle of radius 19 approximately, with its center point at the origin. The sketch after drawing the required slot, circles, and lines is shown in Figure 5-10.

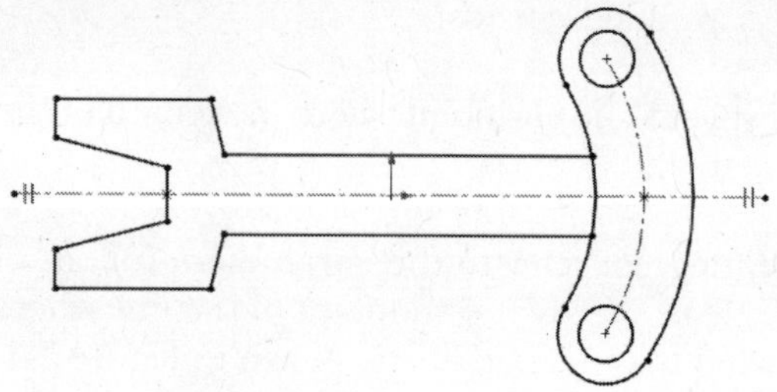

Figure 5-9 Sketch after drawing two circles

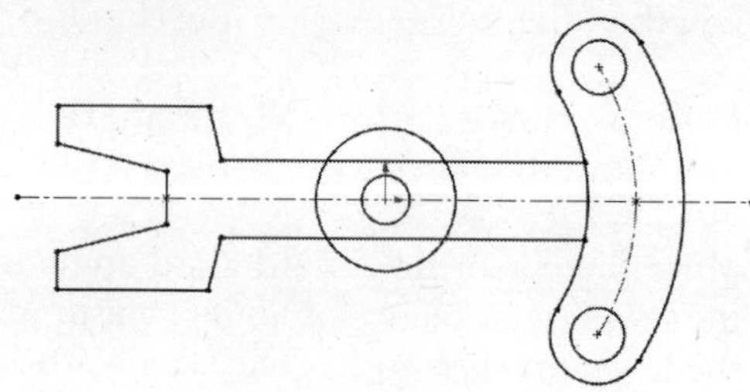

Figure 5-10 Sketch after drawing slots, circles, and lines

Trimming Unwanted Entities

After drawing the sketch, you need to trim some of the unwanted sketched entities using the **Trim Entities** tool.

1. Choose the **Trim Entities** button from the **Sketch CommandManager** to invoke the **Trim PropertyManager**.

2. Choose the **Trim to closest** button from the **Options** rollout of the PropertyManager, if it is not chosen by default; the select cursor is replaced by the trim cursor.

3. Select the entities to be trimmed, refer to Figure 5-11; the entities are dynamically trimmed. Next, exit the tool.

Note

While trimming the unwanted sketches of the slot, the ***SOLIDWORKS*** *message box is displayed with the message* ***This trim operation will destroy the slot entity. Do you want to continue?*** *Choose the* ***OK*** *button to continue the trimming operation.*

As the trim operation destroys the slot entities, you need to apply the tangent and symmetric relations to them.

4. Apply the tangent and symmetric relations to the slot entities by using the **Add Relations PropertyManager**, refer to Figure 5-12. Also, make sure that the center points of both the circles that are having 15 mm diameter merge with the center points of the arcs of the slot.

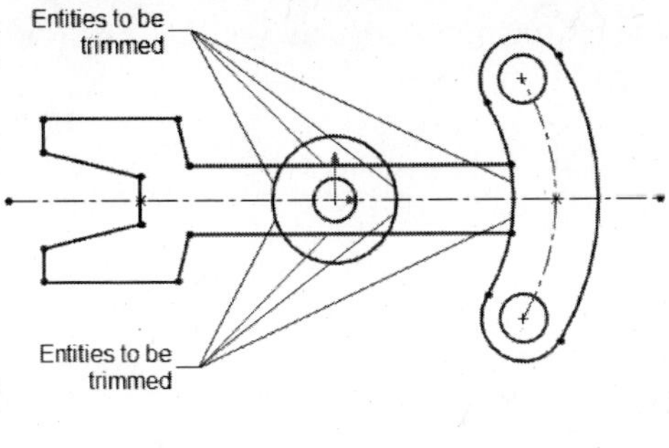

Figure 5-11 The entities to be trimmed

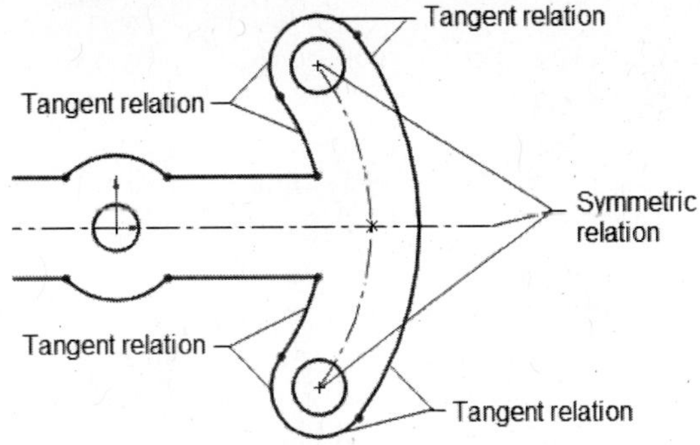

Figure 5-12 Relations to be applied to the slot entities

Filleting Sketched Entities

Next, you need to fillet the sketched entities. Fillets are generally added to avoid the stress concentration at sharp corners.

1. Choose the **Sketch Fillet** button from the **Sketch CommandManager**; the **Sketch Fillet PropertyManager** is displayed. Next, set the value **5** in the **Radius** spinner of the PropertyManager.

2. Select the set of entities one by one to apply fillet, refer to Figure 5-13. Next, exit the **Sketch Fillet** tool. Figure 5-14 shows the sketch after applying fillets of radius 5 mm.

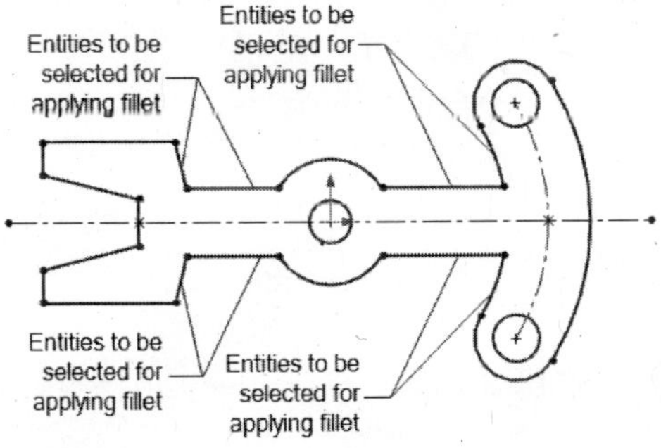

Figure 5-13 The entities to be filleted

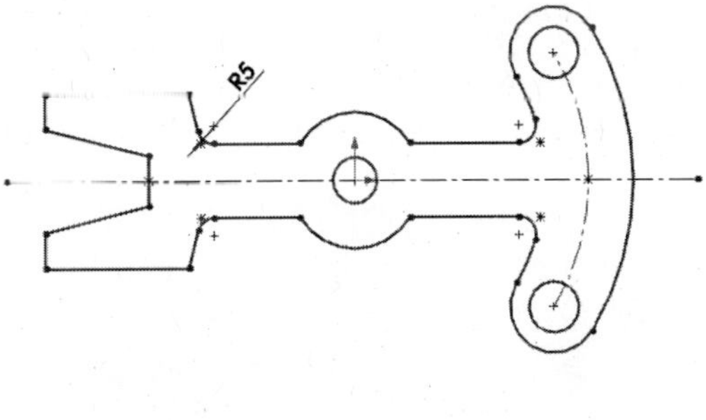

Figure 5-14 Sketch after filleting the sketched entities

Adding Dimensions to the Sketch

Next, you need to apply dimensions to the sketch and fully define it.

1. Choose the **Smart Dimension** button from the **Sketch CommandManager**; the arrow cursor is replaced by the dimension cursor.

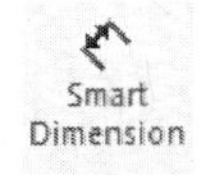

2. Select the construction arc of the slot that is displayed as a construction entity; a radius dimension is attached to the cursor. Move the cursor away from the sketch toward the right and place the dimension; the **Modify** dialog box is displayed.

3. Enter **69** in the **Modify** dialog box and press ENTER, refer to Figure 5-15.

4. Select the upper arc of the slot; a radius dimension is attached to the cursor. Move the cursor away from the sketch toward the right and place the dimension.

5. Enter **13** in the **Modify** dialog box and press ENTER, refer to Figure 5-15.

6. Select the origin and the start point of the construction arc of the slot; a dimension is attached to the cursor. Next, select the endpoint of the construction arc; an angular dimension is attached to the cursor. Place the angular dimension outside the sketch.

Tip
In SOLIDWORKS, you can also apply angular dimensions to an arc by using the ***Smart Dimension*** *tool. To do so, you need to select two endpoints and the center point of the arc.*

7. Enter **60** as the value of the angular dimension in the **Modify** dialog box and press ENTER, refer to Figure 5-15.

8. Select the upper right circle; a diameter dimension is attached to the cursor. Place the dimension outside the sketch.

9. Enter **15** as the value of the diameter dimension in the **Modify** dialog box and press ENTER, refer to Figure 5-15.

10. Select the upper right horizontal line and the lower right horizontal line that coincide with the trimmed circle; a vertical dimension is attached to the cursor. Move the cursor vertically upward and click to place the dimension.

11. Enter **20** in the **Modify** dialog box and press ENTER, refer to Figure 5-15.

12. Select the circle at the origin; a diameter dimension is attached to the cursor. Move the cursor upward and place the dimension outside the sketch.

13. Enter **13** as the value of the diameter dimension in the **Modify** dialog box and press ENTER.

14. Select the outer trimmed circle and place the radius dimension outside the sketch.

15. Enter **19** as the value of the radial dimension in the **Modify** dialog box and press ENTER.

16. Select the upper right inclined line; a dimension is attached to the cursor. Next, select the upper left horizontal line; an angular dimension is attached to the cursor. Place the dimension above the upper left horizontal line, refer to Figure 5-15.

17. Enter **75** as the value of the angular dimension in the **Modify** dialog box and press ENTER.

18. Select the origin and the lower endpoint of the lower right inclined line. Move the cursor vertically downward and place the dimension. Enter **49** in the **Modify** dialog box and press ENTER, refer to Figure 5-15.

19. Select the origin and the middle left vertical line, refer to Figure 5-15. Move the cursor vertically downward and place the dimension below the previously placed dimension.

20. Enter **61** in the **Modify** dialog box and then press ENTER.

21. Select the origin and the lower endpoint of the outer left vertical line, refer to Figure 5-15. Move the cursor vertically downward and place the dimension below the last placed dimension.

22. Enter **90** in the **Modify** dialog box and then press ENTER.

23. Select the upper left and lower left inclined lines, refer to Figure 5-15; an angular dimension is attached to the cursor. Move the cursor horizontally toward the left and place the dimension.

24. Enter **28** as the value of the angular dimension in the **Modify** dialog box and then press ENTER.

25. Select the upper left and the lower left horizontal lines; a linear dimension is attached to the cursor. Move the cursor horizontally toward the left and place the dimension.

26. Enter **50** in the **Modify** dialog box and then press ENTER.

27. Select the lower endpoint of the upper left vertical line and the upper endpoint of the lower left vertical line; a linear dimension is attached to the cursor. Move the cursor horizontally toward the left and click to place the dimension.

28. Enter **30** in the **Modify** dialog box and then press ENTER.

29. Add the remaining dimensions to the sketch and make it a fully defined sketch. Figure 5-15 shows the fully defined sketch.

Tip

*In SOLIDWORKS, you can also fully define a sketch by applying the required relations and dimensions to it automatically using the **Fully Define Sketch** tool. To fully define a sketch, draw the sketch using the standard sketching tools. Next, choose the **Fully Define Sketch** button from the **Display/Delete Relations** flyout in the **Sketch CommandManager**; the **Fully Define Sketch PropertyManager** will be displayed. You can also invoke this PropertyManager by right-clicking in the drawing area and then choosing the **Fully Define Sketch** option from the shortcut menu displayed. Using this PropertyManager, you can make all the entities of a sketch or selected entities of a sketch fully defined by selecting the respective option from the PropertyManager.*

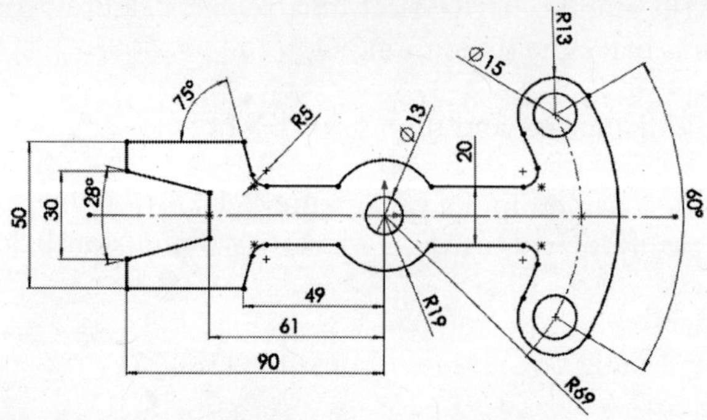

Figure 5-15 Sketch after applying all relations and dimensions

Extruding the Sketch

After creating the sketch, you need to convert it into a base feature. To do so, you need to invoke the **Extruded Boss/Base** tool and extrude the sketch using the parameters given in the tutorial description.

1. Choose the **Features** tab from the **CommandManager** to display the **Features CommandManager** tools.

The **Features CommandManager** provides all the modeling tools that are used in feature-based solid modeling.

2. Choose the **Extruded Boss/Base** button from the **Features CommandManager**; the sketch is automatically oriented to the trimetric view and the **Boss-Extrude PropertyManager** is displayed.

Also, you will notice that the preview of the base feature is displayed in the temporary shaded graphics with the default values, refer to Figure 5-16. Additionally, an arrow will appear in front of the sketch. Note that the closed loops that are available inside the outer loop of the sketch are automatically subtracted from the outer loop while extruding it, refer to Figure 5-16.

The **Extruded Boss/Base** tool is used to add material to the area defined by a sketch.

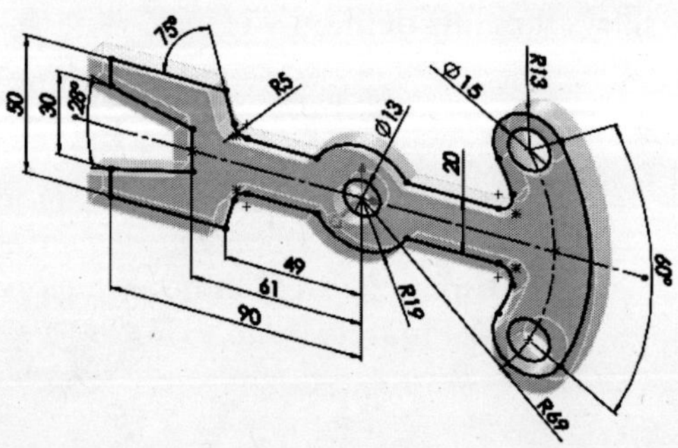

Figure 5-16 Preview of the feature being extruded

3. Make sure that the **Sketch Plane** option is selected in the **Start Condition** drop-down list of the **From** rollout in the **Boss-Extrude PropertyManager**, as shown in Figure 5-17.

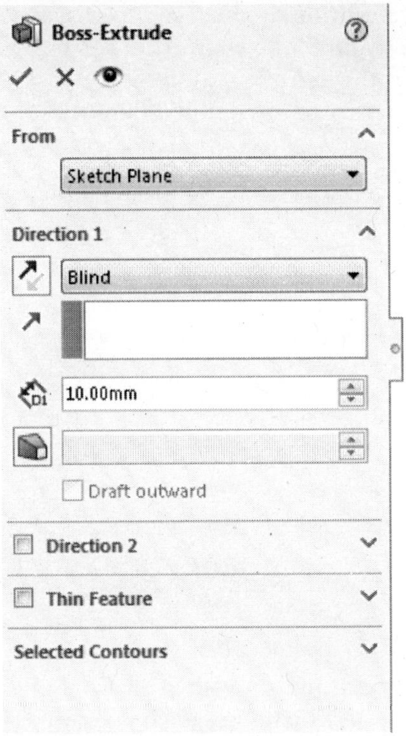

Figure 5-17** The **Boss-Extrude PropertyManager

In the **Boss-Extrude PropertyManager**, the **Sketch Plane** option is selected by default in the **Start Condition** drop-down list of the **From** rollout. Therefore, the resulting extrude feature will start from the sketching plane on which the sketch is drawn. This option is mostly used while creating the extrude feature, refer to Figure 5-16. In SOLIDWORKS, you can also select the **Surface/Face/Plane**, **Vertex**, and **Offset** options from the **Start Condition** drop-down list of the **From** rollout. The **Surface/Face/Plane** option is used to start the extrude feature from a selected surface, face, or a plane, instead of the plane on which the sketch is drawn. Figure 5-18 shows the sketch to be extruded and the face to be selected as the face to start extrusion. Figure 5-19 shows the resulting extrude feature created on the selected face up to a specified depth.

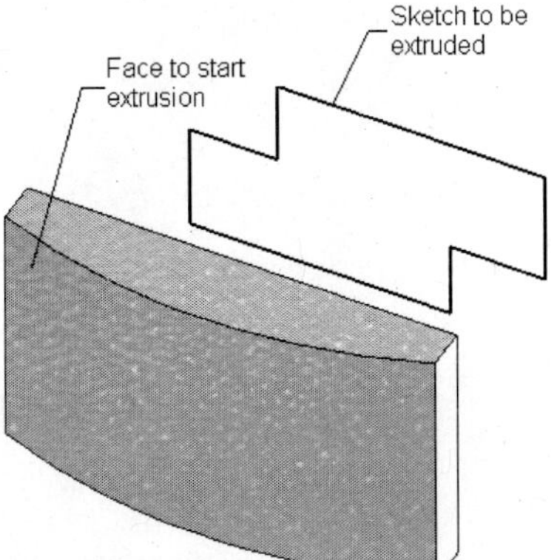

***Figure 5-18** Sketch to be extruded and the reference face selected*

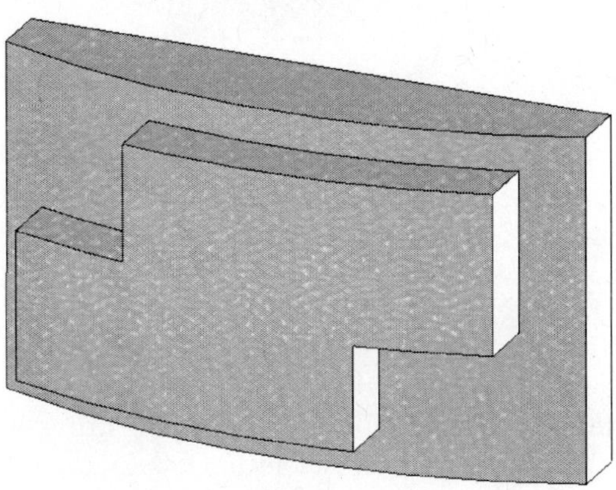

***Figure 5-19** Resulting extruded feature*

The **Vertex** option of the **Start Condition** drop-down list is used to specify a vertex as a reference for starting the extrude feature. Figure 5-20 shows the sketch to be extruded and the vertex to be selected as a reference to start the extrude feature. Figure 5-21 shows the resulting extruded feature created on the selected vertex to the defined depth.

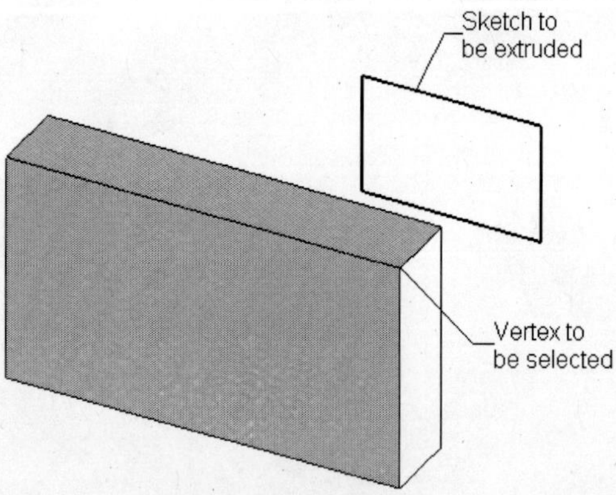

Figure 5-20 *Sketch to be extruded and a reference vertex to be selected*

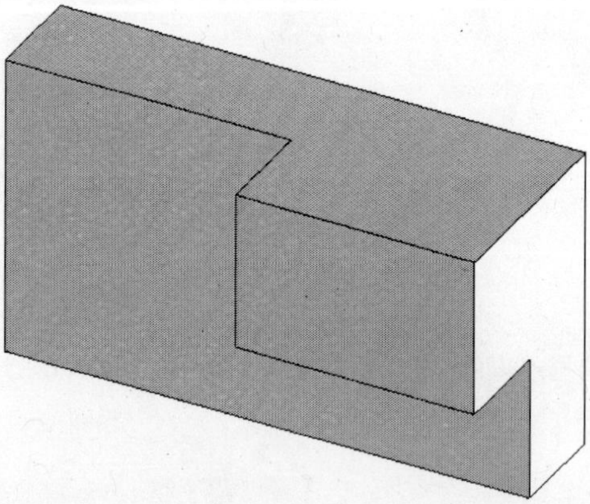

Figure 5-21 *Resulting extruded feature*

The **Offset** option of the **Start Condition** drop-down list is used to start the extrude feature at an offset distance from the plane on which the sketch is drawn. Figure 5-22 shows the preview of a sketch drawn on the front plane and being extruded using the **Offset** option. Figure 5-23 shows the resulting extruded feature created at an offset distance from the sketching plane.

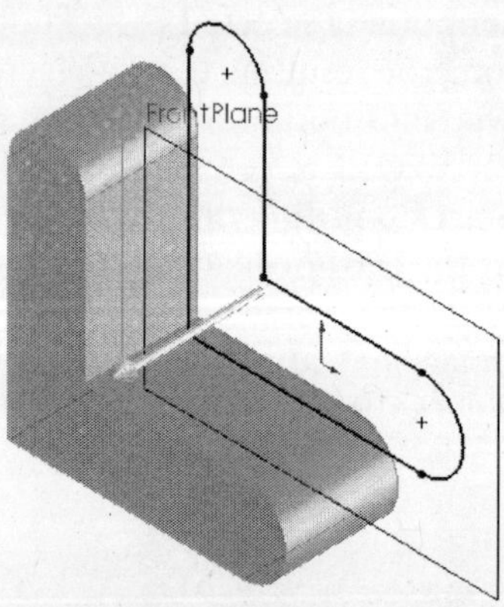

Figure 5-22 *Sketch being extruded using the* ***Offset*** *option*

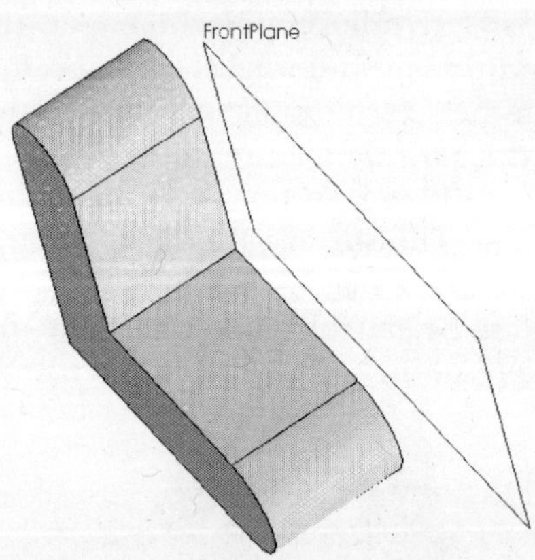

Figure 5-23 *Resulting extruded feature*

4. Make sure that the **Blind** option is selected in the **End Condition** drop-down list of the **Direction 1** rollout of the **Boss-Extrude PropertyManager**.

The **End Condition** drop-down list of the **Direction 1** rollout in the PropertyManager is used to define the termination of extrude features in one direction from the sketching plane. Note that the **Blind** option is selected by default in this drop-down list and is used to define the termination of the extrude features by specifying the depth of extrusion. The depth of extrusion is specified in the **Depth** spinner of the PropertyManager. The other options of this drop-down list are discussed next.

Mid Plane

The **Mid Plane** option of the **End Condition** drop-down list is used to create a feature by extruding the sketch equally in both the directions of the plane on which the sketch is drawn.

Up To Vertex

The **Up To Vertex** option of the **End Condition** drop-down list is used to define the termination of a feature at a virtual plane that is parallel to the sketching plane and passes through the selected vertex. The vertex can be a point on an edge, a sketched point, or a reference point. Figure 5-24 shows a sketch drawn on a plane at an offset distance and Figure 5-25 shows the model in which the sketch is extruded up to the selected vertex.

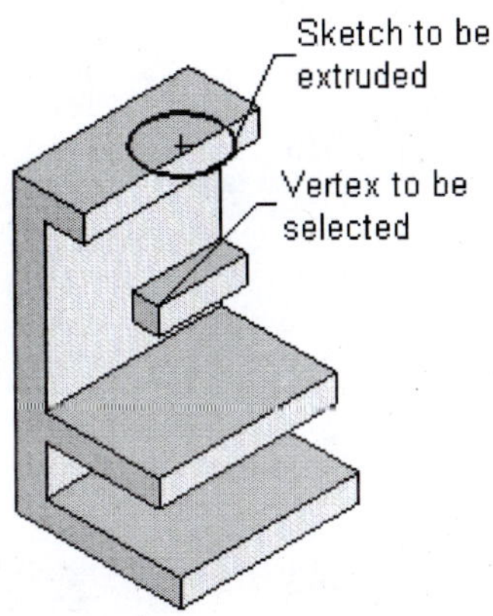

Figure 5-24 Sketch drawn on a plane created at an offset distance and the vertex to be selected

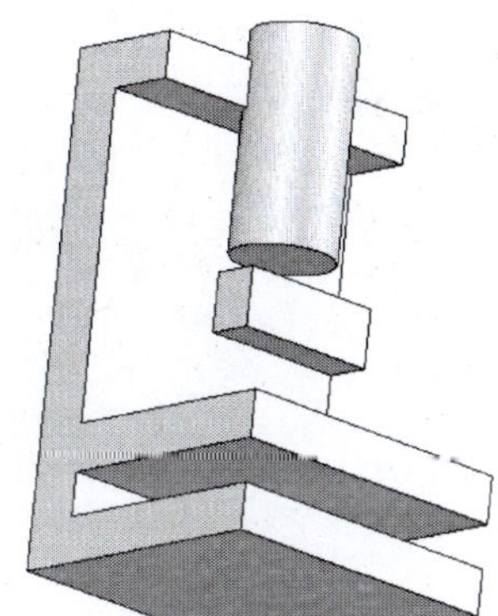

*Figure 5-25 Sketch extruded using the **Up To Vertex** option*

Up To Surface

The **Up To Surface** option of the **End Condition** drop-down list is used to define the termination of a feature up to a selected surface or face. Figure 5-26 shows the sketch drawn at an offset distance and the surface to be selected. Figure 5-27 shows the resulting feature extruded up to the selected surface.

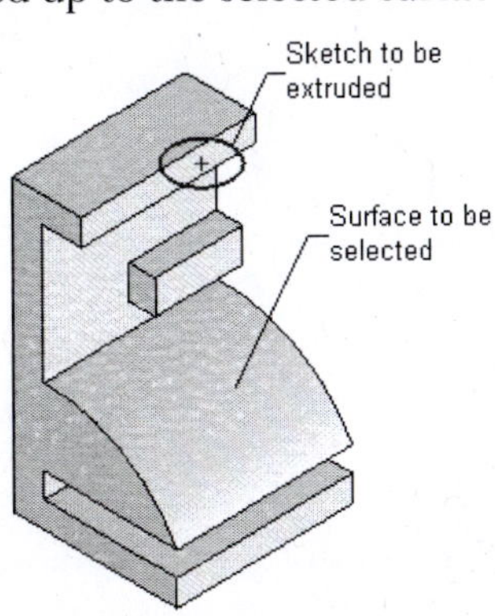

Figure 5-26 Sketch drawn on a plane created at an offset distance and the surface to be selected

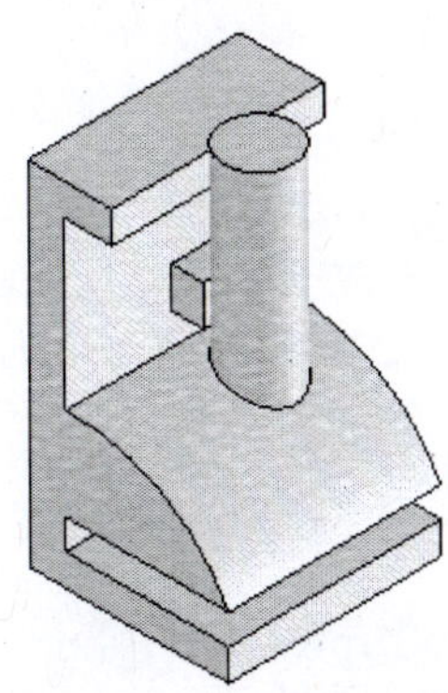

*Figure 5-27 Sketch extruded using the **Up To Surface** option*

Offset From Surface

The **Offset From Surface** option is used to define the termination of a feature on a virtual surface that is created at an offset distance from the selected surface.

Up To Body

The **Up To Body** option is used to define the termination of the extruded feature to another body. Figure 5-28 shows the sketch for the extruded feature and a body up to which the sketch will be extruded. Figure 5-29 shows the resulting feature.

Up To Next

The **Up To Next** option is used to extrude the sketch from the sketching plane to the next surface that intersects the feature. This option will be available in the **End Condition** drop-down list only after you create a base feature.

Through All

The **Through All** option is used to extrude the sketch from the sketching plane to all the existing geometric entities. This option will be available in the **End Condition** drop-down list only after you create a base feature.

5. Set the value of the **Depth** spinner to 10mm.

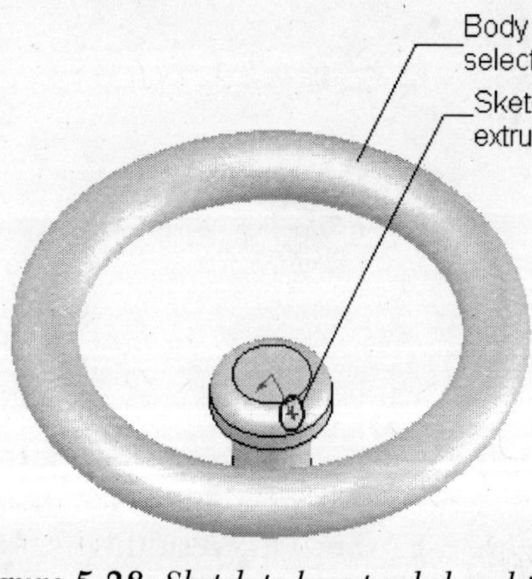

Figure 5-28 *Sketch to be extruded and the body to be selected for the extrude feature*

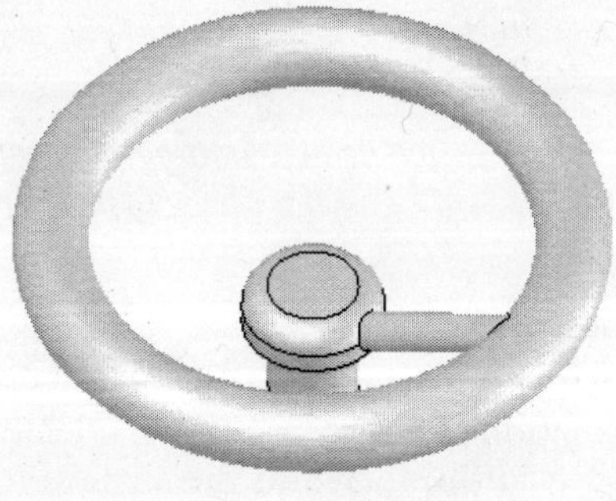

Figure 5-29 *Sketch extruded using the* ***Up To Body*** *option*

> **Tip**
> *In SOLIDWORKS, you can also extrude a sketch to a blind depth by dragging the feature dynamically using the mouse. To do so, move the mouse to the arrow displayed in the preview; the move cursor will be displayed and the color of the arrow will also be changed. Left-click once on the arrow; a scale will be displayed. Now, move the cursor; the value of the depth of extrusion will change dynamically on this scale as you move the cursor. Left-click again to specify the termination of the extruded feature.*

6. Choose the **Draft On/Off** button from the **Direction 1** rollout of PropertyManager to enable the **Draft Angle** spinner.

The **Draft On/Off** button is used to specify a draft angle while extruding a sketch. Applying a draft angle results in tapering of the resulting feature. By default, the feature will be tapered inward. However, if you want to taper the feature outward, you need to select the **Draft outward** check box that is displayed below the **Draft Angle** spinner.

7. Set the value of the **Draft Angle** spinner to 35 deg; the preview of the feature is modified, as shown in Figure 5-30.

   These are the settings for direction 1. Next, you need to specify the settings for direction 2.

8. Select the **Direction 2** check box to invoke the **Direction 2** rollout. As soon as you invoke the **Direction 2** rollout, another arrow is displayed in the preview of the feature. Also, the material is added along the second direction with the default depth value, refer to Figure 5-31.

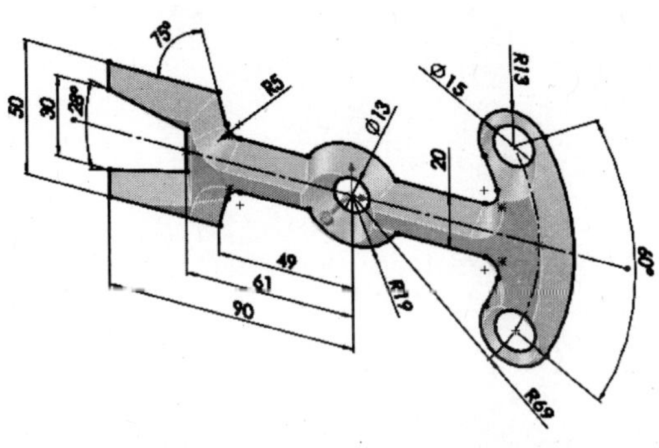

Figure 5-30 Preview of the extrude feature after applying the draft angle

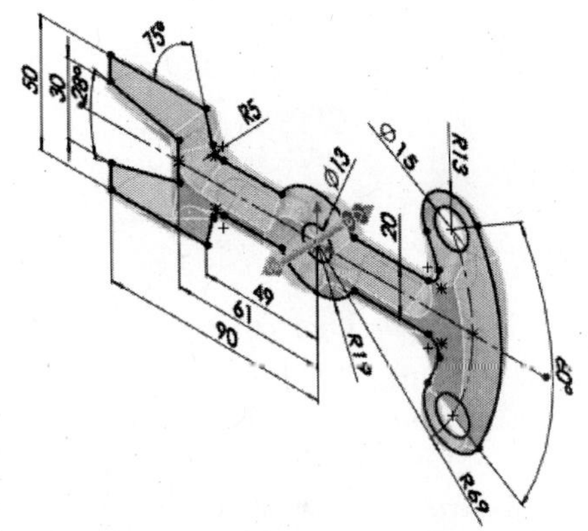

*Figure 5-31 Preview of the extrude feature after invoking the **Direction 2** rollout*

The **Direction 2** rollout is used to extrude a sketch with different values in the second direction of the sketching plane. You can expand this rollout by selecting the check box available in its title bar. This check box will not be enabled, if the **Mid Plane** option is selected in the **End Condition** drop-down list of the **Direction 1** rollout. The options available in the **Direction 2** rollout are similar to the options in the **Direction 1** rollout.

9. Choose the **Draft On/Off** button in the **Direction 2** rollout to turn it off, if it is on. This is because you do not require the draft angle in the second direction.

10. Set **15** in the **Depth** spinner of the **Direction 2** rollout as the depth in the second direction.

11. Choose the **OK** button to create the feature or choose **OK** from the confirmation corner. The feature is created and its name is displayed in the **FeatureManager Design Tree**.

The **FeatureManager Design Tree** that is available on the left side of the drawing area is one of the most important components of SOLIDWORKS screen. It contains information about the default planes, materials, lights, and all other features that are added to a model. When you add features to a model using the modeling tools, the added features are also displayed in the **FeatureManager Design Tree**. It stores and displays all features in hierarchical manner.

It is recommended that you change the view to isometric after creating the feature to view it properly.

12. Choose the **View Orientation** button from the **View (Heads-Up)** toolbar; the **View Orientation** flyout is displayed, refer to Figure 5-32. Next, choose the **Isometric** button from it. The isometric view of the resulting solid model is shown in Figure 5-33.

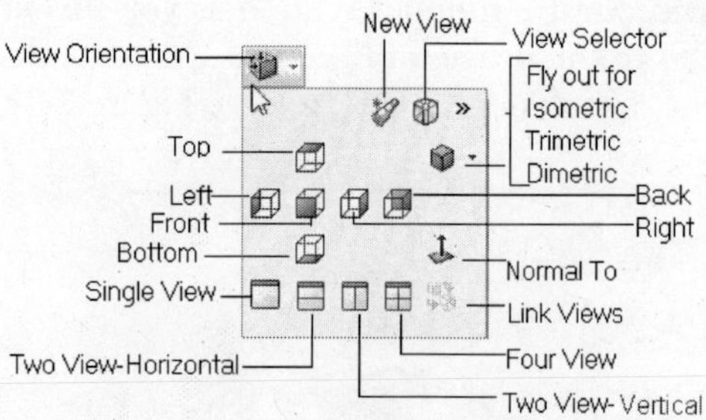

*Figure 5-32 The **View Orientation** flyout*

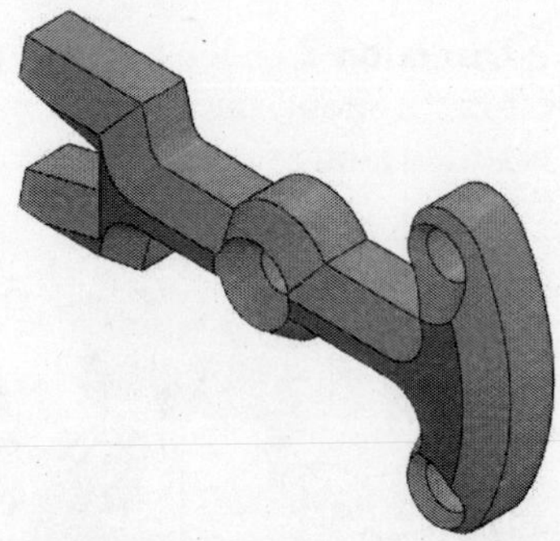

Figure 5-33 Resulting extruded feature

The tools available in the **View Orientation** flyout are used to change the view orientation as per the predefined standard views. This flyout also provides the tools to display a model in two or four viewports.

Displaying the Shadow

As mentioned in the tutorial description, you need to display the shadow of the model, if it is not displayed by default. You can turn on the display of the shadow using the **View (Heads-Up)** toolbar.

1. Choose **View Settings** from the **View (Heads-Up)** toolbar; the **View Setting** flyout is displayed, refer to Figure 5-34. Next, choose the **Shadows In Shaded Mode** button from this flyout to display the model with shadow, as shown in Figure 5-35.

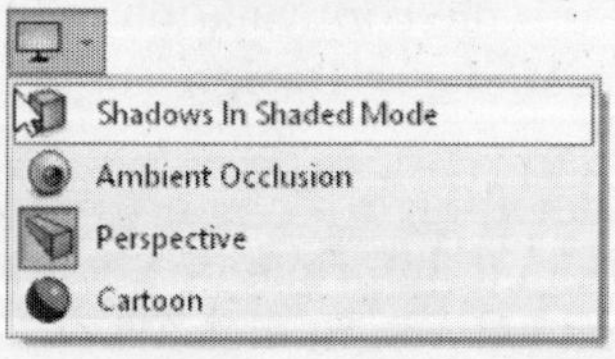

*Figure 5-34 The **View Settings** flyout*

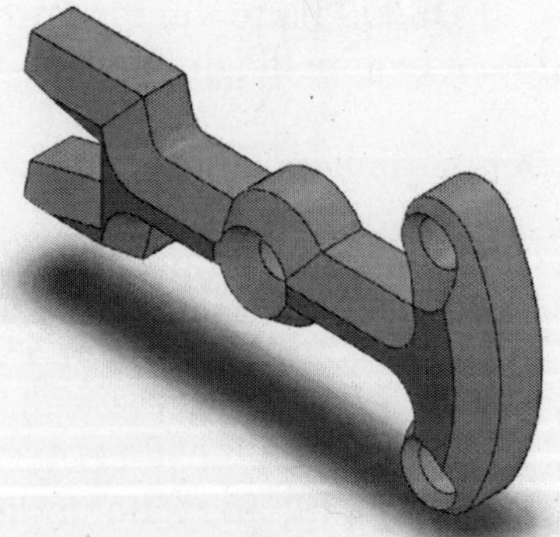

Figure 5-35 Model with the display of shadow turned on

Assigning Materials to the Model

As mentioned in the tutorial description, you need to apply Alloy Steel (SS) material to the model. When you apply material to a model, the physical properties such as Density, Young's modulus, and so on of the selected material are assigned to the model. As a result, when you calculate the mass properties of the model, they will be based on the physical properties of the material applied.

1. Choose **Edit > Appearance > Material** from the SOLIDWORKS menu; the **Material** dialog box is displayed. Alternatively, right-click on the **Material <not specified>** option in the **FeatureManager Design Tree** and choose **Edit Material** from the shortcut menu to invoke the **Material** dialog box.

The **Material** dialog box displays the list of all materials available in the material library of SOLIDWORKS. A number of material families are available in the left area of the **Material** dialog box. When you click on the ‣ sign located on the left of a material family, it displays a list of all materials under that family.

2. Select **Alloy Steel (SS)** from the list of materials available in the **Steel** family; all the properties of the Alloy Steel (SS) material are displayed on the right side of the dialog box.

3. Choose the **Apply** button from the **Material** dialog box and then choose the **Close** button to exit. The model after assigning the material is shown in Figure 5-36.

Figure 5-36 *Model after assigning the Alloy Steel (SS) material*

Determining the Mass Properties of the Model

After assigning the material to the model, you need to calculate the mass properties of the model.

1. Choose the **Mass Properties** tool from the **Evaluate CommandManager**; the **Mass Properties** dialog box with the mass properties of the current model is displayed, as shown in Figure 5-37.

The **Mass Properties** tool is used to determine the mass properties of the part or assembly that is available in the current session. Note that this tool will not be enabled, if there is no solid model available in the current session. The mass properties include density, mass, volume, surface area, center of mass, principal axes of inertia, principal moments of inertia, and moments of inertia.

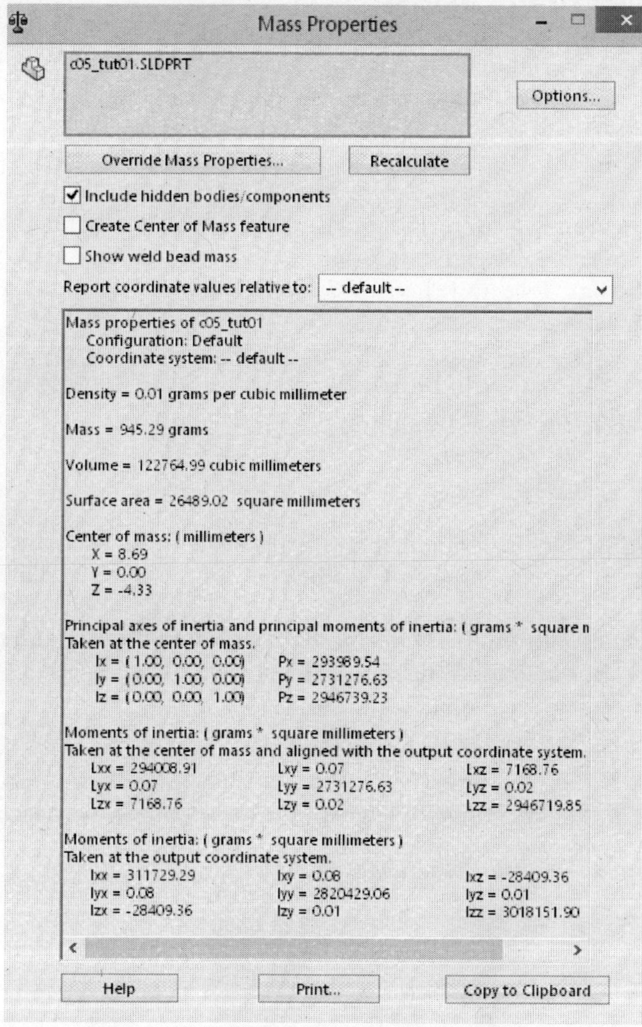

***Figure 5-37** The **Mass Properties** dialog box*

Saving the Model

1. Choose the **Save** button from the Menu Bar to invoke the **Save As** dialog box. Next, browse to *\Documents\SOLIDWORKS Tutorials* and create a new folder with the name *c05*.

2. Enter **c05_tut01** as the name of the model in the **File name** edit box of the **Save As** dialog box and then choose the **Save** button. The model is saved at the location *\Documents\SOLIDWORKS Tutorials\c05*.

3. Choose **File > Close** from the SOLIDWORKS menus to close the document.

Tutorial 2

In this tutorial, you will open the sketch drawn in Tutorial 2 of Chapter 2. Then you will apply the required relations and dimensions to the sketch to make it fully defined. You will also determine the section properties of the sketch and convert it into a revolve feature by revolving the sketch through an angle of 270 degrees, as shown in Figure 5-38. **(Expected time: 45 min)**

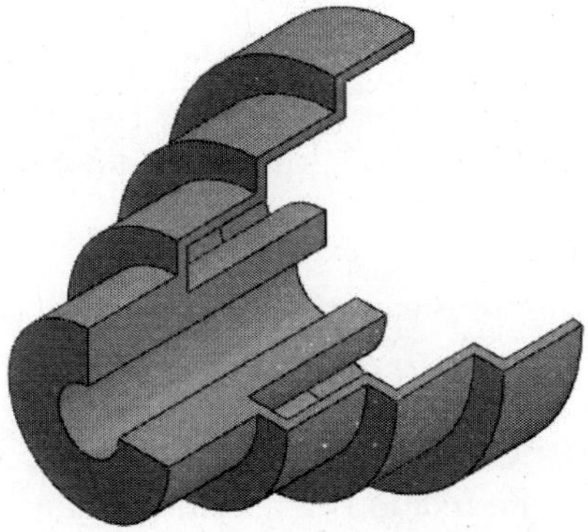

Figure 5-38 *Model for Tutorial 2*

The following steps are required to complete this tutorial:

a. Open Tutorial 2 of Chapter 2, refer to Figure 5-41.
b. Save this document in the *c05* folder with a new name.
c. Apply required relations and dimensions to the sketch, refer to Figures 5-40 through 5-42.
d. Determine the section properties of the sketch, refer to Figure 5-43.
e. Invoke the **Revolved Boss/Base** tool and revolve the sketch through an angle of 270 degrees, refer to Figure 5-44.
f. Change the current view to isometric view and then save the document.
g. Save the model.

Opening Tutorial 2 of Chapter 2

As the required document is saved in the *c02* folder, first you need to open it in SOLIDWORKS 2018.

1. Choose the **Open** button from the SOLIDWORKS menus; the **Open** dialog box is displayed.

The **Open** button is used to open an existing SOLIDWORKS part, assembly, or drawing document. You can also import files from other applications saved with standard file formats by using this button.

2. Browse to the *SOLIDWORKS Tutorials* folder and then double-click on the *c02* folder.

3. Select the **c02_tut02.sldprt** document and then choose the **Open** button from the dialog box to open the selected part in the current session of SOLIDWORKS.

As the sketch was saved in the sketching environment in Chapter 2, it can be opened in the sketching environment.

Saving the Document in c05 Folder

In this section you need to save the document and ensure that the original document of the other chapter is not affected if modifications are made in the current document.

1. Choose the **File > Save As** from the SOLIDWORKS menus; the **Save As** dialog box is displayed.

2. Browse to *\SOLIDWORKS Tutorials\c05* folder and then enter **c05_tut02** as the new name of the document in the **File name** edit box and then choose the **Save** button to save the document.

   The document is saved with the new name and is now displayed in the drawing area, as shown in Figure 5-39.

Applying Relations and Dimensions

As mentioned earlier, some of the relations are automatically applied to the sketch while drawing.

1. Apply the horizontal relation to the horizontal lines and vertical relation to the vertical lines of the sketch, if they are not applied automatically while drawing the sketch. You can apply relations by using the **Add Relations PropertyManager** or the pop-up toolbar that will be displayed after selecting the entity.

2. Apply the equal relation to those entities of the sketch that are of same length, refer to Figure 5-40.

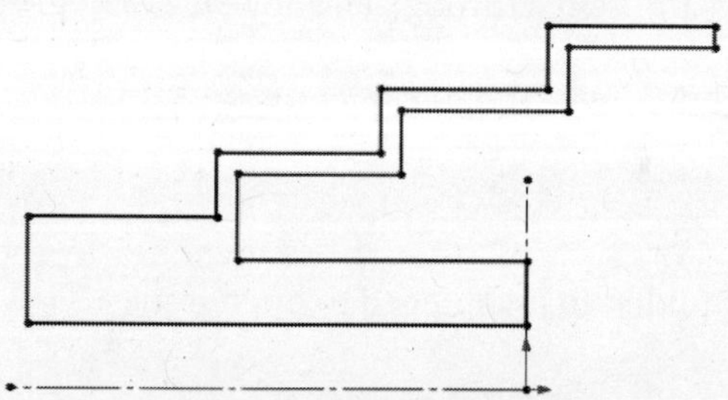

Figure 5-39 *Sketch displayed in the drawing area*

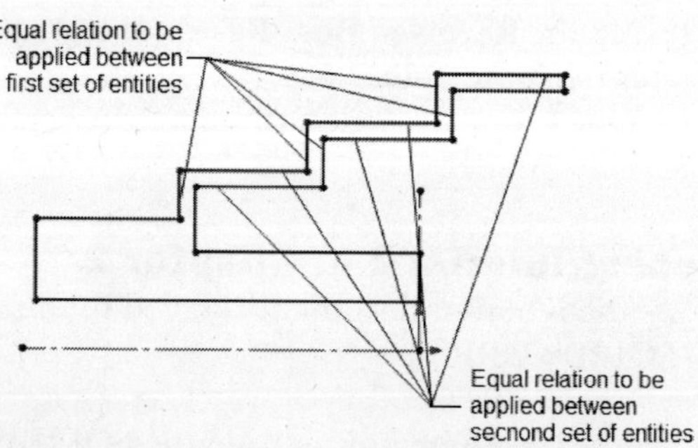

Figure 5-40 *Equal relations to be applied*

3. Invoke the **Smart Dimension** tool from the **Sketch CommandManager** and apply the linear diameter dimensions to the sketch, as shown in Figure 5-41.

   Next, you will apply the horizontal ordinate dimensions to the sketch by using the **Horizontal Ordinate Dimension** tool. You can also use the **Smart Dimension** tool for applying remaining dimensions to the sketch to make it fully defined.

4. Choose the **Horizontal Ordinate Dimension** button from the **Smart Dimension** flyout in the **Sketch CommandManager**.

The **Horizontal Ordinate Dimension** tool is used to dimension the horizontal distance of the selected entities from the specified datum.

Note

When you apply an ordinate dimension, the ***Modify*** *dialog box will not be displayed to modify the dimension value. In this case, to modify dimensions, first you need to place all the ordinate dimensions, exit the tool, and then double-click on the dimensions and modify the values.*

5. Select the upper right vertical line of the sketch as the datum entity from where the remaining entities are to be measured; the dimension value 0 is attached with the cursor.

6. Move the cursor vertically upward to a small distance and place the dimension by clicking the left mouse button, refer to Figure 5-42.

7. Select the other vertical entities of the sketch to apply the ordinate dimensions, refer to Figure 5-42. The fully defined sketch after applying the required relations and dimensions is shown in Figure 5-42.

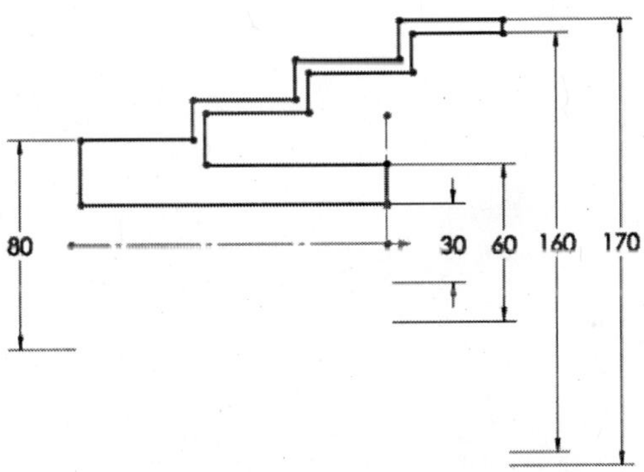

Figure 5-41 Sketch after applying the linear diameter dimensions

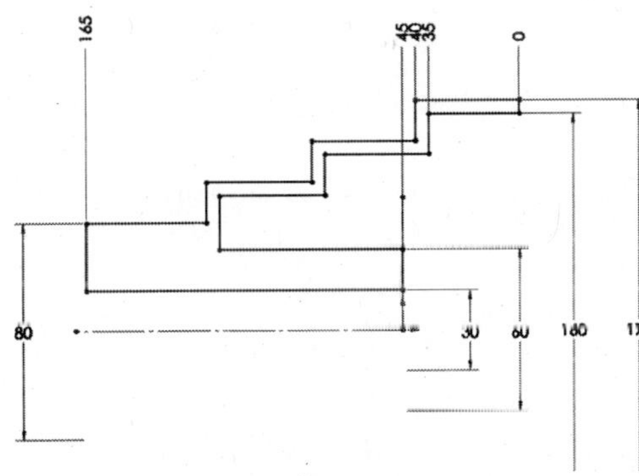

Figure 5-42 Sketch after applying the horizontal ordinate dimensions

Determining the Section Properties of the Sketch

As mentioned in the tutorial description, you need to determine the section properties of the sketch.

1. Choose the **Evaluate** tab available in the **CommandManager** to invoke the **Evaluate CommandManager**.

2. Choose the **Section Properties** button from the **Evaluate CommandManager**; the **Section Properties** dialog box is displayed, as shown in Figure 5-43. Also, a 3D triad is placed at the centroid of the sketch.

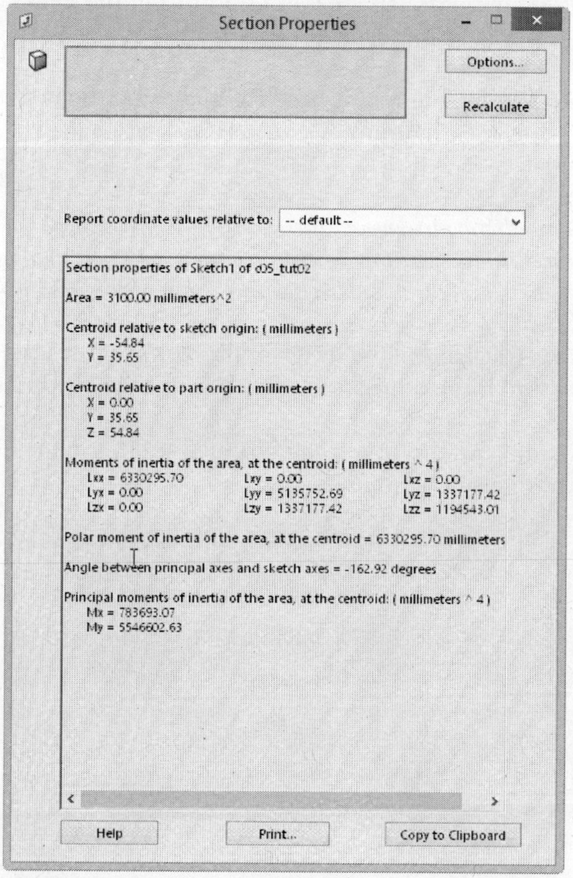

***Figure 5-43** The **Section Properties** dialog box*

The **Section Properties** dialog box displays the section properties of the sketch such as the area, centroid relative to sketch origin, centroid relative to the part origin, moment of inertia, polar moment of inertia, angle between principle axes and sketch axes, and principle moment of inertia.

The **Section Properties** tool enables you to determine the section properties of the sketch in the sketching environment. You can also determine the section properties of the selected planar face in the **Part** mode or in the **Assembly** mode by using this tool.

Note

*The section properties of closed sketches with non-intersecting closed loops can only be determined by using the **Section Properties** tool.*

Revolving the Sketch

Now, you need to convert the sketch into a revolve feature by revolving it through an angle of 270 degrees around the horizontal centerline.

1. Choose the **Features** tab from the **CommandManager** to display the **Features CommandManager**.

2. Choose the **Revolved Boss/Base** button from the **Features CommandManager**; the sketch is automatically oriented in the trimetric view and the **Revolve PropertyManager** is displayed. As the sketch has two centerlines, SOLIDWORKS cannot determine which one of them has to be used as an axis of revolution. As a result, you are prompted to select the axis of revolution.

3. Select the horizontal centerline, which had been used to create linear diameter dimensions, as the axis of revolution; the preview of a complete revolved feature in temporary shaded graphics is displayed in the drawing area. If the preview of the model is not displayed properly in the current view, you need to fit the view of the model into the drawing area.

4. Choose the **Zoom to Fit** button from the **View (Heads-Up)** toolbar or press the **F** key on the keyboard to fit the preview of the model into the drawing area.

5. In the **Direction 1** rollout, select the **Blind** option in the **Revolve Type** drop-down list, if it is not selected by default. Set the value of the **Direction 1 Angle** spinner to **270** and then press the ENTER key; the preview of the revolved model is modified accordingly.

Note

In SOLIDWORKS, you can specify the start and end conditions for a revolve feature similar to that of an extrude feature.

Note that if the horizontal centerline is drawn from left to right, then the direction of revolution has to be reversed to get the required model. You can reverse the direction of revolution by choosing the **Reverse Direction** button that is available at the left side of the **Revolve Type** drop-down list in the PropertyManager.

6. Choose the **OK** button from the **Revolve PropertyManager**; the revolved feature is created.

Tip

In SOLIDWORKS, the right-hand thumb rule is followed for determining the direction of revolution. This rule states that if the thumb of the right hand points in the direction of the axis of revolution, the direction of the curled fingers will determine the default direction of revolution.

7. Choose the **View Orientation** button from the **View (Heads-Up)** toolbar; a flyout is displayed. Choose the **Isometric** option from the flyout to orient the model to isometric view. The isometric view of the final revolved model is shown in Figure 5-44.

Figure 5-44 *Final model for Tutorial 2*

Saving the Model

As the name of the document was specified at the beginning, now you need to choose the **Save** button to save the document.

1. Choose the **Save** button from the Menu Bar to save the model. If the **SOLIDWORKS** warning message box is displayed, choose **Yes** from it to rebuild the model before saving. The model is saved at the location *\Documents\SOLIDWORKS Tutorials\c05*
2. Choose **File > Close** from the SOLIDWORKS menu to close the document.

Tutorial 3

In this tutorial, you will create the model shown in Figure 5-45. The sketch of the model is shown in Figure 5-46. First you will draw the outer loop of the sketch of the model and make it fully defined by applying the required relations and dimensions in the sketching environment. Next, you will convert the outer loop of the sketch into a thin extruded model by adding thickness of 3 mm in the inward direction. The depth of extrusion is 20 mm. After creating the model, add a color of your choice to it. **(Expected time: 45 min)**

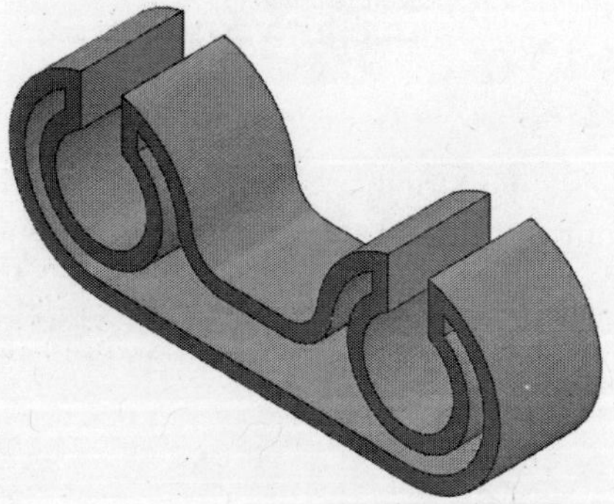

Figure 5-45 *Solid Model for Tutorial 3*

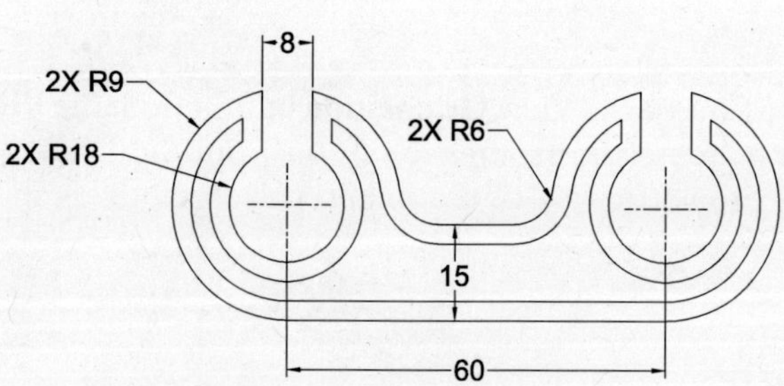

Figure 5-46 *Sketch of the model*

The following steps are required to complete this tutorial:

a. Create the sketch of the model. Apply the required relations and dimensions to make the sketch fully defined, refer to Figure 5-47.
b. Invoke the **Extruded Boss/Base** tool and convert the sketch into a thin extrude feature, refer to Figure 5-48.
c. Apply color to the model, refer to Figure 5-50.
d. Save the model.

Drawing the Sketch

As mentioned in the tutorial description, you will first draw the outer loop of the sketch and then convert it into a thin extrude feature.

1. Start SOLIDWORKS and then invoke a new Part document. Next, choose the **Sketch** button from the **Sketch CommandManager** and then select the **Front Plane** as the sketching plane to invoke the sketching environment.

2. Draw the outer loop of the sketch by using the sketching tools and apply the required relations and dimensions to it, refer to Figure 5-47.

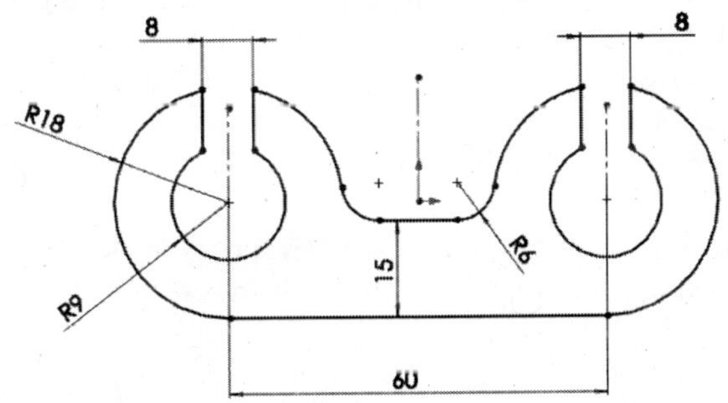

Figure 5-47 *Sketch of the outer loop*

Creating Thin Extrude Feature

Now, you will convert the sketch into a thin extruded feature by adding thickness of 3 mm in the inward direction and depth of 20 mm.

1. Choose the **Features** tab from the **CommandManager** to display the **Features CommandManager**.

2. Choose the **Extruded Boss/Base** button from the **Features CommandManager**; the sketch is automatically oriented in the trimetric view and the **Boss-Extrude PropertyManager** is displayed. Also, the preview of the extrude feature is displayed in the drawing area with the default values.

3. Select the **Mid Plane** option from the **End Condition** drop-down list; the preview of the extrude feature is modified and the material is added to both sides of the sketching plane.

The **Mid Plane** option is used to create a feature by extruding the sketch equally in both the directions of the plane on which the sketch is drawn. If the total depth of the extruded feature is 30 mm, it will be extruded 15 mm toward the front and 15 mm toward the back of the sketching plane.

4. Set the value of the **Depth** spinner to 20 mm.

   As it is evident from Figure 5-45 that the model is a thin extrude feature, therefore you need to invoke the **Thin Feature** rollout of the PropertyManager to add the thickness in the inward direction of the sketch.

5. Select the check box available on the title bar of the **Thin Feature** rollout; the **Thin Feature** rollout is invoked and the preview of the extrude feature is changed to thin extrude feature using the default values.

The thin extruded features can be created using a closed or an open sketch. If the sketch is a closed sketch, the thickness will be specified inside or outside the sketch to create a cavity inside the feature. However, if the sketch is an open sketch, the thickness will be specified below or above the sketch. Also, if the sketch to be extruded is an open sketch, the **Thin Feature** rollout will be invoked automatically on invoking the **Extrude PropertyManager**.

6. Make sure that the **One-Direction** option is selected in the **Type** drop-down list of the **Thin Feature** rollout.

The options provided in the **Type** drop-down list are used to specify the method used for defining the thickness of the thin feature. The **One-Direction** option of this drop-down list is used to add the thickness to one side of the sketch. The **Mid-Plane** option is used to add the thickness equally on both sides of the sketch and the **Two-Direction** option is used to create a thin feature by adding different thicknesses on both sides of a sketch.

7. Set the value of thickness in the **Thickness** spinner to 3; the preview of the feature is modified and the thickness of 3 mm is added in the outward direction.

   Now, you need to reverse the direction of thickness toward the inward direction.

8. Choose the **Reverse Direction** button available on the left of the **Type** drop-down list to reverse the direction of thickness.

9. Choose the **OK** button from the **Boss-Extrude PropertyManager**; the thin extruded feature is created, refer to Figure 5-48. Next, change the orientation of the model to an isometric view by choosing the **Isometric** button from the **View Orientation** flyout. The isometric view of the model after adding thickness and extrusion depth is shown in Figure 5-48.

Figure 5-48 Model after adding thickness and extrusion depth

Adding Color to the Model

As mentioned in the tutorial description that after completing the model, you need to add the color of your choice to it.

1. Choose **Edit > Appearance > Appearance** from the SOLIDWORKS menus; the **color PropertyManager** is displayed on the left side of the drawing area, as shown in Figure 5-49. Ensure that the **Select Part** button is chosen and the name of the part is displayed in the **Selected Entities** area of the **Selected Geometry** rollout of the PropertyManager.

   Note that as soon as the **color PropertyManager** is invoked, the **Appearance, Scenes, and Decals** task pane is also displayed on the right-side of the drawing area.

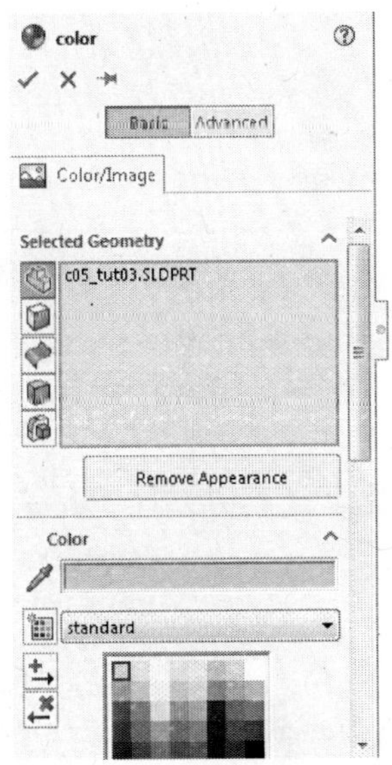

Figure 5-49 The ***color PropertyManager***

In the **color PropertyManager**, the **Selected Geometry** rollout has five buttons on its left, namely **Select Part, Select Faces, Select Surfaces, Select Bodies**, and **Select Features**. These buttons are used as filters for making a selection to assign the color to a model. For example, if you want to assign a color to the face of the model, clear all existing selections from the **Selected Entities** area and then choose the **Select Faces** button from the **Selected Geometry** rollout. As a result, you will be able to select only the faces of the model.

2. Select a color from the **Color** rollout of the PropertyManager; the selected color is displayed in the **Color** display area of the **Color** rollout. You can also set the required color using the **Pick a Color** display area.

Alternatively, you can use the **Red Component of Color, Green Component of Color**, and **Blue Component of Color** spinners to set the color. The color selected in this rollout will be applied to the selected part, features, faces, or bodies.

3. Choose the **OK** button from the PropertyManager; the selected color is applied to the model. Figure 5-50 shows the final model.

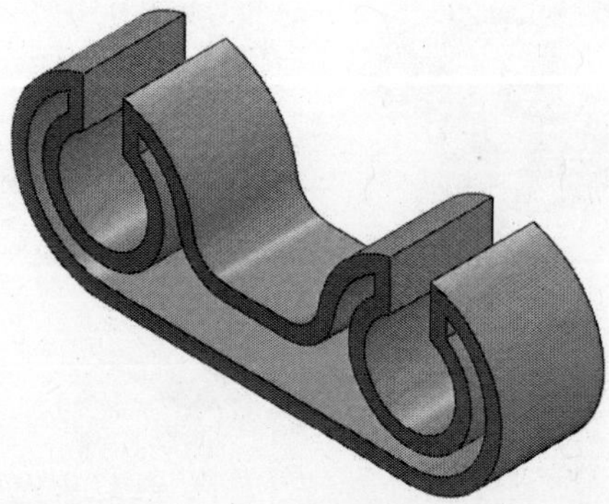

Figure 5-50 *The final model for Tutorial 3*

Saving the Model

Now, you need to save the model in the *c05* folder.

1. Save the model in the *c05* folder with the name *c05_tut03*. The model is saved at the location *\Documents\SOLIDWORKS Tutorials\c05*

2. Choose **File > Close** from the SOLIDWORKS menus to close the document.

Self-Evaluation Test

Answer the following questions and then compare them to those given at the end of this chapter:

1. Which of the following tools is used to apply the horizontal ordinate dimensions?

   (a) **Smart Dimension** (b) **Horizontal Ordinate Dimension**
   (c) **Horizontal Dimension** (d) **Hor Ordinate Dimension**

2. The __________ tool enables you to determine the mass properties of the part or assembly that is available in the current session.

3. The __________ button of the **Boss-Extrude PropertyManager** is used to taper the feature.

4. The __________ check box is used to create a feature with different values in both directions of the sketching plane.

5. The thin extruded feature can be created using a __________ or an __________ sketch.

6. The __________ tool is used to reverse the direction of material.

7. In SOLIDWORKS, a sketch is revolved using the **Boss-Extrude PropertyManager**. (T/F)

8. You can also specify the depth of extrusion dynamically in the preview of the extruded feature. (T/F)

9. In SOLIDWORKS, the right-hand thumb rule is followed for determining the direction of revolution. (T/F)

10. You can invoke the drawing display tools such as **Zoom to Fit** even if the preview of a model is displayed on the screen. (T/F)

Review Questions

Answer the following questions:

1. Which of the following tools is used to determine the section properties of the sketch?

   (a) **Properties** (b) **Sec Properties**
   (c) **Section Properties** (d) None

2. In which of the following features, you can convert an open sketch into solid?

   (a) Thin feature (b) Solid feature
   (c) Both (d) None of these

3. Which of the following tools is used to make a sketch fully defined in SOLIDWORKS?

   (a) **Fully Define Sketch** (b) **Smart Dimension**
   (c) Both (d) None of these

4. When you invoke the **Extruded Boss/Base** tool or the **Revolved Boss/Base** tool, the view is automatically changed to a __________.

5. The thin extruded features are created by invoking the __________ rollout of the PropertyManager.

6. The **Section Properties** tool is available in the __________ **CommandManager**.

7. The __________ option is used to define the termination of a feature on a virtual surface created at an offset distance from the selected surface.

8. In SOLIDWORKS, you can change the appearance of a model by assigning color to it. (T/F)

9. In SOLIDWORKS, you can display the drawing area in multiple viewports. (T/F)

10. If you clear the **Draft outward** check box of the **Boss-Extrude PropertyManager**, the feature will be tapered outward. (T/F)

EXERCISES

Exercise 1

Create the model shown in Figure 5-51. The dimensions of the model are shown in Figure 5-52. The extrusion depth of the model is 35 mm. **(Expected time: 30 min)**

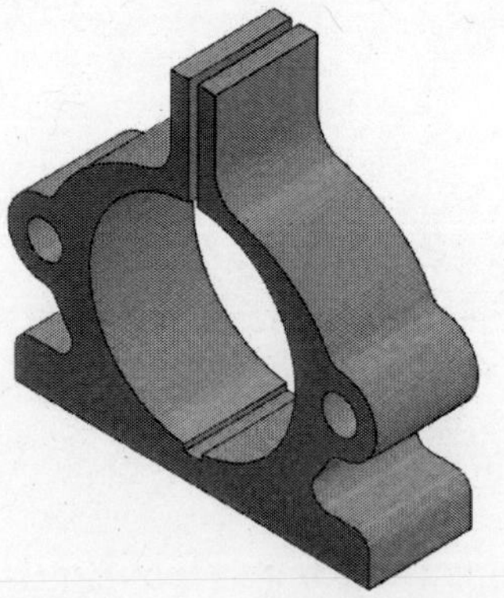

Figure 5-51 Model for Exercise 1

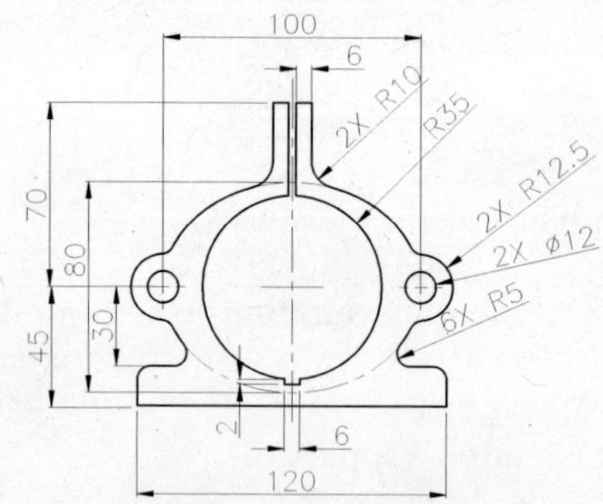

Figure 5-52 *Dimensions of the model for Exercise 1*

Exercise 2

Create the model shown in Figure 5-53. The dimensions of the model are shown in Figure 5-54. The angle of revolution about the axis is 180 degrees. Wall thickness is 1 mm.

(Expected time: 25 min)

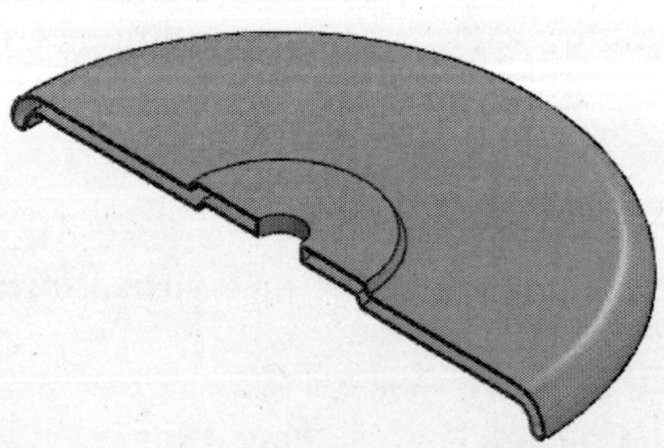

Figure 5-53 *Model for Exercise 2*

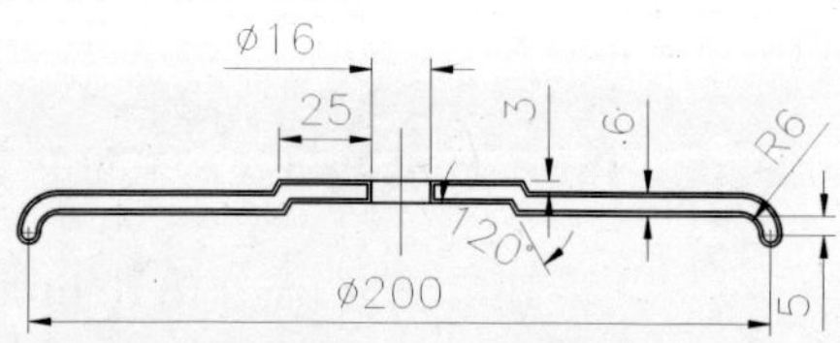

Figure 5-54 *Dimensions of the model for Exercise 2*

Exercise 3

Create the model shown in Figure 5-55. The dimensions of the model are shown in Figure 5-56. After creating the model, apply the copper material to it. Also, determine the mass properties of the model. **(Expected time: 35 min)**

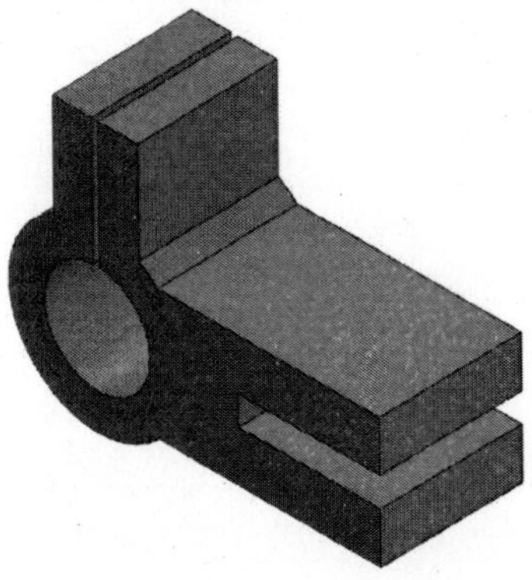

Figure 5-55 Model for Exercise 3

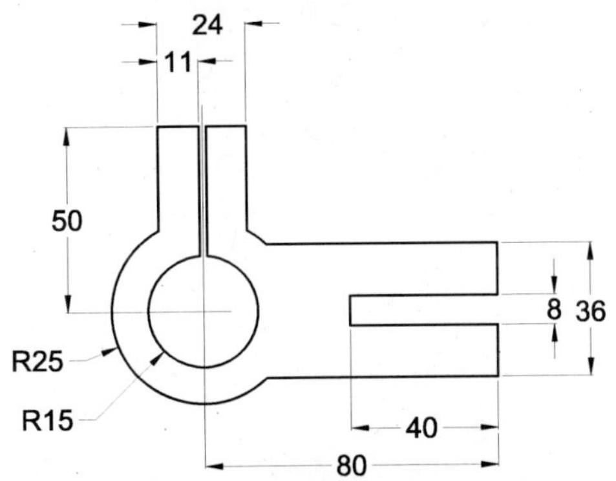

Figure 5-56 *Dimensions of the model for Exercise 3*

Exercise 4

Create the model shown in Figure 5-57. The dimensions of the model are shown in Figure 5-58. **(Expected time: 30 min)**

Figure 5-57 *Model for Exercise 4*

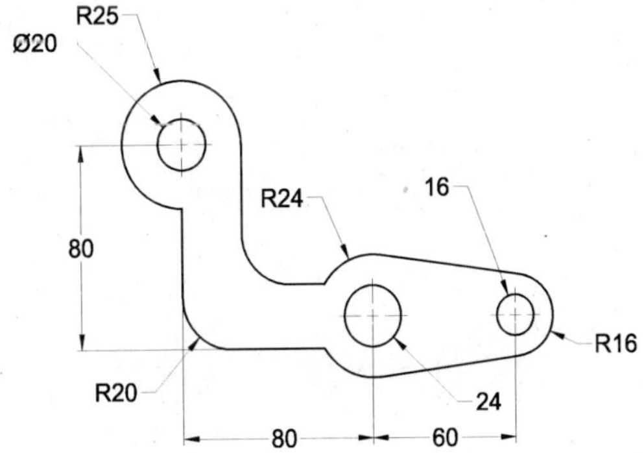

Figure 5-58 *Dimensions of the model for Exercise 4*

Answers to Self-Evaluation Test

1. b, **2. Mass Properties**, **3. Draft On/Off**, **4. Direction 2**, **5.** closed, open, **6. Reverse Direction**, **7.** F, **8.** T, **9.** T, **10.** T

Chapter 6

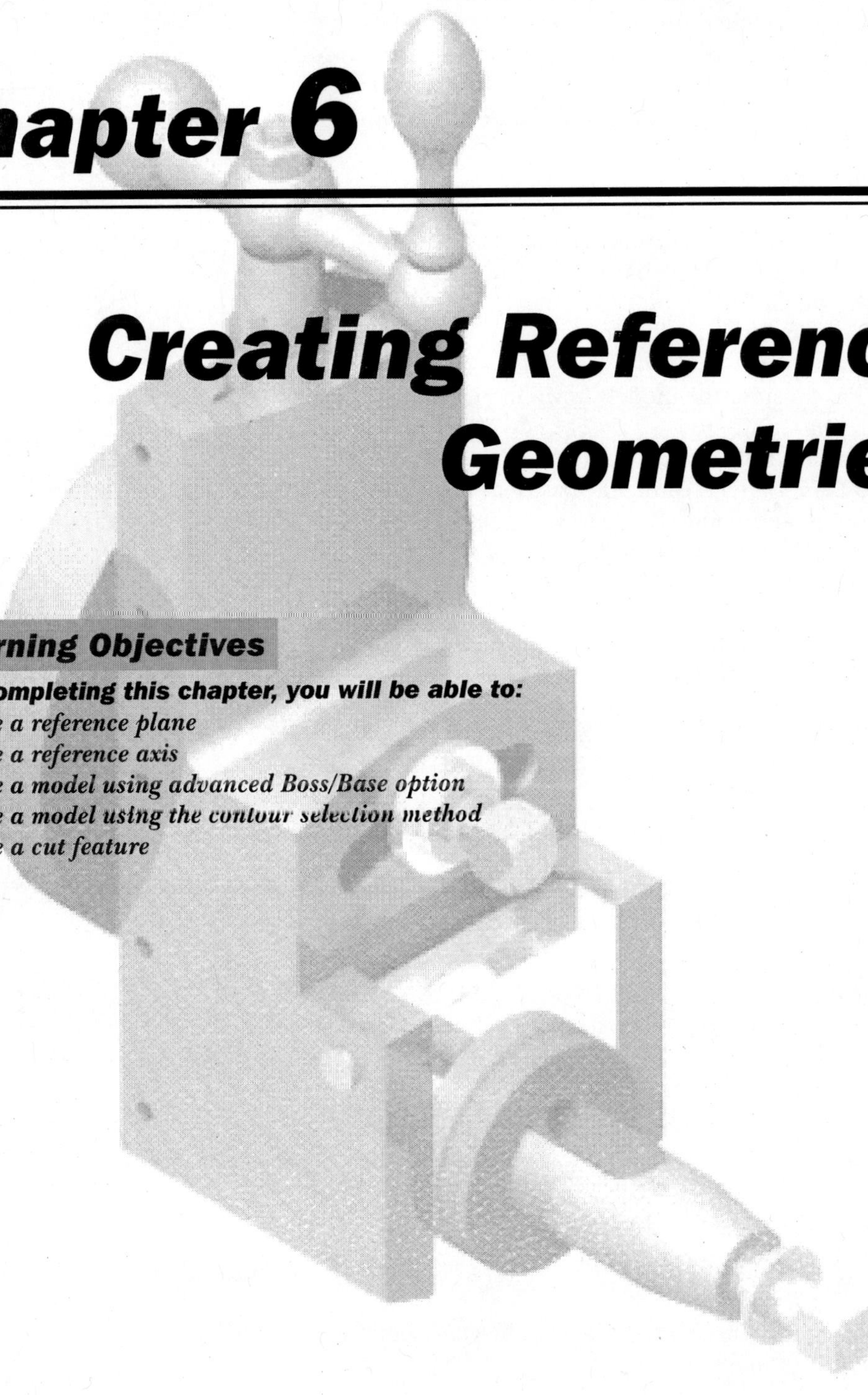

Creating Reference Geometries

Learning Objectives

After completing this chapter, you will be able to:

- *Create a reference plane*
- *Create a reference axis*
- *Create a model using advanced Boss/Base option*
- *Create a model using the contour selection method*
- *Create a cut feature*

IMPORTANCE OF SKETCHING PLANES

In the earlier chapters, you created basic models by extruding or revolving the sketches. All those models were created on a single sketching plane, the **Front Plane**. But most mechanical designs consist of multiple sketched features, referenced geometries, and placed features. These features are integrated together to complete a model. Most of these features lie on different planes. When you start a new SOLIDWORKS document and invoke a sketching plane, you are prompted to select the plane on which you want to draw the sketch. On the basis of design requirements, you can select any plane to create the base feature. To create additional sketched features, you need to select an existing plane or a planar surface, or you need to create a plane that will be used as the sketching plane. For example, consider the model shown in Figure 6-1.

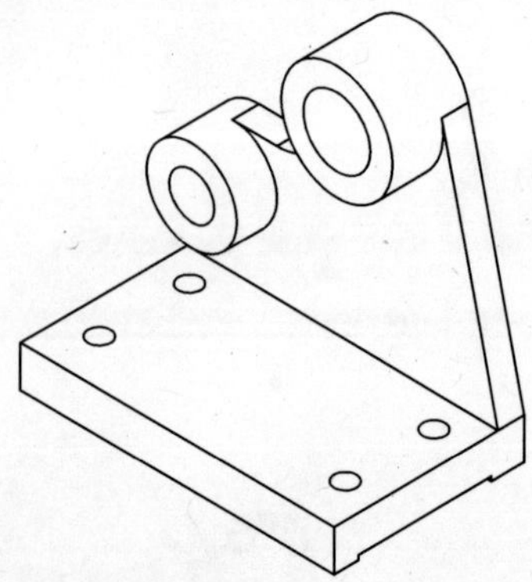

Figure 6-1 *A multifeatured model*

The base feature of this model is shown in Figure 6-2. The sketch for the base feature is drawn on the **Top Plane**. After creating the base feature, you need to create the other sketched features, placed features, and referenced features, refer to Figure 6-3. The boss features and cut features are the sketched features that require sketching planes where you can draw the sketches of the features.

It is evident from Figure 6-3 that the features added to the base feature are not created on the same plane on which the sketch for the base feature is created. Therefore, to draw the sketches of other sketched features, you need to define other sketching planes.

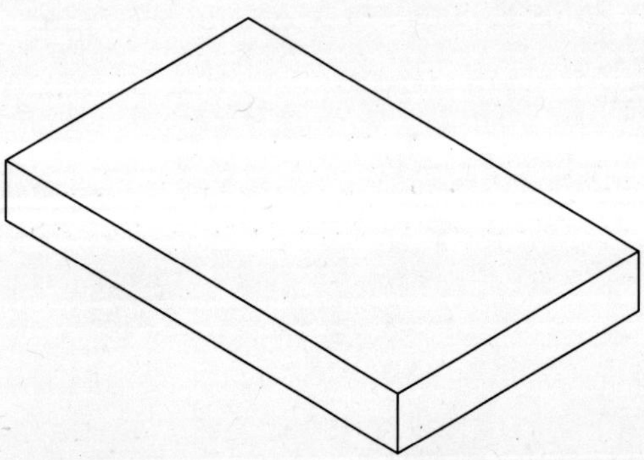

Figure 6-2 *Base feature of the model*

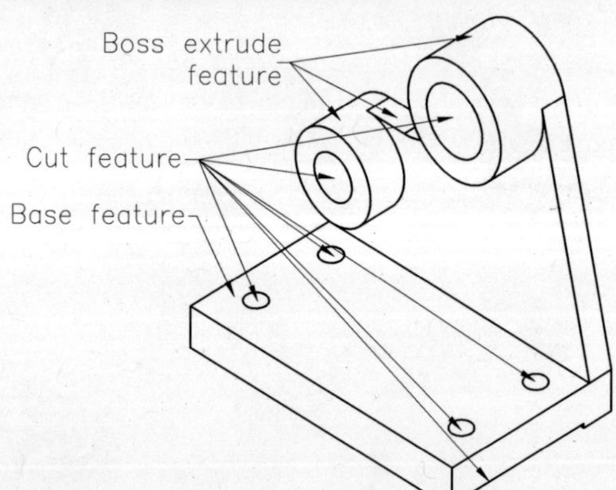

Figure 6-3 *Model after adding other features*

TUTORIALS

Tutorial 1

In this tutorial, you will create the model shown in Figure 6-4. The dimensions of the model are also given in the same figure. **(Expected time: 30 min)**

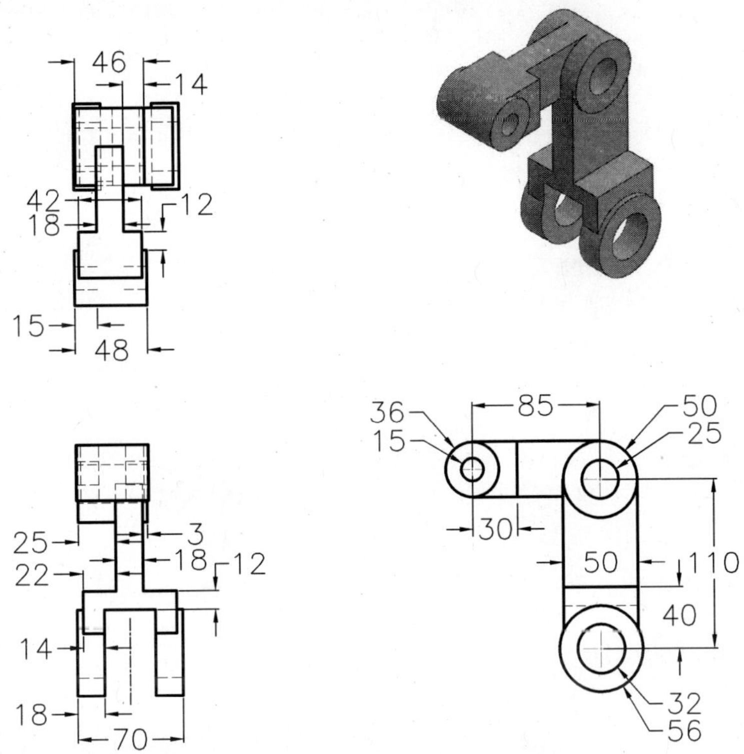

Figure 6-4 *Model and its different views for Tutorial 1*

It is clear from the above figures that the given model is a multi-featured model. It consists of various extrude and cut features. You need to create a separate sketch of each sketched feature for converting them into features.

The following steps are required to complete this tutorial:

a. Create the sketch of the base feature on the **Right Plane** and apply the required relations and dimensions to it, refer to Figure 6-5.
b. Invoke the **Extrude Boss/Base** tool and create the base feature of the model, refer to Figure 6-6.
c. Create the sketch of the second feature on the **Right Plane** and apply the required relations and dimensions to it, refer to Figure 6-7.
d. Invoke the **Extrude Boss/Base** tool and extrude the sketch created for the second feature by using the **Mid Plane** option, refer to Figure 6-8.
e. Create the third and fourth features of the model by using the Contour Selection method, refer to Figures 6-9 through 6-13.
f. Create the fifth feature, which is a extruded cut feature, refer to Figures 6-14 and 6-15.

g. Create a reference plane at an offset distance from the **Front Plane** for creating the sketch of the sixth feature, refer to Figure 6-18.
h. Create the sixth feature of the model, which is also an extruded feature, refer to Figures 6-19 and 6-20.
i. Create a reference plane for creating the sketch of seventh and eighth features, refer to Figure 6-21.
j. Create the seventh and eighth features of the model by using the Contour Selection method, refer to Figures 6-22 through 6-26.
k. Save the document and then close it.

Creating the Base Feature

Now, you will create the base feature of the model, which is an extrude feature.

1. Start a new SOLIDWORKS part document using the **New SOLIDWORKS Document** dialog box.

2. Invoke the sketching environment by selecting the **Right Plane** as the sketching plane and then draw the sketch by using the **Circle** tool. Next, apply the required dimensions to it, as shown in Figure 6-5.

3. Choose the **Extruded Boss/Base** tool from the **Features CommandManager**; the sketch is automatically oriented to the trimetric view and the **Boss-Extrude PropertyManager** is displayed. Also, the preview of the extrude feature, created using the default values, is displayed in the drawing area.

   Now, you will extrude the feature equally on both sides of the sketching plane.

4. Right-click in the drawing area; a shortcut menu is displayed. Next, choose the **Mid Plane** option from it; the preview of the feature is modified and material is added equally in both directions of the sketching plane.

   You can also select the **Mid Plane** option from the **End Condition** drop-down list available in the **Direction 1** rollout of the PropertyManager.

5. Set the value of the **Depth** spinner to 70 mm and then choose the **OK** button from the PropertyManager. The base feature of the model is created.

6. Change the view orientation of the base feature to isometric, if required. Figure 6-6 shows the isometric view of the base feature created.

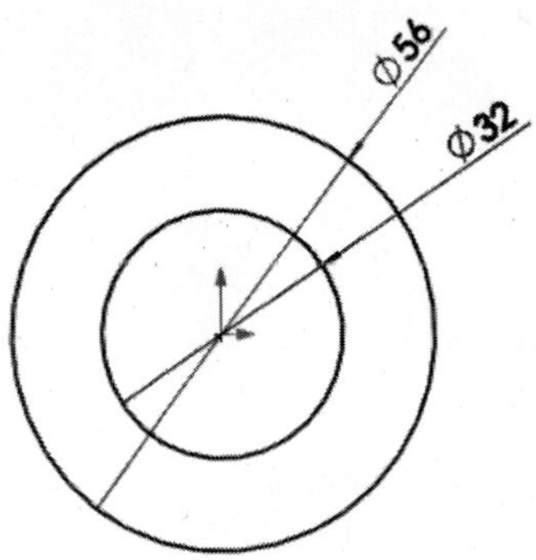

Figure 6-5 Sketch of the base feature

Figure 6-6 The base feature of the model

Creating the Second Feature

Now, you will create the second feature of the model, which is also an extrude feature. To create this feature, you need to first create its sketch on the **Right Pane** and then extrude it by using the **Mid Plane** option.

1. Invoke the sketching environment by selecting the **Right Plane** as the sketching plane. Once the sketching environment is invoked, change the orientation normal to the sketching plane using the **Normal To** tool available in the **View (Heads-Up)** toolbar.

2. Choose the **Convert Entities** tool from the **Sketch CommandManager**; the **Convert Entities PropertyManager** is displayed. Also, you are prompted to select the faces, edges or entities to convert.

3. Select the outer cylindrical edge of the feature with diameter 56; the selected edge is highlighted in blue color.

4. Choose the **OK** button from the PropertyManager; the selected entity is converted into a sketch and displayed in black color.

5. Next, draw the remaining sketch entities of the feature and trim the unwanted entities. Figure 6-7 shows the final sketch. Make sure the sketch is fully defined.

6. Invoke the **Extruded Boss/Base** tool and extrude the sketch upto a depth of 62 mm by using the **Mid Plane** option. Make sure that the **Merge result** check box is selected in the **Boss-Extrude PropertyManager**. Figure 6-8 shows the model after creating the second feature.

As the **Merge result** check box is selected by default in the **Boss-Extrude PropertyManager**, the newly created extrude feature will merge with the parent feature. If you clear this check box, the extrude feature will not merge with the existing feature. As a result, another solid body will be created.

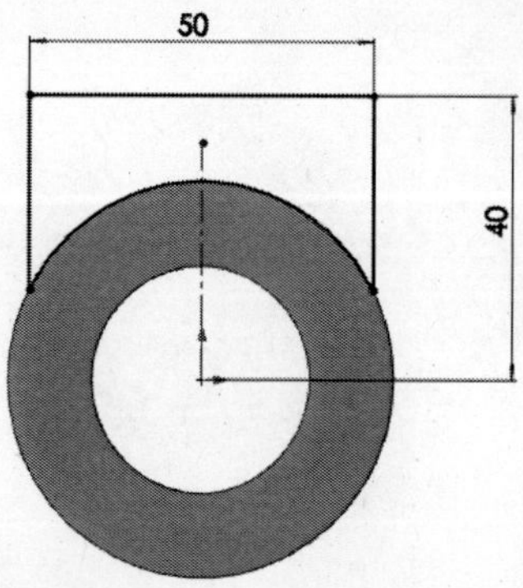

Figure 6-7 Sketch of the second feature

Figure 6-8 Model after creating the second feature

Creating the Third and Fourth Features

Now, you will create the third and fourth features of the model. In conventional method, you need to create separate sketches for both these features and then convert them one by one into features. In this tutorial, you will create a sketch and then convert it into features by selecting different contours of it.

1. Invoke the sketching environment by selecting the **Right Plane** as the sketching plane and then draw the sketch, as shown in Figure 6-9. Do not exit the sketching environment.

   Next, you need to use the contour selection method to create the third and fourth features.

2. Choose the **Extruded Boss/Base** tool from the **Features CommandManager**; the **Boss-Extrude PropertyManager** is displayed on the left side of the drawing area. Since the sketch consists of multiple close contours, the **Selected Contours** rollout of the **Boss-Extrude PropertyManager** is invoked automatically and you are prompted to select a close or open contour. Also, the select cursor is replaced by the contour selection cursor.

3. Move the contour selection cursor toward the bottom close contour of the sketch and then select it when it is highlighted, refer to Figure 6-10; the preview of the feature is displayed in the drawing area. Also, the name of the selected contour is displayed in the selection box of the **Selected Contours** rollout of the PropertyManager.

4. Select the **Mid Plane** option from the **End Condition** drop-down list of the **Direction 1** rollout of the PropertyManager.

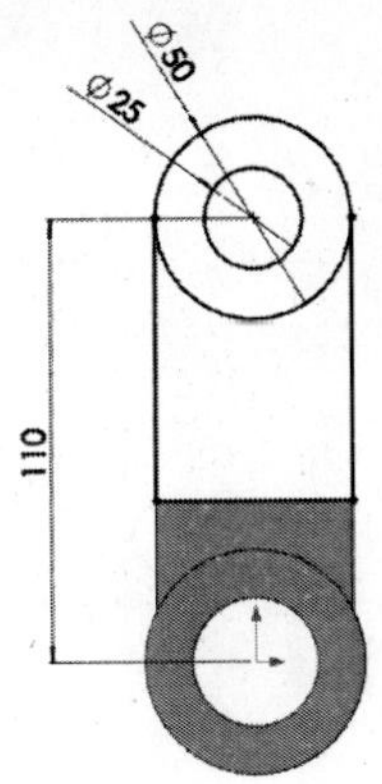

Figure 6-9 Sketch with multiple contours

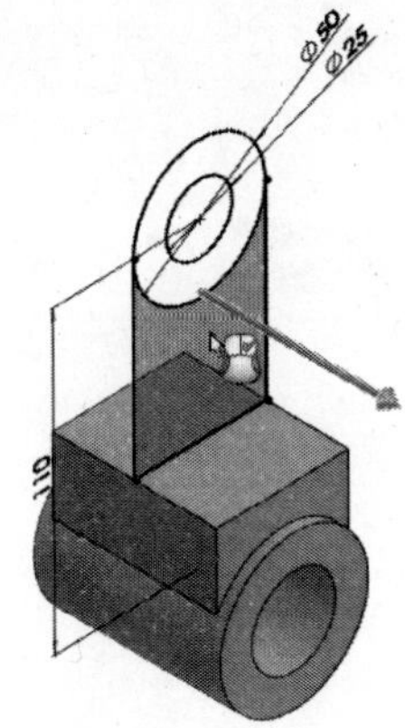

Figure 6-10 The bottom contour of the sketch to be selected

5. Set the value of the **Depth** spinner to 18 mm and then choose the **OK** button from the PropertyManager; the selected contour is extruded. Next, click anywhere in the drawing area to exit from the selection, if any. Figure 6-11 shows the model after creating the third feature.

   Now, you will create the fourth feature of the model by using the same sketch used for creating the third extrude feature.

6. Click on the ▸ sign available on the left of the **Boss-Extrude3** (third extruded feature) node from the **FeatureManager Design Tree**; the node expands and the sketch of the third feature is displayed.

   As mentioned earlier, when you add features to the model using various modeling tools, the same features are also displayed in the **FeatureManager Design Tree**.

7. Select the sketch of the third feature from the **FeatureManager Design Tree**.

8. Choose the **Extruded Boss/Base** button from the **Features CommandManager**; the **Boss-Extrude PropertyManager** is displayed and the **Selection Contours** selection area of the **Selection Contours** rollout is activated in it.

9. Move the cursor toward the closed contour of the sketch formed by two circles and then select it by clicking the left mouse button when it is highlighted, refer to Figure 6-12; the preview of the feature is displayed in the drawing area. Also, the name of the selected contour is displayed in the selection box of the **Selected Contours** rollout of the PropertyManager.

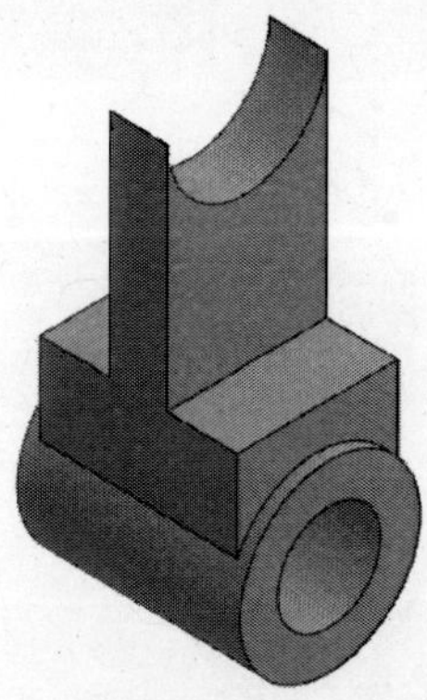

Figure 6-11 Model after creating the third extrude feature by using the contour selection method

Figure 6-12 Contour of the sketch to be selected

10. Make sure that the **Blind** option is selected in the **End Condition** drop-down list in the **Direction 1** rollout.

11. Set the value of the **Depth** spinner to **12** in the **Direction 1** rollout of the PropertyManager.

12. Expand the **Direction 2** rollout of the PropertyManager by selecting the check box available in its title bar.

The **Direction 2** rollout of the PropertyManager is used to extrude a sketch with different values in the second direction of the sketching plane. The options in this rollout are similar to those in the **Direction 1** rollout.

13. Make sure that the **Blind** option is selected in the **End Condition** drop-down list in the **Direction 2** rollout.

14. Set the value of the **Depth** spinner to **34** in the **Direction 2** rollout. Next, choose the **OK** button from the PropertyManager; the extrude feature is created, as shown in Figure 6-13.

Figure 6-13 Model after creating the fourth extrude feature

Creating the Fifth Feature

The fifth feature of the model is a cut feature. Now, you will create a cut feature by using the **Extruded Cut** tool.

1. Choose the **Extruded Cut** tool from the **Features CommandManager**; the **Extrude PropertyManager** is displayed on the left side of the drawing area and you are prompted to select a sketching plane.

The **Extruded Cut** tool is used to remove the material from the model by extruding a sketch. In SOLIDWORKS, you can define a cut feature by extruding a sketch, revolving a sketch, sweeping a section along a path, lofting sections, or by using a surface.

2. Click on the ▸ sign located on the left of the **FeatureManager Design Tree**, which is now displayed in the drawing area. The tree view expands and it displays three default planes and the list of features created in this model.

3. Select the **Front Plane** from the **FeatureManager Design Tree** as the sketching plane; the sketching environment is invoked.

   Now, you will change the current orientation of the model and make it normal to the view.

4. Choose the **View Orientation** button from the **View (Head-up)** toolbar; the **View Orientation** flyout is displayed.

5. Choose the **Normal To** button from the **View Orientation** flyout; the current orientation of the model is changed normal to the view.

The **Normal To** tool is used to reorient the view normal to a selected face or plane.

6. Draw the sketch of the cut feature by using the sketching tools and then apply required relations and dimensions to it, refer to Figure 6-14.

7. Exit the sketcher environment by clicking on **Exit Sketch** from the **Confirmation Corner** available at the upper right corner of the drawing area. As soon as you exit the sketcher environment, the **Cut-Extrude PropertyManager** is displayed. Also, the preview of the cut feature is displayed in the drawing area.

The options in the **Cut-Extrude PropertyManager** are the same as those discussed for the **Boss-Extrude PropertyManager**. The only difference is that the options of the **Cut-Extrude PropertyManager** are used to remove the material from the model.

8. Select the **Through All-Both** option from the **End Condition** drop-down list in the **Direction 1** rollouts of the PropertyManager.

9. Choose the **OK** button from the PropertyManager. Figure 6-15 shows the isometric view of the model after creating the cut feature.

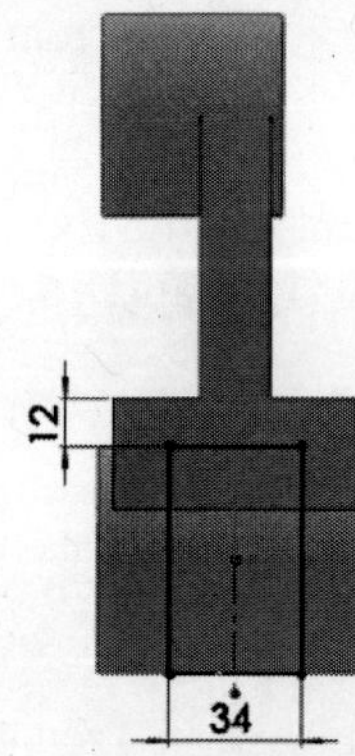

Figure 6-14 Sketch for the cut feature

Figure 6-15 Model after creating the cut feature

Creating the Sixth Feature

The sixth feature of the model is an extrude feature. The sketch of this extrude feature is created by using a reference plane created at an offset distance of 55 mm from the **Front Plane**.

Generally, all engineering components or designs are multi-featured models. As discussed earlier, all features of a model are not created on the same plane on which the base feature is created. Therefore, you need to select one of the default planes or create a new plane that will be used as the sketching plane for the next feature. It is clear from the above discussion that you can use default planes as the sketching plane or you can create reference planes that can be used as the sketching plane.

1. Choose the **Plane** tool from the **Reference Geometry** flyout in the **Features CommandManager**, as shown in Figure 6-16; the **Plane PropertyManager** is displayed, as shown in Figure 6-17.

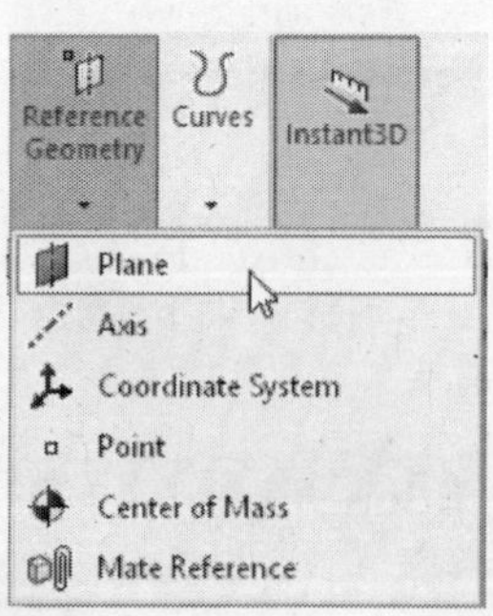

*Figure 6-16 The **Plane** tool in the **Reference Geometry** flyout*

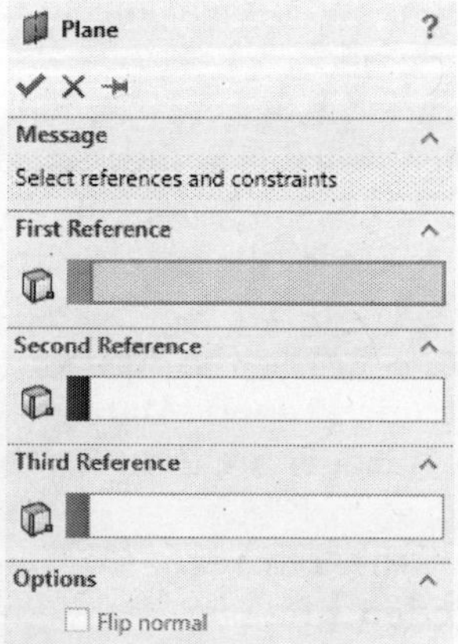

Figure 6-17** The **Plane PropertyManager

The **Plane** tool is used to create reference plane by choosing the respective constraints botton from the PropertyManager. With this tool you can create planes:

- at an offset distance from an existing plane or a planar face
- parallel to an existing plane or a planar face and passing through a point
- at an angle to an existing plane or a planar face
- passing through lines/points
- normal to a curve
- on a non-planar surface
- in the middle of two faces/planes

2. Click on the ▸ sign located on the left of the **FeatureManager Design Tree**, which is now displayed in the graphics area; the tree view expands displaying three default planes and a list of features created in this model.

3. Select the **Front Plane** from the **FeatureManager Design Tree** as the first reference; the preview of the reference plane is displayed in the drawing area. Also, some constraints are displayed in the **First Reference** rollout of the PropertyManager and the **Offset distance** button is chosen by default in it.

   As the **Offset distance** button is chosen by default in the **First Reference** rollout of the PropertyManager; the **Offset distance** spinner, the **Offset Flip** check box, and the **Number of planes to create** spinner are enabled in the PropertyManager.

4. Set the value of the **Distance** spinner to **55** in the **First Reference** rollout of the PropertyManager.

5. Make sure that the value of the **Number of planes to create** spinner is set to 1.

6. Ensure that a message **Fully defined** is displayed in the **Message** rollout of the **Plane PropertyManager**.

7. Choose the **OK** button from the PropertyManager; the reference plane is created at an offset distance of **55** mm from the **Front Plane**, as shown in Figure 6-18.

   Now, you need to invoke the sketching environment by selecting the newly created plane as the sketching plane.

8. Invoke the sketching environment by selecting the newly created plane as the sketching plane.

9. Choose the **Normal To** button from the **View Orientation** flyout of the **View (Heads-Up)** toolbar; the current orientation of the model is changed normal to the view.

10. Draw the sketch of the extrude feature and then apply required relations and dimensions to it, refer to Figure 6-19. Next, exit the sketcher environment.

Figure 6-18 *The plane is created at an offset distance from the* ***Front Plane***

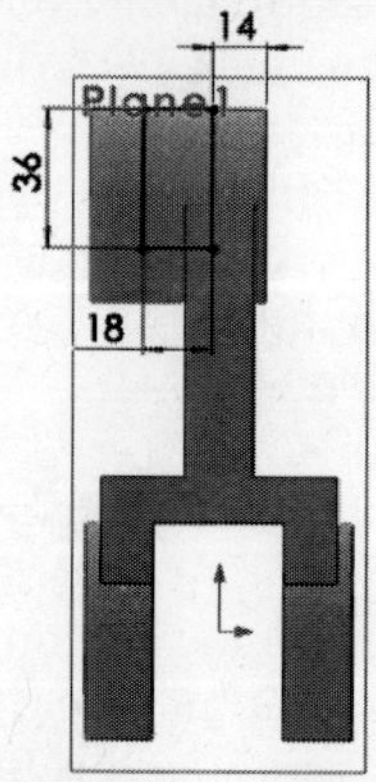

Figure 6-19 *Sketch of the extrude feature*

11. Change the view orientation of the model to isometric by choosing the **Isometric** button from the **View Orientation** flyout.

12. Choose the **Extruded Boss/Base** button from the **Features CommandManager** and then select the sketch from the graphic area; the preview of the extrude feature and the **Boss-Extrude PropertyManager** is displayed.

13. Choose the **Reverse Direction** button available on the left of the **End Condition** drop-down in the **Direction 1** rollout of the PropertyManager.

The **Reverse Direction** button is used to reverse the direction of extrusion.

14. Select the **Up To Next** option from the **End Condition** drop-down in the **Direction 1** rollout of the PropertyManager; the preview of the extrude feature is terminated at the next intersection.

The **Up To Next** option is used to extrude the sketch from the sketching plane to the next surface that intersects the feature.

15. Choose the **OK** button from the PropertyManager; the extrude feature is created.

    Next, you need to hide the reference plane.

16. Select **Plane1** from the **FeatureManager Design Tree** and do not move the cursor; a pop-up toolbar is displayed.

17. Choose the **Hide** button from the pop-up toolbar; the selected reference plane (**Plane1**) is hidden in the graphic area. The model after creating the sixth feature and hiding the reference plane is shown in Figure 6-20.

Figure 6-20 Model after creating the sixth feature

Creating the Seventh and Eighth Features

It is evident from Figure 6-4 that the seventh and eighth features are also extrude features. In conventional method, you first create a separate sketch for each sketched feature and then convert them into features. In this section, you will draw a single sketch and then extrude its close contours one by one by using the contour selection method to create the seventh and eighth features. Also, the sketch used for these features is created by using a reference plane, created at the middle of the planar faces of the fourth feature.

1. Choose the **Plane** button from the **Reference Geometry** flyout in the **Features CommandManager**; the **Plane PropertyManager** is displayed.

2. Select both the planar faces of the fourth feature one by one as the first and second references, respectively, refer to Figure 6-21. Note that as soon as you select the planar faces, the **Mid Plane** button is chosen automatically in the PropertyManager. Also, the preview of the reference plane is displayed in the middle of the selected planar faces, refer to Figure 6-21.

3. Choose the **OK** button from the PropertyManager; the reference plane is created in the middle of the selected planar faces.

   Now, you will create a sketch for the seventh and eight features by selecting the newly created plane as the sketching plane.

4. Invoke the sketching environment by selecting the newly created reference plane as the sketching plane. Next, change the orientation of the model normal to the view by using the **Normal To** button from the **View Orientation** flyout.

5. Draw a sketch with multiple contours and then apply the required relations and dimensions to it, refer to Figure 6-22. Do not exit the sketcher environment.

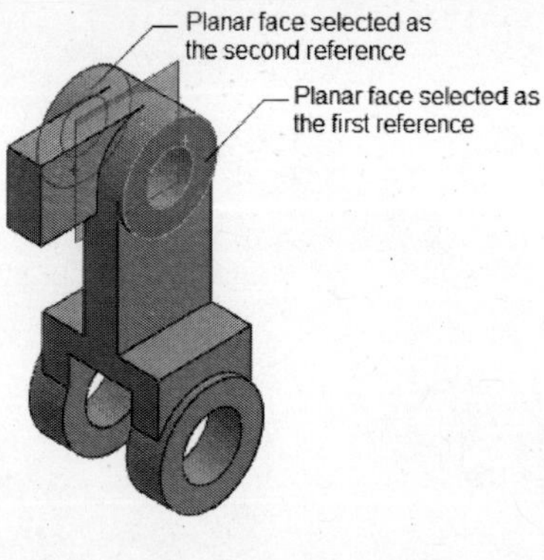

Figure 6-21 The planar faces selected for creating reference plane

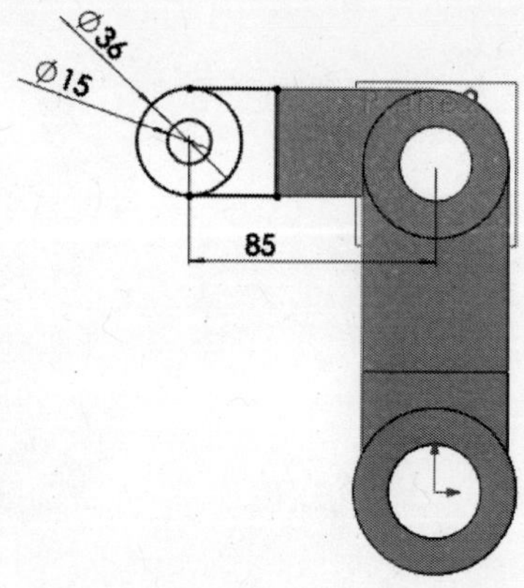

Figure 6-22 Sketch with multiple contours

Next, you need to use the contour selection method to create the seventh and eighth features.

6. Choose the **Extruded Boss/Base** tool from the **Features CommandManager**; the **Boss-Extrude PropertyManager** is displayed on the left of the drawing area. Since the sketch consists of multiple close contours, the **Selected Contours** rollout of the **Boss-Extrude PropertyManager** is invoked automatically and you are prompted to select a close or open contour. Also, the cursor is replaced by the contour selection cursor.

7. Change the current orientation of the model to isometric by choosing the **Isometric** button from the **View Orientation** flyout.

8. Move the contour selection cursor toward the close contour of the sketch and select it when it is highlighted, refer to Figure 6-23; the preview of the feature is displayed in the drawing area. Also, the name of the selected contour is displayed in the selection box of the **Selected Contours** rollout of the PropertyManager.

9. Select the **Mid Plane** option from the **End Condition** drop-down list of the **Direction 1** rollout of the PropertyManager.

10. Set the value of the **Depth** spinner to **42** and then choose the **OK** button from the PropertyManager; the selected contour is extruded. Next, click anywhere in the drawing area to exit selection, if any. Figure 6-24 shows the model after creating the seventh feature.

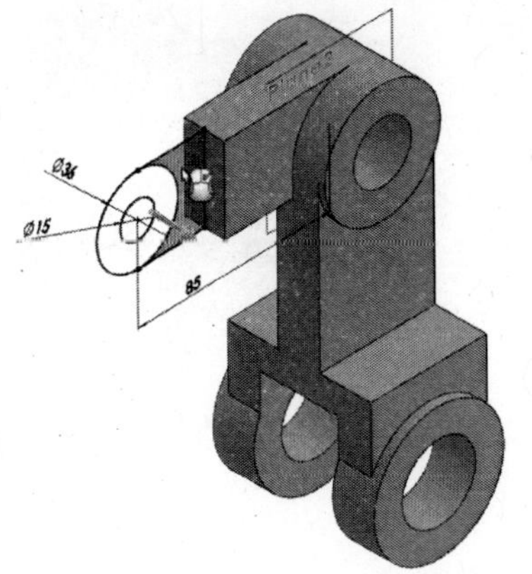

Figure 6-23 Sketch with multiple contours

Figure 6-24 The model after creating the seventh feature

Now, you will create eighth feature of the model by using the same sketch that was used for creating the seventh extrude feature.

11. Click on the ▸ sign available on the left side of the previously created extrude feature (**Boss-Extrude6**) from the **FeatureManager Design Tree**; the node expands and the sketch of the feature is displayed.

12. Select the sketch of the seventh feature from the **FeatureManager Design Tree**.

13. Choose the **Extruded Boss/Base** tool from the **Features CommandManager**; the **Boss-Extrude PropertyManager** is displayed with the **Selection Contours** rollout invoked in it.

14. Move the cursor toward the closed contour of the sketch formed by two circles of diameter 15 and 36, then click and select it when it is highlighted, refer to Figure 6-25. The preview of the feature is displayed in the drawing area. Also, the name of the selected contour is displayed in the selection box of the **Selected Contours** rollout of the PropertyManager.

15. Select the **Mid Plane** option from the **End Condition** drop-down list of the **Direction 1** rollout of the PropertyManager.

16. Set the value of the **Depth** spinner to **48** and then choose the **OK** button from the PropertyManager; the selected contour is extruded. Next, click anywhere in the drawing area to exit the selection, if any.

17. Hide the reference plane in the drawing area. Figure 6-26 shows the final model after all features are created.

Figure 6-25 *Model after creating the third extrude feature by using the contour selection method*

Figure 6-26 *Final model*

Saving the Model

1. Choose the **Save** button from the Menu Bar and save the model with the name *c06_tut01* at the location given below:

   \Documents\SOLIDWORKS Tutorials\c06

2. Choose **File > Close** from the SOLIDWORKS menus to close the document.

Tutorial 2

In this tutorial, you will create the model shown in Figure 6-27. You will use a combination of both the conventional modeling method and the contour selection method to create this model. The dimensions of the model are given in Figure 6-28. **(Expected time: 30 min)**

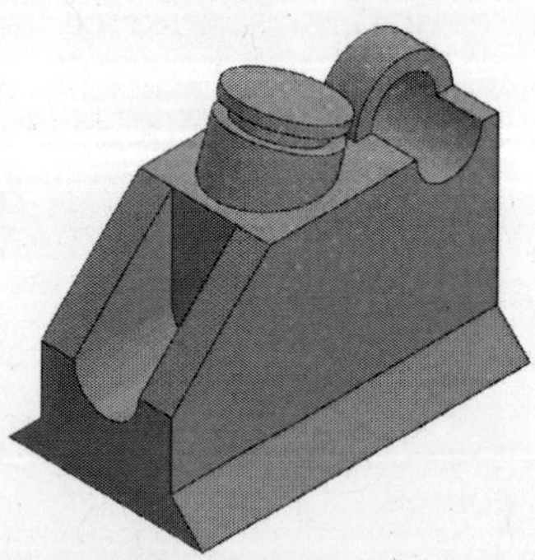

Figure 6-27 *Model for Tutorial 2*

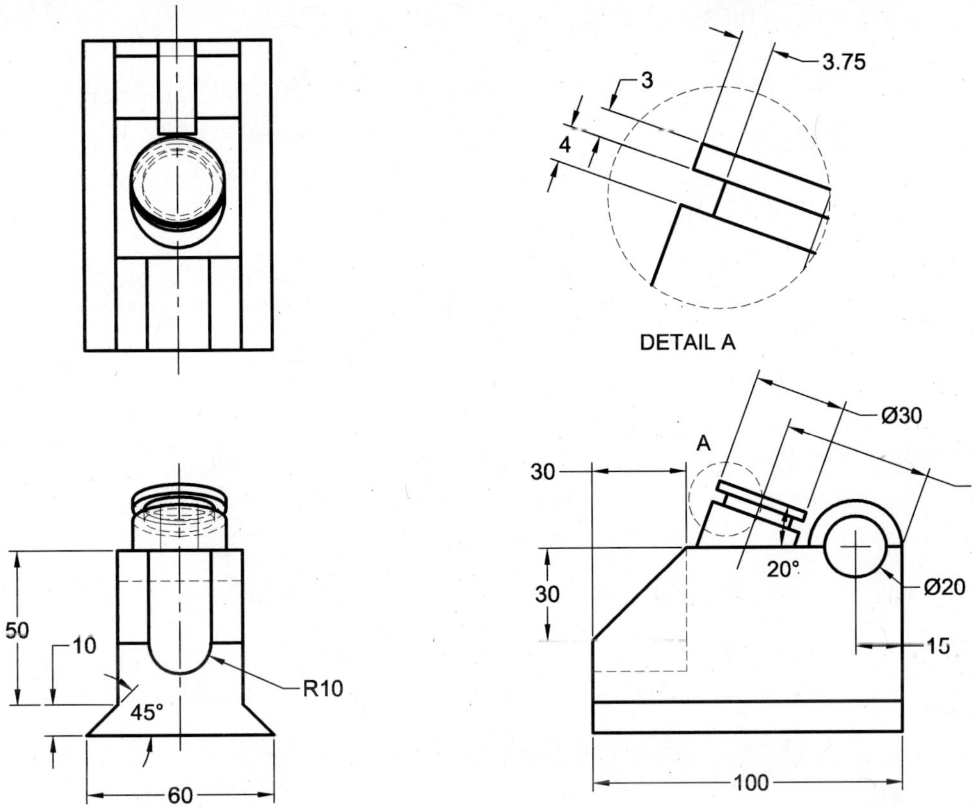

Figure 6-28 *Dimensions for Tutorial 2*

The following steps are required to complete this tutorial:

a. Draw the sketch of the base feature of the model, refer to Figure 6-29.
b. Invoke the **Extruded Boss/Base** tool and create the base feature of the model, refer to Figure 6-30.
c. Create the second feature of the model that is a cut feature, refer to Figures 6-31 and 6-32.
d. Create the third feature of the model that is also a cut feature, refer to Figures 6-33 through 6-35.
e. Create the fourth feature of the model, refer to Figure 6-36.
f. Create the fifth feature of the model, refer to Figures 6-37 and 6-38.
g. Create a reference plane at an angle for creating the sixth feature, refer to Figure 6-39.
h. Create the sixth feature of the model that is an extrude feature, refer to Figures 6-40 and 6-41.
i. Create a reference axis by using the **Axis** tool, refer to Figure 6-42.
j. Create a sketch for the revolve cut feature, refer to Figure 6-43.
k. Invoke the **Revolved Cut** tool and remove the material by revolving the sketch around the reference axis, refer to Figure 6-44.
l. Save and close the document.

Creating the Base Feature

You will create the base feature of the model which is an extrude feature. The sketch of the base feature is created on the **Front Plane**.

1. Start a new SOLIDWORKS part document by using the **New SOLIDWORKS Document** dialog box.

2. Invoke the sketching environment by selecting the **Front Plane** as the sketching plane and then draw the sketch, as shown in Figure 6-29.

3. Choose the **Extruded Boss/Base** tool from the **Features CommandManager**; the sketch is automatically oriented to the trimetric view and the **Boss-Extrude PropertyManager** is displayed. Also, the preview of the extrude feature is displayed in the drawing area.

   Now you will extrude the feature equally on both sides of the sketching plane.

4. Right-click in the drawing area; a shortcut menu is displayed. Next, choose the **Mid Plane** option from it; the preview of the feature is modified and material is added equally in both directions of the sketching plane.

5. Set the value of the **Depth** spinner to **100** mm and then choose the **OK** button from the PropertyManager. The base feature of the model is created.

6. Change the view orientation of the base feature to isometric. Figure 6-30 shows the isometric view of the base feature created.

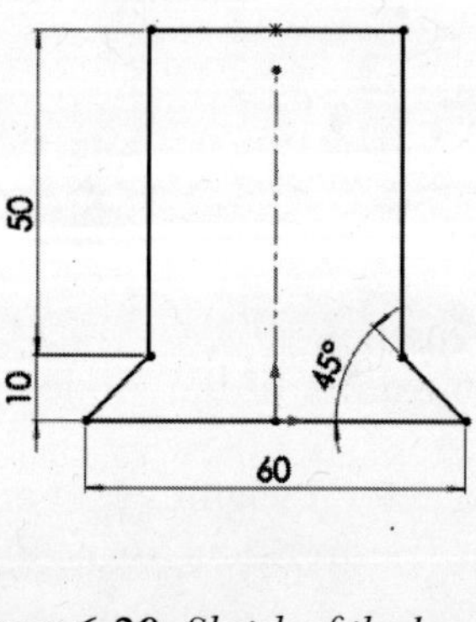

Figure 6-29 *Sketch of the base feature*

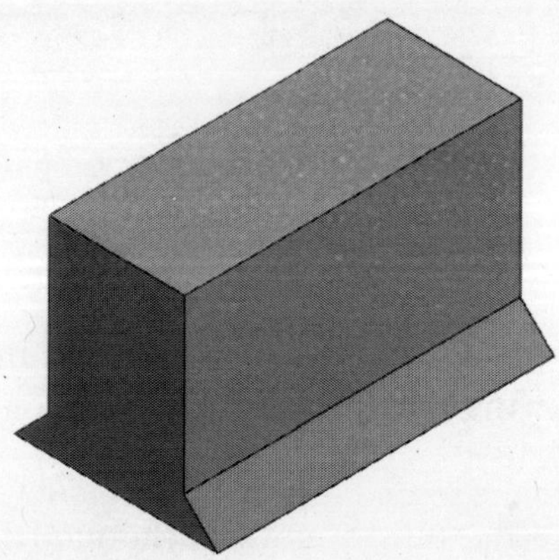

Figure 6-30 *The base feature of the model*

Creating the Second Feature

The second feature of the model is a cut feature, which is created by using the open sketch.

1. Invoke the sketching environment by selecting the right planar face of the base feature as the sketching plane and then draw the sketch of the cut feature, as shown in Figure 6-31.

2. Invoke the **Extruded Cut** tool and then extrude the sketch by using the **Through All** option. Figure 6-32 shows the isometric view of the model after creating the cut feature.

Note

*In this case, you can create a cut feature by extruding an open sketch. This process will work when **Through All - Both** option is selected in the **End Condition** drop-down list of the **Direction1** rollout of the PropertyManager.*

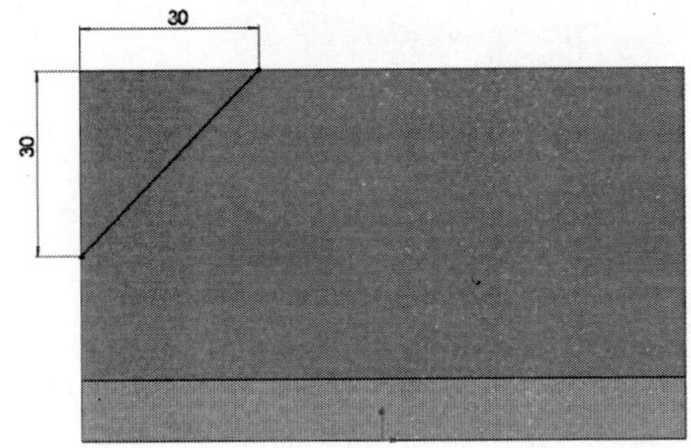

Figure 6-31 *Sketch of the cut feature*

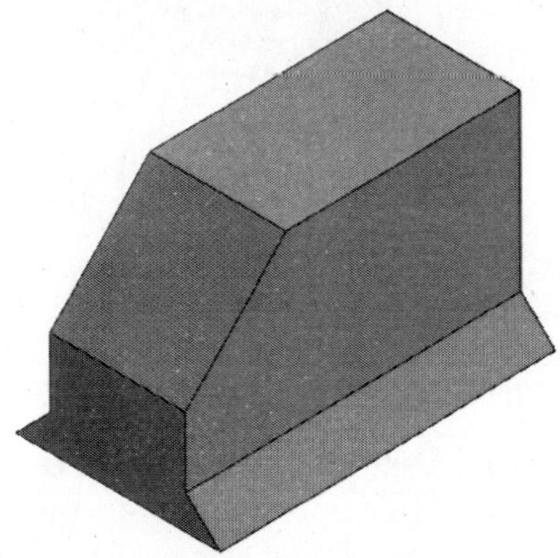

Figure 6-32 *Model after creating the cut feature*

Creating the Third Feature

The third feature of the model is also a cut feature. The sketch of this cut feature is created on the front planar face of the model and extruded by using the **Up To Vertex** option.

1. Invoke the sketching environment by selecting the front planar face of the model as the sketching plane and then draw the sketch, as shown in Figure 6-33. Do not exit the sketching environment.

2. Choose the **Extruded Cut** button from the **Features CommandManager**; the **Cut-Extrude PropertyManager** is displayed on the left of the drawing area. Also, the preview of the model is displayed in the drawing area.

3. Change the current view orientation of the model to isometric.

4. Select the **Up To Vertex** option from the **End Condition** drop-down list in the PropertyManager; the **Vertex** selection area is displayed in the PropertyManager and you are prompted to select a vertex to terminate the extrusion of the cut feature.

The **Up To Vertex** option is used to define the termination of a feature at a virtual plane that is parallel to the sketching plane and passes through the selected vertex. The vertex can be a point on an edge, a sketched point, or a reference point.

5. Select the vertex of the model, as shown in Figure 6-34.

6. Choose the **OK** button from the PropertyManager; the cut feature is created. The isometric view of the model after creating the cut feature is shown in Figure 6-35.

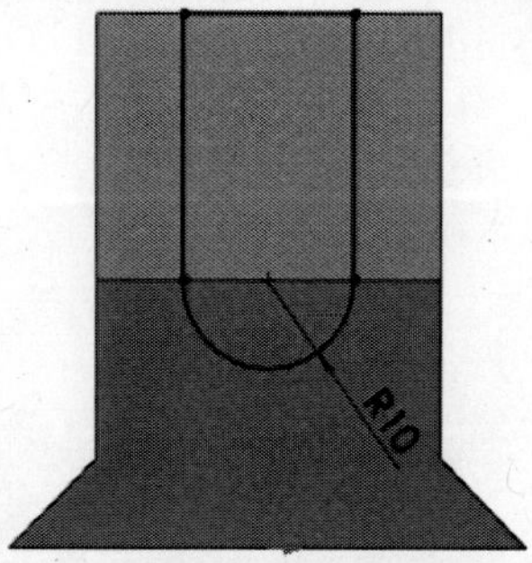

Figure 6-33 Sketch of the cut feature

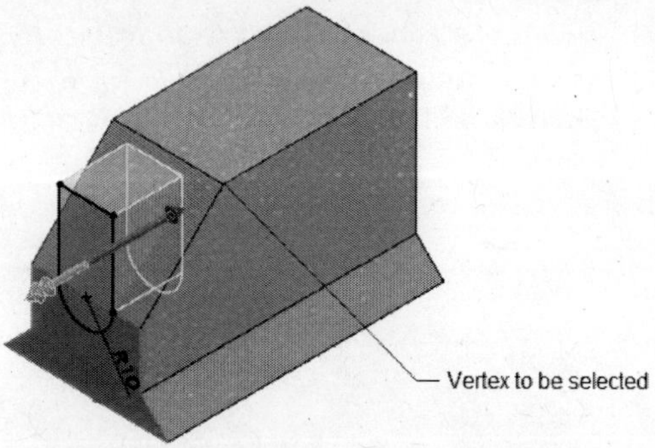

Figure 6-34 Vertex to be selected

Creating the Fourth Feature

The fourth feature of the model is also a cut feature. The sketch of this cut feature is created on the right planar face of the model.

1. Invoke the sketching environment by selecting the right planar face of the model as the sketching plane and draw the sketch of the cut feature. For dimensions of the cut feature, refer to Figure 6-28.

2. Invoke the **Extruded Cut** tool and extrude the sketch by using the **Through All** option as the end condition. The isometric view of the model after creating the fourth feature is shown in Figure 6-36.

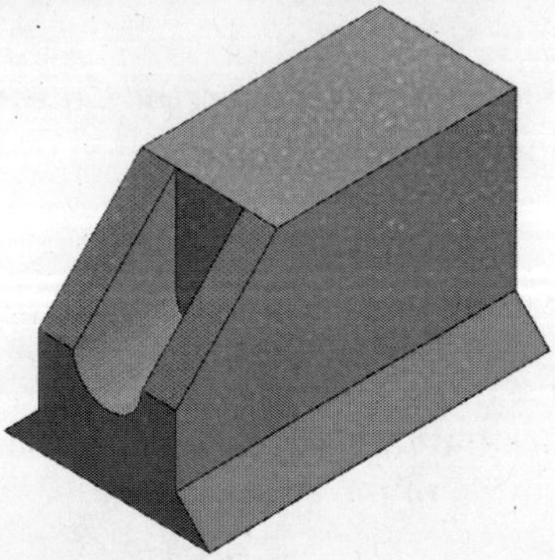

Figure 6-35 Model after creating the third feature

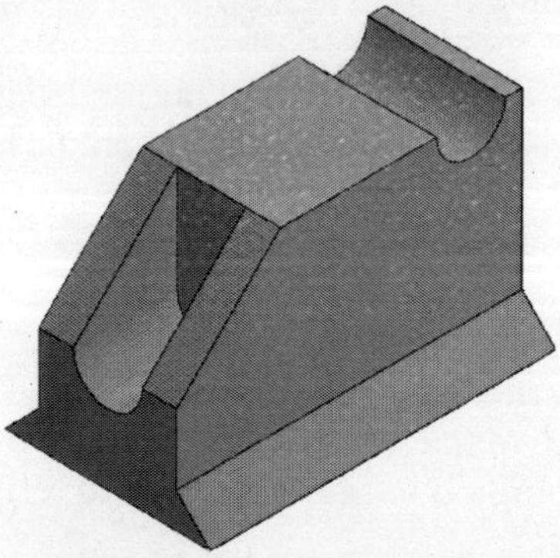

Figure 6-36 Model after creating the fourth feature

Creating the Fifth Feature

The fifth feature of the model is also an extrude feature. The sketch of this extrude feature is created on the **Right Plane**.

1. Invoke the sketching environment by selecting the **Right Plane** as the sketching plane and then draw the sketch of the extrude feature, as shown in Figure 6-37. You may need to change the view normal to the viewing direction by using the **Normal To** tool.

2. Choose the **Extruded Boss/Base** tool from the **Features CommandManager**; the **Boss-Extrude PropertyManager** is displayed. Also, the preview of the extrude feature is displayed in the drawing area.

3. Change the current orientation of the model to isometric.

   Now, you will extrude the feature equally in both sides of the sketching plane.

4. Right-click in the drawing area; a shortcut menu is displayed. Next, choose the **Mid Plane** option from it; the preview of the feature is modified and material is added equally in both directions of the sketching plane.

5. Set the value of the **Depth** spinner to **12** mm and then choose the **OK** button from the PropertyManager; the extrude feature is created, as shown in Figure 6-38.

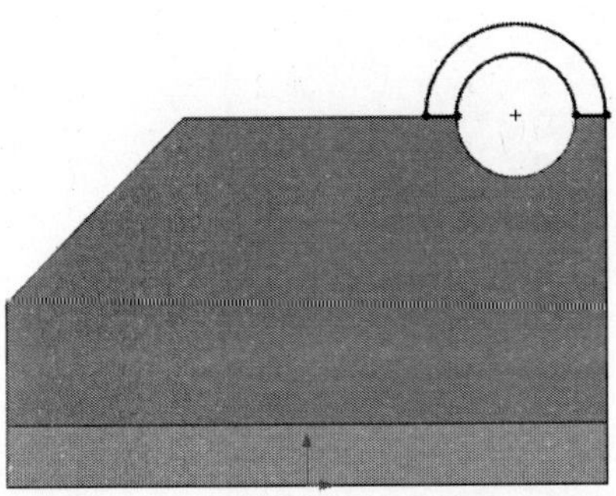

Figure 6-37 Sketch of the extrude feature

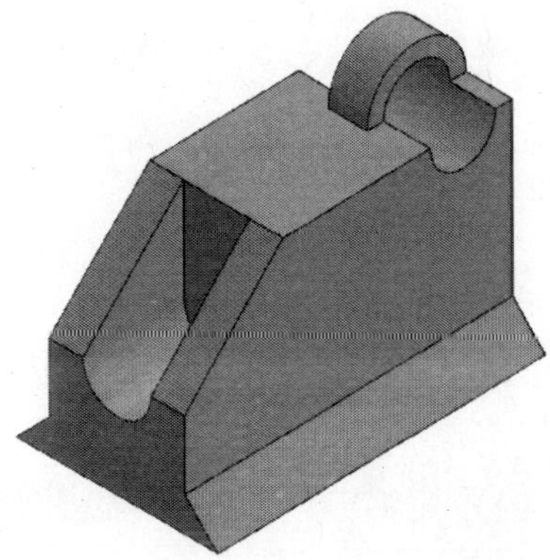

Figure 6-38 Model after creating the fifth feature

Creating the Sixth Feature

The sixth feature of the model is also an extrude feature. The sketch of this extrude feature is created by using a reference plane created at an angle of 20 degrees on the top planar face of the model and passing through the top back horizontal edge of the model.

1. Choose the **Plane** button from the **Reference Geometry** flyout in the **Features CommandManager**; the **Plane PropertyManager** is displayed.

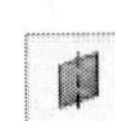

2. Select the top planar face of the model as the first reference; the preview of the reference plane is displayed in the drawing area. Note that by default, the **Offset distance** button is chosen in the **First Reference** rollout. As a result, the preview of the reference plane is displayed at an offset distance.

3. Choose the **At angle** button from the **First Reference** rollout of the PropertyManager; the **Angle** spinner is enabled.

4. Set the value of the **Angle** spinner to 20 degrees in the **First Reference** rollout.

5. Select the top back horizontal edge of the model as the second reference, refer to Figure 6-39.

6. Choose the **OK** button from the PropertyManager; the reference plane is created at an angle of 20 degrees.

   Now, you will create a sketch for the sixth feature by selecting the newly created plane as the sketching plane.

7. Invoke the sketching environment by selecting the newly created reference plane as the sketching plane. Next, change the orientation normal to the view by using the **Normal To** button from the **View Orientation** flyout.

8. Draw the sketch of the feature, refer to Figure 6-40. Next, extrude the sketch upto the next intersecting surface of the model by using the **Up To Next** option. The model after creating the sixth feature is shown in Figure 6-41.

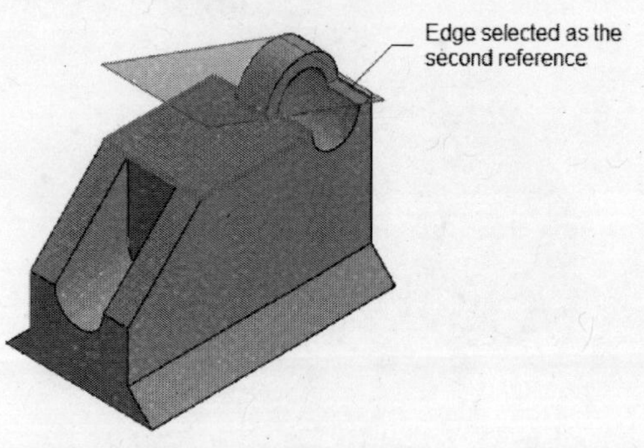

Figure 6-39 *Edge selected as the second reference*

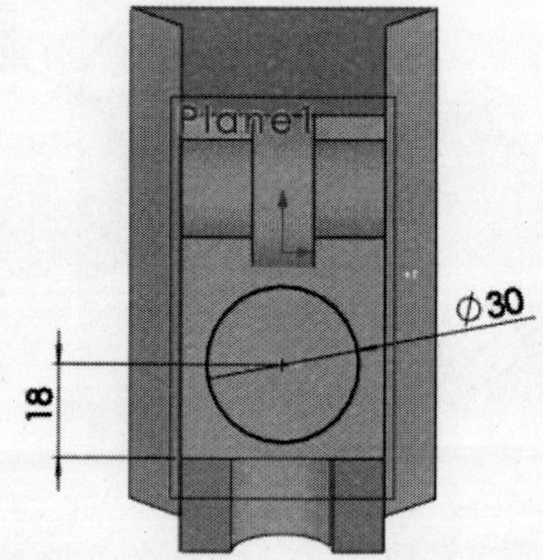

Figure 6-40 *Sketch of the extrude feature*

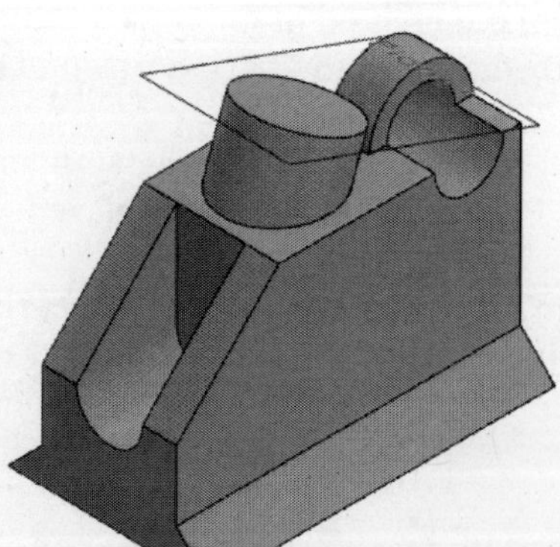

Figure 6-41 *Model after creating the sixth feature*

Creating the Seventh Feature

The seventh feature of the model is a revolved cut feature which will be created by revolving the sketch around an axis. You first need to create reference axis by using the **Axis** tool and then revolve the sketch around it to remove the material.

1. Choose the **Axis** button from the **Reference Geometry** flyout in the **Features CommandManager**, refer to Figure 6-42; the **Axis PropertyManager** is displayed.

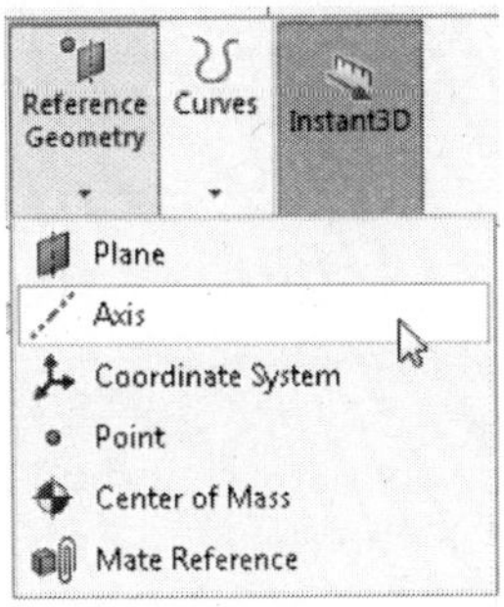

Figure 6-42 The Reference Geometry flyout

The **Axis** tool is used to create a reference axis or a construction axis. These axes are parametric lines passing through a model, feature, or a reference entity. The reference axes are used to create reference planes, coordinates systems, circular patterns, and for applying mates in the assembly. These are also used as a reference while sketching or creating features.

2. Choose the **Cylindrical/Conical Face** button from the **Axis PropertyManager** and then select the cylindrical surface of the previously created feature; the preview of the axis is displayed in the drawing area. Also, the name of the selected face is displayed in the **Reference Entities** selection area of the PropertyManager.

The **Cylindrical/Conical Face** button of this PropertyManager is used to create a reference axis that passes through the centre of a cylindrical or conical face. If you choose the **One Line/Edge/Axis** button from the **Axis PropertyManager**, you can create a reference axis by selecting a sketched line or a construction line, an edge, or a temporary axis. The **Two Planes** button of this PropertyManager is used to create a reference axis at the intersection of two planes. You can also create a reference axis that passes through two points or two vertices by choosing the **Two Points/Vertices** button from the PropertyManager. To create a reference axis that passes through a point and is normal to the selected face/plane, you need to choose the **Point and Face/Plane** button from the **Axis PropertyManager**.

3. Choose the **OK** button from the PropertyManager; the reference axis is created and displayed in the model as well as in the **FeatureManager Design Tree**.

   Now, you can use this reference axis as the axis of revolution to remove the material defined by the sketch geometry.

4. Invoke the sketching environment by selecting the **Right Plane** as the sketching plane and draw the sketch of the revolve cut feature, as shown in Figure 6-43.

   Now, you will remove the material defined by the sketch geometry by using the **Revolved Cut** tool.

5. Choose the **Revolved Cut** button from the **Features CommandManager**; the **Cut-Revolve PropertyManager** is displayed and you are prompted to select the axis of revolution.

The **Revolved Cut** tool is used to remove the material by revolving a sketch around a selected axis. Similar to the revolved boss/base feature, you can define the revolution axis using a centerline, reference axis, or using an entity in the sketch.

6. Select the reference axis from the drawing area as the axis of revolution; the preview of the revolve cut feature is displayed in the drawing area.

7. Change the current orientation of the model to isometric.

8. Make sure that the **Blind** option is selected in the **Revolve Type** drop-down list in the **Direction 1** rollout of the PropertyManager. Also, make sure that the value in the **Angle** spinner is set to 360 degrees.

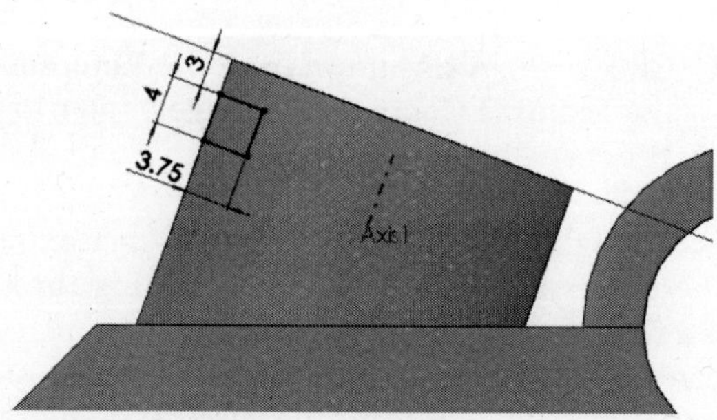

Figure 6-43 Sketch of the revolve cut feature

9. Choose the **OK** button from the **Cut-Revolve PropertyManager**; the revolve cut feature is created, refer to Figure 6-44.

10. Hide the reference axis by selecting it from the **FeatureManager Design Tree** and choosing the **Hide** button from the pop-up toolbar. Similarly, hide the reference plane created at an angle of 20 degrees. The final model after creating all the features is shown in Figure 6-44. The **FeatureManager Design Tree** displaying various features of the model is shown in Figure 6-45.

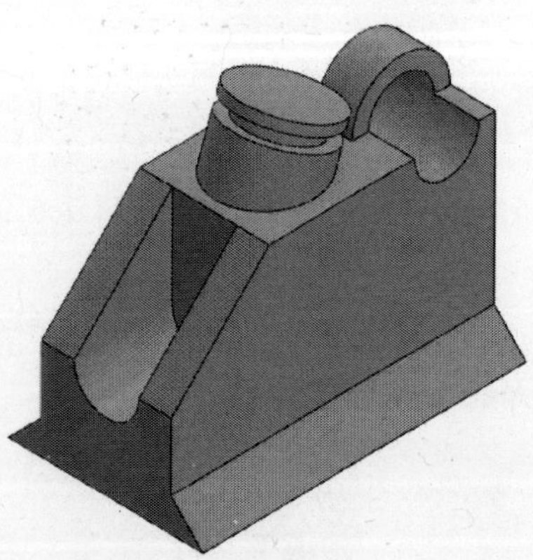

Figure 6-44 Final model for Tutorial 2

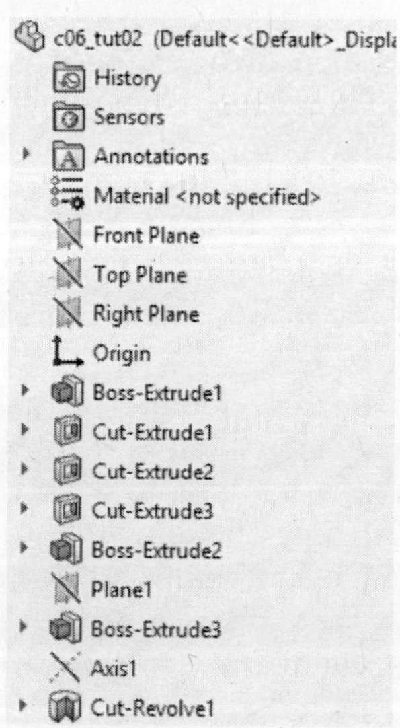

Figure 6-45** The **FeatureManager Design Tree

Saving the Model

1. Choose the **Save** button from the Menu Bar and save the model with the name *c06_tut02* at the location given below:

   \Documents\SOLIDWORKS Tutorials\c06

2. Choose **File > Close** from the SOLIDWORKS menus to close the file.

Tutorial 3

In this tutorial, you will create a model whose dimensions are shown in Figure 6-46. The solid model is shown in Figure 6-47. **(Expected Time: 30 min)**

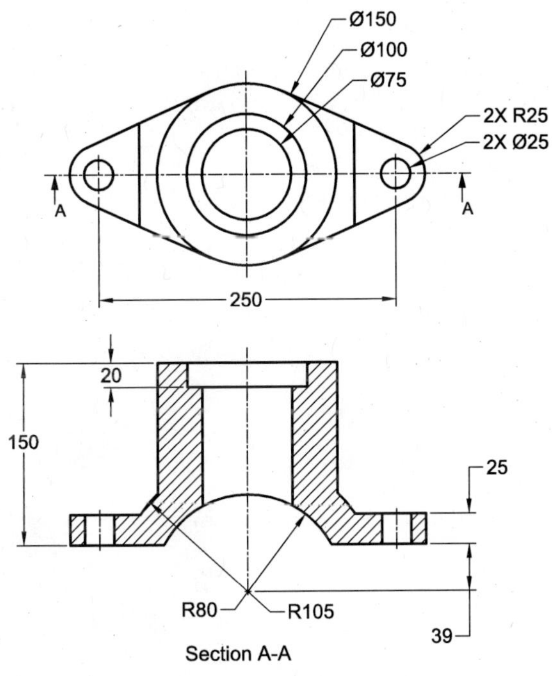

Figure 6-46 Dimensions of the model

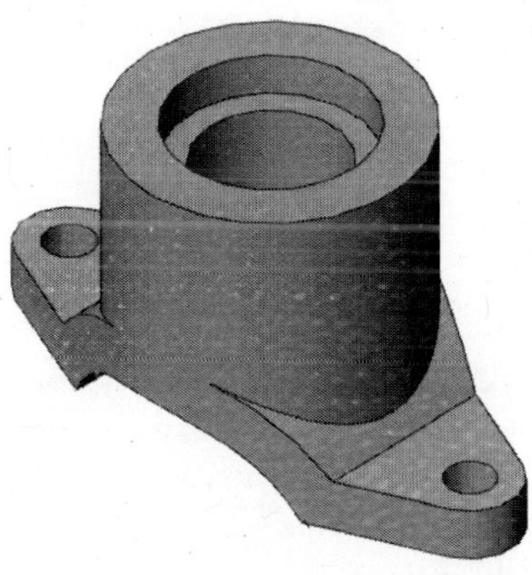

Figure 6-47 Solid model for Tutorial 3

The following steps are required to complete this tutorial:

a. Create the base feature by extruding the sketch drawn on the **Front Plane**, refer to Figures 6-48 and 6-49.
b. Extrude the sketch created on the **Top Plane** to create a cut feature, refer to Figures 6-50 through 6-52.
c. Create a plane at an offset distance of 150 mm from the **Top Plane**.
d. Draw a sketch on the newly created plane and extrude it to the selected surface, refer to Figures 6-53 and 6-54.
e. Create a counterbore hole using the **Revolved Cut** tool, refer to Figures 6-55 and 6-56.

f. Create holes using the extruded cut feature, refer to Figures 6-57 and 6-58.
g. Save and close the document.

Creating the Base Feature

It is evident from the model that its base comprises a complex geometry. Therefore, you first need to create the base feature of the model and then apply the cut feature to get the desired shape. You need to create the base feature on the Front Plane which is the sketching plane. After drawing the sketch, you need to extrude it using the **Mid Plane** option to complete the feature creation.

1. Start a new SOLIDWORKS part document and invoke the **Extruded Boss/Base** tool; you are prompted to select a plane.

2. Select the **Front Plane** and then draw the sketch of the base feature. Apply the required relations and dimensions to the sketch, as shown in Figure 6-48.

3. Exit the sketching environment; the **Boss-Extrude PropertyManager** and the preview of the base feature are displayed. Right-click in the drawing area and choose the **Mid Plane** option from the shortcut menu displayed.

4. Set the value of the **Depth** spinner to **150** in the **Boss-Extrude PropertyManager** and then choose the **OK** button from it. The isometric view of the base feature of the model is shown in Figure 6-49.

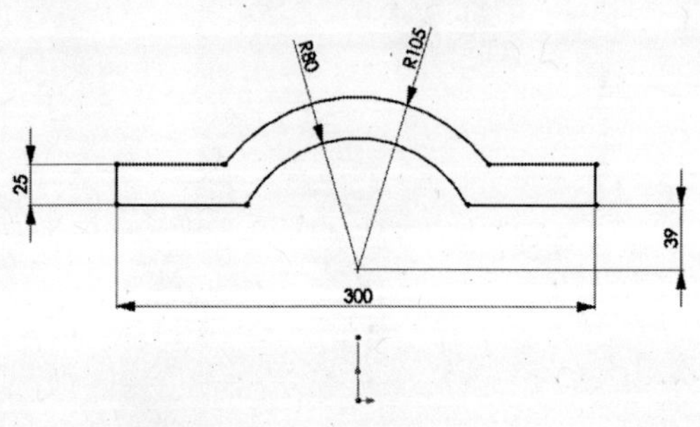

Figure 6-48 *Sketch of the base feature*

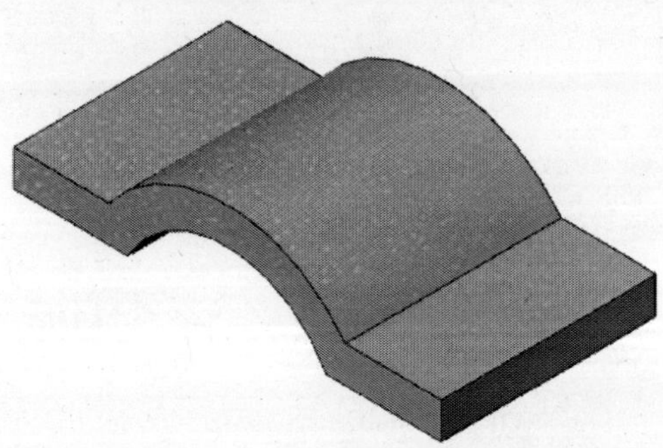

Figure 6-49 *Base feature of the solid model*

Creating the Cut Feature

Now, you need to create a cut feature to get the required shape of the base feature. The sketch for this cut feature is created using a reference plane which is defined tangent to the curved face of the previous feature.

1. Choose the **Plane** tool from the **Reference Geometry** flyout in the **Features CommandManager**; the **Plane PropertyManager** is displayed.

2. Select the upper curved face of the existing feature as the first reference; the **Tangent** button is chosen automatically in the **First Reference** rollout. Now, move the cursor close

to the midpoint of the curved edge of the upper curved face; the midpoint is highlighted in orange, see Figure 6-50. Select this point; the preview of the plane tangent to the curved face and passing through the midpoint of the curved edge is displayed. Next, choose the **OK** button from the PropertyManager; the reference plane is created.

3. Draw the sketch for the cut feature using the standard sketching tools on the previously created plane and then apply the required relations and dimensions to the sketch, as shown in Figure 6-51.

4. Choose the **Extruded Cut** tool from the **Features CommandManager** to invoke the **Cut-Extrude PropertyManager**. Change the current view to the isometric view.

   You will notice that the direction of material removal is not the one as required. Therefore, you need to flip the direction.

5. Select the **Flip side to cut** check box from the dialog box; the direction of the material removal is reversed in the preview.

6. Right-click in the drawing area and choose the **Through All** option from the shortcut menu, and then choose the **OK** button from the **Cut-Extrude PropertyManager**.

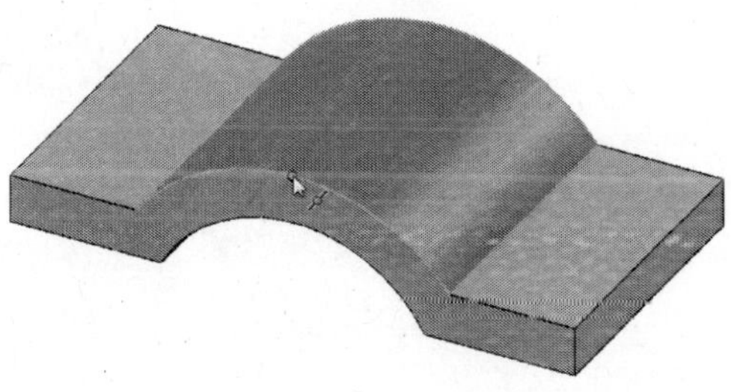

Figure 6-50 *Selecting the midpoint to define the tangent plane*

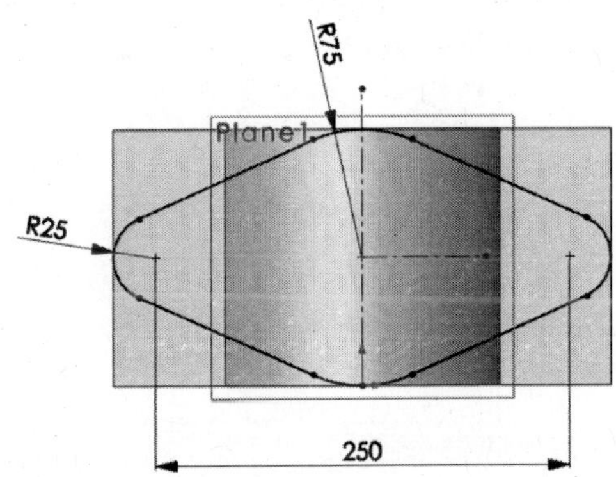

Figure 6-51 *Fully dimensioned sketch for the cut feature*

The reference plane is displayed in the graphic area. Therefore, you need to hide it.

7. Left-click on **Plane1** in the drawing area and choose **Hide** from the pop-up toolbar; the display of the reference plane is turned off. The model after adding the cut feature is shown in Figure 6-52.

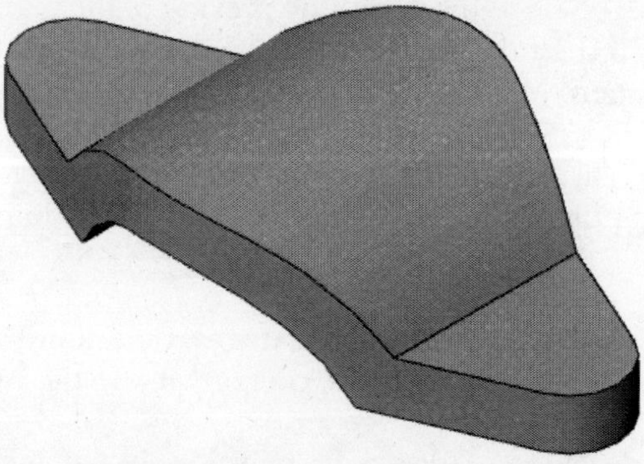

Figure 6-52 Cut feature added to the base feature

Creating a Plane for the Extruded Feature

After creating the base of the model, you need to create a plane at an offset distance of 150 mm from the Top Plane. This newly created plane will be used as the sketching plane for the next feature.

1. Choose the **Plane** tool from the **Reference Geometry** flyout in the **Features CommandManager**; the **Plane PropertyManager** is displayed.

2. Click on the sign located on the left of the **FeatureManager Design Tree** which is now displayed in the drawing area. The tree view expands, displaying the three default planes.

3. Select the **Top Plane** as the first reference and choose the **Offset distance** button from the **First Reference** rollout; the **Offset distance** spinner, the **Offset Flip** check box, and the **Number of planes to create** spinner are displayed in the **Plane PropertyManager**.

4. Set the value of the **Distance** spinner to **150** and choose the **OK** button from the **Plane PropertyManager**; the required plane is created.

Creating the Extruded Feature

After creating the plane at an offset distance from the Top Plane, you need to draw the sketch for the next feature.

1. Select the reference plane which you just created, if it is not already selected, and then invoke the sketching environment. Set the current view normal to the eye view.

2. Draw a sketch of the circle and then apply the required relations to the sketch, as shown in Figure 6-53.

3. Change the current view to isometric and invoke the **Extruded Boss/Base** tool.

   You will observe in the preview that the direction of the feature creation is opposite to the required direction. Therefore, you need to change the direction of the feature creation.

4. Choose the **Reverse Direction** button on the left of the **End Condition** drop-down list to reverse the direction of feature creation; the preview of the feature changes dynamically.

5. Right-click in the drawing area and choose the **Up To Surface** option from the shortcut menu displayed; you are prompted to select a face or a surface to specify the first direction. Also, the **Face/Plane** selection box is displayed below the **End Condition** drop-down list in the **Direction 1** rollout.

6. Select the upper curved surface of the model using the left mouse button. You will observe in the preview that the feature is extruded upto the selected surface.

7. Choose the **OK** button from the **Boss-Extrude PropertyManager**.

   The plane is displayed in the drawing area. Therefore, you need to turn off its display.

8. Select **Plane2** from the **FeatureManager Design Tree** or from the drawing area and choose **Hide** from the pop-up toolbar. The model after creating the extruded feature is shown in Figure 6-54.

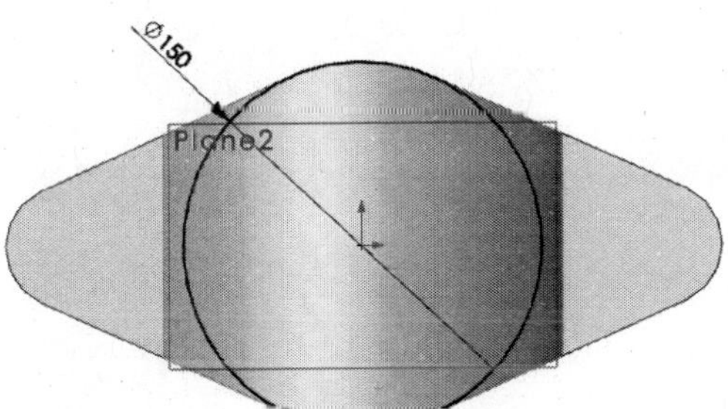

Figure 6-53 *Sketch created on the newly created plane*

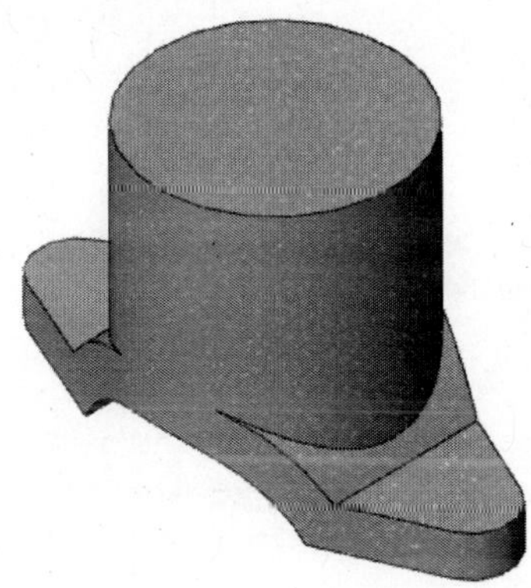

Figure 6-54 *Sketch extruded up to the selected surface*

Creating the Counterbore Hole

Next, you need to create a counterbore hole. It will be created as a revolved cut feature by using a sketch drawn on the Front Plane.

1. Invoke the sketching environment and select **Front Plane** as the sketching plane from the **FeatureManager Design Tree**. Next, orient the sketching plane normal to the view.

2. Draw the sketch of the counterbore hole using the standard sketching tools. Add the required relations and then add the linear diameter dimensions, as shown in Figure 6-55.

3. Set the current view to isometric and then choose the **Revolved Cut** tool from the **Features CommandManager**; the **Cut-Revolve PropertyManager** is displayed.

It is evident from Figure 6-55 that the sketch contains a vertical centerline. Therefore, after invoking the **Cut-Revolve PropertyManager**, SOLIDWORKS has automatically selected the vertical centerline as the axis of revolution. As a result, the preview of the cut feature is displayed in the drawing area in temporary graphics. By default, the value of the angle in the **Direction 1 Angle** spinner is set to **360**. Therefore, you do not need to set the value in the **Angle** spinner.

4. Choose the **OK** button from the **Cut-Revolve PropertyManager**. Figure 6-56 shows the model after creating the revolved cut feature.

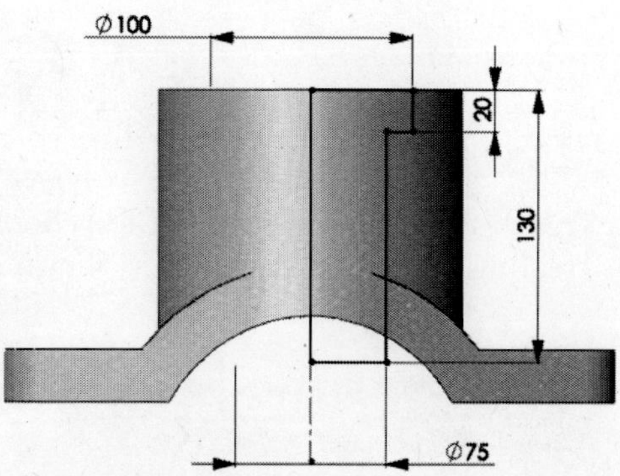

Figure 6-55 *Fully defined sketch for the counterbore hole*

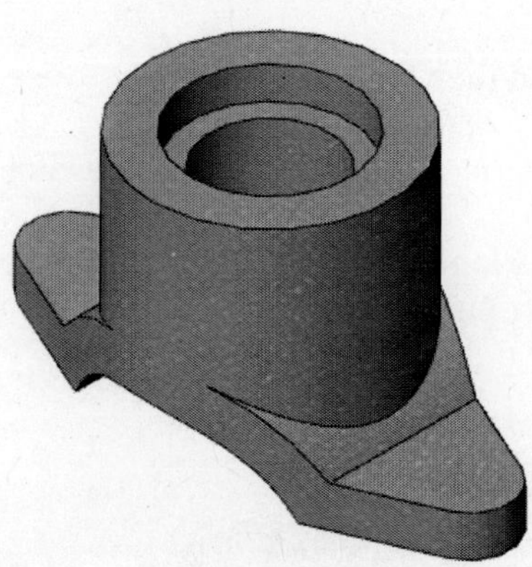

Figure 6-56 *Counterbore hole created using the* ***Revolved Cut*** *tool*

Creating Holes

After creating all the features, you need to create holes using the extruded cut feature to complete the model. The sketch for the cut feature is to be drawn by using the top planar surface of the base feature as the sketching plane.

1. Select the top planar surface of the base feature and invoke the sketching environment. Orient the model such that the selected face of the model is oriented normal to the view.

2. Draw the sketch using the standard sketching tools and apply the required relations and dimensions to it, as shown in Figure 6-57.

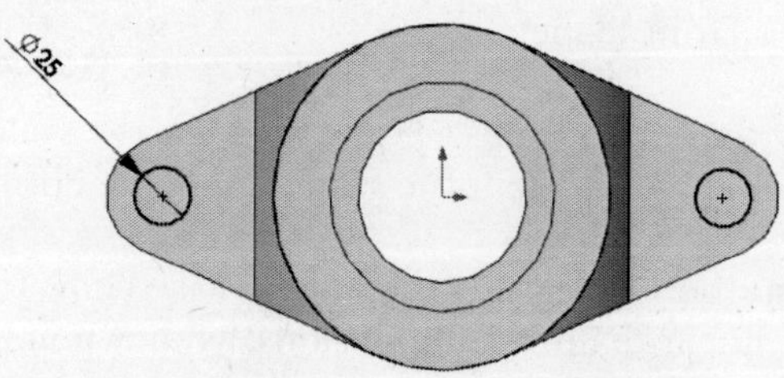

Figure 6-57 *Fully defined sketch for the cut feature*

3. Change the current view to isometric. Choose the **Extruded Cut** tool from the **Features CommandManager**; the **Cut-Extrude PropertyManager** is displayed.

4. Right-click and choose the **Through All** option from the shortcut menu displayed and choose the **OK** button from the **Cut-Extrude PropertyManager**. The final model is shown in Figure 6-58. The **FeatureManager Design Tree** displaying various features of the model is shown in Figure 6-59.

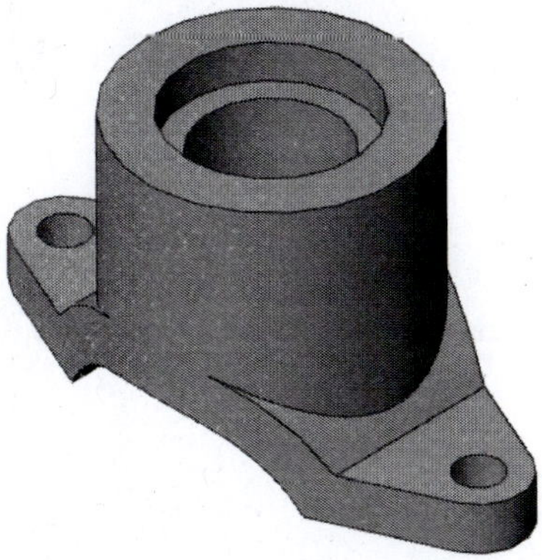

Figure 6-58 *Final model*

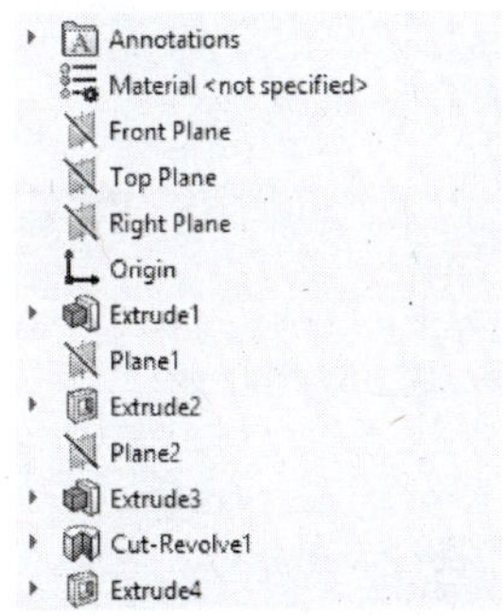

Figure 6-59 *The* ***FeatureManager Design Tree***

Saving the Model

1. Choose the **Save** button from the Menu Bar and save the model with the name *c06_tut03* at the location given below:

   \Documents\SOLIDWORKS Tutorials\c06

2. Choose **File > Close** from the SOLIDWORKS menus to close the file.

Self-Evaluation Test

Answer the following questions and then compare them to those given at the end of this chapter:

1. The __________ option is used to extrude a sketch such that it is upto the next surface.

2. The __________ option in the **End Condition** drop-down list is used to terminate the extruded feature up to another body.

3. You can use the __________ option to create a reference axis that passes through the center point of a cylindrical or conical surface.

4. When you draw a sketch for the first time in the sketching environment, the sketch is drawn on the default plane which is the Front Plane. (T/F)

5. When you start a new SOLIDWORKS part document, SOLIDWORKS provides you with two default planes. (T/F)

6. You need to choose the **Plane** button from the **Features CommandManager** to invoke the **Plane PropertyManager**. (T/F)

7. You cannot create a plane at an offset distance from the selected planar face by using the **Plane PropertyManager**. (T/F)

8. When you create a circular feature, a temporary axis is displayed automatically. (T/F)

Review Questions

Answer the following questions:

1. Which of the following check boxes needs to be selected while creating a feature in a single-body modeling?

   (a) **Combine results** (b) **Fix bodies**
   (c) **Merge results** (d) **Union results**

2. Which of the following buttons is used to add a draft angle to a cut feature?

   (a) **Add Draft** (b) **Create Draft**
   (c) **Draft On/Off** (d) None of these

3. Which of the following PropertyManagers is invoked to create a cut feature by extruding a sketch?

   (a) **Extruded Cut** (b) **Extrude**
   (c) **Extrude-Cut** (d) **Cut**

4. Which of the following options is used to define the termination of feature creation at an offset distance of a selected surface?

   (a) **Distance To Surface** (b) **Normal From Surface**
   (c) **Distance From Surface** (d) **Offset From Surface**

5. Which of the following options is used to define the termination of feature creation to selected surface?

   (a) **To Surface** (b) **Selected Surface**
   (c) **Up To Surface** (d) None of these

6. The __________ option will be available in the **End Condition** drop-down list only after creating a base feature.

7. The __________ check box is used to specify a side from where the material is removed.

8. The __________ check box is used to create an outward draft in a cut feature.

EXERCISES

Exercise 1

Create the solid model shown in Figure 6-60. The dimensions of the model are given in the same figure. **(Expected time: 30 min)**

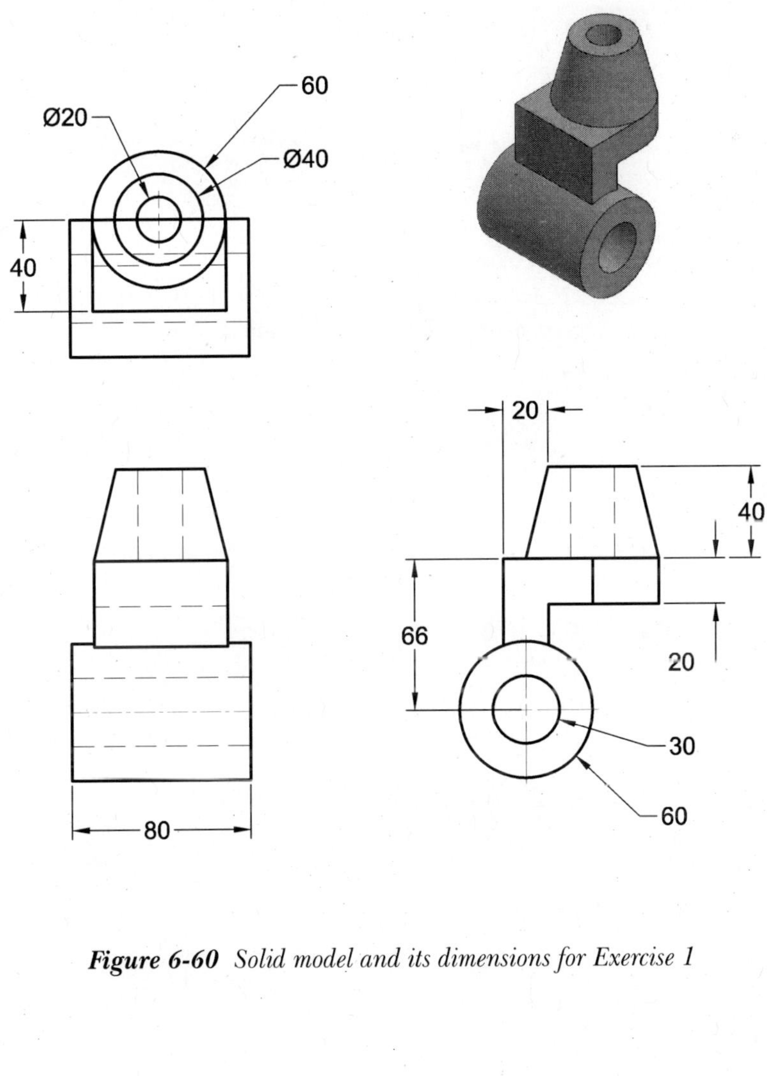

Figure 6-60 *Solid model and its dimensions for Exercise 1*

Exercise 2

Create the model shown in Figure 6-61. The dimensions of the model are given in Figure 6-62.
(Expected time: 30 min)

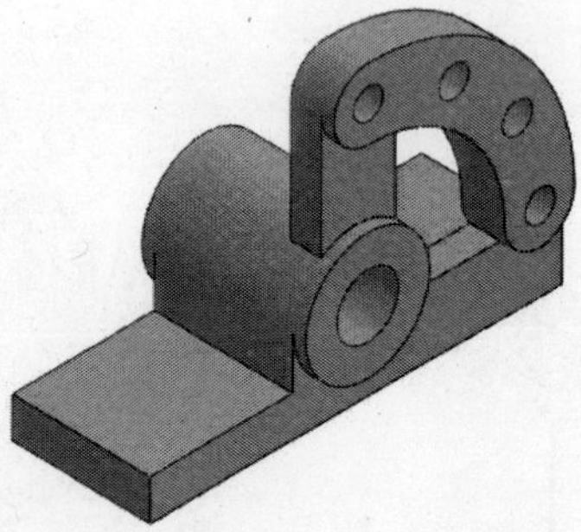

Figure 6-61 *Solid model for Exercise 2*

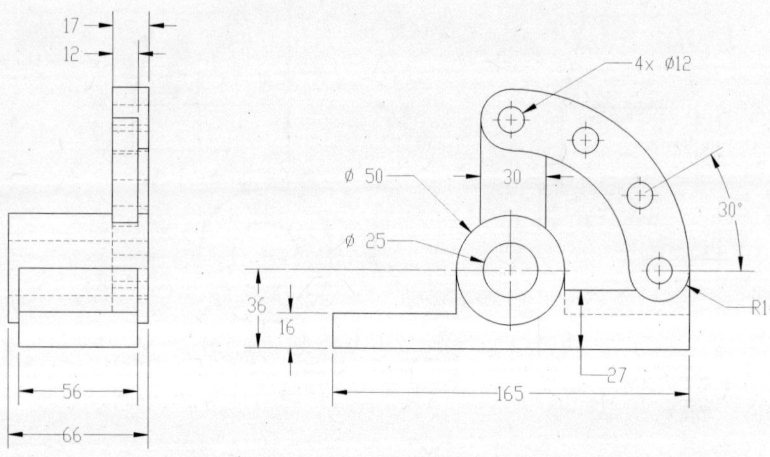

Figure 6-62 *Dimensions for the solid model*

Exercise 3

Create the model shown in Figure 6-63. The dimensions of the model are given in the same figure.
(Expected time: 30 min)

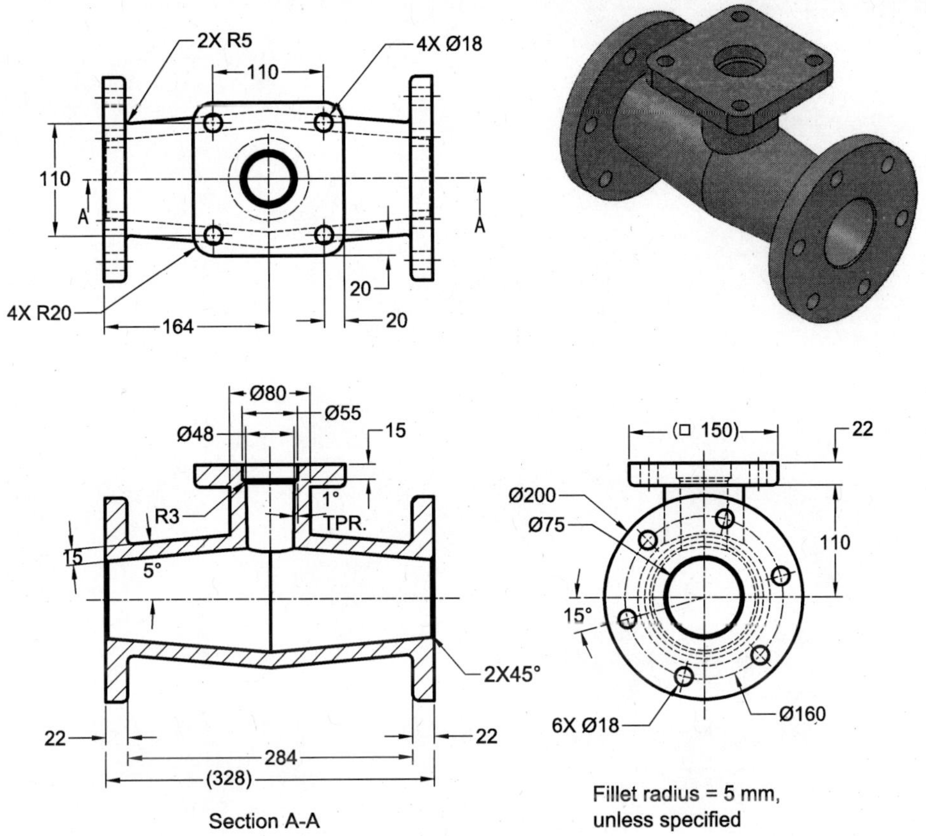

Figure 6-63 *The model and its dimensions for Exercise 3*

Answers to Self-Evaluation Test

1. **Up To Next**, **2.** **Up To Body**, **3.** **Cylindrical/Conical Face**, **4.** F, **5.** F, **6.** T, **7.** F, **8.** F

Chapter 7

Advanced Modeling Tools

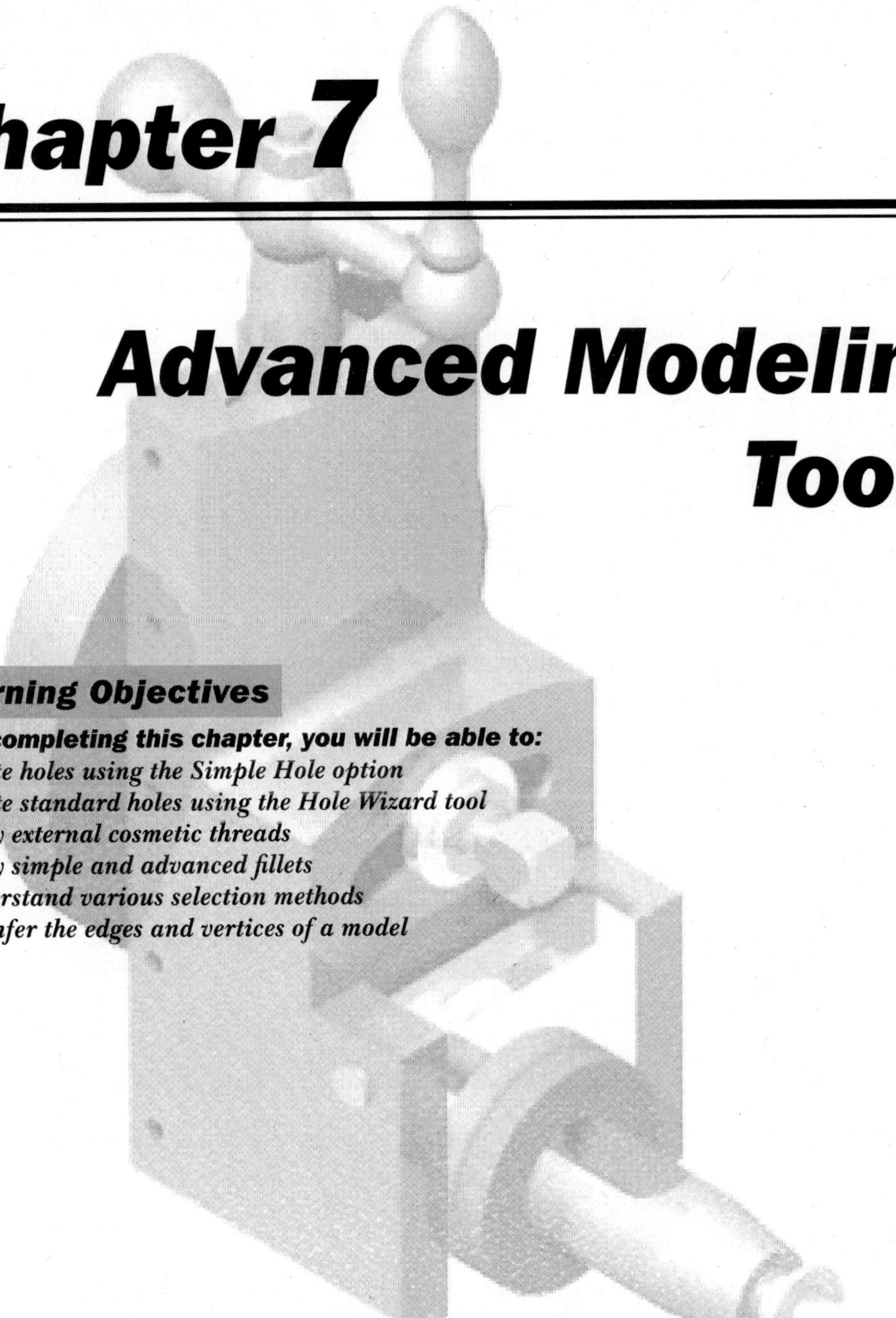

Learning Objectives

After completing this chapter, you will be able to:

- *Create holes using the Simple Hole option*
- *Create standard holes using the Hole Wizard tool*
- *Apply external cosmetic threads*
- *Apply simple and advanced fillets*
- *Understand various selection methods*
- *Chamfer the edges and vertices of a model*

ADVANCED MODELING TOOLS

This chapter discusses various advanced modeling tools available in SOLIDWORKS. These tools assist you in creating an accurate design by capturing the design intent of a model. In previous chapters, you have learned to create a hole using the **Extruded Cut** tool. In this chapter, you will learn how to create holes using the **Simple Hole** and **Hole Wizard** tools. The **Hole Wizard** tool is used to create standard holes, classified based on the industrial standard, screw type, and size. This tool is one of the most used standard industrial virtual hole generation methods available in any CAD packages. You will also learn about some other advanced modeling tools such as the fillet, chamfer, mirror, and pattern.

TUTORIALS

Tutorial 1

In this tutorial, you will create the model shown in Figure 7-1. The dimensions and views of the model are shown in the same figure. **(Expected time: 30 min)**

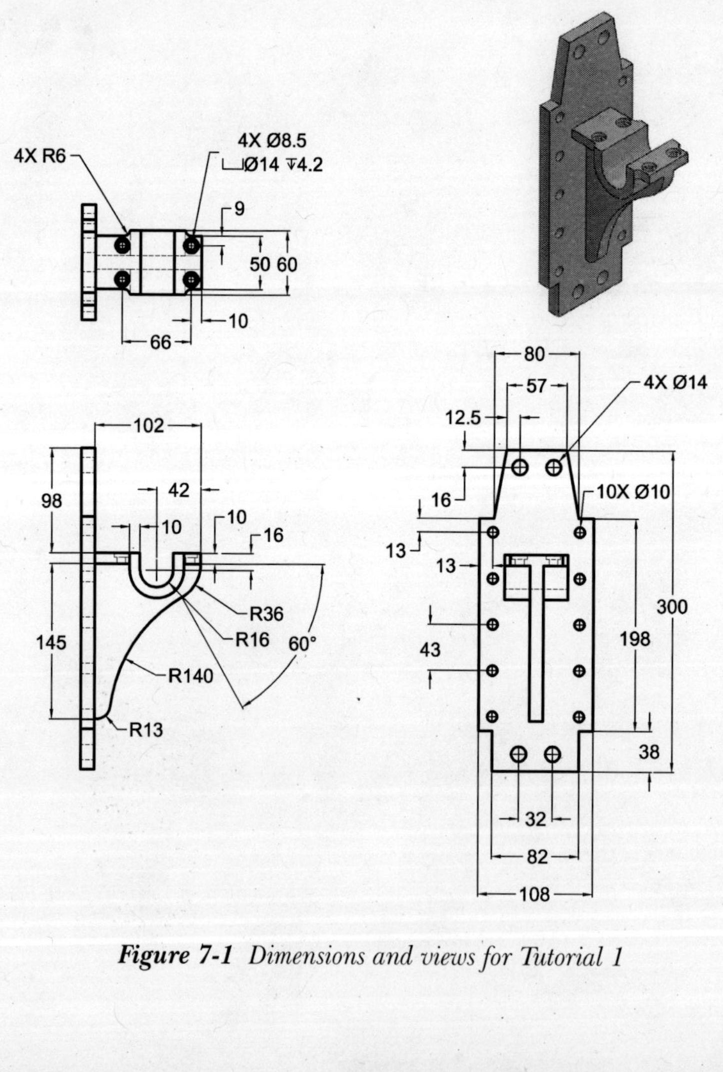

Figure 7-1 *Dimensions and views for Tutorial 1*

The following steps are required to complete this tutorial:

a. Start a new SOLIDWORKS part document and create the base feature of the model on the **Right Plane**, refer to Figure 7-2.
b. Create the second feature, which is an extrude feature, on the right planar face of the base feature, refer to Figures 7-4 and 7-5.
c. Create the cut feature on the top planar face of the second feature, refer to Figures 7-6 and 7-7.
d. Create the mirror copy of the previously created cut feature, refer to Figure 7-8.
e. Create the rib feature using the **Rib** tool, refer to Figure 7-13.
f. Create a simple hole of diameter 10 mm using the **Simple Hole** tool, refer to Figures 7-15 and 7-16.
g. Create a simple hole of diameter 14 mm using the **Simple Hole** tool, refer to Figure 7-17.
h. Create a linear pattern of hole of 10 mm diameter, refer to Figures 7-18 and 7-19.
i. Create a linear pattern of hole of 14 mm diameter, refer to Figure 7-20.
j. Create a counterbore hole, refer to Figures 7-21 through 7-23.
k. Create a linear pattern of counterbore hole, refer to Figure 7-24.
l. Save the model.

Creating the Base Feature

1. Start a new SOLIDWORKS part document using the **New SOLIDWORKS Document** dialog box.

2. Invoke the **Extruded Boss/Base** tool and select the **Right Plane** as the sketching plane.

3. Draw the sketch of the base feature of the model, as shown in Figure 7-2.

4. Exit the sketcher environment; the **Boss-Extrude PropertyManager** is displayed.

5. Make sure that the **Blind** option is selected in the **End Condition** drop-down list of the **Direction 1** rollout of the PropertyManager.

6. Set the value of the **Depth** spinner to 13 mm. Next, choose the **OK** button from the PropertyManager; the base feature of the model is created. The isometric view of the model is shown in Figure 7-3.

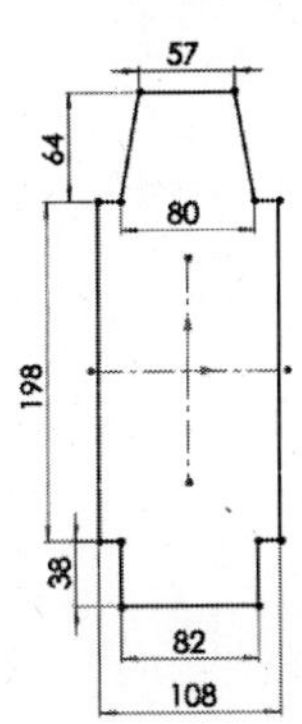

Figure 7-2 *Sketch of the base feature*

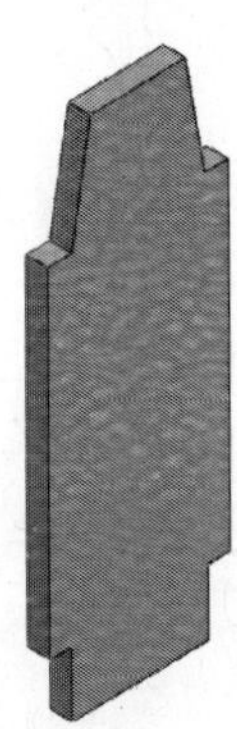

Figure 7-3 *Model after creating the base feature*

Creating the Extrude Feature

The second feature of the model is also an extrude feature. The sketch of this extrude feature will be drawn on the **Front Plane** and extruded by using the **Mid Plane** option.

1. Invoke the **Extruded Boss/Base** tool and select the **Front Plane** as the sketching plane.

2. Draw the sketch of the second feature of the model, as shown in Figure 7-4.

3. Exit the sketcher environment; the **Boss-Extrude PropertyManager** is displayed.

4. Select the **Mid Plane** option from the **End Condition** drop-down list of the **Direction 1** rollout of the PropertyManager.

5. Set the value of the **Depth** spinner to 60 mm. Next, choose the **OK** button from the PropertyManager; the extrude feature is created. The isometric view of the model after creating the second feature is shown in Figure 7-5.

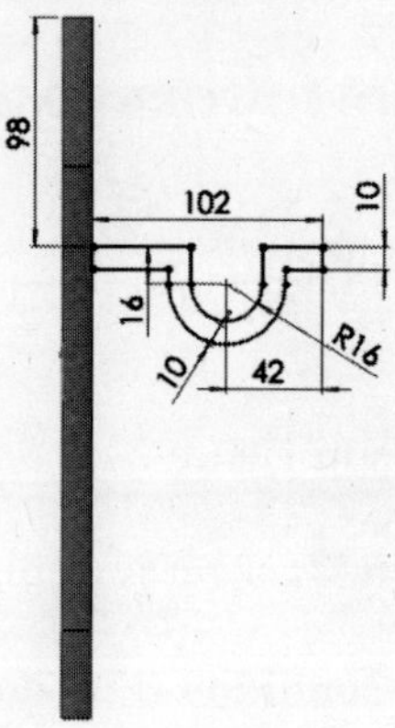

Figure 7-4 Sketch of the base feature

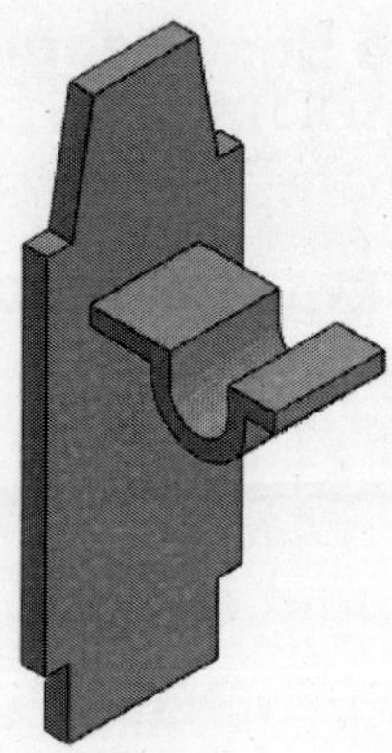

Figure 7-5 Model after creating the base feature

Creating the Cut Feature

The third feature of the model is a cut feature. The sketch of the cut feature will be drawn on the top planar face of the second feature. This sketch will be extruded with the **Through All** option to create the cut feature.

1. Invoke the **Extruded Cut** tool and select the top planar face of the second feature as the sketching plane.

2. Orient the model normal to the sketching plane and draw the sketch for the cut feature using the sketching tools, refer to Figure 7-6.

Note

The sketch of the cut-extrude feature consists of two closed contours.

Now, you will change the current display mode of the model to the **Hidden Lines Visible** mode for better visibility.

3. Choose the **Display Style** button in the **View (Heads-Up)** toolbar; the **Display Style** flyout is displayed.

SOLIDWORKS provides you with various predefined modes to display the model. In SOLIDWORKS, the display modes are grouped together in the **Display Style** flyout.

4. Choose the **Hidden Lines Visible** button from the **Display Style** flyout; the current display mode of the model is changed to hidden lines visible mode, refer to Figure 7-7.

The **Hidden Lines Visible** tool of the **Display Style** flyout is used to display the model in the wireframe mode with hidden edges of the model displayed as dashed lines.

If you choose the **Wireframe** button from the **Display Style** flyout, all hidden edges of the model will be displayed along with the visible edges. Note that in a complex model, it is very difficult to recognize the visible lines and hidden lines, if the **Wireframe** mode is invoked. The **Hidden Lines Removed** tool of this flyout is used to display only the edges of the faces that are visible in the current view of the model. In this case, the hidden edges of the model will not be displayed. The **Shaded With Edges** mode is the default selected mode in which the model remains shaded and the edges of the visible faces of the model are displayed. The **Shaded** mode is similar to the **Shaded With Edges** mode with the only difference that in the **Shaded** mode the edges of the visible faces will not be displayed.

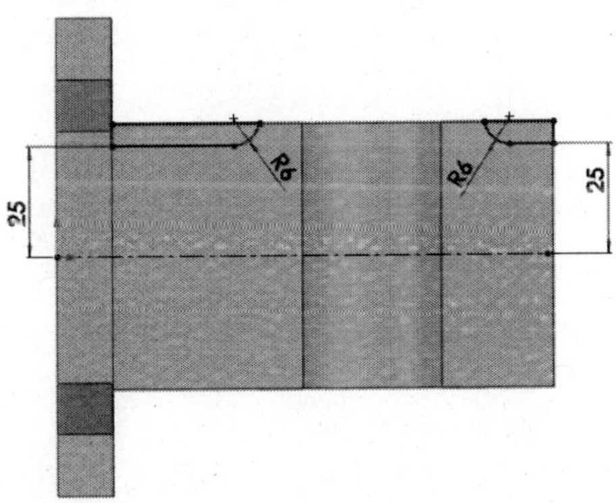

Figure 7-6 *Sketch of the cut-extrude feature*

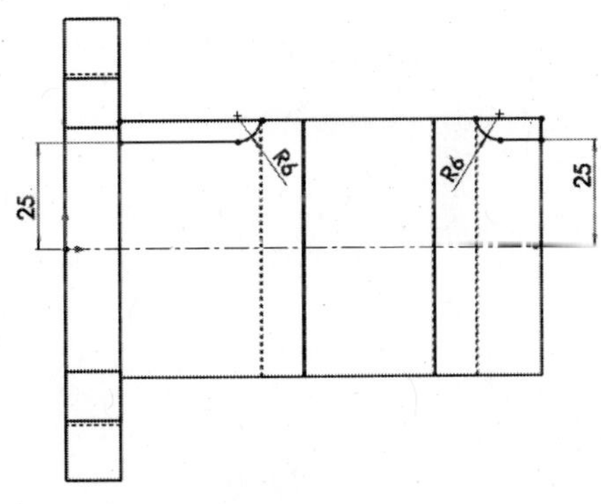

Figure 7-7 *Model displayed in the* ***Hidden Lines Visible*** *mode*

5. Exit the sketching environment; the **Cut-Extrude PropertyManager** is displayed.

   The preview of the cut feature is displayed in the drawing area.

6. Change the view orientation to isometric.

7. Right-click in the drawing area and choose **Through All** from the shortcut menu. Next, choose the **OK** button from the PropertyManager.

8. Change the current display mode of the model to the **Shaded With Edges** display mode, as discussed earlier.

The model after creating the cut feature is shown in Figure 7-8.

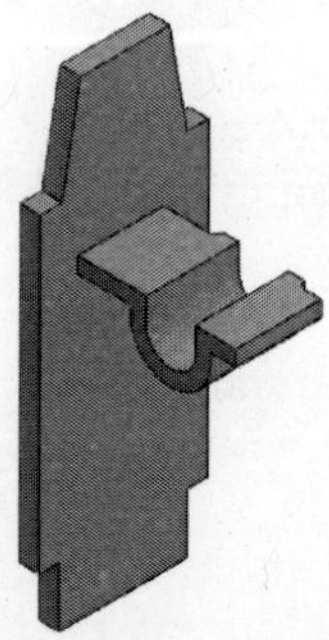

Figure 7-8 *Model after creating the cut feature*

Creating the Mirror Feature

Now you need to create a mirror copy of the last created cut feature by using the **Mirror** tool.

1. Choose the **Mirror** tool from the **Features Command Manager**; the **Mirror Property Manager** is displayed at the left of the drawing area, refer to Figure 7-9. Also, you are prompted to select a plane or a planar face about which the features will be mirrored, followed by the features to be mirrored.

The **Mirror** tool is used to mirror a selected feature, face, or body about a specified mirror plane, which can be a reference plane or a planar face.

The **Mirror Face/Plane** rollout of the **Mirror PropertyManager** is used to specify a plane or planar face about which the features will be mirrored. The **Features to Mirror** rollout of the PropertyManager is used to select the features to be mirrored about the selected plane. The **Faces to Mirror** rollout of the PropertyManager is used to select the faces to be mirrored. Note that the faces selected to be mirrored about the selected plane or planar face must form a close body. In SOLIDWORKS, you can also select bodies to be mirrored by using the **Bodies to Mirror** rollout of the PropertyManager.

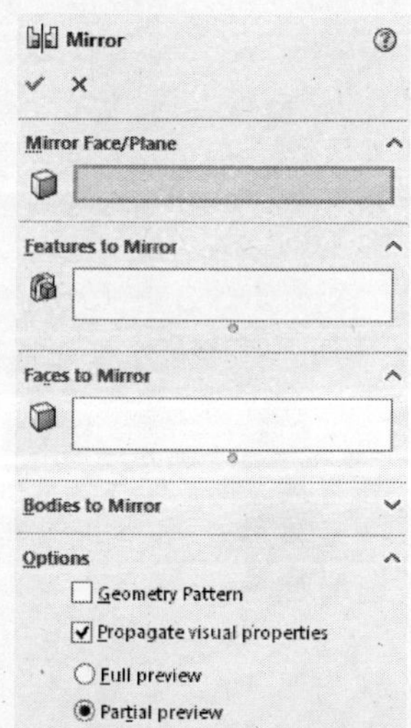

Figure 7-9 *The* ***Mirror PropertyManager***

Note

By default, the ***Geometry Pattern*** *check box is not selected in the* ***Options*** *rollout of the PropertyManager. Therefore, if you mirror a feature that is related to some other entity, the same relationship will be applied to the mirrored feature. Also, the* ***Propagate visual properties*** *check box in the* ***Options*** *rollout is selected by default. As a result, all the visual properties of the mirrored instance are the same as that of its parent feature or the parent body.*

2. Click on the arrow located on the left of the **FeatureManager Design Tree**, which is now displayed in the drawing area; the tree view expands and it displays three defaults planes and the list of all the features created in this model.

3. Select the **Front Plane** as the mirroring plane from the **FeatureManager Design Tree**; the name of the selected plane is displayed in the **Mirror Face/Plane** selection area of the PropertyManager. Also, as soon as you select the mirroring plane, the **Features to Mirror** selection area of the PropertyManager is activated and you are prompted to select features to be mirrored.

4. Select the previously created cut feature as the feature to be mirrored from the **FeatureManager Design Tree**; the preview of the mirrored feature is displayed in the drawing area. Also, the name of the selected feature is displayed in the **Features to Mirror** selection area of the PropertyManager.

5. Choose the **OK** button from the **Mirror PropertyManager**; the mirrored feature of the selected feature is created. The isometric view of the model after creating the mirrored feature is shown in the Figure 7-10.

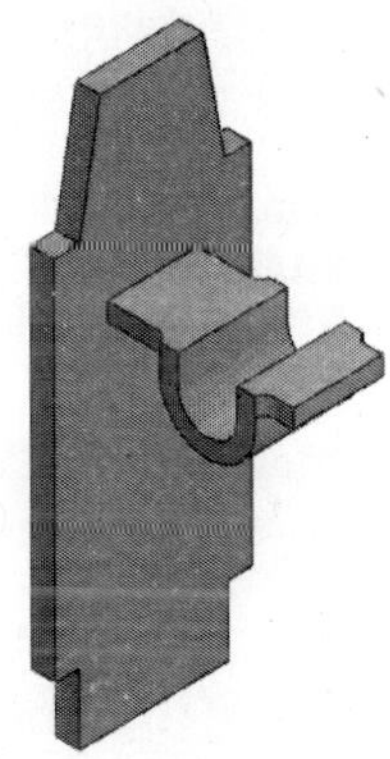

Figure 7-10 *Model after creating the mirrored feature*

Creating the Rib Feature

The fifth feature of the model is a rib feature. The sketch of this rib feature will be created on the **Front Plane**.

1. Invoke the sketcher environment by selecting the **Front Plane** as the sketching plane.

2. Orient the model normal to the sketching plane and draw the sketch for the rib feature using the sketching tools, as shown in Figure 7-11.

3. Choose the **Rib** tool from the **Features CommandManager**; the **Rib PropertyManager** is displayed, refer to Figure 7-12. Also, a preview of the rib feature is displayed in the drawing area.

The **Rib** tool is used to create a rib feature. Ribs are defined as the thin-walled structures that are used to increase the strength of the entire structure of a component so that it does not fail under an increased load. In SOLIDWORKS, the ribs are created using an open sketch as well as a closed sketch.

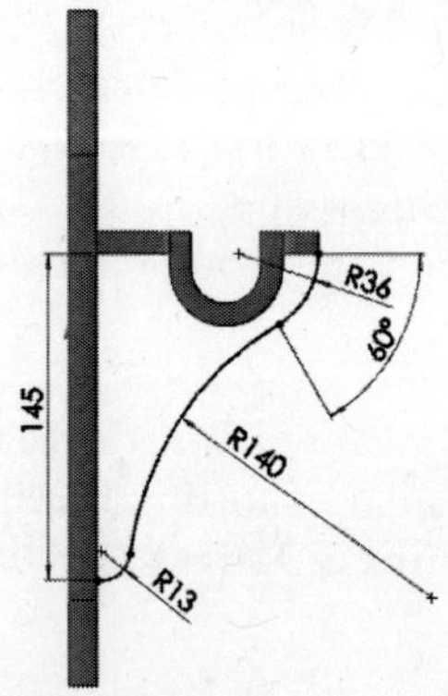

Figure 7-11 *Sketch of the rib feature*

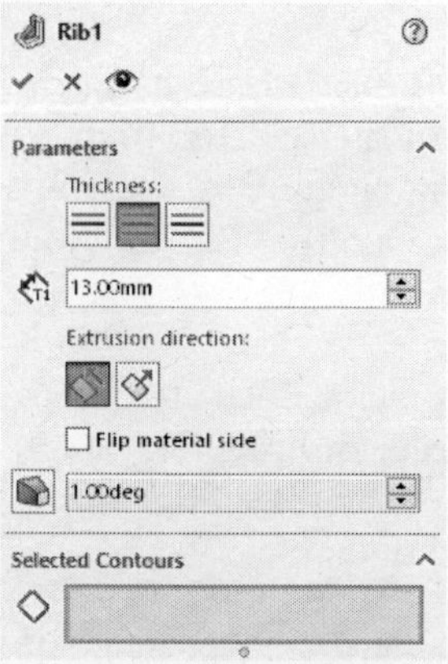

Figure 7-12 *The **Rib PropertyManager***

4. Make sure that the **Both Sides** button is chosen in the **Thickness** area of the **Parameters** rollout of the PropertyManager.

The **Thickness** area in the **Parameters** rollout is used to specify the side of the sketch where the material is to be added as well as the thickness of the rib feature.

Note

*By default, the **Both Sides** button is chosen in the **Thickness** area of the **Parameters** rollout of the PropertyManager. As a result, the rib will be created on both sides of the sketch. You can also choose the **First Side** or **Second Side** button from this area to create ribs on either sides of the sketch.*

5. Set the value of the **Rib Thickness** spinner to **13** mm.

6. Make sure that the **Parallel to Sketch** button is chosen in the **Extrusion direction** area of the PropertyManager.

The **Extrusion direction** area of the PropertyManager is used to specify the method of extrusion to be used for extruding a closed or open sketch. When you invoke the **Rib PropertyManager**, the option that is suitable for creating the rib feature will be activated by default.

The **Parallel to Sketch** button in the **Extrusion direction** area of the PropertyManager is used to extrude the sketch in a direction that is parallel to both the sketch and the sketching plane. However, the **Normal to Sketch** button of this area is used to extrude the sketch in a direction that is normal to both the sketch and the sketching plane.

7. Change the view orientation to isometric.

8. Make sure that the arrow that is displayed with the preview of the rib feature in the drawing area points toward the planar face of the base feature.

Note

*The direction of arrow shows the direction of material addition. You can reverse the direction of material addition by using the **Flip material side** check box of the PropertyManager. You can also left-click on the arrow displayed in the preview to reverse the direction.*

9. Choose the **OK** button from the PropertyManager; the rib feature is created, as shown in Figure 7-13.

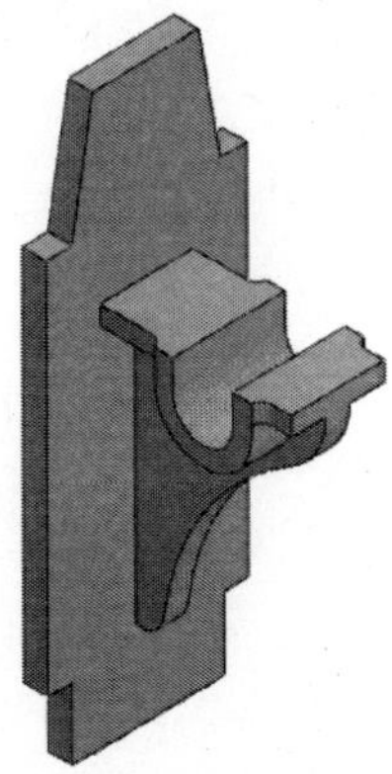

Figure 7-13 *Model after creating the rib feature*

Creating the Hole Feature

Now, you will create hole features of the model. You can create a hole using the **Hole Wizard** tool. However, in this tutorial, you will create hole features arbitrarily on the right planar face of the base feature by using the **Simple Hole** tool and position them later.

Note

*In the previous chapters, you learned to create holes by extruding a circle using the **Extruded Cut** tool. Now, you will learn how to create a hole feature using the **Simple Hole** tool. If you use this tool, you do not need to draw the sketch of the hole. The holes created using this tool act as placed features.*

1. Select the right planar face of the base feature as the placement plane for the hole feature.

2. Choose **Insert > Features > Simple Hole** from the SOLIDWORKS menus; the **Hole PropertyManager** is displayed, refer to Figure 7-14. Also, the preview of the hole feature is displayed in the drawing area with the default values.

3. Select the **Through All** option from the **End Condition** drop-down list of the **Direction 1** rollout in the PropertyManager to specify the feature termination. You can also right-click in the drawing area and select the **Through All** option from the shortcut menu displayed.

4. Set the value of the **Hole Diameter** spinner to **10** mm in the **Direction 1** rollout of the PropertyManager. Next, choose the **OK** button; the hole feature of the specified diameter is created arbitrarily on the right planar face of the base feature.

Since the hole feature is placed arbitrarily on the right planar face of the base feature, you need to define its position.

5. Select **Hole1** from the **FeatureManager Design Tree**; a pop-up toolbar is displayed.

6. Choose the **Edit Sketch** button from the pop-up toolbar; the sketcher environment is invoked. Now, apply required dimensions to locate the hole feature, refer to Figure 7-15.

7. Exit the sketcher environment. Next, press the CTRL + B keys or choose the **Rebuild** button from the Menu Bar to rebuild the model. The isometric view of the model after creating the hole feature is shown in Figure 7-16.

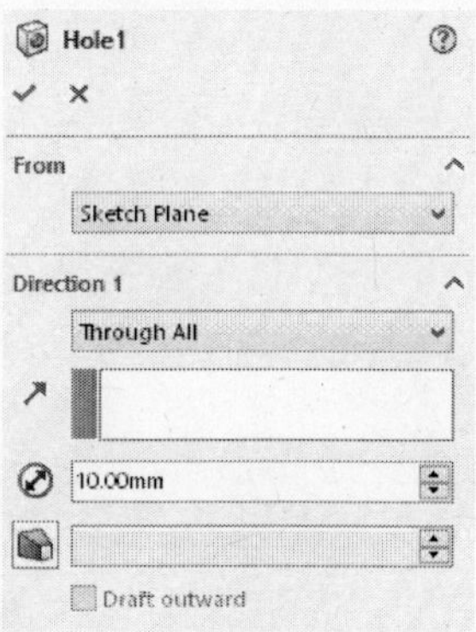

Figure 7-14 *The* ***Hole PropertyManager***

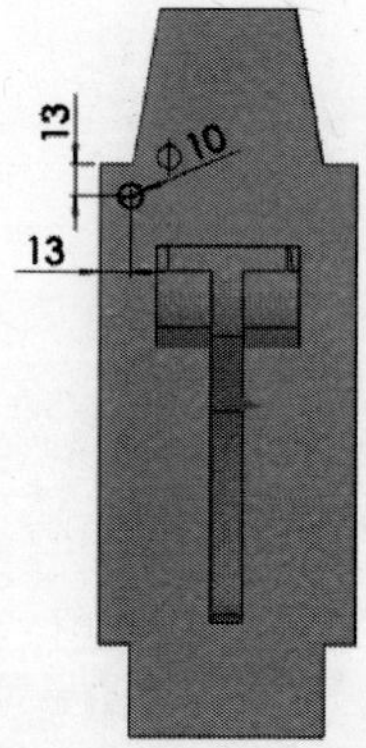

Figure 7-15 *Placement for the hole feature*

8. Use the same procedure as discussed above to create the second hole feature of diameter 14 mm on the top left corner of the right planar face of the base feature. Refer to Figure 7-1 for the placement of the second hole feature. The isometric view of the model after creating both hole features is shown in the Figure 7-17.

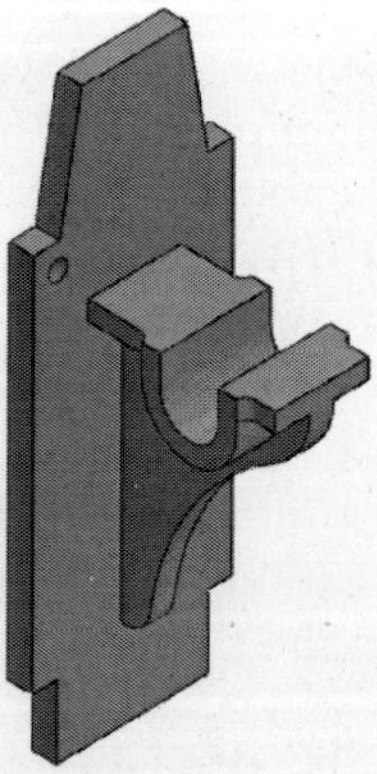

Figure 7-16 *Model after creating the first hole feature*

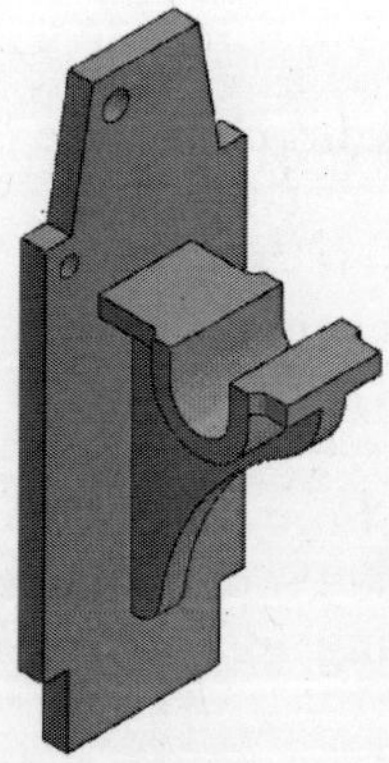

Figure 7-17 *Model after creating the second hole feature*

Patterning the Features

After creating the hole features, you need to pattern them one by one using the **Linear Pattern** tool. First, you will create the linear pattern of the hole having 10 mm diameter and then you will create the linear pattern of the hole having 14 mm diameter.

1. Choose the **Linear Pattern** tool from the **Features CommandManager**; the **Linear Pattern PropertyManager** is displayed. Also, you are prompted to select an edge or an axis for the direction reference.

The **Linear Pattern** tool is used to create pattern instances of selected features in linear directions. Using this tool, you can create linear pattern of selected features, faces, and bodies.

2. Select a vertical linear edge of the base feature as the first direction reference for creating the linear pattern of the hole having 10 mm diameter; the name of the selected edge is displayed in the **Pattern Direction** selection area of the **Direction 1** rollout in the PropertyManager. Also, the **Direction 1** callout is attached to the selected edge, refer to Figure 7-18.

The callout has two edit boxes, one to define the number of instances and the other to define the spacing between two instances.

As soon as you select the first direction reference, the **Pattern Direction** selection area of the **Direction 2** rollout in the PropertyManager is activated. As a result, you are prompted to select an edge or an axis for the second direction reference.

3. Set the value of the **Spacing** spinner to 43 and the **Number of Instances** spinner to 5 in the **Direction 1** rollout of the PropertyManager.

Tip

You can also define the spacing between two instances and number of instances in one direction by using the respective edit boxes of the callout that is attached to the edge selected for defining the linear direction.

4. Select a horizontal linear edge of the base feature as the second direction reference for creating the linear pattern of the hole which has 10 mm diameter; the name of the selected edge is displayed in the **Pattern Direction** selection area of the **Direction 2** rollout in the PropertyManager. Also, the **Direction 2** callout is attached to the selected edge, refer to Figure 7-18.

5. Set the value of the **Spacing** spinner to **82** and the **Number of Instances** spinner to **2** in the **Direction 1** rollout of the PropertyManager.

As soon as you select the second direction reference, the **Features to Pattern** selection area of the **Features to Pattern** rollout in the PropertyManager is activated. As a result, you are prompted to select features to be patterned.

6. Select **Hole1** from the **FeatureManager Design Tree** which has diameter 10 mm as the feature to pattern; the name of the selected hole feature is displayed in the **Features to Pattern** selection area of the PropertyManager. Also, a preview of the linear pattern is displayed in the drawing area, refer to Figure 7-18.

Note

*If needed, you can also reverse the pattern direction by choosing the **Reverse Direction** button available at the left of the **End Condition** drop-down list in the respective rollouts of the PropertyManager. Alternatively, you can click the left mouse button on the arrow whose direction needs to be reversed. The direction of arrow defines the direction of pattern creation.*

Tip

*In SOLIDWORKS, you can also skip some of the instances from the pattern by using the **Instances to Skip** rollout of the **Linear Pattern PropertyManager**. To do so, expand the **Instances to Skip** rollout of the PropertyManager; pink dots will be displayed at the center of all the pattern instances except the parent instance. Next, move the cursor to the pink dot of the instance to be skipped and then click on it; the preview of that instance will disappear from the drawing area. Also, the position of the skipped instance in the form of a matrix will be displayed in the **Instances to Skip** selection area of the PropertyManager. You can resume the skipped instance by again clicking on the dot or by deleting the name of the instance from the **Instances to Skip** selection area.*

7. Choose the **OK** button from the PropertyManager; a linear pattern of the selected hole feature is created, as shown in Figure 7-19.

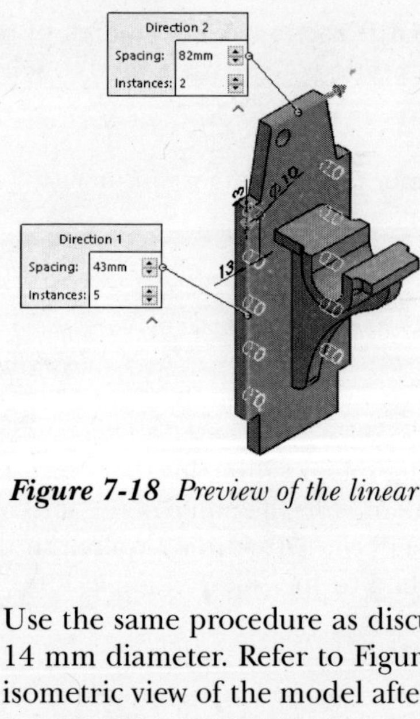

Figure 7-18 *Preview of the linear pattern*

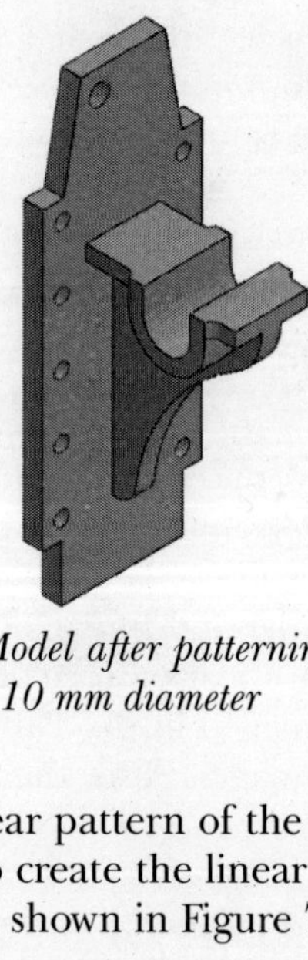

Figure 7-19 *Model after patterning the hole feature that has 10 mm diameter*

8. Use the same procedure as discussed above to create a linear pattern of the hole that has 14 mm diameter. Refer to Figure 7-2 for the parameters to create the linear pattern. The isometric view of the model after creating linear patterns is shown in Figure 7-20.

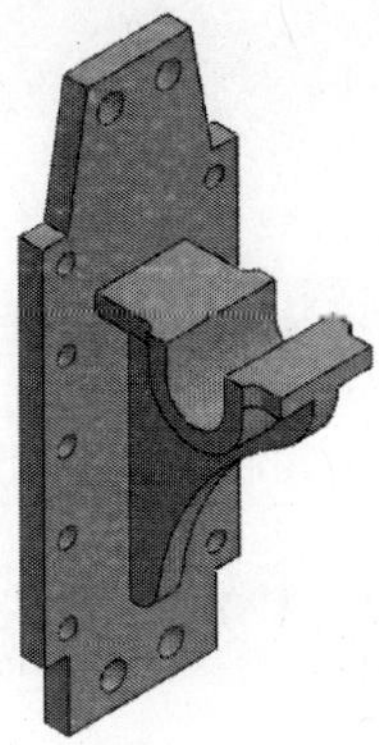

Figure 7-20 Model after patterning both the hole features

Creating the Counterbore Hole

Next, you need to create the counterbore hole of the model. First, you will create an instance of the counterbore hole by using the **Hole Wizard** tool and then pattern it by using the **Linear Pattern** tool.

1. Choose the **Hole Wizard** tool from the **Features CommandManager**; the **Hole Specification PropertyManager** is displayed.

The **Hole Wizard** tool is used to add standard holes such as the counterbore, countersink, drilled, tapped, and pipe tap holes. You can also add a user-defined counterbore drill hole, simple hole, simple drilled hole, tapered hole, and so on by using this tool. You can control all the parameters of the holes, including the termination options. You can also modify the holes according to your requirement after placing them.

2. Choose the **Counterbore** button from the **Hole Type** rollout of the PropertyManager.

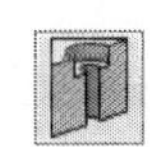

The buttons in the **Hole Type** rollout of the PropertyManager are used to define the type of standard hole to be created.

3. Select the **ANSI Metric** option from the **Standard** drop-down list of the **Hole Type** rollout PropertyManager.

The **Standard** drop-down list of the **Hole Type** rollout of the PropertyManager is used to specify the industrial dimensioning and hole standards.

4. Select the **Socket Button Head Cap Screw - ANSI B18.3.4M** option from the **Type** drop-down list of the **Hole Type** rollout.

The **Type** drop-down list of the **Hole Type** rollout of the PropertyManager is used to define the type of fastener to be inserted in the hole.

Note

*The standard holes that are created using the **Hole Wizard** tool depend on the type and the size of the fastener to be inserted in the hole.*

5. Select the **M8** option from the **Size** drop-down list of the **Hole Specifications** rollout in the PropertyManager.

The **Size** drop-down list of the **Hole Specifications** rollout is used to define the size of the fastener to be inserted in the hole that you are creating by using the **Hole Wizard** tool.

6. Select the **Show custom size** check box to customize the size of the counterbore hole and then enter the following parameters in the **Hole Specification** rollout:

   Through Hole Diameter: **8.5 mm** Counterbore Diameter: **14 mm**
   Counterbore Depth: **4.2 mm**

The **Show custom sizing** check box of the **Hole Specifications** rollout is used to create a user-defined hole feature.

7. Make sure that the **Through All** option is selected in the **End Condition** drop-down list of the **End Condition** rollout in the PropertyManager.

The **End Condition** drop-down list of the **End Condition** rollout in the PropertyManager is used to define the termination of the hole feature.

After specifying the parameters for the counterbore hole, you need to define its placement position.

8. Choose the **Positions** tab from the **Hole Specification PropertyManager**; you are prompted to select a face on which you want to place the hole.

9. Select the top planar face of the second extruded feature as the placement face for the counterbore hole. As soon as you select the placement face, the preview of the hole feature is displayed attached with the cursor and you are prompted to use dimensions and other sketching tools to position the center of the holes.

10. Click the left mouse button anywhere on the top planar face of the second extruded feature to define an arbitrary location for the placement of the hole feature, refer to Figure 7-21.

11. Choose the **Smart Dimension** button from the **Sketch CommandManager** and apply the dimensions, refer to Figure 7-22. Next, exit the **Smart Dimension** tool.

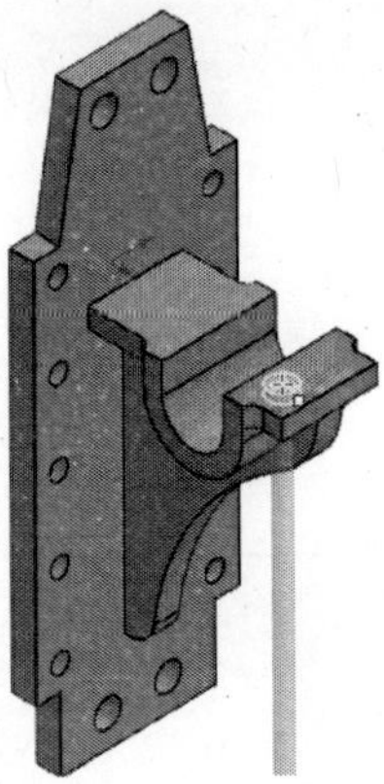

Figure 7-21 Preview of the counterbore hole

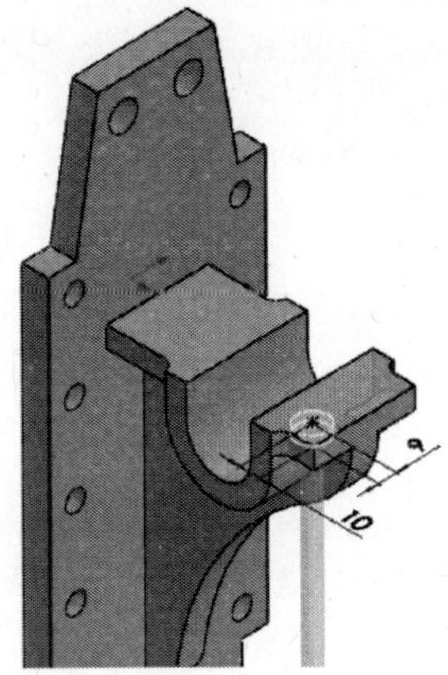

Figure 7-22 The preview of the counterbore hole after defining its placement position

12. Choose **OK** from the **Hole Position PropertyManager** to end the feature creation and click anywhere in the drawing area. Figure 7-23 shows the model after creating the counterbore hole.

Patterning the Counterbore Hole

After creating the first instance of the counterbore hole, you need to pattern it by using the **Linear Pattern** tool to create other instances of the counterbore hole.

1. Invoke the **Linear Pattern PropertyManager** by choosing the **Linear Pattern** button from the **Features CommandManager** and create a linear pattern of the counterbore hole, as shown in Figure 7-24. Refer to Figure 7-1 for its parameters.

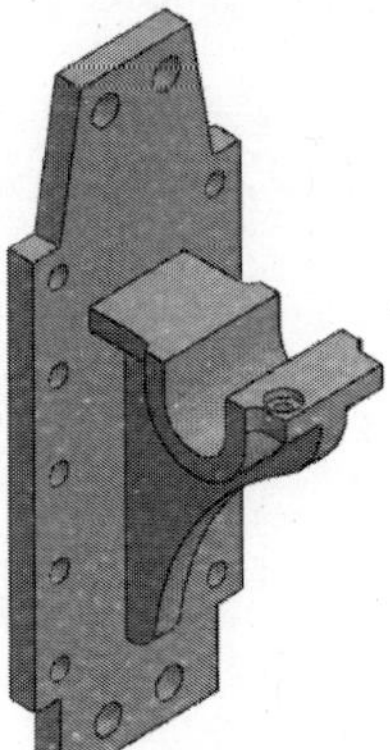

Figure 7-23 Model after creating the first instance of the counterbore hole

Figure 7-24 Final model after creating all the features

Saving the Model

Next, you need to save the document.

1. Choose the **Save** button from the Menu Bar and save the document with the name *c07_tut01* at the location given next.

   \Documents\SOLIDWORKS Tutorials\c07

2. Choose **File > Close** from the SOLIDWORKS menus to close the file.

Tutorial 2

In this tutorial, you will create the model shown in Figure 7-25. The dimensions of the model are shown in the same figure. Also, you will create a section view of the model using the **Section View** tool. **(Expected time: 30 min)**

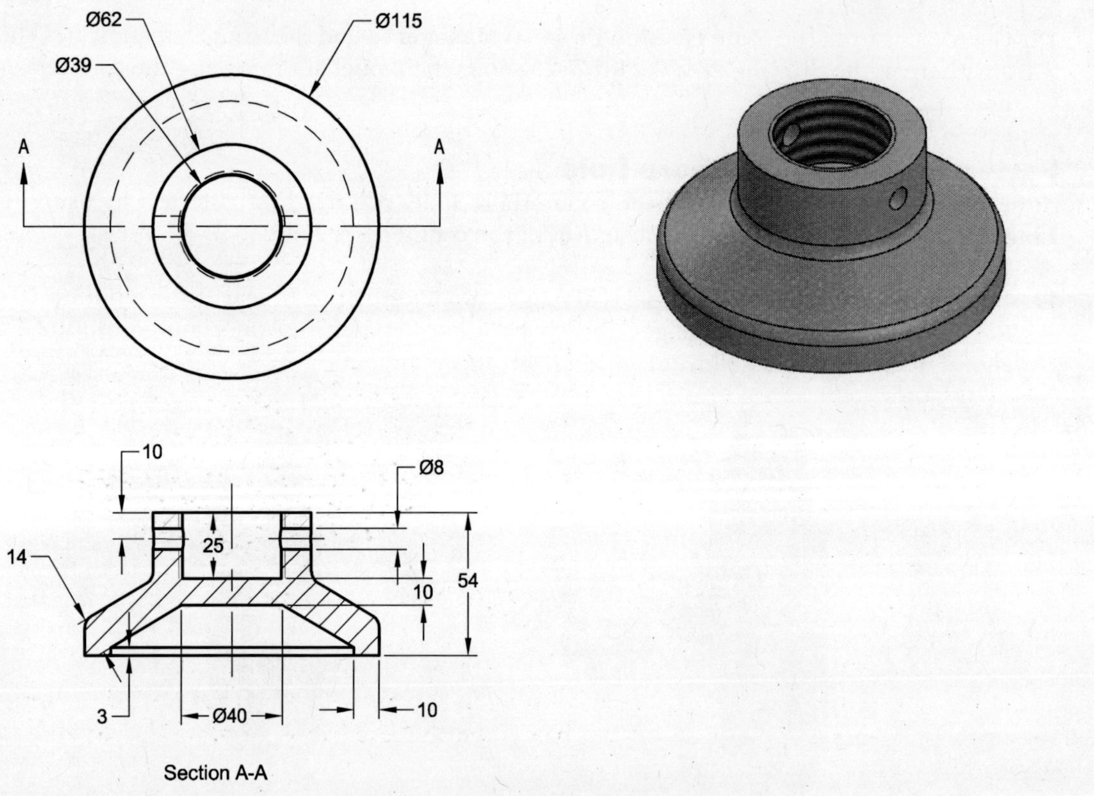

***Figure 7-25** Dimensions and views for Tutorial 2*

The following steps are required to complete this tutorial:

a. Create the base feature of the model by revolving the sketch, refer to Figures 7-26 and 7-27.
b. Create the cut feature, refer to Figure 7-28.
c. Apply cosmetic threads, refer to Figure 7-30 and then change its display style to shaded cosmetic threads, refer to Figure 7-31.
d. Add a fillet to the base feature, refer to Figure 7-34.
e. Display the section view of the model, refer to Figure 7-35.
f. Save the model.

Creating the Base Feature

The base feature of the model is a revolve feature.

1. Start a new SOLIDWORKS part document and then invoke the sketcher environment by selecting the **Front Plane** as the sketching plane.

2. Draw the sketch of the revolve feature, as shown in Figure 7-26.

3. Invoke the **Revolved Boss/Base** tool and revolve the sketch by selecting its vertical centerline as the axis of revolution. The isometric view of the model after creating the revolved feature is shown in Figure 7-27.

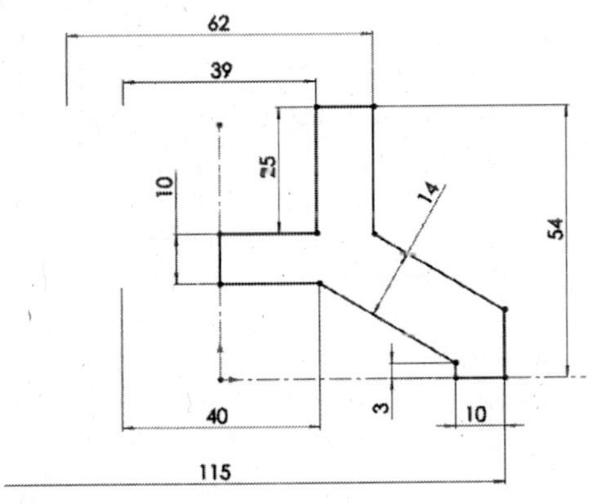

Figure 7-26 *Sketch of the base feature*

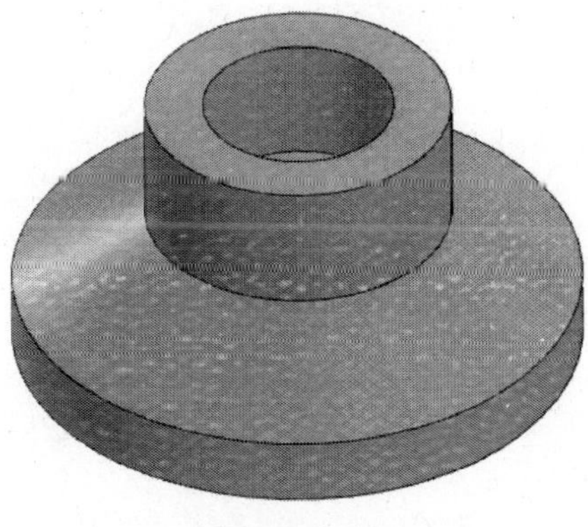

Figure 7-27 *Model after creating the base feature*

Creating the Cut Feature

The second feature of the model is a cut feature. The sketch of the cut feature will be drawn on the **Right Plane** and then you will extrude it by using the **Through All** option in both the directions of the sketching plane.

1. Invoke the **Extruded Cut** tool and select the **Right Plane** as the sketching plane to invoke the sketcher environment.

2. Orient the model normal to the sketching plane and draw a circle of diameter 8 mm using the **Circle** tool. Refer to Figure 7-25 for the placement of the circle.

3. Exit the sketching environment; the **Cut-Extrude PropertyManager** is displayed. Also, the preview of the cut feature is displayed in the drawing area with the default values of the **Blind** option.

4. Change the view orientation to isometric. Next, select the **Through All- Both** option from the **End Conditon** drop-down lists in the **Direction 1** rollout.

5. Choose the **OK** button from the PropertyManager; the cut feature is created, as shown in Figure 7-28.

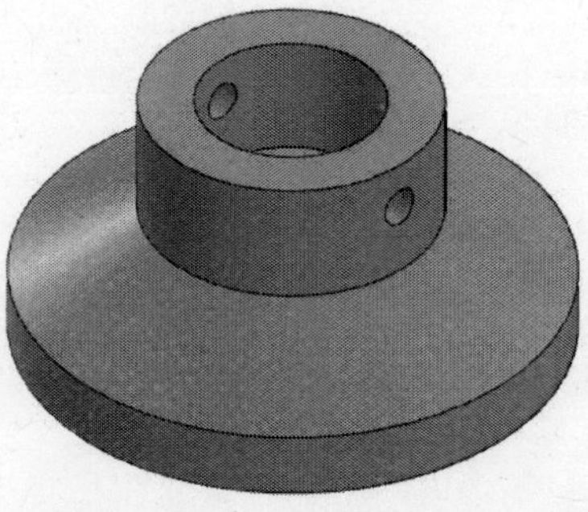

Figure 7-28 *Model after creating the cut feature*

Applying Cosmetic Threads

It is evident from Figure 7-25 that the cosmetic threads are required in the top inner circular edge of the model. The cosmetic threads are applied by using the **Cosmetic Thread** tool. These threads are used to schematically represent threads.

1. Choose **Insert > Annotations > Cosmetic Thread** from the SOLIDWORKS menus; the **Cosmetic Thread PropertyManager** is displayed. Also, you are prompted to select the edges and set of parameters for applying the cosmetic threads.

The **Cosmetic Thread** tool is used for schematic representation of threads in the circular face of the model.

Note

Generally, the creation of threads in a model is avoided as it results in a complex geometry. The views generated from the models having complex geometry are difficult to understand. Therefore, it is better to avoid creating threads in the model, and add the cosmetic threads instead. It is also recommended that you use the cosmetic threads to get the thread convention in the drawing views.

2. Select the top circular inner edge of the model, refer to Figure 7-29; the name of the selected edge is displayed in the **Circular Edges** selection area of the PropertyManager.

3. Select the **ANSI Metric** option from the **Standard** drop-down list of the PropertyManager.

4. Select the **Machine Threads** option from the **Type** drop-down list of the PropertyManager.

5. Make sure **M42x3.0** is selected in the **Size** drop-down list and the **Up to Next** option is selected in the **End Condition** drop-down list of the PropertyManager.

6. After defining all parameters for the cosmetic threads in the **Cosmetic Thread PropertyManager**, choose the **OK** button to exit it. The cosmetic threads are applied to the model and represented by a circle, as shown in Figure 7-30.

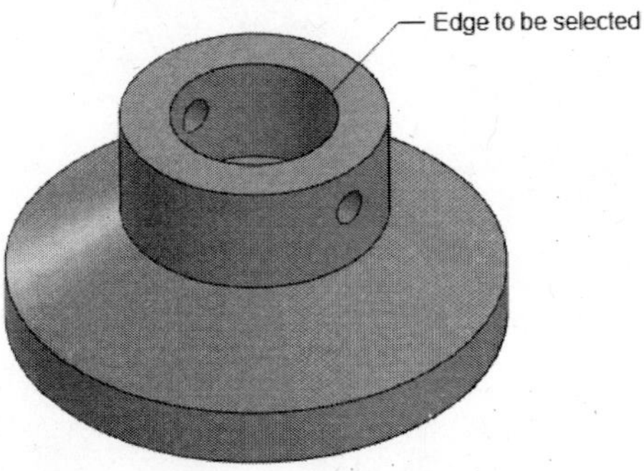

Figure 7-29 *Edge to be selected*

Figure 7-30 *The model after applying cosmetic threads*

As it is evident from Figure 7-25 that the cosmetic threads are displayed in the shaded mode. Therefore, you also need to display the cosmetic threads in the shaded mode.

7. Invoke the **System Options - General** dialog box by choosing the **Options** button from the Menu Bar.

8. Choose the **Document Properties** tab from this dialog box; the **System Options - General** dialog box is changed to the **Document Properties - Drafting Standard** dialog box.

9. Select the **Detailing** option from the left side area of the dialog box; the options related to the detailing are displayed on the right side of the dialog box.

10. Select the **Shaded cosmetic threads** check box from the **Display filter** area of the dialog box.

11. Choose the **OK** button from the dialog box; the cosmetic threads applied to the model are displayed in the shaded mode, as shown in Figure 7-31.

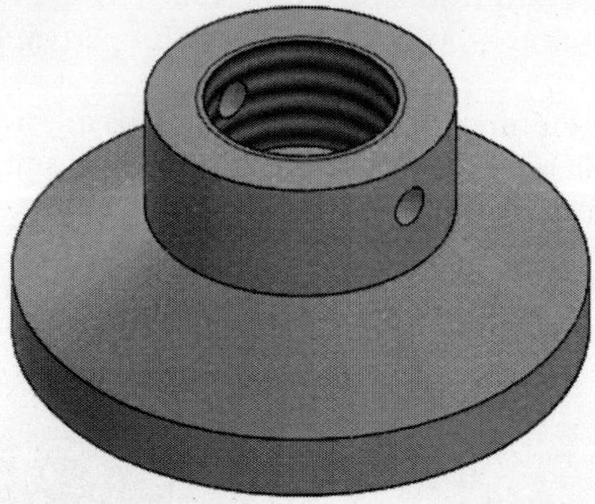

Figure 7-31 *Model after displaying the cosmetic threads in the shaded mode*

Tip

You can also edit the cosmetic threads after applying them to the circular face of the model. To edit the cosmetic threads applied to a feature, expand the node corresponding to that feature in the ***FeatureManager Design Tree*** *and then select the* ***Cosmetic Thread****; a pop-up toolbar will be displayed. Choose the* ***Edit Feature*** *option from the pop-up toolbar to display the* ***Cosmetic Thread PropertyManager*** *for editing the parameters of the selected cosmetic thread.*

Creating the Fillet Features

After creating all the features, you need to add fillets to the model by using the **Fillet** tool.

1. Choose the **Fillet** tool from the **Features CommandManager**; the **Fillet PropertyManager** is displayed, refer to Figure 7-32. Also, you are prompted to select edges, faces, features, or loops to create fillet.

Note

If on choosing the ***Fillet*** *tool from the* ***Features CommandManager****, the* ***FilletXpert PropertyManager*** *is displayed then you need to choose the* ***Manual*** *button from it to display the* ***Fillet PropertyManager****.*

The **Fillet** tool is used to remove the sharp corners by adding or removing material from the corners based on the selected edge reference. In SOLIDWORKS, you can create different types of fillets such as constant radius fillet, variable radius fillet, face fillet, and full round fillet by selecting the respective radio buttons from the **Fillet Type** rollout of the **Fillet PropertyManager**.

2. Make sure that the **Constant Size Fillet** button is chosen in the **Fillet Type** rollout of the PropertyManager, as shown in Figure 7-32.

3. Select the edges of the model from the drawing area, refer to Figure 7-33. You can select multiple edges for creating a set of fillet with same size. As soon as you select the edges of the model, a preview of the fillet with the default values and the radius callout are displayed in the drawing area.

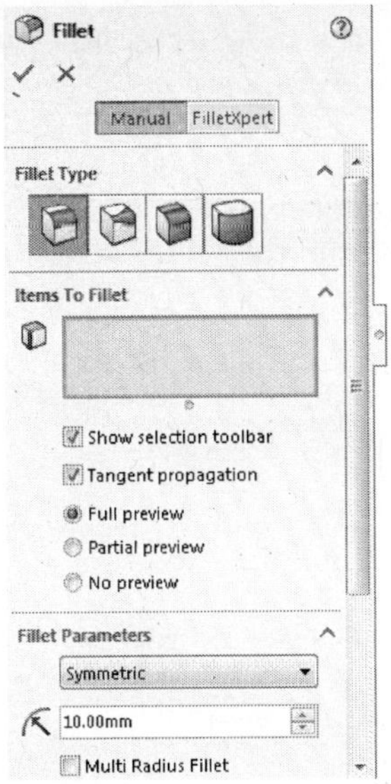

*Figure 7-32 Partial view of the **Fillet PropertyManager***

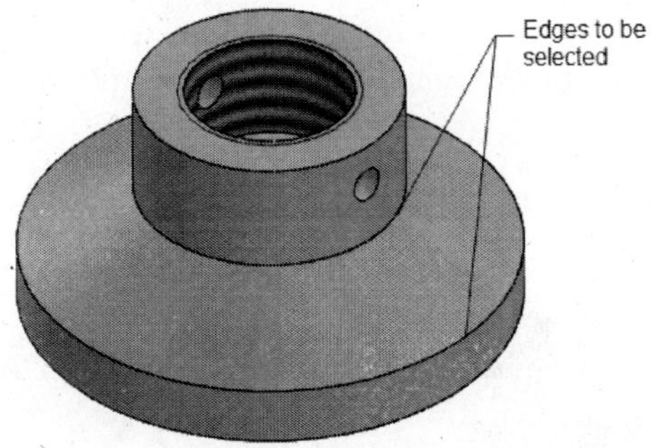

Figure 7-33 Edges to be selected

Note

*You can also define different fillet radius for the edges by selecting the **Multiple radius** check box in the **Fillet PropertyManager** and specifying the appropriate radius.*

4. Set the value in the **Radius** spinner to **5** and choose the **OK** button from the **Fillet PropertyManager**. Figure 7-34 shows the model after adding the fillets.

Displaying the Section View of the Model

Next, you need to display the section view of the model. The section view of the model will be created using the **Section View PropertyManager**.

1. Orient the model to the isometric view.

2. Choose the **Section View** button from the **View (Heads-Up)** toolbar; the **Section View PropertyManager** is displayed with the **Front Plane** selected as the default section plane. As a result, the preview of the section view by using the **Front Plane** as the section plane is displayed in the drawing area along with the handle at the center of the section plane.

You can manipulate the section plane by using the spinners available in the **Section 1** rollout of the PropertyManager. You can also drag the handle that is displayed at the center of the section plane for dynamically adjusting the offset distance of the section plane.

Tip

*If you need to select the **Right Plane** or the **Top Plane** as the section plane, choose the respective buttons from the **Section 1** rollout of the **Section View PropertyManager**.*

The **Section View** tool is used to display the section view of the model by cutting it using a plane or a face. You can also save the section view with a name to generate the section view directly on the drawing sheet in the drawing environment.

3. Choose the **OK** button from the **Section View PropertyManager** to display the section view of the model. The section view of the model is shown in Figure 7-35.

4. Again choose the **Section View** button from the **View (Heads-Up)** toolbar to return to the full view mode.

Saving the Model

1. Save the part document with the name *c07_tut02* at the following location:

   \Documents\SOLIDWORKS Tutorials\c07

2. Choose **File> Close** from the SOLIDWORKS menu to close the document.

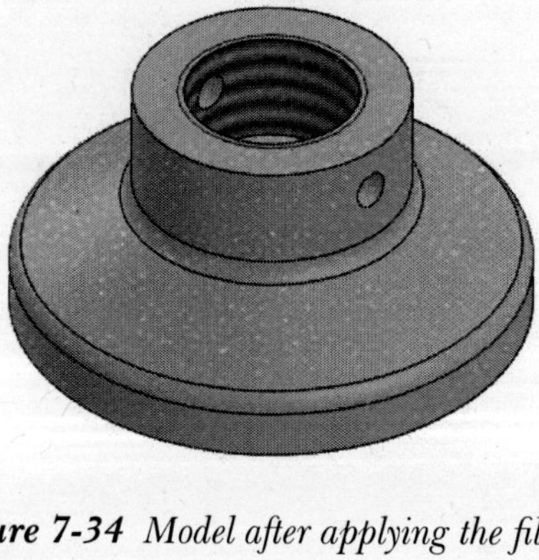

Figure 7-34 *Model after applying the fillets*

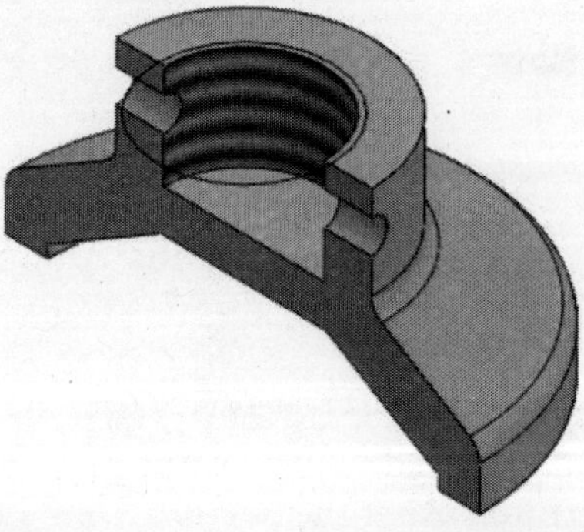

Figure 7-35 *Section view of the model*

Tutorial 3

In this tutorial, you will create the model shown in Figure 7-36. The views and dimensions of the model are shown in Figure 7-37. You will first create a sketch of the top view of the model and then extrude it by selecting different contours in it. **(Expected time: 45 min)**

Figure 7-36 Model for Tutorial 3

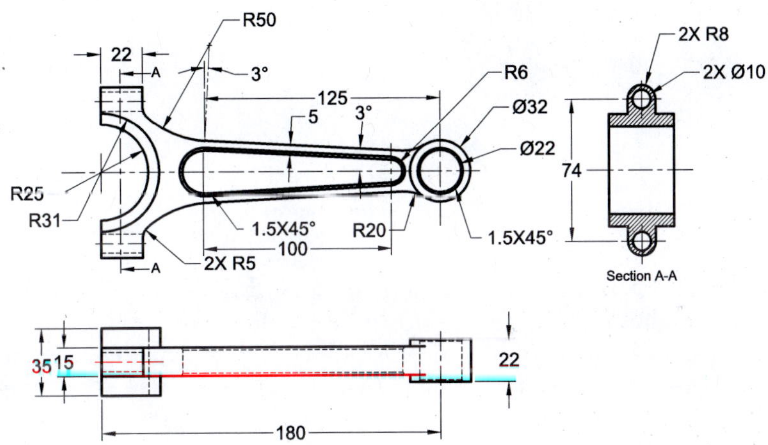

Figure 7-37 Dimensions and views for Tutorial 3

The following steps are required to complete this tutorial:

a. Create the sketch of the top view of the model, refer to Figure 7-38.
b. Invoke the **Extrude Boss/Base** tool and extrude the selected contour, refer to Figures 7-39 and 7-40.
c. Select the other set of contours and extrude them to the required distance, refer to Figures 7-41 and 7-42.
d. Select the other set of contours and extrude them to the required distance, refer to Figure 7-43.
e. Create the full round fillets, refer to Figures 7-45 through 7-47.
f. Create the user-defined hole by using the **Hole Wizard** tool, refer to Figure 7-49.
g. Create the mirror image of the previously created user-defined hole, refer to Figure 7-50.
h. Create the chamfer features, refer to Figure 7-54.
i. Save the model.

Creating the Sketch of the Model

1. Start a new SOLIDWORKS part document using the **New SOLIDWORKS Document** dialog box.

   As mentioned in the tutorial description, you will draw the sketch of the top view of the model and extrude it by selecting its different contours. You can also create this model by creating a separate sketch for each sketch based feature and then converting them into features.

2. Invoke the sketcher environment by selecting the **Top Plane** as the sketching plane and draw the sketch of the base feature, as shown in Figure 7-38. Exit the sketching environment.

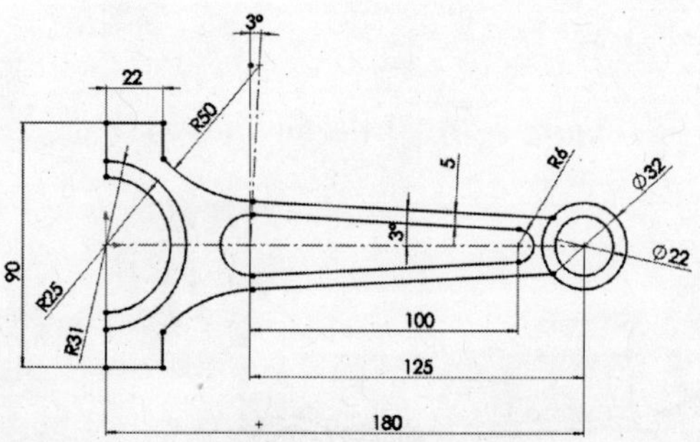

Figure 7-38 *Sketch of the top view of the model*

Selecting and Extruding the Contours of the Sketch

You need to use the contour selection method to create the model. Therefore, you first need to select one of the contours from the given sketch and then extrude it. For a better view, you can also orient the sketch to the isometric view.

1. Choose the **Isometric** button from the **View Orientation** flyout in the **View (Heads-Up)** toolbar; the sketch is displayed in the isometric view. 

2. Right-click in the drawing area to invoke a shortcut menu. Expand the shortcut menu, if required. Next, choose the **Contour Select Tool** option from the shortcut menu; the select cursor is replaced by the contour selection cursor and the selection confirmation corner is displayed.

3. Select the sketch and then select the close contour, refer to Figure 7-39.

Note

As evident from Figure 7-39, a centerline is dividing the contours of the sketch. You may need to press the CTRL key for selecting the close contours of the sketch.

4. Choose the **Extruded Boss/Base** tool from the **Features CommandManager**; the **Boss-Extrude PropertyManager** is invoked and the preview of the base feature is displayed in the drawing area.

Also, the name of the selected contour is displayed in the selection box of the **Selected Contours** rollout.

5. Right-click in the drawing area to display the shortcut menu. Next, choose the **Mid Plane** option from it.

6. Enter **15** in the **Depth** spinner and choose the **OK** button; the selected contour is extruded, as shown in Figure 7-40.

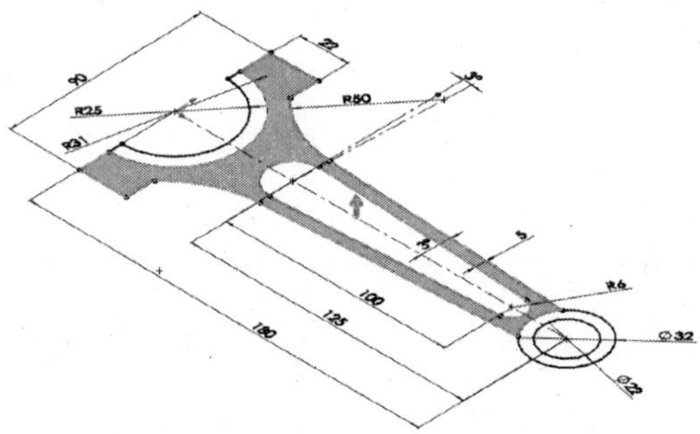

Figure 7-39 The closed area selected as a contour

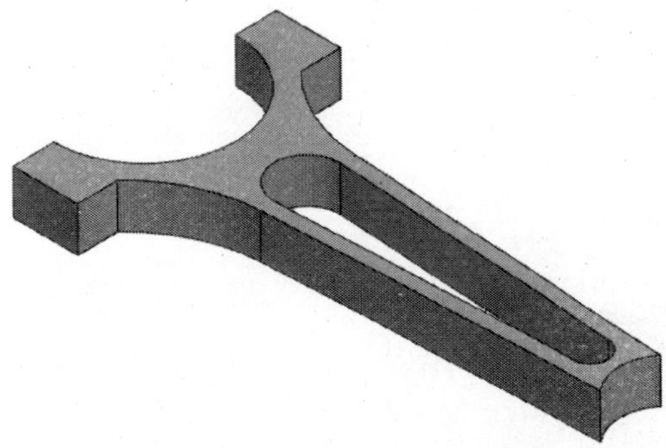

Figure 7-40 Model after extruding the contour

7. Select the sketch from the **FeatureManager Design Tree** and then right-click in the drawing area to invoke a shortcut menu. Next, choose the **Contour Select Tool** option from the shortcut menu.

8. Select the close contour of the sketch, refer to Figure 7-41. Next, invoke the **Extruded Boss/Base** tool and extrude the sketch upto the depth of 22 mm by using the **Mid Plane** option, as shown in Figure 7-42.

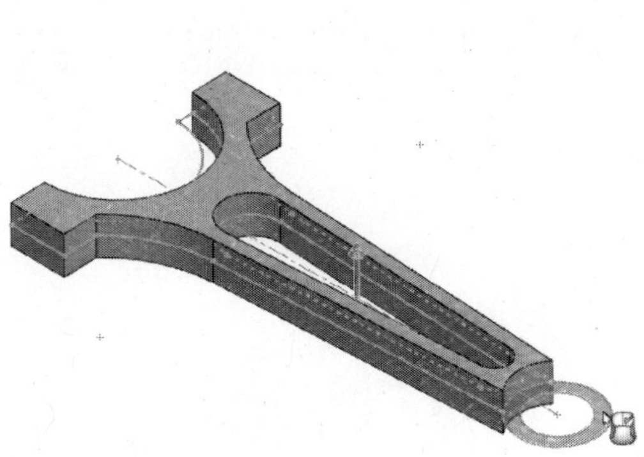

Figure 7-41 Contour selected for extrusion

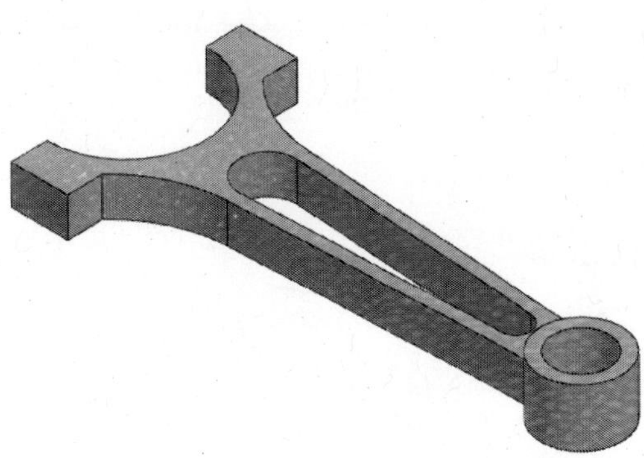

Figure 7-42 Model after extruding contours of the sketch

9. Similarly, extrude the other contours of the sketch. The model after extruding all contours of the sketch is shown in Figure 7-43.

Figure 7-43 Model after extruding all the contours of the sketch

Creating the Fillet Features

After creating the extrude features, you need to add full round fillets to the model.

1. Choose the **Fillet** tool from the **Features CommandManager**; the **Fillet PropertyManager** is displayed.

2. Select the **Full Round Fillet** button from the **Fillet Type** rollout of the **PropertyManager**; the **Face Set 1**, **Center Face Set**, and **Face Set 2** selection areas are displayed in the **Items To Fillet** rollout of the PropertyManager. Note that the **Face Set 1** selection box is activated by default in this rollout.

3. Select a face as the face set 1, refer to Figure 7-44.

4. Click on the **Center Face Set** selection box to activate it. Now, select the side face of the model as the center face set, refer to Figure 7-44.

5. Activate the **Face Set 2** selection box and then select the face as the face set 2, refer to Figure 7-44. Preview of the full round fillet on the selected face sets is displayed in the drawing area with their respective callouts, as shown in Figure 7-45.

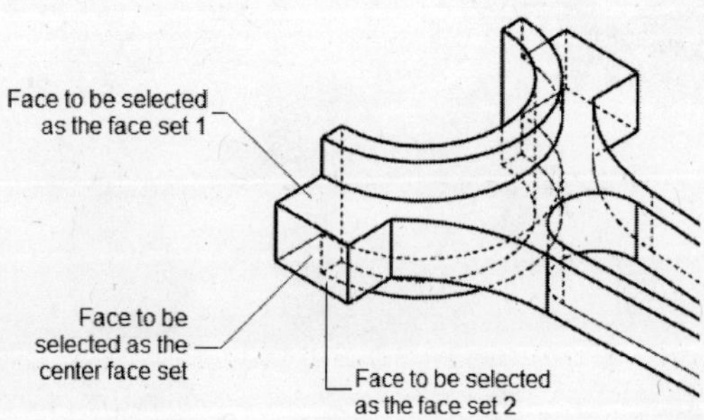

Figure 7-44 Faces to be selected

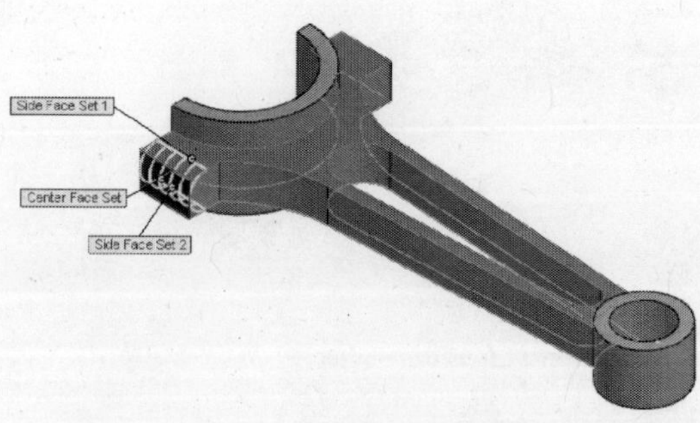

Figure 7-45 Preview of the full round fillet

Note

In Figure 7-44, the display state of the model has been changed to Hidden Lines Visible display state by choosing the ***Hidden Lines Visible*** *button from the* ***Display Style*** *flyout of the* ***View (Heads-Up)*** *toolbar.*

6. Choose the **OK** button from the **PropertyManager**; the full round fillet is created, as shown in Figure 7-46.

7. Similarly, create the full round fillets on the other side feature of the model, as shown in Figure 7-47.

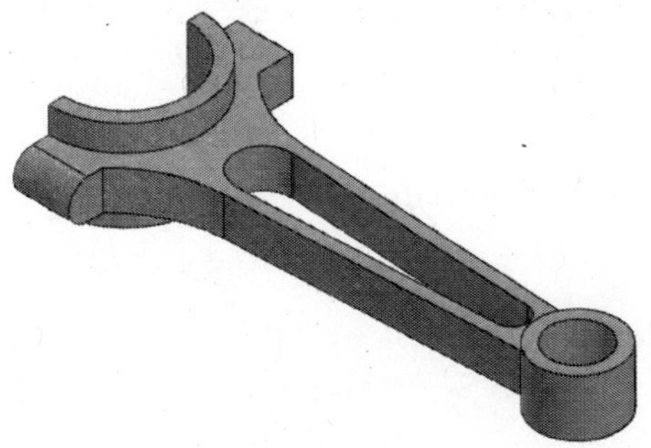

Figure 7-46 *Model after creating the full round fillet on one side*

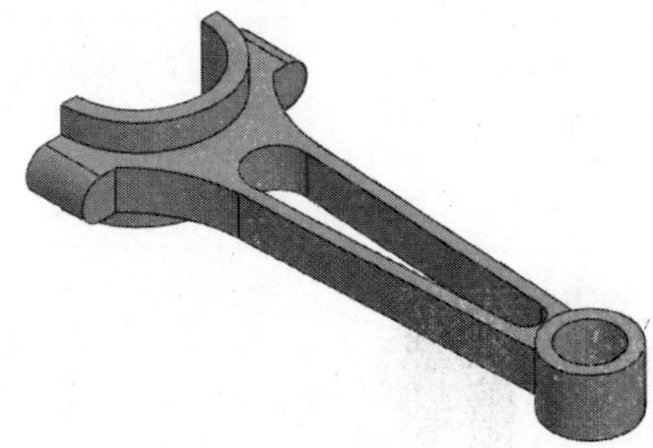

Figure 7-47 *Model after creating full round fillet on the other side*

Creating the User-Defined Holes Using the Hole Wizard Tool

Next, you will create a user-defined hole by using the **Hole Wizard** tool. First you will create a hole on one side of the model by using the **Hole Wizard** tool and then mirror it on the other side of the model by using the **Mirror** tool.

1. Choose the **Hole Wizard** tool from the **Features CommandManager**; the **Hole Specification PropertyManager** is displayed.

The **Hole Wizard** tool is used to create standard holes such as the counterbore, countersink, drilled, tapped, and pipe tap holes. You can also create a user-defined counterbore drill hole, simple hole, simple drilled hole, tapered hole, and so on by using this tool. You can control all the parameters of the holes, including the termination options. You can also modify the holes according to your requirement after placing them.

2. Choose the **Legacy Hole** button from the **Hole Type** rollout of the PropertyManager.

The **Legacy Hole** button is used to create a user-defined hole.

3. Make sure that the **Simple** option is selected in the **Type** drop-down list of the PropertyManager.

4. Double-click in the **Value** field of the **Diameter** in the **Section Dimensions** rollout of the PropertyManager; an edit box is displayed. Enter **10** in the edit box.

5. Select the **Through All** option from the **End Condition** drop-down list of the **End Condition** rollout of the PropertyManager.

   After specifying the parameter for the user-defined hole, you need to specify its placement position.

6. Choose the **Positions** tab from the **Hole Specification PropertyManager**; you are prompted to select a face on which you want to place the hole.

7. Select the planar face of the model as shown in Figure 7-48. As soon as you select the placement face, the preview of the hole feature is attached with the cursor and you are prompted to use dimensions and other sketching tools to position the center of the holes.

8. Click the left mouse button on the planar face when the cursor snaps to the center point of the semi-circular edge of the feature and coincident relation is displayed below the cursor.

Note

If the cursor does not snap to the center point of the semi-circular edge, move the cursor toward the semi-circular edge to highlight its center point. When the center point is highlighted, click on it.

9. Choose **OK** from the **Hole Position PropertyManager** to end the feature creation and click anywhere in the drawing area. Figure 7-49 shows the model after creating the user-defined hole.

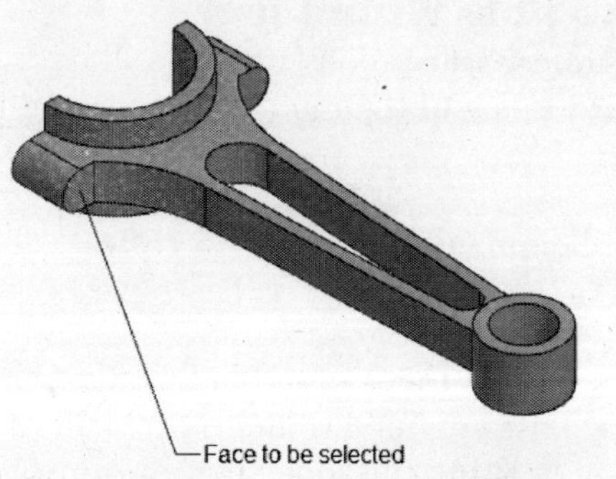

Figure 7-48 *Face to be selected*

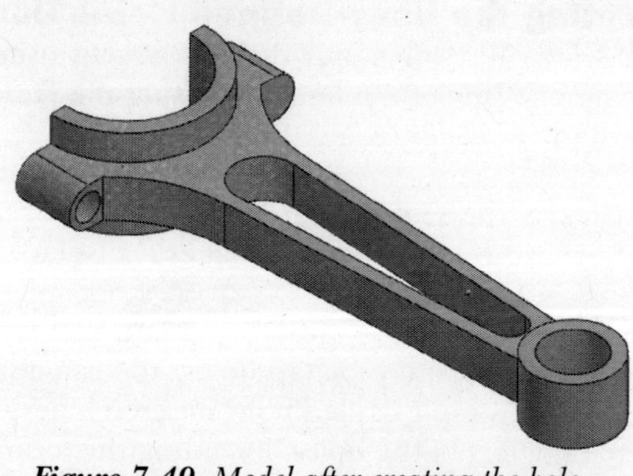

Figure 7-49 *Model after creating the hole*

Mirroring the Feature

Now, you need to create a mirror copy of the last created cut feature by using the **Mirror** tool.

1. Choose the **Mirror** button from the **Features CommandManager**; the **Mirror PropertyManager** is displayed on the left of the drawing area. Also, you are prompted to select a plane or a planar face about which the features need to be mirrored.

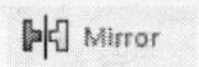

2. Select the **Front Plane** as the mirroring plane from the **FeatureManager Design Tree** and then select the previously created hole feature as the feature to be mirrored; the preview of the mirror feature is displayed in the drawing area.

3. Choose the **OK** button from the PropertyManager; the mirror copy of the hole feature is created, as shown in Figure 7-50.

Creating the Chamfer Features

The next feature that you need to add to this model is a chamfer feature.

1. Choose the **Chamfer** tool from the **Fillet** flyout of the **Features CommandManager**, refer to Figure 7-51; the **Chamfer PropertyManager** is displayed, refer to Figure 7-52.

Chamfering is a process in which the sharp edges of the model are beveled in order to reduce the area of stress concentration. This process also eliminates the undesirable sharp edges and corners of the model.

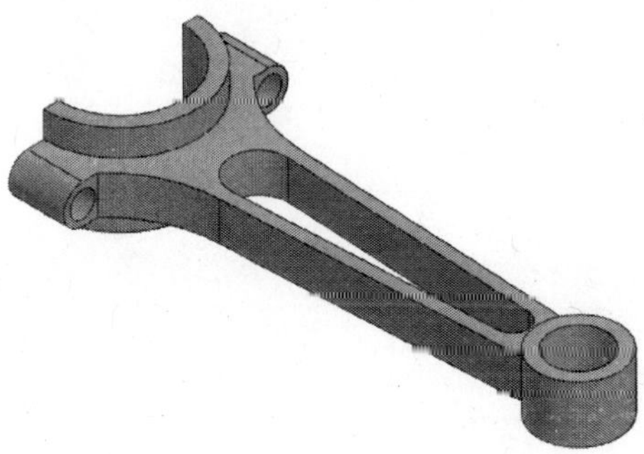

Figure 7-50 Model after mirroring the hole

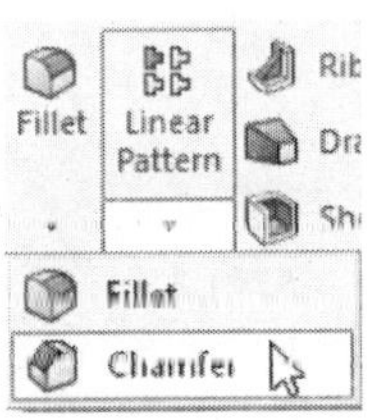

*Figure 7-51 The **Fillet** flyout*

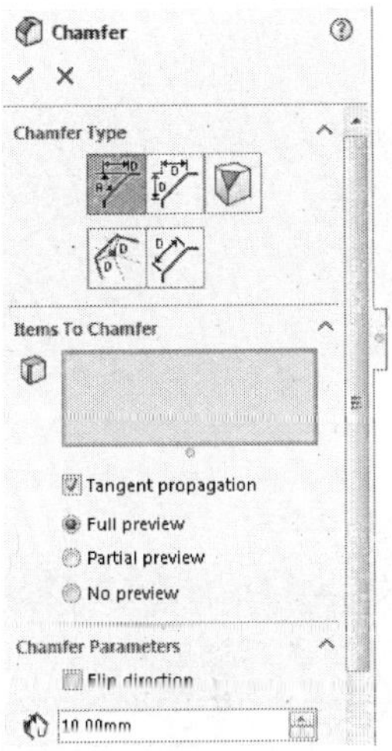

*Figure 7-52 The **Chamfer PropertyManager***

2. Select the **Angle distance** radio button from the **Chamfer Parameters** rollout of the PropertyManager.

By default, the **Angle distance** radio button is selected. Therefore, after selecting the edge to be chamfered, the distance and angle callouts are displayed in the drawing area. Set the value of the distance and angle in the **Distance** and **Angle** spinners of the PropertyManager or enter the values directly in the **Distance** and **Angle** callouts. The **Flip direction** check box of the **Chamfer PropertyManager** is used to specify the direction of the distance measurement. You can also flip the direction by clicking on the arrow in the drawing area.

If you select the **Distance Distance** radio button from the **Chamfer Parameters** rollout, the **Distance** spinner is displayed in which you can specify chamfer distance to create the chamfer. Also, you can specify the chamfer method by selecting an option from the **Chamfer Method** drop-down list. The **Offset Face chamfer** option creates a chamfer by offsetting the faces adjacent to the selected edges. And, the **Face Face chamfer** option blends non-adjacent and non-continuous faces.

3. Set the value of the **Distance** spinner to **1.5** and the **Angle** spinner to **45** in the PropertyManager.

4. Make sure that the **Tangent propagation** check box is selected in the PropertyManager.

The **Tangent propagation** check box is selected by default. Therefore, the edges that are tangent to the selected edge are selected automatically.

5. Select the edges of the model one by one to apply the chamfer, refer to Figure 7-53; the preview of the chamfer features is displayed in the drawing area.

6. Choose the **OK** button from the PropertyManager. The isometric view of the final model after creating the chamfer features is shown in Figure 7-54.

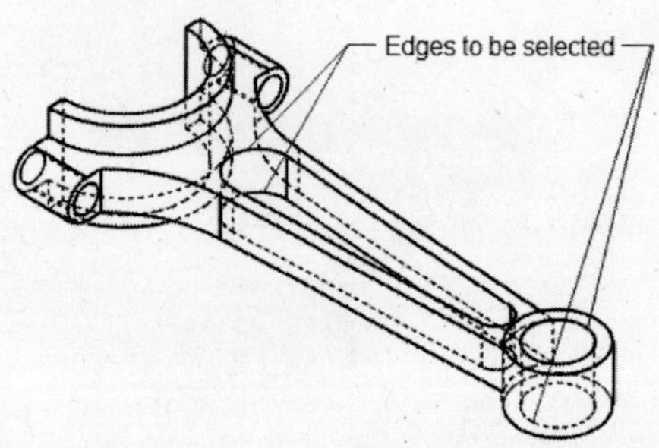

Figure 7-53 *Edges to be selected*

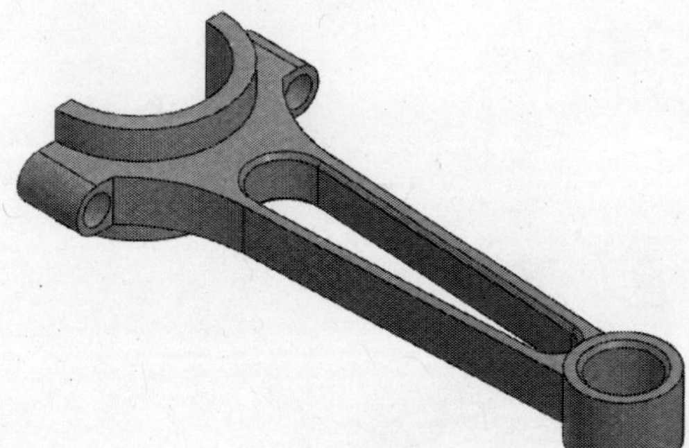

Figure 7-54 *Final model for Tutorial 3*

Saving the Model

1. Save the part document with the name *c07_tut03* at the location given next.

   \Documents\SOLIDWORKS Tutorials\c07

2. Choose **File > Close** from the SOLIDWORKS menus to close the document.

Self-Evaluation Test

Answer the following questions and then compare them to those given at the end of this chapter:

1. If you want to specify different distances while creating a chamfer, clear the ________ check box.

2. The ________ radio button is used to apply the full round fillet feature.

3. The ________ tool is used to create a rib feature.

4. The ________ tool is used for the schematic representation of threads on a circular face of the model.

5. You can create standard counterbore, countersink, and tapped holes using the **Hole PropertyManager**. (T/F)

6. The hole features created using the **Hole Wizard** tool and the **Hole PropertyManager** are not parametric. (T/F)

7. You cannot define a user-defined hole using the **Hole Wizard** tool. (T/F)

8. You cannot preselect the edges or faces for creating a fillet feature. (T/F)

Review Questions

Answer the following questions:

1. Which of the following options, when selected, does not require a radius to create a fillet feature?

   (a) **Face fillet with hold line** (b) **Constant radius fillet**
   (c) **Variable radius fillet** (d) **Full round fillet**

2. Which PropertyManager is displayed by default when you choose the **Hole Wizard** button from the **Features CommandManager**?

   (a) **Hole** (b) **Hole Definition**
   (c) **Hole Wizard** (d) **Hole Specification**

3. The __________ option is used to add standard holes to a model.

4. After specifying all parameters of a hole feature using the **Hole Specification PropertyManager**, the __________ tab is chosen to specify the placement of the hole feature.

5. The__________ **PropertyManager** is used to modify the fillets created at corners.

6. The __________ button from the **Hole Specifications** rollout is used to define a standard drilled hole.

7. By default, the __________ radio button is selected in the **Chamfer PropertyManager**.

8. The__________ check box from the **Display filter** area of the **Document Properties - Detailing** dialog box is used to display cosmetic treads in shaded mode.

EXERCISES

Exercise 1

Create the model shown in Figure 7-55. The views and dimensions of the model are shown in Figure 7-56. **(Expected time: 30 min)**

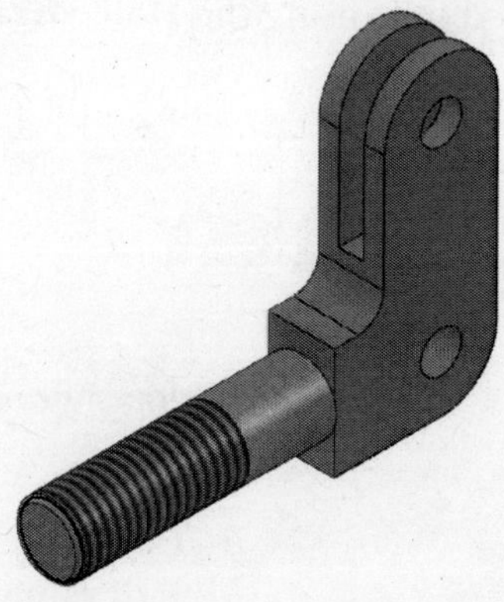

Figure 7-55 *Solid model for Exercise 1*

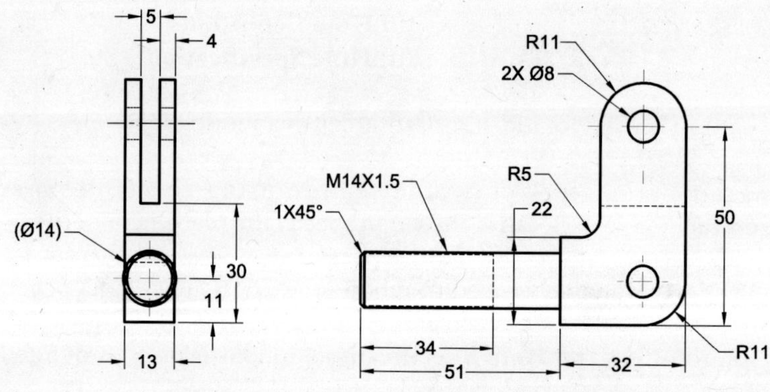

Figure 7-56 *Views and dimensions for Exercise 1*

Exercise 2

Create the model shown in Figure 7-57. The views and dimensions of the model are shown in Figure 7-58. **(Expected time: 30 min)**

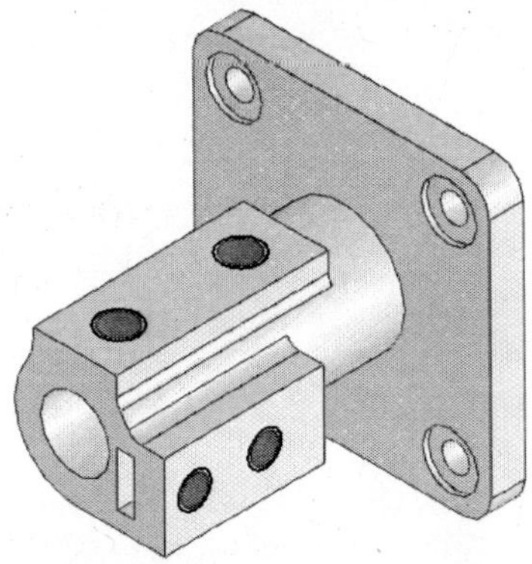

Figure 7-57 *Solid model for Exercise 2*

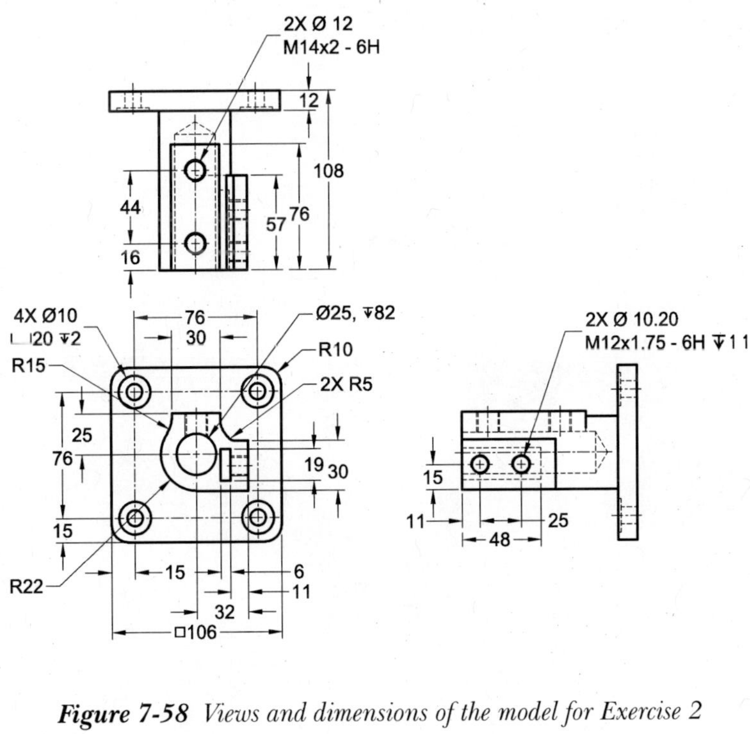

Figure 7-58 *Views and dimensions of the model for Exercise 2*

Answers to Self-Evaluation Test

1. Equal distance, **2.** Full round fillet, **3.** Rib, **4.** Cosmetic Thread, **5.** F, **6.** F, **7.** F, **8.** F

Chapter 8

Advanced Modeling Tools-II

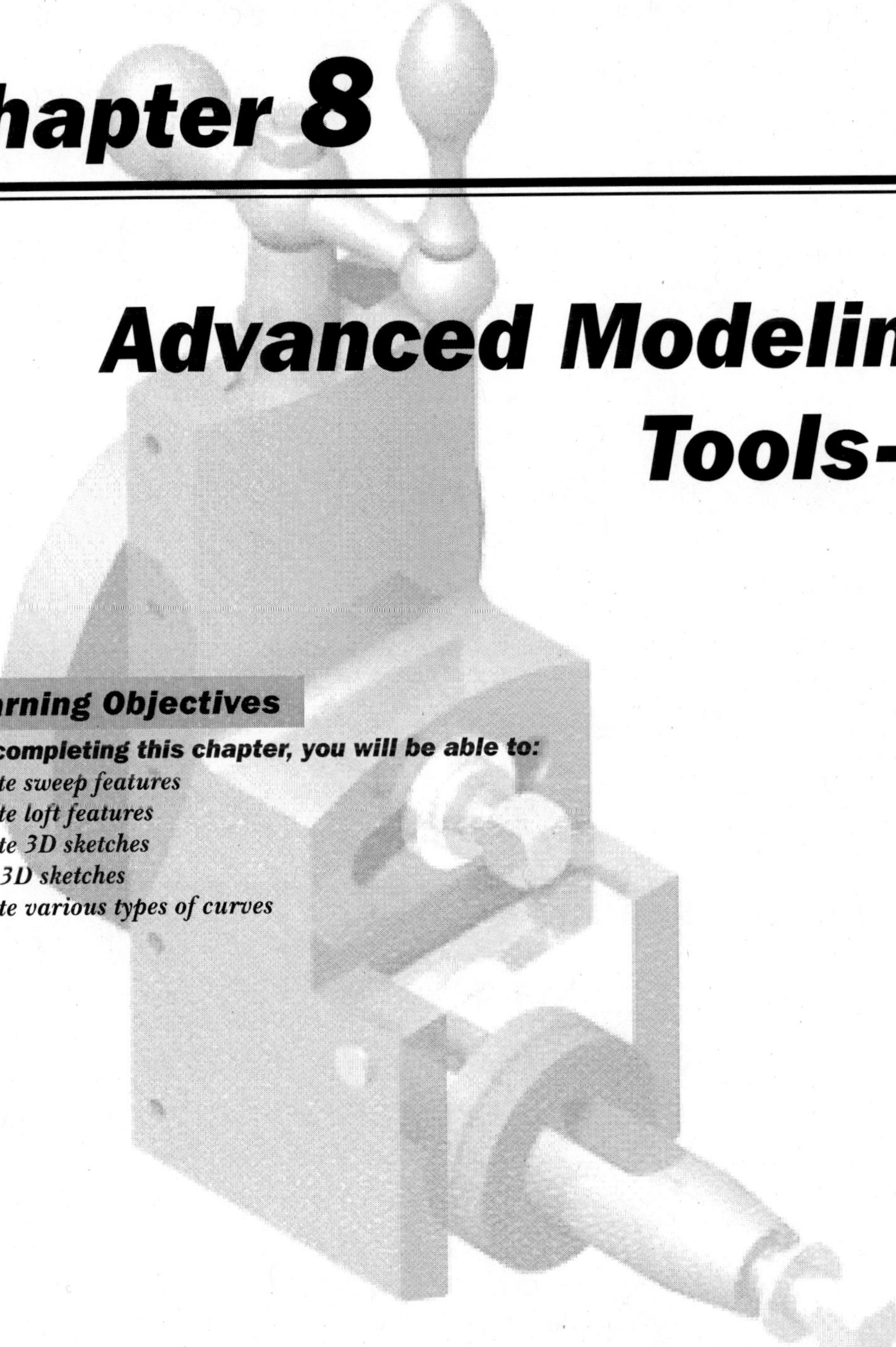

Learning Objectives

After completing this chapter, you will be able to:

- *Create sweep features*
- *Create loft features*
- *Create 3D sketches*
- *Edit 3D sketches*
- *Create various types of curves*

ADVANCED MODELING TOOLS

In the earlier chapters, some of the advanced modeling tools were discussed. In this chapter, you will learn about some more advanced modeling tools such as shell, sweep, loft, draft, curves, 3D sketches, and so on.

TUTORIALS

Tutorial 1

In this tutorial, you will create the model shown in Figure 8-1. The dimensions of the model are shown in the same figure. **(Expected time: 45 min)**

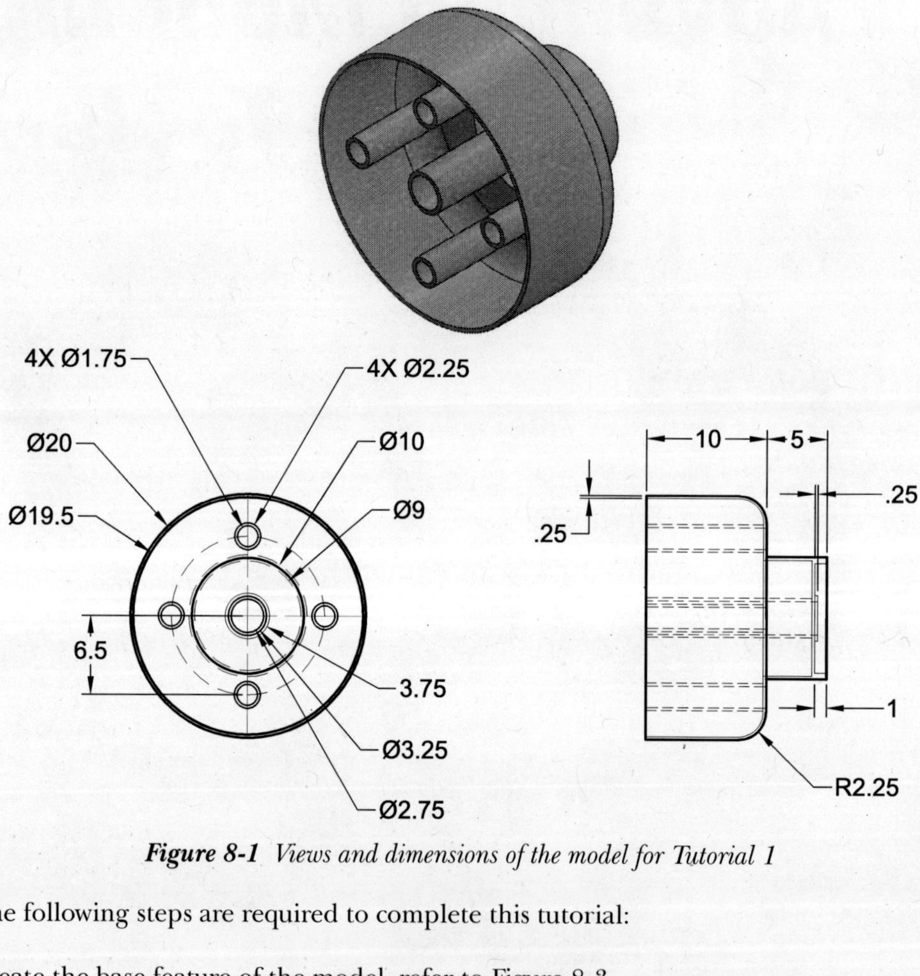

Figure 8-1 *Views and dimensions of the model for Tutorial 1*

The following steps are required to complete this tutorial:

a. Create the base feature of the model, refer to Figure 8-3.
b. Create second, third, fourth, and fifth features of the model, refer to Figures 8-4 through 8-7.
c. Create the hole feature, refer to Figures 8-8 and 8-9.
d. Create the circular pattern of the hole feature, refer to Figure 8-10.

e. Create the fillet feature, refer to Figure 8-11.
f. Create the shell feature, refer to Figure 8-12.
g. Save the model.

Creating the Base Feature

The base feature of the model is an extrude feature and the sketch of this feature is created on the Front Plane.

1. Start a new SOLIDWORKS part document using the **New SOLIDWORKS Document** dialog box.

2. Invoke the sketching environment by selecting the Front Plane as the sketching plane and draw the circle of diameter 10 mm, as shown in Figure 8-2. Next, exit the sketching environment and change the view to isometric.

3. Invoke the **Extruded Boss/Base** tool and extrude the sketch upto a depth of 5 mm. The model after creating the base feature is shown in Figure 8-3.

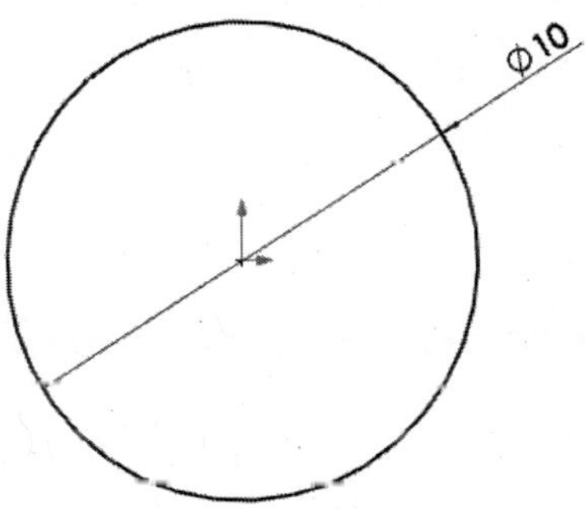

Figure 8-2 *Sketch of the base feature*

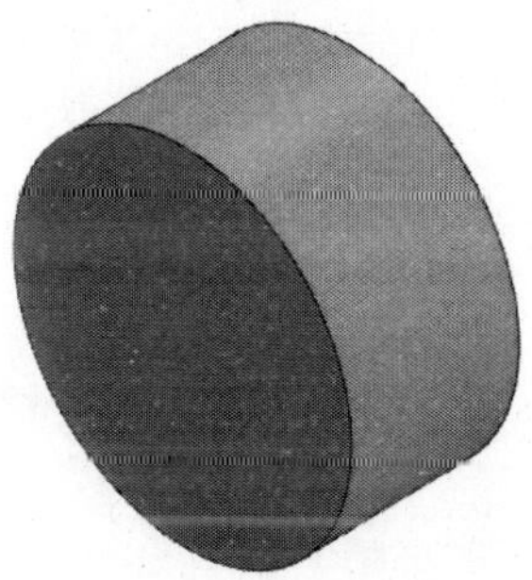

Figure 8-3 *Base feature of the model*

Creating the Second, Third, Fourth, and Fifth Features

Now, you need to create the second, third, fourth, and fifth features of the model.

1. Invoke the sketching environment by selecting the front planar face of the base feature as the sketching plane.

2. Draw a circle of diameter 20 mm. Next, invoke the **Extruded Boss/Base** tool and extrude the sketch upto a depth of 10 mm. The model after creating the second feature is shown in Figure 8-4.

   After creating the second feature, you need to create the third feature of the model.

3. Create the third feature of the model which is a cut feature. The sketch of this feature is created on the back planar face of the base feature. Figure 8-5 shows the rotated view of the model after creating the third feature. For dimensions, refer to Figure 8-1.

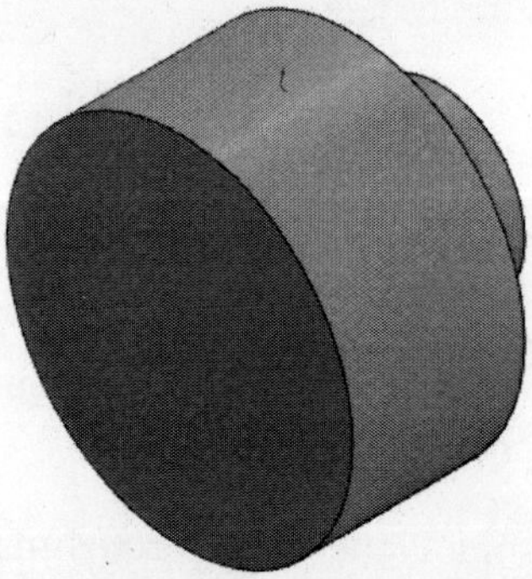

Figure 8-4 Model after creating the second feature

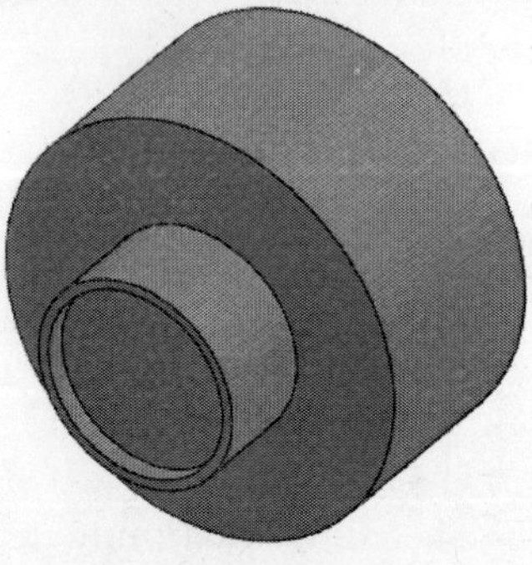

Figure 8-5 Model after creating the third feature

Next, you will create the fourth feature of the model.

4. Create the fourth feature of the model which is an extrude feature. The rotated view of the model after creating the fourth feature is shown in Figure 8-6. For dimensions, refer to Figure 8-1.

   Next, you will create the fifth feature of the model.

5. Create the fifth feature of the model which is a cut feature. The rotated view of the model after creating the cut feature is shown in Figure 8-7. For dimensions, refer to Figure 8-1.

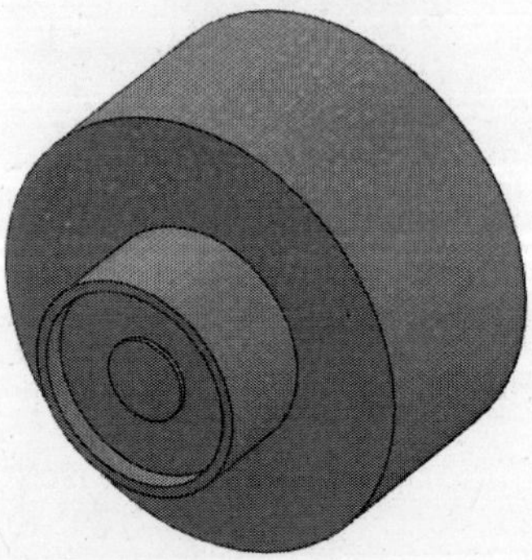

Figure 8-6 Model after creating the fourth feature

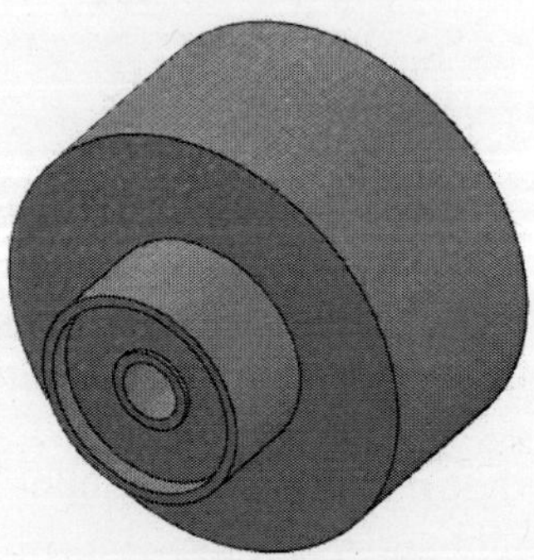

Figure 8-7 Model after creating the fifth feature

Creating the Hole Feature

The sixth feature of the model is a hole feature which is created by using the **Simple Hole** tool. You can also create this feature by using the **Extruded Cut** tool.

1. Choose **Insert > Features > Simple Hole** from the SOLIDWORKS menus; the **Hole PropertyManager** is displayed.

2. Change the view orientation of the model to isometric and select the front planar face of the model as the placement face for the hole feature; the preview of the hole feature is displayed.

3. Set the value of the **Hole Diameter** spinner to 1.75 mm. Next, select the **Through All** option from the **End Condition** drop-down list of the PropertyManager.

4. Choose the **OK** button from the PropertyManager; the hole feature is created arbitrarily on the selected face.

   Now, you need to position the hole feature.

5. Select the hole feature from the **FeatureManager Design Tree**; a pop-up toolbar is displayed.

6. Choose the **Edit Sketch** button from the pop-up toolbar; the sketching environment is invoked. Next, apply the required relation and dimension to position the center point of the hole feature, refer to Figure 8-8.

7. Exit from the sketching environment. The isometric view of the model after creating the hole feature is shown in Figure 8-9.

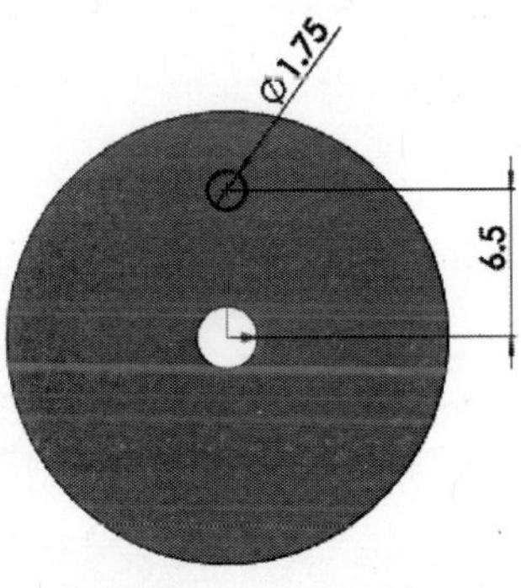

Figure 8-8 *The sketch of the hole feature*

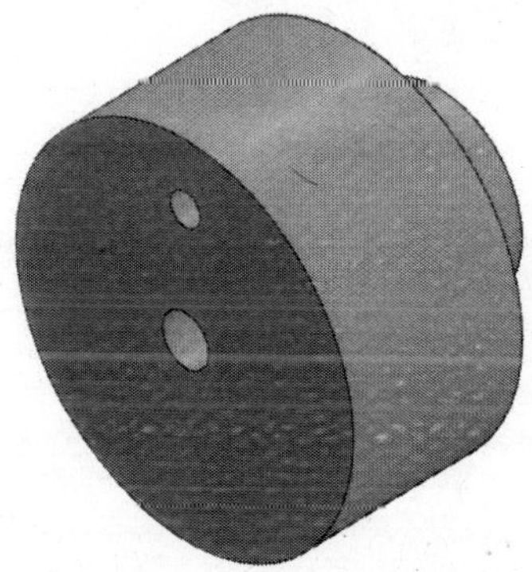

Figure 8-9 *Model after creating the hole feature*

Creating the Circular Pattern of the Hole Feature

After creating the hole feature, you need to create its other instances by using the **Circular Pattern** tool.

1. Choose the **Circular Pattern** tool from the **Linear Pattern** flyout in the **Features CommandManager**; the **CirPattern PropertyManager** is displayed.

2. Select the previously created hole feature from the **FeatureManager Design Tree**.

3. Click on the **Pattern Axis** selection area of the **Direction1** rollout of the PropertyManager to activate it and then select the circular edge of the model; the preview of the circular pattern of the hole feature is displayed.

4. Set the value of the **Number of Instances** spinner to **4** and make sure the **Equal spacing** check box is selected.

5. Choose the **OK** button from the PropertyManager; the hole feature is patterned, as shown in Figure 8-10.

Creating the Fillet Feature

Now, you need to create the fillet feature by using the **Fillet** tool.

1. Invoke the **Fillet Property Manager** and create the fillet feature of radius 2.25 mm. The model after creating the fillet feature is shown in Figure 8-11.

Figure 8-10 Model after patterning the feature

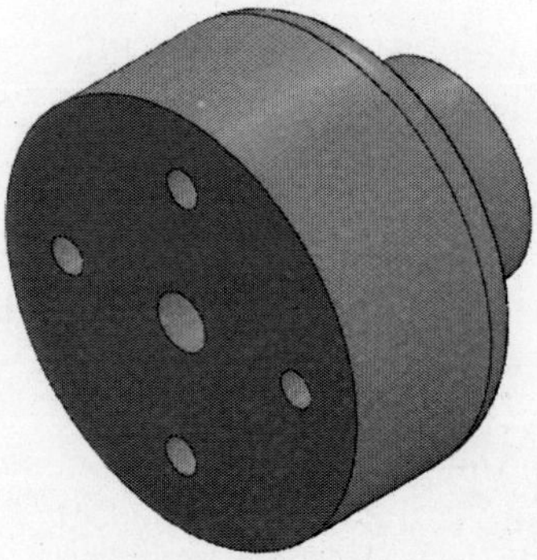

Figure 8-11 Model after creating the fillet feature

Creating the Shell Feature

It is evident from Figure 8-2 that you need to create a thin-walled structure. This will be created using the **Shell** tool.

1. Choose the **Shell** button from the **Features CommandManager**; the **Shell1 PropertyManager** is displayed and you are prompted to select the faces to be removed.

The **Shell** tool is used to scoop out the material from the model, leaving behind a thin-walled hollow model with walls of a specified thickness and cavity inside. Also, the selected face or the faces of the model are removed in this operation. If you do not select a face to remove, a closed hollow model will be created. You can also specify multiple thicknesses to the walls.

2. Select the front planar face of the model as the face to be removed; the name of the selected face is displayed in the **Faces to Remove** selection box of the **Shell1 PropertyManager**. Also, this face is highlighted in blue in the graphic area.

3. Set the value of the **Thickness** spinner to **0.25**.

Note

If the thickness of the shell feature is more than the radius of the fillet feature, the fillet will not be included in the shell feature. As a result, sharp edges are created after adding the fillet. The same is true in case of chamfer feature. The face selected to be removed in the shell feature can be a planar face or a curved face.

4. Select the **Show preview** check box, if it is not selected by default to view the preview of shell feature.

5. Make sure that the **Shell outward** check box is cleared in the **Parameters** rollout of the PropertyManager to create the shell feature on the inner side of the model.

Note
*If the **Shell outward** check box is selected, the shell feature will be created on the outer side of the model.*

6. Choose the **OK** button from the PropertyManager; the shell feature of uniform wall thickness is created, as shown in Figure 8-12.

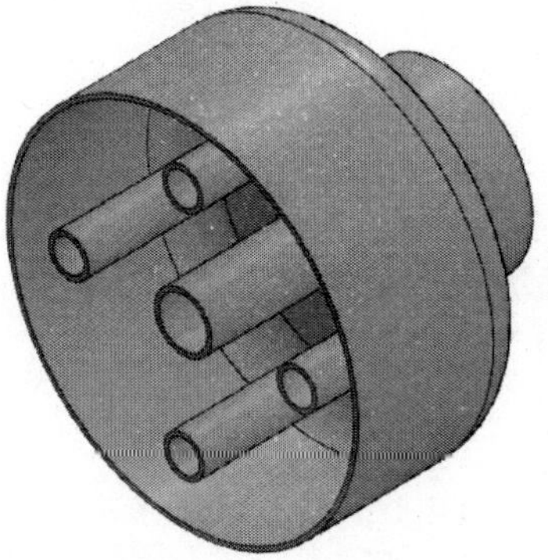

Figure 8-12 *Final model after creating the shell feature*

Tip
*You can also create a shell feature with different wall thickness. To do so, after selecting the faces to be removed and specifying the thickness value in the **Thickness** spinner of the **Parameters** rollout, click once in the **Multi-thickness Faces** selection box to activate the selection mode. Next, select the faces for which you want to specify different thicknesses. Set the thickness value using the **Multi-thickness(es)** spinner and choose the **OK** button.*

Saving the Model

1. Save the model with the name *c08_tut01* at the location given next.

   \Documents\SOLIDWORKS Tutorials\c08

2. Choose **File > Close** from the SOLIDWORKS menus to close the file.

Tutorial 2

In this tutorial, you will create the model shown in Figure 8-13. The dimensions of the model are shown in the same figure. **(Expected time: 45 min)**

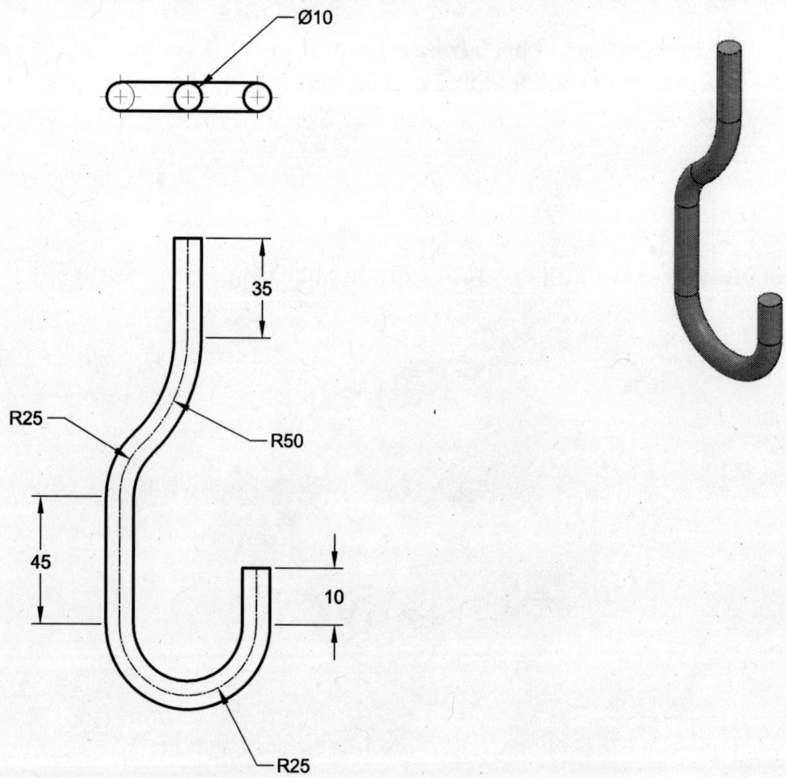

Figure 8-13 *Views and dimensions of the model for Tutorial 2*

The following steps are required to complete this tutorial:

a. Create the path for the sweep feature, refer to Figure 8-14.
b. Create the profile for the sweep feature.
c. Sweep the profile along the path, refer to Figure 8-16.
d. Save the model.

Creating the Path for the Sweep Feature

It is evident from the Figure 8-13 that the model is created by using a sweep feature. In SOLIDWORKS, you can create a sweep feature by using the **Swept Boss/Base** tool. To create the sweep feature, you first need to create its path and profile. A profile is a section for the sweep feature and a path is the course taken by the profile while creating the sweep feature.

1. Start a new SOLIDWORKS part document using the **New SOLIDWORKS Document** dialog box.

2. Invoke the sketching environment by selecting the **Front Plane** as the sketching plane. Next, draw the sketch of the path for the sweep feature, as shown in Figure 8-14.

3. Exit from the sketching environment and change the view to isometric.

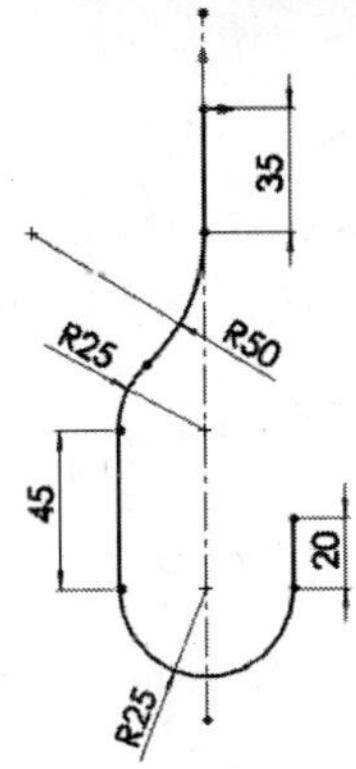

Figure 8-14 *Sketch of the path*

Creating the Profile for the Sweep Feature

After creating the path for the sweep feature, you need to create its profile. To create the profile, first you need to create a reference plane normal to the path and then select it as the sketching plane. However, in this tutorial, you can create the profile of the sweep feature on the **Top Plane**, as it is normal to the path created for the sweep feature.

Tip
It is not necessary that the sketch drawn for the profile of a sweep feature should intersect the path. However, a plane on which the profile is drawn should lie at one of the endpoints of the path.

1. Invoke the sketching environment by selecting the **Top Plane** as the sketching plane and draw a circle of diameter 10 mm. Note that the center point of the circle is at the origin of the plane.

2. Exit from the sketching environment after drawing the profile of the sweep feature.

Creating the Sweep Feature

After drawing the path and profile, you can create a sweep feature by using the **Swept Boss/Base** tool.

1. Change the current view of the model to isometric.

2. Choose the **Swept Boss/Base** button from the **Features CommandManager**; the **Sweep PropertyManager** is displayed, refer to Figure 8-15. Note that the **Profile** selection area is activated in the **Profile and Path** rollout of the PropertyManager. As a result, you are prompted to select the profile for the sweep feature.

The **Swept Boss/Base** tool is one of the most important advanced modeling tools. This tool is used to extrude a closed profile along an open or a closed path. Therefore, you need a profile and a path to create a sweep feature. A profile is a section for the sweep feature and a path is the course taken by the profile while creating the sweep feature. The profile has to be a sketch, but the path can be a sketch, curve, or an edge.

3. Select the circle as the profile for the sweep feature; the circle is highlighted and the **Profile** callout is attached with the circle in the graphic area. Also, its name is displayed in the **Profile** selection area and the **Path** selection area is activated automatically in the PropertyManager. As a result, you are prompted to select the sweep path after selecting the profile.

4. Select the path for the sweep feature; the selected path is highlighted and the **Path** callout is also displayed. Also, the preview of the sweep feature is displayed in the graphic area.

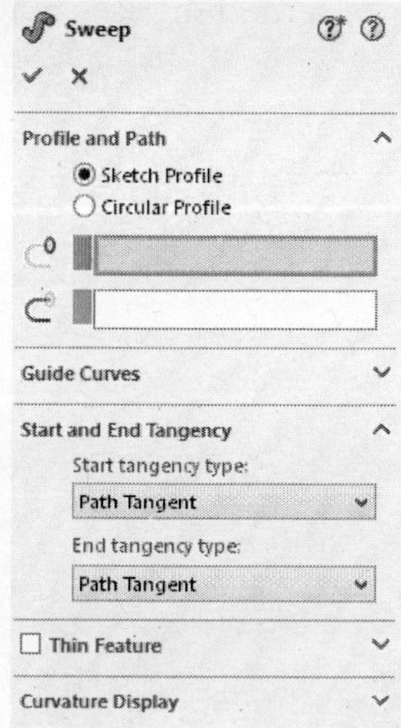

Figure 8-15 The Sweep PropertyManager

The **Start/End Tangency** rollout in the **Sweep PropertyManager** is used to define the tangency conditions at the start and end of a feature.

5. Accept all the default options available in the **Sweep PropertyManager** and then choose the **OK** button; the final model is created, as shown in Figure 8-16.

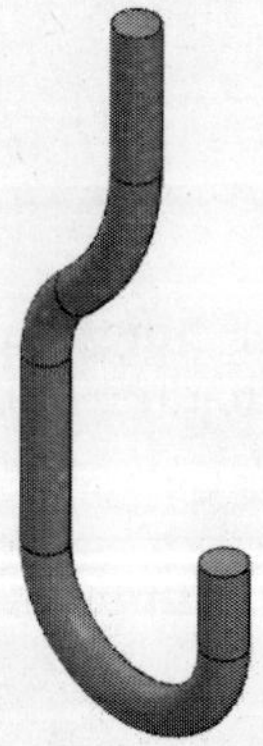

Figure 8-16 Model after creating the sweep feature

> **Tip**
> *You can also create a thin sweep feature by specifying the thickness of the sweep feature in the **Thin Feature** rollout of the **Sweep PropertyManager**. The options in this rollout are the same as those discussed in the earlier chapters, where the process of extruding and revolving the thin features was discussed.*

Saving the Model

1. Save the model with the name *c8_tut02* at the location given next.

\Documents\SOLIDWORKS Tutorials\c8

2. Choose **File > Close** from the SOLIDWORKS menus to close the file.

Tutorial 3

In this tutorial, you will create the model shown in Figure 8-17. The dimensions of the model are also shown in the same figure. **(Expected time: 30 min)**

The following steps are required to complete this tutorial:

a. Create the path for the sweep feature by using the **Project Curve** tool, refer to Figures 8-18 through 8-22.
b. Create the profile for the sweep feature.
c. Sweep the profile along the path, refer to Figure 8-24.
d. Save the model.

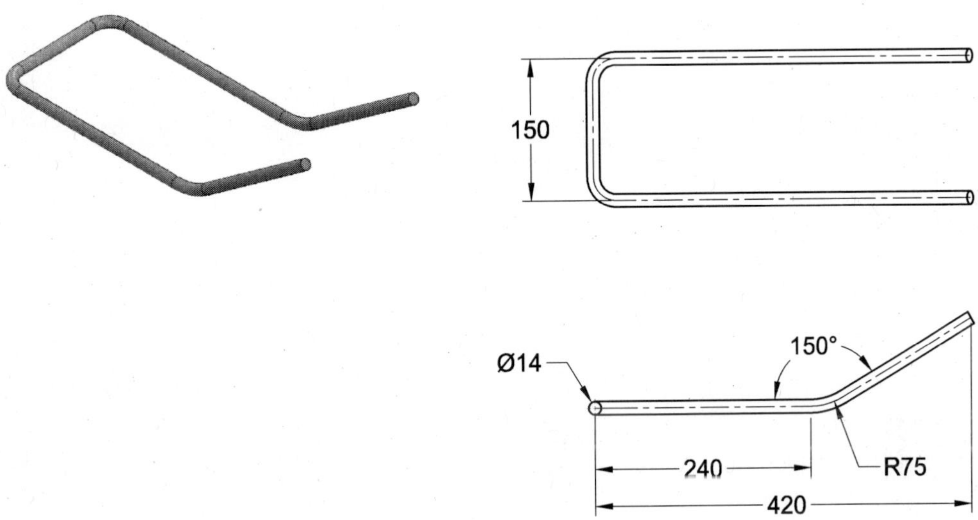

***Figure 8-17** Views and dimensions of the model for Tutorial 3*

Creating the Path for the Sweep Feature

It is evident from Figure 8-17 that the model needs to be created by sweeping a profile along the 3D path. In this tutorial, you will create the 3D path of the sweep feature by projecting a sketched entity on another sketched entity using the **Sketch on sketch** projection type of the **Project Curve** tool. However, you can also create 3D path by using the tools available in the 3D sketcher environment of SOLIDWORKS. You will learn more about the 3D sketcher environment later in this chapter.

1. Start a new SOLIDWORKS part document using the **New SOLIDWORKS Document** dialog box.

   Now, you need to create two sketches on different planes to project onto one another.

2. Invoke the sketching environment by selecting the **Top Plane** as the sketching plane for creating the first sketch to be projected.

3. Draw the sketch, as shown in Figure 8-18. Next, exit from the sketcher environment.

   After creating the first sketch, you need to create another sketch to be projected.

4. Invoke the sketcher environment by selecting the **Front Plane** as the sketching plane and draw the sketch, as shown in Figure 8-19. Next, exit from the sketching environment and change the view to isometric.

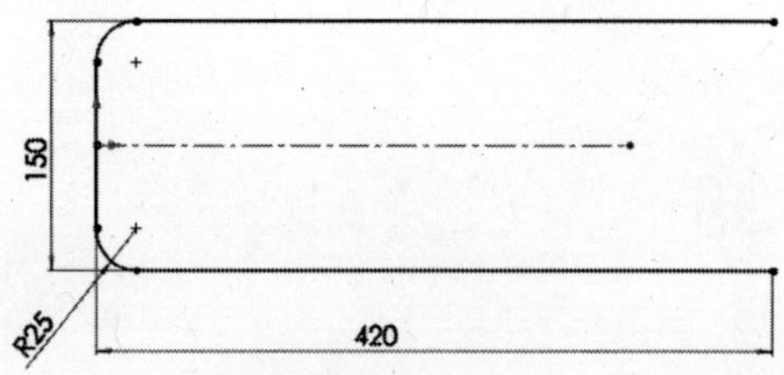

Figure 8-18 *The sketch created on the* ***Top Plane***

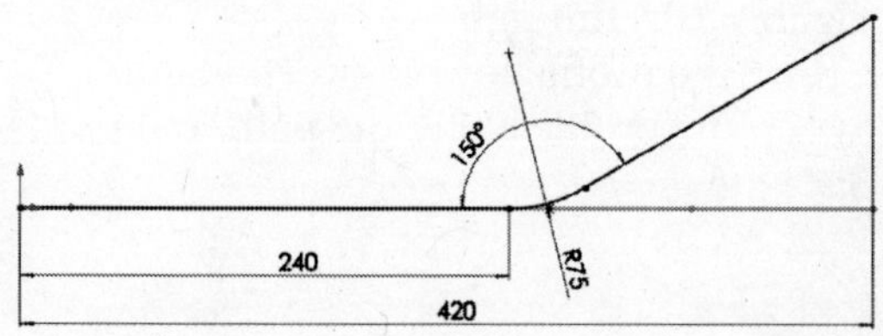

Figure 8-19 *The sketch created on the* ***Front Plane***

Now, you need to create the 3D path for the sweep feature by projecting the previously created sketched entities onto one another by using the **Project Curve** tool.

5. Choose the **Project Curve** button from the **Curves** flyout of the **Features CommandManager**, refer to Figure 8-20; the **Projected Curve PropertyManager** is displayed, refer to Figure 8-21.

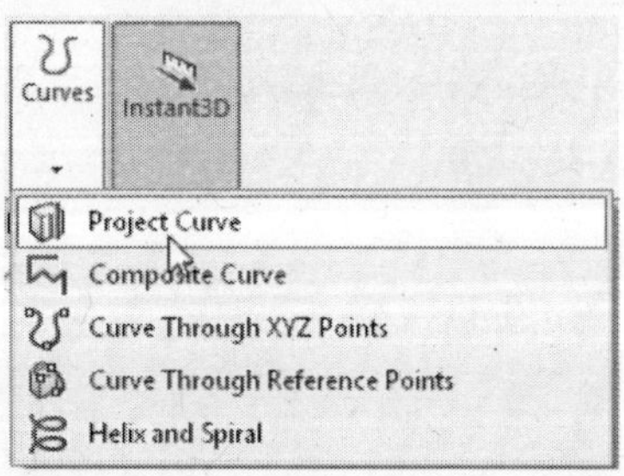

Figure 8-20 *The* ***Curves*** *flyout*

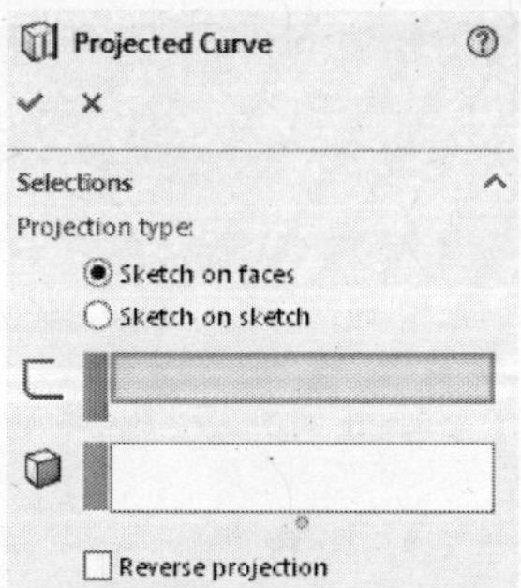

Figure 8-21 *The* ***Projected Curve PropertyManager***

You can create various types of curves in SOLIDWORKS. These curves are mostly used to create complex shapes using the **Swept Boss/Base** and **Lofted Boss/Base** tools. In SOLIDWORKS, you can create curves by using different tools and these tools are grouped in the **Curves** flyout in the **Features CommandManager**, as shown in Figure 8-20.

The **Project Curve** tool is used to project a closed/open sketched entity on one or more than one planar or curved faces. You can also project a sketched entity on another sketched entity to create a 3D curve. To create a projected curve, draw at least two sketches or a single sketch and at least one feature that do not lie on the same plane.

6. Make sure that the **Sketch on sketch** radio button in the **Project Type** area of the **Selections** rollout in the PropertyManager is selected. You are prompted to select two sketches to project onto another.

The **Sketch on sketch** radio button is used to project a sketched entity on another sketched entity to create a 3D curve. However, the **Sketch on faces** radio button of the **Projection Type** area is used to project a sketch on a planar or curved face.

7. Select both the previously created sketches from the graphic area one by one; the names of the selected sketches are displayed in the **Sketches to Project** selection area of the PropertyManager. Also, the preview of the 3D curve is displayed in the graphic area.

8. Choose the **OK** button from the PropertyManager; the 3D curve is created, as shown in Figure 8-22.

Creating the Profile for the Sweep Feature

After creating the path for the sweep feature, you need to create its profile. As discussed earlier, a profile is a section for the sweep feature and a path is the course taken by the profile while creating the sweep feature. To create the profile, first you need to create a reference plane normal to the path and then select this plane as the sketching plane for creating the profile for the sweep feature.

1. Invoke the **Plane PropertyManager** and create a plane normal to the path and coincident to the endpoint of a curve, as shown in Figure 8-23.

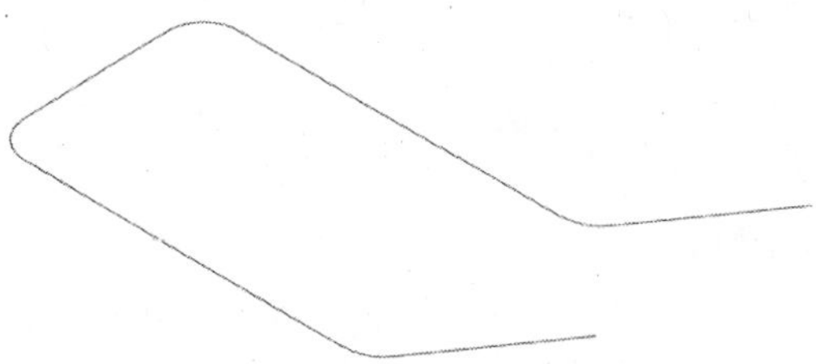

Figure 8-22 *The 3D curve created by projecting the sketches*

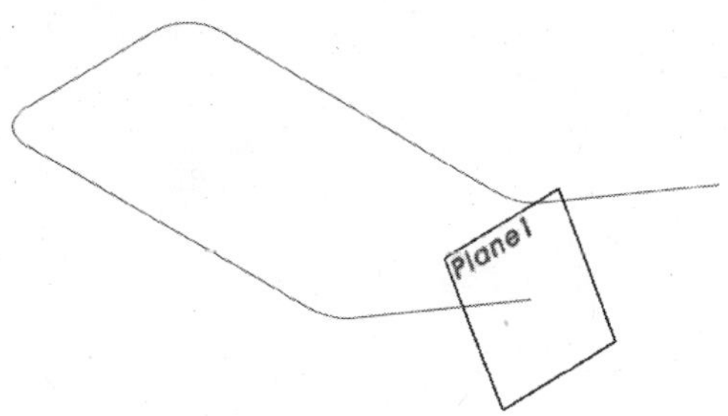

Figure 8-23 *Plane created normal to the path*

2. Invoke the sketching environment by selecting the newly created plane as the sketching plane.

3. Draw the sketch of the profile of the sweep feature using the **Circle** tool. The center of the circle is at the origin of the new plane and the diameter of the circle is 14 mm.

4. Exit from the sketcher environment after drawing the profile of the sweep feature.

Creating the Sweep Feature

After drawing the path and profile, you can create a sweep feature by using the **Swept Boss/Base** tool.

1. Change the current view of the model to isometric.

2. Choose the **Swept Boss/Base** button from the **Features CommandManager**; the **Sweep PropertyManager** is displayed. Also, you are prompted to select the profile for the sweep feature.

3. Select the circle as the profile for the sweep feature; the circle is highlighted and the **Profile** callout is attached to the circle in the graphic area. Also, its name is displayed in the **Profile** selection area and the **Path** selection area is activated automatically in the PropertyManager. As a result, you are prompted to select the sweep path after selecting the profile.

4. Select the path for the sweep feature; the selected path is highlighted and the **Path** callout is also displayed in the graphic area. Also, the preview of the sweep feature is displayed in the graphic area.

5. Accept all default options available in the **Sweep PropertyManager** and then choose the **OK** button; the sweep feature is created. Figure 8-24 shows the final model after hiding the reference plane.

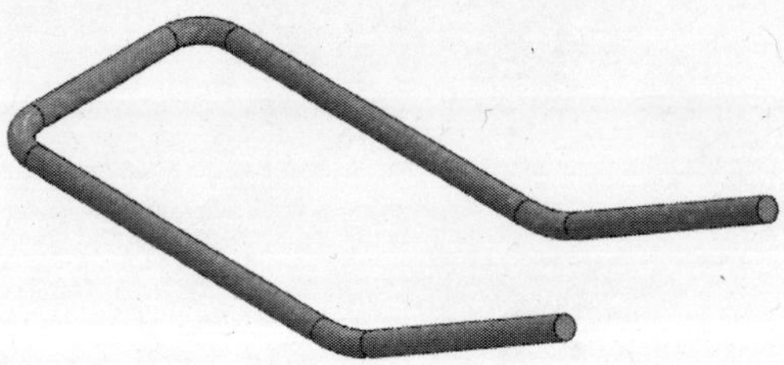

Figure 8-24 *Final model of Tutorial 3*

Saving the Model

1. Save the model with the name *c8_tut03* at the location given next:

   \Documents\SOLIDWORKS Tutorials\c8

2. Choose **File > Close** from the SOLIDWORKS menus to close the file.

Tutorial 4

In this tutorial, you will create the chair frame shown in Figure 8-25. The dimensions of the chair frame are also shown in the same figure. **(Expected time: 30 min)**

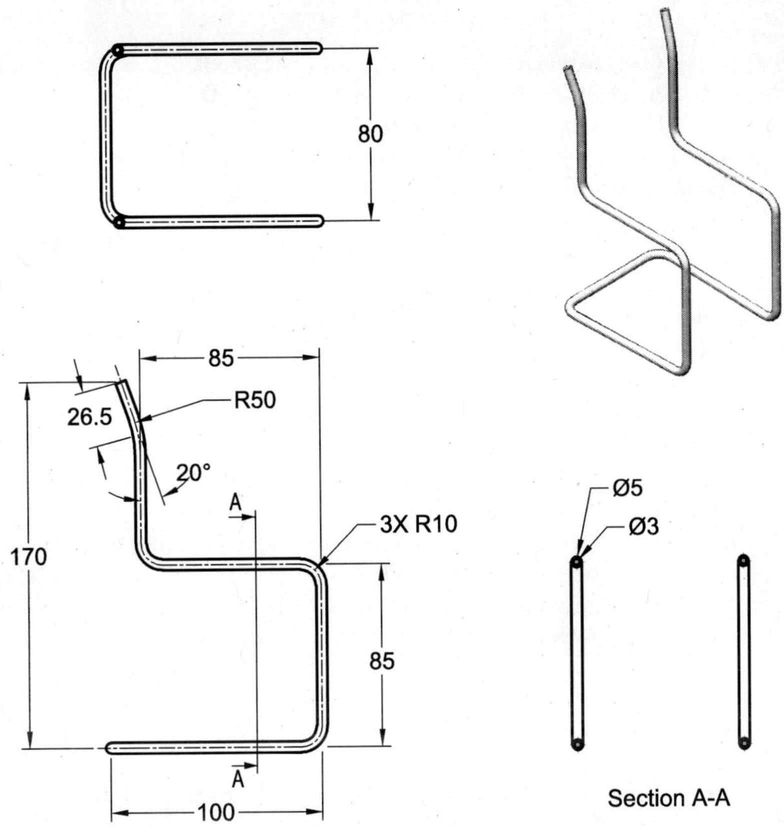

Figure 8-25 *Views and dimensions of the model for Tutorial 4*

The following steps are required to complete this tutorial:

a. Invoke the 3D sketching environment and then draw the sketch of a 3D path. Create only the left half of the 3D path in the 3D sketching environment, refer to Figure 8-27.
b. Select the **Front Plane** as the sketching plane and draw the sketch of the profile.
c. Sweep the profile along the 3D path using the **Thin Feature** option, refer to Figure 8-28.
d. Mirror the sweep feature using the **Front Plane**, refer to Figure 8-29.
e. Save the model.

Creating the Path for the Sweep Feature Using the 3D Sketching Environment

It is evident from Figure 8-25 that the model needs to be created by sweeping a profile along the 3D path. Therefore, you need to create a path for the sweep feature in the 3D sketching environment.

1. Start a new SOLIDWORKS part document.

2. Create a plane at an offset distance of 40 mm from the **Front Plane**.

3. Change the current view to isometric.

4. Choose the **3D Sketch** button from the **Sketch** flyout of the **Sketch CommandManager**, refer to Figure 8-26 or choose **Insert > 3D Sketch** from the SOLIDWORKS menus; the 3D sketching environment is invoked. Also, the origin is displayed in red and the confirmation corner is displayed on the top right corner of the drawing area. The sketching tools that can be used in the 3D sketching environment are also highlighted.

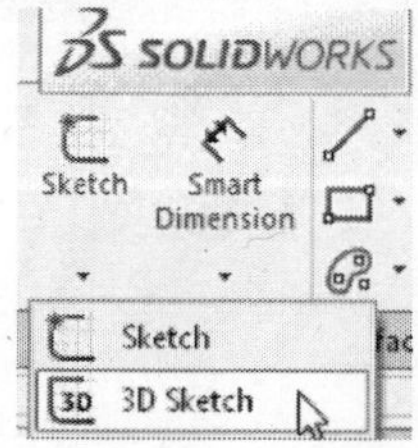

***Figure 8-26** The **Sketch** flyout*

You need to draw the left half of the sketch as the path of the sweep profile.

5. Invoke the **Line** tool from the **Sketch CommandManager**; the **Insert Line PropertyManager** is displayed. Also, the select cursor is replaced by the line cursor with **XY** displayed at its bottom.

   The **XY** symbol displayed below the line cursor indicates that the line will be sketched in the XY plane. You can toggle between the default planes using the TAB key. On doing so, the orientation of the coordinate system also modifies with respect to the current plane. Move the cursor to the location from where you want to start sketching.

   You need to draw the first line in the ZX plane. Therefore, you need to toggle the plane before you start creating the sketch.

6. Press the TAB key twice to switch to the ZX plane.

7. Move the line cursor to the origin. When a red dot is displayed, click to specify the start point of the line.

> **Tip**
> *You can also toggle the plane after specifying the start point of the line.*

8. Move the cursor in the positive Z direction of the triad; a small triad with Z appears below the cursor indicating that you are drawing the line along the **Z** direction. Click to specify the endpoint of the line, when a value close to 40 is displayed above the cursor; a rubber-band line is attached to the cursor.

9. Move the cursor toward the right along the infinite line, indicating the X axis. Click to specify the endpoint of the line when a value close to 100 is displayed above the cursor.

10. Press the TAB key to switch over to the XY plane. Move the cursor vertically upward.

11. Click to specify the endpoint of the line when the value above the cursor is close to 85.

12. Similarly, draw the remaining part of the sketch, and then add the required relations and dimensions to it.

13. Apply the **On Plane** relation between the upper endpoint of the 3D sketch and Plane1. The final sketch is displayed in Figure 8-27.

14. Exit the 3D sketching environment by using the confirmation corner.

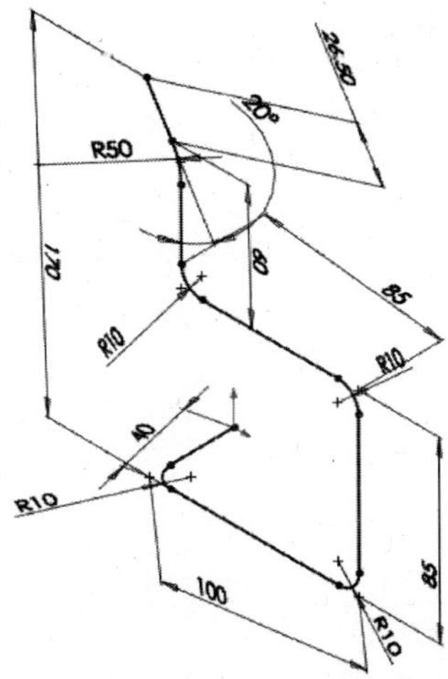

Figure 8-27 Sketch of the 3D path

Sweeping the Profile along the 3D Path Using the Circular Profile

As discussed earlier, a sweep feature is created by sweeping the profile along the 3D path. In SOLIDWORKS 2018, you can directly create a Circular profile.

1. Choose the **Swept Boss/Base** button from the Features CommandManager; the **Sweep PropertyManager** is displayed. 

2. Select Circular Profile radio button under Profile and Path in Sweep PropertyManager.

3. Select the 3D sketch as the path for the sweep feature; the name of the path is displayed in the selection box and set value in Diameter Spinner to 5mm. The Path callout and the preview of the sweep feature are also displayed in the graphic area. As is evident from Figure 8-28, the frame of the chair is made up of a hollow pipe. Therefore, you need to create a thin sweep feature to create a hollow chair frame.

4. Choose the **Thin Feature** option rollout and set the value in the **Thickness** spinner to **1mm**.

   By default, the thickness is provided in the outer direction of the sketch. You can also make a thin feature inside the sketch. To do so, you need to choose the **Reverse Direction** button.

5. Choose the **Reverse Direction** button from the **Thin Features** rollout to reverse the direction of the thin feature creation in the inside direction of the sketch.

6. Choose the **OK** button from the **Sweep PropertyManager** to end the creation of the feature.

The model after creating the sweep feature is displayed in Figure 8-28.

7. Mirror the sweep feature about the **Front Plane** by using the **Mirror** tool. The model after mirroring is shown in Figure 8-29.

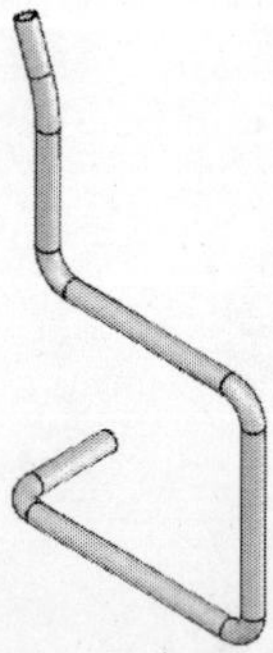

Figure 8-28 *Sweep feature created by sweeping a profile along a 3D path*

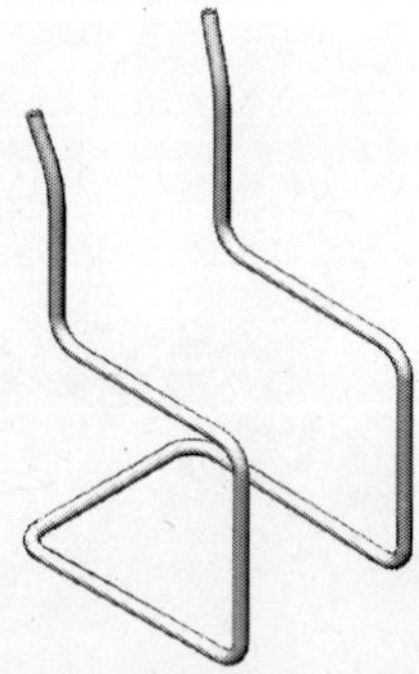

Figure 8-29 *The final model*

Saving the Model

1. Save the model with the name *c8_tut04* at the location given next.

   \Documents\SOLIDWORKS Tutorials\c8

2. Close the document.

Tutorial 5

In this tutorial, you will create the model shown in Figure 8-30. The dimensions of the model are shown in Figure 8-31. **(Expected time: 30 min)**

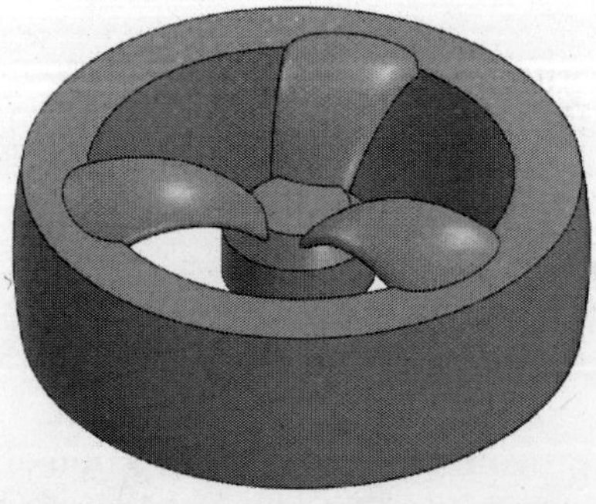

Figure 8-30 *Model for Tutorial 5*

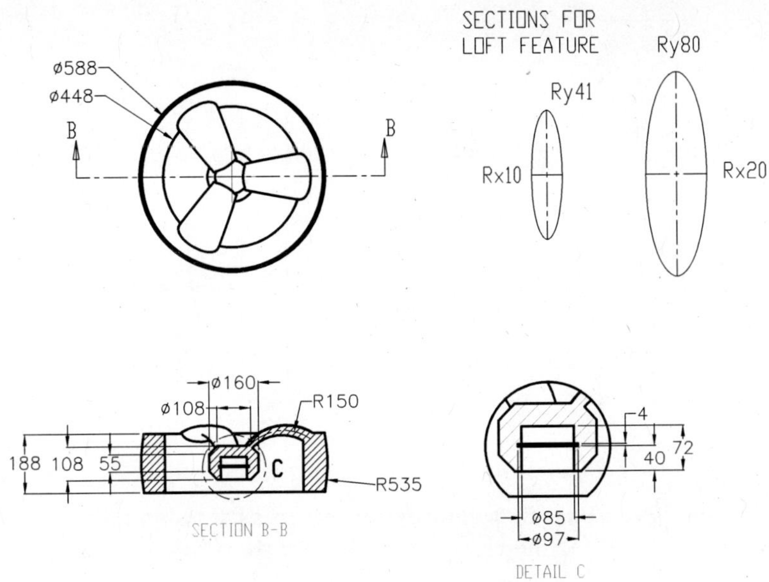

Figure 8-31 Views and dimensions of the model for Tutorial 5

The following steps are required to complete this tutorial:

a. Create a revolve feature as the base feature of the model, refer to Figures 8-32 and 8-33.
b. Create the loft feature by blending two sections along a specified path, refer to Figures 8-34 through 8-41.
c. Create the circular pattern of the loft feature, refer to Figure 8-42.
d. Save the model.

Creating the Base Feature

You will create the base feature of the model which is a revolve feature.

1. Start a new SOLIDWORKS part document and invoke the sketching environment by selecting the **Front Plane** as the sketching plane.

2. Draw the sketch of the revolve feature, as shown in Figure 8-32.

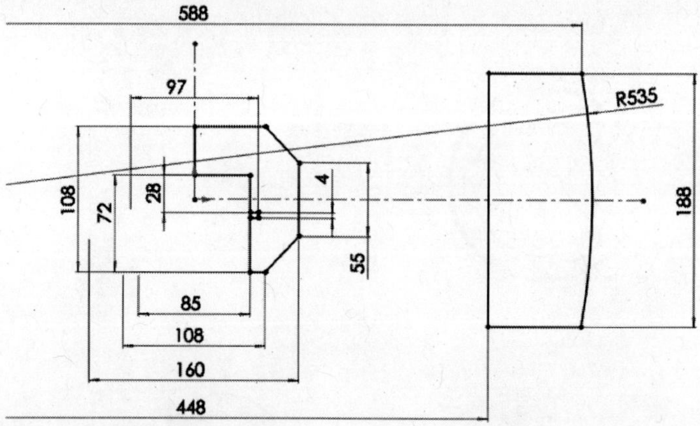

Figure 8-32 Sketch of the revolve feature

3. Choose the **Revolved Boss/Base** button from the **Features CommandManager**; the sketch is automatically oriented in the trimetric view and the **Revolve PropertyManager** is displayed.

   As the sketch shown in Figure 8-32 has two center lines, SOLIDWORKS cannot determine which one of them should be used as the axis of revolution. As a result, you are prompted to select the axis of revolution.

4. Select the vertical center line as the axis of revolution; the preview of the revolve feature is displayed in the graphic area with the default option.

5. Make sure the **Blind** option is selected in the **Revolve Type** drop-down list and the value of the **Direction 1 Angle** edit box is set to 360 degrees.

6. Choose the **OK** button from the PropertyManager; the revolve feature is created, as shown in Figure 8-33.

Creating the Loft Feature

The second feature of the model is the loft feature created by using the **Lofted Boss/Base** tool. The loft features are created by blending more than one similar or dissimilar sections together to get a free-form shape. These similar or dissimilar sections may or may not be parallel to each other. In this tutorial, you will create a loft feature by blending two sections along a specified path. Therefore, first you need to create a path and then sections for creating the loft feature.

1. Invoke the sketching environment by selecting the **Front Plane** as the sketching plane for creating the path that will specify the transition of the sections.

2. Change the current display style of the model to hidden lines visible by choosing **Display Style > Hidden Lines Visible** from the **View (Heads-Up)** toolbar. Next, change the current orientation of the model normal to the view.

3. Create the sketch of the path, as shown in Figure 8-34.

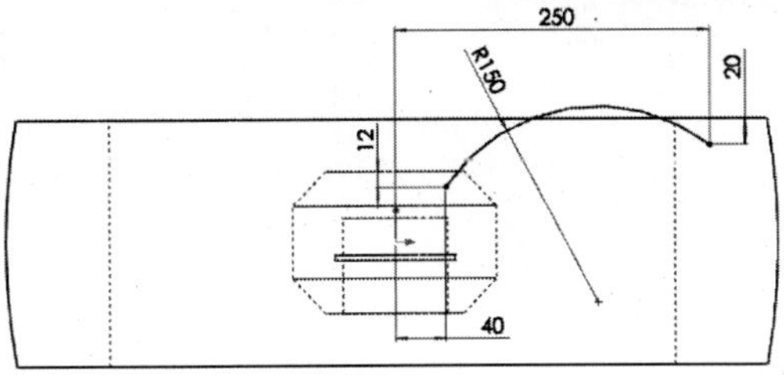

Figure 8-33 *Model after creating the revolve feature*

Figure 8-34 *The sketch of the path*

After creating the path, you need to create sections for creating the loft feature. In this tutorial, you need to create reference planes normal to the path at its both ends for creating the loft sections.

4. Change the current display style of the model to shaded with edges.

5. Invoke the **Plane PropertyManager** and then select the path that was created previously as the first reference for creating the plane. Next, select one of its end point as the second reference; the preview of the reference plane is created. Next, choose the **OK** button from the PropertyManager.

6. Similarly, create another reference plane normal to the path and coincident to the other endpoint of the path. Figure 8-35 shows the isometric view of the model after creating the reference planes.

After creating the reference planes, you need to create loft sections on it.

7. Select the reference plane, refer to Figure 8-36, to invoke the sketching environment and then create the elliptical section, as shown in Figure 8-37. Then, exit from the sketching environment.

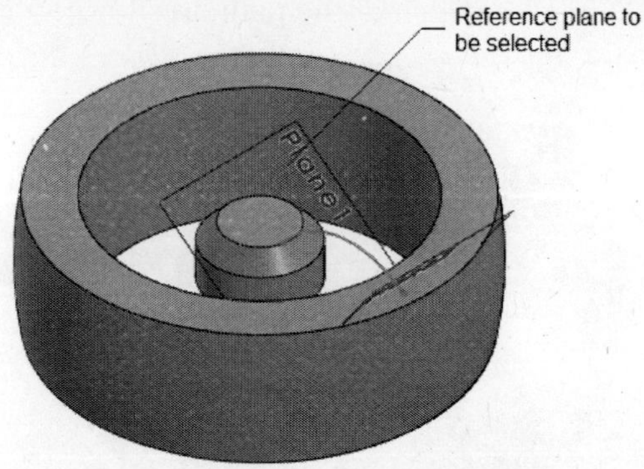

Figure 8-35 *The reference planes created on the endpoints of the path*

Figure 8-36 *The reference plane to be selected*

8. Again, invoke the sketching environment by selecting the second reference plane that was created previously as the sketching plane and then draw the second section of the loft feature, as shown in Figure 8-38. Next, exit from the sketching environment.

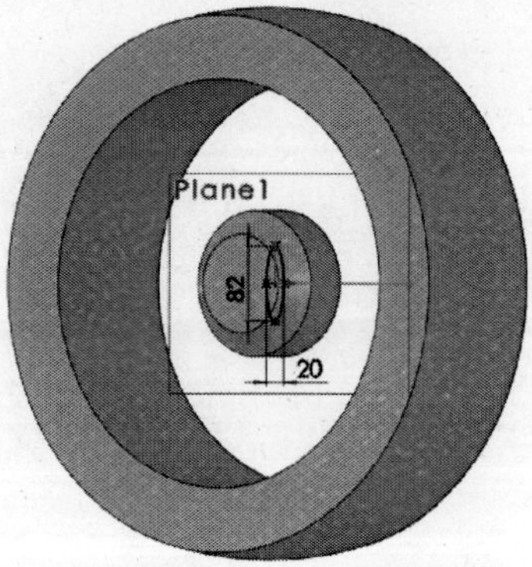

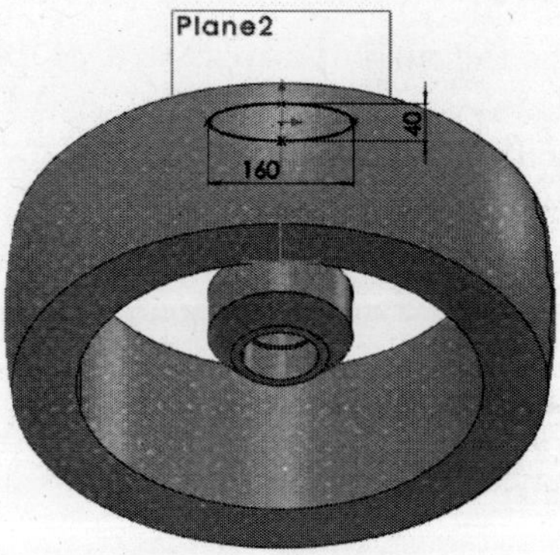

Figure 8-37 *The first section created for the loft feature*

Figure 8-38 *The second section created for the loft feature*

Now, you will create the loft feature by blending the previously created sections along the path by using the **Lofted Boss/Base** tool.

9. Choose the **Lofted Boss/Base** button from the **Features CommandManager**; the **Loft PropertyManager** is displayed. Also, you are prompted to select at least two profiles.

As discussed earlier, the **Lofted Boss/Base** tool is used to create a loft feature by blending more than one similar or dissimilar sections together to get a free-form shape. These similar or dissimilar sections may or may not be parallel to each other. Note that the sections for the solid lofts should be closed sketches.

10. Select both the sections from the graphic area one by one; the preview of the loft feature along with a connector is displayed in the graphic area, as shown in Figure 8-39. Also, the names of the selected sections or profiles are displayed in the **Profile** selection area of the **Profiles** rollout in the **Loft PropertyManager**.

Note

By default, a mesh is displayed in the preview of the loft feature. You can turn off this mesh by right-clicking in the graphic area and then choosing ***Mesh Preview > Clear All Meshed Faces*** *from the shortcut menu displayed.*

If the start and end loft sections are circular, elliptical, or closed spline sections, then only one controller will be displayed with the preview of the loft feature. You can also add more connectors to manipulate the loft feature. Connectors can be added to the straight profiles or curved profiles. To add a connector, right-click on the sketch at a location where you want to add the connector; a shortcut menu is displayed. Now, choose the ***Add Connector*** *option from the shortcut menu; a connector will be added to the loft feature.*

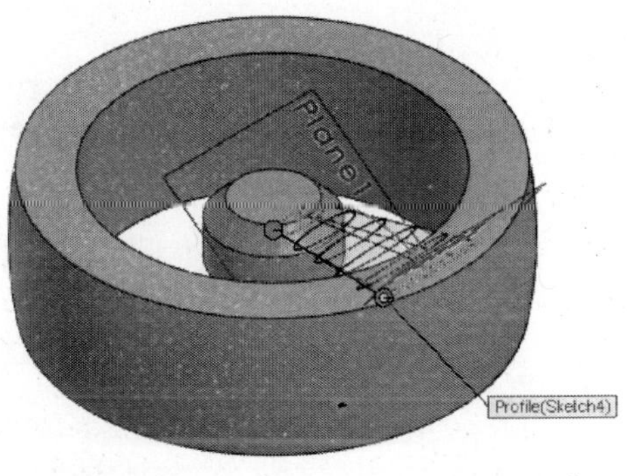

Figure 8-39 *The preview of the loft feature*

11. Click on the down arrow displayed at the right of the **Centerline Parameters** rollout in the **Loft PropertyManager** to expand it.

The **Centerline Parameters** rollout is used to create a loft feature by blending two or more than two sections along a specified path.

12. Select the path created earlier from the graphic area for specifying the transition of loft feature; the preview of the loft feature is modified accordingly, as shown in Figure 8-40.

13. Accept the other default parameters and then choose the **OK** button from the PropertyManager; the loft feature is created. Next, hide the reference planes for clarity. Figure 8-41 shows the model after hiding the reference planes and creating the loft feature.

Tip

The loft feature can be reshaped using the handles of the connector that appear as filled circles in the preview. To do so, press and hold the left mouse button on a handle, drag the cursor to specify a new location, and then release the left mouse button to place the connector. The process of controlling the loft shape using the connectors is known as Loft Synchronization.

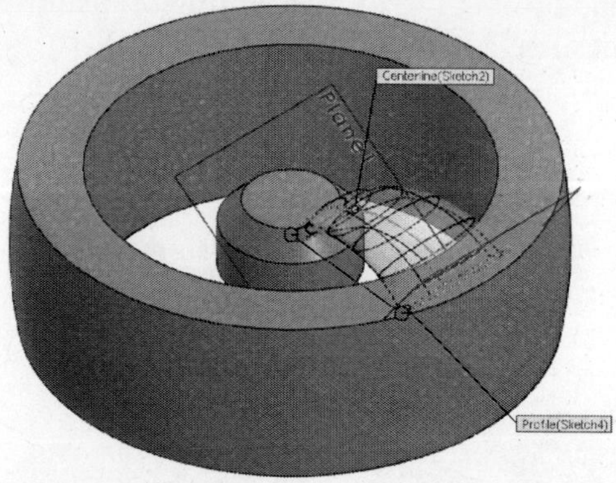

Figure 8-40 *The preview of the loft feature after selecting the path* ***Figure 8-41*** *Model after creating the loft feature*

Patterning the Loft Feature

After creating the loft feature, you need to pattern it using the **Circular Pattern** tool.

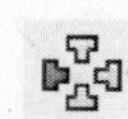

1. Choose the **Circular Pattern** button from the **Linear Pattern** flyout in the **Features CommandManager**; the **Circular Pattern PropertyManager** is displayed.

2. Select the loft feature from the graphic area as the feature to pattern or from the **FeatureManager Design Tree**; the name of the loft feature is displayed in the **Features to Pattern** selection area of the **Features to Pattern** rollout of the PropertyManager.

3. Click on the **Pattern Axis** selection area of the **Parameters** rollout in the PropertyManager to activate it and then select the circular edge of the base feature; the preview of the circular pattern of the loft feature is displayed in the graphic area.

4. Set the value of the **Number of Instances** spinner to **3** and make sure that the **Equal spacing** check box is selected in the **Parameters** rollout of the PropertyManager.

5. Choose the **OK** button from the PropertyManager; the loft feature is patterned in circular manner. Figure 8-42 shows the isometric view of the final model after creating the loft feature.

Saving the Model

1. Save the model with the name *c8_tut05* at the location given next.

   \Documents\SOLIDWORKS Tutorials\c8

2. Close the document.

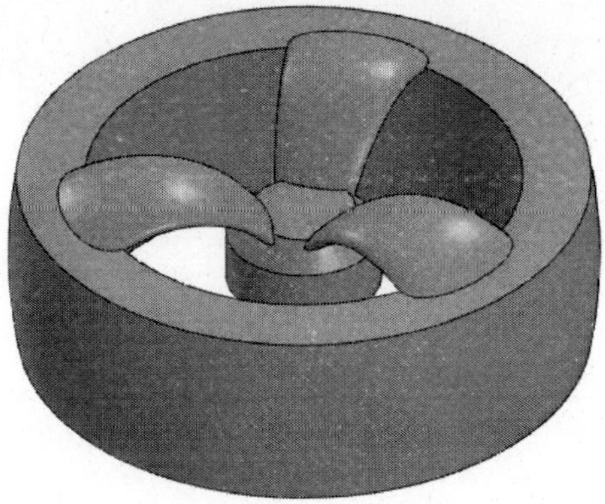

Figure 8-42 Final model for Tutorial 5

Tutorial 6

In this tutorial, you will create the model shown in Figure 8-43. The dimensions of the model are shown in Figure 8-44. **(Expected time: 30 min)**

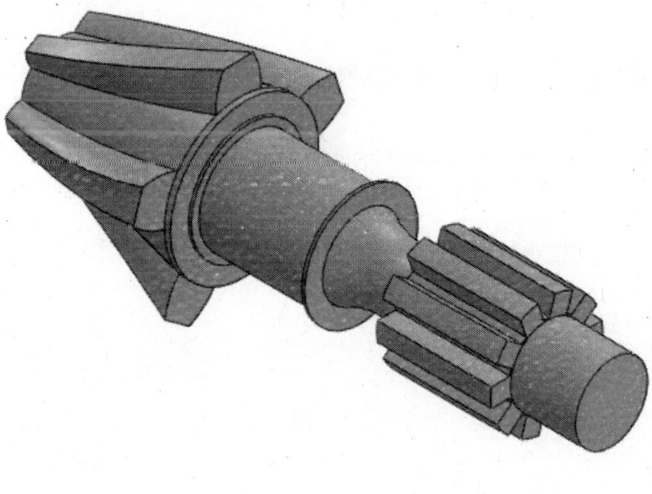

Figure 8-43 Model for Tutorial 6

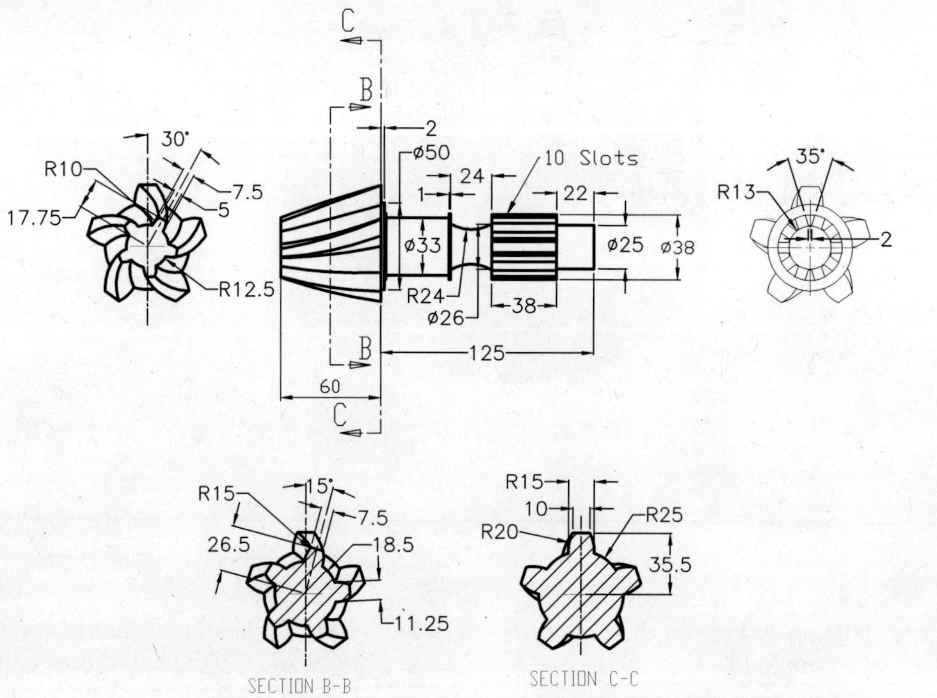

***Figure 8-44** Views and dimensions of the model for Tutorial 6*

The following steps are required to complete this tutorial:

a. Create a revolve feature as the base feature of the model, refer to Figures 8-45 and 8-46.
b. Create the extrude cut feature, refer to Figure 8-49.
c. Create the circular pattern of the extruded cut feature, refer to Figure 8-50.
d. Create the loft feature, refer to Figures 8-51 through 8-57.
e. Save the model.

Creating the Base Feature

You will create the base feature of the model, which is a revolve feature.

1. Start a new SOLIDWORKS part document and invoke the sketching environment by selecting the **Front Plane** as the sketching plane.

2. Draw the sketch of the revolve feature, as shown in Figure 8-45.

3. Choose the **Revolved Boss/Base** button from the **Features CommandManager**; the sketch is automatically oriented in the trimetric view and the **Revolve PropertyManager** is displayed. Also, the preview of the revolve feature is displayed in the graphic area. As the sketch has only one centerline, SOLIDWORKS

automatically selects the centerline as the axis of revolution. As a result, the preview of the feature is displayed in the drawing area.

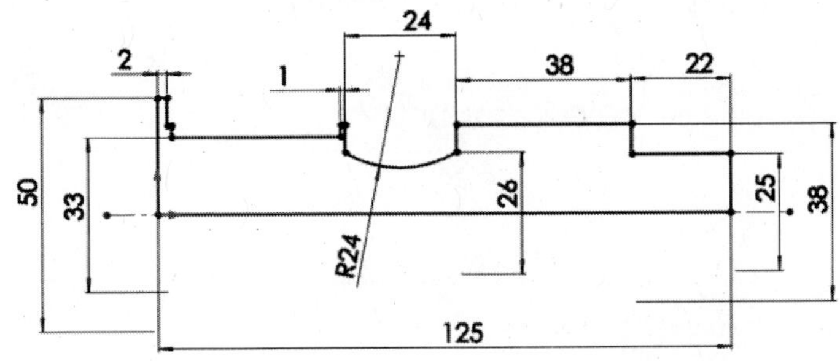

Figure 8-45 Sketch of the revolve feature

4. Make sure that the **Blind** option is selected from the **Revolve Type** drop-down list and the value of the **Direction 1 Angle** edit box is set to 360-degree.

5. Choose the **OK** button from the PropertyManager; the revolve feature is created, as shown in Figure 8-46.

Creating the Cut Feature

The second feature of the model is a cut feature created by using the **Extruded Cut** tool.

1. Invoke the sketching environment by selecting the face of the model as the sketching plane, refer to Figure 8-47.

Figure 8-46 Model after creating the revolve feature

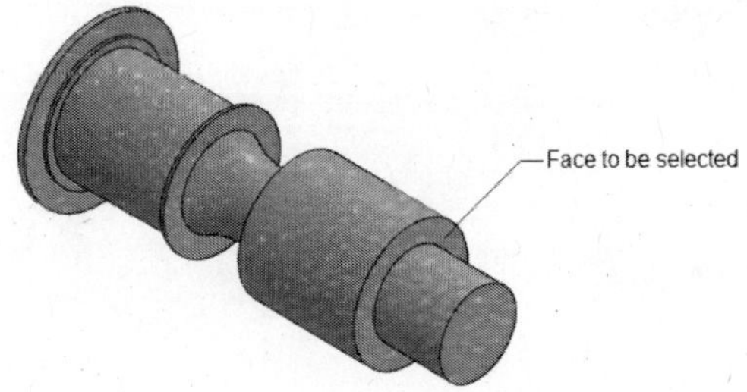

Figure 8-47 The face to be selected as the sketching plane

2. Draw the sketch of the cut feature, as shown in Figure 8-48, and then exit from the sketcher environment.

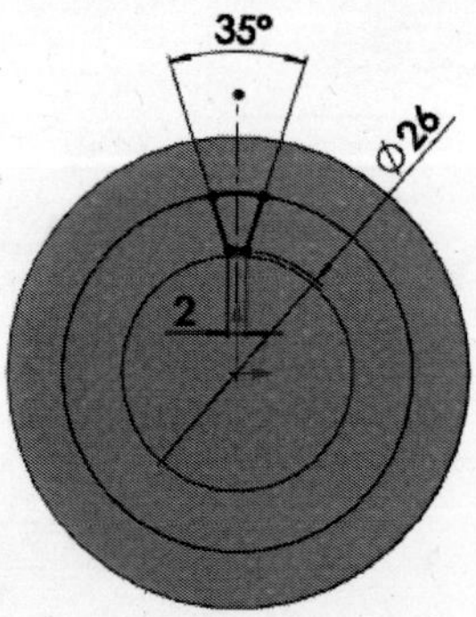

Figure 8-48 Sketch of the cut feature

3. Invoke the **Extruded Cut** tool and extrude the sketch up to the next surface that intersects the feature by using the **Up To Next** option. The isometric view of the model after creating the cut feature is shown in Figure 8-49.

After creating the cut feature, you need to pattern it using the **Circular Pattern** tool.

4. Invoke the **Circular Pattern** tool and pattern the cut feature in a circular manner to create its 10 instances. The model after creating the circular pattern is shown in Figure 8-50.

Figure 8-49 Model after creating the cut feature

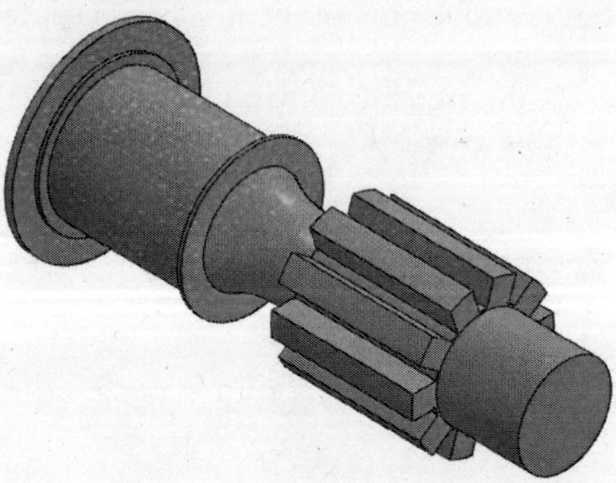

Figure 8-50 Model after patterning the cut feature in circular manner

Creating the Loft Feature

The next feature of the model is the loft feature created by using the **Lofted Boss/Base** tool. As discussed earlier, the loft features are created by blending more than one similar or dissimilar sections together to get a free-form shape. In this tutorial, you will create a loft feature by blending three sections.

1. Invoke the sketching environment by selecting the back planar face of the base feature as the sketching plane, refer to Figure 8-51.

2. Draw the sketch of the first section of the loft feature, as shown in Figure 8-52. Next, exit from the sketcher environment.

   It is evident from Figure 8-44 that the distance between first and second section of the loft feature is 30 mm. Therefore, for creating the second section of the loft feature, first you need to create a reference plane at an offset distance of 30 mm from the back planar face of the base feature.

3. Create a reference plane at an offset distance of 30 mm from the back planar face of the base feature. Figure 8-53 shows the model after creating the reference plane.

4. Invoke the sketcher environment by selecting the newly created plane as the sketching plane and draw the sketch of the second section of the loft feature, as shown in Figure 8-54.

> **Tip**
> *You can use the **Convert Entities**, **Rotate** and **Scale** tools to create the sketch. The scale value for the sketch will be 0.75 and the rotation angle will 15 degree. After creating the sketch, you need to provide the required dimensions and relations to make the sketch fully-defined.*

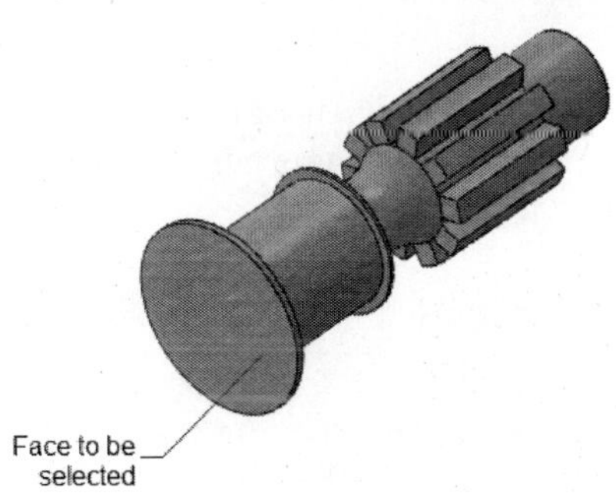

Figure 8-51 *Face to be selected*

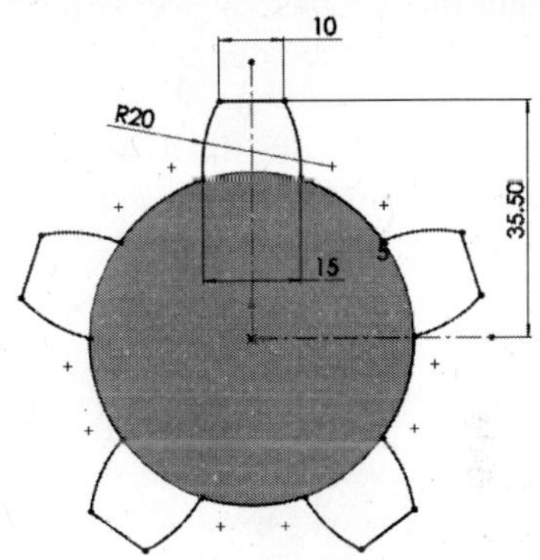

Figure 8-52 *First section of the loft feature*

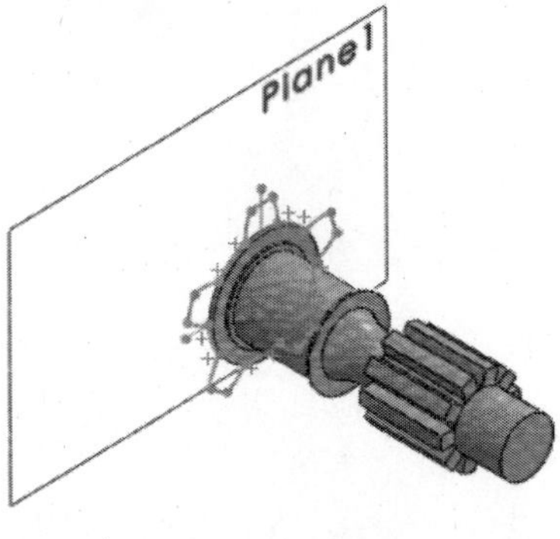

Figure 8-53 *Reference plane created at an offset distance*

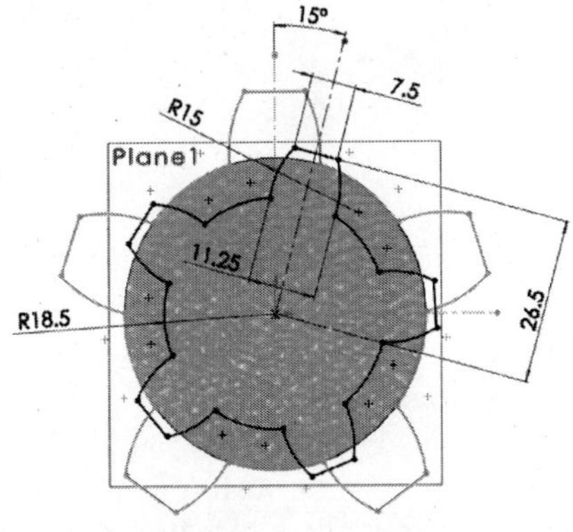

Figure 8-54 *Second section of the loft feature*

Now, you need to create a reference plane at an offset distance of 60 mm from the back planar face of the base feature for creating the third section of the loft feature.

5. Create a reference plane at an offset distance of 60 mm from the back planar face of the base feature.

6. Invoke the sketcher environment by selecting the newly created plane as the sketching plane and draw the sketch of the third loft feature, as shown in Figure 8-55.

After creating the sections, you need to create the loft feature by blending all the sections using the **Lofted Boss/Base** tool.

7. Choose the **Lofted Boss/Base** button from the **Features CommandManager**; the **Loft PropertyManager** is displayed. Also, you are prompted to select at least two profiles.

As discussed earlier, the **Lofted Boss/Base** tool is used to create loft features by blending more than one similar or dissimilar sections together to get a free-form shape. These similar or dissimilar sections may or may not be parallel to each other. Note that the sections for the solid lofts should be closed sketches.

8. Select the sections from the graphic area one by one; the preview of the loft feature along with a connector is displayed in the graphic area, as shown in Figure 8-56. Also, the name of the selected sections or profiles are displayed in the **Profile** selection area of the **Profiles** rollout in the **Loft PropertyManager**.

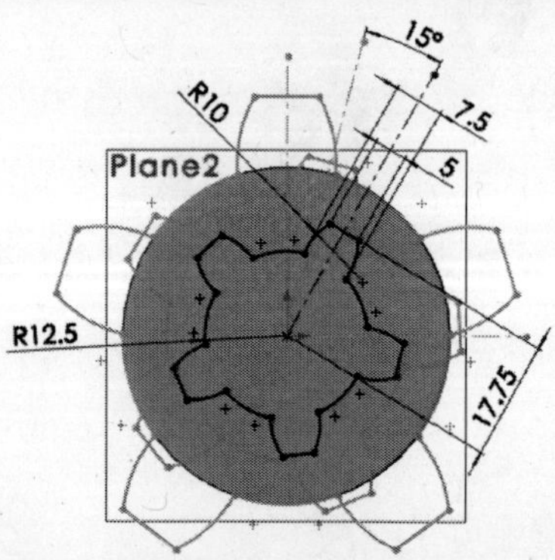

Figure 8-55 *Third section of the loft feature*

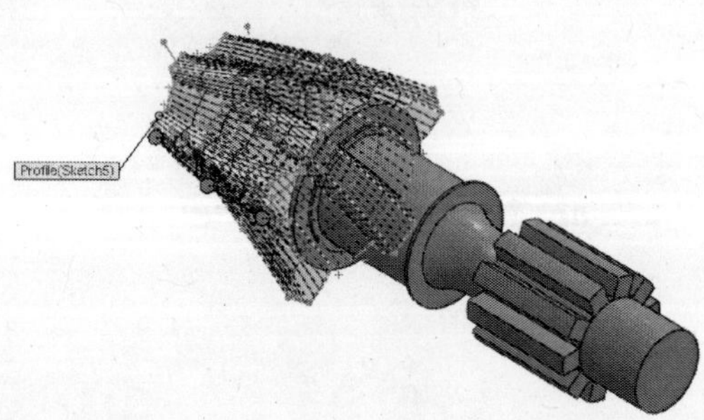

Figure 8-56 *Preview of the loft feature*

You can also create a thin loft feature by defining the thin parameters in the **Thin Feature** rollout of the PropertyManager.

9. Accept the other default parameters and then choose the **OK** button from the PropertyManager; the loft feature is created. Figure 8-57 shows the model after hiding the reference planes and creating the loft feature.

Note that if the shape of the teeth profile is not similar to the shape shown in Figure 8-57 then you need to change it by using the green connector points.

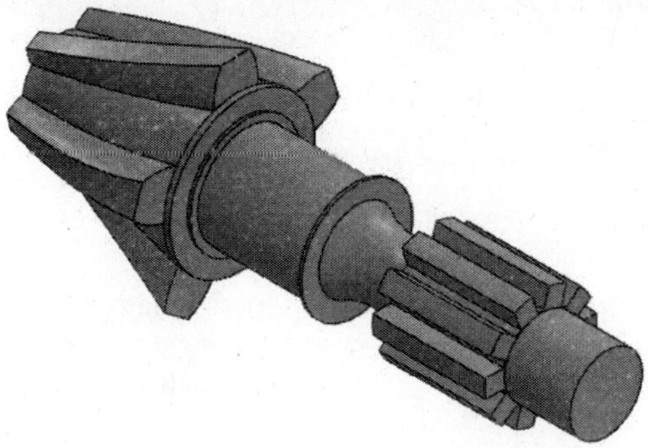

Figure 8-57 Final model of Tutorial 6

Saving the Model

1. Save the model with the name *c8_tut06* at the location given next.

   \Documents\SOLIDWORKS Tutorials\c8

2. Close the document.

Self-Evaluation Test

Answer the following questions and then compare them to those given at the end of this chapter:

1. The __________ **PropertyManager** is used to create a loft feature.

2. You need to apply the __________ relation between a sketch and a guide curve for sweeping a profile along a path using guide curves.

3. The __________ tool is used to project a closed/open sketched entity on one or more than one planar or curved faces.

4. You need a profile and a path to create a sweep feature. (T/F)

5. At least two sections are required to create a loft feature. (T/F)

6. You cannot sweep a closed profile along a closed path. (T/F)

7. You cannot create a thin sweep feature. (T/F)

8. You can create a loft feature by using open sections. (T/F)

Review Questions

Answer the following questions:

1. Which of the following buttons is used to invoke the 3D sketching environment?

   (a) **2D Sketch** (b) **3D Sketching Environment**
   (c) **3D Sketch** (d) **Sketch**

2. Which of the following rollouts in the **Sweep PropertyManager** is used to define the tangency?

   (a) **Start/End Tangency** (b) **Tangency**
   (c) **Options** (d) None of these

3. Which of the following buttons in the **Guide Curves** rollout is used to display sections while creating the sweep feature with guide curves?

   (a) **Preview Sections** (b) **Show Sections**
   (c) **Sections** (d) **Preview**

4. In the __________ rollout, you can define the tangency at the start and end sections of the sweep feature.

5. The __________ rollout is used to create a thin loft feature.

6. You need to invoke the __________ dialog box to create a spiral curve.

7. The __________ **PropertyManager** is used to project a curve on a surface.

8. The __________ radio button of the **Projected Curve PropertyManager** is used to project a sketched entity on another sketched entity to create a 3D curve.

EXERCISES

Exercise 1

Create the model of the Upper Housing, as shown in Figure 8-58. The dimensions of the model are shown in Figure 8-59. **(Expected time: 1 hr)**

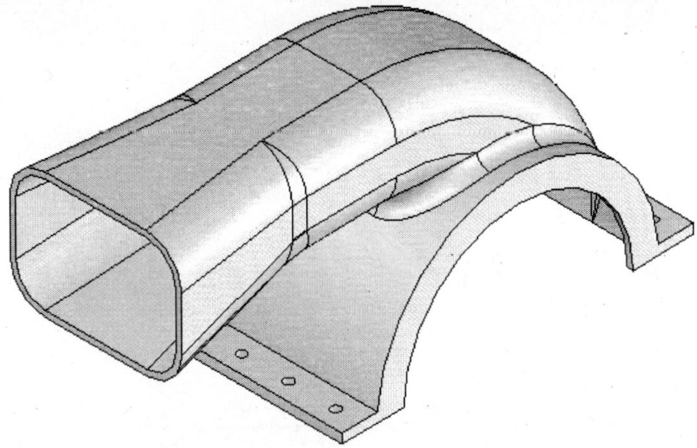

Figure 8-58 *Model of the Upper Housing*

Tip

This model is divided into three major parts. The first part is the base and is created by extruding the sketch to a distance of 80 mm using the ***Mid Plane*** *option.*

The second part of this model is the right portion of the discharge venturi and is created using the sweep feature.

The third part of this model is the left portion of the discharge venturi created using the loft feature. You need to create the first section of the loft feature on the planar face of the sweep feature created earlier. The second section will be created on a plane at an offset distance of the planar face of the sweep feature created earlier. Create a loft feature using the two sections created earlier. The other features needed to complete the model are fillets, hole, pattern, and so on.

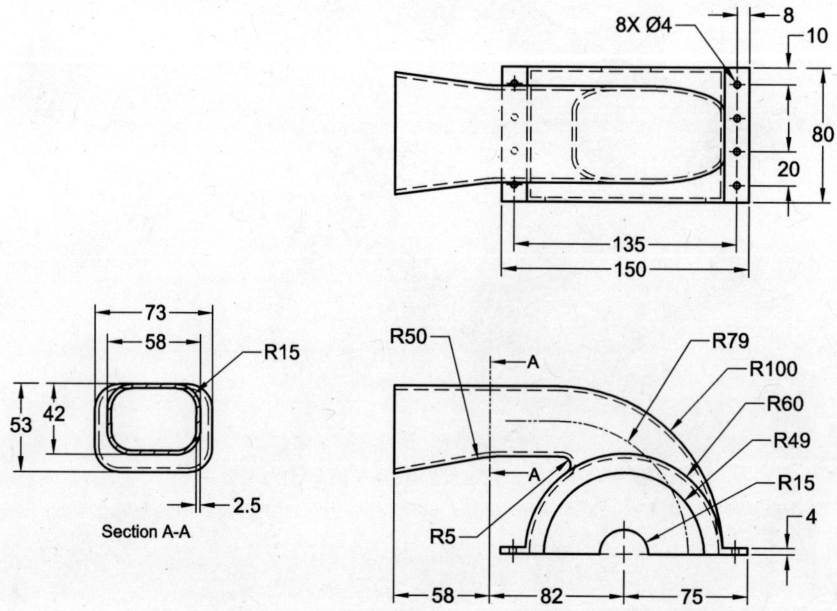

Figure 8-59 Dimensions of the Upper Housing

Exercise 2

In this tutorial, you will create the model shown in Figure 8-60. The dimensions of the model are shown in the same figure. The hidden lines in the top and side views are suppressed for clarity.
(Expected time: 45 min)

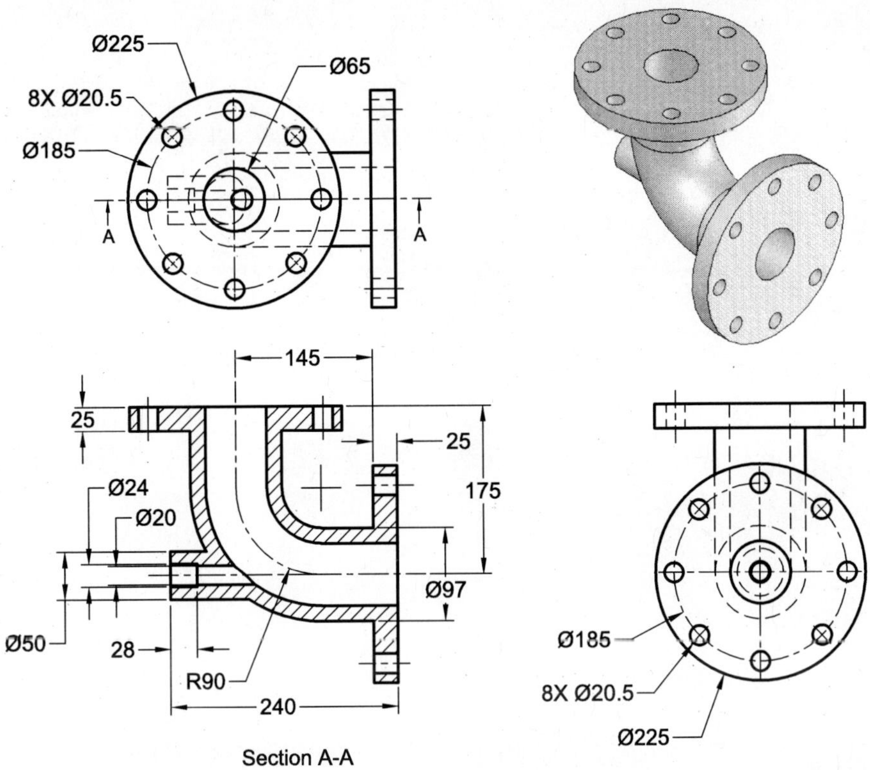

Figure 8-60 *Views and dimensions of the model for Exercise 2*

Answers to Self-Evaluation Test

1. Loft, **2.** Coincident, **3.** Project Curve, **4.** T, **5.** T, **6.** F, **7.** F, **8.** T

Chapter 9

Assembly Modeling

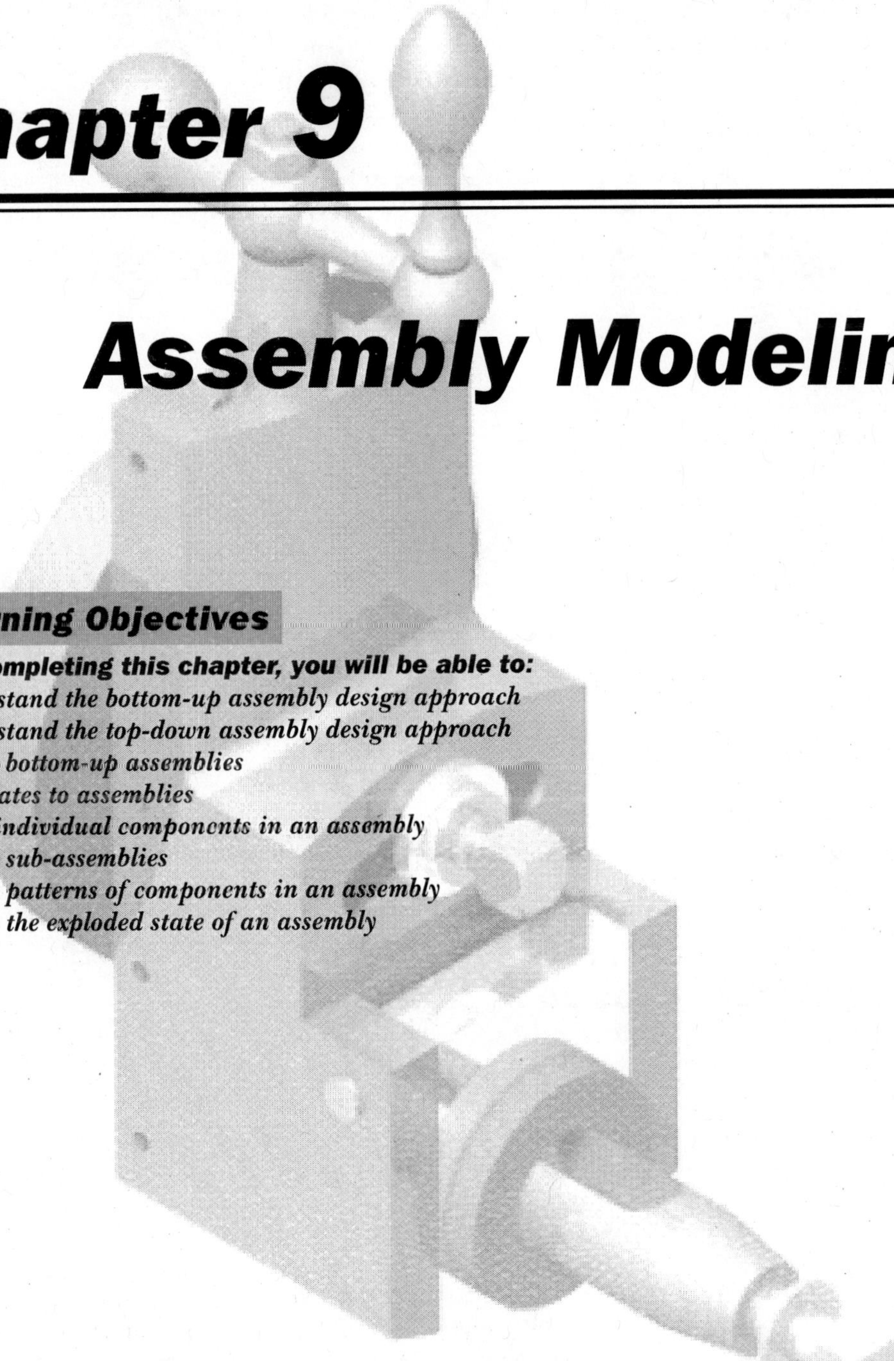

Learning Objectives

After completing this chapter, you will be able to:

- *Understand the bottom-up assembly design approach*
- *Understand the top-down assembly design approach*
- *Create bottom-up assemblies*
- *Add mates to assemblies*
- *Move individual components in an assembly*
- *Create sub-assemblies*
- *Create patterns of components in an assembly*
- *Create the exploded state of an assembly*

ASSEMBLY MODELING

An assembly design consists of two or more components assembled together at their respective work positions by using parametric relations. In SOLIDWORKS, these relations are called mates. Mates allow you to constrain the degrees of freedom of components at their respective work positions. To start the **Assembly** mode of SOLIDWORKS, invoke the **New SOLIDWORKS Document** dialog box and then choose the **Assembly** button, refer to Figure 9-1. Next, choose the **OK** button to create a new assembly document. On doing so, a new SOLIDWORKS document will open in the **Assembly** mode and the **Begin Assembly PropertyManager** will be invoked along with **Open** dialog box. The **Begin Assembly PropertyManager** is shown in Figure 9-2.

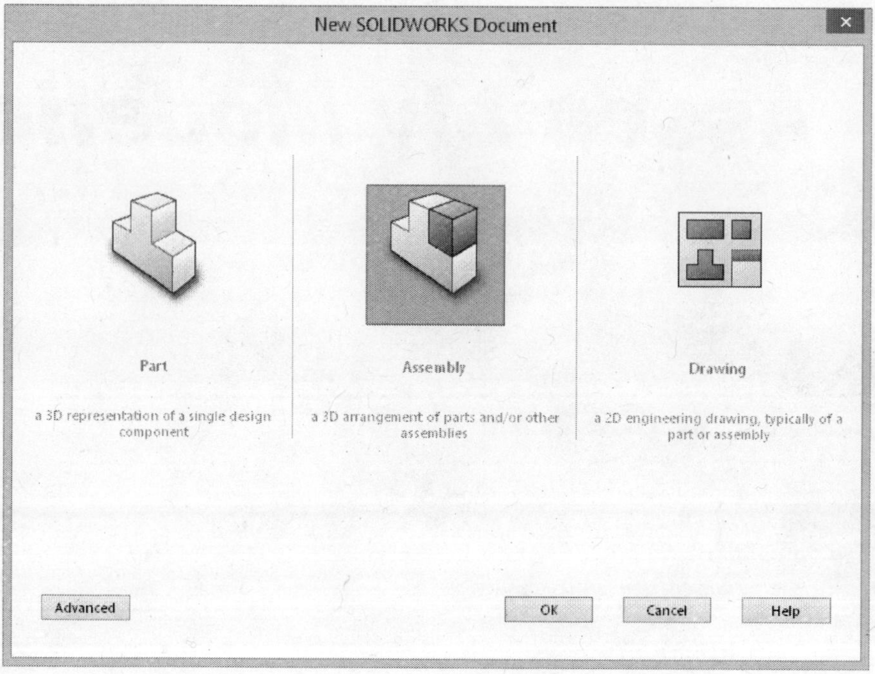

***Figure 9-1** The **Assembly** button chosen in the **New SOLIDWORKS Document** dialog box*

Types of Assembly Design Approach

In SOLIDWORKS, assemblies are created using two types of design approaches: bottom-up approach and top-down approach. These approaches are discussed next.

Bottom-up Assembly Design Approach

The bottom-up assembly design approach is the traditional and the most widely preferred approach of assembly design. In this approach, all components are created as separate part documents, and then they are placed and referred in the assembly as external components.

In this type of approach, components are created in the **Part** mode and saved as the *.sldprt* documents. After creating and saving all components of the assembly, start a new assembly document (*.sldasm*) and insert the components in it using the tools provided in the **Assembly** mode. After inserting the components, assemble them using the assembly mates.

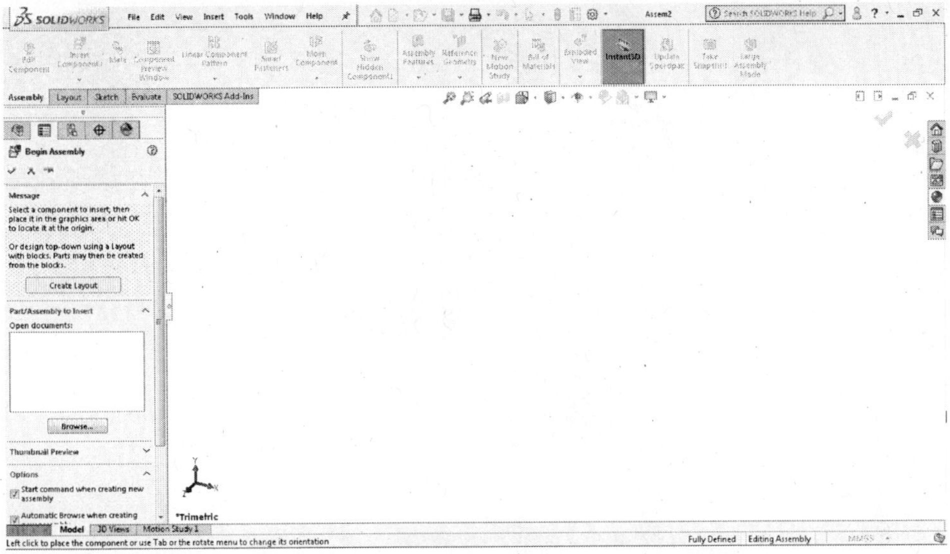

*Figure 9-2 The **Assembly** mode with the **Begin Assembly PropertyManager***

The main advantage of using this approaches is that the view of the part is not restricted because there is only a single part in the current file. Therefore, this approach allows you to concentrate on the complex individual features. It is also preferred while handling large assemblies or assemblies with complex parts.

Top-down Assembly Design Approach

In the top-down assembly design approach, the components are created in the same assembly document, but they are saved as separate part files. Therefore, the top-down assembly design approach is entirely different from the bottom-up design approach. In this approach, you will start your work in the assembly document and the geometry of one part will help in defining the geometry of the other part.

Note

You can also create an assembly with a combination of bottom-up and top-down assembly approaches.

TUTORIALS

Tutorial 1

In this tutorial, you will create all components of Tool Vise assembly and then assemble them. The Tool Vise assembly is shown in Figure 9-3. The dimensions of various components of the assembly are given in Figures 9-4 through 9-9. **(Expected time: 2 hr 45 min)**

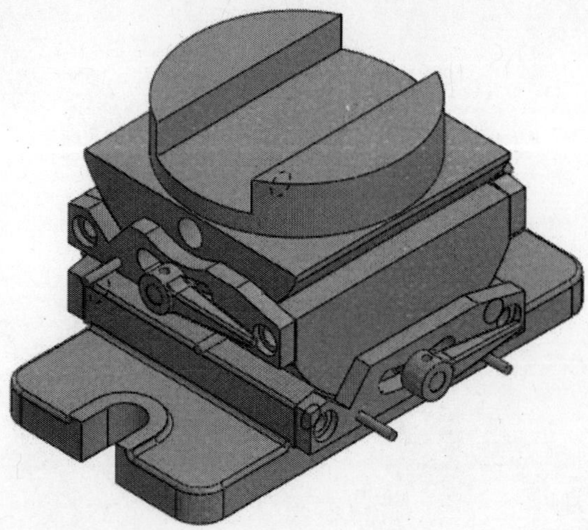

Figure 9-3 Tool Vise assembly

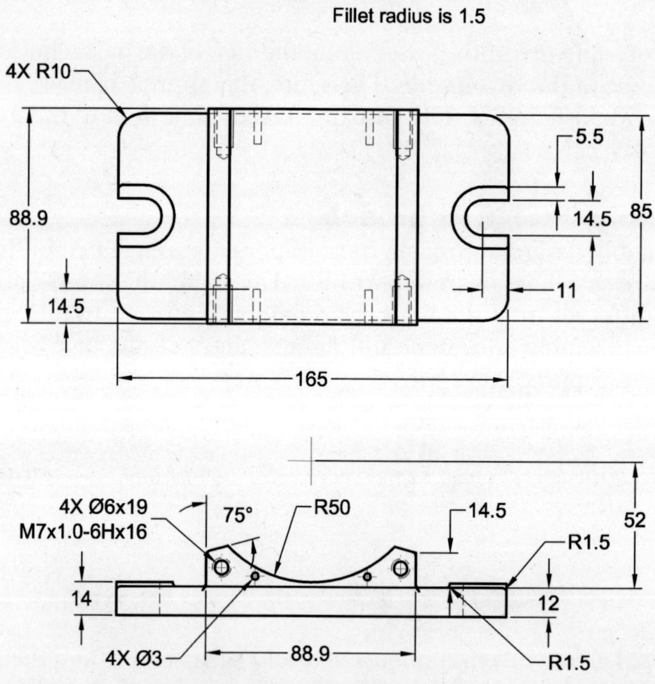

Figure 9-4 Orthographic views and dimensions of the Saddle

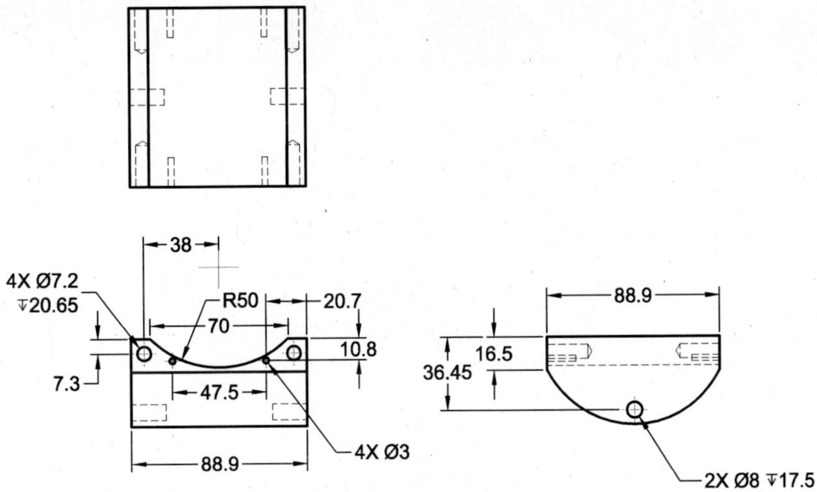

Figure 9-5 *Orthographic views and dimensions of the Center Member*

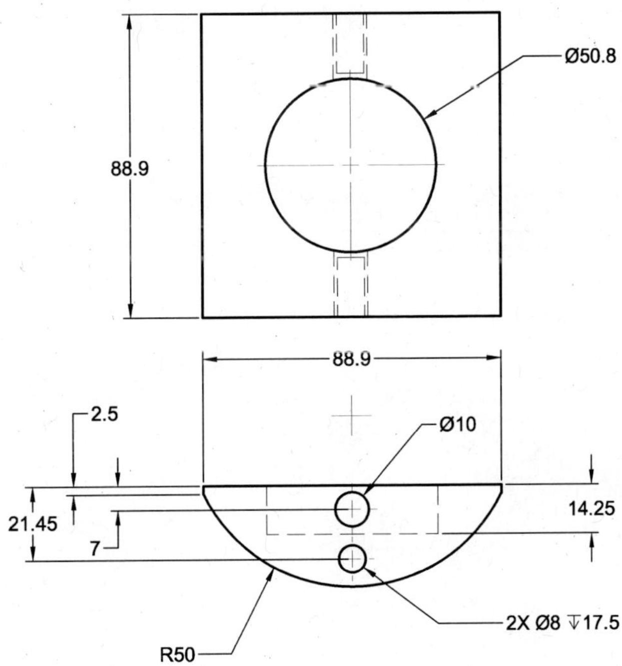

Figure 9-6 *Orthographic views and dimensions of the Upper Member*

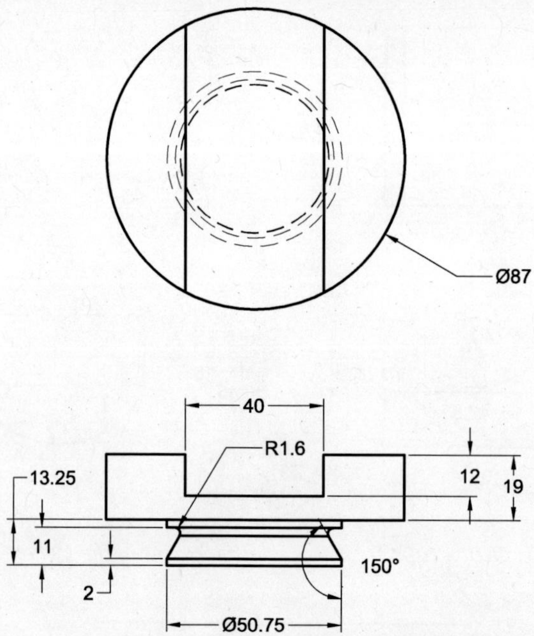

Figure 9-7 Orthographic views and dimensions of the Top Holder

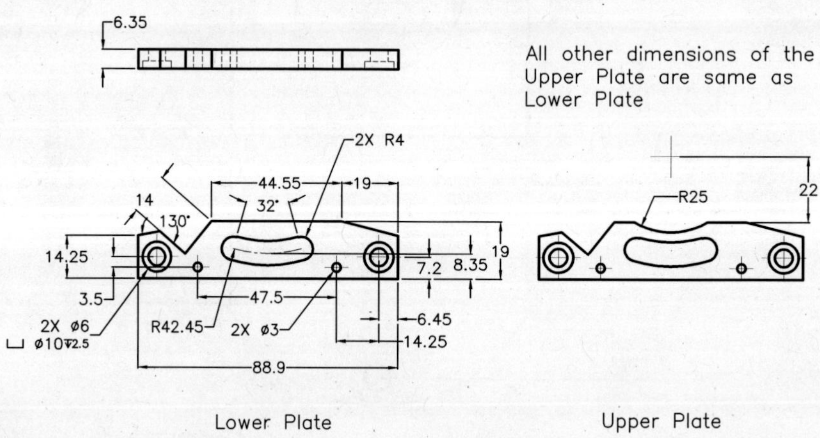

Figure 9-8 Orthographic views and dimensions of the Upper and Lower Plate

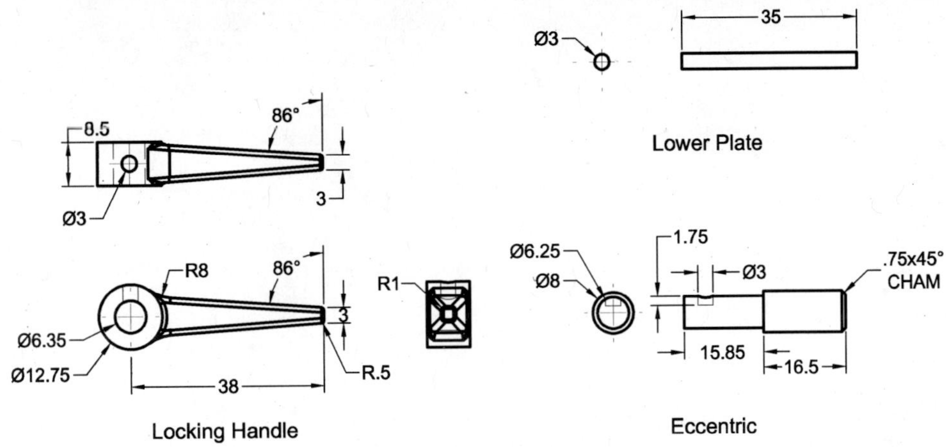

Figure 9-9 *Orthographic views and dimensions of the Locking Handle, Eccentric, and Lower Plate*

The following steps are required to complete this tutorial:

a. Create all components as individual part documents and save them at the location *\Documents\SOLIDWORKS Tutorials\c09\Tool Vise.*
b. Insert the Saddle component and place it at the origin of the **Assembly** environment, refer to Figure 9-21.
c. Insert the Center Member in the **Assembly** environment. Apply mates between the Saddle and the Center Member, refer to Figures 9-22 through 9-27.
d. Insert the Upper Member in the **Assembly** environment. Apply mates between the Center Member and the Upper Member, refer to Figures 9-28 and 9-29.
e. Insert the Tool Holder in the **Assembly** environment. Apply mates between the Upper Member and the Tool Holder, refer to Figures 9-30 through 9-32.
f. Insert the remaining components of the assembly in the **Assembly** environment and apply the required mates to assemble them with the other components of the assembly, refer to Figures 9-33 through 9-40.
g. Save the assembly.

Creating Components

As discussed in the tutorial description, first you need to create all the components of the Tool Vise assembly as individual part documents in the **Part** environment and then assemble them in the **Assembly** environment.

First, you will create the Saddle of the assembly.

1. Start a new part document of SOLIDWORKS and create the base feature of the Saddle on the Top Plane, as shown in Figure 9-10. For dimensions, refer to Figure 9-4.

2. Create the second feature of the model that is an extrude feature, as shown in Figure 9-11. For dimensions, refer to Figure 9-4.

Figure 9-10 *Base feature of the Saddle*

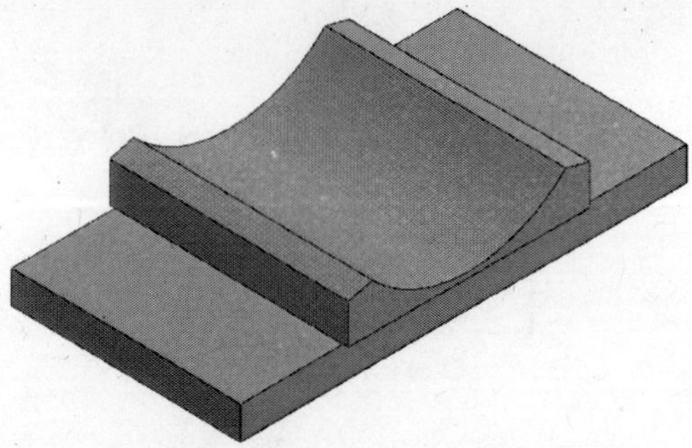

Figure 9-11 *Second feature of the Saddle*

3. Create the third feature of the model, which is a cut feature, using the **Extruded Cut** tool, as shown in Figure 9-12. For dimensions, refer to Figure 9-4.

4. Create the fourth feature of the model that is an extrude feature, as shown in Figure 9-13. For dimensions, refer to Figure 9-4.

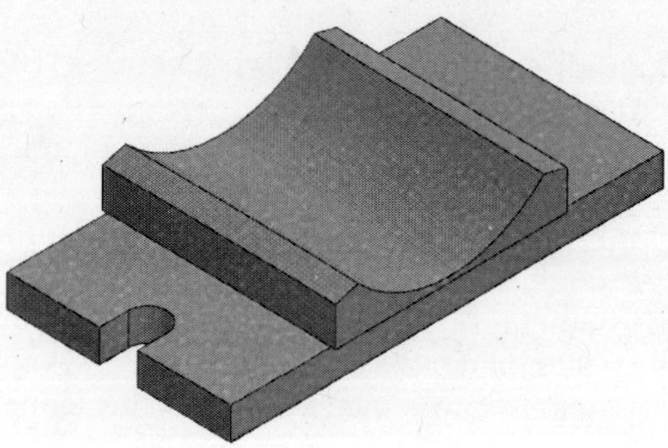

Figure 9-12 *Model after creating the cut feature*

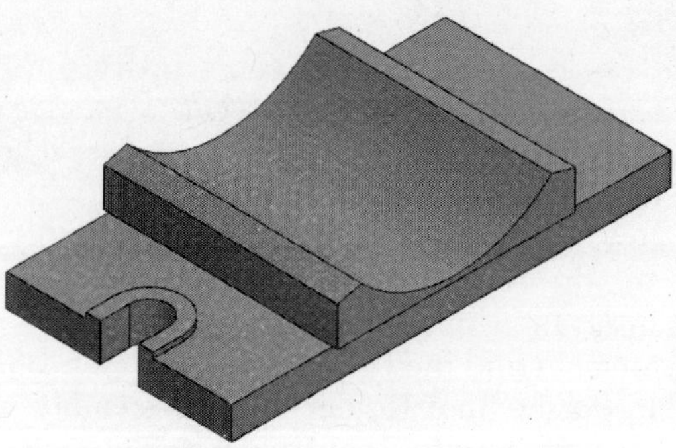

Figure 9-13 *Model after creating the fourth feature*

5. Create the fifth feature of the model by mirroring the third and fourth features, as shown in Figure 9-14.

6. Create the tapped hole of M7.0 x 1.0 by using the **Hole Wizard** tool, refer to Figure 9-15. Next, create its three instances by using the **Mirror** tool, as shown in Figure 9-16.

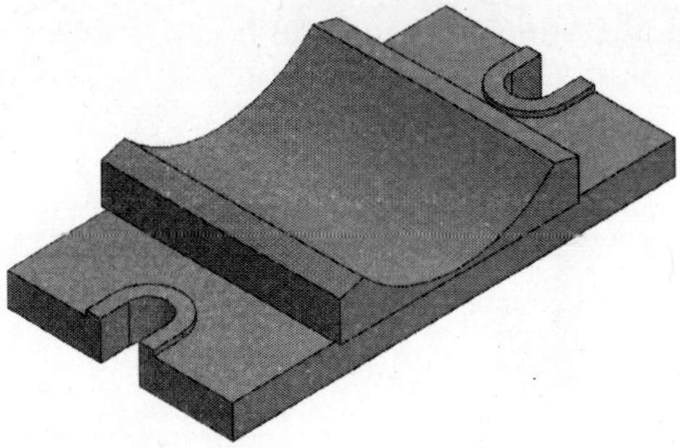

Figure 9-14 Model after creating the mirror feature

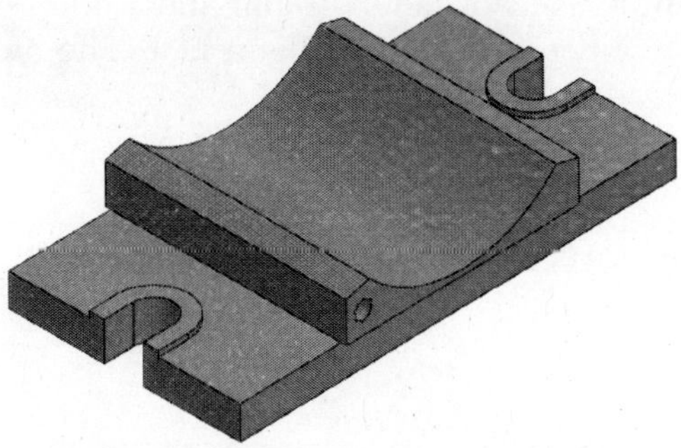

Figure 9-15 Model after creating the tapped hole

Note

In Figure 9-16, the display style of the model has been changed to hidden lines visible for better understanding of the model.

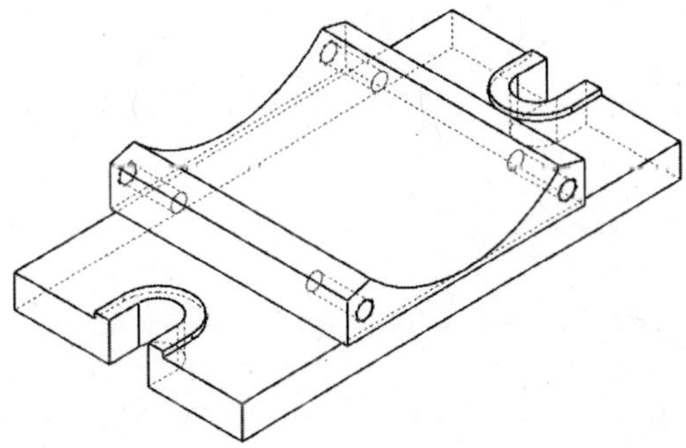

Figure 9-16 Model after creating all the instances of the tapped hole

7. Create a simple hole of diameter 3mm by using the **Simple Hole** tool, as shown in Figure 9-17. Next, create its three instances by using the **Mirror** tool, as shown in Figure 9-18.

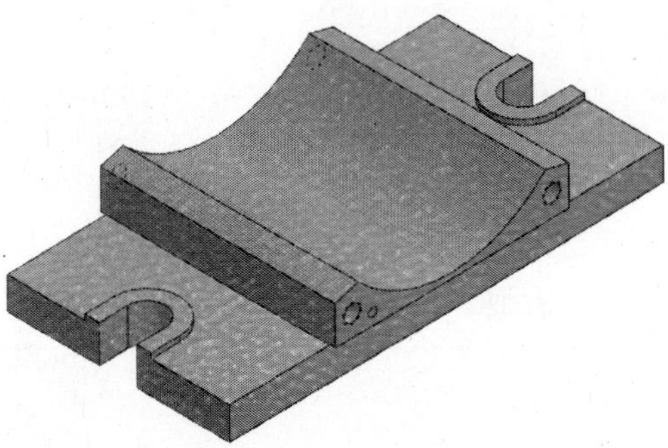

Figure 9-17 Model after creating the simple hole

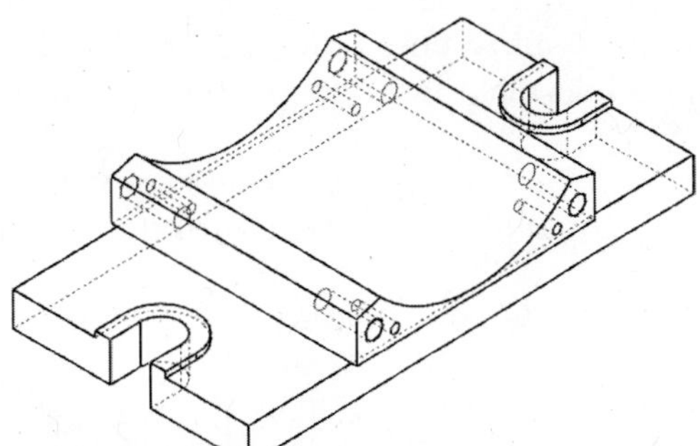

Figure 9-18 Model after creating all instances of the simple hole

8. Apply fillets of radius 10mm and 1.5mm on the respective edges of the model by using the **Fillet** tool, refer to Figure 9-4. The final model after applying the fillets is shown in Figure 9-19.

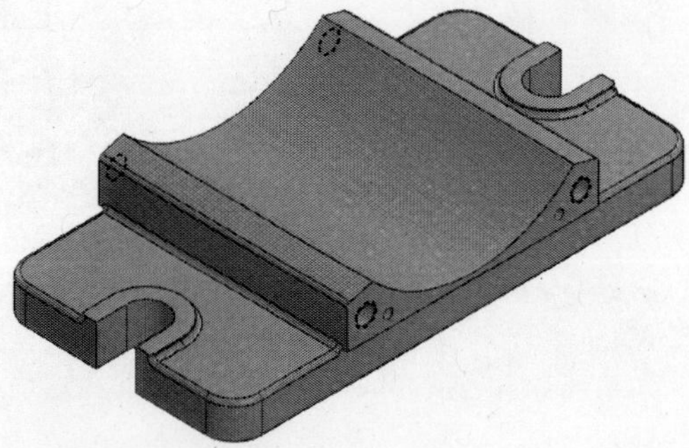

Figure 9-19 *Final model of the Saddle*

After creating the model, you need to save it.

9. Save the model at the location *\Documents\SOLIDWORKS Tutorials\c09\Tool Vise* with the name *Saddle*.

10. Similarly, create all other components of the Tool Vise assembly as separate part documents. Specify the names of components as mentioned in Figures 9-5 through 9-9. Save the files at the location *\Documents\SOLIDWORKSTutorials\c09\Tool Vise*.

Inserting the First Component into the Assembly

After creating all components of the Tool Vise assembly, you need to start a new SOLIDWORKS assembly document to assemble them.

1. Start SOLIDWORKS and then invoke the **New SOLIDWORKS Document** dialog box.

2. Choose the **Assembly** button from this dialog box and then choose the **OK** button; the **Assembly** environment is invoked with the **Begin Assembly PropertyManager** and **Open** dialog box. The **Assembly** environment of SOLIDWORKS is shown in Figure 9-20.

   Now, you need to insert the first component of the Tool Vise assembly, which is Saddle, in the **Assembly** environment by using the **Begin Assembly PropertyManager**.

The **Begin Assembly PropertyManager** is used to insert the components in the **Assembly** environment. This PropertyManager will be displayed only when you start a new assembly document. The **Message** rollout of this PropertyManager displays the working procedure.

3. Choose the **Browse** button from the **Part/Assembly to Insert** rollout to display the **Open** dialog box. Next, browse to the location *\Documents\SOLIDWORKS Tutorials\c09\Tool Vise*.

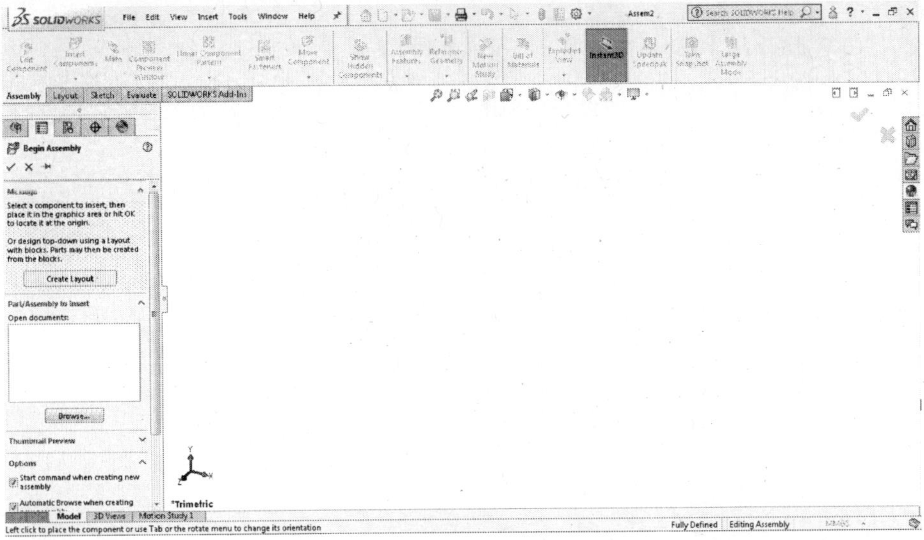

Figure 9-20** The **Assembly** environment with the **Begin Assembly PropertyManager

4. Double-click on the Saddle; preview of the Saddle is displayed attached with the cursor in the **Assembly** environment. Also, the name of the selected component is displayed in the **Open documents** display area of the **Part/Assembly to Insert** rollout in the PropertyManager. Note that as you move the component cursor, the Saddle moves along with it.

   It is recommended to place the first component of the assembly at the assembly origin.

5. Choose the **OK** button from the **Begin Assembly PropertyManager** to place the Saddle origin coincident to the origin of the assembly document. Alternatively, you can click anywhere in the graphics window to place it.

Tip

*If the component to be inserted is opened in another window, it will be listed in the **Open documents** display area of the **Begin Assembly PropertyManager**. To insert the component from this display area, select it and move the cursor to the graphics window; the component will be attached to the cursor. Left-click to place the component in the **Assembly** environment. Also, to preview the selected component, expand the **Thumbnail Preview** rollout of the PropertyManager.*

*Also, to place multiple components or multiple instances of the same component, choose the **Keep Visible** button available at the top in the **Begin Assembly PropertyManager** and select placement points in the graphics window.*

Note

*When you place the first component in the assembly using the bottom-up assembly design approach, it is fixed by default. Therefore, there is no need to apply a mate to the fixed component. To add mates to a fixed component, you first need to float the component. To do so, select the component from the drawing area or from the **FeatureManager Design Tree**. Next, right-click to invoke the shortcut menu and then choose the **Float** option.*

6. Change the view orientation to isometric. Figure 9-21 shows the **Assembly** environment after inserting the first component of the assembly.

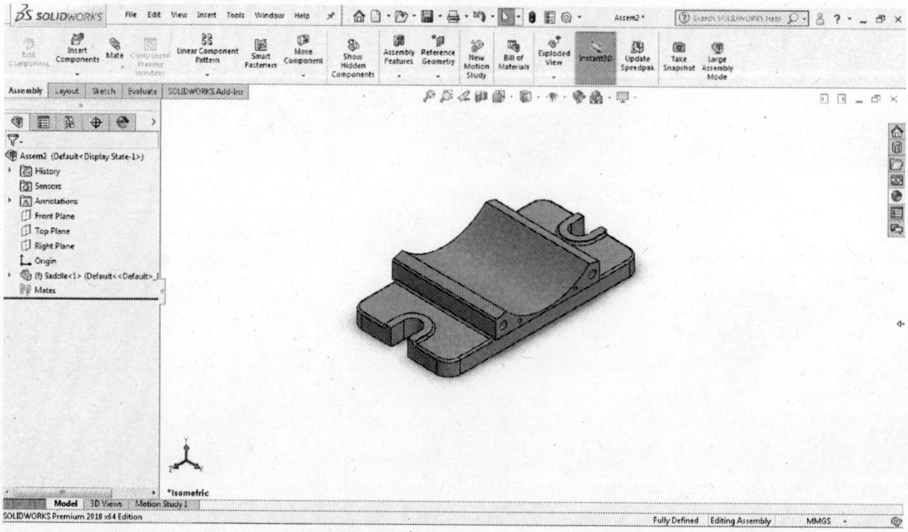

*Figure 9-21 The **Assembly** environment after inserting the first component*

Note

*When you insert a component in an assembly, it is displayed in the **FeatureManager Design Tree**. The naming convention of the first component is **(f) Name of Component <1>**. In this convention, **(f)** indicates that the component is fixed and you cannot move it. Next, the name of the component will be displayed. The **<1>** symbol denotes the serial number of the same component in the entire assembly.*

*The **(-)** symbol before the name of the component implies that the component is floating and is under-defined. You need to apply the required mates to the component to fully define it. You will learn more about assembly mates later in this chapter. The **(+)** symbol implies that the component is over-defined. If no symbol appears before the name of the component, then the component is fully defined.*

Inserting and Assembling the Second Component

After placing the first component in the **Assembly** environment, you need to insert the Center Member and then assemble it with the Saddle by applying the required mates.

1. Click on the **Assembly** tab available in the **CommandManager** to display the **Assembly CommandManager**.

2. Choose the **Insert Components** button from the **Assembly CommandManager**; the **Insert Component PropertyManager** is displayed along with the **Open** dialog box.

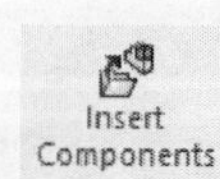

The **Insert Component PropertyManager** is used to insert components in the **Assembly** environment. As discussed earlier, you can also insert the components by using the **Begin Assembly PropertyManager**. However, the **Begin Assembly PropertyManager** will be displayed only when you start a new assembly document.

3. Double-click on the Center Member; the preview of the component is displayed along with the component cursor. Next, click the left mouse button to place the component in the Assembly environment such that it does not interfere with the existing component. Figure 9-22 shows the Assembly environment after inserting the second component.

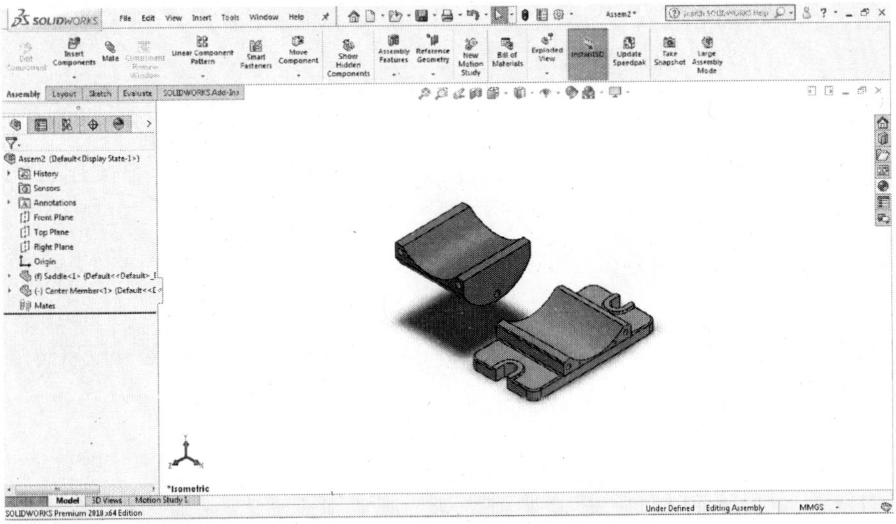

Figure 9-22 *The assembly environment after inserting the second component*

Note that the **(-)** symbol is displayed before the name of the component in the **FeatureManager Design Tree**. It implies that the component is floating and under-defined. Now, you need to apply the required mates to it by using the **Mate** tool.

4. Choose the **Mate** button from the **Assembly CommandManager**; the **Mate PropertyManager** is displayed.

The **Mate** tool is used to assemble the components by applying mates. Mates help you to precisely place and position the component with respect to other components and surroundings in the assembly by constraining their degrees of freedom.

5. Select the face of the Saddle, refer to Figure 9-23; the name of the selected face is displayed in the **Entities to Mate** selection area of the **Mate Selections** rollout of the **Mate PropertyManager**. Next, select the face of the Center Member, refer to Figure 9-23; the **Mate** pop-up toolbar is displayed with the **Concentric** button chosen, refer to Figure 9-24. Also, preview of the assembly with the concentric mate applied to it is displayed in the graphics area.

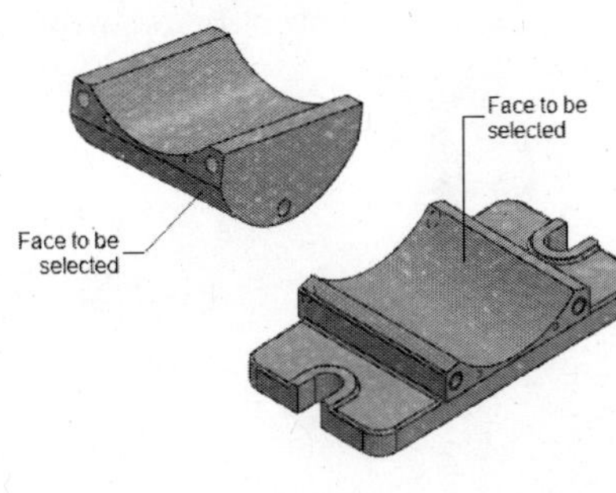

Figure 9-23 *Faces to be selected*

Note

For selecting the face of the Center Member component, you may need to rotate it individually in the ***Assembly*** *environment by using the* ***Rotate Component*** *tool available in the* ***Move Component*** *flyout of the* ***Assembly CommandManager****.*

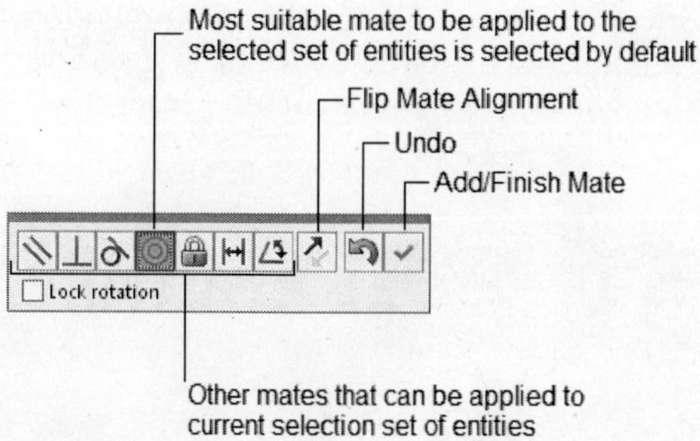

Figure 9-24 *The* ***Mate*** *pop-up toolbar*

The **Mate** pop-up toolbar displays the mates that can be applied to the current selection set. Also, the most suitable mate that can be applied is selected by default in it.

6. Choose the **Add/Finish Mate** button from the **Mate** pop-up toolbar; the concentric mate is applied between the selected faces.

   After applying the concentric mate between the selected faces, the **Mate PropertyManager** is still displayed on the left of the graphics area.

7. Apply the coincident mate between the right planar faces of the Saddle and the Center Member, refer to Figure 9-25. Similarly, apply the coincident mate between the front planar faces of the components, refer to Figure 9-26.

8. Exit the **Mate PropertyManager**. Figure 9-27 shows the **Assembly** environment after assembling the first two components.

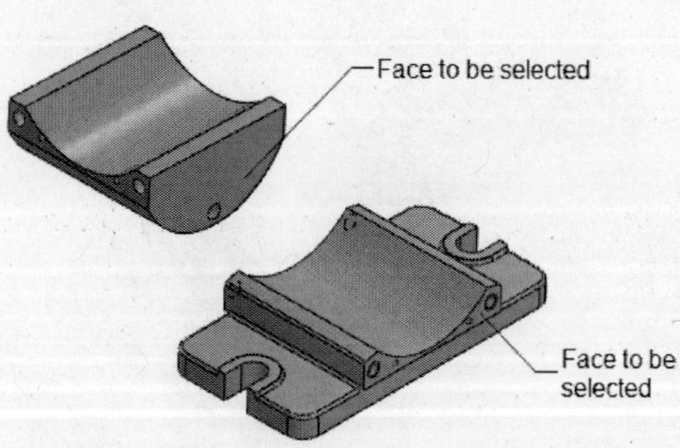

Figure 9-25 *Faces to be selected*

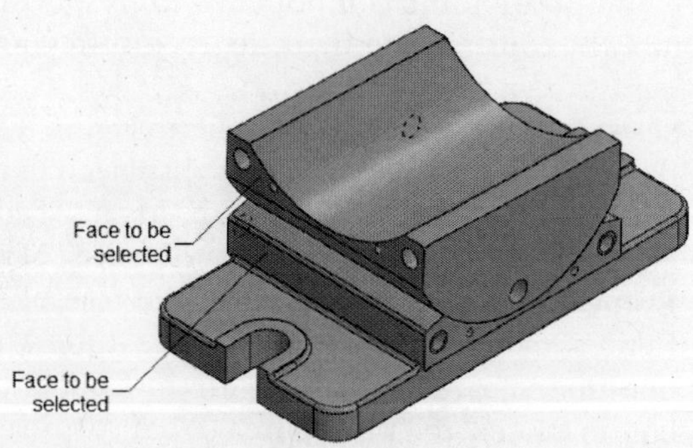

Figure 9-26 *Faces to be selected*

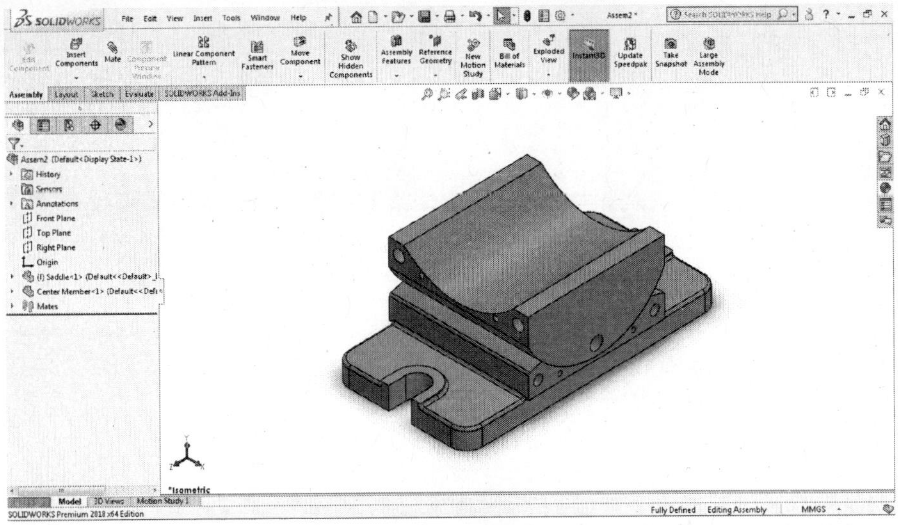

*Figure 9-27 The **Assembly** environment after assembling the first two components*

Inserting and Assembling the Third Component

Now, you need to place the third component that is the Upper Member in the **Assembly** environment and apply the required mates to assemble it with the assembly.

1. Choose the **Insert Components** button from the **Assembly CommandManager**; the **Insert Components PropertyManager** is displayed.

2. Choose the **Browse** button from the **Part/Assembly to Insert** rollout of the PropertyManager; the **Open** dialog box is displayed.

3. Double-click on the Upper Member; the preview of the component is attached with the component cursor. Next, place the component in the **Assembly** environment such that it does not interfere with the existing components by clicking the left mouse button.

4. Choose the **Mate** button from the **Assembly CommandManager**; the **Mate PropertyManager** is displayed.

5. Rotate the assembly by pressing and dragging the middle mouse button and select the bottom semi-circular face of the Upper Member. Next, select the upper semi-circular face of the Center Member; the **Mate** pop-up toolbar is displayed with the **Concentric** button chosen. Also, the preview of the assembly with the concentric mate applied is displayed in the graphics area.

6. Choose the **Add/Finish Mate** button from the **Mate** pop-up toolbar; the concentric mate is applied between the selected faces.

7. Similarly, apply the coincident mate between the front planar faces of the Center Member and the Upper Member, refer to Figure 9-28. Next, apply the coincident mate between the right planar faces of the components, refer to Figure 9-29.

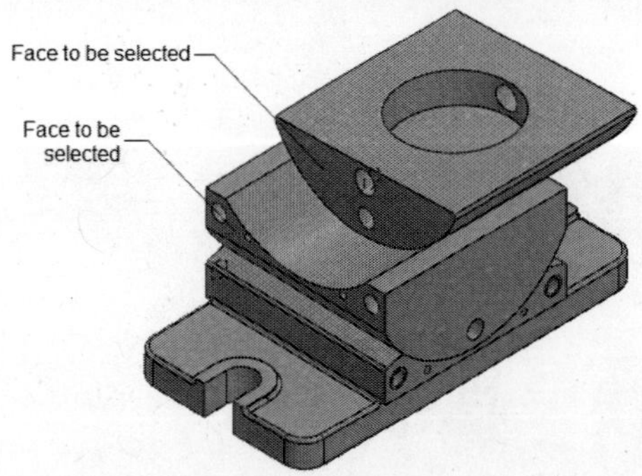

Figure 9-28 Faces to be selected

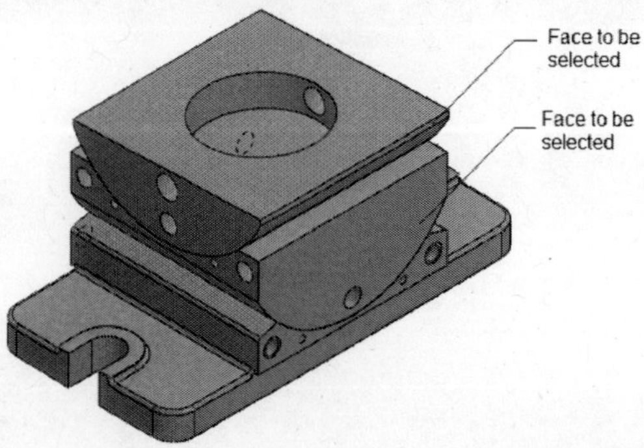

Figure 9-29 Faces to be selected

8. Exit the **Mate PropertyManager**.

Inserting and Assembling the Fourth Component

Now, you need to place the Top Holder in the **Assembly** environment and apply the required mates to assemble it.

1. Insert the Top Holder component in the **Assembly** environment by using the **Insert Components** tool.

2. Invoke the **Mate PropertyManager** by choosing the **Mate** button. Next, rotate the assembly by pressing and dragging the middle mouse button and then select the cylindrical face of the Upper Member and the Top Holder, refer to Figure 9-30; the **Mate** pop-up toolbar is displayed with the **Concentric** button chosen.

3. Choose the **Add/Finish Mate** button of the **Mate** pop-up toolbar; the concentric mate is applied between the selected faces.

4. Select the top planar face of the Upper Member of the assembly and then select the planar face of the Top Holder, refer to Figure 9-31; the **Mate** pop-up toolbar is displayed with the **Coincident** button chosen. Note that if the faces are not visible, you need to move the Top Holder using the **Move Component** tool from the **Assembly CommandManager**.

5. Choose the **Add/Finish Mate** button from the **Mate** pop-up toolbar; the coincident mate is applied between the selected faces. Next, exit the PropertyManager. Figure 9-32 shows the **Assembly** environment after assembling the Top Holder component.

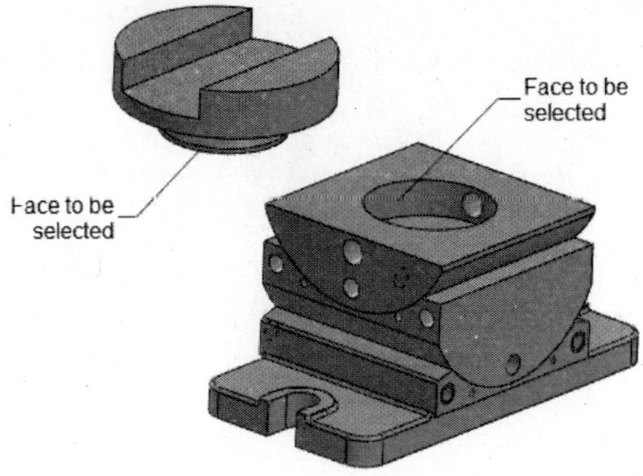

Figure 9-30 Faces to be selected

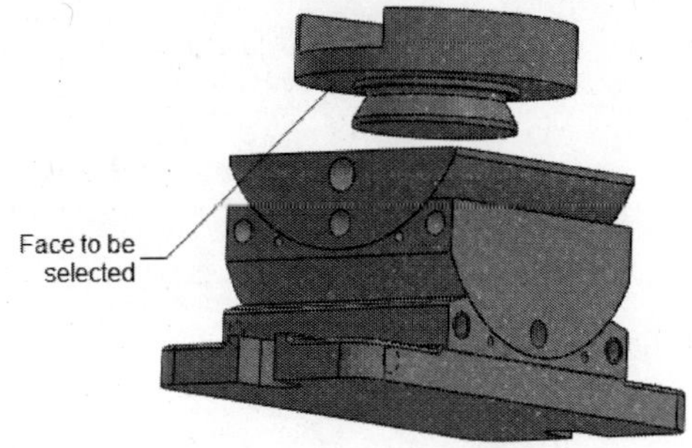

Figure 9-31 Face to be selected

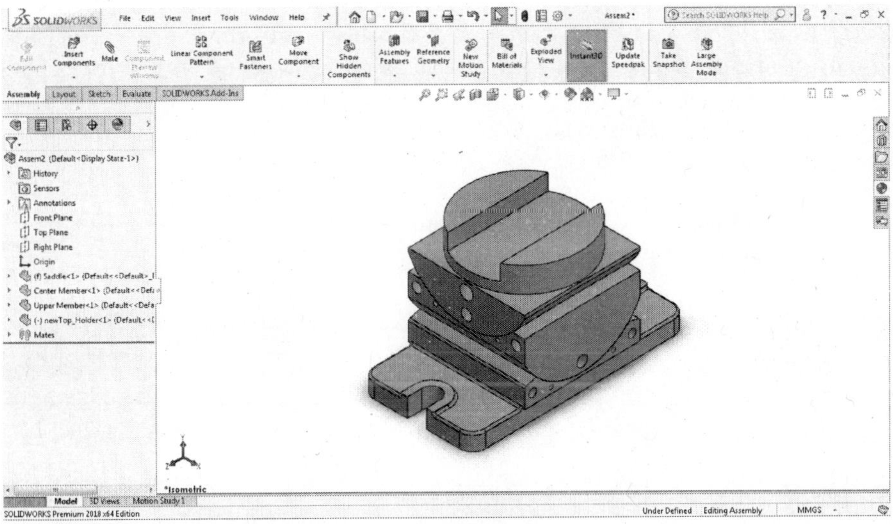

*Figure 9-32 The **Assembly** environment after assembling the Top Holder*

Inserting and Assembling the Remaining Components

Now, you need to assemble the remaining components of the Tool Vise assembly.

1. Insert the Lower Plate component in the **Assembly** environment by using the **Insert Components** tool.

2. Invoke the **Mate** tool and assemble the Lower Plate by applying the required mates. Figure 9-33 shows the assembly after assembling the Lower Plate.

3. Similarly, insert one more instance of the Lower Plate in the **Assembly** environment and then assemble it, refer to Figure 9-34.

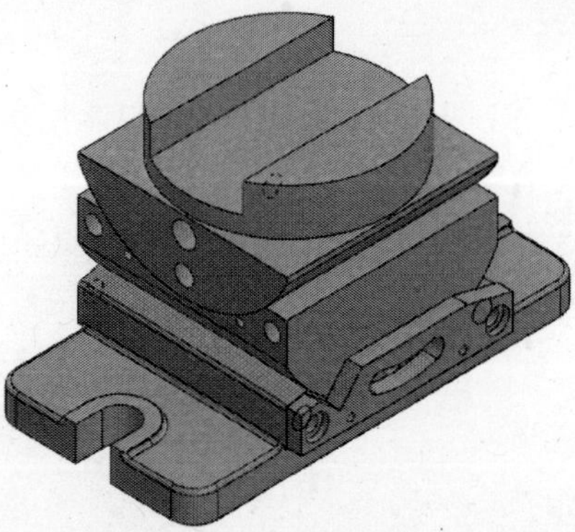

Figure 9-33 Assembly after assembling the first instance of the Lower Plate

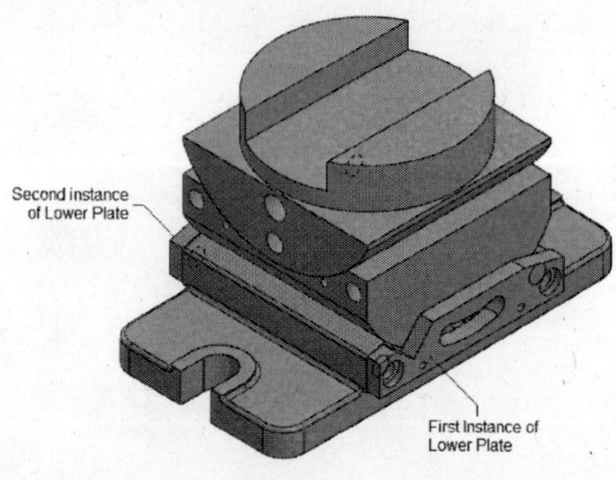

Figure 9-34 Assembly after assembling the second instance of the Lower Plate

4. Insert the Upper Plate component in the **Assembly** environment by using the **Insert Components** tool and then assemble it with the assembly, as shown in Figure 9-35.

5. Similarly, insert the second instance of the Upper Plate and assemble it with the assembly components, refer to Figure 9-36.

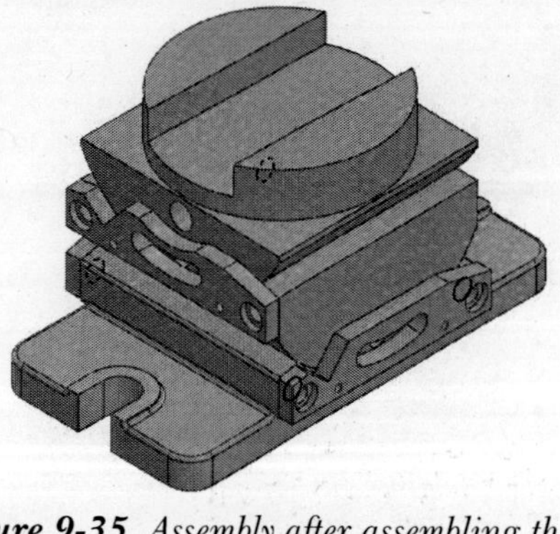

Figure 9-35 Assembly after assembling the first instance of the Upper Plate

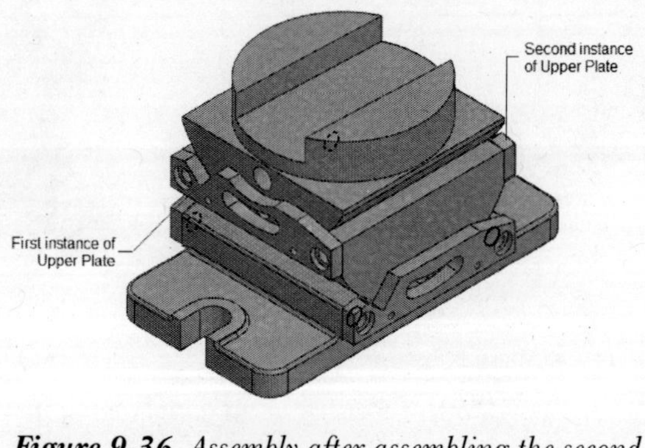

Figure 9-36 Assembly after assembling the second instance of the Upper Plate

Now, you need to insert four instances of Eccentric component in the **Assembly** environment to assemble them with the assembly.

6. Invoke the **Insert Component PropertyManager** and then choose the **Keep Visible** button available at the top right corner of the PropertyManager.

The **Keep Visible** button is used to keep the PropertyManager invoked even after the task is completed so that you can perform the same task multiple times.

7. Choose the **Browse** button from the **Part/Assembly to Insert** rollout of the PropertyManager; the **Open** dialog box is displayed.

8. Double-click on the Eccentric component; the preview of the component is attached with the component cursor. Next, place the component in the **Assembly** environment such that it does not interfere with the existing components; the other instance of the same component is attached with the cursor. Also, you are prompted to place the second instance of the selected component.

   After placing the first instance of the Eccentric component in the **Assembly** environment, the **Insert Component PropertyManager** is still invoked. This is because you have chosen the **Keep Visible** button from the PropertyManager to keep it visible.

9. Place the second instance of the Eccentric component in the **Assembly** environment such that it does not interfere with the existing components. Similarly, place the other two instances of the Eccentric component. Next, exit the PropertyManager by choosing the **OK** button from it.

   After placing the four instances of the Eccentric component in the **Assembly** environment, you need to assemble them with the other components of the assembly by applying the required mates.

10. Invoke the **Mate** tool and assemble all the four instances of the Eccentric component by applying the required mates. You can rotate the Eccentric component by using the **Rotate Component** tool from the **Assembly CommandManager**, if required. Figure 9-37 shows the top view of the assembly after assembling all the Eccentric components and Figure 9-38 shows isometric view of the assembly after assembling all the Eccentric components.

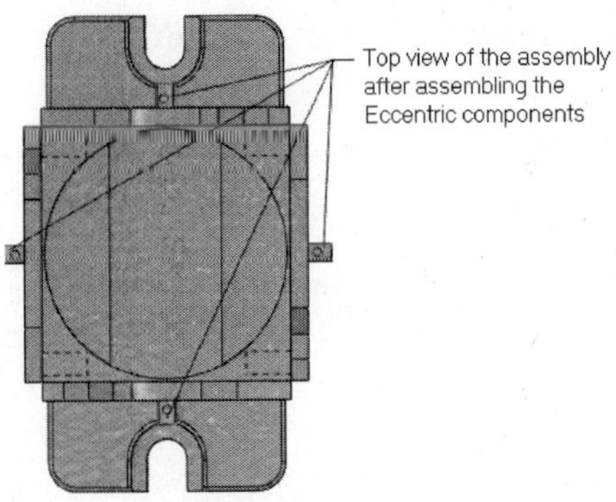

Figure 9-37 *Top view of the assembly after assembling the four instances of Eccentric*

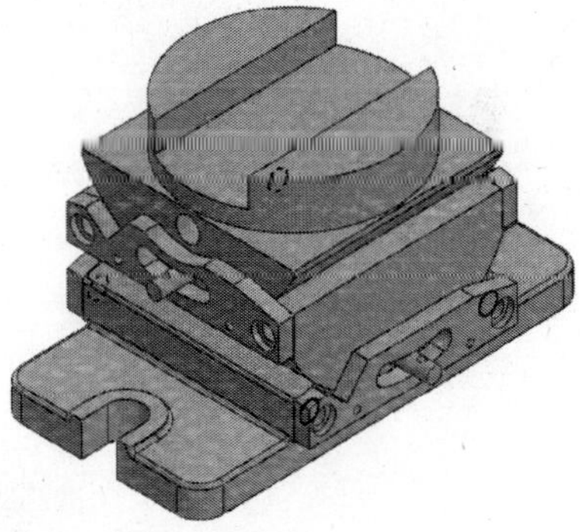

Figure 9-38 *Isometric view of the assembly after assembling the four instances of Eccentric*

11. Similarly, assemble the eight instances of the Drill Rod and four instances of the Lock Handle. Figure 9-39 shows the top view of the assembly after assembling all these components with the other components of the assembly and Figure 9-40 shows the isometric view of the final assembly.

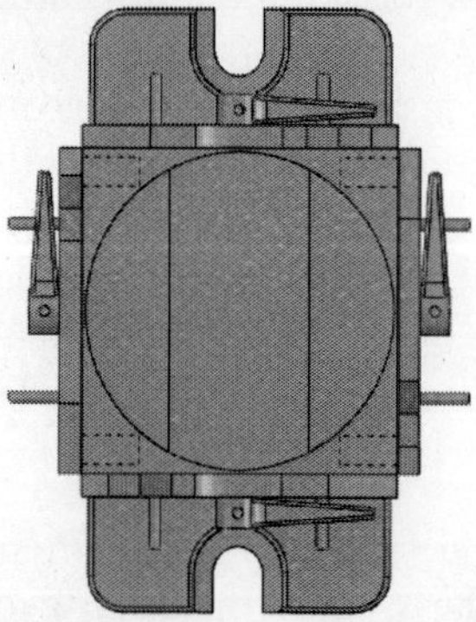

Figure 9-39 Top view of the final assembly

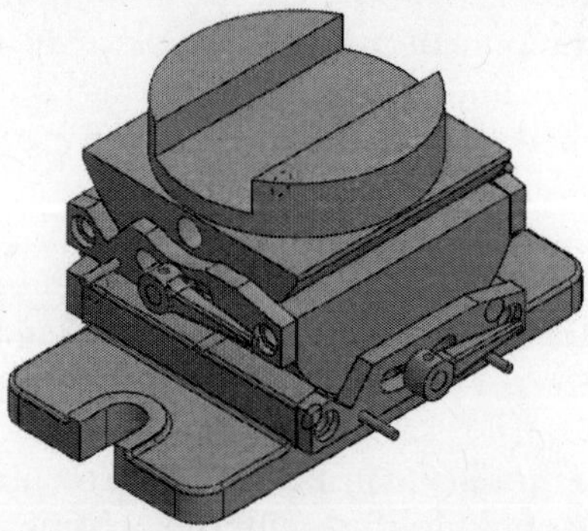

Figure 9-40 Isometric view of the final assembly

12. Save the assembly document with the name *Tool Vise* at the location *\Documents\SOLIDWORKS Tutorials\c09\Tool Vise*.

Tutorial 2

In this tutorial, you will create all components of the Pipe Vice assembly and then assemble them. The Pipe Vice assembly is shown in Figure 9-41. The dimensions of various components of this assembly are shown in Figures 9-42 and 9-43. **(Expected time: 2 hr 45 min)**

Figure 9-41 Pipe Vice assembly

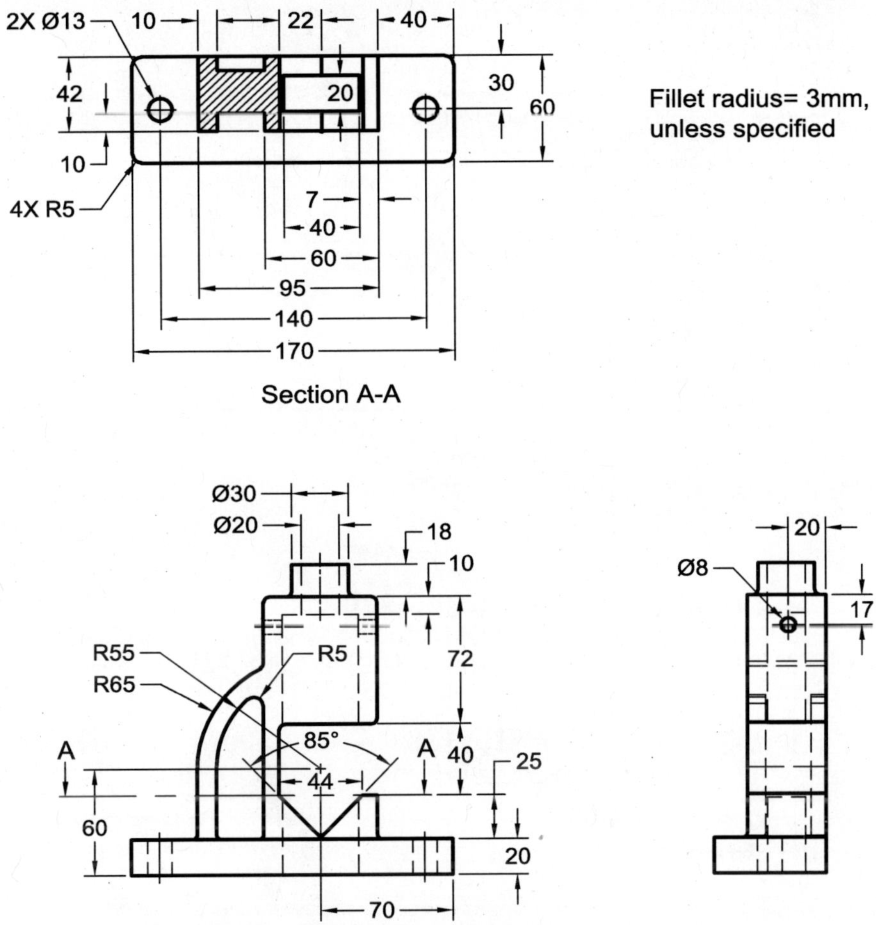

Figure 9-42 *Views and dimensions of the base*

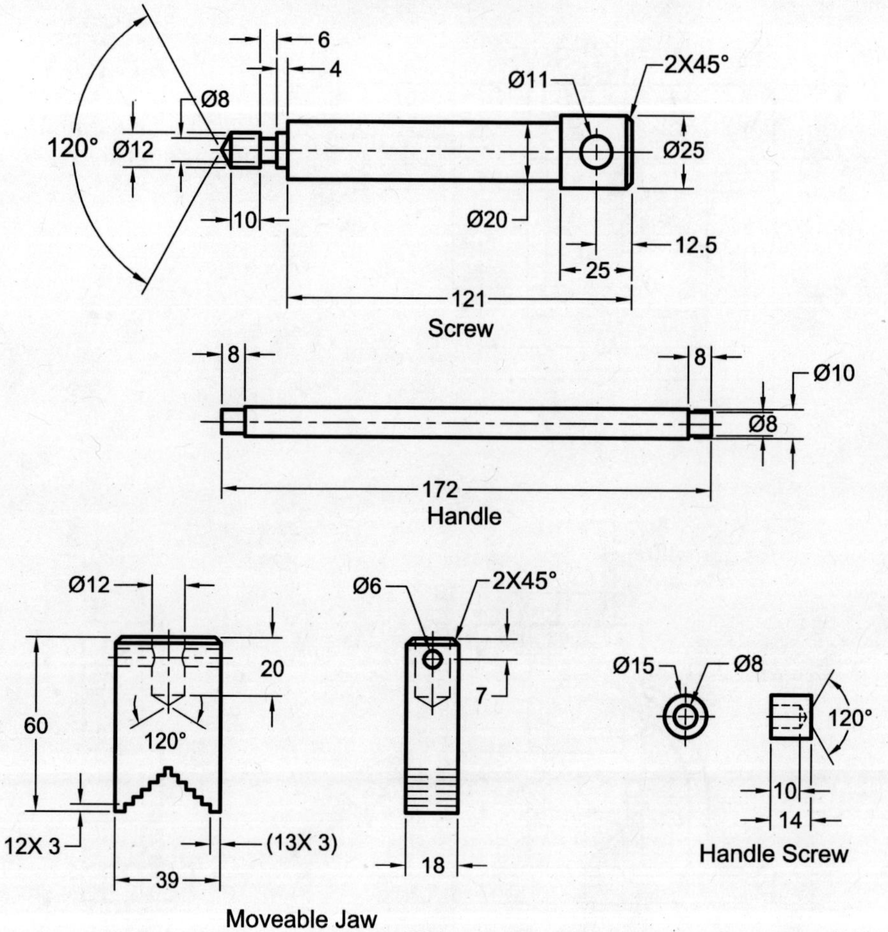

Figure 9-43 Views and dimensions of the Screw, Handle, Moveable Jaw, and Handle Screw

You will create all components of the Pipe Vice assembly as separate part documents. After creating the parts, you will assemble them in the assembly document. In this tutorial, you need to use the bottom-up approach for creating the assembly.

The following steps are required to complete this tutorial:

a. Create all components as separate part documents and then save them. The part documents will be saved at *\Documents\SOLIDWORKS Tutorials\c09\Pipe Vice*.
b. Place the Base at the origin of the assembly.
c. Place the Moveable Jaw and the Screw in the assembly. Apply mates between the Moveable Jaw and the Screw, refer to Figure 9-45.
d. Assemble the Moveable Jaw and the Screw with the Base, refer to Figures 9-46 and 9-47.
e. Save the assembly.

Creating Components

1. Create all components of the Pipe Vice assembly as separate part documents. Specify the names of the files as used in Figures 9-42 and 9-43. Save the documents at the location *\Documents\SOLIDWORKS Tutorials\c09\Pipe Vice*.

Inserting First Component into the Assembly

After creating all components of the Pipe Vice assembly, you need to start a new SOLIDWORKS assembly document.

1. Start a new SOLIDWORKS assembly document; the **Begin Assembly PropertyManager** is displayed along with the **Open** dialog box.

2. Choose the **Browse** button from the **Part/Assembly to Insert** rollout to display the **Open** dialog box. Next, open the **Pipe Vice** folder and double-click on the Base component.

3. Choose the **OK** button from the **Begin Assembly PropertyManager** to place the Base origin coincident to the origin of the assembly document.

4. Change the view orientation to isometric.

Inserting and Assembling the Components

After placing the first component in the assembly environment, you need to place the Moveable Jaw and the Screw in the assembly environment. After placing these components, you need to apply the required mates.

1. Choose the **Insert Components** button from the **Assembly CommandManager**. Then, choose the **Keep Visible** button from the PropertyManager to keep it visible. Next, invoke the **Open** dialog box by choosing the **Browse** button from the **Part/Assembly to Insert** rollout.

2. Double-click on the Moveable Jaw. Place the component in the assembly environment such that it does not interfere with the existing component.

3. Similarly, place the Screw in the assembly environment and choose the **OK** button from the **Insert Component PropertyManager**. Figure 9-44 shows the Moveable Jaw, Screw, and Base placed in the assembly environment.

   Now, you need to assemble the Screw with the Moveable Jaw. Therefore, you need to fix the Moveable Jaw.

4. Select the Moveable Jaw from the drawing area or from the **FeatureManager Design Tree** and then right-click to invoke the shortcut menu.

5. Choose the **Fix** option from the shortcut menu; the Moveable Jaw becomes fixed and you cannot move or rotate it.

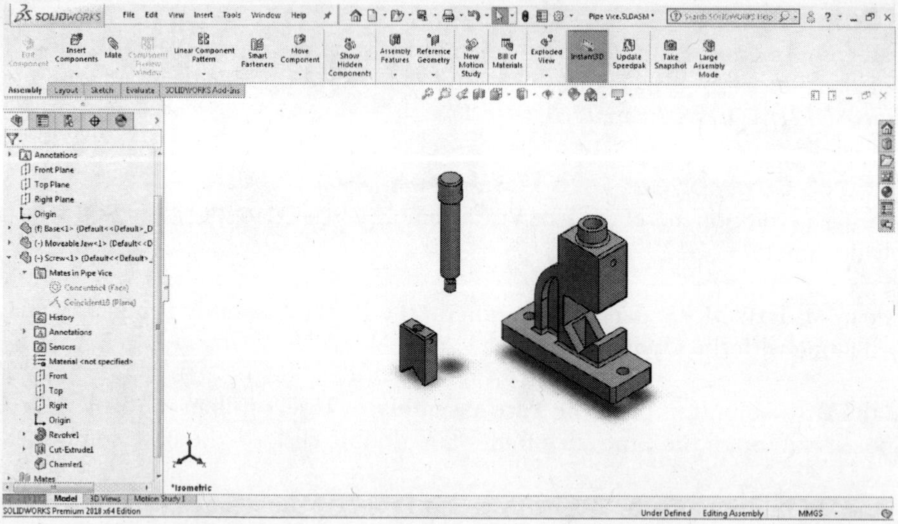

Figure 9-44 The Moveable Jaw, Screw, and Base placed in the assembly environment

Now, you will assemble the Screw with the Moveable Jaw by using the **Smart Mates** option.

6. Choose the **Move Component** button from the **Assembly CommandManager**; the **Move Component PropertyManager** is displayed.

The **Move Component** tool is used to move the individual unconstrained component in the assembly document without affecting the position and location of the other components.

Tip

*In the **Assembly** environment of SOLIDWORKS, you can also move the component placed in an assembly without invoking any tool. To move an individual component, press and hold the left mouse button on the component and drag the cursor. Release the left mouse button to place the component at the desired location.*

7. Choose the **SmartMates** button from the **Move** rollout of the **Move Component PropertyManager**; the current PropertyManager is changed to **SmartMates PropertyManager**.

The **SmartMates PropertyManager** is used to apply Smart Mates to the components in order to assemble them in the **Assembly** environment. Smart Mates are the most attractive feature of the assembly design environment in SOLIDWORKS. Smart Mates technology speeds up the design process in the **Assembly** environment of SOLIDWORKS.

8. Double-click on the lowermost cylindrical face of the Screw; the Screw appears transparent.

9. Drag the cursor to the hole located on the top of the Moveable Jaw by pressing the left mouse button. Next, release the left mouse button as soon as the concentric symbol is displayed below the cursor; the **Mate** pop-up toolbar is displayed with the **Concentric** button chosen.

10. Choose the **Add/Finish Mate** button from the **Mate** pop-up toolbar. Next, select the Screw and move it up, so that it is not inside the Moveable Jaw.

11. Right-click in the drawing area and then choose the **Clear Selections** option from the shortcut menu to clear the current selection.

12. Rotate the assembly and double-click on the lower flat face of the Screw; the Screw appears transparent.

13. Rotate the model again and drag the cursor toward the top planar face of the Moveable Jaw by pressing the left mouse button. Next, release the left mouse button as soon as the coincident symbol is displayed below the cursor; the **Mate** pop-up toolbar is displayed with **Coincident** button chosen.

14. Choose the **Add/Finish Mate** button from the **Mate** pop-up toolbar. The coincident mate is applied between the selected faces.

15. Choose the **OK** button from the **SmartMates PropertyManager**. Next, change the current view of the assembly to isometric view. Figure 9-45 shows the Screw after applying mates.

    Next, you need to assemble the Screw and the Moveable Jaw with the Base.

16. Select the Moveable Jaw, invoke the shortcut menu, and then choose the **Float** option from it. Now, you can move the Moveable Jaw and the Screw assembled to it.

Figure 9-45 *The Screw assembled with the Moveable Jaw*

17. With the ALT key pressed, select the cylindrical face of the Screw and move the Screw toward the hole created on the top face of the Base. Now add the concentric mate between them.

18. Invoke the **Mate PropertyManager** and then select the front planar face of the Moveable Jaw and the front planar face of the Base.

19. Choose the **Parallel** button from the **Mate** pop-up toolbar and then choose the **Add/Finish Mate** button to add the **Parallel** mate between the selected faces.

20. Select the faces, as shown in Figure 9-46.

21. Choose the **Parallel** button from the **Mate** pop-up toolbar. Next, expand the **Advanced Mates** rollout of the **Parallel1 PropertyManager** displayed at the left of the graphics area.

22. Choose the **Distance** button from **Advanced Mates** rollout of the PropertyManager; the **Distance, Maximum Value**, and **Minimum Value** edit boxes are enabled.

The **Distance** button available in the **Advanced Mates** rollout of the **Mate PropertyManager** is used to create to and fro motion between the components.

Note

The maximum distance by which the two selected faces can be moved apart is specified in the ***Distance*** *spinner and the same values will be displayed in the* ***Maximum Value*** *edit box as well. To move the selected faces in to and fro motion, you need to specify the minimum distance in the* ***Minimum Value*** *edit box.*

23. Enter **65** and **5** in the **Maximum Value** and **Minimum Value** edit boxes, respectively. Next, choose the **OK** button twice to exit the PropertyManager. Figure 9-47 shows the assembly document after assembling the Moveable Jaw and Screw with the Base component of the assembly.

24. Similarly, assemble the other components of the Pipe Vice assembly. Figure 9-47 shows the final Pipe Vice assembly.

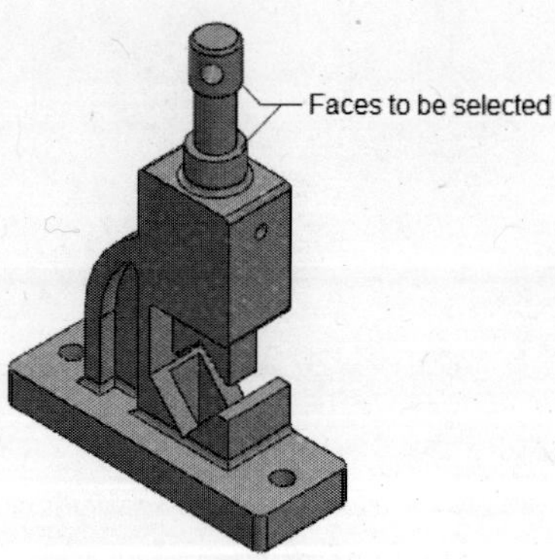

Figure 9-46 *Faces to be selected*

Figure 9-47 *Final Pipe Vice assembly*

25. Save the assembly document at the location *\Documents\SOLIDWORKS\c09\Pipe Vice.*

Tutorial 3

In this tutorial, you will create the Radial Engine assembly shown in Figure 9-48. This assembly will be created in two parts: sub-assembly and main assembly. You will also create the exploded state of the assembly and then create the explode line sketch. The exploded state of the assembly is displayed in Figure 9-49. The views and dimensions of all the components of this assembly are displayed in Figures 9-50 through 9-53. **(Expected time: 3 hr)**

Figure 9-48 *The Radial Engine assembly*

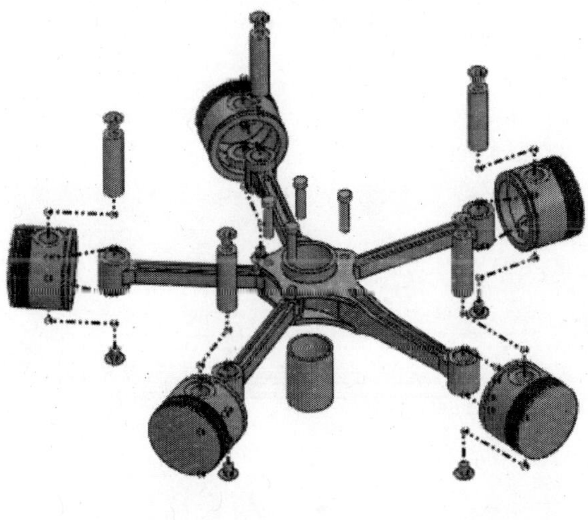

Figure 9-49 *Exploded view of the assembly*

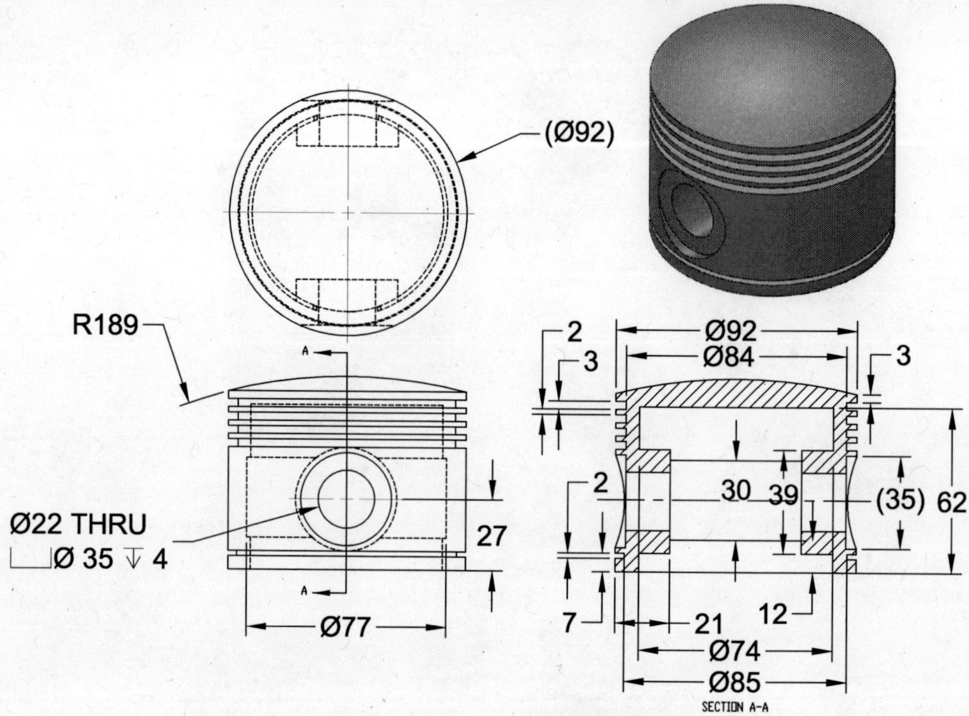

Figure 9-50 *Views and dimensions of the Piston*

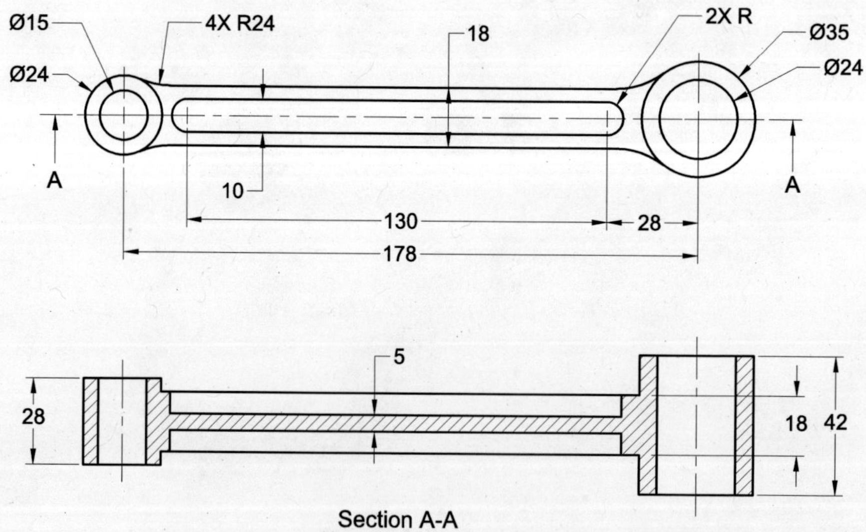

Figure 9-51 *Views and dimensions of the Articulated Rod*

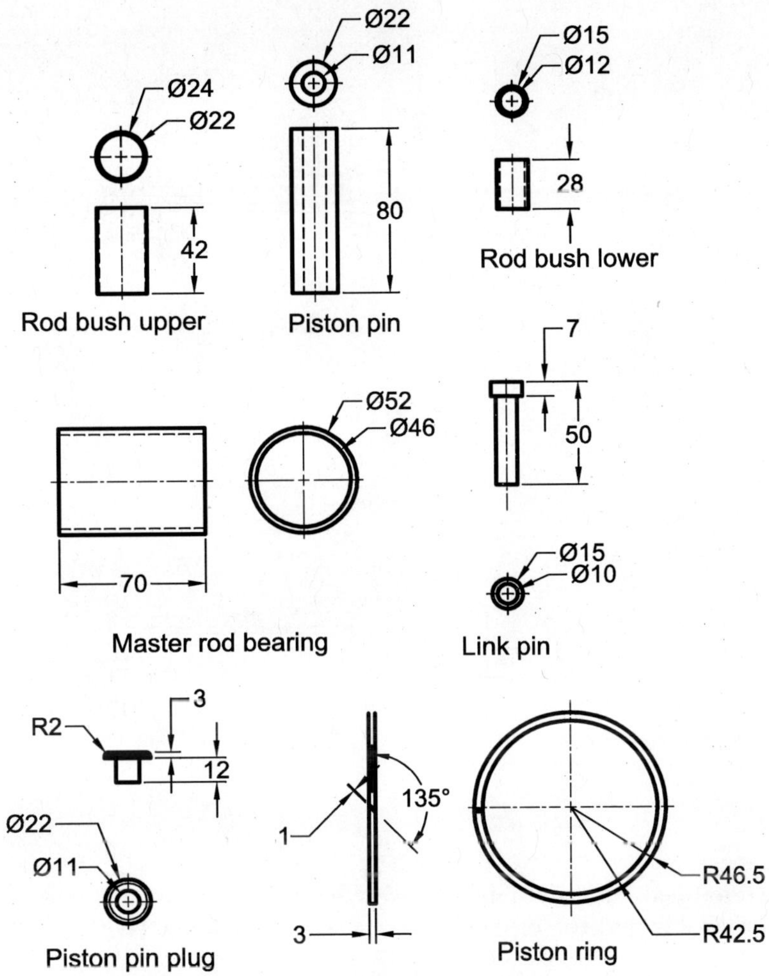

Figure 9-52 *Views and dimensions of other components*

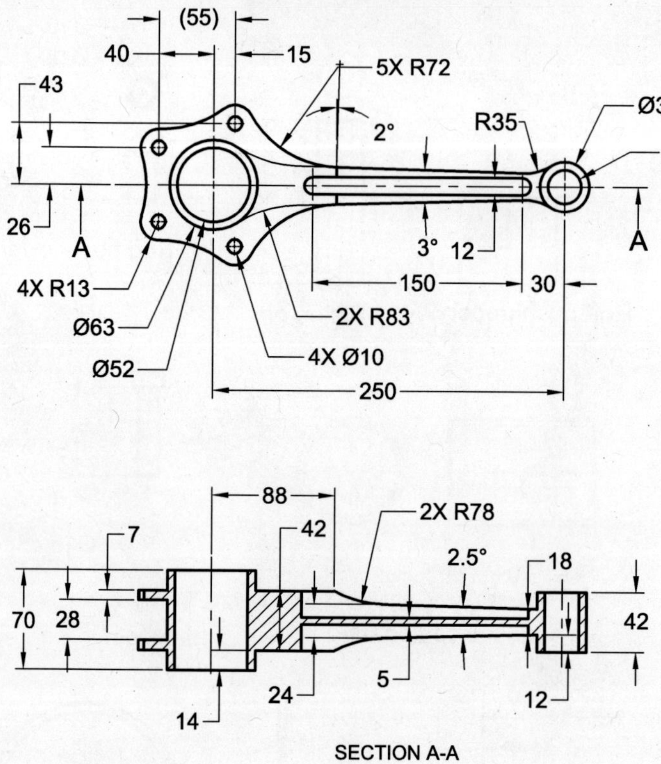

***Figure 9-53** Views and dimensions of the Master Rod*

You need to break this assembly into two parts because it is a large assembly. One will be the sub-assembly and the other will be the main assembly. First, you need to create the sub-assembly consisting of Articulated Rod, Piston, Piston Rings, Piston Pin, Rod Bush Upper, Rod Bush Lower, and Piston Pin Plug. Next, you need to create the main assembly by assembling the Master Rod with the Piston, Piston Rings, Piston Pin, Rod Bush Upper, and Piston Pin Plug. Finally, you will assemble the sub-assembly with the main assembly.

The following steps are required to complete this tutorial:

a. Create all components of the assembly in the **Part** mode and save them in the *Radial Engine Assembly* folder.
b. Start a new assembly document and assemble the components to complete the sub-assembly, refer to Figures 9-54 through 9-57.
c. Start a new assembly document and assemble the components of the main assembly, refer to Figure 9-58.
d. Assemble the sub-assembly in the main assembly, refer to Figures 9-59 through 9-64.
e. Create the exploded view of the assembly and then create the explode line sketch, refer to Figures 9-65 through 9-71.
f. Save the assembly.

Creating the Components

1. Create a folder with the name *Radial Engine Assembly* in the *\Documents\SOLIDWORKS Tutorials\c09* folder. Create all components in the individual part documents and save them in this folder.

Note

While creating the Master Rod, make sure that the holes on the left of the Master Rod are created using the sketch-driven pattern. This is done because while assembling the Link Pin, you need to create the derived pattern of the Link Pin using the sketch-driven pattern feature.

Creating the Sub-assembly

As discussed earlier, you need to first create the sub-assembly and then assemble it with the main assembly.

1. Start a new SOLIDWORKS assembly document and exit the **Begin Assembly PropertyManager**. Next, save the assembly document with the name **Piston Articulation Rod Sub-assembly** in the same folder in which the parts are saved.

2. First place the Articulated Rod at the origin of the assembly and then place the other components such as Piston, Piston Pin, Piston Pin Plug, Rod Bush Upper, and Rod Bush Lower in the assembly document.

3. Apply the required mates to assemble these components. Figure 9-54 shows the sequence for assembling the components. In this figure, the exploded view and the explode line sketch are given only for your reference. The assembly after assembling the Articulated Rod, Piston, Piston Pin, Piston Pin Plug, Rod Bush Upper, and Rod Bush Lower is shown in Figure 9-55.

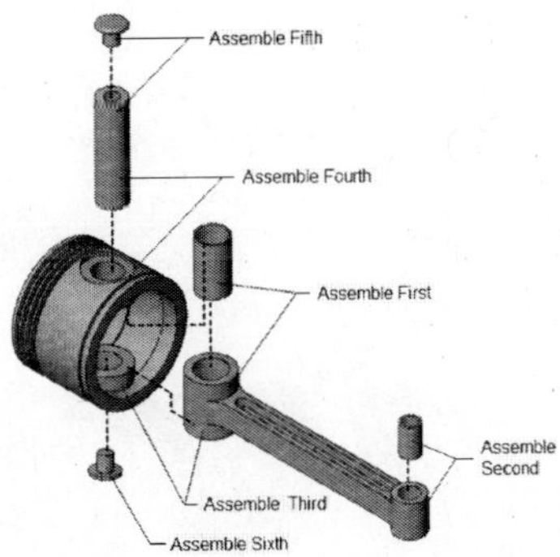

***Figure 9-54** Assembly of the Articulated Rod, Piston, Piston Pin, Piston Pin Plug, Rod Bush Upper, and Rod Bush Lower*

***Figure 9-55** Assembly after assembling the components*

It is clear from the assembly that you need to assemble four instances of the Piston Ring. You will assemble only one instance of the Piston Ring at the uppermost groove of the ring and then create a local linear pattern.

4. Insert the Piston Ring in the assembly environment and assemble the Piston Ring at the uppermost groove of the Piston using the assembly mates, refer to Figure 9-56.

Note

In this assembly, the color of the Piston Ring is changed. To change the color, select the Piston Ring; a pop-up toolbar is displayed. Choose the ***Appearances*** *button from the pop-up toolbar; a flyout is displayed. Choose the name of the component; the* ***color PropertyManager*** *is displayed. Set the color using the option available in this PropertyManager.*

Next, you need to create the local linear pattern of the Piston Ring.

5. Choose the **Linear Component Pattern** button from the **Assembly CommandManager**; the **Linear Pattern PropertyManager** is displayed.

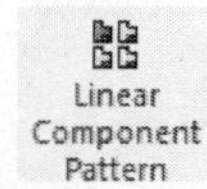

6. Select any one of the horizontal edges of the Articulated Rod to define the direction of pattern creation.

7. Click once in the **Components to Pattern** selection box and select the Piston Ring from the graphics area; the preview of the linear pattern with the default settings is displayed in the graphics area.

8. Choose the **Reverse Direction** button to reverse the direction of the pattern creation, if required.

9. Set **5** in the **Spacing** spinner and **4** in the **Number of Instances** spinner.

10. Choose the **OK** button from the **Linear Pattern PropertyManager**; the sub-assembly after patterning the Piston Ring is shown in Figure 9-57.

11. Save and close the assembly document.

Figure 9-56 *First instance of the Piston Ring assembled with the Piston*

Figure 9-57 *Sub-assembly after patterning the Piston Ring*

Creating the Main Assembly

Next, you need to create the main assembly and then assemble the sub-assembly with it.

1. Start a new SOLIDWORKS assembly document and exit the **Begin Assembly PropertyManager**. Now, save it with the name *Radial Engine assembly* in the same folder in which the parts are saved.

2. First, place the Master Rod at the origin of the assembly and then place the Piston, Piston Pin, Piston Pin Plug, Piston Ring, Rod Bush Upper, and Master Rod Bearing in the current assembly document.

3. Assemble all components of the main assembly using the assembly mates. Note that you need to create a linear pattern of the Piston Ring. Also, you need to assemble two instances of the Piston Pin Plug in the assembly. Figure 9-58 shows the main assembly after assembling all the components.

Assembling the Sub-assembly with the Main Assembly

Next, you need to place the sub-assembly in the main assembly and then assemble them together.

1. Choose the **Insert Components** button from the **Assembly CommandManager**; the **Insert Component PropertyManager** is displayed.

2. If the sub-assembly document is not opened, choose the **Browse** button in the **Part/Assembly to Insert** rollout; the **Open** dialog box is displayed.

3. Select **Assembly (*.asm, *.sldasm)** from the **Files of type** drop-down list.

4. Double-click on the **Piston Articulated Rod Sub-assembly** sub-assembly and place it in the main assembly. Figure 9-59 shows the sub-assembly and the main assembly placed together.

Figure 9-58 *Components assembled in the main assembly*

Figure 9-59 *Sub-assembly and the main assembly placed together*

5. Assemble the sub-assembly with the main assembly using the assembly mates. Figure 9-60 shows the assembly structure that will help you in assembling the instances of the sub-assembly.

   Figure 9-61 shows all instances of the sub-assembly assembled with the main assembly.

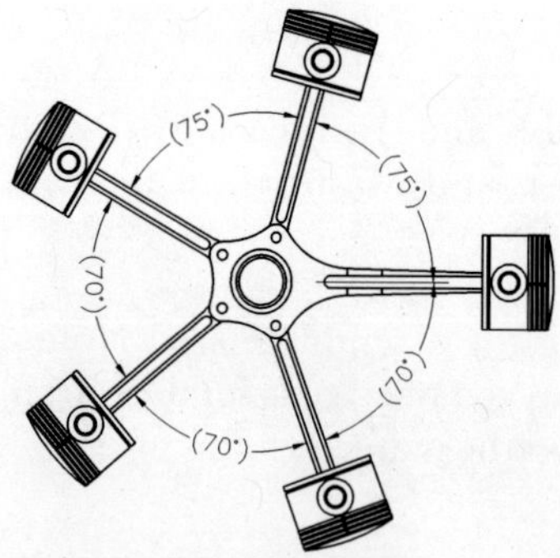

Figure 9-60 *Components assembled in the main assembly*

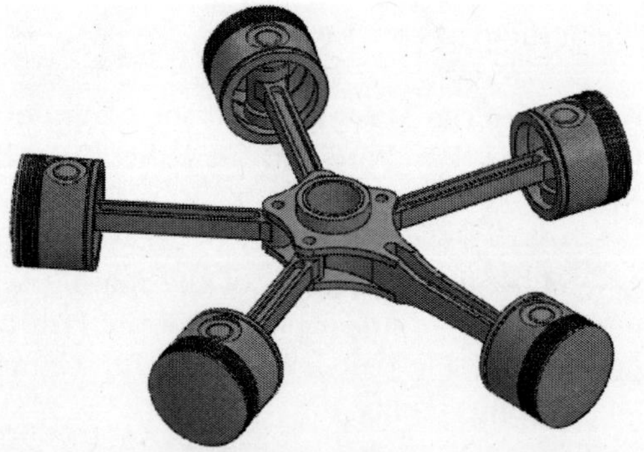

Figure 9-61 *Sub-assembly assembled with the main assembly*

> **Tip**
> *You can create more than one instance of the sub-assembly. To do so, press and hold the CTRL key, select and drag the sub-assembly from the* ***FeatureManager Design Tree,*** *and then release the left mouse button.*

Assembling the Link Pin

After assembling the sub-assembly with the main assembly, you need to assemble the Link Pin with the main assembly.

1. Place the Link Pin in the current assembly environment. Assemble the Link Pin with the main assembly using the assembly mates. Figure 9-62 shows the first instance of the Link Pin assembled with the main assembly.

   As discussed earlier, the other instances of the Link Pin will be assembled using the pattern-driven pattern feature of the holes created on the left of the master rod.

Figure 9-62 *The first instance of the Link Pin assembled with the main assembly*

2. Choose the **Pattern Driven Component Pattern** button from the **Linear Component Pattern** flyout of the **Assembly CommandManager**, refer to Figure 9-63; the **Pattern Driven PropertyManager** is displayed.

The **Pattern Driven Component Pattern** tool is used to pattern the instances of the components to be used in an existing pattern feature created while creating the component in the **Part** environment.

3. Select the Link Pin from the main assembly; its name is displayed in the **Components to Pattern** selection box.

4. Click once in the **Driving Feature or Component** selection box to activate the selection mode.

5. Select any one of the hole instances from the master rod; the name of the sketch pattern feature is displayed in the **Driving Feature or Component** selection box and the preview of the resulting pattern is also displayed.

6. If the instances are not placed properly, choose the **Select Seed Position** button and select the correct seed feature.

7. Choose the **OK** button from the **Pattern Driven PropertyManager**.

   Figure 9-64 shows the final assembly.

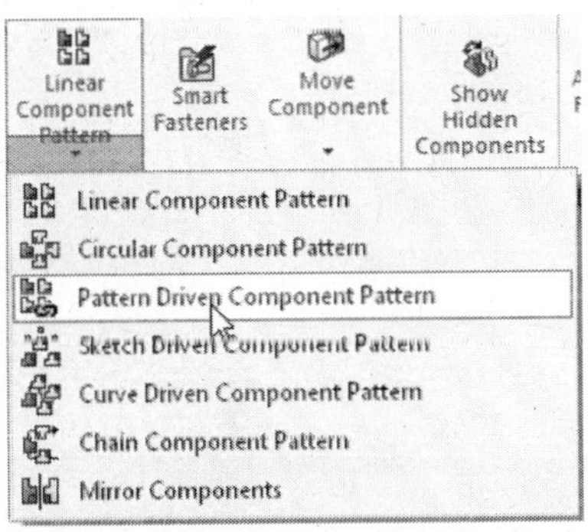

***Figure 9-63** The **Pattern Driven Component Pattern** button*

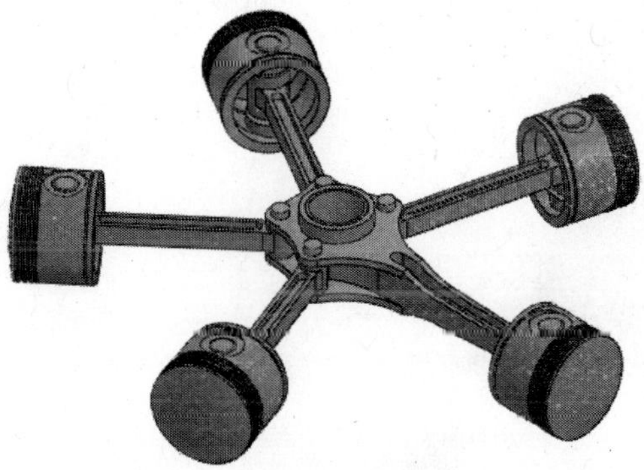

***Figure 9-64** The final assembly*

Note
The number of instances of the component pattern is automatically modified when you change the number of instances of the pattern feature that were used to derive the component pattern. This indicates the associative nature of the derived component pattern.

Exploding the Assembly

After creating the assembly, you need to explode it using the **Exploded View** tool. You can explode the subassembly and it is reflected in the main assembly.

1. Open the *Piston Articulate Rod Sub-assembly* in the separate graphics window. To do so, select a Piston Articulation Rod Sub-assembly from the **FeatureManager Design Tree**; a pop-up

toolbar is displayed. Next, choose the **Open Subassembly** button from the pop-up toolbar to open the selected sub-assembly in a separate graphics window.

2. Choose the **Exploded View** button from the **Assembly CommandManager**; the **Explode PropertyManager** is displayed. Ensure that all check boxes available in the PropertyManager are cleared.

The **Exploded View** tool is used to create an exploded state of the assembly.

3. Select the top face of the Piston Pin Plug; the triad is displayed, refer to Figure 9-65.

4. Select the arrow of the triad that is normal to the selected plane.

5. Set the value of the **Explode Distance** spinner to **170**, and then choose the **Apply** button; the selected instances of the Piston Pin Plug are exploded and the components are removed from the selection set. Also, the sequence of explosion is displayed in the **Existing explode steps** list box of the **Explode Steps** rollout of the PropertyManager.

6. If the Piston Pin Plug is moved downward, choose the **Reverse direction** button on the left of the **Explode Direction** edit box in the **Settings** rollout and then choose **Done**. Next, choose the **OK** button. The Figure 9-66 shows the sub-assembly after exploding the Piston Pin Plug.

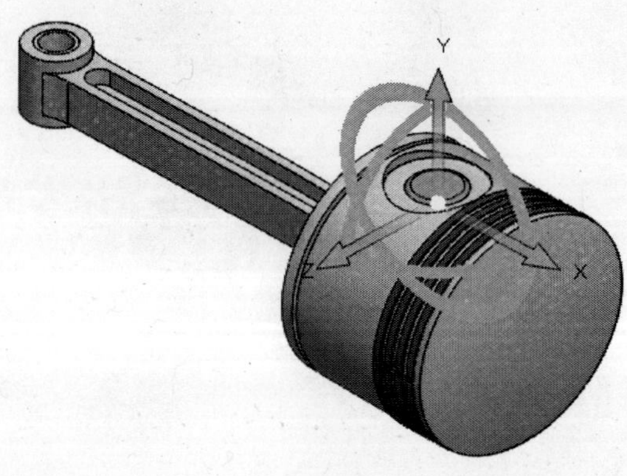

***Figure 9-65** Triad displayed after selecting the top face of the Piston Pin Plug*

***Figure 9-66** Sub-assembly after exploding the Piston Pin Plug*

Now, you need to explode the Piston Pin of the assembly.

7. Select the top planar face of the Piston Pin from the graphics area; the triad is displayed.

8. Select the arrow of the triad that is normal to the selected plane.

9. Set the value of the **Explode Distance** spinner to **150** and then choose the **Apply** button; the selected instances of the Piston Pin are exploded and the components are removed from the selection set. Also, the sequence of explosion is displayed as **Explode Step2** in the **Existing explode steps** list box of the **Explode Steps** rollout.

10. If the Piston Pin is moved downward, choose the **Reverse direction** button on the left of the **Explode Direction** edit box in the **Settings** rollout and then choose **Done**. Next, choose the **OK** button.

> **Tip**
> *When the triad is displayed on selecting the face, you can select an arrow to specify the direction and drag the arrow to relocate the component.*

11. Similarly, explode other components of the sub-assembly, refer to Figure 9-67.

12. Save the sub-assembly and open the main assembly document; the **SOLIDWORKS** message box is displayed stating that the models in the assembly have changed and would you like to rebuild them. Choose **Yes** to save and rebuild the sub-assembly.

13. Choose the **Exploded View** button from the **Assembly CommandManager**; the **Explode PropertyManager** is displayed. Ensure that all check boxes of the PropertyManager are cleared.

14. Explode the components of the main assembly, refer to Figure 9-68.

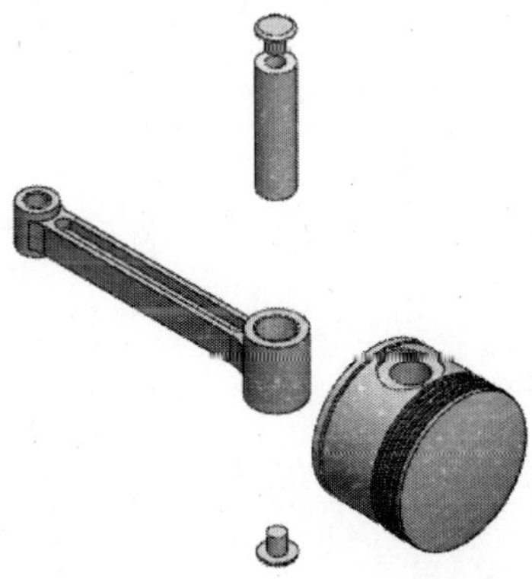

Figure 9-67 *Sub-assembly after exploding the components*

Figure 9-68 *View after exploding the components of the main assembly*

Next, you need to explode the parts of the remaining sub-assemblies in the main assembly document.

15. Select all sub-assemblies from the drawing area and then choose the **Reuse Sub-assembly Explode** button in the **Explode PropertyManager**; all sub-assemblies are exploded.

The **Re-use Sub-assembly Explode** button is chosen to reuse the exploding steps of a sub-assembly in the current assembly.

16. Choose **OK** to exit the **Explode PropertyManager**. The assembly after exploding the components is shown in Figure 9-69.

Figure 9-69 Final exploded assembly

Creating the Explode Line Sketch

After exploding the assembly, you need to create the explode line sketch of the exploded state of the assembly.

1. Choose the **Explode Line Sketch** button from the **Assembly CommandManager**; the **Route Line PropertyManager** is displayed and you are prompted to select a cylindrical face, planar face, vertex, point, arc, or line entities.

The **Explode Line Sketch** tool is used to create exploded lines. The explode lines are the parametric axes that display the direction of explosion of the components in an exploded state.

2. Choose the **Keep Visible** button, if not chosen automatically, from the **Route Line PropertyManager** to keep the PropertyManager visible on the screen.

3. Select the cylindrical face of a Piston Pin Plug, refer to Figure 9-70, as the first selection; the name of the selected face is displayed in the **Items To Connect** selection box. Also, the preview of the explode line sketch is displayed at the center of the selected face.

4. Select the other cylindrical faces to create the explode line sketch, refer to Figure 9-70.

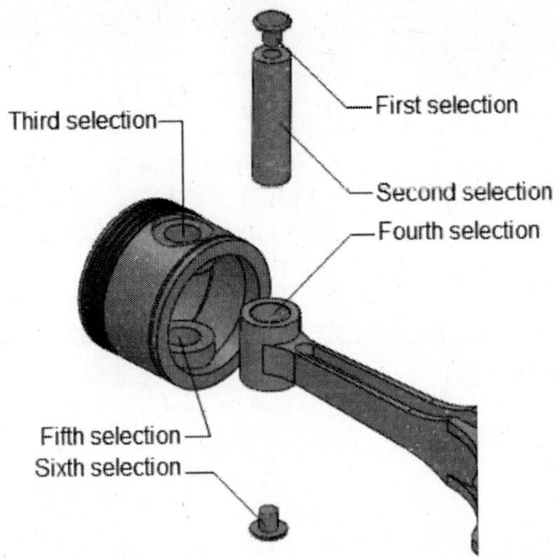

Figure 9-70 *Faces to be selected to create the explode line sketch*

5. Next, choose the **OK** button; an exploded line is created.

6. Similarly, create exploded lines between the other parts of the exploded assembly. Figure 9-71 shows the assembly after creating the explode line sketch.

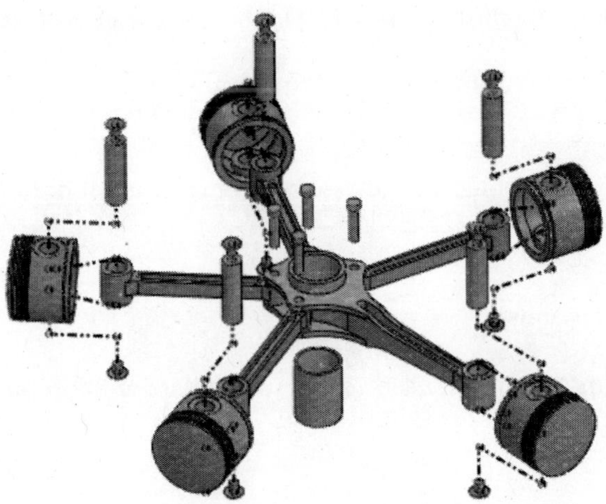

Figure 9-71 *Explode line sketch created for the exploded state of the assembly*

Now, you will animate the exploded view of the assembly.

7. Select the name of the main assembly from the **FeatureManager Design Tree** and right-click; a shortcut menu is displayed.

8. Choose the **Animate collapse** option from the shortcut menu to view the animation of the exploded view.

9. Save and close the assembly document.

Self-Evaluation Test

Answer the following questions and then compare them to those given at the end of this chapter:

1. Choose the __________ button from the **Assembly CommandManager** to invoke the **Rotate Component PropertyManager**.

2. The component patterns created using an existing pattern feature are known as __________ patterns.

3. To create the explode line sketch, choose the __________ button from the **Assembly CommandManager**.

4. The bottom-up assembly design approach is the traditional and the most widely preferred approach used for assembly design. (T/F)

5. In the top-down assembly design approach, all components are created in the same assembly document. (T/F)

6. The **Coincident** mate is generally applied to make two planar faces coplanar. (T/F)

7. The most suitable mates that can be applied to the current selection set are displayed in the **Mate** pop-up toolbar. (T/F)

8. You cannot create sub-assemblies in the assembly environment of SOLIDWORKS. (T/F)

Review Questions

Answer the following questions:

1. Which of the following options is used to open a sub-assembly separately in the separate assembly document?

   (a) **Modify** (b) **Edit**
   (c) **Open Part** (d) **Open Assembly**

2. Which of the following methods is widely used for adding mates to the components in an assembly?

   (a) **Smart Mates** (b) **Mate PropertyManager**
   (c) By dragging from part document (d) None of these

3. Which of the following buttons is used to make the **Mate Component PropertyManager** available after applying a mate to selected entities?

   (a) **Help** (b) **OK**
   (c) **Keep Visible** (d) **Cancel**

4. The names of the selected entities are displayed in the _________ selection box of the **Mate Component PropertyManager**.

5. The exploded state of an assembly is created using the _________ tool.

6. The _________ button is chosen in the **Explode PropertyManager** to reuse the exploded steps of a sub-assembly in the current assembly.

7. The _________ button of the pop-up toolbar is used to change the appearance of a component.

8. The _________ option is used to change the state of a component from fix to floating.

EXERCISES

Exercise 1

Create all components of the Fixture assembly and assemble them. The Fixture assembly is shown in Figure 9-72. After creating the assembly, explode it and create the explode line sketch, refer to Figure 9-73. The dimensions of various components of this assembly are given in Figures 9-74 through 9-78. Note that all dimensions are in inches. **(Expected time: 1 hr)**

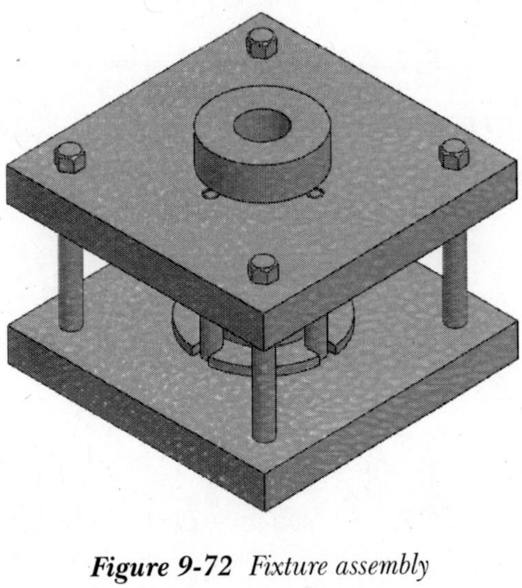

Figure 9-72 *Fixture assembly*

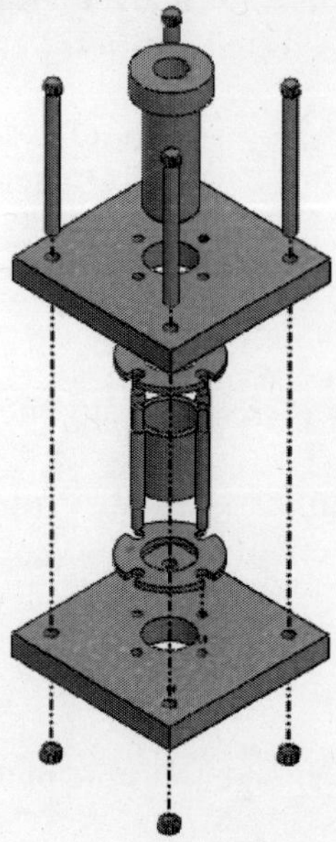

Figure 9-73 Exploded view of the assembly

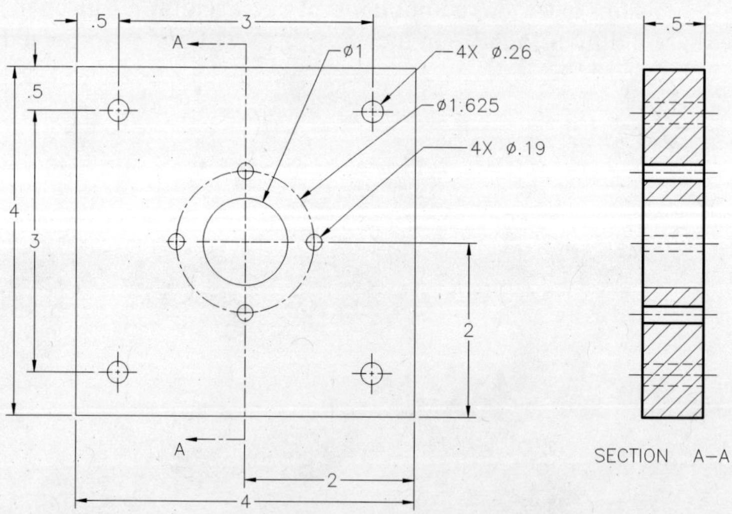

Figure 9-74 Dimensions of the End Plate

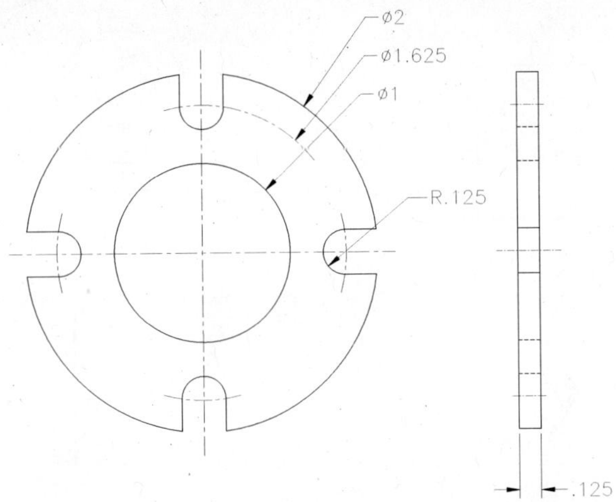

Figure 9-75 Dimensions of the Disk

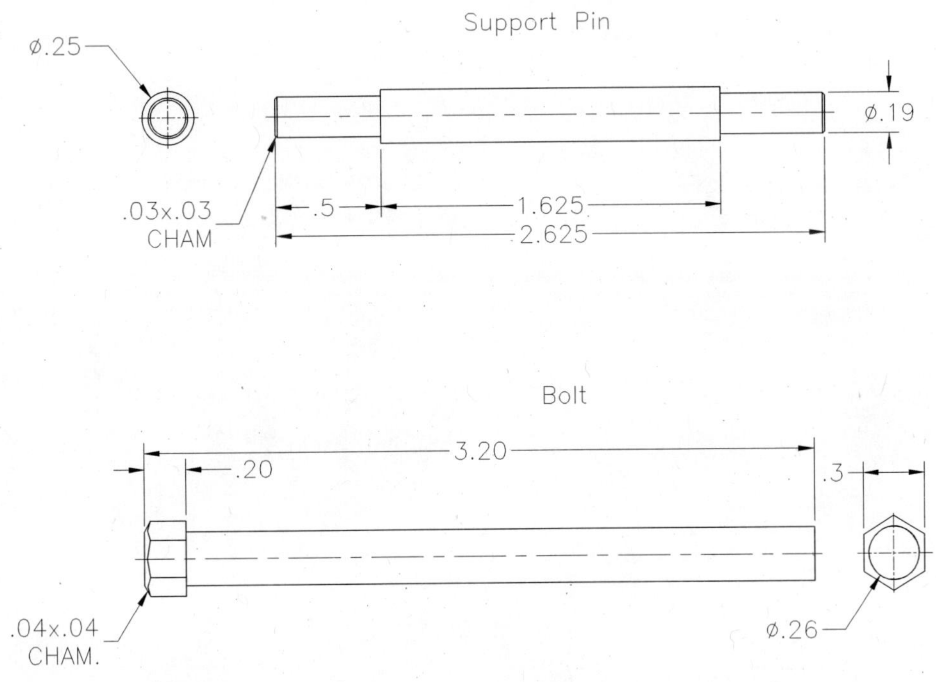

Figure 9-76 Dimensions of the Support Pin and the Bolt

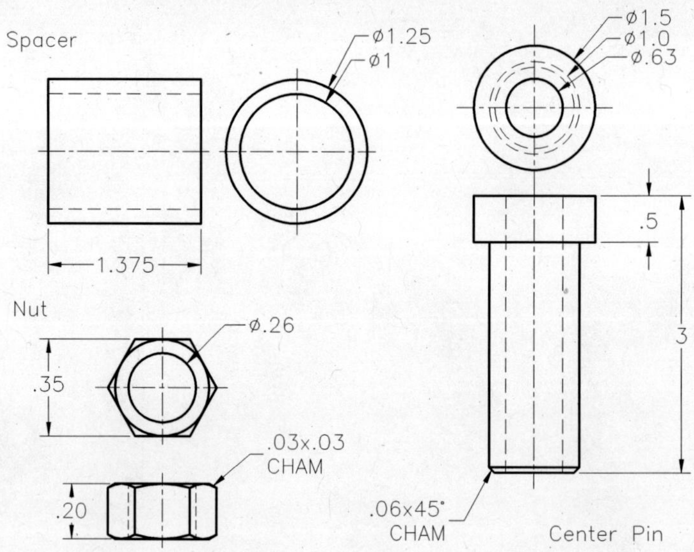

Figure 9-77 *Dimensions of the Spacer, Center Pin, and Nut*

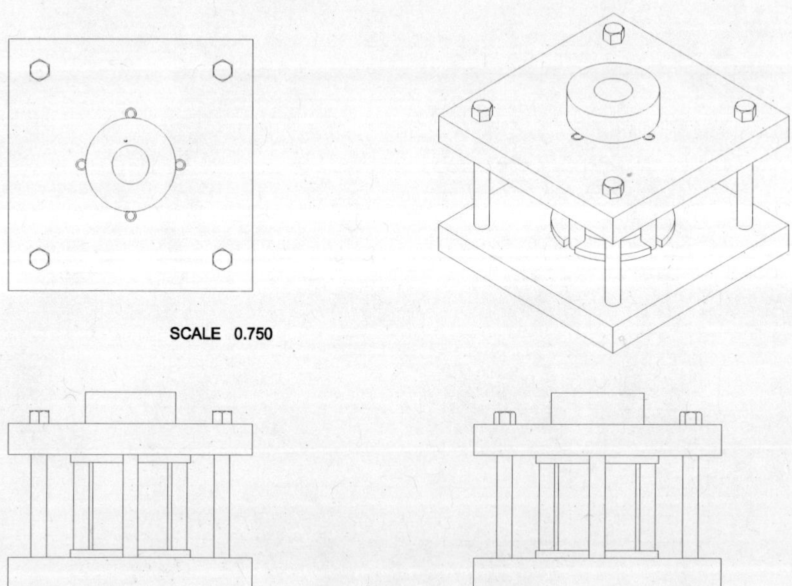

Figure 9-78 *Drawing views of the Fixture assembly*

Exercise 2

Create all components of the Blower assembly and assemble them. The Blower assembly is shown in Figure 9-79. The exploded view of the assembly is given in Figure 9-80 for reference. The dimensions of various components of this assembly are given in Figures 9-81 through 9-86. Note that all dimensions are in inches. **(Expected time: 1 hr)**

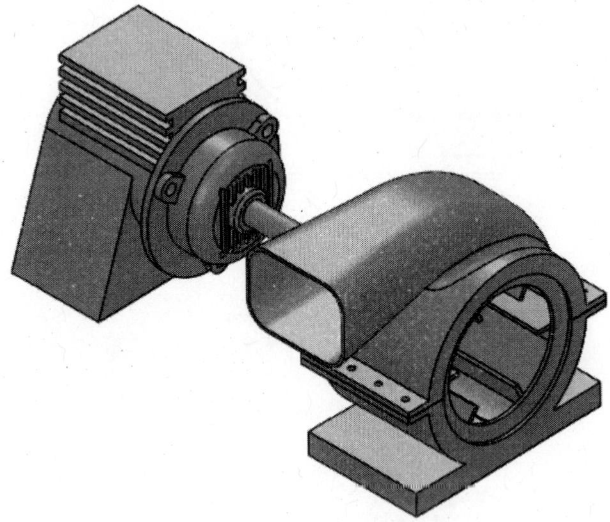

Figure 9-79 *Dimensions of the Blower*

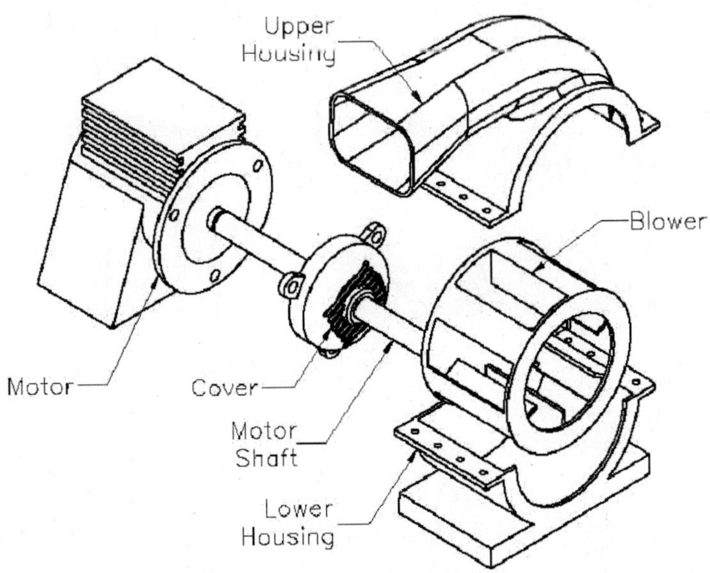

Figure 9-80 *Exploded view of the Blower assembly*

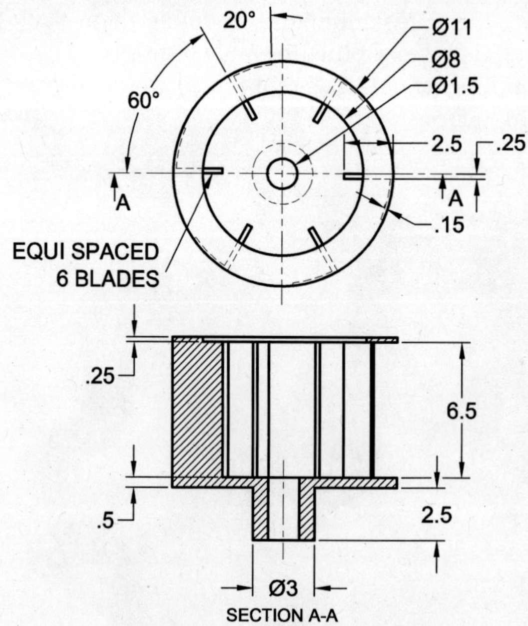

Figure 9-81 Dimensions of the Blower

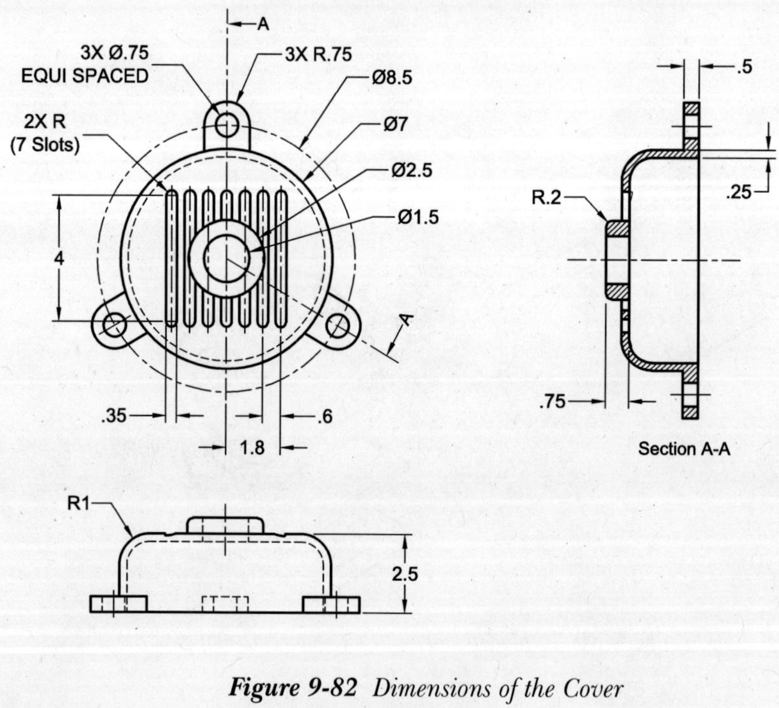

Figure 9-82 Dimensions of the Cover

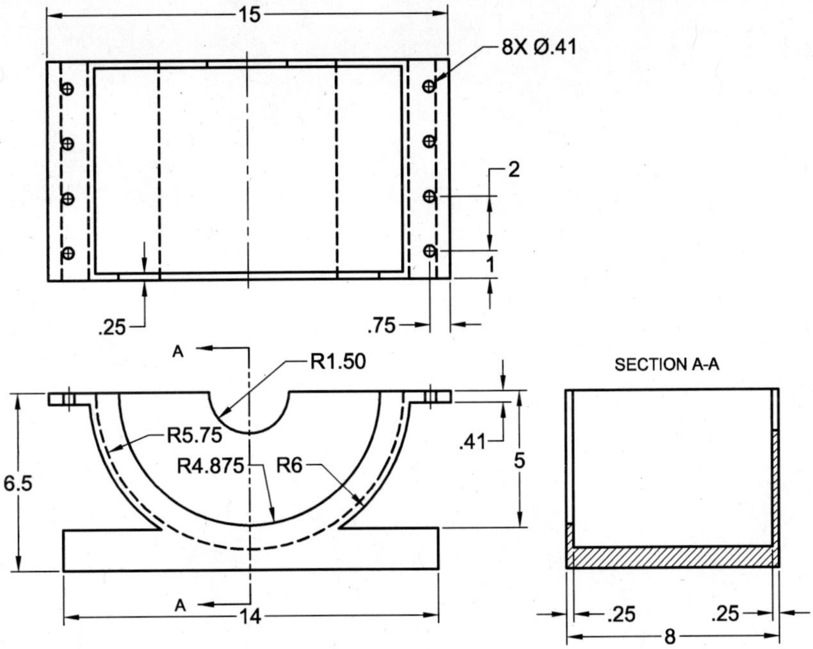

Figure 9-83 *Dimensions of the Lower Housing*

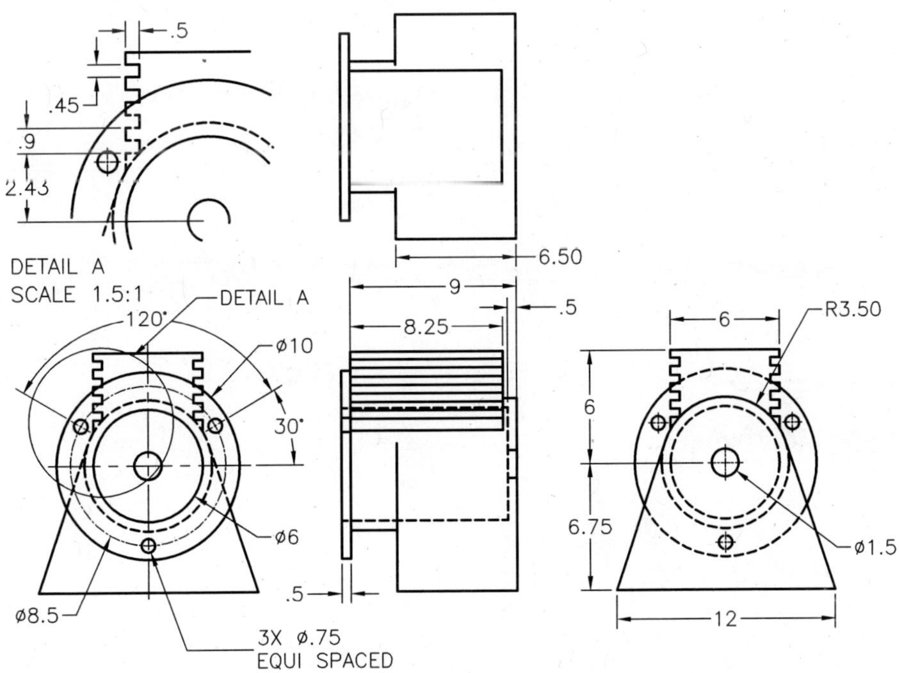

Figure 9-84 *Dimensions of the Motor*

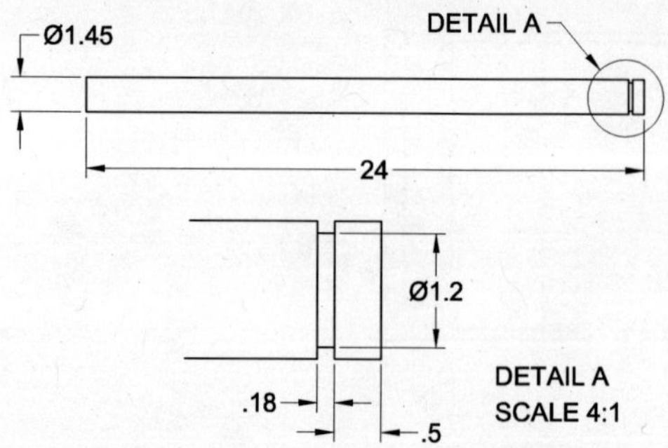

Figure 9-85 Dimensions of the Motorshaft

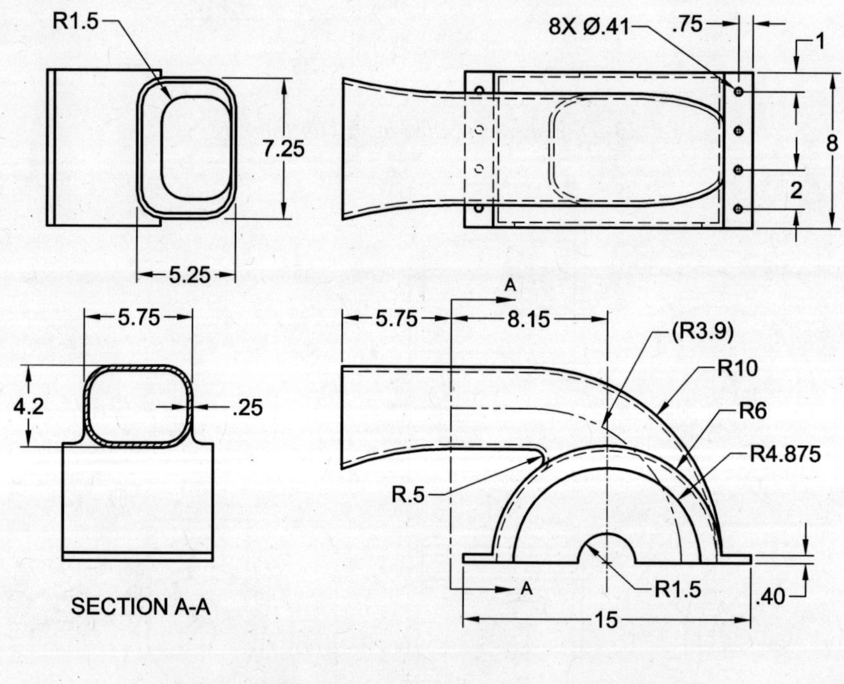

Figure 9-86 Dimensions of the Blower Upper Housing

Answers to Self-Evaluation Test

1. Rotate Component, **2.** Feature Driven, **3. Explode Line Sketch**, **4.** T, **5.** T, **6.** T, **7.** T, **8.** F

Chapter 10

Working with Drawing Views

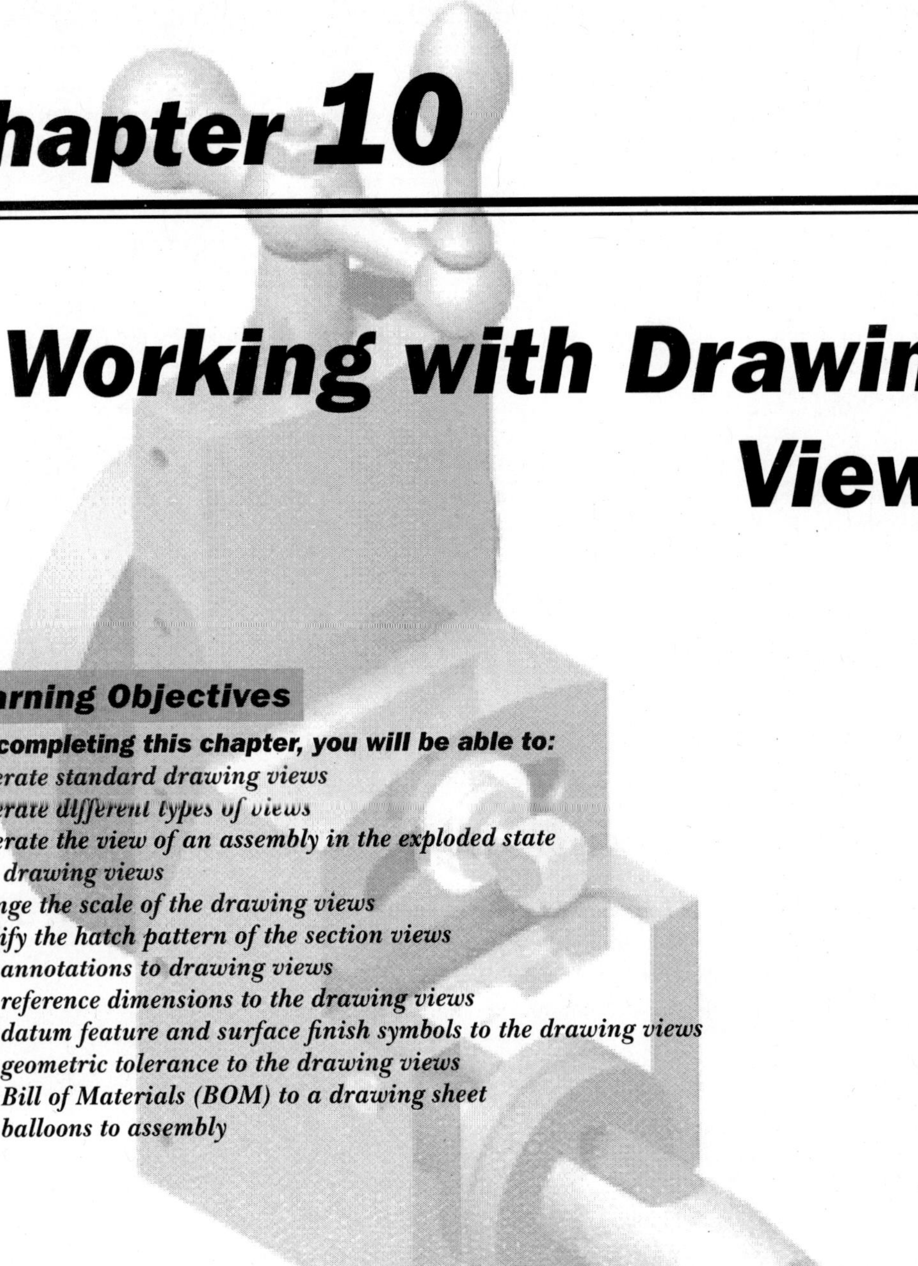

Learning Objectives

After completing this chapter, you will be able to:

- *Generate standard drawing views*
- *Generate different types of views*
- *Generate the view of an assembly in the exploded state*
- *Edit drawing views*
- *Change the scale of the drawing views*
- *Modify the hatch pattern of the section views*
- *Add annotations to drawing views*
- *Add reference dimensions to the drawing views*
- *Add datum feature and surface finish symbols to the drawing views*
- *Add geometric tolerance to the drawing views*
- *Add Bill of Materials (BOM) to a drawing sheet*
- *Add balloons to assembly*

THE DRAWING MODE

After creating the solid models or assemblies, you need to generate the two-dimensional (2D) drawing views. These views are the important for all manufacturing systems because at the shop floor or the machine floor, the machinist needs the 2D drawing for manufacturing. SOLIDWORKS provides a specialized environment, known as the **Drawing** mode, which has all the tools required to generate and modify the drawing views and add dimensions and annotations to them. In other words, you can create the final shop floor drawing in this mode.

You can also sketch the 2D drawings in the **Drawing** mode of SOLIDWORKS using the sketching tools provided in this mode. In other words, there are two types of drafting methods available in SOLIDWORKS: Generative and Interactive. Generative drafting is a technique of generating the drawing views by using a solid model or an assembly. Interactive drafting is a technique of sketching the drawing views in the **Drawing** mode by using the sketching tools. In this chapter, you will learn about generating the drawing views of parts or assemblies by using generative drafting method.

One of the major advantages of working in SOLIDWORKS is that this software has bidirectional associative property. This property ensures that the modifications made in a model in the **Part** mode are reflected in the **Assembly** and **Drawing** modes, and vice versa.

TUTORIALS

Tutorial 1

In this tutorial, you will generate the front view, top view, right view, aligned section view, detail view, and isometric view of the model created in Tutorial 5 of Chapter 8. Use the Standard A4 Landscape sheet format for generating these views. **(Expected time: 30 min)**

The following steps are required to complete this tutorial:

a. Copy the part document of Tutorial 5 of Chapter 8 in the folder of the current chapter.
b. Open the copied part document and start a new drawing document from the part document.
c. Select the standard A4 landscape sheet format and generate the parent view, refer to Figure 10-4.
d. Generate the projected views using the **Projected View** tool, refer to Figure 10-4.
e. Generate the aligned section view using the **Aligned Section View** tool, refer to Figures 10-5 through 10-7.
f. Generate the detail view, refer to Figure 10-8.
g. Save and close the drawing document.

Copying and Opening the Part Document

1. Create a folder with the name *c10* in the *SOLIDWORKS Tutorials* directory and copy *c08_tut05.sldprt* from *\Documents\SOLIDWORKS Tutorials\c08*.

2. Start SOLIDWORKS and open the part document that you copied in the *c10* folder.

Starting a New Drawing Document

To generate the drawing views, you need to start a new drawing document. There are two methods to start a drawing document in SOLIDWORKS. The first method to start a drawing document is by using the **New SOLIDWORKS Document** dialog box and the second method is by using the option available in the Part or Assembly document.

In this tutorial, you will start a new drawing document from the Part document. In this way, the model in the Part document is automatically selected and you can generate its drawing views.

1. Choose the **Make Drawing from Part/Assembly** button from the **New** flyout of the Menu Bar, refer to Figure 10-1; the **Sheet Format/Size** dialog box is displayed, as shown in Figure 10-2.

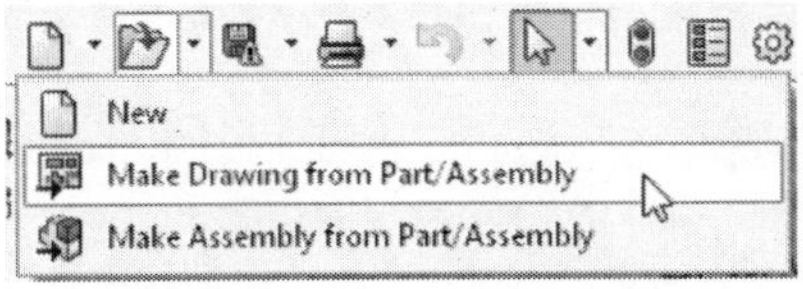

***Figure 10-1** The **Make Drawing from Part/Assembly** button in the **New** flyout*

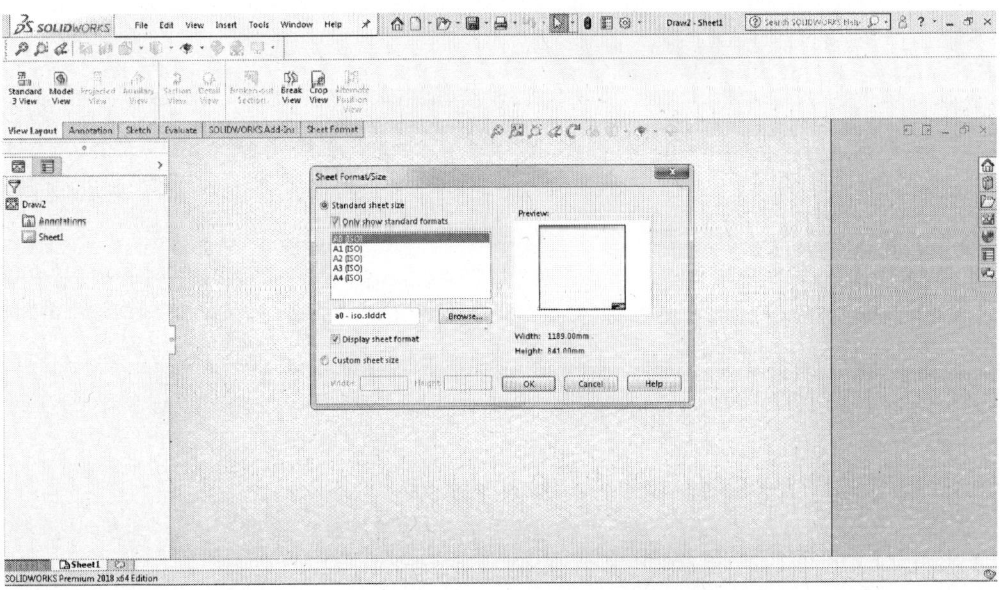

***Figure 10-2** The initial screen of the drawing document with the **Sheet Format/Size** dialog box*

> **Tip**
> *You can also start a drawing document by using the **New SOLIDWORKS Document** dialog box. To do so, invoke the **New SOLIDWORKS Document** dialog box by choosing the **New** button from the Menu Bar. Next, choose the **Drawing** button and then the **OK** button from the dialog box.*

2. Clear the **Only show standard formats** check box, if it is selected by default. Next, select the **A4 (ANSI) Landscape** sheet from the list box in this dialog box and choose the **OK** button;

a new drawing document is started with the standard A4 sheet and the **View Palette** task pane is displayed on its right, as shown in Figure 10-3. By default, the model of Tutorial 5 of Chapter 8 is displayed in the **View Palette** task pane for generating the drawing views.

The **Sheet Format/Size** dialog box is used to select the desired format and size of the sheet. You can select the predefined standard sheet size template from the list box of the dialog box. Also, you can customize the size of the sheet as per your requirement by selecting the **Custom sheet size** radio button. As soon as you select this radio button, the **Width** and **Height** edit boxes are enabled for entering the desired width and height of the sheet.

Tip

*If you choose the **Cancel** button from the **Sheet Format/Size** dialog box, a blank custom sheet of 431.80 mm × 279.40 mm will be inserted in the drawing document.*

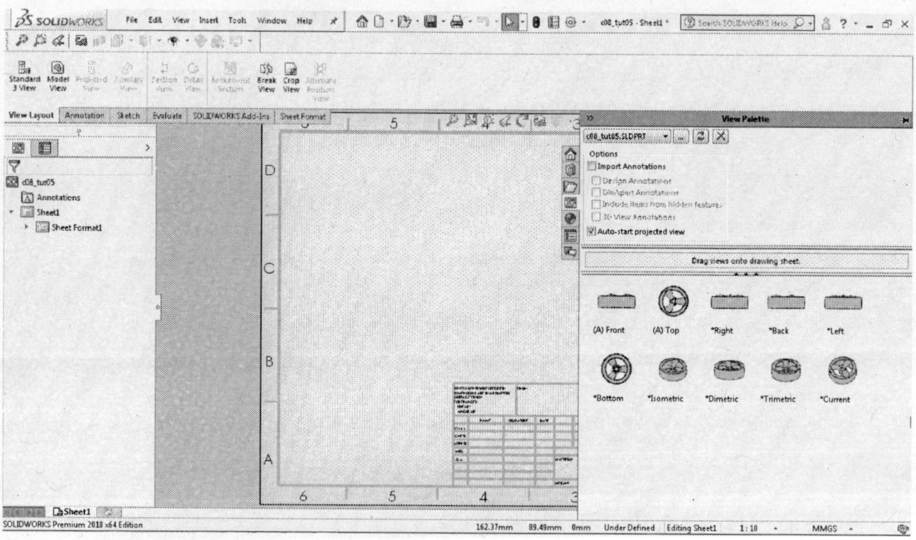

Figure 10-3 *A new drawing document with the **View Palette** task pane*

Generating the Parent and Projected Views

Before you proceed to generate the drawing views, you need to confirm whether the projection type for the current sheet is set to third angle.

1. Click anywhere on the sheet to close the **View Palette** task pane. Select **Sheet1** from the **FeatureManager Design Tree** and right-click on it; a shortcut menu is displayed. Next, choose the **Properties** option from the shortcut menu; the **Sheet Properties** dialog box is displayed.

2. Select the **Third angle** radio button from the **Type of projection** area, if it is not selected by default. Choose the **Apply Changes** button and close the dialog box.

3. Choose the **View Palette** tab to view the **View Palette** task pane.

4. Select the **Front** view from the **View Palette** task pane, drag it to the middle left of the drawing sheet, and then drop the view at this location to place it, refer to Figure 10-4.

   The front view is generated and placed at this location. This view is generated at a 1:10 scale. Note that the **Projected View PropertyManager** is invoked automatically and the preview of the projected view is attached to the cursor.

5. Move the cursor to the top of the front view and specify a point to place the top view, refer to Figure 10-4. The top view of the model is generated and the preview of another projected view with the front view as the parent view is attached to the cursor.

6. Similarly, move the cursor horizontally toward the right and then move it upward; the preview of the isometric view is displayed. Specify a point to place the isometric view.

7. Choose the **OK** button from the **Projected View PropertyManager** to exit from it.

   The current location of the isometric view of the model is such that it may interfere with the aligned section view that you need to place next. Therefore, you need to move the isometric view close to the top right corner of the drawing sheet.

8. Move the cursor over the isometric view; the bounding box of the view is displayed in orange color.

9. Click the left mouse button to select the view; the border of the view is highlighted in a different color.

10. Move the cursor over one of the borderlines of the view; the cursor changes to the move cursor.

11. Press and hold the left mouse button and drag the view close to the upper right corner of the drawing sheet. The drawing sheet after generating and moving the isometric view is shown in Figure 10-4.

Note

*In Figure 10-4, the display style of the front and top views is Hidden Lines Visible and the display style of isometric view is also Hidden Lines Visible. To change the display style of a view, select it; the **Drawing View PropertyManager** will be displayed. Next, select the required display style from the **Display Style** rollout of the PropertyManager.*

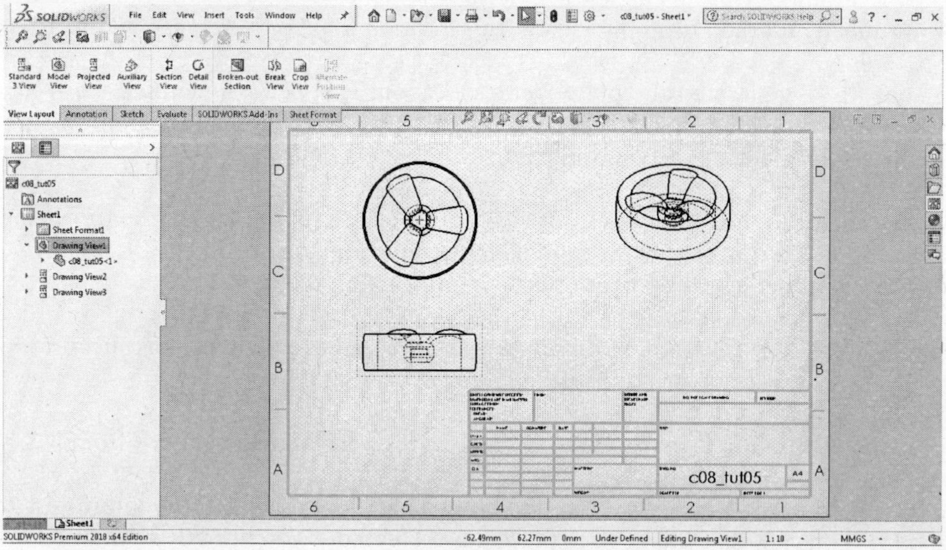

Figure 10-4 Drawing sheet after generating the front, top, and isometric views

Tip

You can turn on/off the origins displayed in the drawing views by using the ***View (Heads-Up)*** *toolbar.*

Generating the Aligned Section View

Next, you need to generate the aligned section view using the **Section View** tool.

1. Choose the **Section View** tool from the **View Layout CommandManager**; the **Section View Assist PropertyManager** is displayed, refer to Figure 10-5.

2. Choose the **Aligned** button from the **Cutting Line** rollout of the PropertyManager to create an aligned section view; the aligned section line is attached to the cursor. Also, you are prompted to specify the three points for defining the aligned section line.

3. Click at the center of the Top view to specify the first point. You are prompted to specify the second point.

4. Move the cursor in the vertically upward direction and click to specify the second point when the vertical symbol appears. As soon as you specify the second point, the first reference line of the aligned section line will be created, refer to Figure 10-6.

5. Click to specify the second reference line, refer to Figure 10-6.

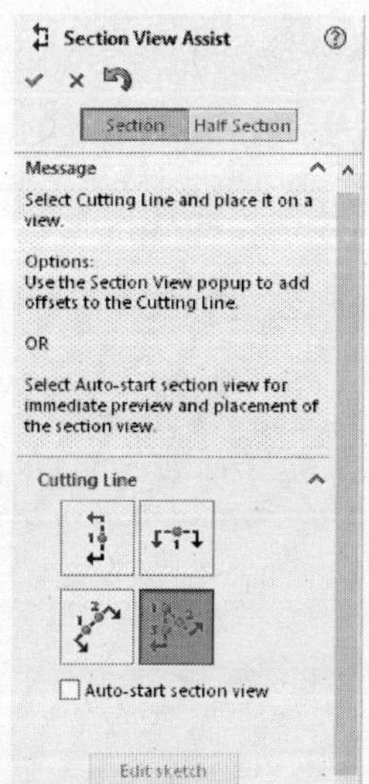

Figure 10-5 The ***Section View Assist PropertyManager***

6. Choose the **Edit sketch** button from the **Section View Assist PropertyManager**; the sketching mode is activated.

7. Choose the **Smart Dimension** tool from the **Sketch CommandManager** and specify the angle between the two reference lines as **150** degree. Figure 10-6 shows the two reference lines after specifying the angle of 150 degrees.

8. Choose the **Exit Sketch** button available at the top right of the drawing area; the preview of the aligned section view is attached to the cursor.

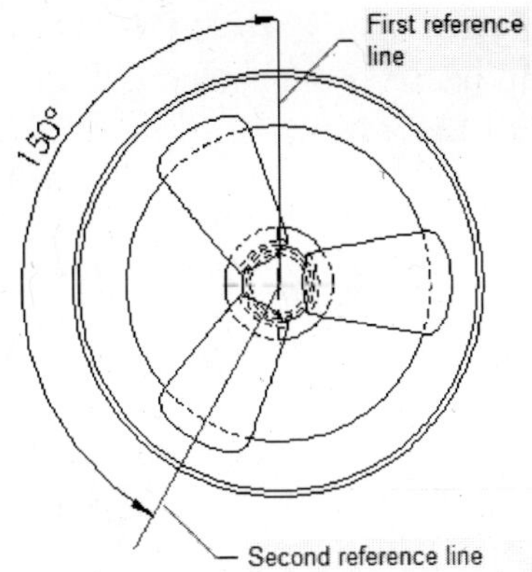

Figure 10-6 Reference lines after specifying the dimension value of 150

9. Move the cursor to the right of the top view and place the aligned section view, refer to Figure 10-7.

10. Click anywhere on the sheet to deselect the selected view and exit from the PropertyManager. The sheet after generating the aligned section view is shown in Figure 10-7.

Note

When you generate the section view of an assembly or a component, a hatch pattern is applied to the sectioned portion of features or components. The hatch pattern is based on the material assigned to the components in the part document.

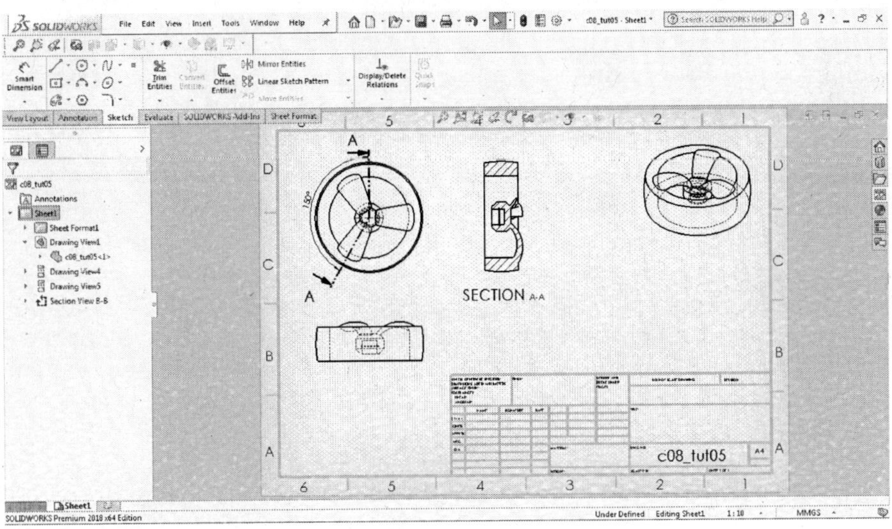

Figure 10-7 Drawing sheet after generating the aligned section view

Modifying the Hatch Pattern of the Aligned Section View

The gap between the hatching lines in the aligned section view is large. Therefore, you need to modify the spacing.

1. Select the hatch pattern from one of the sections in the aligned section view; the **Area Hatch/Fill PropertyManager** is displayed.

The **Area Hatch/Fill** tool is used to modify the default hatch patterns.

2. Clear the **Material crosshatch** check box; the **Hatch Pattern**, **Hatch Pattern Scale**, and **Hatch Pattern Angle** options are enabled.

The **Material crosshatch** check box is selected to apply the hatch pattern based on the material assigned to the model. On clearing this check box, you can change the type of the hatch pattern.

3. Make sure that the **Hatch** radio button is selected in the **Properties** rollout of the PropertyManager.

The **Hatch** radio button is selected to apply the standard hatch patterns to the section view. On selecting this radio button, some options available in the **Area Hatch/Fill PropertyManager** are enabled to define the properties of the hatch pattern.

4. Enter the value **1.5** in the **Hatch Pattern Scale** edit box and then exit the PropertyManager by choosing the **OK** button; the gap between the hatching lines in the aligned section view is changed accordingly.

The **Hatch Pattern Scale** edit box is used to specify the scale factor of the standard hatch pattern selected from the **Hatch Pattern** drop-down list. When you change the scale factor using this edit box, the preview displayed in the **Preview** area updates dynamically.

Generating the Detail View

Next, you need to generate the detail view of the center circular feature of the model. Before doing so, you need to activate the view from which you will derive the detail view.

1. Activate the aligned section view by selecting it. Next, choose the **Detail View** button from the **View Layout CommandManager**; the **Detail View PropertyManager** is displayed and you are prompted to sketch a circle to continue viewing the creation. Also, the cursor is replaced by the circle cursor.

2. Draw a small circle on the center circular feature of the model in the aligned section view, refer to Figure 10-8. As you draw the circle, the detail view is attached to the cursor.

3. Place the attached detail view on the right side of the drawing sheet above the title block, refer to Figure 10-8.

4. Select the **Use custom scale** radio button in the **Scale** rollout of the **Detail View PropertyManager**. Then, select the **1:5** option from the drop-down list available below the **Use custom scale** radio button.

5. Make sure that the **Pin position** check box is selected in the **Detail View** rollout. Choose the **OK** button from the **Detail View PropertyManager**.

The **Pin position** check box of the **Detail View** rollout of the PropertyManager is used to pin the position of the detail view. If you select the **Full outline** check box in this rollout, the detail view will be displayed with the complete outline of the closed profile.

You may need to move the drawing view and its label such that the view does not overlap the title block. Figure 10-8 shows the final drawing sheet displayed after generating the detail view from the aligned section view.

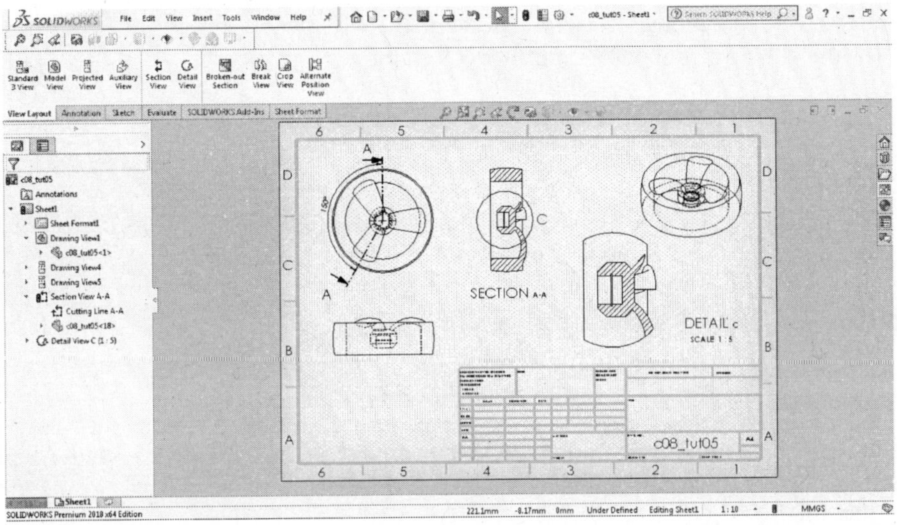

***Figure 10-8** The detail view derived from the aligned section view*

Saving the Drawing

1. Choose the **Save** button from the Menu Bar and save the drawing file with the name *c10_tut01* at the location given below:

   \Documents\SOLIDWORKS Tutorials\c10

2. Choose **File > Close** from the SOLIDWORKS menus to close this document. Also, close the part file of Tutorial 5 of Chapter 8.

Tutorial 2

In this tutorial, you will generate the drawing view of the Tool Vise assembly created in Tutorial 1 of Chapter 9. You will generate the top view, section front view, and isometric view of the assembly in the exploded state. You will also generate the Bill of Materials (BOM) of the assembly and then add balloons to the isometric view in the exploded state.

(Expected time: 45 min)

The following steps are required to complete this tutorial:

a. Copy the folder of the Tool Vise assembly from Chapter 9 to the *c10* folder.
b. Create the exploded view of the Tool Vise assembly, refer to Figure 10-9.
c. Start a new drawing document from the assembly document using A4 landscape sheet format and generate the top view, refer to Figure 10-10.
d. Generate the section view using the **Section View** tool, refer to Figure 10-11.
e. Generate the isometric view and change the state of the isometric view to the exploded state, refer to Figure 10-12.
f. Set the anchor on the drawing sheet where the BOM will be attached.
g. Generate BOM, refer to Figure 10-14.
h. Add balloons to the isometric view, refer to Figure 10-15.
i. Save and close the drawing and assembly documents.

Copying the Folder of the Tool Vise Assembly

First, you need to copy the folder of the Tool Vise assembly to the *c10* folder.

1. Copy the folder of the Tool Vise assembly from *\Documents\SOLIDWORKS\c09* folder to the folder *c10*.

Creating the Exploded View of the Assembly

Before proceeding further to generate the drawing views of the assembly, you need to create the exploded state of the assembly in the **Assembly** mode.

1. Open the Tool Vise assembly in SOLIDWORKS and create the exploded state as well as the explode lines by using the **Exploded View** and **Explode Line Sketch** tools respectively, as shown in Figure 10-9.

Note

In Figure 10-9, the rotated view of the Tool Vise assembly has been given for its clear visualization.

It is recommended that whenever you create an exploded state of an assembly, you must revert to the collapsed state. If you save the assembly in the exploded state, then whenever you generate the drawing views of the assembly, the view will be generated in the exploded state.

2. Right-click on the *Tool Vise* assembly in the **FeatureManager Design Tree** to invoke the shortcut menu. Next, choose the **Collapse** option from the shortcut menu displayed to unexplode the assembly.

3. Save the assembly.

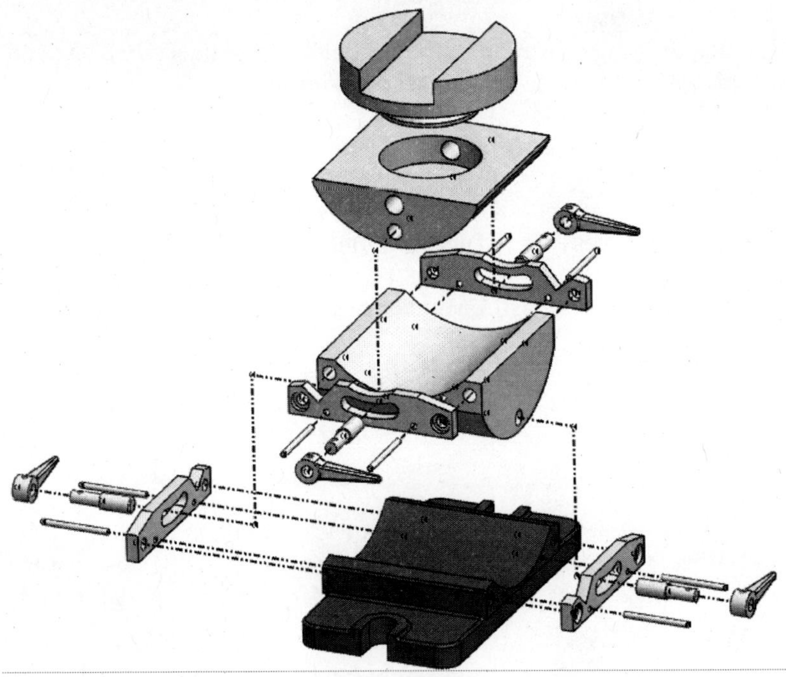

Figure 10-9 Exploded view of the assembly with explode lines

Starting a New Drawing Document from the Assembly Document

As mentioned earlier, you can also start a drawing document from the assembly document.

1. Choose **New > Make Drawing from Part/Assembly** from the Menu Bar; the **Sheet Format/Size** dialog box is displayed.

2. Select the **A4 (ANSI) Landscape** sheet from the list box in this dialog box and choose the **OK** button; a new drawing document is started with the standard A4 sheet and the **View Palette** task pane is displayed automatically on the right side of the drawing area.

   By default, the *Tool Vise* assembly is selected for generating the drawing views.

3. Select **Sheet1** from the **FeatureManager Design Tree** and right-click on it; a shortcut menu is displayed.

4. Choose the **Properties** option from the shortcut menu; the **Sheet Properties** dialog box is displayed.

5. Select the **Third angle** radio button from the **Type of projection** area. Choose the **Apply Changes** button to set the current projection type to the third angle projection and close the dialog box.

Generating the Top View

After starting a new drawing document with the standard A4 sheet size, you need to generate the top view of the assembly by using the **Model View** tool.

1. Choose the **Model View** button from the **View Layout CommandManager**; the **Model View PropertyManager** is displayed. As the Tool Vise assembly is already opened in the assembly document of the current session of SOLIDWORKS, its name is displayed in the **Part/Assembly to Insert** rollout of the PropertyManager.

2. Double-click on *Tool Vise* in the **Part/Assembly to Insert** rollout of the PropertyManager; a rectangular box is attached to the cursor.

3. Choose the **Top** button from the **Standard views** area in the **Orientation** rollout of the **Model View PropertyManager**.

Tip

*You can change the orientation of the model view even after placing it. To do so, double-click on the required view; the **Model View PropertyManager** will be displayed. Select the required view from the **Orientation** rollout; the orientation of the view will be automatically modified.*

4. Select the **Use custom scale** radio button from the **Scale** rollout of the PropertyManager.

5. Select the **User Defined** option from the drop-down list available below the **Use custom scale** radio-button. Note that as soon as you select this option from the drop-down list, the **Scale** edit box below it is enabled.

6. Enter the value of the scale factor to **1:3** in the **Scale** edit box and then select the **Preview** check box from the **Orientation** rollout; the preview of the top view of the assembly is displayed inside the rectangle attached to the cursor.

Note

*The views generated in the **Drawing** mode of SOLIDWORKS are automatically scaled on the basis of the size of the sheet. However, you can further modify the scale factor as discussed in the above steps, if required.*

In this tutorial, after generating the Top view, you need to generate the section front view, right view, and the isometric view of the assembly, instead of its projection views. Therefore, you need to clear the **Auto-start projected view** check box.

7. Clear the **Auto-start projected view** check box in the **Options** rollout of the PropertyManager.

If the **Auto-start projected view** check box is selected in the **Options** rollout of the PropertyManager, the **Projected View** tool will automatically be invoked to generate the projected view immediately after placing the model view.

8. Choose the **Hidden Lines Removed** button from the **Display Style** rollout.

9. Place the view close to the top left corner of the drawing sheet, refer to Figure 10-10. Click anywhere on the sheet to exit the PropertyManager.

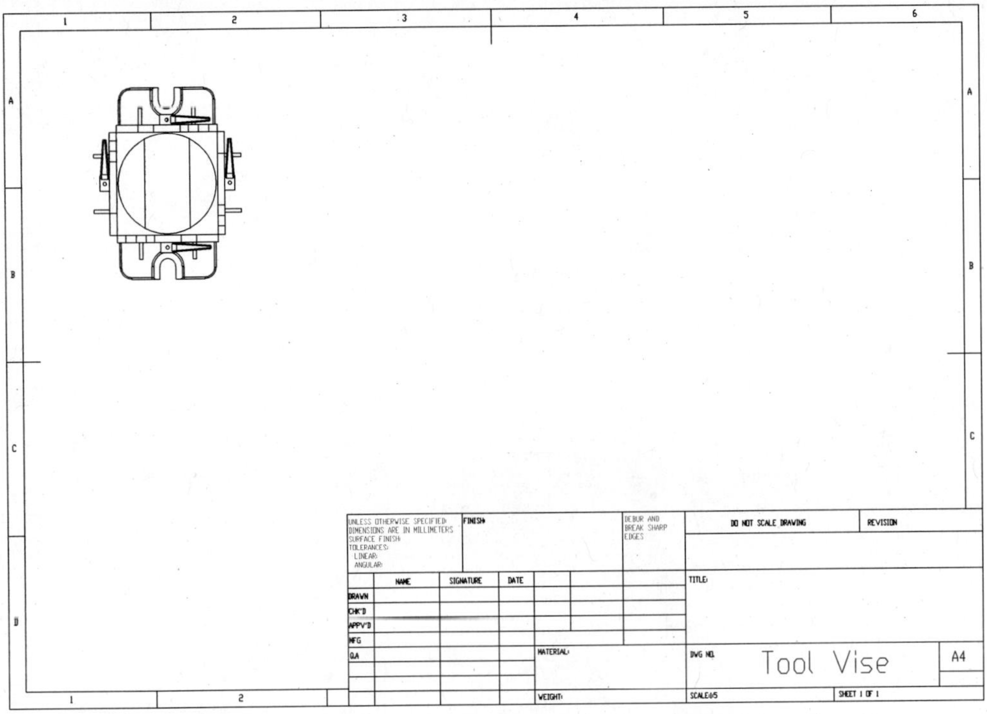

*Figure 10-10 Top view generated using the **Model View** tool*

Creating the Sectioned Front View

Next, you need to generate the sectioned front view that is derived from the top view.

1. Choose the **Section View** tool from the **View Layout CommandManager**; the **Section View Assist PropertyManager** is displayed.

2. Choose the **Horizontal** button from the **Cutting Line** rollout in the PropertyManager; the horizontal section line is attached to the cursor.

3. Click at the center of the Tool Vise to specify the position of the cutting line; the **Section View** pop-up toolbar is displayed.

4. Choose the **OK** button from the pop-up toolbar and then choose the **OK** button from the **Section View** window displayed next; you are prompted to specify the position for the section view.

5. Move the cursor in downward direction and click to specify the position for the section view, as shown in Figure 10-11. Next, click anywhere in the drawing area.

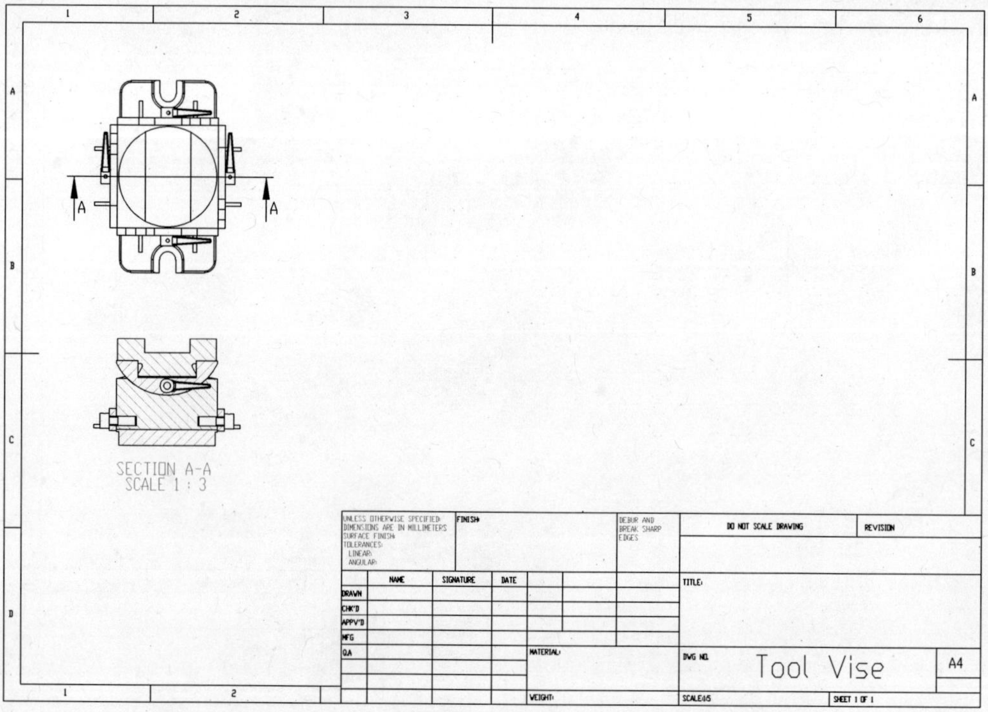

***Figure 10-11** Section view generated using the **Section View** tool*

Tip

While placing the section view, you will observe that the view is aligned to the direction of arrows on the section line. To remove this alignment, press and hold the CTRL key and move the view to the desired location. Now, select a point in the drawing sheet to place the view.

Creating the Isometric View of the Assembly in the Exploded State

The last view to be generated is the isometric view of the assembly in the exploded state.

1. Choose the **Model View** button from the **View Layout CommandManager**; the **Model View PropertyManager** is displayed. As the Tool Vise assembly is already opened in the assembly document of the current session of SOLIDWORKS, its name is displayed in the **Part/Assembly to Insert** rollout of the PropertyManager.

2. Double-click on *Tool Vise* in the **Part/Assembly to Insert** rollout of the PropertyManager; a rectangular box is attached to the cursor.

3. Make sure that the **Isometric** button is chosen in the **Orientation** rollout of the PropertyManager.

4. Set the scale factor of the drawing view to **1:3**.

5. Choose the **Hidden Lines Removed** button from the **Display Style** rollout. Next, click the left mouse button to place the view, refer to Figure 10-12.

6. Right-click on the view to invoke the shortcut menu. Choose the **Properties** option from the shortcut menu; the **Drawing View Properties** dialog box is displayed.

7. Select the **Show in exploded or model state** check box in the **View Properties** tab of the **Drawing View Properties** dialog box and choose the **OK** button.

8. Move the views to place them in the drawing sheet, refer to Figure 10-12.

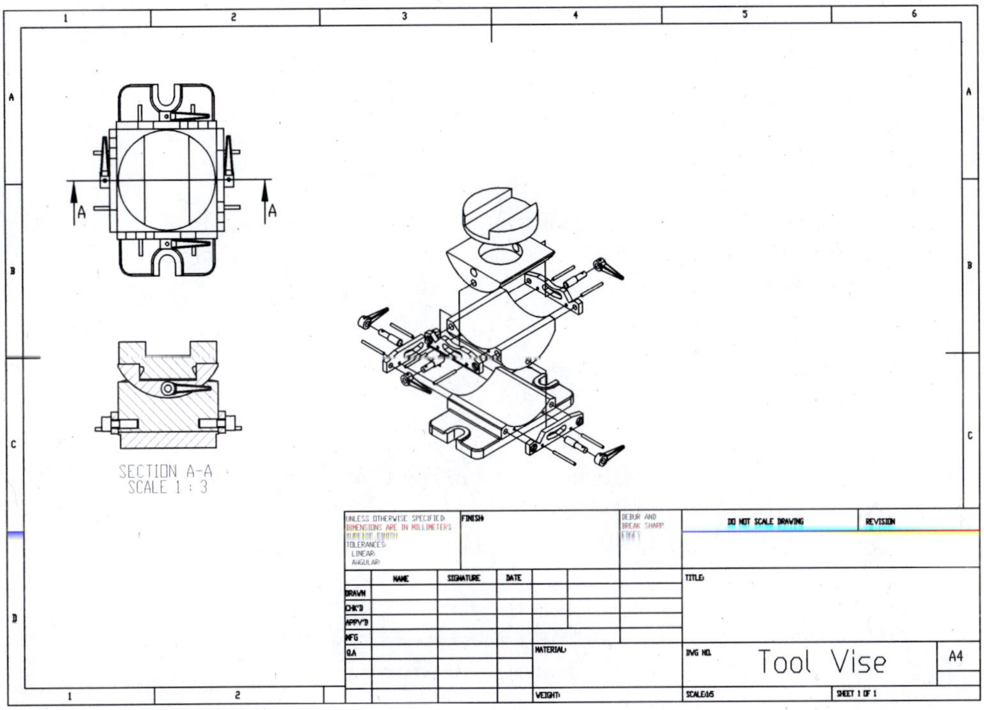

***Figure 10-12** Drawing sheet after generating the isometric view in the exploded state*

Setting the Anchor for the BOM

Before generating the BOM, you need to set its anchor. The anchor is a point on the drawing sheet with which one of the corners of the BOM coincides. By default, the anchor is defined at the top left corner of the drawing sheet. But in this tutorial, you need to add the BOM on the top right corner of the drawing sheet. Therefore, you need to set the anchor before generating the BOM.

1. Expand **Sheet1** from the **FeatureManager Design Tree** and then expand **Sheet Format1**.

2. Select the **Bill of Materials Anchor1** option from the expanded **Sheet Format1** node and then right-click to invoke a shortcut menu. Next, choose the **Set Anchor** option from it; the drawing views will disappear from the sheet.

3. Specify the anchor point on the inner top right corner of the drawing sheet; a point is placed at the selected location.

After you specify the anchor point, the drawing views are displayed automatically in the sheet.

Generating the BOM

Next, you need to generate the BOM. The Bill of Materials (BOM) is a table that displays a list of components used in an assembly. This table can also be used to provide information related to the number of components in an assembly, their names, quantity, and any other information required to assemble the components. Remember that the sequence of parts displayed in the BOM depends on the sequence in which they were inserted in the assembly document. The BOM, placed in the drawing document, is parametric. Therefore, if you add or delete a part from the assembly in the assembly document, the change will be reflected in the corresponding BOM in the drawing document. But before generating the BOM, you need to set its text parameters.

1. Invoke the **Document Properties - Drafting Standard** dialog box. To do so, choose the **Options** button from the Menu Bar; the **System Options - General** dialog box is displayed. Next, choose the **Document Properties** tab from this dialog box.

2. Choose **Annotations > Notes** from the area on the left of the dialog box. Next, choose the **Font** button from the **Text** area of the dialog box; the **Choose Font** dialog box is displayed.

3. Select the **Points** radio button from the **Height** area and set the value of the font size to **9** in the list box. Next, choose the **OK** button from the **Choose Font** dialog box.

4. Similarly, change the text height of balloons to **12** points.

5. Select the isometric drawing view from the drawing sheet and then click on the **Annotation** tab of the **CommandManager** to invoke the **Annotation CommandManager**.

6. Choose the **Bill of Materials** tool from the **Tables** flyout of the **Annotation CommandManager**, refer to Figure 10-13; the **Bill of Materials PropertyManager** is displayed.

7. Make sure that the **Attach to anchor point** check box is selected in the **Table Position** rollout of the PropertyManager.

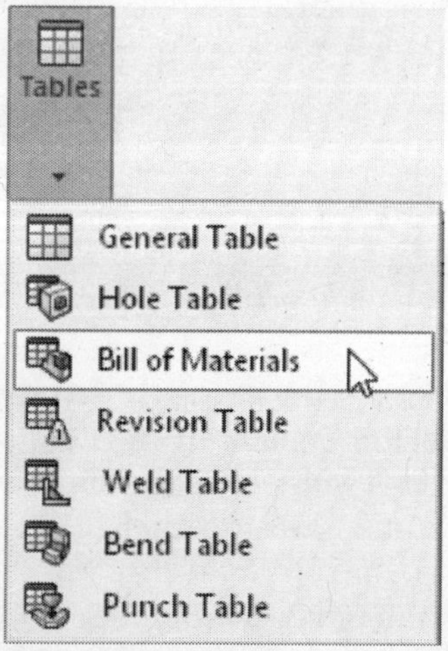

***Figure 10-13** The **Bill of Materials** tool in the **Tables** flyout*

8. Accept all other default options of the **Bill of Materials PropertyManager** and then choose the **OK** button; the BOM is displayed in the drawing area at the default anchor point position.

Note that in your case the location of BOM in the drawing area may be different from the one shown in Figure 10-14. As discussed earlier, it depends upon the anchor point location. You can change the anchor point of the BOM table, as required. To do so, expand the **Sheet format** node by clicking on the expand ▸ sign available on its left. Next, right-click on the **Bill of Material Anchor** option from the expanded **Sheet Format** node; a shortcut menu is displayed. Now, choose the **Set Anchor** option from the shortcut menu; you will be prompted to specify the anchor point location. Click on the required location in the drawing sheet; the anchor point is specified at the specified location.

9. Select the top left corner of BOM table; **Bill of Material PropertyManager** is displayed. Select the **Top Right** button from the **Table Position** rollout and then the **Close Dialog** button from the PropertyManager.

   You will notice that the **Description** column is also displayed in the BOM. As this column is not required, you need to delete it.

10. Move the cursor over the **Description** heading and right-click on it; a shortcut menu is displayed. Choose **Delete > Column** from the shortcut menu; the column is deleted. The drawing sheet after generating the BOM and deleting the **Description** column is displayed in Figure 10-14.

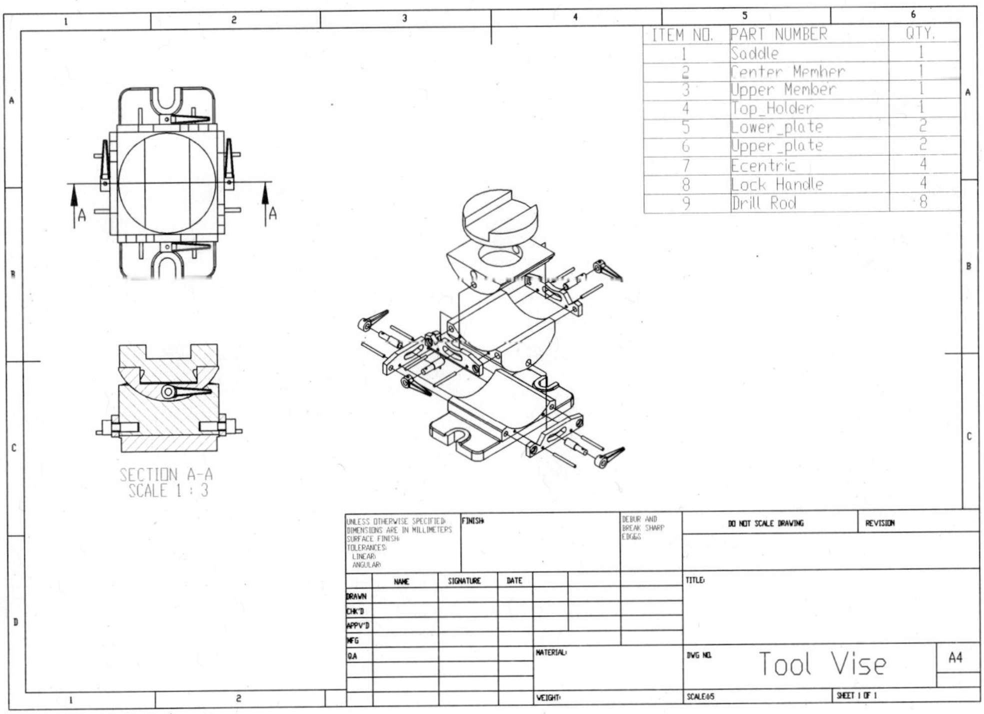

Figure 10-14 Drawing sheet after generating the BOM

Adding Balloons to the Components

After generating the BOM, you need to add balloons to the components.

1. Select the isometric drawing view and then choose the **AutoBalloon** button from the **Annotation CommandManager**; the balloons are automatically added to all the components in the isometric view and the **Auto Balloon PropertyManager** is also displayed.

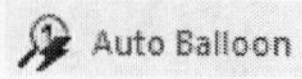

The **AutoBalloon** tool is used to add the balloons automatically on the selected drawing view.

> **Tip**
> *In SOLIDWORKS, you can also add balloons manually by using the* ***Balloon*** *tool. To do so, choose the* ***Balloon*** *tool from the* ***Annotation CommandManager****; the* ***Balloon PropertyManager*** *will be displayed. Set the properties of the balloon using the options in the* ***Settings*** *rollout of the PropertyManager. Next, select the components from the assembly drawing view to add the balloons. If you select the face of a component, the balloon will have a filled circle at the attachment point. However, if you select an edge of the component, the balloon will have a closed filled arrow.*

2. Make sure that the **Ignore multiple instances** check box is selected in the **Balloon Layout** rollout of the PropertyManager to ignore the multiple instances of any component.

3. Choose the **Layout Balloons to Circular** button from the **Balloon Layout** rollout; the preview of the balloons layout is changed to circular.

   If the balloons overlap any drawing view, BOM, and Title block, you need to move them to avoid intersections.

4. Move the cursor over a balloon and then press the left mouse button. Next, drag the cursor toward the isometric view in the sheet such that balloon does not overlap any drawing view, BOM, and Title block of the sheet and then release the left mouse button. You can also individually shift any overlapping balloon later.

5. Select the **2 Character** option from the **Size** drop-down list in the **Balloon Settings** rollout. Next, choose **OK** to close this **PropertyManager**. Figure 10-15 shows the drawing sheet after adding the balloons.

Saving the Drawing

Next, you need to save the drawing file.

1. Choose the **Save** button from the Menu Bar and save the drawing document with the name *c10_tut02* at the location given below:

   \Documents\SOLIDWORKS Tutorials\c10\Tool Vise

2. Close the drawing and assembly files.

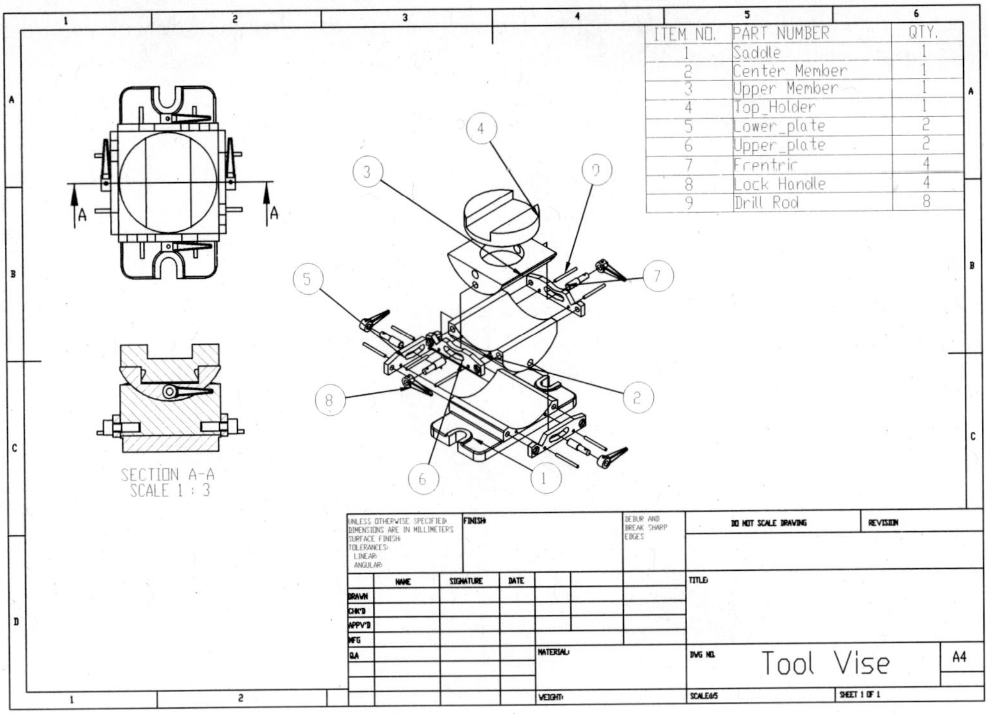

Figure 10-15 Final drawing sheet after adding balloons

Tutorial 3

In this tutorial, you will first open the drawing created in Tutorial 1 of this chapter and then generate dimensions and add annotations to it. Next, you will change the display of the isometric view to the shaded mode. **(Expected time: 30 min)**

The following steps are required to complete this tutorial:

a. Open the drawing document created in Tutorial 1 of this chapter and save it with a different name.
b. Configure the font settings and generate the dimensions using the **Model Items** tool.
c. Arrange the dimensions and delete the unwanted ones, refer to Figures 10-18 and 10-19.
d. Add the datum symbol and geometric tolerance to the drawing views, refer to Figures 10-20 and 10-21.
e. Change the model display state of the drawing views, refer to Figure 10-22.

Opening and Saving the Drawing Document

You need to open the drawing document created in Tutorial 1 of this chapter in the SOLIDWORKS window and save it with a different name.

1. Open the *c10_tut01.slddrw* document from the folder of the current chapter in the SOLIDWORKS window.

2. Choose **File > Save As** from the SOLIDWORKS menus and save the document with the name *c10_tut03* in the same folder. Figure 10-16 shows the drawing sheet in which you need to add dimensions and annotations.

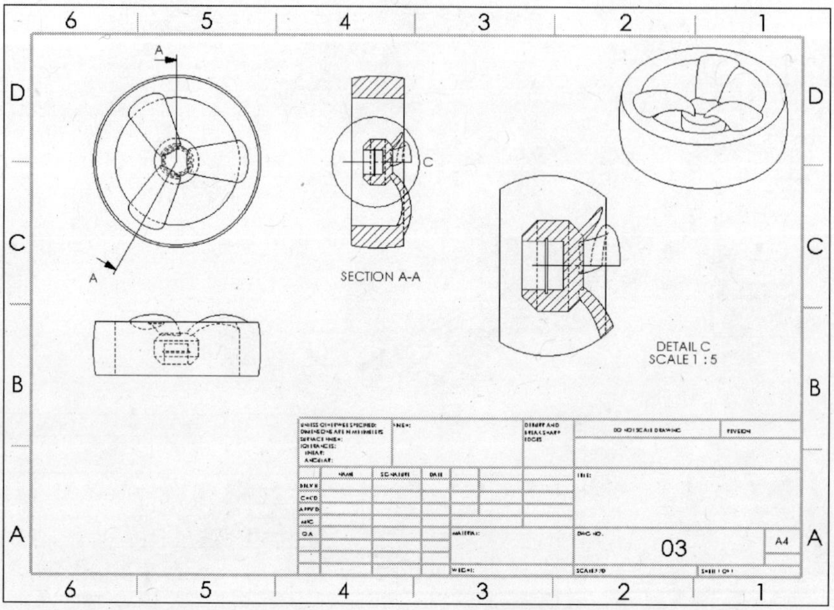

Figure 10-16 *Drawing sheet for adding dimensions and annotations*

Applying the Document Settings

Before generating the dimensions of the model, you need to configure the document settings. These settings will allow the dimensions and other annotations in the current sheet to be viewed properly.

1. Invoke the **Document Properties - Drafting Standard** dialog box. Choose the **Annotations > Notes** from the area on the left.

2. Choose the **Font** button from the **Text** area of the dialog box; the **Choose Font** dialog box is invoked.

3. Select the **Points** radio button from the **Height** area and set the value of the font size to **9** in the list box.

4. Choose the **OK** button from the **Choose Font** dialog box.

5. Choose the **Dimensions** option from the area on the left; the related options are displayed on the right.

6. Set the values of height, width, and length of the arrows as **1**, **3**, and **6** in their respective edit boxes in the **Arrows** area.

7. Choose **Views > Section** from the left of the dialog box; the related options are displayed on the right. Set the values of height, width, and length of the section arrows as **2**, **4**, and **8** in their respective edit boxes in the **Section/view size** area.

8. Choose the **OK** button from the **Document Properties** dialog box.

Generating the Dimensions

Next, you need to generate the dimensions using the **Model Items** tool.

1. Select the top view of the drawing sheet. Next, choose the **Model Items** button from the **Annotation CommandManager**; the **Model Items PropertyManager** is displayed and the name of the selected view is displayed in the **Source/Destination** rollout.

The **Model Items** tool is used to generate the annotations that are added while creating the model in the **Part** mode.

> **Tip**
> *If you do not select any view for generating the dimensions using the **Model Items** tool, all dimensions will be displayed in all views. Sometimes, the dimensions may overlap each other. Therefore, you need to select the view in which you have to generate the dimensions and then you need to invoke the **Model Items** tool.*

2. Select the **Entire model** option from the **Source** drop-down list.

The **Entire model** option is used to import the annotations of the entire model to the selected drawing view. However, the **Selected feature** option of the **Source** drop-down list is used to import the annotations only from the selected feature or features.

3. Choose the **OK** button from the **Model Items PropertyManager**; the dimensions of the entire model, which can be displayed in the selected view, are generated.

   Note that the generated dimensions are scattered arbitrarily on the drawing sheet. Therefore, you need to arrange the dimensions by moving them to the required locations.

4. Select all dimensions by dragging a window around them; the **Dimension Palette rollover** button will be displayed near the cursor.

5. Move the cursor over this button; the **Dimension Palette** window is displayed, refer to Figure 10-17.

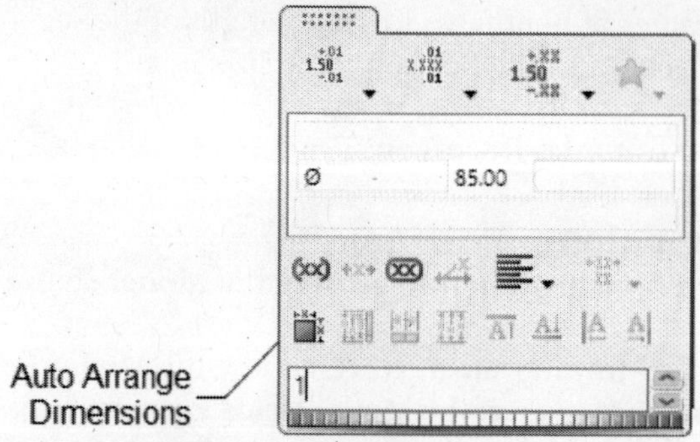

***Figure 10-17** The **Dimension Palette** window*

6. Choose the **Auto Arrange Dimensions** button from this palette; the dimensions will be arranged at equal distance. Now, click in the drawing sheet to exit the window.

7. Select the dimensions one by one and drag them to the desired location, refer to Figure 10-18. You can reverse the direction of arrowheads by clicking on the control points displayed on them. The diameter dimensions 85, 97, 108, and 160 need to be deleted from the top view because these dimensions need to be added in the detailed view of the drawing sheet later.

8. Select the diameter dimension 85 from the top view of the drawing sheet and press the DELETE key; the selected dimension is deleted from the top view. Similarly, delete the diameter dimension values 97, 108, and 160. The drawing view after arranging the dimensions and deleting the diameter dimensions is shown in Figure 10-18.

   Note that if the dimension arrowheads are displayed as not filled, you need to change the arrowheads to filled arrowheads.

9. Drag a window around all dimensions such that they are enclosed inside it. Next, release the left mouse button; all the dimensions are selected and the **Dimension PropertyManager** is displayed.

10. Choose the **Leaders** tab and select the Filled Arrow option from the **Style** drop-down list in the **Witness/Leader Display** rollout. Choose the **Close Dialog** button to close the **Dimension PropertyManager**; the arrowheads are changed to the filled arrowheads.

11. Select the detailed view from the drawing sheet and generate the dimensions using the **Model Items** tool in the **Annotation CommandManager**. Next, arrange the dimensions by using the **Dimension Palette** window.

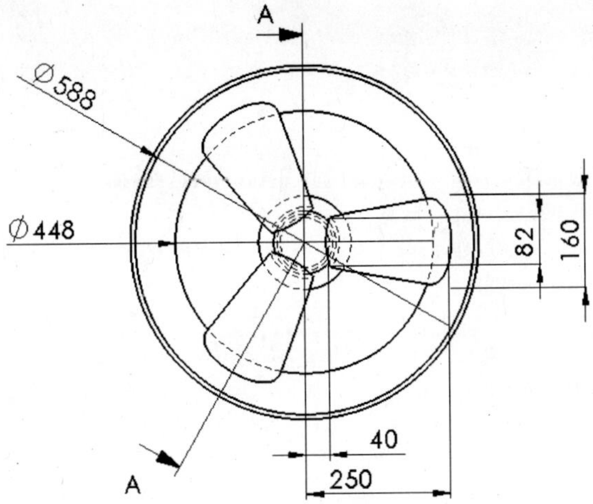

Figure 10-18 *Top view after generating and arranging the dimensions*

12. Delete the unwanted dimensions from the view and then arrange the remaining dimensions by dragging them to the desired locations. The drawing view after arranging and deleting the dimensions is shown in Figure 10-19.

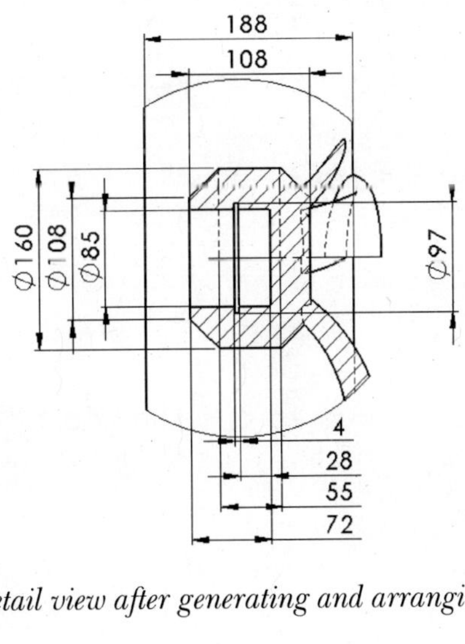

Figure 10-19 *Detail view after generating and arranging the dimensions*

Tip

*In SOLIDWORKS, you can also add reference dimensions to the drawing views in the **Drawing** mode by using the **Smart Dimension** tool, as discussed in the earlier chapters.*

Adding the Datum Feature Symbol to the Drawing View

After generating the dimensions, you need to add the datum feature symbol to the drawing view. The datum feature symbols are used as datum reference for adding the geometric tolerance to the drawing views.

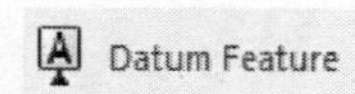

1. Select the edge of the outer cylindrical feature from the top view and then choose the **Datum Feature** button from the **Annotation CommandManager**; the **Datum Feature PropertyManager** is displayed and a datum callout is attached to the cursor.

2. Place the datum feature symbol at an appropriate location, refer to Figure 10-20.

3. Choose the **OK** button from the **Datum Feature PropertyManager**.

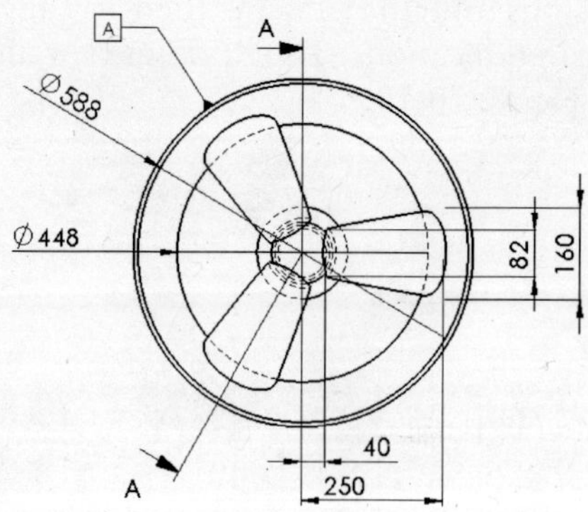

Figure 10-20 *Datum feature symbol added to the top view*

Adding the Geometric Tolerance to the Drawing View

After defining the datum feature symbol, you need to add the geometric tolerance to the drawing view.

1. Select the circular edge that has a diameter of 448 mm from the top view and then choose the **Geometric Tolerance** button from the **Annotation CommandManager**; the **Properties** dialog box is displayed. Also, a callout is attached to the cursor.

   The **Properties** dialog box is used to specify the parameters of the geometric tolerance.

2. Select the down arrow in the **Symbols** drop-down list in the first row; the **Symbols** flyout is displayed.

3. Choose the **Concentricity** option from this flyout and then enter **0.02** in the **Tolerance 1** edit box.

4. Enter **A** in the **Primary** edit box to define the primary datum reference. Note that as you specify the parameters in the **Properties** dialog box, the preview of the geometric tolerance will be modified dynamically in the drawing sheet.

5. Choose the **OK** button from the **Properties** dialog box; the geometric tolerance is attached to the selected circular edge. You may need to move the geometric tolerance, if it overlaps the dimensions. Figure 10-21 shows the drawing view after adding and rearranging the geometric tolerance.

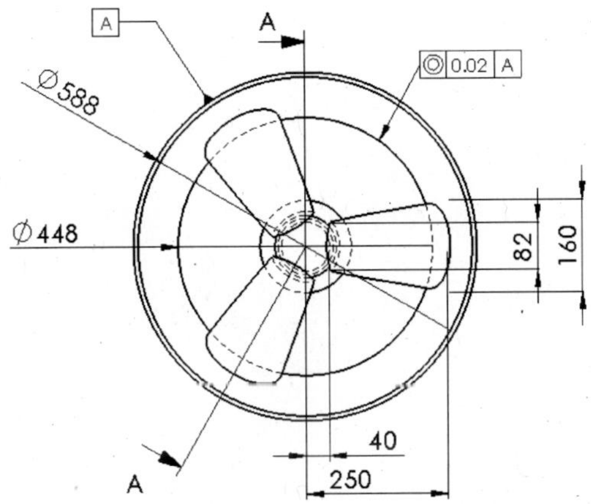

Figure 10-21 *Geometric tolerance added to the drawing view*

Tip
In SOLIDWORKS, you can add the surface finish symbols to the edges or the faces in the drawing views using the ***Surface Finish*** *tool available in the* ***Annotation CommandManager****.*

You can also generate hole callouts for the holes that are created in the ***Part*** *mode using the* ***Simple Hole*** *tool, the* ***Hole Wizard*** *tool, or the* ***Extruded Cut*** *tool.*

Changing the View Display Options

After adding all annotations to the drawing views, you need to change the display setting of the isometric view.

1. Select the isometric view in the drawing sheet; the **Drawing View PropertyManager** is displayed.

2. Choose the **Shaded With Edges** button from the **Display Style** rollout of the PropertyManager; the display style of the isometric view is changed to Shaded With Edges display style. Figure 10-22 shows the final drawing sheet after changing the display view settings.

3. Save and close the drawing document.

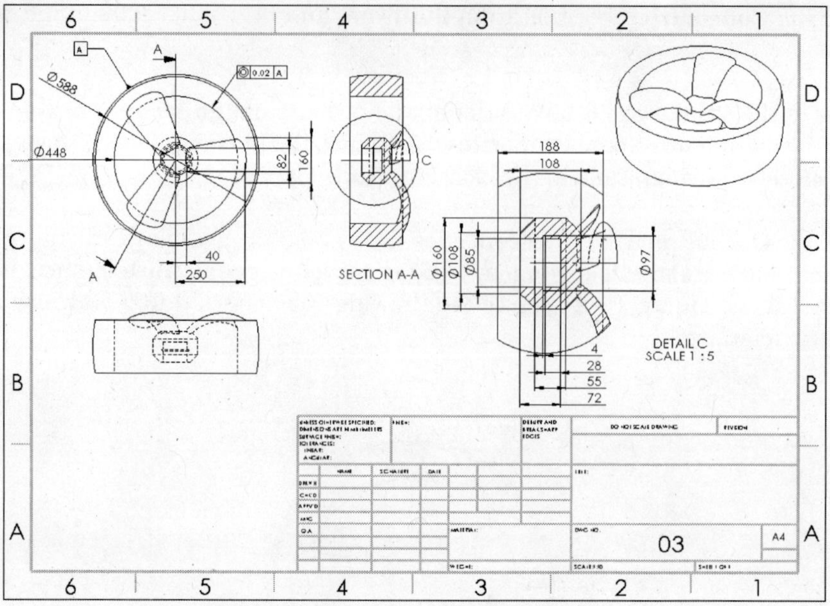

Figure 10-22 Final drawing sheet

Self-Evaluation Test

Answer the following questions and then compare them to those given at the end of this chapter:

1. To start a new drawing document from the part document, choose the __________ button from the **New** flyout.

2. The __________ check box available in the **Detail View** rollout of the **Detail View PropertyManager** is used to display the complete outline of the closed profile in the detail view.

3. To change the scale of the drawing views, first select the drawing view and then select the __________ radio button from the **Scale** rollout.

4. The __________ tool is used to add balloons automatically to the components of the assembly in the drawing view.

5. The __________ tool is used to create hole callouts.

6. The **Standard sheet size** radio button is selected by default in the **Sheet Format/Size** dialog box. (T/F)

7. If you want to use the empty sheet without any margin lines or a title block, then select the **Display sheet format** check box in the **Sheet Format/Size** dialog box. (T/F)

8. In SOLIDWORKS, you cannot add annotations while creating the parts. (T/F)

Review Questions

Answer the following questions:

1. In which shape is the detail view boundary displayed by default?

   (a) Circle (b) Ellipse
   (c) Rectangle (d) None

2. Which **PropertyManager** is invoked to add balloons manually to the selected drawing view?

   (a) **AutoBalloon** (b) **Balloon**
   (c) **Properties** (d) **Center Mark**

3. The __________ tool is used to add reference dimensions to the drawing views.

4. The __________ tool is used to add surface finish symbols to the drawing views.

5. The __________ dialog box is used to modify the hatch pattern of a section view.

6. The __________ check box needs to be cleared to modify the scale of the hatch pattern.

7. In SOLIDWORKS, you cannot modify the hatch pattern angle. (T/F)

8. In SOLIDWORKS, you can modify the hatch pattern scale. (T/F)

EXERCISE

Exercise 1

In this exercise, you will generate the front view, top view, and isometric view in the exploded state of the assembly created in Exercise 1 of Chapter 9. You will also generate the Bill of Materials (BOM) of the assembly and then add balloons to the isometric view in the exploded state, as shown in Figure 10-23. Use the Standard A4 Landscape sheet format for generating these views. **(Expected time: 30 min)**

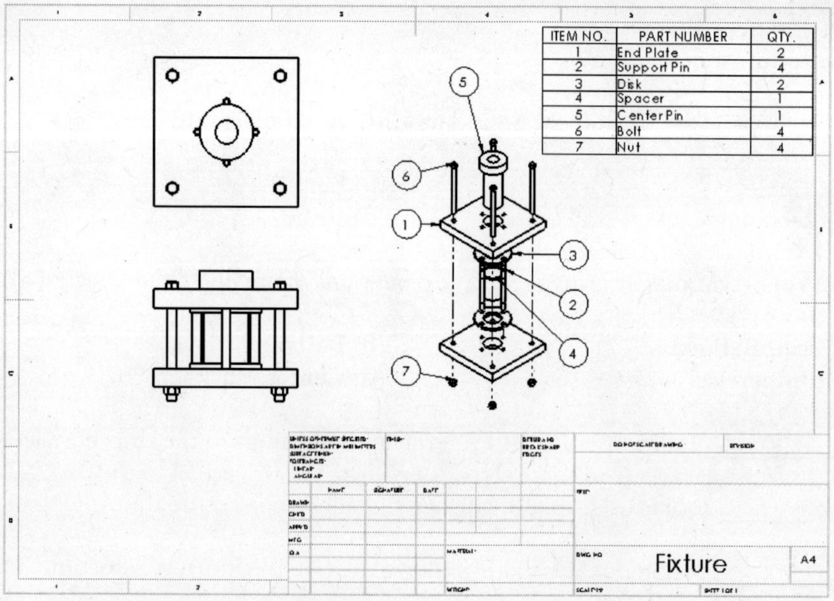

Figure 10-23 *Drawing sheet for Exercise 1*

Answers to Self-Evaluation Test

1. Make Drawing from Model/Assembly, **2.** Full outline, **3.** Use custom scale, **4.** AutoBalloon, **5.** Hole Callout **6.** T, **7.** T, **8.** T

Chapter 11

Introduction to FEA and SOLIDWORKS Simulation

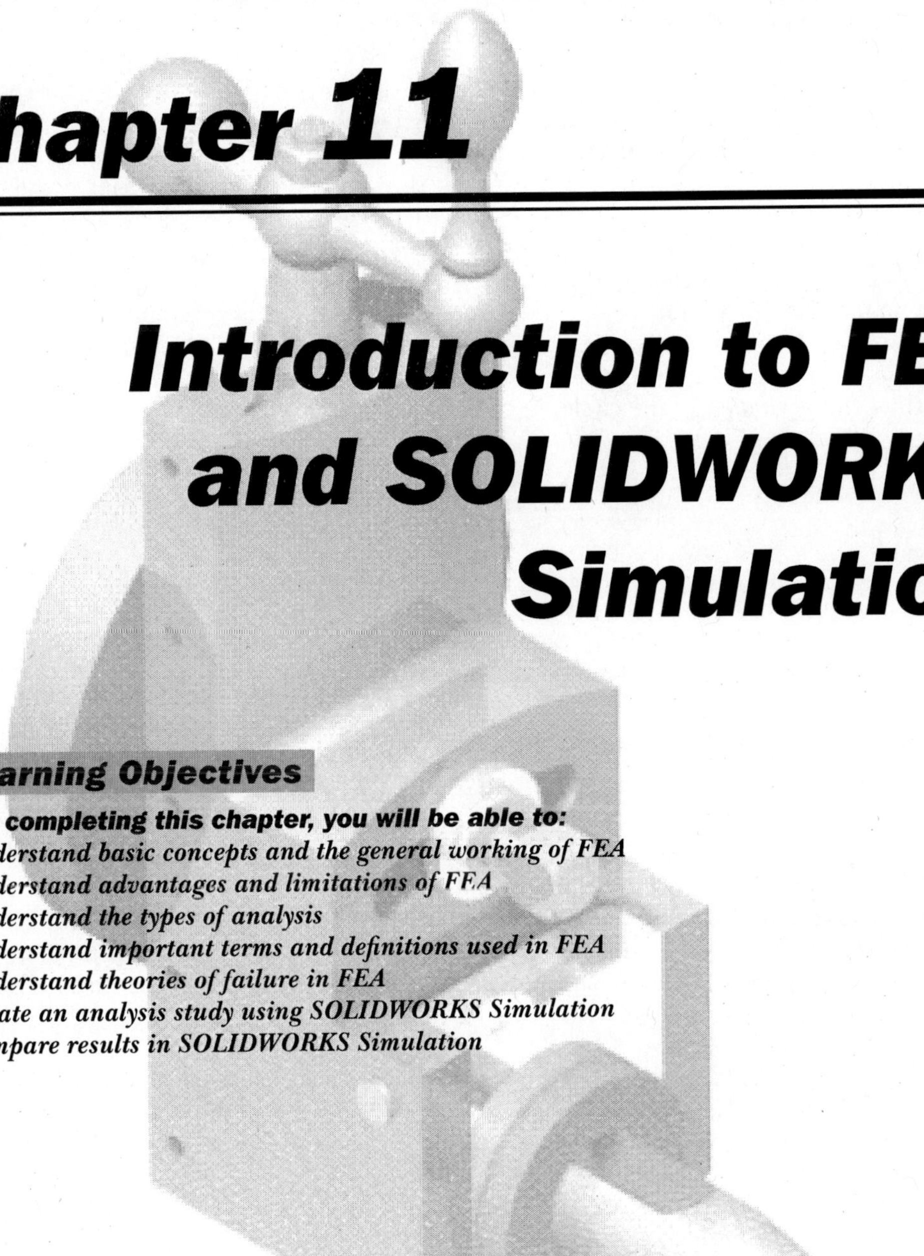

Learning Objectives

After completing this chapter, you will be able to:

- *Understand basic concepts and the general working of FEA*
- *Understand advantages and limitations of FEA*
- *Understand the types of analysis*
- *Understand important terms and definitions used in FEA*
- *Understand theories of failure in FEA*
- *Create an analysis study using SOLIDWORKS Simulation*
- *Compare results in SOLIDWORKS Simulation*

INTRODUCTION TO FEA

The finite element analysis (FEA) is a computational technique that is used to obtain approximate solutions to the boundary value problems in engineering. In this analysis, a numerical technique called the finite element method (FEM) is used to solve boundary value problems. FEA involves a computer model of a design that is loaded and analyzed for specific results. The finite element analysis was first introduced by Richard Courant in 1943. He used the Ritz method of numerical analysis and minimization of variational calculus for getting approximate solutions to vibration systems. Later, the academic and industrial researchers created the finite element method for structural analysis.

The concept of FEA can be explained through a simple example of measuring the perimeter of a circle. To measure the perimeter of a circle without using the conventional formula, divide the circle into equal segments, as shown in Figure 11-1. Next, join the start point and endpoint of each of these segments by a straight line. Now, you can easily measure the length of straight line, and thus, the perimeter of the circle.

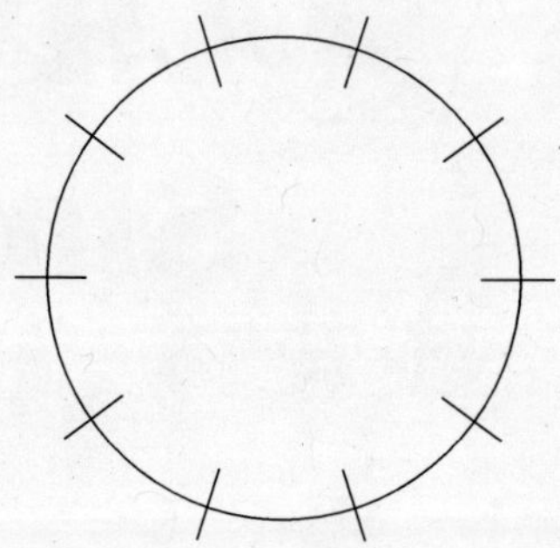

Figure 11-1 *The circle divided into equal segments*

If you divide the circle into four segments only, you will not get accurate results. For more accurate results, divide the circle into more number of segments. However, with more segments, the effort required would be more. The same concept applies to FEA also and therefore, there is always a compromise between accuracy and speed while using this method. This makes it an approximate method.

The FEA was first developed to be used in the aerospace and nuclear industries where the safety of structures is crucial. Nowadays, the simplest of the products rely on the FEA for their design evaluation.

The FEA verifies a design in accordance with the proposed specifications and loading conditions prior to manufacturing. The design is modeled using the discrete building blocks called elements. Each element has some equations that describe how it responds to certain loads. The sum of the responses of all the elements in the model gives the total response of the design.

General Working of FEA

Better knowledge of FEA will help you build more accurate models. It will also help you understand the backend working of a software. A simple model is discussed here to give you a brief overview of FEA.

Figure 11-2 shows a spring assembly that represents a simple two-spring element model. These two springs are connected in series and one of the springs is fixed at the left endpoint, refer to Figure 11-2. The stiffness of the springs is represented by spring constants K_1 and K_2. The endpoints of each spring is restricted to the displacement or the translation in the X direction only. The change in position from the undeformed state of each endpoint can be defined by the variables X_1 and X_2. The forces acting on each endpoint of the springs are represented by F_1 and F_2.

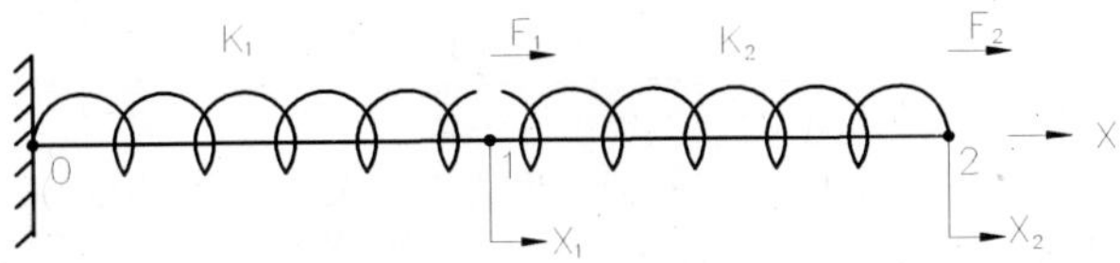

***Figure 11-2** Representation of a two-spring assembly*

To develop a model that can predict the state of this spring assembly, you can use the linear spring equation given below:

$$F = KX$$

If you use the spring parameters defined above and assume a state of equilibrium, the following equations can be written for the state of each endpoint:

$$F_1 - X_1K_1 + (X_2 - X_1)K_2 = 0$$
$$F_2 - (X_2 - X_1)K_2 = 0$$

Therefore,

$$F_1 = (K_1 + K_2)X_1 + (-K_2)X_2$$
$$F_2 = (-K_2)X_1 + K_2X_2$$

If the above set of equation is written in matrix form, it will be as follows:

$$\begin{matrix} F_1 \\ F_2 \end{matrix} = \begin{matrix} K_1 + K_2 & -K_2 \\ -K_2 & K_2 \end{matrix} \quad \begin{matrix} X_1 \\ X_2 \end{matrix}$$

In the above mathematical model, if the spring constants (K_1 and K_2) are known and forces (F_1 and F_2) are defined, then you can determine the resultant deformed shape (X_1 and X_2). Alternatively, if the spring constants (K_1 and K_2) are known and the deformed shapes (X_1 and X_2) are defined, then the resulting forces (F_1 and F_2) can be determined.

This type of spring system may be complicated to define, but it involves most of the key terminologies used in FEA. These FEA terminologies are discussed next.

1. Stiffness Matrix
2. Degrees of Freedom
3. Boundary Conditions

Stiffness Matrix

The stiffness matrix represents the resistance offered by a body to withstand the load applied. In the previous equation, the following part represents the stiffness matrix (K):

$$\begin{matrix} K_1 + K_2 & -K_2 \\ -K_2 & K_2 \end{matrix}$$

This matrix is relatively simple because it comprises only one pair of spring, but it turns complex when the number of springs increases.

Degrees of Freedom

Degrees of freedom of an object is defined as the number of independent parameters that define its movement. In the previous example, you are only concerned with the displacement and forces. By making one endpoint fixed, one degree of freedom for displacement is restricted. So, now the model has two degrees of freedom. The number of degrees of freedom in a model determines the number of equations required to solve the mathematical model.

Boundary Conditions

The boundary conditions are used to eliminate the unknowns in a system. A set of equations that is solvable is meaningless without the input. In the previous example, the boundary condition was $X_0 = 0$, and the input forces were F1 and F2. In either ways, the displacements could have been specified in place of forces as boundary conditions and the mathematical model could have been solved for the forces. In other words, the boundary conditions help you reduce or eliminate unknowns in the system.

The FEA technique needs the finite element model (FEM) for its final solution as it does not use the solid model. FEM consists of nodes, keypoints, elements, material properties, loading, and boundary conditions.

Nodes, Elements, and Element Types

Before proceeding further, you must be familiar with commonly used terms such as nodes, elements, and element types. These terms are discussed next.

Nodes

An independent entity in space is called a node. Nodes are similar to the points in geometry and represent the corner points of an element. You can change the shape of an element by moving the nodes in space. The shape of a node is shown in Figure 11-3.

Elements

An element is an entity into which the system under study is divided. An element shape is specified by nodes. The shape (area, length, and volume) of an element depends on the nodes with which it is made. An element (triangular shaped) is shown in Figure 11-3.

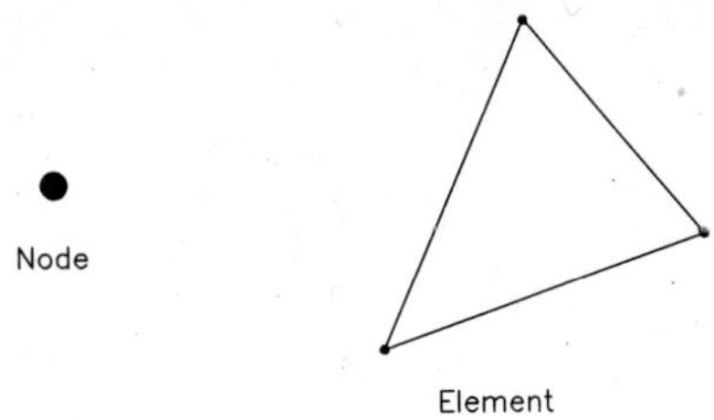

Figure 11-3 A node and an element

Element Types

The following are the basic types of the elements:

Point Element

A point element is in the form of a point and therefore has only one node.

Line Element

A line element has the shape of a line or curve, therefore a minimum of two nodes are required to define it. There can be higher order elements that have additional nodes (at the middle of the edge of the element). The element that does not have a node at the middle of the edge of the element is called a linear element. The elements with node at the mid of the edges are called quadratic or second order elements. Figure 11-4 shows some line elements.

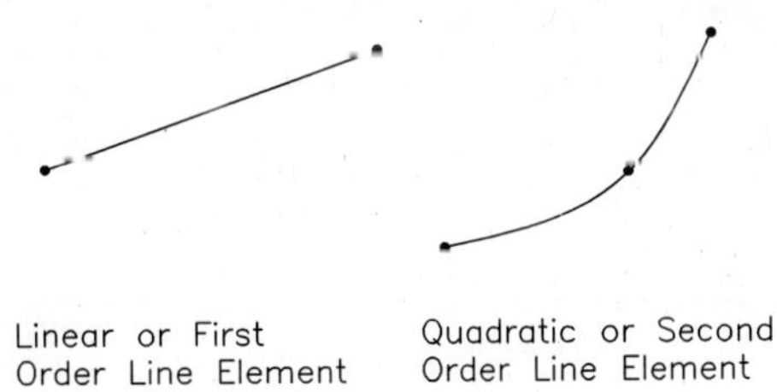

Figure 11-4 The line elements

Area Element

An area element has the shape of a quadrilateral or a triangle, therefore it requires a minimum of three or four nodes to define it. Some area elements are shown in Figure 11-5.

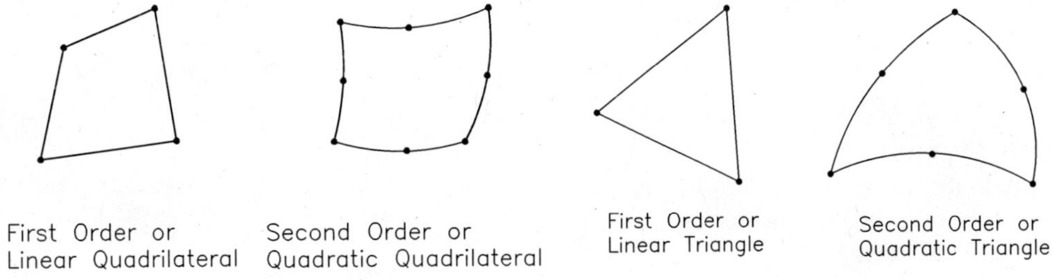

Figure 11-5 The area elements

Note

In this chapter, only the basic introduction of element types has been covered.

Volume Element

A volume element has the shape of a hexahedron (8 nodes), wedge (6 nodes), tetrahedron (4 nodes), or a pyramid (5 nodes). Some of the volume elements are shown in Figure 11-6.

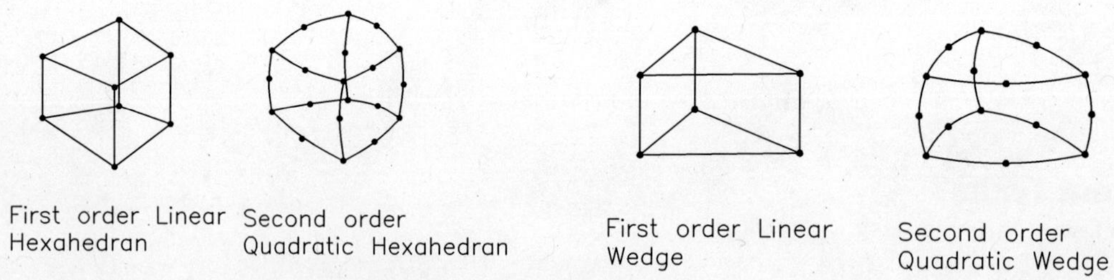

Figure 11-6 *The volume elements*

Areas for Application of FEA

FEA is a very important tool for designing. Some of the areas of its use are listed below:

1. Structural strength design
2. Structural interaction with fluid flows
3. Shock analysis
4. Acoustics
5. Thermal analysis
6. Vibrations
7. Crash simulations
8. Fluid flows
9. Electrical analysis
10. Mass diffusion
11. Buckling problems
12. Dynamic analysis
13. Electromagnetic analysis
14. Coupled analysis.

General Procedure of Conducting Finite Element Analysis

To conduct the finite element analysis, you need to follow certain steps. These steps are given next.

1. Set the type of analysis to be carried out.
2. Create or import the model.
3. Define the element type.
4. Divide the given problem into nodes and elements (generate a mesh).
5. Apply material properties and boundary conditions.
6. Solve the unknown quantities at nodes.
7. Interpret the results.

FEA through SOLIDWORKS Simulation

In SOLIDWORKS Simulation, the general process of finite element analysis is divided into three main phases, namely preprocessor, solution, and postprocessor, refer to Figure 11-7.

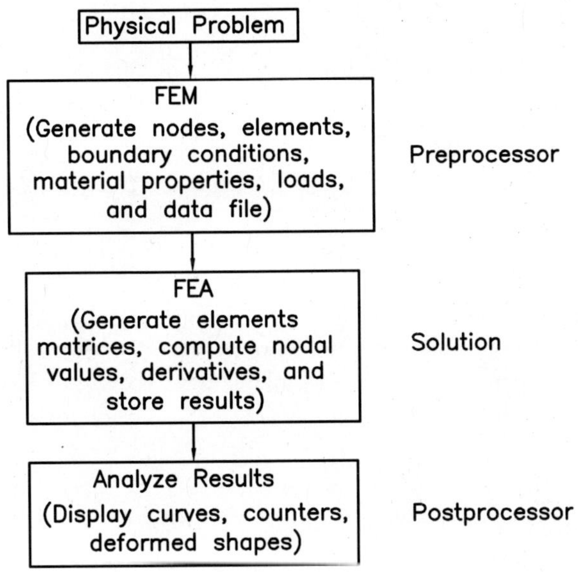

Figure 11-7 *FEA through SOLIDWORKS Simulation*

Preprocessor

The preprocessor is a program that processes the input data to produce the output that is used as input to the subsequent phase (solution). Following are the input data that needs to be given to the preprocessor:

1. Analysis type (structural or thermal, static or dynamic, and linear or nonlinear)
2. Element type
3. Real constants
4. Material properties
5. Geometric model
6. Meshed model
7. Loadings and boundary conditions

The input data will be preprocessed for the output data and preprocessor will generate the data files automatically with the help of users. These data files will be used by the subsequent phase (solution), refer to Figure 11-7.

Solution

Solution phase is completely automatic. The FEA software generates the element matrices, computes nodal values and derivatives, and stores the resulting data in files. These files are further used by the subsequent phase (postprocessor) to review and analyze the results through graphic display and tabular listings, refer to Figure 11-7.

Postprocessor

The output of the solution phase (result data files) is in the numerical form and consists of nodal values of the field variable and its derivatives. For example, in structural analysis, the output is nodal displacement and stress in the elements. The postprocessor processes the result data and displays it in graphical form to check or analyze the result. The graphical output gives detailed information about the resultant data. The postprocessor phase is automatic and generates the graphical output in the form specified by the user, refer to Figure 11-7.

Effective Utilization of FEA

Some prerequisites for effective utilization of FEA from the perspective of engineers and FEA software are discussed next.

Engineers

An engineer who wants to work with this tool must have sound knowledge of Strength of Materials (for structural analysis), Heat Transfer, Thermodynamics (for thermal analysis), and a good analytical/designing skill. Besides this, the engineer must have a fair knowledge of advantages and limitations of the FEA software being used.

Software

The FEA software should be selected based on the following considerations:

1. Analysis type to be performed.
2. Flexibility and accuracy of the tool.
3. Hardware configuration of your system.

Nowadays, the CAE / FEA software can simulate the performance of most of the systems. In other words, anything that can be converted into a mathematical equation can be simulated using the FEA techniques. Usually, the most popular principle of GIGO (Garbage In Garbage Out) applies to FEA. Therefore, you should be very careful while giving/accepting the inputs for analysis. The careful planning is the key to a successful analysis.

Advantages and Limitations of FEA Software

Following are the advantages and limitations of FEA software:

Advantages

1. It reduces the amount of prototype testing; thereby, saving the cost and time involved in performing design testing.
2. It gives graphical representation of the result of analysis.
3. The finite element modeling and analysis are performed by the preprocessor phase and the solution phase, which if done manually will consume a lot of time and in some cases, may be impossible to carry out.
4. Variables such as stress and temperature can be measured at any desired point in the model.
5. It helps optimize the design.
6. It is used to simulate the designs that are not suitable for prototype testing such as surgical implants (artificial knees).
7. It helps you create more reliable, high quality, and competitive designs.

Limitations

1. It provides approximate solutions.
2. FEA packages are costly.
3. Qualified personnel are required to perform the analysis.
4. The results give solutions but not remedies.
5. Features such as bolts, welded joints, and so on cannot be accommodated in the model. This may lead to approximation and errors in the result obtained.
6. For more accurate result, more computer space and time are required.

KEY ASSUMPTIONS IN FEA

There are four basic assumptions that affect the quality of the solution and must be considered before carrying out the finite element analysis. These assumptions are not comprehensive, but cover a wide variety of situations applicable to the problem. Make sure to use only those assumptions that apply to the analysis under consideration.

Assumptions Related to Geometry

1. Displacement values will be small so that a linear solution is valid.
2. Stress behavior outside the area of interest is not important, so the geometric simplifications in those areas will not affect the outcome.
3. Only internal fillets in the area of interest will be included in the solution.
4. Local behavior at the corners, joints, and intersection of geometries is of primary interest therefore no special modeling of these areas is required.
5. Decorative external features will be assumed insignificant for the stiffness and performance of the part and will be omitted from the model.
6. The variation in mass due to the suppressed features is negligible.

Assumptions Related to Material Properties

1. Material properties will remain in the linear region and nonlinear behavior of the material property is not considered while using the linear analysis. For example, it is assumed that the stiffness of material will remain constant under operating conditions and material has a constant stress-strain relationship (Hooke's Law).
2. Material properties are not affected by the load rate.
3. The component is free from surface imperfections that can produce stress risers.
4. All simulations will assume room temperature unless specified otherwise.
5. The effects of relative humidity or water absorption on the material used will be neglected.
6. No compensation will be made to account for the effect of chemicals, corrosives, wears or other factors that may have an impact on the long term structural integrity.

Assumptions Related to Boundary Conditions

1. Displacements will be small so that the magnitude, orientation, and distribution of the load remains constant throughout the process of deformation.
2. Frictional loss in the system is considered to be negligible.
3. All interfacing components will be assumed rigid.
4. The portion of the structure being studied is assumed a part, that is, separate from the rest of the system. As a result, the reaction or input from the adjacent features is neglected.

Assumptions Related to Fasteners

1. Residual stresses due to fabrication, preloading on bolts, welding, or other manufacturing or assembly processes will be neglected.
2. All the welds between the components will be considered ideal and continuous.
3. The failure of fasteners will not be considered.
4. Loads on the threaded portion of the parts is supposed to be evenly distributed among the engaged threads.
5. Stiffness of bearings, radially or axially, will be considered infinite or rigid.

Note

The assumption for non linear analysis is different from linear analysis in FEA. Although most of the nonlinear analyses are based on material's changing stiffness, the origin of nonlinear behavior can be different. The nonlinearity can occur due to nonlinear material or nonlinear geometry.

TYPES OF ANALYSIS

The following types of analysis can be performed using FEA software:

1. Structural analysis
2. Thermal analysis
3. Fluid flow analysis
4. Electromagnetic field analysis
5. Coupled field analysis

Structural Analysis

In structural analysis, first the nodal degrees of freedom (displacement) are calculated and then the stress, strains, and reaction forces are calculated from the nodal displacements. The classification of the structural analysis is shown in Figure 11-8.

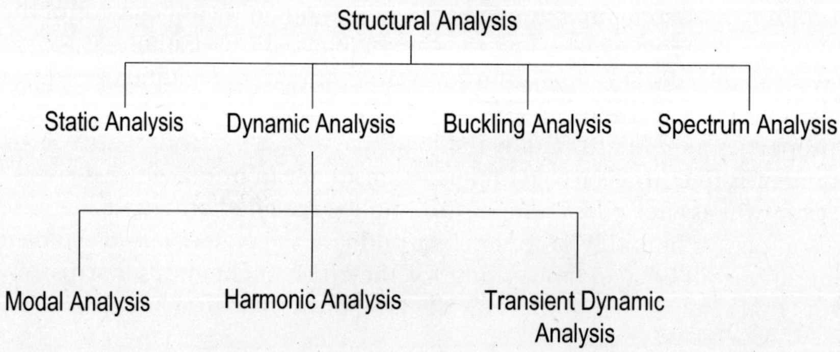

Figure 11-8 *Types of structural analysis*

Static Analysis

In static analysis, the load or field conditions do not vary with respect to time, and therefore, it is assumed that the load or field conditions are applied gradually not suddenly. The system under analysis can be linear or nonlinear. Inertia and damping effects are ignored in structural analysis. In structural analysis, the following matrices are solved:

[K] x [X]= [F]

where,

K = Stiffness Matrix
X = Displacement Matrix
F = Load Matrix

The above equation is called as the force balance equation for the linear system. The Stiffness Matrix [K] is constant for a linear system. The loadings that can be applied in a static analysis include:

1. Externally applied forces and pressures
2. Steady-state inertial forces (such as gravity or rotational velocity)
3. Imposed (non-zero) displacements
4. Temperatures (for thermal strain)
5. Fluences (for nuclear swelling)

The outputs that can be expected from a FEA software are given next.

1. Displacements
2. Strains
3. Stresses
4. Reaction forces

Dynamic Analysis

In dynamic analysis, the load or field conditions do vary with time. The assumption here is that the load or field conditions are applied suddenly. The system can be linear or nonlinear. The dynamic loads include oscillating loads, impacts, collisions, and random loads. The dynamic analysis is classified into the following three main categories:

Modal Analysis

It is used to calculate the natural frequency and mode shape of a structure.

Harmonic Analysis

It is used to calculate the response of the structure to harmonically time varying loads.

Transient Dynamic Analysis

It is used to calculate the response of the structure to arbitrary time varying loads.

In dynamic analysis, the following matrices are solved:

For the system without any external load:

[M] × Double Derivative of [X] + [K] × [X]= 0

where,

M = Mass Matrix
K = Stiffness Matrix
X = Displacement Matrix

For the system with external load:

$$[M] \times \text{Double Derivative of } [X] + [K] \times [X] = [F]$$

where,

K = Stiffness Matrix
X = Displacement Matrix
F = Load Matrix

The above equations are called as force balance equations for a dynamic system. By solving the above set of equations, you will be able to extract the natural frequencies of a system. The load types applied in a dynamic analysis are the same as those in the static analysis. The outputs that can be expected from a software are:

1. Natural frequencies
2. Mode shapes
3. Displacements
4. Strains
5. Stresses
6. Reaction forces

All the outputs mentioned above can be obtained with respect to time.

Spectrum Analysis

This is an extension of the modal analysis and is used to calculate the stress and strain due to the response of the spectrum (random vibrations).

Buckling Analysis

This type of analysis is used to calculate the buckling load and the buckling mode shape. Slender structures and structures with slender part loaded in the axial direction buckle under relatively small loads. For such structures, the buckling load becomes a critical design factor.

Thermal Analysis

Thermal analysis is used to determine the temperature distribution and related thermal quantities such as:

1. Thermal distribution
2. Amount of heat loss or gain
3. Thermal gradients
4. Thermal fluxes

All the primary heat transfer modes such as conduction, convection, and radiation can be simulated. You can perform two types of thermal analysis, steady-state and transient.

Steady State Thermal Analysis

In this analysis, the system is studied under steady thermal loads with respect to time.

Transient Thermal Analysis

In this analysis, the system is studied under varying thermal loads with respect to time.

Fluid Flow Analysis

This analysis is used to determine the flow distribution and temperature of a fluid or gas. SOLIDWORKS Flow simulation program is used to simulate the laminar and turbulent flow, compressible and electronic packaging, automotive design, and so on.

The outputs that can be expected from the fluid flow analysis are:

1. Velocities
2. Pressures
3. Temperatures
4. Film coefficients

Electromagnetic Field Analysis

This type of analysis is used to determine the magnetic fields in electromagnetic devices. The types of electromagnetic analyses are:

1. Static analysis
2. Harmonic analysis
3. Transient analysis

Coupled Field Analysis

This type of analysis considers the mutual interaction between two or more fields. It is impossible to solve the fields separately because they are interdependent. Therefore, you need a program that can solve both the physical problems by combining them.

For example, if a component is exposed to heat, you may first require to study the thermal characteristics of the component and then the effect of the thermal heating on the structural stability.

Alternatively, if a component is bent into a different shape using one of the metal forming processes and then subjected to heating, the thermal characteristics of the component will depend on the new shape of the component and therefore the shape of the component has to be predicted through structural simulations first. This is called as coupled field analysis.

LINEAR ANALYSIS

Linear analysis is undertaken when an object is expected to behave linearly. In other words, it follows the Hooke's Law which states that within the elastic limit, stress is directly proportional to strain, refer to Figure 11-9. Also, the material that undergoes linear analysis experiences elastic deformation and will return to its original configuration or shape after the load has been removed from it. In linear analysis, the following factors are calculated:

1. Displacements and stresses due to static loads
2. Natural frequency and mode shapes of the model
3. Natural frequency and mode shapes of the model with load stiffening
4. Maximum displacement and stress due to a spectrum-type load
5. Statistical response of a system (displacements and stresses) due to random vibration, noise, or spectrum density

6. Steady state response (displacements and stresses) due to harmonic or sinusoidal load or acceleration
7. Displacements and stresses over time due to loads that will vary in a known fashion
8. Load that causes the model to buckle due to geometric instability
9. Response of the model due to shock

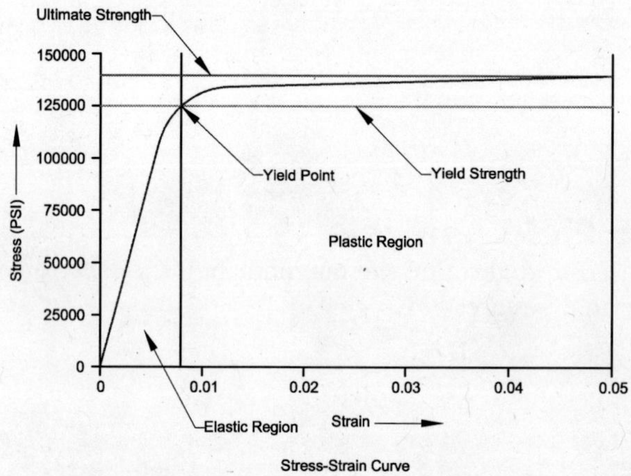

Figure 11-9 *The Stress and Strain Curve*

NONLINEAR ANALYSIS

The Nonlinear Analysis method is used when relationship between load and response becomes nonlinear. Generally this analysis is performed in the following situations to get more accurate results.

1. When the maximum stress exceeds the yield stress for the material or when the material is non linear such as Rubber, Plastics
2. When the deformations are larger than 1/20th of the part's largest dimension
3. When Stress stiffening or stress softening occurs
4. When dynamic or inertial effects are prominent
5. When the load direction/magnitude vary due to the deflection of the model
6. When material is experiencing creep or viscoelasticity

Consider the following equation;

$$[K] \times [X] = [F]$$

In this equation, the Stiffness Matrix [K] is not constant in nonlinear system and depends on either Nonlinear Material or Nonlinear Geometry. There are three types of nonlinearity:

1. Material
2. Geometric
3. Boundary (contact)

In non-linear analysis, you can calculate:

1. Displacements and stresses due to static loads
2. Displacements, velocities, accelerations, and stresses over time due to dynamic loads
3. Natural frequencies and mode shapes of the model
4. Displacements and stresses before and after the model has collapsed

IMPORTANT TERMS AND DEFINITIONS

Some of the important terms and definitions used in FEA are discussed next.

Strength

When a material or body is subjected to an external load, it offers resistance to prevent the deformation in the body. This resistance is offered by the material by the virtue of its strength.

Load

The external force acting on a body is called the load.

Stress

The resistance offered by a body against the deformation is called stress. The stress is induced in the body when the load is applied to it. Stress is calculated as load per unit area.

$$p = F/A$$

Where,

p = Stress in N/mm^2
F = Applied Force in Newton
A = Cross-Sectional Area in mm^2

The material can undergo various types of stresses. These stresses are discussed next.

Tensile Stress

If the resistance offered by a body is against the increase in length, the body is said to be under tensile stress.

Compressive Stress

If the resistance offered by a body is against the decrease in length, the body is said to be under compressive stress. Compressive stress is just the reverse of tensile stress.

Shear Stress

Shear stress exists when two materials tend to slide in any typical plane of shear on application of force parallel to that plane.

Shear Stress = Shear resistance (R) / Shear area (A)

Strain

When a body is subjected to a load (force), its length undergoes a change. The ratio of the change in length to the original length of the member is called strain. If the body returns to its original shape on removing the load, the strain is called as elastic strain. If the metal remains distorted, the strain is called as plastic strain. The strain can be of three types, namely, tensile, compressive, or shear strain.

Strain (ε) = Change in Length (*dl*) / Original Length (*l*)

Elastic Limit

The maximum stress that can be applied to a material without producing permanent deformation is known as the elastic limit of the material. If the stress is within the elastic limit, the material will return to its original shape and dimension when the external stress is removed.

Hooke's Law

It states that the stress is directly proportional to the strain, within the elastic limit.

Stress / Strain = Constant (within the elastic limit)

Young's Modulus or Modulus of Elasticity

In case of axial loading, the ratio of intensity of tensile or compressive stress to the corresponding strain is constant. This ratio is called Young's modulus and it is denoted by E.

$$E = p/\varepsilon$$

Where,

p = Stress
ε = strain

Shear Modulus or Modulus of Rigidity

In case of shear load, the ratio of shear stress to the corresponding shear strain is constant. This ratio is called shear modulus and it is denoted by C, N, or G.

Ultimate Strength

The maximum stress that a material can withstand when it is subjected to an external load is called its ultimate strength.

Factor of Safety

The ratio of the ultimate strength to the estimated maximum stress in ordinary use (design stress) is known as factor of safety. It is necessary that the design stress is well below the elastic limit and to achieve this condition, the ultimate stress should be divided by a 'factor of safety'.

Lateral Strain

If a cylindrical rod is subjected to an axial tensile load, the length (*l*) of the rod will increase (*dl*) and the diameter (ϕ) of the rod will decrease ($d\phi$). In short, the longitudinal stress will not only produce a strain in its own direction, but will also produce a lateral strain. The ratio *dl/l* is called the longitudinal strain or linear strain and the ratio $d\phi/\phi$ is called the lateral strain.

Poisson's Ratio

The ratio of lateral strain to the longitudinal strain is constant, within the elastic limit. This ratio is called as Poission's ratio and is denoted by 1/m. For most of the metals, the value of the 'm' lies between 3 and 4.

Poisson's ratio = Lateral Strain / Longitudinal Strain = 1/m

Bulk Modulus

If a body is subjected to equal stresses along the three mutually perpendicular directions, the ratio of the direct stresses to the corresponding volumetric strain is found to be constant for a body, when the deformation is within a certain limit. This ratio is called the bulk modulus and is denoted by K.

Creep

At elevated temperatures and constant stress or load, many materials continue to deform but at a slow rate. This behavior of materials is called creep. At a constant stress and temperature, the rate of creep is approximately constant for a long period of time. After this period and after a certain amount of deformation, the rate of creep increases, thereby causing fracture in the material. The rate of creep is highly dependent on both the stress and the temperature.

Classification of Materials

Materials are classified into three main categories: elastic, plastic, and rigid. In case of elastic materials, the deformation disappears on the removal of load. In plastic materials, the deformation is permanent. A rigid material does not undergo any deformation when subjected to an external load. However, in actual practice, no material is perfectly elastic, plastic, or rigid. The structural members are designed such that they remain in elastic conditions under the action of working loads. All engineering materials are grouped into three categories that are discussed next.

Isotropic Material

In case of Isotropic materials, the material properties do not vary with direction which means it has same material properties in all directions. The material properties are defined by Young's modulus and Poisson's ratio.

Orthotropic Material

In case of Orthotropic material, the material properties vary with change in direction and are specified in three orthogonal directions. It has three mutually perpendicular planes of material symmetry. The material properties are defined by three separate Young's modulus and Poisson's ratios.

Anisotropic Material

In case of Anisotropic material, the material properties vary with change in direction. But in this case, there is no plane of material symmetry.

THEORIES OF FAILURE

The following are the theories of failure.

von Mises Stress Failure Criterion

The von Mises stress criterion is also called Maximum distortion energy theory. The theory states that a ductile material starts yielding at a location when the von Mises stress becomes equal to the stress limit. In most cases, the yield strength is used as the stress limit.

Maximum Shear Stress Failure Criterion

The Maximum Shear Stress failure criterion is based on the Maximum Shear Stress theory. This theory predicts failure of a material when the absolute maximum shear stress reaches the stress that causes the material to yield in a simple tension test. The Maximum Shear Stress criterion is used for ductile materials.

Maximum Normal Stress Failure Criterion

This criterion is used for brittle materials. It assumes that the ultimate strength of the material in tension and compression is the same. This assumption is not valid in all cases. For example, cracks considerably decrease the strength of a material in tension while their effect is not significant in compression, as in this case, the cracks tend to close. Brittle materials do not have a specific yield point and hence it is not recommended to use the yield strength to define the stress limit for this criterion.

INTRODUCTION TO SOLIDWORKS SIMULATION

Welcome to the world of Computer Aided Engineering (CAE) with SOLIDWORKS Simulation. SOLIDWORKS Simulation is an analysis system, fully integrated with SOLIDWORKS. SOLIDWORKS is one of the products of SOLIDWORKS Corporation which is a part of Dassault Systemes. SOLIDWORKS also works as a platform software for a number of software. This implies that you can also use other compatible software within the SOLIDWORKS window. There are a number of software provided by the SolidWorks Corporation which can be used as add-ins with SOLIDWORKS.

Some of the software that can be used on SOLIDWORKS work platform are listed next.

1. Autotrace
2. eDrawings
3. PhotoView 360
4. ScanTo3D
5. SOLIDWORKS Design Checker
6. SOLIDWORKS Motion
7. SOLIDWORKS Routing
8. SOLIDWORKS Simulation
9. SOLIDWORKS Toolbox Library
10. SOLIDWORKS Toolbox Utilities
11. SOLIDWORKS Utilities
12. CircuitWorks
13. SOLIDWORKS Workgroup PDM 2018
14. TolAnalyst
15. SOLIDWORKS Part Reviewer

SOLIDWORKS Simulation is a registered trademark of Structural Research & Analysis Corporation. It is provided with fast solvers enabling you to solve even the most complicated analysis problems with great ease and in short period of time. In SOLIDWORKS Simulation, you can perform various analyses such as static analysis, frequency analysis, buckling analysis, thermal analysis, design scenario analysis, fatigue analysis, and optimization analysis.

The following is the list of analyses that you can perform using SOLIDWORKS Simulation.

1. Structural analysis
2. Frequency analysis
3. Buckling analysis
4. Thermal analysis
5. Fluid flow analysis
6. Dynamic analysis
7. Fatigue analysis
8. Design Scenario analysis
9. Optimization analysis

GETTING STARTED WITH SOLIDWORKS SIMULATION

To start with SOLIDWORKS Simulation, you need to install SOLIDWORKS and SOLIDWORKS Simulation.

After installing the software, double-click on the SOLIDWORKS icon; the SOLIDWORKS window will be displayed and the **SOLIDWORKS Resources** task pane will be displayed on its right, refer to Figure 11-10.

Note that, by default, the SOLIDWORKS Simulation tools will not be added in the work environment of SOLIDWORKS. In order to activate SOLIDWORKS Simulation, choose **Tools** from the SOLIDWORKS menus; a menu will be displayed. Select **Add-Ins** from the menu; the **Add-Ins** window will be displayed. Select both the check boxes, in the front and back of the **SOLIDWORKS Simulation** in the **Add-Ins** window and choose **OK**. Next, start the new part document in SOLIDWORKS by using the **New SOLIDWORKS Document** dialog box. Note that now the **Simulation** menu is added in the SOLIDWORKS menus and the **Simulation** tab is added in the **CommandManager**.

***Figure 11-10** The **SOLIDWORKS** window*

TUTORIALS

Tutorial 1

In this tutorial, consider a rectangular plate of alloy steel material with cutout. The dimensions and the boundary conditions of the plate are shown in Figure 11-11. It is fixed at one end and loaded on the other. Under the given load and constraints, plot the deformed shape. Also, determine the principal stresses and the von Mises stresses.

In this tutorial, you will perform two cases on the rectangular plate. In Case-1, you will apply uniform load of 15 Ibf on one end of the plate and in Case-2, you will apply a load of 1 Ibf on both corners of the right edge of the plate and 5 Ibf at the middle of the right edge of the plate. **(Expected time: 45 min)**

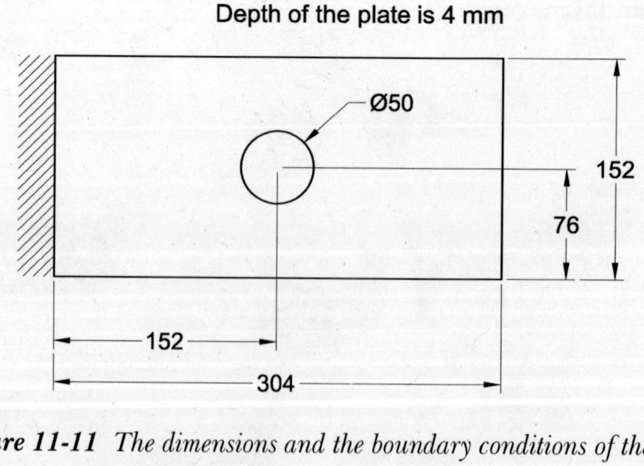

***Figure 11-11** The dimensions and the boundary conditions of the plate*

The following steps are required to complete this tutorial:

a. Add the SOLIDWORKS Simulation in the SOLIDWORKS and start a new part file.
b. Create the model, as shown in Figure 11-12.
c. Start a new static study.
d. Apply the material.
e. Apply constraints and loads.
f. Create mesh and run the analysis.
g. View the results.
h. Create new case study.
i. Generate report.
j. Compare reports.

Adding the SOLIDWORKS Simulation to SOLIDWORKS and Starting a New Part File

1. Start SOLIDWORKS and then choose **Tools > Add-Ins** from the SOLIDWORKS menus; the **Add-Ins** window is displayed. Next, select the check box both in the left and right of **SOLIDWORKS Simulation** and then choose the **OK** button.

2. Start the new part document by using the **New SOLIDWORKS Document** dialog box. Note that the **Simulation** menu is added to the SOLIDWORKS menus and the **Simulation** tab is added to the **CommandManager**.

   Now, you need to create the model of the rectangular plate with a circular cutout for analysis.

Creating the Model for Analysis

1. Create the rectangular plate, as shown in Figure 11-12. For dimensions, refer to Figure 11-11.

Figure 11-12 *Model for analysis*

Starting a New Study

Since you want to determine the principal stresses and von Mises stresses, you need to start a static analysis.

1. Choose the **Simulation** tab from the **CommandManager**; the **Simulation CommandManager** is displayed, refer to Figure 11-13.

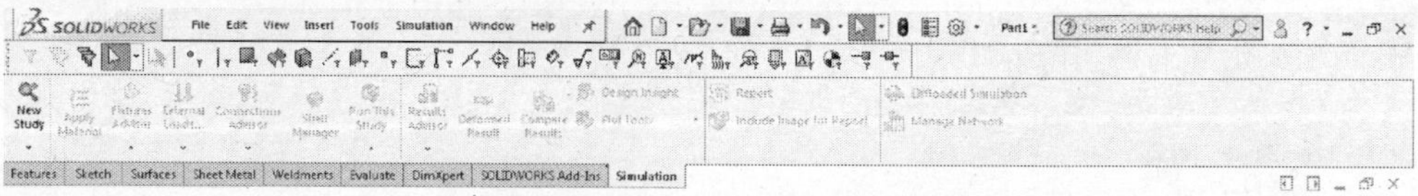

Figure 11-13 The Simulation CommandManager

Note

If the ***Simulation*** *tab is not added in the* ***CommandManager*** *by default, you can customize it. To do so, right-click on a tab in the* ***CommandManager****; a shortcut menu is displayed. Choose* ***Simulation*** *from this shortcut menu; the* ***Simulation*** *tab is added to the* ***CommandManager****.*

2. Choose the **New Study** tool from the **New Study** flyout in the **Simulation CommandManager**, refer to Figure 11-14; the **Study PropertyManager** is displayed, as shown in Figure 11-15.

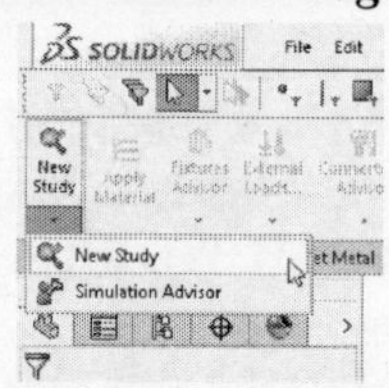

Figure 11-14 *The* ***New Study*** *flyout*

The **Study PropertyManager** allows you to carry out new simulation studies. Using this PropertyManager, you can perform a static study to calculate the response of bodies on which loads are applied slowly; a frequency study to calculate the natural frequencies and mode shapes of bodies; a buckling study to calculate the buckling modes and critical buckling loads of bodies; a thermal study to calculate the temperature distribution in bodies due to conduction, convection, and radiation; a drop test study to evaluate the effect on a part or an assembly when it drops on a rigid or flexible planar surface; a fatigue study to calculate the total life, damage, and load factors due to cyclic loading; a nonlinear study to calculate the nonlinear response of bodies due to applied loads; a linear dynamic study to calculate the response of bodies by accumulating the contribution of each mode to the loading environment. In linear dynamic study, loads are not applied slowly and they change with time or frequency. You can also create a pressure vessel design study by using this PropertyManager to combine the results of static studies with the desired factors.

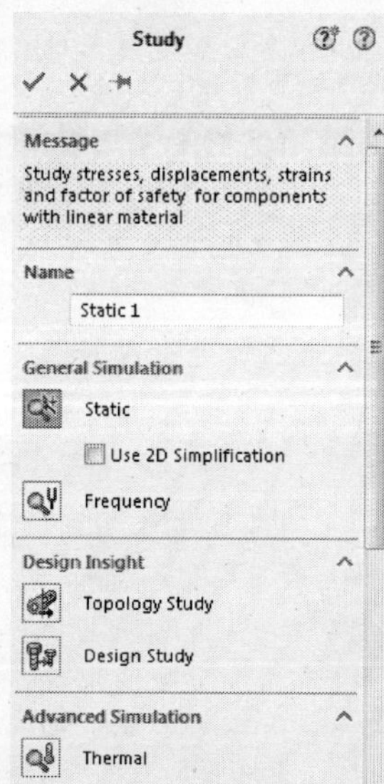

Figure 11-15 *The* ***Study PropertyManager***

3. Choose the **Static** button, if it is not chosen and then enter the name of the study as **Case-1** in the **Name** edit box of the PropertyManager. Next, choose **OK**; a new tree named **Case-1** is added to the **FeatureManager Design Tree**, refer to Figure 11-16.

Applying the Material

Now you need to apply the alloy steel material to the rectangular plate.

1. Choose the **Apply Material** button from the **Simulation CommandManager**; the **Material** dialog box is displayed.

2. Expand the **SOLIDWORKS Materials** node of the **Material** dialog box. Next, expand the **Steel** sub-node under it and choose the **Alloy Steel** material; all the properties of the selected material are displayed on the right side of the dialog box.

3. Choose the **Apply** button from the dialog box; the alloy steel material is applied to the model. Next, close the **Material** dialog box.

Applying Constraints

After applying material to the model, you need to apply constraints to fix one edge of the model.

1. Choose the **Fixed Geometry** button from the **Fixtures Advisor** flyout of the **Simulation CommandManager**, refer to Figure 11-17; the **Fixture PropertyManager** is displayed on the left of the drawing area.

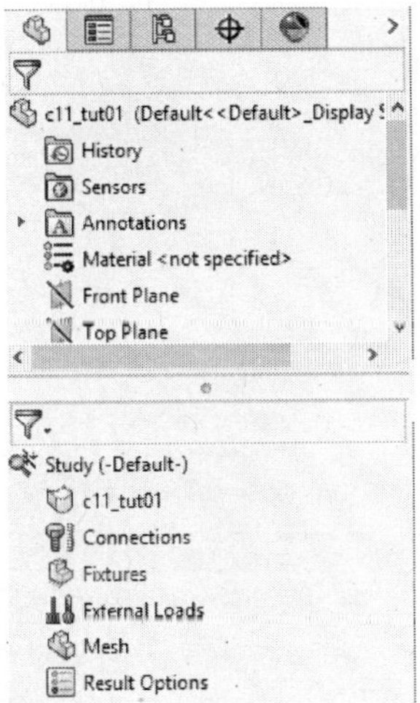

Figure 11-16 The FeatureManager Design Tree

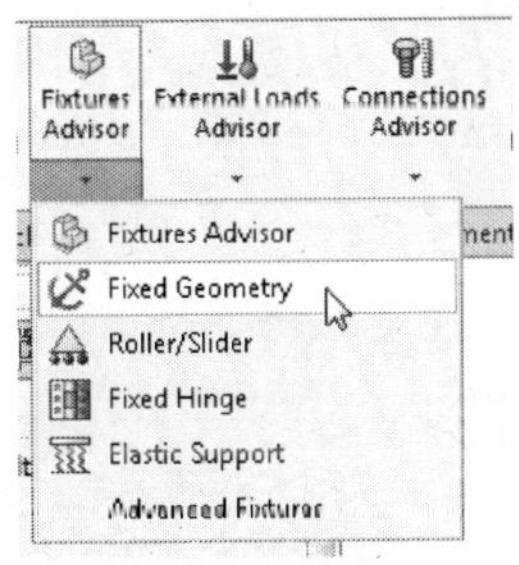

Figure 11-17 The Fixtures Advisor flyout

2. Make sure that the **Fixed Geometry** button is chosen in the **Standard (Fixed Geometry)** rollout of the PropertyManager.

3. Rotate the model such that you can select the left face of the model. Next, select the left face of the model; the left selected face of the model is fixed and the fixed geometry callout is attached to the selected face, as shown in Figure 11-18.

4. Choose the **OK** button from the PropertyManager; the selected face is fixed.

Figure 11-18 The left face of the model selected

Applying Loads

After applying the material and constraints to the model, you need to apply a uniform force along the right edge of the model in vertically downward direction.

1. Choose **Force** from the **External Loads Advisor** flyout of the **Simulation CommandManager**, refer to Figure 11-19; the **Force/Torque PropertyManager** is displayed on the left of the drawing area.

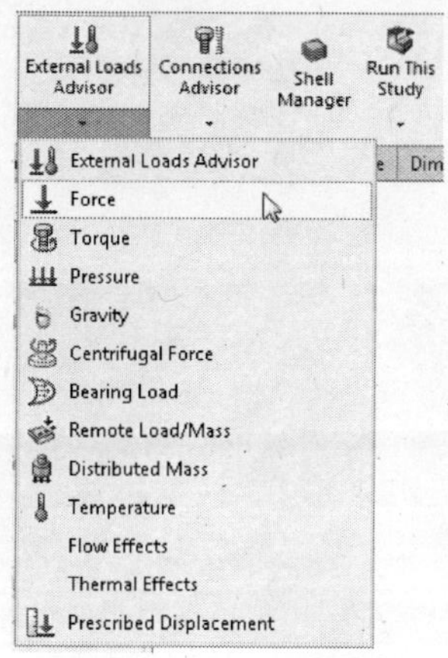

*Figure 11-19 The **External Loads Advisor** flyout*

2. Make sure that the **Force** button is chosen in the **Force/Torque** rollout of the PropertyManager.

3. Select the top right edge of the model to apply the force, refer to Figure 11-20; the force is applied on the selected edge. Also, the force callout is attached to the selected edge.

   Now, you need to specify the direction of force.

4. Select the **Selected direction** radio button from the **Force/Torque** rollout of the PropertyManager; the **Face, Edge, Plane for Direction** selection box is displayed in the **Force/Torque** rollout.

5. Select a vertical edge of the model to apply the force in the vertical direction. You can reverse the direction of the applied force by selecting the **Reverse direction** check box from the **Force** rollout, if needed.

6. Select **English (IPS)** from the **Unit** drop-down list of the **Units** rollout in the PropertyManager.

7. Enter **15** in the **Along Edge** edit box of the **Force** rollout.

8. Accept the other default settings and choose **OK** from the PropertyManager to apply the load. Figure 11-20 shows the model with constraints and loads.

Figure 11-20 Model after applying constraints and loads

Creating Mesh

After applying the constraints and loads, you need to create mesh.

1. Choose the **Create Mesh** button from the **Run This Study** flyout of the **Simulation CommandManager**, refer to Figure 11-21; the **Mesh PropertyManager** is displayed.

2. Accept all the default settings and choose the **OK** button from the PropertyManager; mesh is created in the model, as shown in Figure 11-22.

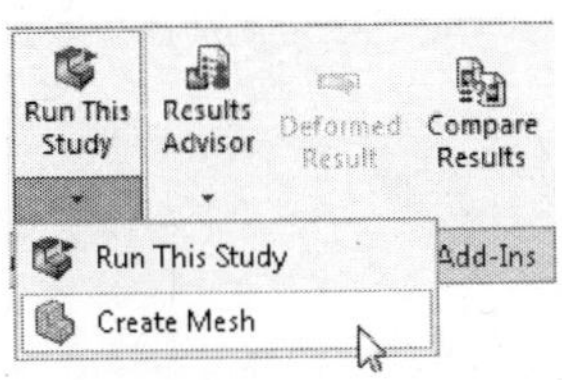

***Figure 11-21** The **Run This Study** flyout*

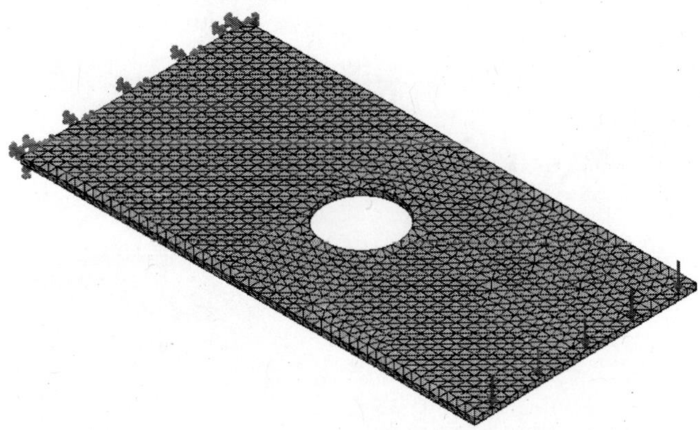

Figure 11-22 The model after meshing

Running Analysis

Now, you need to run the analysis on the model.

1. Choose the **Run This Study** button from the **Simulation CommandManager**; the **Case-1** window is displayed and the process of solving the FE model gets started. Once the analysis process is completed, a new node named **Results** is added to the **FeatureManager Design Tree**. Also, the resultant model is displayed in the drawing area with the von Mises stress contour, as shown in Figure 11-23.

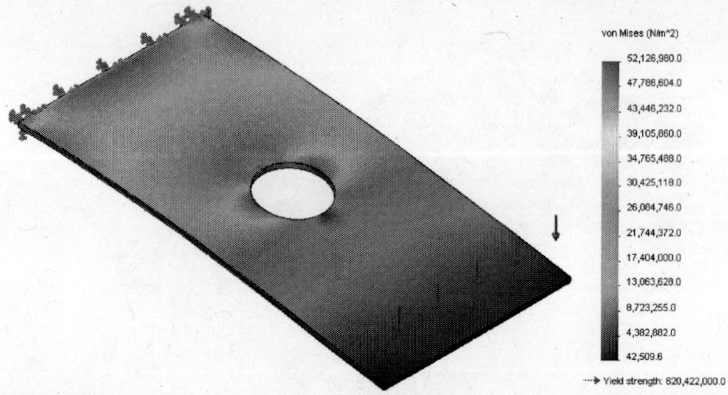

Figure 11-23 *The resultant model with von Mises stress contour*

Viewing the Results

Next, you will view the von Mises stress and displacement contour.

1. Double-click on the **Stress1(-von Mises-)** under the **Results** node to display the von Mises stress contour, if it is not displayed by default, refer to Figure 11-23. The areas in red have maximum stress and the areas in blue are least stressed.

2. Similarly, double-click on the **Displacement1 (-Res disp-)** under the **Results** node to view the displacement plots. Figure 11-24 shows the displacement contour. The areas in red have maximum displacement and the areas in blue have minimum displacement.

Figure 11-24 *The displacement contour*

3. To animate the displacement plot, right-click on **Displacement1 (-Res disp-)** under the **Results** node; a shortcut menu is displayed. Choose the **Animate** option from the menu; animation starts with default settings and the **Animation PropertyManager** is displayed at the left of the screen. Using the PropertyManager, you can change the settings according to your requirement.

Creating a New Case Study

In SOLIDWORKS Simulation, you can also create multiple studies and then compare them with each other. In this session, you will duplicate Case-1 study to create a new case study.

1. Right-click on the **Case-1** tab at the bottom of the screen; a shortcut menu is displayed.

2. Choose the **Copy Study** option from shortcut menu; the **Copy Study PropertyManager** is displayed.

3. Enter the study name as **Case-2** in the **Study name** edit box and select **Case-1** in the **Source Study** drop-down.

4. Select the **Static** button from the **Target Study** rollout and choose the **OK** button from the **Copy Study PropertyManager**; the **Case Study-2** tab is created and all the parameters of the previous study, such as materials, constraints, and loads are added to this study.

   Now, you need to apply two loads on the top right edge of the model. One load of 1 lbf at both the corners and another of 5 lbf at the middle of the top right edge.

5. Activate the **Faces, Edges, Vertices, Reference Points for Force** selection area of the **Force/Torque** rollout of the PropertyManager. Next, right-click on it and choose **Clear Selections** from the shortcut menu displayed.

6. Select both the top corner vertices of the top right edge of the model one by one, refer to Figure 11-25; the arrows pointing vertically downward are displayed on the selected vertices, indicating the direction of force applied. Also, a callout is attached to the vertex selected first with the default value of the force applied.

7. Enter **1** in the **Along Edge** edit box of the **Force** rollout; the concentrated load of 1 lb is applied on both the selected vertices, refer to Figure 11-25. Next, choose the **OK** button from the PropertyManager.

   Next, you need to apply a load of 5 lbf at the midpoint of the top right edge. To do so, first you need to create a reference point at that location.

8. Invoke the **Features CommandManager** and then choose the **Point** button from the **Reference Geometry** flyout; the **Point PropertyManager** is displayed. Next, create a point at the middle of the top right edge by selecting the midpoint and right side face; and then exit the PropertyManager.

9. Right-click on the **External Loads** node available in the **FeatureManager Design Tree** and choose **Force** from the shortcut menu displayed; the **Force/Torque PropertyManager** is displayed.

10. Select the point created by using the **Point PropertyManager**; the force callout with the default force value is attached with the selected point, refer to Figure 11-26.

11. Select the **Selected direction** radio button from the **Force/Torque** rollout of the PropertyManager and then select the vertical edge of the model to specify the direction of

force vertically; an arrow is displayed on the selected point, pointing vertically downward, indicating the direction of the force applied, refer to Figure 11-26.

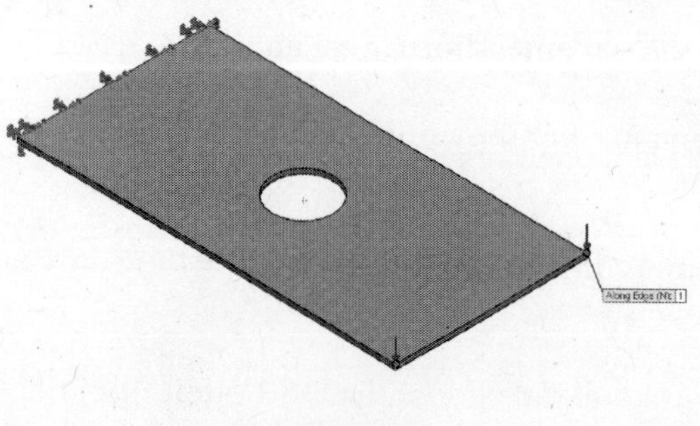

***Figure 11-25** Load applied on both the vertices*

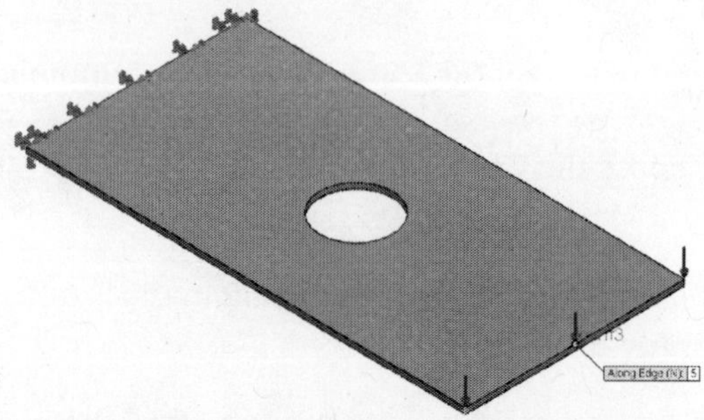

***Figure 11-26** Load applied on middle point*

12. Make sure the **English (IPS)** option is selected in the **Unit** drop-down list of the **Units** rollout. Next, enter **5** lb as the force value and then select the **OK** button.

13. Run the analysis; the **Results** node is modified and the von Mises stress contour is displayed in the drawing area, as shown in Figure 11-27. You can view the plots and compare the results with Case-1.

***Figure 11-27** The von Mises stress contour of Case-2*

Generating the Report

Now, you need to generate the individual report for Case-1 and Case-2.

1. Activate the Case-1 study by clicking on the **Case-1** tab available at the bottom of the screen.

2. Choose the **Report** button from the **Simulation CommandManager**; the **Report Options** dialog box is displayed.

3. In the **Report sections** area, select the check boxes corresponding to the sections that you want to add in the report.

   You can also add information in the header of the report such as designer, company, URL, logo, and so on by using the respective edit boxes of the dialog box. These edit boxes are enabled after you select their respective check boxes. For example, to add the designer information in the header of the report, select the **Designer** check box available in the **Header information** area of the dialog box; the **Designer** edit box will be enabled and you can enter the name of the designer in the edit box.

4. After entering all the required information in the **Report Options** dialog box, choose the **Publish** button to generate the report in the Word document. As soon as the analysis report is generated and displayed in the Word document, the **Report** node is added to the **FeatureManager Design Tree**. After viewing the report, you can close it.

> **Tip**
> *After closing the report, you can again invoke it by double-clicking on its name displayed under the* ***Report*** *node of the* ***FeatureManager Design Tree.***

5. Similarly, generate the report for Case-2 study. After viewing the report you can close it.

Comparing the Results

Now, you can compare both the results side by side using the **Compare Results** tool.

1. Choose the **Compare Results** tool from the **Simulation CommandManager**; the **Compare Results PropertyManager** is displayed.

The **Compare Results** tool is used to compare multiple results side by side on single screen.

2. Select the **The current study** radio button from the **Options** rollout of the PropertyManager; all the studies of the current model will be displayed under the **Studies** node with a tick mark on their left in the PropertyManager.

   You can exclude a study from the current comparison set of studies by clearing the check box corresponding to that study.

The **The current study** radio button allows you to compare the studies created in the current model. If you want to view the results of multiple plots of the current study of the model, you need to select the **All studies in this configuration** radio button from the **Compare Results PropertyManager**. Note that upto four result plots can be selected to display in split windows.

3. Choose the **OK** button from the **Compare Results PropertyManager**; the **Case-1** and **Case-2** studies are displayed in the single window for comparison, as shown in Figure 11-28. After comparing both the studies, you need to save the model.

4. Save the model with the name *c11_tut01* at the location *\Documents\SOLIDWORKS Tutorials\c11*.

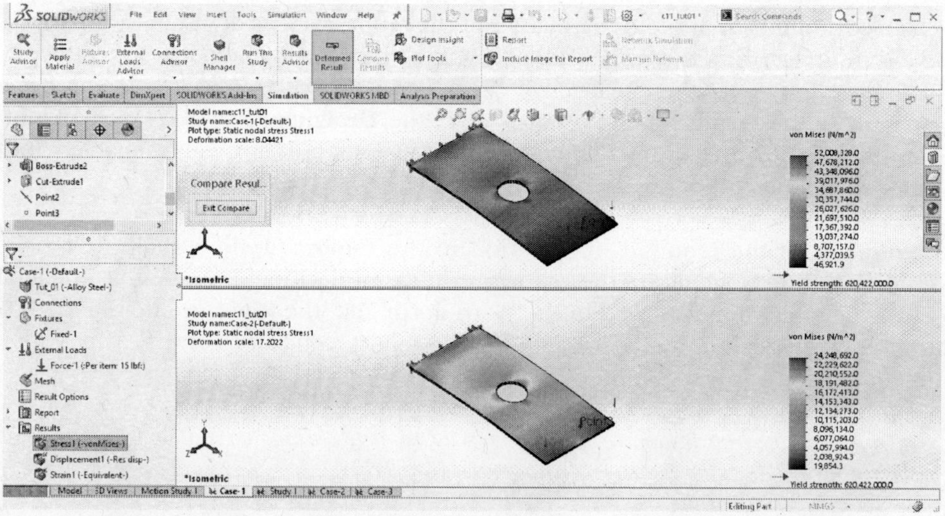

***Figure 11-28** The **Case-1** and **Case-2** studies displayed on the screen*

Tutorial 2

In this tutorial, you will analyze the effect of loads on the bracket model that is created in Tutorial 1 of Chapter 7. Refer to Figure 11-29 for the boundary conditions. Consider that the bracket is of Alloy Steel (SS) material and its back face is fixed. You need to determine the von Mises stresses under the load of 5 N. **(Expected time: 30 min)**

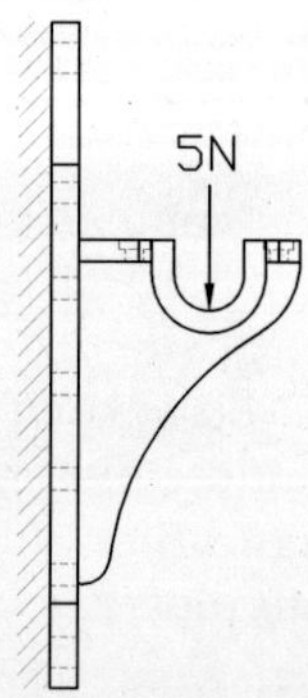

***Figure 11-29** The boundary conditions of the bracket*

The following steps are required to complete this tutorial:

a. Open the model created in Tutorial 1 of chapter 7 and save it with new name in *c11* folder.
b. Start a new static study.

c. Apply material, constraints, and loads.
d. Create mesh and run the analysis.
e. Generate the report.

Opening and Saving the Model

As the required document is saved in the *c07* folder, you need to open it first in SOLIDWORKS 2018 and then you can save it in the current folder.

1. Open the model created in Tutorial 1 of chapter 7 and then save it with the name *c11_tut02* at the location *\Documents\SOLIDWORKS Tutorials\c11*.

Starting a New Study

Since you want to determine the von Mises stresses, you need to start a static analysis.

1. Choose the **Simulation** tab from the **CommandManager**; the **Simulation CommandManager** is displayed.

2. Choose the **New Study** tool from the **New Study** flyout in the **Simulation CommandManager**; the **Study PropertyManager** is displayed.

3. Choose the **Static** button, if it is not chosen and then enter the name of the study as **Bracket** in the **Study Name** edit box of the PropertyManager. Next, choose **OK**; a new tree named **Bracket** is added to the **FeatureManager Design Tree**.

Applying the Material

Now, you need to apply the alloy steel material to the model.

1. Choose the **Apply Material** button from the **Simulation CommandManager**; the **Material** dialog box is displayed.

2. Expand the **SOLIDWORKS Materials** node of the **Material** dialog box. Next, expand the **Steel** sub-node under it and choose the **Alloy Steel (SS)** material. All the properties of the selected material are displayed on the right side of the dialog box.

3. Choose the **Apply** button from the dialog box; the alloy steel material is applied to the model. Next, close the **Material** dialog box.

Applying Constraints

After applying the material to the model, you need to apply constraints to fix one edge of the model.

1. Choose the **Fixed Geometry** button from the **Fixtures Advisor** flyout of the **Simulation CommandManager**; the **Fixture PropertyManager** is displayed at the left of the drawing area.

2. Make sure that the **Fixed Geometry** button is chosen in the **Standard (Fixed Geometry)** rollout of the PropertyManager.

3. Rotate the model and select the back face of the model; the selected face is fixed and the fixed geometry callout is attached to it, as shown in the Figure 11-30.

4. Choose the **OK** button from the PropertyManager.

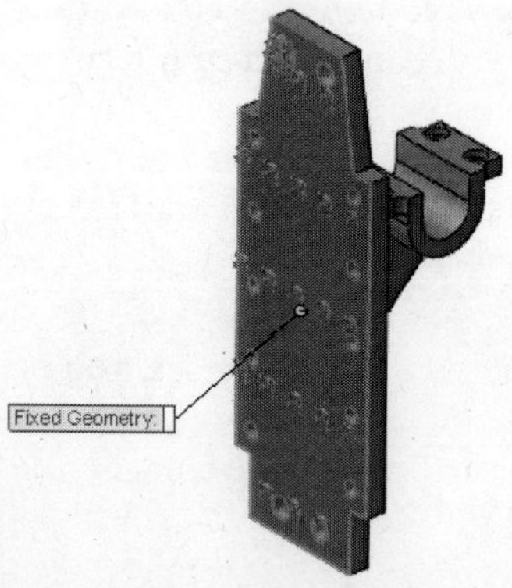

Figure 11-30 *The back face of the model is fixed*

Applying Loads

After applying the material and constraints to the model, you need to apply load.

1. Choose the **Force** button from the **External Loads Advisor** flyout of the **Simulation CommandManager**; the **Force/Torque PropertyManager** is displayed on the left of the drawing area.

2. Make sure that the **Force** button is chosen in the **Force/Torque** rollout of the PropertyManager.

3. Select the top semi-circular face of the model to apply the force, refer to Figure 11-31; the force is applied on the selected edge. Also, the force callout is attached to the selected edge.

   Now, you need to specify the direction of force.

4. Select the **Selected direction** radio button from the **Force/Torque** rollout of the PropertyManager; the **Face, Edge, Plane for Direction** selection box is displayed in the **Force/Torque** rollout.

5. Select the vertical edge of the model to apply force vertically.

   If the direction of the applied force is vertically upward, you need to reverse it to vertically downward.

6. Select the **Reverse direction** check box from the **Force** rollout of the PropertyManager to reverse the direction of the force applied.

7. Select **SI** from the **Unit** drop-down list of the **Units** rollout in the PropertyManager.

8. Enter **5** in the **Along Edge** edit box of the **Force** rollout.

9. Accept the other default settings and choose **OK** to apply the load. Figure 11-31 shows the trimetric view of the model.

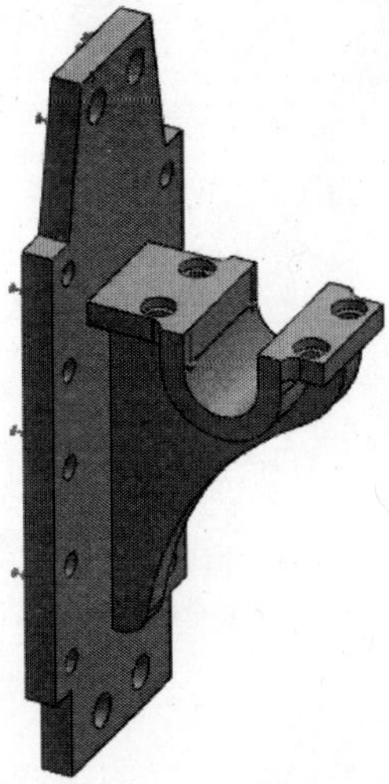

Figure 11-31 *Model after applying boundary condition and load*

Creating Mesh

After applying the boundary condition and load, you need to create mesh.

1. Choose the **Create Mesh** button from the **Run This Study** flyout of the **Simulation CommandManager**; the **Mesh PropertyManager** is displayed.

2. Accept all the default settings and choose the **OK** button from the PropertyManager; the **Mesh Progress** window is displayed. Once the process of meshing is done, the meshed model is displayed in the drawing area, as shown in Figure 11-32.

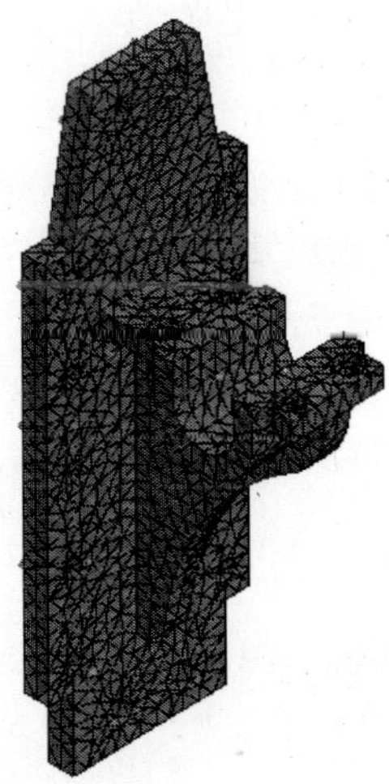

Figure 11-32 *The model after meshing*

Running Analysis

Now, you need to run the analysis on the model.

1. Choose the **Run This Study** button from the **Simulation CommandManager**; the **Bracket** window is displayed and the process of solving the FE model is started. Once the analysis process is completed, a new node named **Results** is added to the **FeatureManager Design Tree**. Also, the resultant model is displayed in the drawing area with the von Mises stress contour, as shown in Figure 11-33.

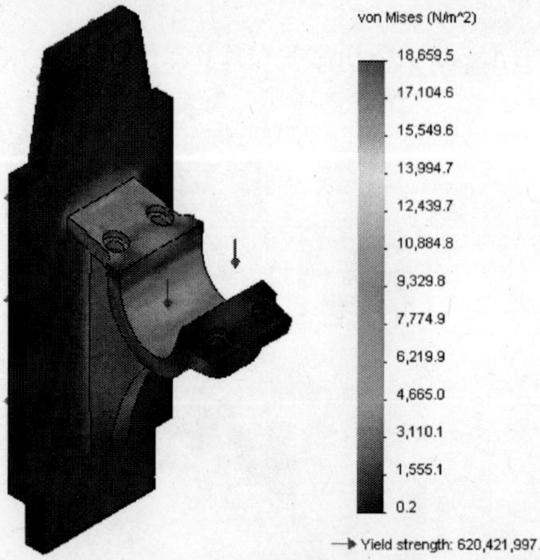

***Figure 11-33** The resultant model with von Mises stress contour*

> **Tip**
> *To animate the displacement plot, right-click on the **Displacement1 (-Res disp-)** under the **Results** node; a shortcut menu will be displayed. Select the **Animate** option; the animation starts with the default settings. Also, the **Animation PropertyManager** is displayed on the left of the screen enabling you to change the settings according to your requirement.*

Generating the Report

Now, you need to generate the report.

1. Choose the **Report** button from the **Simulation CommandManager**; the **Report Options** dialog box is displayed.

2. Select all the sections that you want to add in the report by selecting their respective check boxes available in the **Report sections** area of the dialog box.

   As discussed earlier, you can also add information such as designer, company, URL, logo, and so on in the header of the report. To do so, you need to add information in the respective edit boxes of the dialog box that will be enabled after selecting the check box corresponding to them.

3. After entering all the required information in the **Report Options** dialog box, choose the **Publish** button to generate the report in the Word format. As soon as the analysis report is generated and displayed in Word document, the **Report** node is added to the **FeatureManager Design Tree**. After viewing the report, you can close it.

4. Save and close the file.

Tip

*After closing the report, you can further open it by double-clicking on its name displayed under the **Report** node of the **FeatureManager Design Tree**.*

Tutorial 3

In this tutorial, you will perform static analysis on a frame shown in Figure 11-34. The dimensions, boundary conditions, and load applied on the frame are shown in Figure 11-34. The frame to be built is made up of hollow aluminum (5052-H38) tubing of 0.5 inch and 40 schedule.

(Expected time: 1 hr)

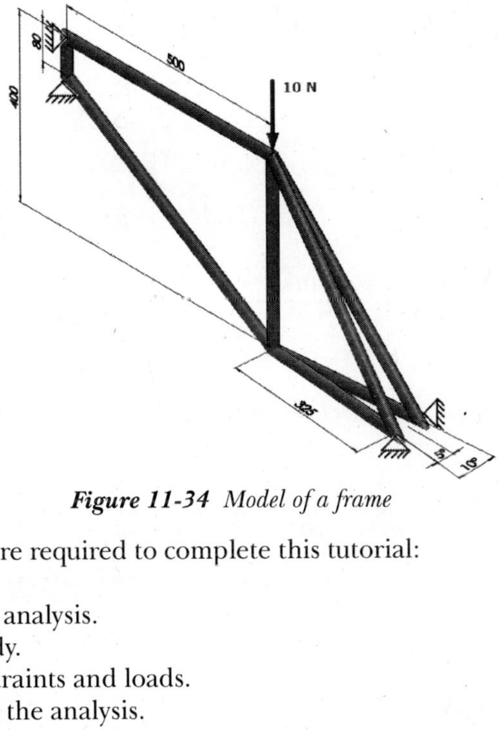

Figure 11-34 *Model of a frame*

The following steps are required to complete this tutorial:

a. Create the model for analysis.
b. Start a new static study.
c. Apply material, constraints and loads.
d. Create mesh and run the analysis.
e. View the results.

Creating Model for Analysis

1. Start the new SOLIDWORKS part document and then invoke the **3D Sketch** tool from the **Sketch** flyout of the **Sketch CommandManager**, refer to Figure 11-35; the 3D sketch environment is invoked.

Figure 11-35 *The **Sketch** flyout*

2. Create the 3D sketch frame of the bicycle model, as shown in Figure 11-36. Next, exit the 3D sketch environment. You can also download the 3D sketch frame of the bicycle model from ***www.cadcim.com***.

Note

The method of creating 3D Sketches is explained in Chapter 8 of this textbook.

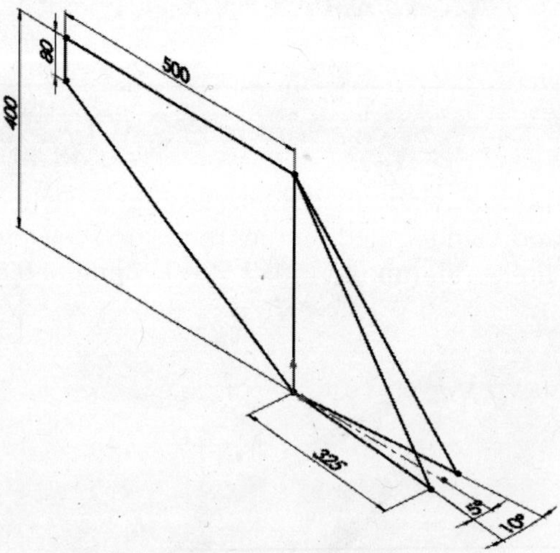

***Figure 11-36** The 3D sketch frame*

3. Invoke the **Weldments CommandManager** by choosing the **Weldments** tab from the **CommandManager**.

Note

*If the **Weldments** tab is not added in the **CommandManager** by default, you can customize it.*

The SOLIDWORKS provides you with the options to create the weldment structure in which the members are grouped together to form a complex structure. In SOLIDWORKS, the weldment structures are created by using the tools available in the **Weldments CommandManager**. You can use the 2D and 3D sketches to define the basic framework for creating the weldment structure.

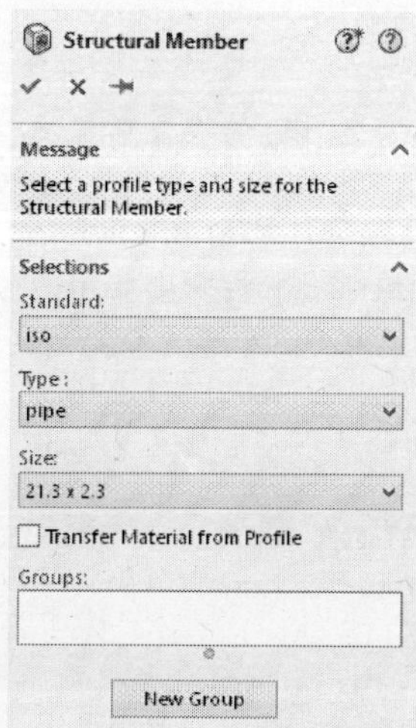

Figure 11-37** The **Structural Member PropertyManager

After creating the 3D sketch frame of the model, you need to create the weldment structure by using the **Structural Member** tool of the **Weldments CommandManager**.

4. Choose the **Structural Member** tool from the **Weldments CommandManager**; the **Structural Member PropertyManager** is displayed, as shown in Figure 11-37.

The **Structural Member** tool is used to create structural members by sweeping a pre-defined profile along the user-defined path.

5. Select **ansi inch** from the **Standard** drop-down list of the **Selections** rollout in the PropertyManager.

6. Select **pipe** from the **Type** drop-down list and **0.5 sch 40** from the **Size** drop-down list of the **Selections** rollout of the PropertyManager.

7. Click in the **Groups** selection area of the PropertyManager to activate it. Next, select the first set of entities as the entities of the first group, refer to Figure 11-38; a preview of the structural members is displayed in the drawing area, as shown in Figure 11-39. Also, a group is created in the **Groups** selection area of the PropertyManager.

8. Make sure that the **Apply corner treatment** check box is selected in the **Settings** rollout of the **Structural Member PropertyManager**. Next, choose the **End Miter** button available below the **Apply corner treatment** check box if not already selected.

9. Clear the **Merge miter trimmed bodies** check box of the **Settings** rollout. Next, set the value in the **Gap between Connected Segments in Same Group** edit box to **0**.

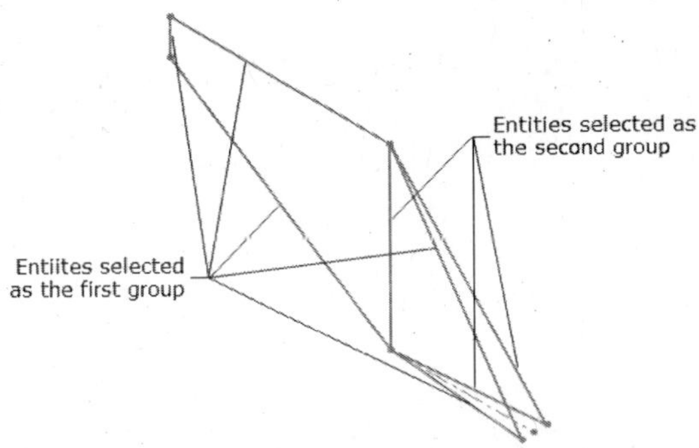

Figure 11-38 Different set of entities to be selected

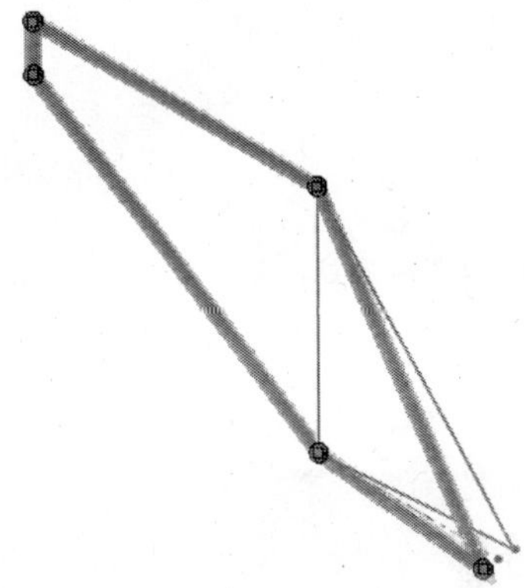

Figure 11-39 The preview of the structural members

Note

In SOLIDWORKS, you can create a weldment structure that contains one or more groups. All the members of a group are treated as a single unit. You can select parallel or continuous line segments in a group. Also, the weldment profile of all the groups within a structural member feature remains same.

10. Choose the **New Group** button from the **Structural Member PropertyManager** to create a new group of structural members; the new group is added in the **Groups** selection area of the PropertyManager.

11. Select the other set of entities as the entities of the second group, refer to Figure 11-38; the preview of the structural members is displayed in the drawing area. Also, a new group is created in the **Groups** selection area of the PropertyManager.

12. Make sure that the **Apply corner treatment** check box is selected in the **Settings** rollout of the **Structural Member PropertyManager**. Next, choose the **End Miter** button available below the **Apply corner treatment** check box.

13. Clear the **Merge miter trimmed bodies** check box of the **Settings** rollout. Next, set the value in the **Gap between Connected Segments in Same Group** edit box to **0**.

14. Choose the **OK** button from the **Structural Member PropertyManager**; the weldment structure is created, as shown in Figure 11-40.

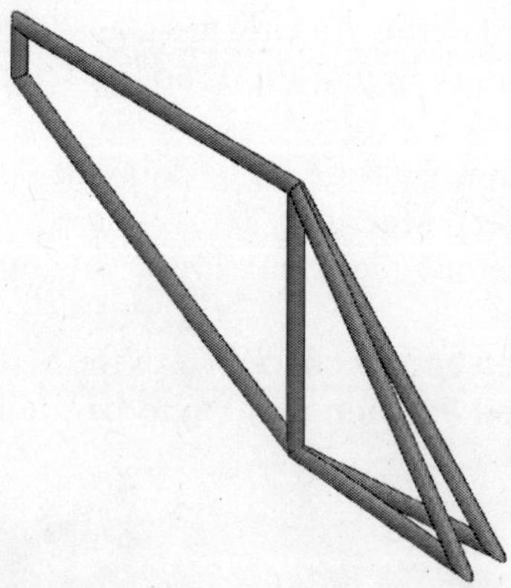

Figure 11-40 *The weldment structure of the bicycle frame*

Starting a New Study

Now, you need to start a new analysis study.

1. Choose the **Simulation** tab from the **CommandManager**; the **Simulation CommandManager** is displayed.

2. Choose the **New Study** tool from the **Study Advisor** flyout in the **Simulation CommandManager**; the **Study PropertyManager** is displayed.

3. Choose the **Static** button, if it is not chosen by default, and then enter the name of the study as **Bicycle Frame** in the **Name** edit box of the PropertyManager. Next, choose **OK**; a new tree named **Bicycle Frame** is added to the **FeatureManager Design Tree**. Also, joints are displayed in the drawing area, as shown in Figure 11-41.

   A joint is displayed at the free end of a structural member or at the intersection of two or more structural members.

Note

Pink color joints will be displayed where two or more structural members are intersecting and the light green color joints will be displayed in a structural member at its end and mid points.

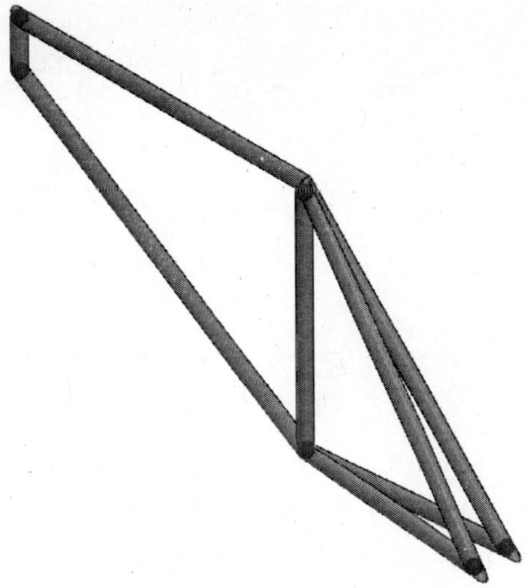

Figure 11-41 *The weldment structure with joints*

Applying the Material

Now, you need to apply the aluminium material to the frame.

1. Choose the **Apply Material** tool from the **Simulation CommandManager**; the **Material** dialog box is displayed.

2. Expand the **SOLIDWORKS Materials** node in the **Material** dialog box. Next, expand the **Aluminium Alloys** node under the **SOLIDWORKS Materials** node.

3. Select the **5052-H38** material; all the properties of the selected material are displayed in the right side of the dialog box.

4. Choose the **Apply** button from the dialog box; the selected material is applied to the model. Next, close the **Material** dialog box.

Applying Constraints

1. Choose the **Fixed Geometry** tool from the **Fixtures Advisor** flyout of the **Simulation CommandManager**; the **Fixture PropertyManager** is displayed.

2. Make sure that the **Fixed Geometry** button is chosen in the **Standard (Fixed Geometry)** rollout of PropertyManager.

3. Select four joints one by one from the drawing area, refer to Figure 11-42; the symbol of fixed geometry is displayed on the joints. Next, choose the **OK** button from the PropertyManager; the degree of freedom of the selected joints is restrained. Figure 11-43 shows the weldment structure after applying constraints.

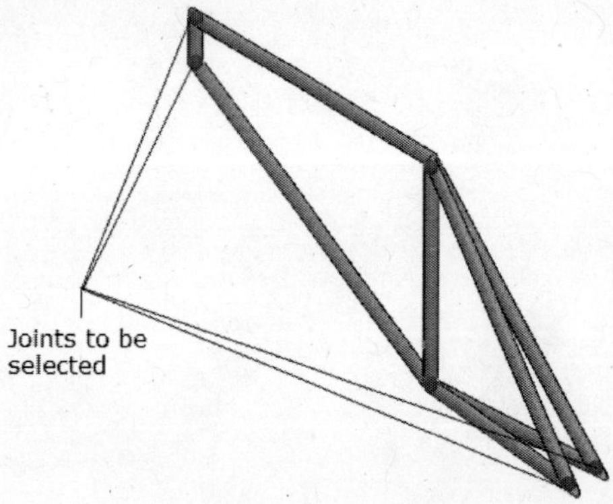

Figure 11-42 *Joints to be selected*

Figure 11-43 *The weldment structure after applying the fixed constraint*

Applying Loads

After applying the material and constraints to the model, you need to apply loads.

1. Choose the **Force** button from the **External Loads Advisor** flyout of the **Simulation CommandManager**; the **Force/Torque PropertyManager** is displayed on the left of the drawing area.

2. Choose the **Joints** button available at the left of the **Joint** selection area of the **Selection** rollout of the PropertyManager.

3. Select the joint displayed on the top of the middle vertical member of the frame from the drawing area to apply the force.

4. Click on the **Face, Edge, Plane for Direction** selection area in the **Selection** rollout of the PropertyManager to activate it.

   Now, you need to specify the direction of force.

5. Select the **Top Plane** from the **FeatureManager Design Tree** and then select **SI** from the **Unit** drop-down list of the **Units** rollout in the PropertyManager.

6. Choose the **Normal to Plane** button from the **Force** rollout of the PropertyManager; the **Normal to Plane** edit box is enabled.

7. Enter **10** in the **Normal to Plane** edit box of the **Force** rollout. Next, select the **Reverse Direction** check box to reverse the direction of force to vertically downward.

8. Choose the **OK** button from the PropertyManager. Figure 11-44 shows the structural frame after applying the load.

Creating Mesh

After applying the boundary condition and load, you need to create mesh.

1. Choose the **Create Mesh** button from the **Run This Study** flyout of the **Simulation CommandManager**; the **Mesh PropertyManager** is displayed.

2. Accept all the default settings and choose the **OK** button from the PropertyManager; the **Mesh Progress** window is displayed. Once the process of meshing is done, the meshed model is displayed in the drawing area, as shown in Figure 11-45.

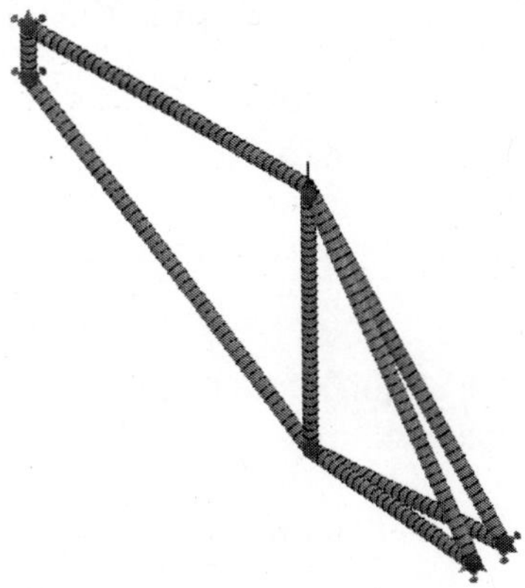

Figure 11-44 *Structure after applying the load*

Figure 11-45 *Structure after meshing*

Running Analysis

Now, you need to run the analysis on the model.

1. Choose the **Run This Study** button from the **Simulation CommandManager**; the **Bracket** window is displayed and the solution process is started. Once the analysis is completed, a new node named **Results** is added to the **FeatureManager Design Tree**. Also, the resultant structure is displayed in the drawing area with the stress contour, as shown in Figure 11-46.

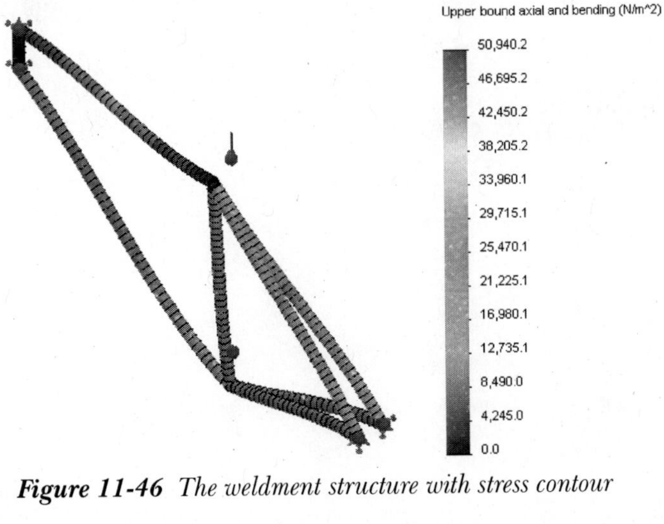

Figure 11-46 *The weldment structure with stress contour*

Viewing the Results

Viewing the stress and displacement contours is same as discussed in previous tutorials. In this tutorial, you will learn to find out the safety factor of the design.

1. Right-click on the **Results** node; a shortcut menu is displayed. Next, select the **Define Factor Of Safety Plot** option from it; the **Factor of Safety PropertyManager** is displayed, as shown in Figure 11-47. By default, the **Automatic** option is selected in the **Criterion** drop-down list of the **Step 1 of 3** rollout in the PropertyManager.

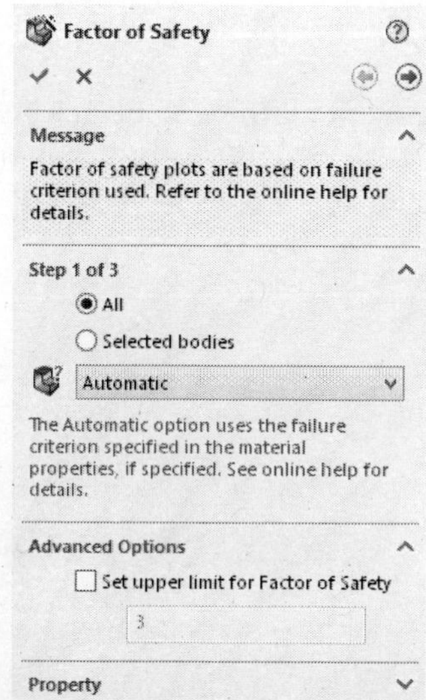

Figure 11-47** The **Factor of Safety PropertyManager

The **Criterion** drop-down list provides you with the options to specify the failure criteria for safety. You can select the **Max von Mises stress, Max shear stress (Tresca), Mohr-Coulomb stress, Max Normal stress,** or **Automatic** option as the failure criteria for safety.

The **Automatic** option of the **Criterion** drop-down list is the most appropriate failure criterion across all element types.

2. Accept the default settings and choose the **Next** button from the PropertyManager; the **Step 1 of 3** rollout is replaced by the **Step 2 of 3** rollout in the PropertyManager.

   By default, the value in the **Multiplication factor** edit box in the **Step 2 of 3** rollout is set to 1.

The **Multiplication factor** edit box allows you to specify a multiplication factor for calculating the selected stress limit. For example, if you apply a factor of 0.6 to a yield strength stress limit of 2000 psi, the factor of safety will be 0.6 x 2000 = 1200 psi for the stress limit.

3. Accept the default settings and then choose the **Next** button to go the step 3. Choose **OK** to accept and exit the PropertyManager; the factor of safety plot is displayed, as shown in Figure 11-48.

   Now, you need to save the model.

4. Save the model with the name *c11_tut03* at the location *\Documents\SOLIDWORKS Tutorials\c11*.

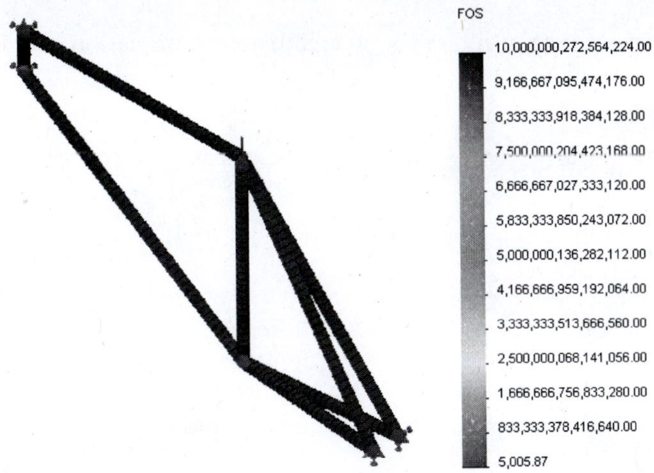

Figure 11-48 *The weldment structure with FOS*

Self-Evaluation Test

Answer the following questions and then compare them to those given at the end of this chapter:

1. Which of the following tools is used to generate the reports of studies created in a model?

   (a) **Generate** (b) **Create Report**
   (c) **Report** (d) **Reports**

2. Which of the following drop-down lists provides you with the options for specifying the failure criteria of safety?

   (a) **Criterion safety** (b) **Create Report**
   (c) **Criterion** (d) **Reports**

3. The external force acting on a body is called _________.

4. The von Mises stress criterion is also called _________ theory.

5. You can invoke the **Study PropertyManager** by choosing the _________ tool.

6. The multiplication factor is used for calculating the selected _________ limit.

7. In the dynamic analysis, the load or field conditions vary with time. (T/F)

8. The Model Analysis is used to calculate the natural frequency and mode shape of a structure. (T/F)

9. In SOLIDWORKS Simulation, you cannot reverse the direction of applied load. (T/F)

10. The **Study PropertyManager** allows you to create a new simulation study. (T/F)

Review Questions

Answer the following questions:

1. In SOLIDWORKS Simulation, which of the following tools is used to compare the studies of a model?

   (a) **Compare Results** (b) **Result**
   (c) **Compare** (d) None of these

2. In SOLIDWORKS, which of the following CommandManagers is used to create weldment structures?

   (a) **Weldment** (b) **Weldments**
   (c) **Weld** (d) None of these

3. The __________ tool is used to apply material to a model.

4. The __________ tool is used to create mesh in a model.

5. The __________ radio button in the **Compare Results PropertyManager** needs to be selected to compare the studies created in the current model.

6. In SOLIDWORKS Simulation, the general process of finite element analysis is divided into three main phases, __________, __________, and __________.

7. In SOLIDWORKS Simulation, you can not create multiple case studies for a model. (T/F)

8. The maximum shear stress failure criterion is based on the maximum shear stress theory. (T/F)

9. In SOLIDWORKS Simulation, you can also create a study with non-uniform load. (T/F)

10. In SOLIDWORKS, you can create a weldment structure that contains one or more groups. (T/F)

EXERCISE

Exercise 1

In this exercise, you will perform static analysis on a model shown in Figure 11-49. The dimensions, boundary conditions, and load applied on the frame are shown in Figure 11-50. The model is made up of alloy steel material.

(Expected time: 1 hr)

Figure 11- 49 The model for Exercise 1

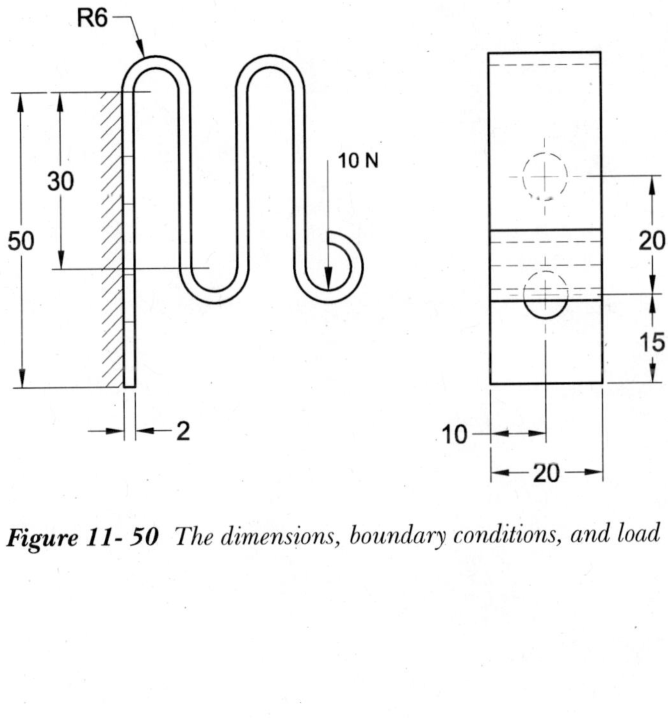

Figure 11- 50 The dimensions, boundary conditions, and load

Answers to Self-Evaluation Test

1. c, **2.** c, **3.** load, **4.** maximum distortion energy, **5. New Study**, **6.** stress, **7.** T, **8.** T, **9.** F, **10.** T

Chapter 12

Introduction to Mold Design

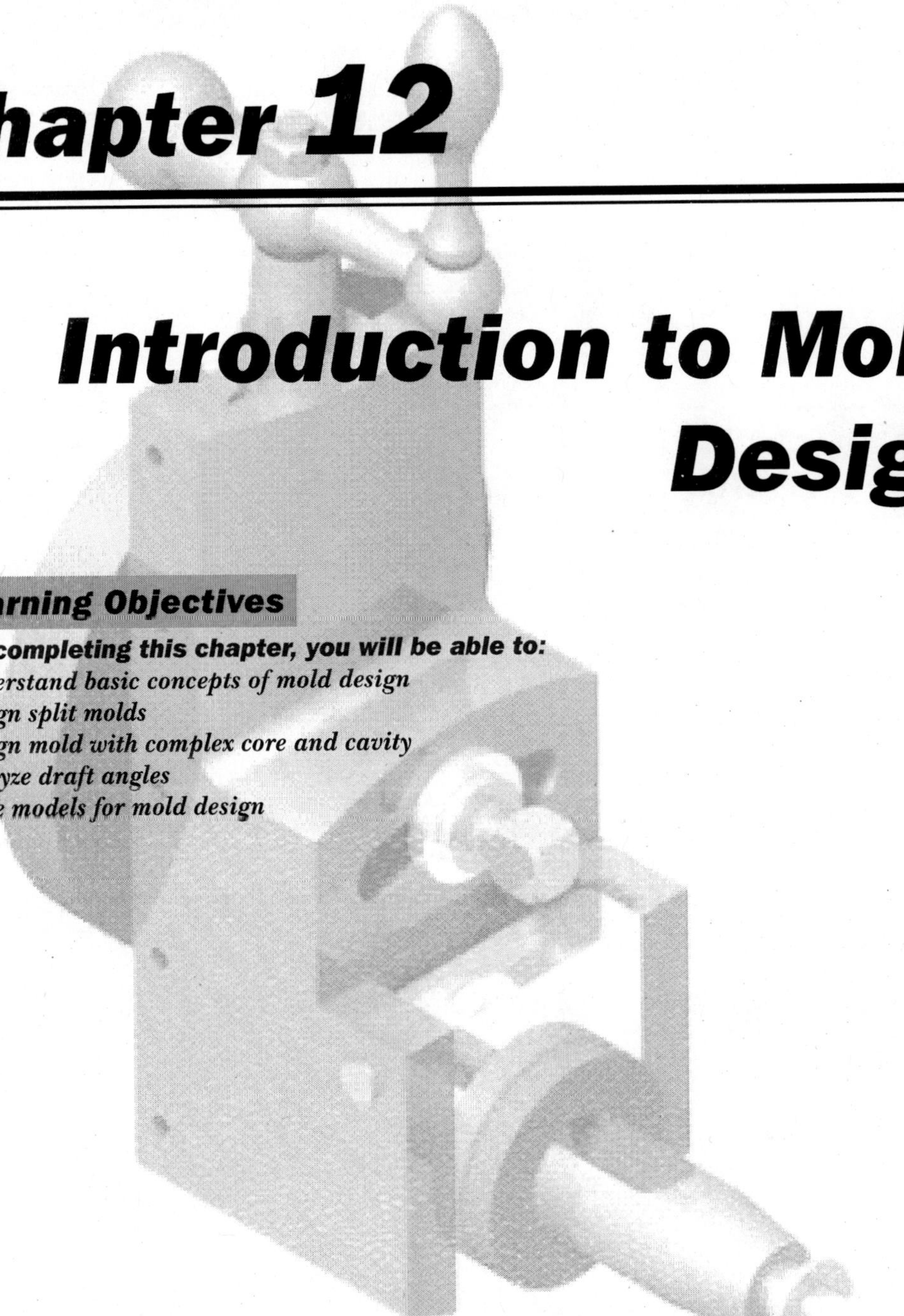

Learning Objectives

After completing this chapter, you will be able to:

- *Understand basic concepts of mold design*
- *Design split molds*
- *Design mold with complex core and cavity*
- *Analyze draft angles*
- *Scale models for mold design*

INTRODUCTION TO MOLD DESIGN

In this chapter, you will learn about the tools that you can use to design the molds for a cast or plastic molded components. Generally, the complete mold design consists of designing of mold base, gates and runners, ejection mechanism, and core and cavity. But in the mold design using SOLIDWORKS, you will only learn about designing of core and cavity which means extraction of core and cavity from a part created. You will also learn about creating the inserts for extracting the core and cavity of complex parts. Figure 12-1 shows a soap case created in the **Part** mode of SOLIDWORKS. Figure 12-2 shows the core for manufacturing this part and Figure 12-3 shows the respective cavity.

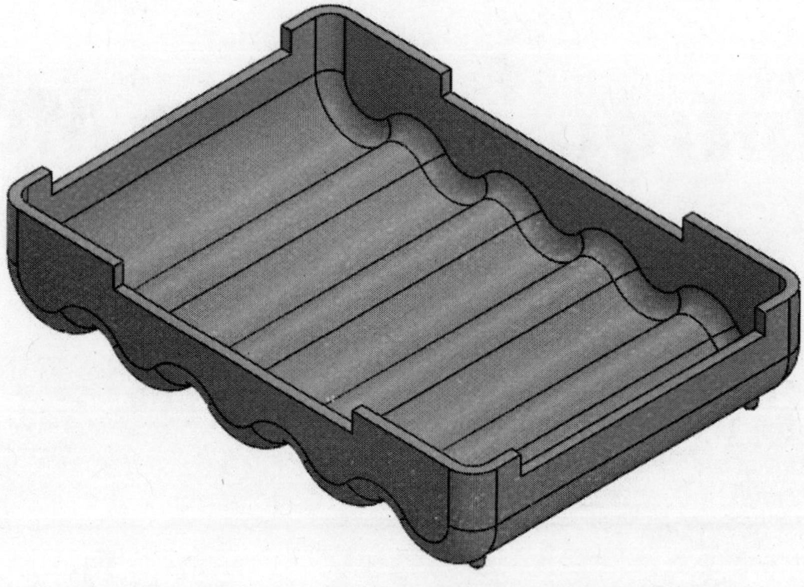

Figure 12-1 *Soap case created in the part mode of SOLIDWORKS*

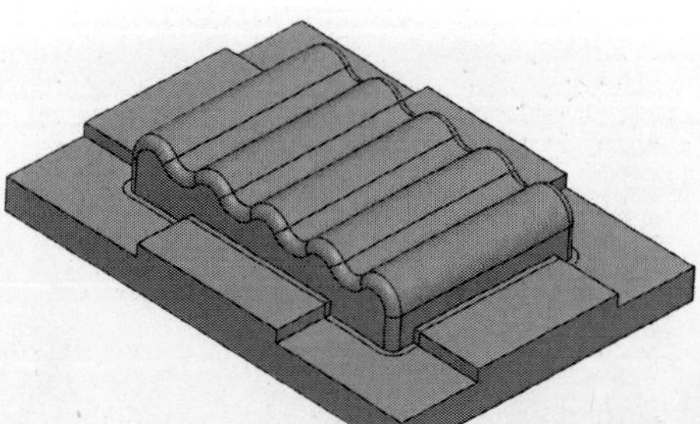

Figure 12-2 *Core of the mold for manufacturing*

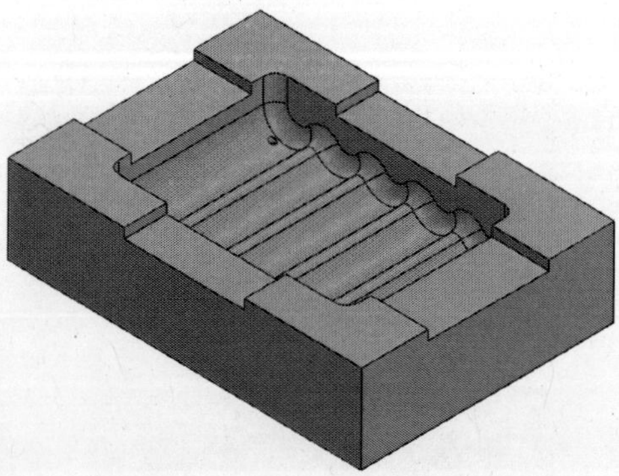

Figure 12-3 *Cavity of the mold for manufacturing*

Before you learn about mold design, it is necessary that you first learn about some of the major terms and definitions related to mold design.

Mold Assembly

Mold assembly is an assembly created by assembling a number of parts such as top plate, back plate, core back plate, cavity back plate, ejector mechanism, guide bushes, guide pillars, fasteners, cooling mechanism, and so on. The complete molds are designed by considering the part to be molded. Its design also depends on the complexity of the part.

Cavity

The cavity is the female part of the mold and remains hollow from inside. The molten metal or the molten plastic is poured into it so that it can take the shape of the cavity to create the component.

Core

The core is the male part of the mold and it defines the area where the molten metal should not reach. The core generally helps in defining the holes, pockets, and other cut out features of a part while molding.

Parting Line

Parting line is a line from where the molds split and open in their respective directions. Figure 12-4 shows an assembly of core and cavity with the parting line. Figure 12-5 shows the exploded view of the core and cavity assembly with the component that will be created using this combination of core and cavity.

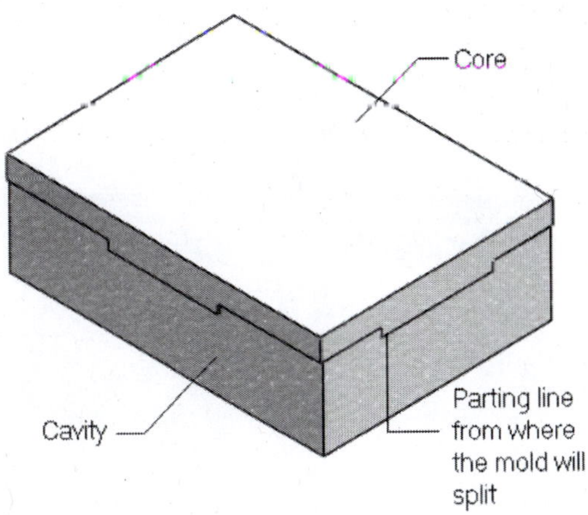

Figure 12-4 Assembly of core and cavity with the parting line

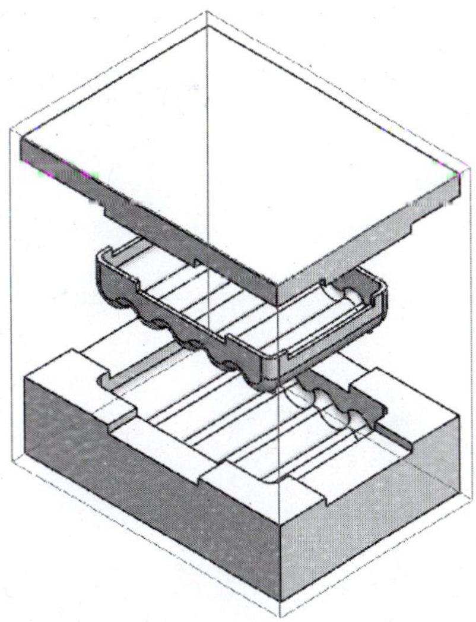

Figure 12-5 Exploded view of the core and cavity assembly

Scale Factor

Scale factor is defined as the amount by which the molded or cast component shrinks, depending on the type of material and the shape of the mold. The scale factor is defined in terms of percentage.

Draft Angle

In the molded or cast component, the draft angles are of great importance. It is very important to add draft in the core and cavity because if the faces of the core and cavity do not have any draft angle, then you cannot take out the molded or cast component from the mold. Therefore, it is very important that you add the required draft angles to the component in the Part mode so that the same draft is also added in the core and cavity.

Note

Sometimes, you may need to place some inserts in the mold. Inserts are placed where you need to restrict the flow of metal in the mold. While designing a mold in SOLIDWORKS, you need to create inserts using the top-down assembly approach.

TUTORIALS

Tutorial 1

In this tutorial, you will extract the core and cavity of a plastic cover shown in Figure 12-6. The resultant core is displayed in Figure 12-7 and the cavity is displayed in Figure 12-8. Figure 12-9 shows the exploded view of the assembly of the Mold Base. Figure 12-10 shows the views and dimensions of the plastic cover. Figure 12-11 shows the dimensions of the core plate. The dimensions of the cavity plate are displayed in Figure 12-12. **(Expected time: 2 hr)**

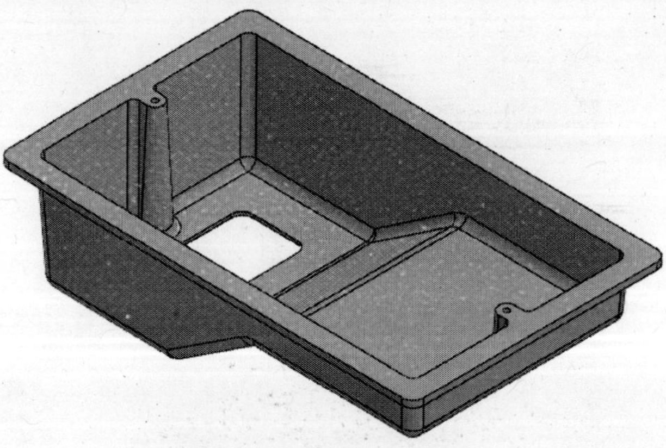

Figure 12-6 *Plastic cover*

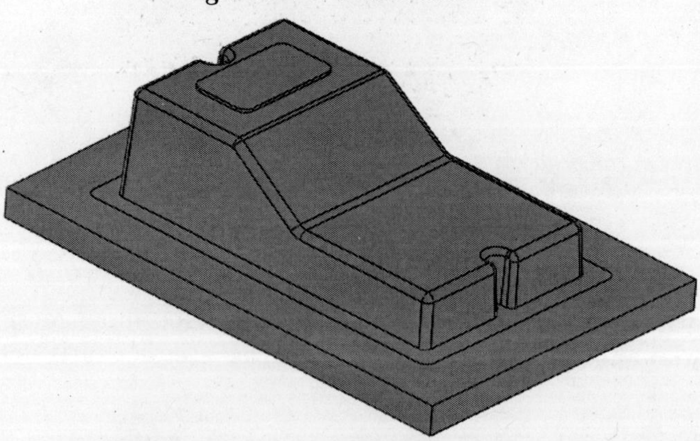

Figure 12-7 *Core of the plastic cover*

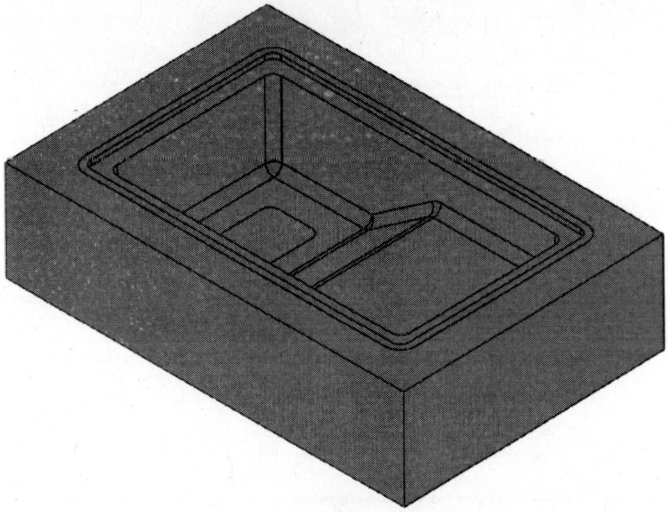

Figure 12-8 *Cavity of the plastic cover*

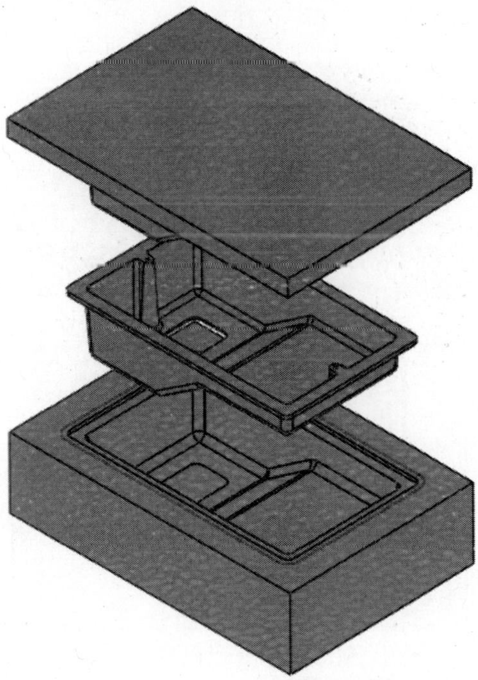

Figure 12-9 *Exploded view of the mold base assembly*

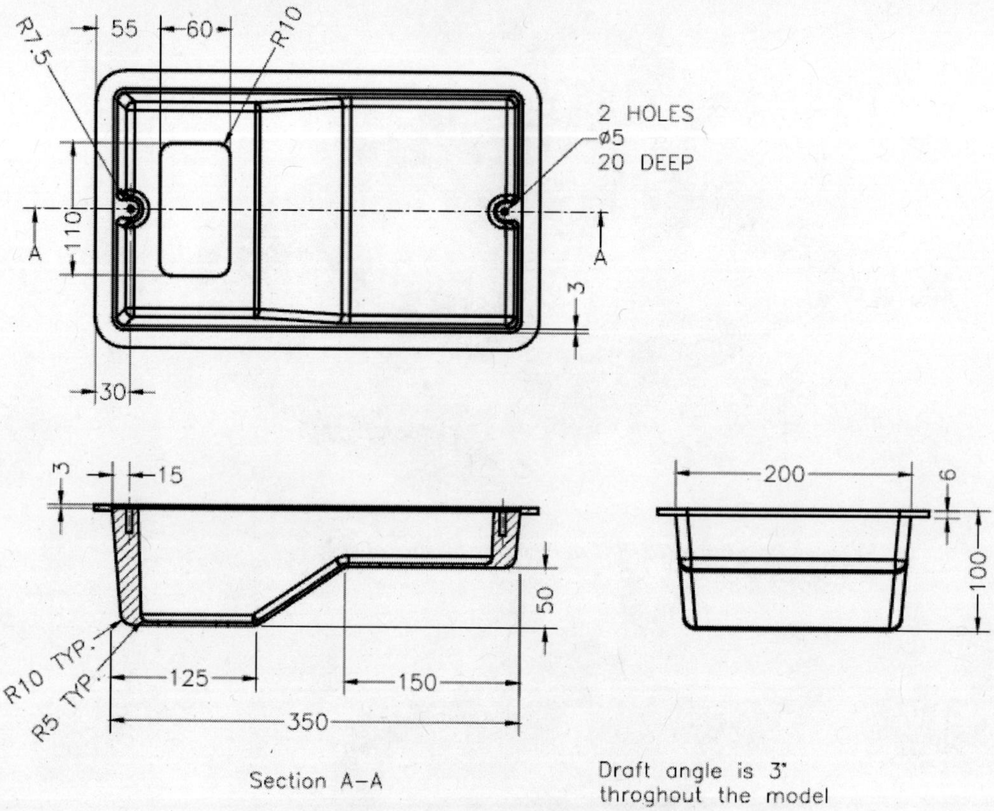

Figure 12-10 Views and dimensions of the plastic cover

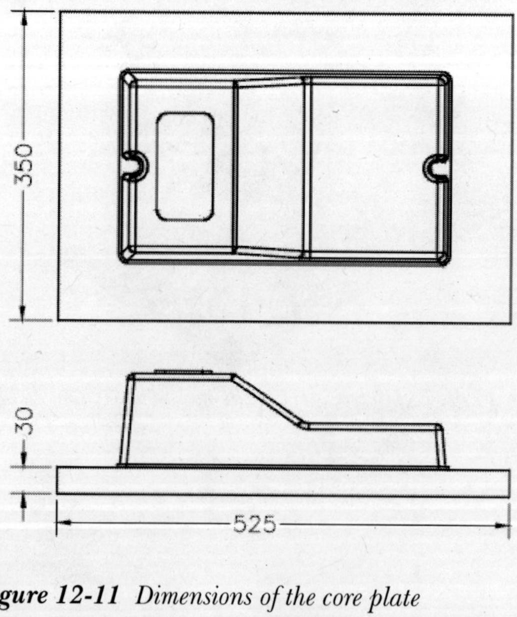

Figure 12-11 Dimensions of the core plate

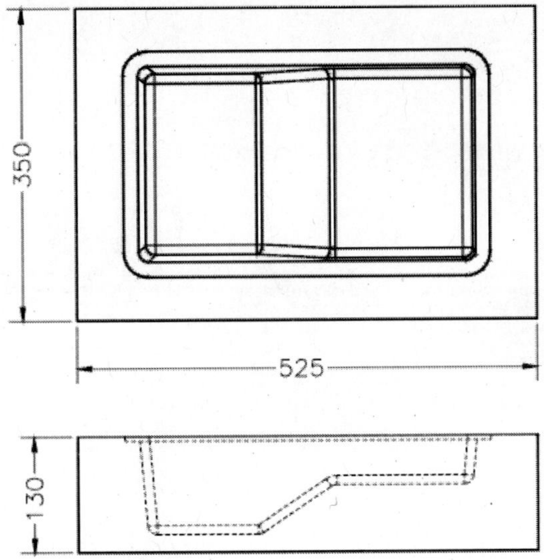

Figure 12-12 *Dimensions of the cavity plate*

The following steps are required to complete this tutorial:

a. Create the new SOLIDWORKS document and then the model of the plastic cover, refer to Figure 12-13.
b. Analyze the model for draft angles using the Draft analysis.
c. Scale the model.
d. Create the shut off surfaces, refer to Figures 12-14 and 12-15.
e. Create a new SOLIDWORKS document in the Assembly mode and place the plastic cover in the assembly document.
f. Using the top-down approach, extract the core and cavity of the plastic cover, refer to Figures 12-20 through 12-24.
g. Explode the assembly, refer to Figure 12-25.

Creating the Plastic Cover

First, you need to create the plastic cover in the Part mode of SOLIDWORKS.

1. Create a new SOLIDWORKS document in the Part mode.

2. Using the standard modeling tools, create the model of the plastic cover. For dimensions, refer to Figure 12-10.

3. Save the model. Figure 12-13 shows the final model created using the standard modeling tools.

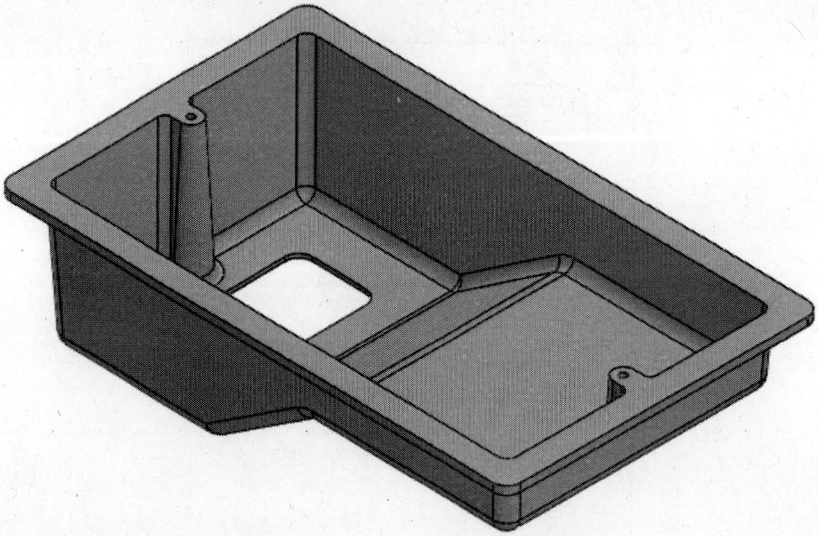

Figure 12-13 *Final model of the plastic cover*

Analyzing the Model for Draft Angles

As discussed earlier, before extracting the core and cavity, you need to make sure that the required draft angles are applied to the model so that the component is easily removed from the model after solidification. Therefore, you will analyze the model using the **Draft Analysis** tool.

Note

*If **Mold Tools CommandManager** is not available, you need to add it by customizing the CommandManagers.*

1. Choose the **Draft Analysis** button from the **Mold Tools** toolbar. The **Draft Analysis PropertyManager** is displayed.

First, you need to select the direction of pull along which the mold will be pulled out.

2. Select the top face of the plastic cover to define the direction of pull. Choose the **Reverse Direction** button available on left of the **Direction of Pull** selection box.

You will notice that the faces having the positive draft and the negative draft are displayed in green and red color respectively. Also, some small faces are displayed in yellow color, suggesting that the draft angle is required on these faces. Since these faces are very small in height as compared to other faces of the part, therefore the draft angle is not required on them. You will also notice that the hole placed on one of the top faces of the part also displays its inner faces in yellow color. But you do not need to add draft to the inner faces of these holes because these holes will not be included in the core. These type of holes are drilled in the final molded part.

If any face other than the faces having minor thickness are displayed in yellow, then you need to add the required draft angle on those faces.

3. Choose the **OK** button from the **Draft Analysis PropertyManager**.

Scaling the Model

After analyzing the model for draft angles, you need to scale the model. As discussed earlier, the scaling of the model is done in order to create the core and cavity larger than the component to be manufactured, as the components shrinks after solidification. The scale factor always depends on the material to be used for molding or casting and also on the type of mold.

1. Choose the **Scale** button from the **Mold Tools** toolbar to invoke the **Scale PropertyManager**.

2. Select the model and then set the value of the scale factor in the **Scale Factor** spinner to 1.1.

3. Choose the **OK** button from the **Scale PropertyManager**.

4. Invoke **Planar Surface** tool and select all the edges, as shown in Figure 12-14. Next, create the shutoff surface and then close the **Planar Surface PropertyManager**. Model after creating the shutoff surface using the **Planar Surface** tool is shown in Figure 12-15.

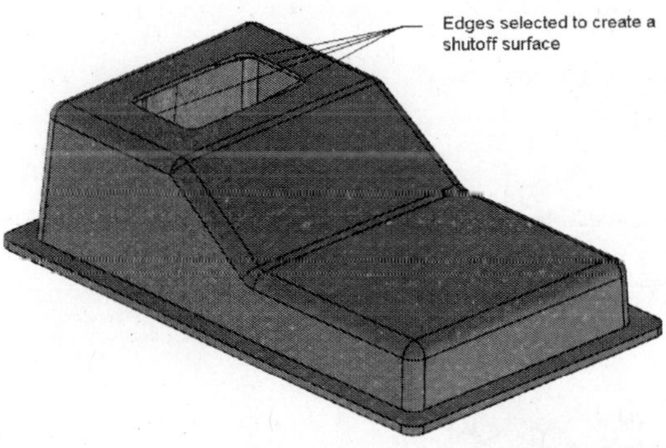

***Figure 12-14** Edges selected to create a shutoff surface*

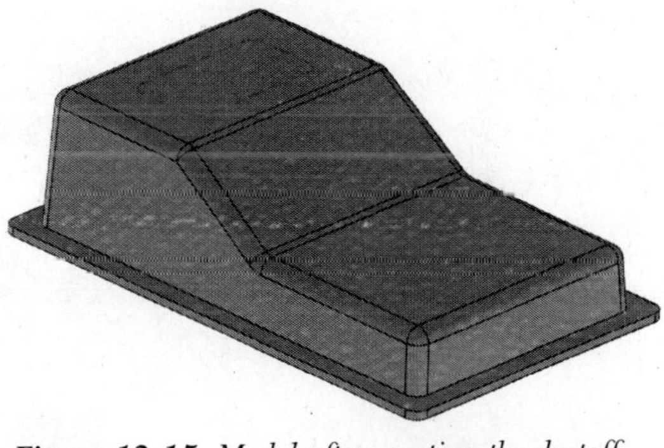

***Figure 12-15** Model after creating the shutoff surface*

5. Similarly, using the **Planar Surface** tool, create the shutoff surfaces on the edges of the holes created on one of the top faces of the model.

6. After creating the surfaces, save the model.

Creating the Interim Assembly

After finalizing the model, you need to create an interim assembly. Using this interim assembly and the top-down approach, you will extract the core and cavity of the model. To create the interim assembly, you first need to create a new SOLIDWORKS document in the Assembly mode.

1. Create a new SOLIDWORKS document in the Assembly mode.

2. Place the Plastic Cover coincident to the assembly origin.

3. Save the assembly file with the name Mold base.

Extracting the Cavity

After creating the interim assembly, you need to extract the cavity. For extracting the cavity, you will use the top-down approach of the assembly. For extracting the cavity, you need to create a new SOLIDWORKS document in the part mode.

1. Choose **Insert > Component > New Part** from the menu bar.

2. Select the **Front Plane** from the **FeatureManager Design Tree** to place the new component.

   As you place the component, the plastic cover is displayed in transparent and the sketching environment in invoked. Right-click on the new part node added in **FeatureManager Design Tree** and rename the part as cavity.

3. Exit the sketching environment.

4. Using the **Radiate Surface** tool, create a radiated surface with the radiate distance of 9 mm, refer to Figure 12-16.

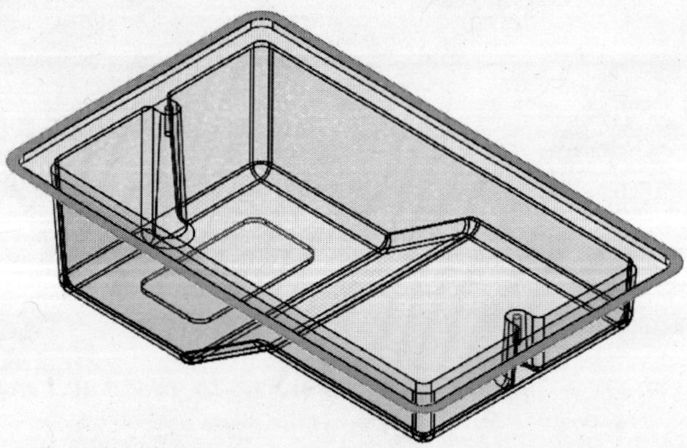

Figure 12-16 *After creating the radiated surface*

Remember that if you have created shutoff surfaces in the model, there will be no seed surface. You need to select all the other faces of the model and the radiated surface as the surface to knit.

5. Invoke the **Knit Surface** tool to knit the radiated surface with all the outer faces of the Plastic Cover. To do so, you need to select all the outer faces of the model as well as the radiated surface as the surfaces to knit. In this case, you will not select any surface as the seed surface. Also, select all the shutoff surfaces, including the shutoff surface on the bottom face of the plastic cover. After selecting the surfaces, choose the **OK** button from the **Knit Surface PropertyManager**.

6. Select the Plastic cover from the **FeatureManager Design Tree** and invoke the shortcut menu. Choose the **Hide Components** option from the shortcut menu. The resultant surface body is displayed in Figure 12-17.

   Next, you need to create a plane at an offset distance from the radiated surface and then create the sketch of the cavity on the newly created plane. Then, extrude the sketch of the cavity up to the knitted surface.

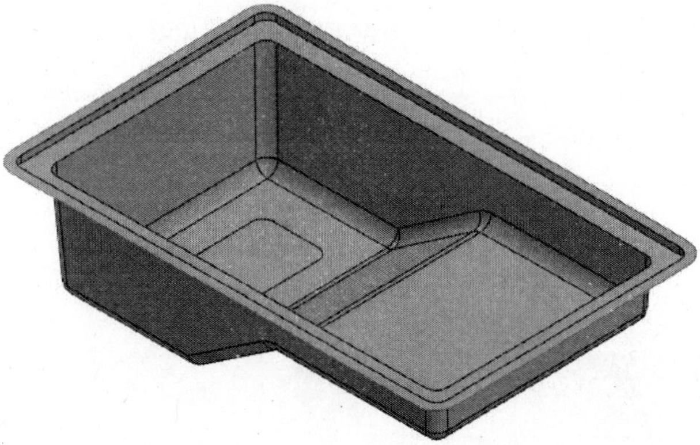

Figure 12-17 *Resultant knitted surface after hiding the plastic cover*

7. Create a new plane vertically downwards at an offset distance of 130 mm from the radiated surface.

8. Create the sketch on the newly created plane for creating the solid cavity with help of the **Convert Entities** tool, as shown in Figure 12-18.

9. Now, using the **Up To Surface** option, extrude the sketch up to the knitted surface.

10. Hide the knit surface.

   The resultant cavity is displayed in Figure 12-19.

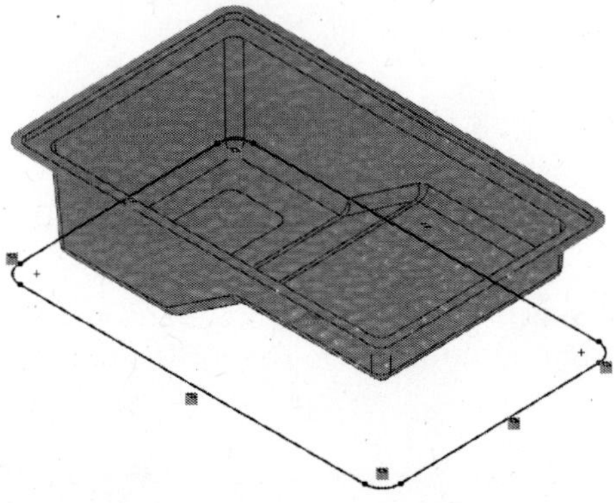

Figure 12-18 *Sketch for the cavity*

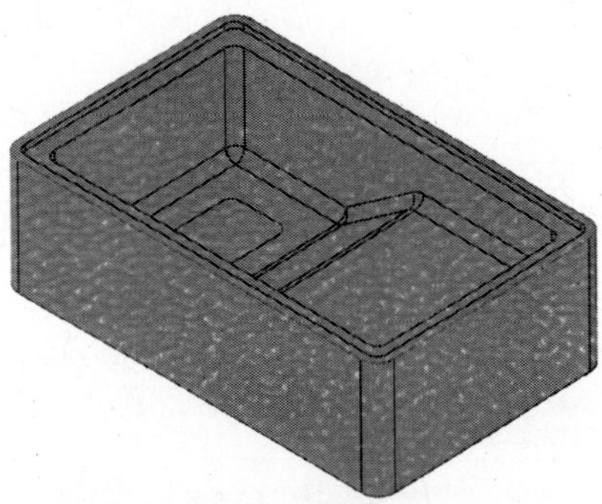

Figure 12-19 *Resultant cavity*

Next, you need to create the cavity plate. This plate will be created by extruding a rectangular sketch to a distance of 130 mm.

11. Select the bottom face of the cavity as the sketching plane and invoke the sketching environment.

12. Create the rectangular sketch of dimension 525 × 350.

13. Extrude the sketch to a distance of 130 mm by selecting the desired contour from the **Selected Contours** rollout.

14. Save the assembly.

Figure 12-20 shows the final cavity plate.

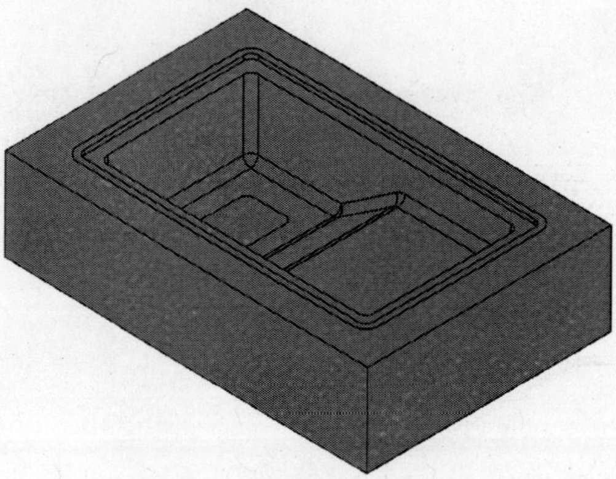

Figure 12-20 *Final cavity plate*

Extracting the Core

Next, you need to extract the core from the plastic cover. The core will also be extracted using the top-down approach of the assembly. Before proceeding further, you need to hide the cavity and unhide the plastic cover.

1. Hide the Cavity and unhide the plastic cover.

2. Choose **Insert > Component > New Part** from the menu bar.

3. Select the **Front plane** from the **FeatureManager Design Tree** to place the new component.

   As you place the component, the plastic cover is displayed in transparent and the sketcher environment in invoked. Right-click on the new part node added in **FeatureManager Design Tree** and rename the part as core.

4. Exit the sketcher environment.

5. Create a radiated surface as created earlier.

6. Now, knit all the internal surfaces of the plastic cover with the radiated surface.

7. Hide the plastic cover.

   The resultant extracted surface is displayed in Figure 12-21.

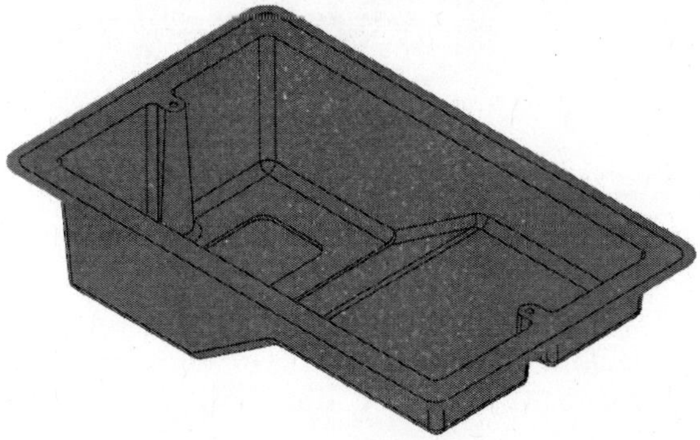

Figure 12-21 *Resultant extracted surface*

8. Now, create a plane at an offset distance of 30 mm from the top face of the extracted surface.

9. Select the newly created plane as the sketching plane and create the sketch of the core using **Convert Entities** tool, as shown in Figure 12-22.

10. Extrude the sketch up to the knitted surface and hide it. Figure 12-23 shows the resultant core extracted from the plastic cover.

11. Now, create the core plate by extruding the sketch created on the top face of the Core.

12. Save the assembly.

    The final Core is displayed in Figure 12-24.

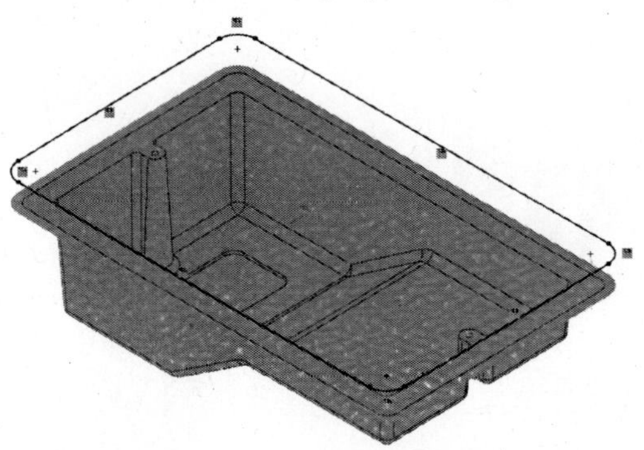

Figure 12-22 *Sketch for creating the Core*

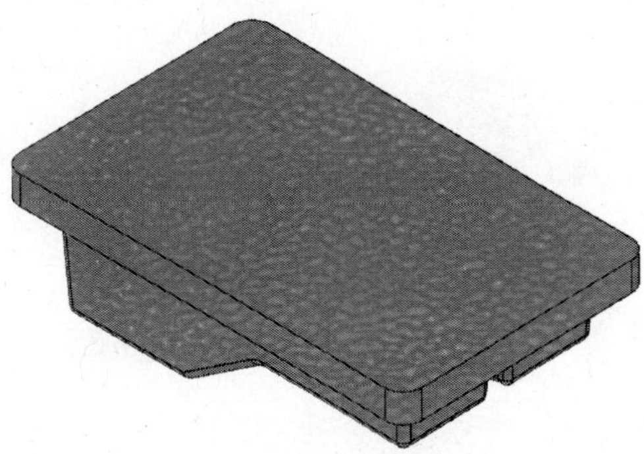

Figure 12-23 *Resultant Core*

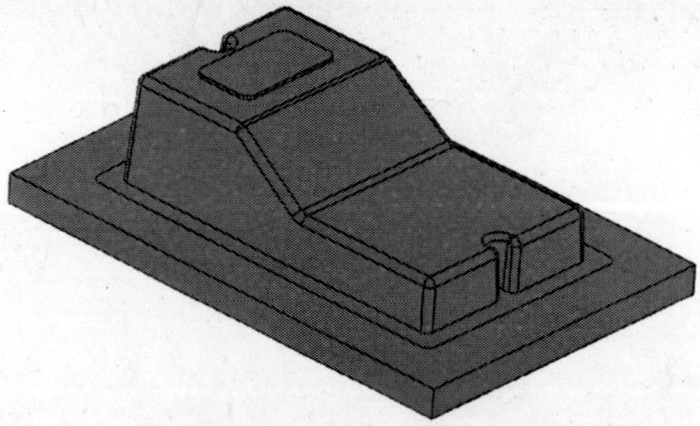

Figure 12-24 Rotated view of the core

Creating the Exploded View of the Assembly

After extracting the core and cavity of the plastic cover, you need to create the exploded view of the Mold base assembly. For creating the exploded view of the Mold base assembly, first you need to unhide the cavity and the plastic cover.

1. Unhide the cavity and plastic cover.

2. Using the **Exploded View** option from **Assembly CommandManager**, explode the Mold base assembly, refer to Figure 12-25.

3. Save the assembly.

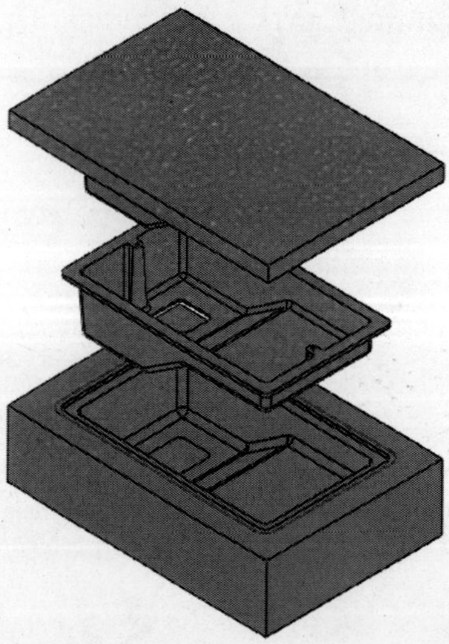

Figure 12-25 Exploded view of the Mold base assembly

Tutorial 2

In this tutorial, you will extract the core and cavity of the cover shown in Figure 12-26. The other side of the cover is displayed in Figure 12-27. The core of the cover is displayed in Figure 12-28 and the cavity in Figure 12-29. The first insert to be inserted in the mold is displayed in Figure 12-30. The second insert is also the same as displayed in Figure 12-30. Figure 12-31 shows the exploded view of the Mold base assembly. Figure 12-32 shows the views and dimensions of the cover. Figure 12-33 shows the views and dimensions of the core. Figure 12-34 shows the views and dimensions of the cavity. Figure 12-35 shows the views and dimensions of the insert. After creating the Mold base assembly, you will also create the exploded view of the assembly.

(Expected time: 3 hr)

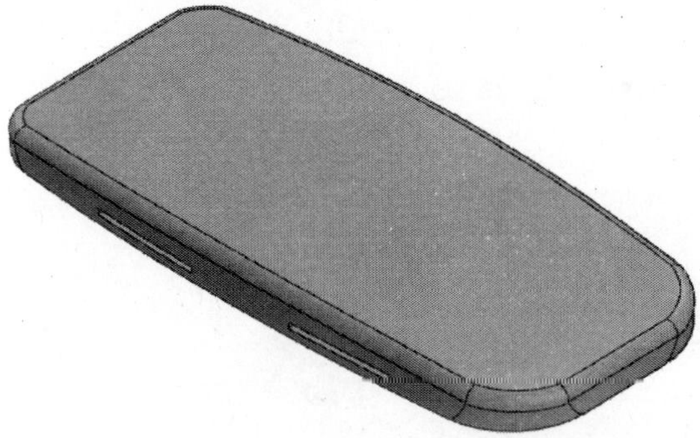

Figure 12-26 *Isometric view of the cover*

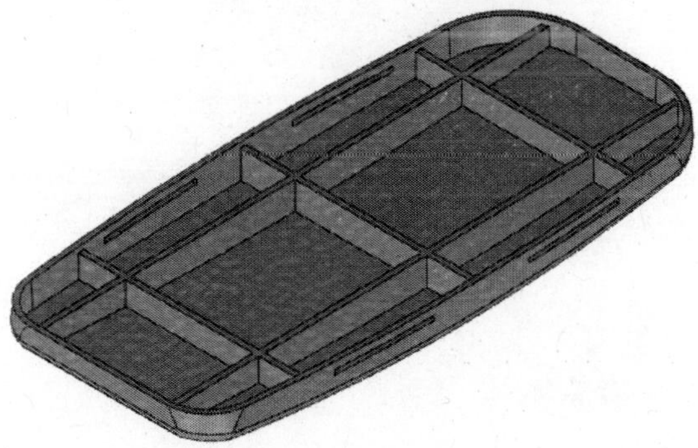

Figure 12-27 *Rotated view of the cover*

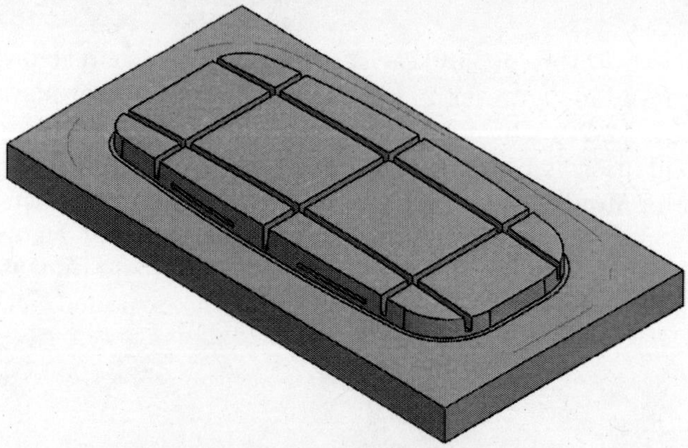

Figure 12-28 *Isometric view of the core*

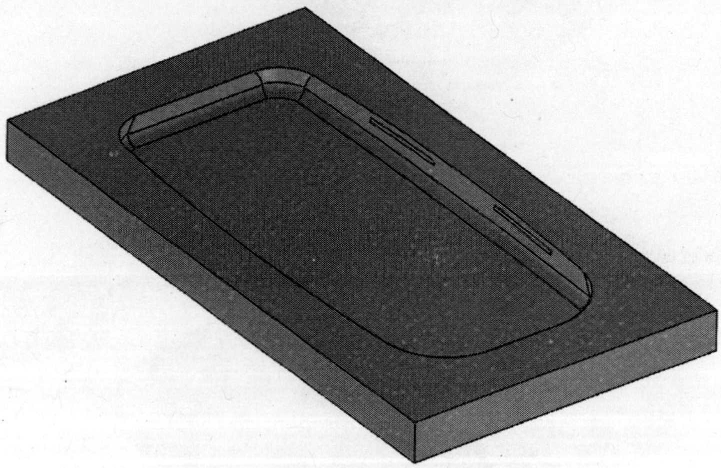

Figure 12-29 *3D view of the cavity*

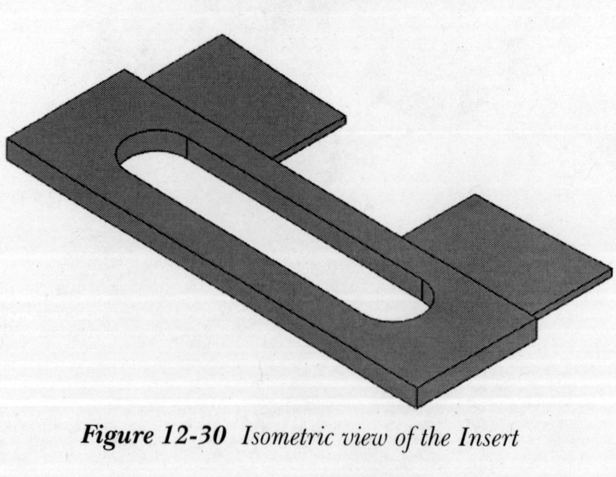

Figure 12-30 *Isometric view of the Insert*

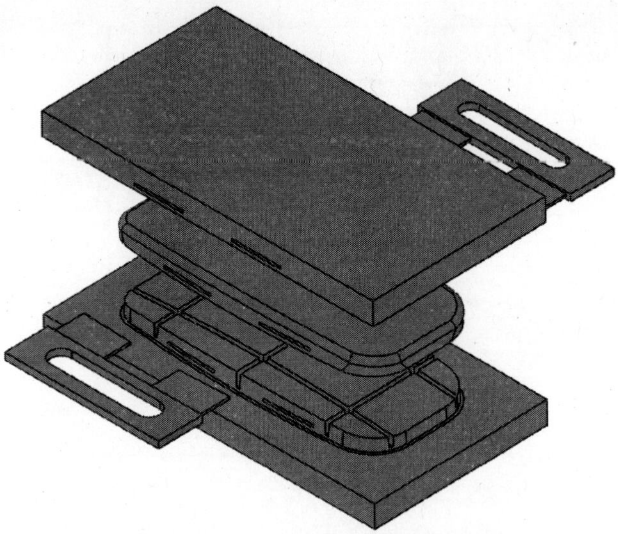

Figure 12-31 Exploded view of the Mold Base assembly

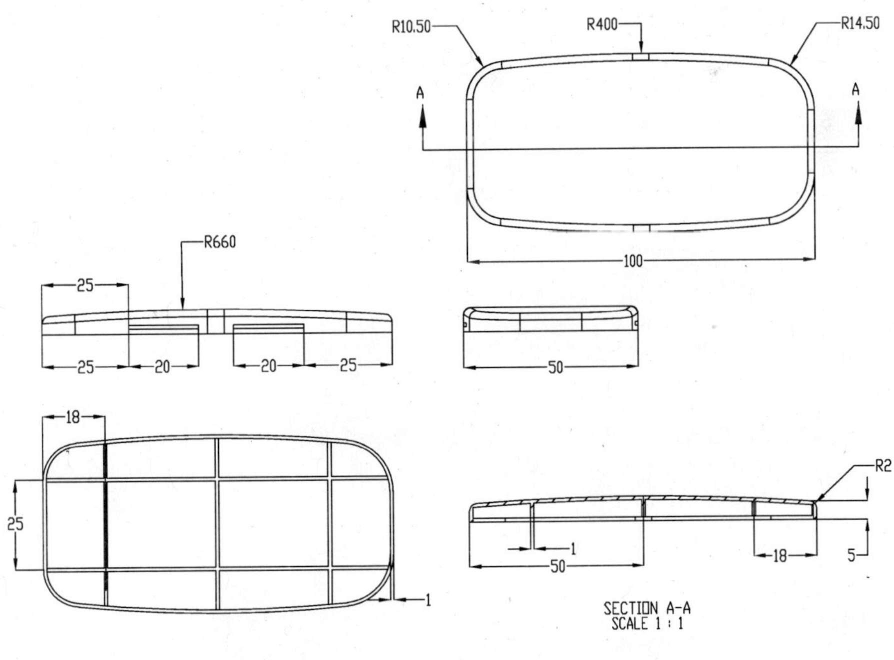

Figure 12-32 Views and dimensions of the cover

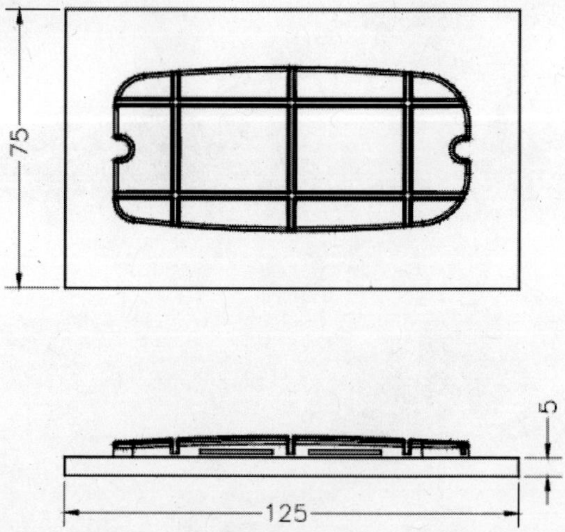

Figure 12-33 Views and dimensions of the core

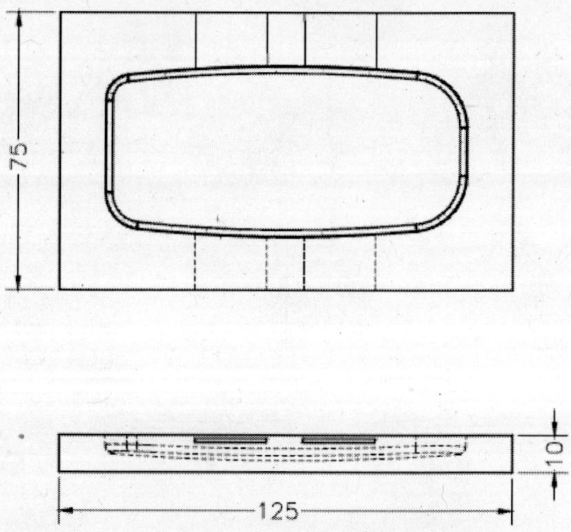

Figure 12-34 Views and dimensions of the cavity

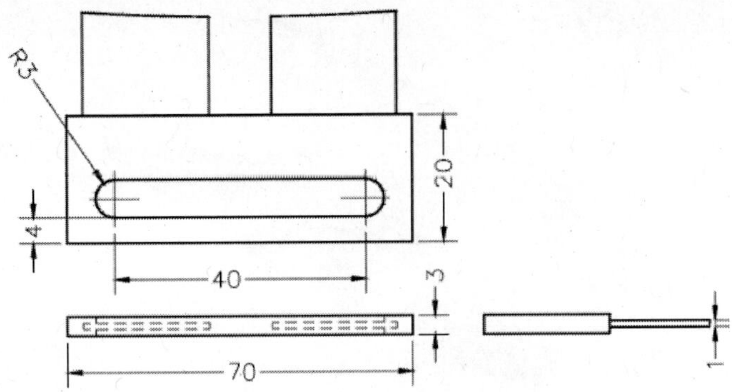

Figure 12-35 *Views and dimensions of the insert*

The following steps are required to complete this tutorial:

a. Create a new SOLIDWORKS document in the Part mode and using the standard modeling tools, create the model of the cover, refer to Figure 12-36.
b. Analyze the model for the draft angles.
c. Scale the model.
d. Create the shutoff surfaces.
e. Create the interim assembly.
f. Extract the core, refer to Figure 12-37.
g. Extract the cavity, refer to Figure 12-38.
h. Create the slots in the cavity for the insertion of inserts, refer to Figure 12-39.
i. Using the top-down approach, create the inserts, refer to Figures 12-40 and 12-41.
j. Create the exploded view of the assembly, refer to Figure 12-43.

Creating the Cover Part

First, you need to create the model of the cover plate. For creating the model, create a new SOLIDWORKS document in the Part mode.

1. Create a new SOLIDWORKS document in the Part mode.

2. Using the standard modeling tools, create the model of the cover. The completed model of the cover is displayed in Figure 12-36.

Analyzing the Draft Angles

After creating the model, you need to analyze the model for draft angles using the **Draft Analysis** tool.

1. Invoke the **Draft Analysis** tool from the **Mold Tools** toolbar to display the **Draft Analysis PropertyManager**. Using this tool, analyze the draft angles in the model. If some faces of the model are displayed in yellow, then you need to add the draft angles on those faces.

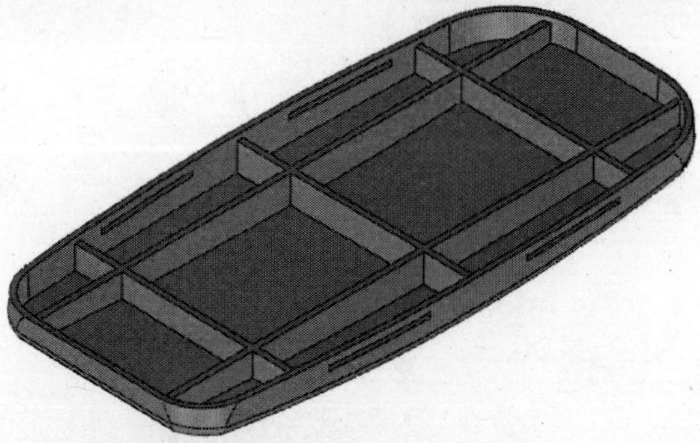

Figure 12-36 Model of the cover

Note
If some part of the middle portion of the curved face is displayed in yellow, you can ignore that.

Scaling the Model

After analyzing the model for draft angles and adding the drafts as required, you need to scale the model.

1. Invoke the **Scale PropertyManager**.
2. Select the model and then set the value of the scale factor in the **Scale Factor** spinner to 1.1.
3. Choose the **OK** button from the **Scale PropertyManager**.

Creating the Shutoff Surfaces

After scaling the model, you need to create the shutoff surfaces. Using the **Filled Surface** tool, shut the openings on the outer front face and on the inner front face.

Similarly, shut the openings on the outer back face and on the inner back face using the **Filled Surface** tool.

Creating the Interim Assembly

After creating and saving the part model, you need to create an interim assembly. In this interim assembly, you will extract the core and cavity using the top-down approach.

1. Create a new SOLIDWORKS document in the Assembly mode.
2. Save the assembly with the name Mold base.
3. Place the cover part coincident to the assembly origin.

Extracting the Core

For extracting the core, first you need to place a new SOLIDWORKS part document in the assembly.

1. Choose **Insert > Component > New Part** from the menu bar.

2. Select the **Front Plane** from the **FeatureManager Design Tree** to place the new component.

   As you place the component, the cover is displayed in transparent and the sketching environment is invoked.

3. Right-click on the new part node added in **FeatureManager Design Tree** and rename the part as Core.

4. Exit the sketching environment.

5. Using the **Radiate Surface** tool, create the radiated surface using the outer edges of the bottom face of the Cover.

6. Now, using the **Knit Surface** tool, knit all the inner surfaces of the cover with the radiated surface to create a single knitted surface.

7. Hide the cover and create a new offset plane vertically downwards at a distance from the radiated surface.

8. Select the newly created plane as the sketching plane and invoke the sketching environment.

9. Create the sketch of the core and extrude it up to the knitted surface.

10. Select the bottom face of the core and invoke the sketching environment.

11. Create the sketch of the core plate and extrude it to the required depth.

12. Now, return to the assembly environment and save the assembly.

    The final core is shown in Figure 12-37.

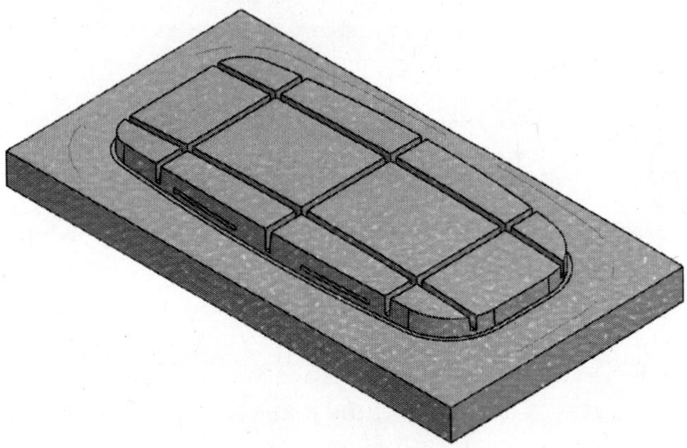

Figure 12-37 *Final core*

Extracting the Cavity

After extracting the core, you need to the extract the cavity. The cavity will also be extracted using the same procedure that was used to extract the core. For this, you first need to create a new component in the assembly.

1. Choose **Insert > Component > New Part** from the menu bar.

2. Select the **Front PSlane** from the **FeatureManager Design Tree** to place the new component.

   As you place the component, the cover is displayed in transparent and the sketcher environment is invoked. Right-click on the new part node added in **FeatureManager Design Tree** and rename the part as core.

3. Exit the sketcher environment.

4. Create the radiated surface and knit the radiated surface with the outer surfaces of the part.

5. Now, create a plane vertically upward at an offset distance of 10 mm from the radiated surface.

6. Select the newly created plane and invoke the sketching environment.

7. Create the sketch of the cavity and then extrude the sketch up to the knitted surface.

8. Add the remaining features to create the final cavity plate, refer to Figure 12-38.

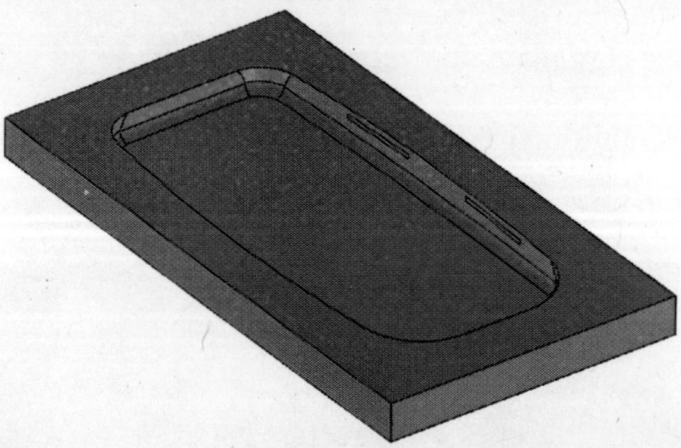

Figure 12-38 *Cavity displayed after hiding the cover*

Next, you need to create the slots in the cavity that will be used to place the inserts. The slots will be created by extruding a sketch created on the front face of the cavity using the cut option. The sketch of the slots will be created by using the **Convert Entities** tool on the edges of the slots of the cover.

9. Select the front face of the cavity as the sketching plane and invoke the sketching environment.

10. Choose the **Convert Entities** tool and select the edges of two slots displayed on the front face of the cover.

11. Invoke the **Cut-Extrude PropertyManager** and extrude the sketch using the **Through All** option.

12. Return to the assembly environment and save the assembly.

    The final cavity after creating the slots is displayed in Figure 12-39.

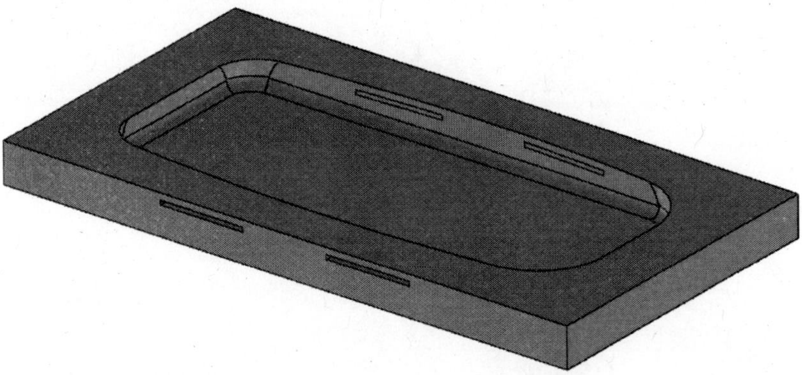

Figure 12-39 *Cavity after creating the slots*

Creating Insert

After extracting the core and cavity, you need to create the insert that will be used to restrict the flow of molten material in the portion where the insert is placed. This in turn will create the slot in the molded plastic component. The insert will also be created as a separate part using the top-down approach.

1. Choose **Insert > Component > New Part** from the menu bar.

2. Select the **Front plane** from the **FeatureManager Design Tree** to place the new component.

   Right-click on the new part node added in **FeatureManager Design Tree** and rename the part as insert 1.

3. Exit the sketching environment.

4. Select the front face of the cavity as the sketching plane and invoke the sketching environment.

5. Using the **Convert Entities** tool, select the edges of the slots placed on the front face of the cavity.

6. Extrude the sketch up to the inner front curved face of the cover. The assembly after creating the sketch of the base feature of the insert is shown in Figure 12-40.

7. Using the standard modeling tools, create the back plate of the insert.

   Figure 12-41 shows the assembly after creating the insert.

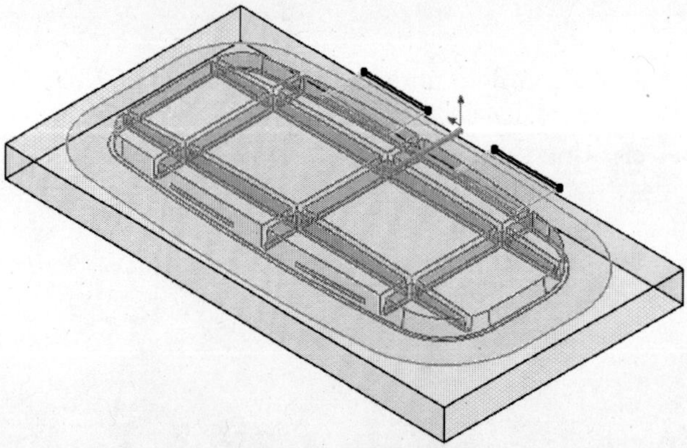

Figure 12-40 *Base feature of the insert*

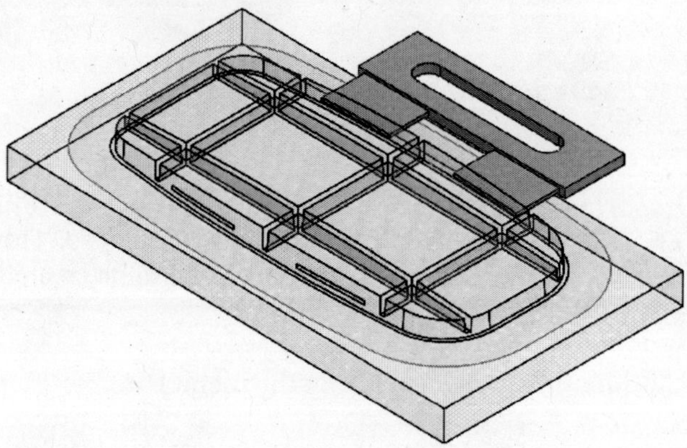

Figure 12-41 *Assembly after completing the insert*

Similarly, create the another insert. The final Mold base assembly is shown in Figure 12-42.

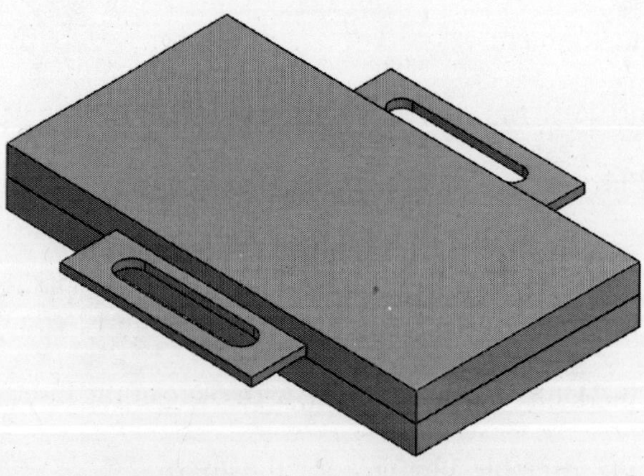

Figure 12-42 *Final Mold base assembly*

Next, you need to create the exploded view of the assembly, refer to Figure 12-43.

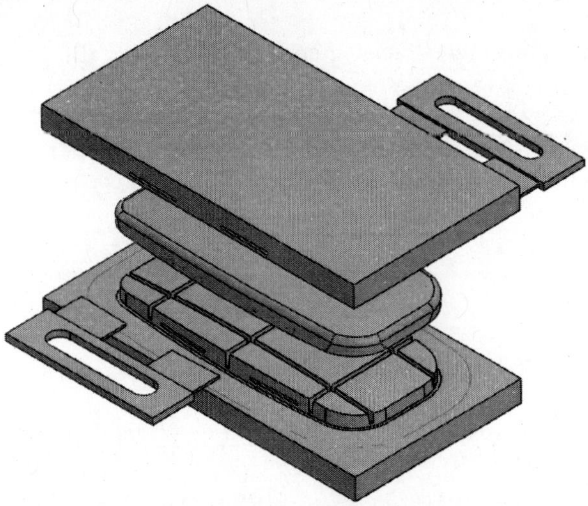

***Figure 12-43** Exploded view of the Mold base assembly*

Self-Evaluation Test

Answer the following questions and then compare them to those given at the end of this chapter:

1. The _________ is the female part of the mold, it is hollow from inside and the molten metal or the model plastic is poured into it so that it can take the shape of the cavity to create the component.

2. The _________ is the male part of the mold and it defines the area where the molten metal should not reach.

3. The cavity is created using the _________ tool.

4. The options available in the _________ drop-down list provided in the **Scale Parameters** area of the **Cavity PropertyManager** are used to define the origin about which you need to scale the cavity.

5. For creating the derived components, you need to choose the _________ from the **File** menu in menu bar.

6. If the **Mold Tools** toolbar is not available by default, then choose **View > Toolbars >Mold Tools** from the menu bar to display this toolbar. (T/F)

7. To invoke the **Scale PropertyManager**, you need to choose the **Scale** tool from the **Mold Tools** toolbar. (T/F)

8. The **Uniform scaling** check box is not selected by default and the model is uniformly scaled. (T/F)

9. You need to select the **Find steep faces** check box to analyze the positive steep faces and the negative steep faces. (T/F)

10. You can analyze the draft angle by choosing the **Calculate** button from the **Analysis Parameters** rollout in the **Draft Analysis PropertyManager**. (T/F)

Review Questions

Answer the following questions:

1. The __________ tool is used to analyze the draft angles of the model.

2. For scaling the model, you need to invoke the __________ tool.

3. Using the options available in the __________ drop-down list, you can specify the direction along which you can scale the model.

4. The __________ tool is used to analyze the draft angles.

5. The __________ check box is selected to display color variations specifying the draft angles on the model in the **Draft Analysis PropertyManager**.

6. You can create a radiated surface by using the __________ tool.

7. The **Gradual transition** check box available in the **Color Settings** rollout of **Draft Analysis PropertyManager** is used to display color variations specifying the draft angles on the model. (T/F)

8. The **Face classification** check box available in the **Analysis Parameters** rollout is used to refine the draft analysis depending on the type of draft. (T/F)

9. Using the **Scale Factor** spinner, you can not specify the scale factor for scaling the model. (T/F)

10. The **Find steep faces** check box is selected to analyze the positive steep faces and the negative steep faces. (T/F)

EXERCISE

Exercise 1

In this exercise, you will extract the core and cavity of the model, refer to Figure 12-44 and Figure 12-45. Before proceeding further, you need to modify the model by deleting the lip created as an extruded feature and then add the required draft angles to the model. **(Expected time: 2 hr)**

Download the input file for this exercise from *www.cadcim.com*. The complete path for downloading the file is as follows:

CAD/CAM>Solidworks Tutorial> SOLIDWORKS 2018: A Tutorial Approach> Input Files

Figure 12-44 *Model for creating mold with core and cavity*

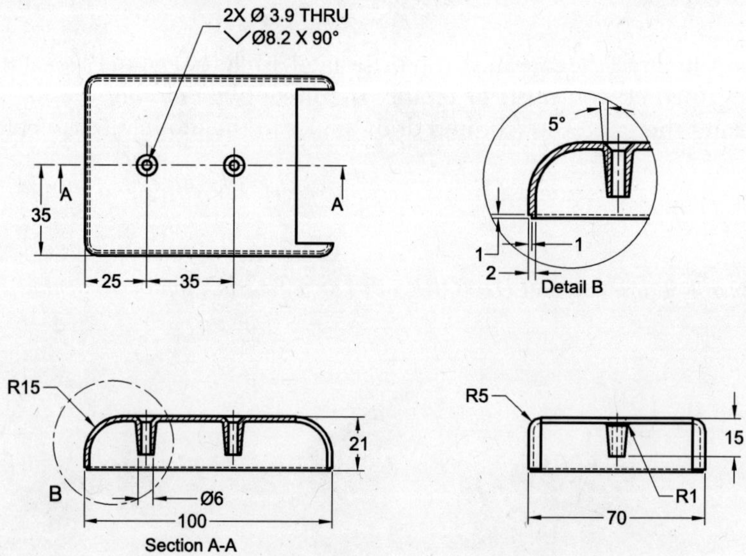

Figure 12-45 *Top view, front section view, and right side view with dimensions*

Answers to Self-Evaluation Test

1. cavity, **2.** core, **3. Cavity**, **4. About**, **5. Derive Component Part**, **6.** T, **7.** T, **8.** F, **9.** T, **10.** T

Student Projects

Student Project 1

Create all components of the Double Bearing assembly and then assemble them, as shown in Figure 1. Figure 2 shows the exploded view of the assembly. The dimensions of the components are given in Figures 3 through 5. **(Expected time: 1hr 45 min)**

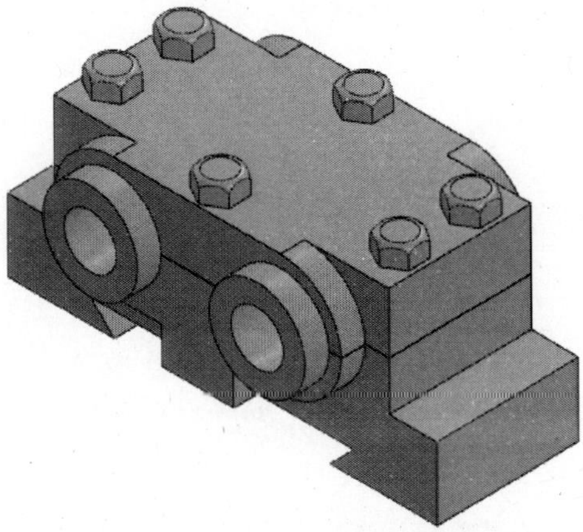

Figure 1 *Double Bearing assembly*

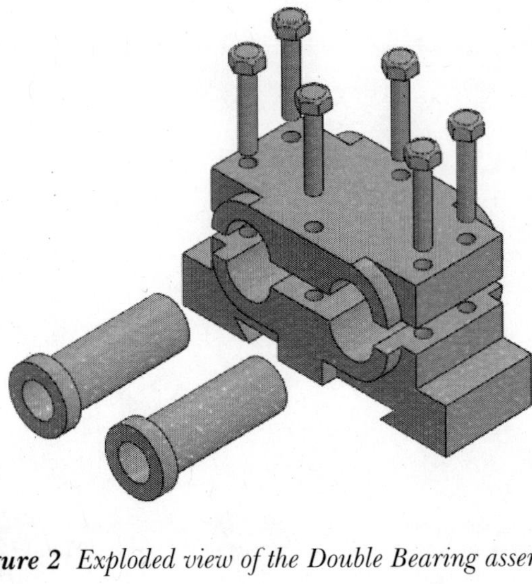

Figure 2 *Exploded view of the Double Bearing assembly*

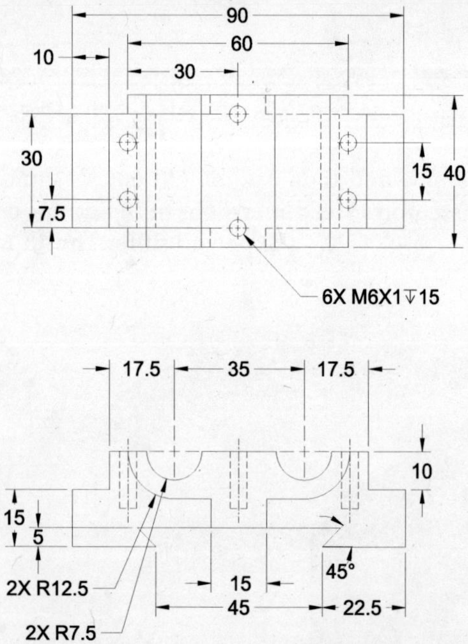

Figure 3 Top and Front views of the Base

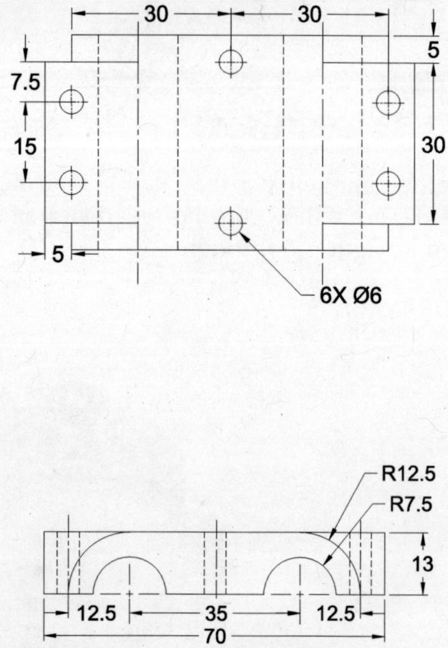

Figure 4 Top and Front views of the Cap

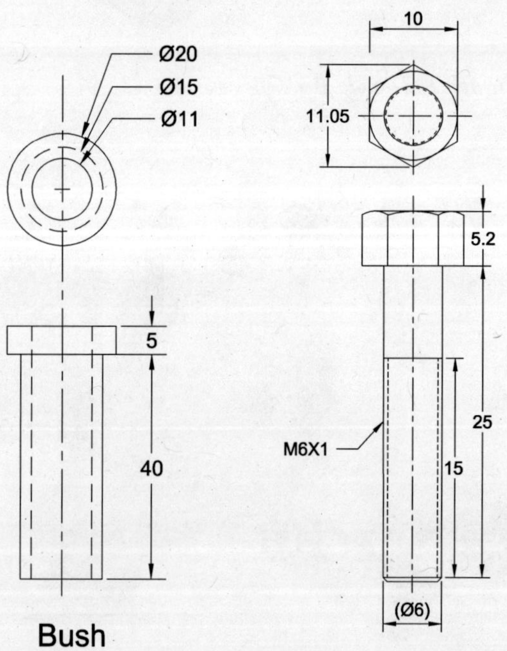

Figure 5 Top and Front views of Bush and Bolt

Index

Symbols

A

B

C

D

E

F

N

O

P

R

S

T

U

CAD/CAM/CIM/GIS/ANIMATION/CIVIL BOOKS

by **Prof. Sham Tickoo** (Purdue University, USA and Autodesk Authorised Author)

NX Nastran 9
For Designers
ISBN 978-93-8655-122-1
Price: ₹ 899/-

NX 11
for Designers
ISBN 978-93-8655-124-5
Price: ₹ 1099/-

Mold Design
Using NX 11
ISBN 978-93-8728-406-7
Price: ₹ 599/-

Siemens NX 12.0
for Designers
ISBN 978-93-8728-407-4
Price: ₹ 1099/-

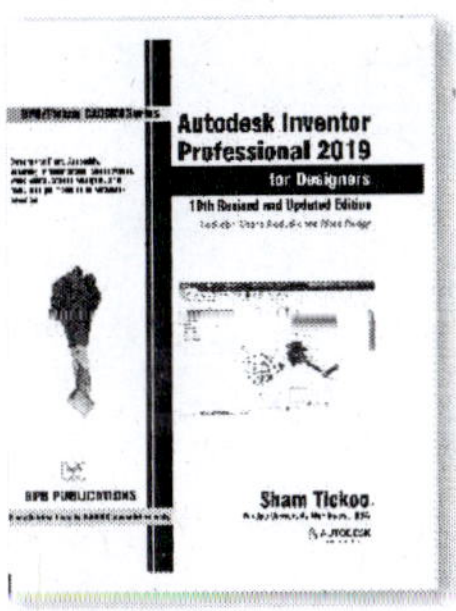

Autodesk Inventor Professional 2019
For Designers
ISBN 978-93-8817-629-3
Price: ₹ 1299/-

Autodesk Inventor Professional 2018
For Designers
ISBN 978-93-8655-164-1
Price: ₹ 1199/-

Autodesk Inventor Professional 2017
For Designers
ISBN 978-93-8655-126-9
Price: ₹ 1299/-

Autodesk FUSION 360
A Tutorial Approach
ISBN 978-93-8728-441-8
Price: ₹ 599/-

Solid Edge ST 10
For Designers
ISBN 978-93-8728-410-4
Price: ₹ 1099/-

Solid Edge ST 9
For Designers
ISBN 978-93-8655-120-7
Price: ₹ 1099/-

Solid Works 2017
For Designers
ISBN 978-93-8655-121-4
Price: ₹ 1299/-

Solid Works Simulation 2016
A Tutorial Approach
ISBN 978-93-8655-175-7
Price: ₹ 499/-

Available on **www.bpbonline.com** and all leading book stores.

bpb PUBLICATIONS | #1 Publisher of Computer Books | 62 Years of Excellence | OVER 90 Million Books Sold Worldwide